A TEXAS SCRAP-BOOK

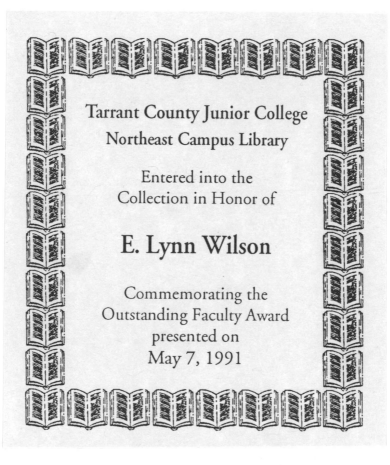

Tarrant County Junior College
Northeast Campus Library

Entered into the
Collection in Honor of

E. Lynn Wilson

Commemorating the
Outstanding Faculty Award
presented on
May 7, 1991

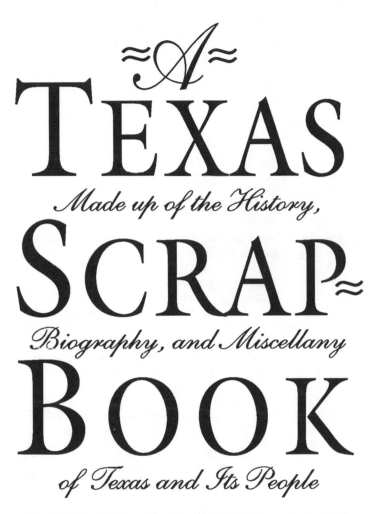

A TEXAS

Made up of the History,

SCRAP-

Biography, and Miscellany

BOOK

of Texas and Its People

BY D. W. C. BAKER — 1875

WITH A NEW INTRODUCTION BY
ROBERT A. CALVERT

Texas State Historical Association

Library of Congress Cataloging-in-Publication Data
Baker, D. W. C. (DeWitt Clinton), 1832–1881.
  A Texas scrap-book : made up of the history, biography, and miscellany of Texas
and its people / compiled by D. W. C. Baker ; with a new introduction by Robert
Calvert.
      p.   cm.   — (Fred H. and Ella Mae Moore Texas history reprint series.)
  Reprint. Originally published: New York : A. S. Barnes, 1875.
  Includes bibliographical references and index.
  ISBN 0-87611-108-8. — ISBN 0-87611-109-6 (pbk.)
  1. Texas—History. 2. Texas—Biography. 3. Texas—History—To 1846. I. Title. II.
Series.
F386.B17   1991
976.4—dc20   91-23059
                                                                       CIP

                    10 9 8 7 6 5 4 3 2 1

Published by the Texas State Historical Association in Cooperation with the Center for
Studies in Texas History at The University of Texas at Austin.

This book is in the Texas State Historical Association's Fred H. and Ella Mae Moore
Texas History Reprint Series.

The Barker Texas History Center at the University of Texas at Austin provided the
copy of *A Texas Scrap-Book* used to reprint this edition.

The paper used in this book meets the minimum requirements of the American National Standard for Permanence of Paper for Printed Library Materials, Z39.48—1984

The Fred H. and Ella Mae Moore
Texas History Reprint Series

The Texas Revolution
By William C. Binkley

Through Unexplored Texas
By W. B. Parker
With a new introduction by
George B. Ward

Spanish Explorers in the
Southern United States,
1528–1543
Edited by Frederick W. Hodge and
Theodore H. Lewis

A Ranchman's Recollections
By Frank S. Hastings
With a new introduction by
David J. Murrah

A Comprehensive History of Texas, 1685–1897
By Dudley Goodall Wooten

The History of Texas
By David B. Edward
With a new introduction by
Margaret S. Henson

Report on the United States and Mexican
Boundary Survey
By Major William H. Emory
With a new introduction by
William H. Goetzmann

Texas
By Mary Austin Holley
With a new introduction by
Marilyn McAdams Sibley

Army Exploration in the
American West, 1803–1863
By William H. Goetzmann
With a new introduction by the author

A Texas Scrap-Book
by D. W. C. Baker
With a new introduction by Robert A. Calvert

*The publication of this series is made possible by a gift from Fred H.
and Ella Mae Moore and the Mobil Foundation, Inc.*

DeWitt Clinton Baker by unknown photographer. Courtesy Austin History Center, Austin Public Library.

INTRODUCTION

Anecdotal evidence suggests that *A Texas Scrap-Book* may be the book requested most by the patrons of the Eugene C. Barker Texas History Center at the University of Texas at Austin.[1] DeWitt Clinton (Clint) Baker would undoubtedly have been surprised. The volume that he compiled was his second venture into book publishing and, like his first, failed to earn him any money. Although he may have continued to write poetry and essays for possible publication and for the entertainment of his family, he never again authored any books.[2]

Born on November 23, 1832, in Gorham, Maine, a small community near Portland, Clint was second of the four children of Dr. Symonds William and Mary Anne (Watson) Baker. D. W. C. Baker attended Gorham Academy and Bowdin College in Brunswick, Maine. His father, a physician, also educated him at home. Clint must have had an academic bent. He tutored students briefly at Gorham Academy, was reputed to have read and written five languages, and sent articles and poems back to the Portland paper after he left Maine.[3]

---

[1]Ron Tyler, Director of the Texas State Historical Association, asked Ralph L. Elder, head of Public Services at the Barker Center, which book in the Texas collection was asked for the most. He cited D. W. C. Baker (comp.), *A Texas Scrap-Book. Made up of the History, Biography, and Miscellany of Texas and Its People* (New York: A. S. Barnes and Co., 1875).

[2]Baker published *A Brief History of Texas from its earliest settlement. To which is appended the Constitution of the state* (New York: A. S. Barnes and Co., 1873). Note Baker's own poems that he included in the *Scrap-Book*, on pp. 378 and 386 for example. He evidently published poems and essays in the Portland (Maine) *Transcript* and elsewhere. "DeWitt Clinton Baker (Pioneer Lay Leader)," Biographical File, Austin History Center (cited hereafter as AHC).

[3]Austin *American-Statesman*, Apr. 23, 1971; John P. G. McKenzie, "Dewitt Clinton Baker School (a brief history thereof)," John P. G. McKenzie/DeWitt Baker School, AF Public Schools-Junior High (typescript; AHC). McKenzie wrote this to commemorate the school's fiftieth anniversary. Four-page handwritten sketch of D. W. C. Baker (author unknown), DeWitt Clinton Baker Papers (AHC).

Dr. S. W. Baker went to San Antonio in 1848 to settle the estate of his younger brother, Joseph Baker, who had come to San Felipe de Austin in 1831, where he taught school and served as the secretary of the *ayuntamiento*. Joseph had won fame in Texas participating in the Battle of San Jacinto, and he was elected to the House of Representatives from the Bexar district in 1837. He held office as primary court judge in Austin and as chief justice of Bexar County. At the time of his death in July 1846, he worked as a translator in the General Land Office. The reputation of the Baker family preceded it to Austin.[4]

News that Mary had died on February 7, 1849, reached S. W. Baker during his absence. Her death convinced him to stay in Texas. Eventually Dr. Baker became superintendent of the Asylum for the Blind. In spring 1849, Clint decided to follow his father to Austin. First he journeyed to New York and then sailed to Galveston, arriving on June 18, 1850. He went from there to Houston and then by stagecoach to Austin. In the capital city he joined his father's pharmacy business and began training to be a physician. Evidently wanderlust overtook the young man, and he left Austin briefly in 1853 to work on a surveying crew on the Fisher-Miller land tract. He returned to Austin the next year and became a prominent druggist and businessman. He owned a drugstore on the corner of Ninth Street and Congress Avenue, which he operated first with his father and then by himself and with other partners until ill health overtook him in 1878 and he retired. He died on April 17, 1881, and was buried in Oakwood Cemetery, Austin.[5]

---

[4]Austin *American-Statesman*, Apr. 23, 1971; Copy of the family tree with dates of arrival in Texas of some of the Baker family, DeWitt Clinton Baker Biographical File (AHC); Walter Prescott Webb, H. Bailey Carroll, and Eldon Stephen Branda (eds.), *The Handbook of Texas* (3 vols.; Austin: Texas State Historical Association, 1952, 1976), I, 100. DeWitt Clinton Baker wrote a short sketch of his uncle in *A Texas Scrap-Book* (pp. 272–273); p. 566 lists Baker as first sergeant in Mosely Baker's company, and p. 582 recounts Joseph's death.

[5]Austin *Statesman*, Apr. 19, 1881; Webb, Carroll, and Branda (eds.), *Handbook of Texas*, I, 99; Mrs. Sarah B. Trufant to DeWitt Clinton Baker [Jr.?], Aug. 20, 1920, DeWitt Clinton Baker Biographical File, (AHC); Nellie Baker Franklin to E. W. Winkler, May 28, 1936, DeWitt Clinton Baker Biographical File (Eugene C. Barker Texas History Center, University of Texas, Austin). In this

In his twenty-five years as a businessman, Baker rose to prominence in the Austin community. He met his wife-to-be, Mary Elizabeth Graham, at a ball at the governor's mansion. Mary Elizabeth was the daughter of Dr. Beriah Graham, a leading physician, who tended to Sam Houston's family when he was in Austin. In 1859 Houston appointed Graham superintendent of the state lunatic asylum. Reappointed by governors A. J. Hamilton and E. M. Pease, Graham went on to become treasurer of the state during E. J. Davis's administration. The young couple were married on May 28, 1861. The marriage produced nine children. Dr. Graham gave the Bakers land at 2620 Rio Grande, where they built a house that became an Austin showpiece. "Honeysuckle Glen," as the home was called, remained in the Baker family until it was sold in 1968 to Alpha Delta Phi sorority.[6]

Clint's family must have played an important role in his rise to prominence in the small city of Austin. Obviously his father and father-in-law contributed to his financial development. Like many successful young businessmen with the right family connections, Baker devoted time and energy to civic affairs. He helped found the first library association, which was probably the forerunner to the development of the Austin Public Library, and served as its treasurer. He participated actively in a local literary club, contributing essays to the meetings; from these literary clubs public library associations frequently sprung. He gathered data on the weather and sent it to Washington, D.C., where the information was incorporated into the monthly meteorological reports. He joined Saint David's Episcopal Church and as an active layman was the senior warden and superintendent of Sunday schools. In addition to these volunteer activities, he served the city as alderman in 1867 and briefly as city treasurer

collection are copies of the notice of Baker's funeral service and his death certificate. See letterhead on letter from D. W. C. Baker to A. S. Barnes, Aug. 11, 1875, Baker Papers (AHC); Money and Morrison (comps.), *General Dictionary of the City of Austin, Texas for 1877–1878* (Houston: Money and Morrison, n.d.), 68; McKenzie, "DeWitt Clinton Baker School (a brief history thereof)" (AHC).

[6]"Dewitt Clinton Baker (Pioneer Lay Leader)," Biographical File (AHC); Webb, Carroll, and Branda (eds.), *Handbook of Texas*, I, 714; Austin *American-Statesman*, Apr. 23, 1971.

in 1871. After his retirement from the drugstore, he was appointed to the city's internal revenue department, where he was employed at the time of his death.[7]

D. W. C. Baker was fairly typical of what historians later described as urban progressives. Many of these city progressives linked education with urban and economic advancement. Here, too, Baker combined interests, family connections, and civic responsibility. Thomas Baker, his uncle, had been an English instructor at Bowdin College, which might have been part of the school's attraction to young Clint. Thomas also migrated to Austin and taught English at the Austin Collegiate Female Institute from 1857 until his death in 1873. DeWitt Clinton Baker lectured to his brother's students on occasion and further established himself as a leader in education. Clint had tutored students in Maine, written for the Portland newspaper, and demonstrated a wide-ranging intellectual interest in a variety of scientific and literary subjects. His reputation, sense of civic duty, and membership in a family committed to public endeavors must have encouraged him to take an active role in the creation of the Austin public schools.[8]

In 1864 fellow citizens elected D. W. C. Baker to the post of school trustee in Travis County. Both prestige as a local educator and possible family connections influenced Governor E. J. Davis to appoint Baker to the state examining board in 1872. The examiners were charged with certifying teachers as to their competence. Re-

---

[7]Austin *Statesman*, Apr. 19, 1881; Austin *American-Statesman*, Dec. 18, 1955; McKenzie, "Dewitt Clinton Baker School (A brief history thereof)" (AHC); Handwritten Sketch of D. W. C. Baker, Baker Papers (AHC); "DeWitt Clinton Baker (Pioneer Lay Leader)," Biographical File (AHC); Webb, Carroll, and Branda (eds.), *Handbook of Texas*, I, 99.

[8]Mary Starr Barkley, *History of Travis County and Austin, 1839–1899* (Austin: Steck and Company, 1963), 156, 163–169. Handwritten Sketch of D. W. C. Baker, Baker Papers, cites lectures on chemistry (AHC). For definition of southern progressivism see Dewey W. Grantham, *Southern Progressivism: The Reconciliation of Progress and Tradition* (Knoxville: University of Tennessee Press, 1983), 279, which includes a cryptic remark about the impact of volunteer societies on demands for efficiency and reform of public institutions. Although progressivism is a later occurrence chronologically, varieties of urban progressivism, of course, extended from the Age of Industrialism onward.

gardless of whether a school were private or public, to qualify in meeting state-mandated student attendance requirements its teachers had to be certified as competent by school examiners and endorsed by the district school boards. Baker was the inspector of the schools for Travis and Hays counties until 1873 when the post was abolished. Supposedly the responsibility of examining teachers increased Baker's disillusionment with the lack of regularized education for students. After the Constitution of 1875 almost abolished the public school system, Baker involved himself in the organization of a new graded school for Austin. The common schools that functioned after 1875 were a combination of private and public enterprises. Pupils were assigned to specific classes or grades based upon their academic abilities. These newly organized schools were the beginnings of the current school system, and in 1878 Baker was president of the Board of Trustees, which in modern terms is school superintendent. In 1902, in recognition of his public service and his pioneering contributions to creating Austin's public school system, the city changed the name of the Hyde Park School to the DeWitt Clinton Baker School. It was moved in 1911 and renamed Baker Junior High. The Austin school district now uses the Baker school for administrative and educational purposes.[9]

Baker's tenure on the school's examining board involved him in the process of Republican attempts to institute the state's first public school system. The E. J. Davis administration passed a very controversial school law in 1871 that established compulsory school attendance, certified teachers, and aimed for uniform textbooks. Tradition has it that white Texans objected to the law, maintaining that the cost of education was too high, that it provided for the education of African Americans, and that the proposed law created a central-

[9]Mary Starr Barkley, *History of Travis County and Austin*, 175, 179, 182; Austin *American-Statesman*, Dec. 18, 1955; McKenzie, "DeWitt Clinton Baker School (a brief history thereof)" (AHC). McKenzie lists 1864 as the date of Baker's election as trustee. The handwritten sketch of Baker in the Baker Papers lists the date as 1854. In either case Baker was interested in public education throughout his adult life. The job of state examiners is discussed in Anita Louise White, "The Teacher in Texas: 1836–1879" (Ph.D. diss., Baylor University, 1972), 132–134.

ized school system that allowed the state government too much power. Quite probably, however, Democrats were able to use the school legislation of 1871 for partisan political ends by identifying the act as a Republican attempt to create wasteful patronage positions. Progressive educational leaders such as Baker may have been traditional Democrats who recognized the need for school reform and thus cooperated with early attempts to bring about educational uniformity. He could also have been sympathetic with the Davis administration, since his father-in-law was the state treasurer in 1872.[10]

Whichever the case, Baker supported the concept of a unified curriculum. The state board adopted the required textbooks for the established courses. Baker recognized the need for a standard textbook on Texas history. With this in mind, he wrote *A Brief History of Texas from Its Earliest Settlement. To which Is Appended the Constitution of the State. For Schools,* which was published by A. S. Barnes and Company in 1873. The company contracted for a wide range of textbooks for public schools. Its United States history book was adopted by the Board of Education for use in all Texas schools.[11] It was not clear if Barnes approached Baker or if the latter contacted the company. Nevertheless Baker secured a contract from A. S. Barnes and Company to write a history of Texas intended for primary-school use.[12] The state board adopted Baker's book in January 1873.[13] By the time the book appeared, the 1871 law had been modified so as to return textbook adoptions back to local school boards. The action caused the publisher to lament that "Our

---

[10]Frederick Eby, *The Development of Education in Texas* (New York: The MacMillan Co., 1925), 157–168; Carl H. Moneyhon, "Public Education and Texas Reconstruction Politics," *Southwestern Historical Quarterly,* XCII (Jan., 1989), 394–395. For further descriptions of the school laws of 1871 and 1873, see William Michael White, "History of Education in Texas, 1860–1884" (Ph.D. diss., Baylor University, 1969), 205–207.

[11]The list of books adopted by the State Board of Education can be found in *First Annual Report of the Superintendent of Public Instruction of the State of Texas, 1871* (Austin: J. G. Tracey, State Printer, 1872), 105–106.

[12]A copy of the contract can be found in the DeWitt Clinton Baker Biographical File (AHC).

[13]Handwritten Sketch of D. W. C. Baker, Baker Papers (AHC), 3.

misfortune was a modification in the school laws, and we fear the book [*A Brief History*] will never reach copyright." [14]

The revision of the school law in 1873, which passed over Davis's veto, began the dismantling of the public school system. The Democrats gained control of the legislature in 1874, and by 1876 had returned control of the curriculum and the adoption of textbooks to local schoolteachers, with the approval of the school trustees.[15] Barnes wrote to Baker that *A Brief History of Texas* sold only about 400 copies.[16] White Texans had complained vigorously in the 1870s that the books adopted by the Republican school board expressed anti-southern views. Since there were no uniform textbook adoptions, one cannot be certain that Baker's textbook did not sell some copies later. Certainly its biases do not seem to be anti-southern. But possibly the imprimatur given by the Republicans meant that the book never achieved wide favor in Texas. The book was not reprinted, for example, whereas a competitor published later, Homer S. Thrall's *A History of Texas, From The Earliest Settlement to the Year 1876; With an Appendix Containing the Constitution of the State. For Use in the Schools, and for the General Reader*, was revised and updated in 1885.[17]

Lore has it that while researching his *Brief History of Texas*, Baker collected so much information that he decided to author another book.[18] That does not seem very likely; *A Texas Scrap-Book* seemed to have been designed from its origins as a subscription book.[19] It

---

[14]A. S. Barnes to DeWitt Clinton Baker, Aug. 3, 1875, Baker Papers (AHC). By copyright Barnes meant paying off the cost of publication.

[15]Frederick Eby (comp.), *Education in Texas: Source Materials*, University of Texas Bulletin #1824, Apr. 25, 1918 (Austin, Texas), 700; Stewart Dean Smith, "Schools and Schoolmen: Chapters in Education in Texas, 1870–1900" (Ph.D. diss., University of North Texas, 1974), 20–26.

[16]A. S. Barnes to DeWitt Clinton Baker, Aug. 3, 1875, Baker Papers (AHC).

[17]Homer S. Thrall, *A History of Texas* . . . (1876; rev. ed., New York: University Publishing Co., 1885).

[18]Austin *American-Statesman*, Apr. 23, 1971.

[19]D. W. C. Baker (comp.), *A Texas Scrap-Book. Made up of the History, Biography, and Miscellany of Texas and Its People* (New York: A. S. Barnes and Co., 1875).

was fairly common during the period after the Civil War to compile books that could be sold to a given number of subscribers in advance, guaranteeing thus the cost of production and some profit to the author/compiler. Baker approached A. S. Barnes in fall 1874 with a proposal for the *Scrap-Book*. Barnes did not express much enthusiasm for the project. He pointed out that the company usually did not do such publications, but that if Baker could secure 500 subscribers willing to pay $4.00 in advance, the company would undertake the project. The book was not to exceed 800 pages. By November the two parties had reached a tentative agreement: Baker would enroll 500 subscribers at $5.00 each, he and the company would split the cost of the engraving plates, and he could control the sale of the book for a year after its publication. Later the publisher and author would quarrel over how the proceeds from the sale of the book should be divided.[20]

Spring 1875 witnessed the collaborators sparring about the progress of the book. Baker had not secured the requisite number of subscribers, and Barnes was willing to extend more time to the author but was unwilling to push forward with the publication of the book until money was forthcoming. The publisher pointed out that it would take $2,500 to cover present expenses. By mid-March Barnes agreed to hasten the book's completion, both on the promise that Baker had commitments and to protect the funds that the company had already invested. It was clear that neither the book nor the specimen pages for advertising purposes would be printed as quickly as Baker wished.[21]

By that summer, the partners were bickering. Barnes hired N. R. Richardson of New York to do the engravings for the book. Early on the publisher assured Baker of the engraver's competence and inquired about how Clint wanted the book laid out. Evidently instructions were not clear. The compiler turned down the first sample engravings, probably because they were incorrectly sized and because the paper stock was of an inferior quality. It was possible that

---

[20]A. S. Barnes to Baker, Oct. 19, Nov. 4, Dec. 23, 1874, Baker Papers (AHC).
[21]Barnes to Baker, Jan. 5, Mar. 5, Mar. 19, 1875, ibid.

Barnes was overly optimistic about the time needed for the engravings, though he later denied any culpability for the delay in publishing the *Scrap-Book*, instead calling the engraving mix-up an error. Indeed the problems with the engravings, according to Barnes, cost the company an additional $1,000.[22] Specimen pages came out that summer and were circulated in Austin and Houston as examples of the soon-to-be published book.[23] The July 1 publishing deadline, however, was not met.

Barnes, in turn, discovered that co-owners of the company wanted to publish *A Texas Scrap-Book* with an A. S. Barnes imprint. It was not clear why this decision was made, but Barnes clearly disapproved of it, describing the "literature" in the book as "sub-par." He told Baker, moreover, that no earlier protests about the book's contents had been lodged because the selections were *"none of our business"* (emphasis Barnes). Now, however, the book was to carry the company imprint, and he felt that Baker should agree to change part of the selections in future editions. The "dialogue on p. 346 *etc.*, for instance," Barnes continued, "is very profane, and we hope for your own sake and the dignity that should attach to such a book you will authorize a modification before the next edition." The publication of the book was now slated for mid-September.[24]

The expense of the specimen pages was one of many contentions between Barnes and Baker as the quarrel over the book changed from format to finances. Barnes wrote to Baker that the company had $2,258.48 of its own money in the book. Presumably that figure did not include staff costs. The publisher urged Baker to canvas the state. "Can't we place a copy on every centre table in Texas?" Barnes asked. "Please," he pleaded, "do not desert us now in this critical period."[25] But Baker was not particularly sympathetic with the plight

---

[22]Barnes to Baker, n.d. (probably January 1875), June 5, 30, July 21, Sept. 15, 1875, ibid.

[23]D. W. C. Baker (comp.), "Specimen Pages: A Texas Scrap-Book. Made up of the History, Biography, and Miscellany of Texas and Its People" (New York: Published for Author, 1875).

[24]Barnes to Baker, Aug. 3, Sept. 3 (quotations), 1875, Baker Papers (AHC).

[25]Barnes to Baker, Sept. 15, Sept. 21 (quotation), 1875, ibid.

of A. S. Barnes and Company. Although promised in July, the book was published in September 1875, and the first copies did not reach Clint until October. He explained later that the delay in publishing the book caused many of his original subscribers to cancel the purchase agreements. Since some of the subscribers backed out, Clint had cash-flow problems. Consequently, he wanted to receive the books in lots of 125 with thirty-day billing. The company desired cash, which, it asserted, the publishing agreement specified. Having no choice, since Baker was the outlet for the volume, Barnes relented and mailed the books in lots of 125 before he received the money.[26]

It was apparent by winter that *A Texas Scrap-Book* was not to be a successful financial venture. Both parties were dismayed by the failure of the book to sell, and each blamed the other. Baker believed, as many authors do about their publishers, that the company did not adequately publicize his book. Consequently he spent $154.10 of his own money to take out advertisements in newspapers in Austin, Dallas, Houston, Jefferson, Galveston, San Antonio, and Waco. The publisher also refused to send books to agents other than Baker unless they paid cash, maintaining that it was the responsibility of the compiler to furnish books on credit to prospective sellers. The company contended that the author did not work hard enough at selling the book. By early spring the rancor and disappointment engendered by the book's lack of success spilled over into quarrels about how many books had been sold and how the fees for the sale of these books should be split.[27]

Baker argued that he controlled the sale of the book for one year. He should thus receive a discount fee of 33 percent for each book he sold, plus a 10 percent author's fee, which he described as a copyright fee. The company maintained that the copyright fee did not go into effect until the cost of plates for the engravings was recovered. The collaborators also came to no decision about how

---

[26]Baker to A. S. Barnes and Co., Jan. 10, 1879, ibid.; Barnes to Baker, Sept. 15, 1875, ibid.

[27]Barnes to Baker, Dec. 2, 17, 1875, ibid.; Undated list of advertisements and list of books sent to newspapers for review (probably December 1875), ibid.; Barnes to Baker, Feb. 10, Apr. 29, 1876, ibid.

advertising costs, including the specimen pages, were determined and who was responsible for them. Baker's refusal to remit money for the books he had received until they were sold complicated the issue.[28]

Accounts had not been settled by the new year. Indeed they had worsened. Barnes wrote to Baker that he was "not well pleased at the tone of your recent favor."[29] That spring the author notified the publisher that he had contacted his attorney and wished to settle the account. Barnes responded that no account could be settled unless Baker agreed that he would not receive an author's fee of 10 percent. In reply to a query by Baker about advertising and other obligations, the publisher wrote, "To ask if the enterprise was not to be a mutual risk. We did not so understand it and for that reason asked for the guarantee."[30]

Events, however, were coming to a close. Baker had saved all the correspondence from the company. He notified Barnes that letters sent to him in the first stages of the project gave the author control of sales of the book with no stipulation concerning payment for the plates. Barnes confessed as much in March 1877, writing "we see indeed that our unguarded correspondence" failed to spell out shared costs. He went on to add, "As matters are we can only throw ourselves upon your mercy reminding you of the heavy loss we have sustained on both your books."[31] No mercy was forthcoming. Baker paid for the 500 copies he received at a 43 percent discount, and eventually Barnes even dropped claims for the advertising costs of *A Texas Scrap-Book*. He closed out the first disputes by defending the publishing house, writing, "Remember, doctor, that you alone have received any income from the book. Our connection with it and the previous one, has only brought us trouble and loss," and adding that, "We regret on your account as well as our own that your ventures have both failed but do not think any other house could

---

[28]Barnes to Baker, June 17, Aug. 14, Sept. 1, 1976, ibid.

[29]Barnes to Baker, Jan. 5, 1877, ibid. By "favor," Barnes meant "request."

[30]Baker to Barnes, Mar. 2, 1877, ibid.; Barnes to Baker, Mar. 17, Apr. 11 (quotation), 1877, ibid.

[31]Barnes to Baker Mar. 30, 1877, ibid.

have served you more successfully or faithfully than Yours Truly A. S. Barnes."[32]

The issue of the plates did not die. Baker learned that N. D. Thompson and Company intended to publish a history of Texas. He wrote to Barnes suggesting that the publisher contact the St. Louis company and sell them the rights to *A Texas Scrap-Book*, "that it could be got into the hands of those who make a business of publishing subscription books" and make money for all the parties involved.[33] Instead A. S. Barnes and Company sold the plates to N. D. Thompson and Company, and all but four of the thirty-two engravings in *A Texas Scrap-Book* were used by Homer S. Thrall in another subscription book, *A pictorial history of Texas, from the earliest visits of European adventurers, to A. D. 1879. . . .*[34] Thrall selected one of the illustrations, that of Thomas J. Rusk, to be used in the 1885 edition of his textbook.[35] Of the ninety-five engravings in *A pictorial history of Texas*, about 31 percent came from the *Scrap-Book*, with no attribution.

The failure of an author to identify the origin of illustrations in a book was not an unusual practice. Baker took some illustrations for the *Scrap-Book* from his history of Texas and did not identify those. In some cases, indeed, where he attributed the source of an engraving in his textbook, he dropped the attribution when he used the same illustration in the *Scrap-Book*.[36] Both men also modified a few of the original titles of engravings used in other books when they reprinted the illustrations, if they were not simply portraits, thus further confusing the source of the materials.[37]

---

[32]Barnes to Baker, Jan. 17, 1879, ibid.

[33]Baker to Barnes, Feb. 22, 1879, ibid.

[34]Homer S. Thrall, *A pictorial history of Texas* . . . (St. Louis: N. D. Thompson and Co., 1879).

[35]The engraving appears on p. 264 in *A Texas Scrap-Book* and on p. 140 in Thrall's *A History of Texas.* . . . The four Thrall did not use appear on pp. 35, 143, 371, and 500 in *A Texas Scrap-Book*.

[36]Four engravings appear in both books. "Indians" appears in Baker's *A Brief History of Texas* . . . (p. 101) and is attributed to *Monteith's Comprehensive Geography,* and the same engraving is used on p. 132 of the *Scrap-Book*, with no attribution to either source.

[37]The changes were not major but rather a slight modification of the plate.

Baker was not outraged by N. D. Thompson and Company's intended use of the plates but rather of the failure of A. S. Barnes and Company to notify him of their sale. When he discovered in December 1878 that a forthcoming book would contain illustrations that appeared in the *Scrap-Book*, he wrote to Barnes asking if the publisher knew of this and what business deals if any had been negotiated.[38] Barnes, Baker, and N. D. Thompson exchanged letters over the next few months. Baker pointed out that some of the illustrations had appeared elsewhere—he referred to a life of Houston as well as the history textbook—but most, he maintained, had been collected by him for exclusive use in *A Texas Scrap-Book*. He asserted that to sell the plates without the text eliminated any chance of marketing the remaining copies of his book. He demanded that A. S. Barnes and Company pay him $500 for the copyright to the plates. Failing to do so, he said, meant that he would do everything necessary to prevent the sale of the *A pictorial history of Texas*.[39] No record exists of the final settlement reached. Presumably Baker was either satisfied or gave up hope of redress, because evidence of correspondence among the parties ended in 1879, Thrall published his book that year, and it was reprinted in 1883 by the same company.[40]

A Texas Scrap-Book, on the other hand, was not reprinted until the Steck Company did a facsimile edition in the twentieth century.[41] It has thus always been a rare item. Part of the problem in determining the exact count of the first edition was the haphazard nature of its publication. Much of the confusion over fees and costs

---

"The Capitol at Austin" in *A Texas Scrap-Book* (p. 120) was entitled "The Capitol at Austin in 1870" in *A pictorial history of Texas* . . . (p. 623), or, for example, Baker's "Texas Indians" (p. 132) was entitled by Thrall simply "Indians" (p. 83).

[38] Baker to Barnes, Dec. 24, 1878, Baker Papers (AHC).

[39] Baker to Barnes, Jan. 10, Feb. 22, Mar. 18, 1879, ibid.; N. D. Thompson to Barnes, Feb. 26, 1879, ibid.; Barnes to N. D. Thompson and Co., Mar. 1, 1879, ibid.

[40] The new edition described itself as revised and enlarged. Homer S. Thrall, *A pictorial history of Texas* . . . (1879; rev. ed., St. Louis: N. D. Thompson and Co., 1883).

[41] The title page of the reprint describes the book as "A Facsimile Reproduction of the Original." The book, published in Austin by the Steck Company in 1935, is an exact replication of the original edition with no introduction or index.

between A. S. Barnes and D. W. C. Baker arose from the rather informal agreements reached about the publishing of the *Scrap-Book*. It seems probable that Barnes issued no formal contract to Baker. The latter saved his copy of the contract for *A Brief History of Texas*, but either did not receive or did not save one for the *Scrap-Book*. He did keep the incoming correspondence from Barnes about the prospective subscription volume, but again Baker retained no copies of his letters to the publisher until it appeared that lawsuits might occur. The manner in which he kept the letters leads one to infer that no binding contract was issued. Consequently there was no record of how many actual books A. S. Barnes and Company printed.

Barnes told Baker in June 1876 that the company had sold fewer than twenty-five books. The next year Barnes wrote to Baker that he had one hundred copies of cloth and fifteen bound in sheepskin on hand. These books were shipped to Baker in 1878, after the first round of negotiations ended, by H. A. Wilkins who was a publisher and partner of A. S. Barnes. Wilkins ran the New Orleans office, which did publish subscription books, and he kept that branch's business affairs separate from Barnes and the publishing of textbooks, which were published in New York and Chicago. It was Wilkins's objections that placed the Barnes and Company imprint on the *Scrap-Book*. Baker told N. D. Thompson and Company in 1879 that he had sold 525 copies and that Barnes and Company had sold none. It cannot be determined how many books were actually sold, but an estimate would be, by the time of Clint's death in 1881, no more than about 550. He had been ill since 1878 and would not likely have hawked the *Scrap-Book*. As a publisher of textbooks, Barnes had no network of agents to sell literature. The outside estimate of the press run would be no more than 625 books bound in cloth (the 525 sold by Clint, 25 by A. S. Barnes, and the 100 shipped in 1878) and 25 in leather. The latter figure assumes that Clint wanted about 10 leather copies for his own use.[42]

---

[42]Barnes to Baker, June 17, 1876, Apr. 11, 1877, Baker Papers (AHC); Baker to H. A. Wilkins, Mar. 8, 1878, ibid.; Baker to N. D. Thompson and Co., Mar. 1, 1879, ibid. There is a "copy one" of the leather edition in the Baker Papers.

One suspects that Baker was right in assessing that the failure of the book was at least partially due to Barnes's inexperience in publishing subscription books and in not realizing how to sell items other than textbooks. Yet Barnes probably assumed that Baker wanted a vanity book and that the publisher was printing the book as job work. That attitude would explain why neither of the parties insisted on an iron-clad contract. But Baker intended to make money from the book. It is arranged as many subscription books of the day were, when one assumed that leisure time would be spent in casual reading. Collected from a wide range of sources, Baker included in the volume anecdotes, poems, speeches, statistics, and descriptions of flora, fauna, and the weather. He also included in the *Scrap-Book* long lists of individuals and some biographical sketches of those who died in wars or served at San Jacinto or played some other role in Texas history. He knew that the best way to sell a book was to put enough names in it so that relatives and friends of those included in the text might buy a copy. Little did the compiler realize that the listings, sketches, and statistical collections would be of value to researchers in the next century.

One major liability of *A Texas Scrap-Book* for researchers and readers, however, has been the difficulty in ferreting out the information in the book. As most subscription books, indeed as most books published in the nineteenth century, the original edition included no index. The Steck Company facsimile reproduction of the book also omitted an index. Nineteenth-century readers may have been willing to casually and slowly work their way through a 657-page collection of diverse materials, but most twentieth-century readers are not. Today readers want quick access to the materials they wish to read or facts they wish to know. Recognizing that Richard Morrison published an *Index to D. W. C. Baker's* A Texas Scrap-

---

Baker gave it to his eldest daughter. He probably received some consequently in one of the early shipments, and, since he paid A. S. Barnes and Company for 500 copies, the discrepancy in figures between 500 and 525 could well be those sheepskin copies. A. S. Barnes and Company stationary lists the Chicago and New York offices as handling their publications for schools and cites the New Orleans office as a subscription publisher. Wilkins told Baker that there was no financial overlapping among the offices.

Book in 1984.[43] Mr. Morrison has been kind enough to allow the Texas State Historical Association to include his index in this edition. Both those who use this book and the Association are in his debt.

Most of us would probably agree with Barnes that much of the literature in the book is not first rate. But after perusing the book and the index, one suspects that all readers will find some items of interest for information and for fun reading. And if one would like to sample the sort of writing that won for the late nineteenth century a reputation for over-sentimentality, then turn to the section on poetry. The prose in *A Texas Scrap-Book* represents much of what Texans were like at the time: patriotic, maudlin, colorful, and insensitive about race and ethnic groups. Moreover, as Baker hints in the preface, with the passing of the Republic and the population growth after the Civil War, white Texans were anxious to romanticize and glorify their past. Baker attempted to compile selections that captured nostalgia for an older pioneer life many Texans thought was ending. The book stands as both an historical document and a research tool. Students of Texas history will welcome the new easier access to the book and its contents. With this reprinting of *A Texas Scrap-Book*, some other book should now become the most frequently requested item in the Barker Texas History Center.

ROBERT A. CALVERT
COLLEGE STATION, TEXAS

---

[43]Richard Morrison, *Index to D. W. C. Baker's* A Texas Scrap-Book (Austin: W. M. Morrison Books, 1984).

STEPHEN H. AUSTIN.

See p. 253.

A

TEXAS SCRAP-BOOK.

MADE UP OF THE

HISTORY, BIOGRAPHY, AND MISCELLANY

OF

TEXAS AND ITS PEOPLE.

COMPILED BY

D. W. C. BAKER.

HIC DOMUS, HÆC PATRIA EST.—*Virgil.*

———————

A. S. BARNES & COMPANY,

NEW YORK, CHICAGO AND NEW ORLEANS.

PREFACE.

THE compiler of this volume has for many years been impressed with the conviction that much of deep interest connected with the history of our State would be lost, unless carefully gathered up by one whose heart should be in the work.

As year by year has passed away, and one after another of the active participators in the eventful scenes of 1835–6, has been gathered to his fathers, source after source of information has been taken away from us.

Many incidents of surpassing interest have never been written down, and much that would be prized by our posterity can never be given to them. With these thoughts the writer has for years been collecting whatever of interest he could find relating to the history, biography, and miscellany of Texas and its people ; and now, with a view of offering to his fellow citizens of this State a book which will embalm the memory of the past, and enshrine it in the heart of the present, he has compiled this work. Much that is in the following pages has never been published. Some of it has been published in local papers, or periodicals, and has never been reproduced.

A portion of it will be considered to possess but little literary merit. But let it be remembered that in many instances these little pieces are the only legacies by which to perpetuate the memory of those who have gone forever. This book is not offered to the world as a model of literary excellence, but as an urn in which is gathered the ashes of the days gone by. That portion of it which is devoted to biography, has been made as complete as possible, but there are, doubtless, some omitted who should be here.

The notices are confined to those who came to Texas before the revolution of 1836, and who have passed away, with one or two exceptions, among which is Colonel F. W. Johnson, of the heroes of San Antonio.

A complete list of the Governors of Texas, with biographical notices, will be found an interesting and valuable feature of the "Scrap-Book."

In this connection, the undersigned begs leave to tender his grateful acknowledgments to Governor E. M. Pease, Swante, Palm, Colonel F. W. Johnson, and others, who have kindly aided him in his work.

The Constitution and By-Laws of the Texas Veteran Association, also, a Complete List of all Living Texas Veterans, and a list of all who have died or have been killed since 1828 is appended.

This volume, which is the result of much patient labor, is now offered to an indulgent and discriminating public.

D. W. C. BAKER.

AUSTIN, December, 1874.

CONTENTS.

PART I.

HISTORICAL.

PAGE

Early Spanish Missions in Texas 17
Historical Notes collected from Registers of Old Mission of San Antonio Valero 18
The Name Texas... 19
Geography of Texas 20
A Compend of Texas History 23
The Anahuac, or Opening Campaign of the Texan Revolution 24
Battle of Velasco, in 1832 30
The Celebrated Indian Fight of 1831... 35
Storming of San Antonio de Bexar, in 1835... 37
Historical Reminiscences—Memorial from Texas Convention of April, 1833 39
    The Convention of 1836... 53
    Declaration of Texan Independence.................................. 55
    Names, etc., of the Signers of the Texan Declaration of Independence 58
A Declaration adopted by the General Consultation of Texas, November, 1835........ 60
A Declaration of Independence made at Goliad, December 20, 1835................ 61
Battle of Concepcion 65
Early History of Texas—Campaign of 1835 67
First Sunday School in Texas 69
The Texas Navy.. 77
Expedition West, under Johnson, Grant, and Morris 80
First breaking out of the Texas Revolution at Gonzales............................ 83
Texas.. 86
Austin's First Colony.. 88
Momentous Incident of the Texas Revolution—Reconciliation of Austin and Wharton. 89
The Grass Fight.. 92
Military Events of Texas... 92
The Battle of San Jacinto 95
Revolutionary Incidents—Burning of Vince's Bridge................................ 98
Early History of Texas 101
The Fall of the Alamo... 106

PAEG

Monument erected to the Heroes of the Alamo 112
Names Inscribed on Monument 113
Description of the Monument 114
Ground Plan and Description of the Alamo. 115
The Babe of the Alamo 116
Seat of Government. 118
Historical Statistics concerning Texas. 120
Early History of Texas. 122
Death of Big Foot. 124
Dawson's Defeat 124
Santa Fé Expedition of 1841 126
Battle of Mier 127
Texas Indians 132
Description of Old Goliad, or La Bahia 135
Scene on the Battle-field of Salado 136
Texas Indian Wars—Scalping of Wilbarger in 1834 138
      The Morgan Massacre 140
      Bryant's Fight and Defeat. 141
The Archive War—A Leaf from the History of Austin 142
Fannin's Massacre 144
The Carankawa Indians 145
Texas History 147
Comache Fight at San Antonio. 154
Another Chapter of our Early History. 155
Incidents of Texas History 157
Adventures of a Texan Volunteer. 160
A Relic of the Texas Revolution. 165
More of the Texas Revolution. 169
A Reminiscence of the Mexican war of 1846. 172
Judicial Organization of Austin's Colony 175
      Civil Regulations. 175
      Fees 177
      Criminal Regulations. 177
La Salle. 179
Speech of Honorable Guy M. Bryan 181
Old Fort Parker. 198
Letter from Stephen F. Austin to the Senate of Texas 202
Speech of Colonel Charles De Morse 204
Official Account of the Fall of Bexar, and Surrender of General Cos. 218
Revolution of Texas in 1812 224
Philip Nolan. 229
The Last of the Alabamas 236
Waco—A Leaf from its History 237
Aboriginal Antiquities of Texas 238
Fannin's Massacre—Account of the Georgia Battalion. 242

PART II.

BIOGRAPHY.

PAGE

DISTINGUISHED TEXANS.

Stephen F. Austin.. 253
Sam Houston... 255
David G. Burnett.. 257
Mirabeau B. Lamar... 258
Anson Jones... 259
Lorenzo de Zavalla.. 259
Baron de Bastrop.. 260
Don Erasmo Seguin... 260
Benjamin R. Milam... 260
William B. Travis... 261
J. W. Fannin.. 262
David Crockett.. 262
Thomas J. Rusk.. 264
Dr. Branch T. Archer.. 265
William H. Wharton.. 267
John A. Wharton... 267
Patrick C. Jack... 267
William H. Jack... 267
Dr. James B. Miller... 267
Sidney Sherman.. 268
Edward Burleson... 268
Frank W. Johnson.. 269
James Bowie... 269
J. B. Bonham.. 270
James Hamilton.. 270
E. M. Moore... 270
Thomas Green.. 270
Albert Sidney Johnston.. 271
Ben McCulloch... 271
Mosly Baker... 272
G. W. Hockley... 272
Memucan Hunt.. 272
Thomas William Ward... 272
Joseph Baker.. 272
Dr. Francis Moore... 273
George W. Smyth... 273
Albert C. Horton.. 273
R. M. Williamson.. 274
Wylie Martin.. 274
Benjamin C. Franklin.. 274

PAGE

DISTINGUISHED TEXANS.

Henry Smith 274
Baily Hardeman 275
David Thomas.. 275
Robert Potter.. 275
Joshua Fletcher 275
John Rice Jones.. 275
James W. Robinson 275
Samuel P. Carson 276
Thomas J. Chambers... 276
Thomas Jefferson Green.. 276
Hugh D. McLeod 276
Alexander Somerville 277
Lieutenant-Colonel Ward 277
Felix Huston 277
Dr. James Grant... 277
Peter W. Grayson.. 278
Robert Morris 278
"Deaf Smith".. 278
Asa Brigham... 278
James Collingsworth.. 278
Philip Dimmitt.. 279
W. S. Fisher... 279
S. Rhoads Fisher 279
Richard Ellis.. 279
Samuel M. Williams.. 279
Thomas F. McKinney 279
Michael B. Menard... 280
Oliver Jones 280
Jesse Grimes 280
Kenneth Lewis Anderson... 280
Martin Parmer... 280
Henry Karnes.. 281

REMINISCENCES OF EARLY TEXANS.

Captain Henry S. Brown.. 282
Captain Randal Jones.. 284
Sketch of the Life of Henry Castro 286
John Austin.. 287
W. T. Austin 287
Collin McKinney... 287
James G. Swisher.. 287
Sam Maverick... 287
Andrew Briscoe.. 287
Ira Ingram.. 288
Sterling C. Robertson.. 288
Warren D. C. Hall 289

PAGE

REMINISCENCES OF EARLY TEXANS—Continued.

George C. Childress.. 289
Jose Antonio Navarro... 289
Robert Wilson.. 289
Thomas J. Hardeman.. 289
Colonel Barnard E. Bee... 289
R. R. Royal.. 290
Benjamin Fort Smith.. 290
James Kerr... 290
John Caldwell.. 292
Matt Caldwell.. 292

BIOGRAPHIES OF GOVERNORS OF TEXAS.

James Pinckney Henderson... 293
George T. Wood... 293
P. Hansboro Bell... 293
Elisha M. Pease.. 294
Hardin R. Runnels.. 294
Edward Clark... 294
Frank R. Lubbock... 294
Pendleton Murrah... 295
A. J. Hamilton... 295
J. W. Throckmorton... 296
Edmund J. Davis.. 296
Richard Coke... 297
W. B. Ochiltree.. 298
Major Valentine Bennett.. 298

BIOGRAPHICAL NOTICES OF DECEASED JUDGES OF THE SUPREME COURT OF THE
STATE OF TEXAS.

John Hemphill.. 300
Abner S. Lipscomb.. 300
Royal F. Wheeler... 301

PART III.

MISCELLANY.

Houston's First Inaugural Address.................................... 305
Sudden Floods in Texas... 308
M. De Saligny.. 310
Anecdote of David G. Burnet.. 310
Anecdote of Stephen F. Austin.. 311
Fred Dawson.. 312
Governor Bell and Captain S——.. 312

                                                                    PAGE.
Another Unpublished Anecdote of General Sam Houston...................... 313
A Bear Fight.. 313
A Pig meddles in Diplomacy... 315
Judge Burnet's Oration at the Funeral of John A. Wharton................ 315
Aaron Burr... 318
Ellis F. Bean 322
Texas Sports.. 325
Floods in the Colorado... 327
Extract from General Houston's Proclamation, December 12, 1835.......... 328
San Jacinto.. 329
A Texas Prairie in Spring-time... 330
A Prairie Sunset 330
Houston's Letter to Santa Anna, March, 1842............................ 331
From Governor Smith's Address.. 332
President Burnet's Proclamation, June 20, 1836......................... 332
Houston to Santa Anna, March, 1842..................................... 333
The Flag of the Lone Star.. 334
From President Lamar's Message, November, 1840......................... 335
Speech of D. S. Kaufman, welcoming M. de Saligny, November 17, 1840..... 335
From a speech of Honorable Forbes Britton, November 21, 1857........... 336
From the Remarks of Chief-Justice Hemphill on the death of General James Hamilton,
        December, 1857.. 337
From the Eulogy on Honorable James Webb, by Honorable J. C. Wilson, November,
        1836.. 337
Extract from Address by Stephen F. Austin, in Louisville, Kentucky, March, 1836..... 338
Hymn of the Alamo 338
From the Valedictory Address of President Anson Jones, at Inauguration of New State
        Government, February 19, 1849................................. 339
From Report of Committee on Foreign Relations, June 20, 1845 340
The Lone Star of Texas... 341
Ad. Lawrence's Ride.. 342
The Currency during the War of 1861-'65................................ 345
Last Days of the Trans-Mississippi Department 348
Mexican Revolutions.. 350
Another Anecdote of General Houston.................................... 352
Copy of Letter by J. W. Fannin, a few days before his capture.......... 353
Dawson and Sims 354
Texas Independence... 355
Lafitte 356
Meteorology of Texas... 358
Texan Scenery.. 359
The Wild Man of the Woods.. 361
The Mothers of Texas... 366
Adventures of a Young Texan.. 368
The Soldier's Sweet Home... 374
Up! Men of Texas... 375
Leave it! Ah no—the land is our own................................... 376

	PAGE
My Childhood's Home	377
The Tolling Bell	378
Lament for a Stolen "Pet"	380
Reply to a Lament for a Stolen Pet	382
Laurel and Cypress	386
The Texas Soldier's Address to his Flag	387
I'm thinking of the Soldier	388
Always New	389
To my Sleeping Wife	390
The Marble Lily	392
Texan Hymn	395
Ode to San Jacinto	396
Lone Star of the South	398
Texas, our Home	400
Love and Latin	403
The Last Tear I shed	404
Naval Heroes	405
Texan Song of Liberty	406
The Lone Star of Texas	407
A Garnered Memory	408
An Escape from the Alamo	410
The Writing on the Wall	413
The Mier Prisoner's Lament	417
The Texas Ranger	418
On the Death of David Crockett	419
My Early Days	420
The Girl with the Calico Dress	421
Mary	422
Resurgam	423
Little Babies	424
Lines in Memory of Midshipman A. J. Bryant	426
Sunbeams	428
The Best	428
The Night before the Wedding	430
Swedish Poetry—The Viking	432
Not Dead, but gone before	436
The Texan's Song of Liberty	437
The Golden Opportunity	438
Epitaph of the Texas Dead	440
Boys, Rub your Steels	440
Character of David G. Burnet	441
Texas Minerals	442
Outline of the leading Characteristics of Texas	447
Wichita and Wilbarger Counties	461
Unsettled Regions on the Western Limits of Texas and to the Pacific Railroad to Guaymas, etc.	464
The Pan-handle of Texas	468
Game in Texas	474

PAGE

Same Subject—Continued 479
The Yellow Fever in Texas in 1867.......... 487
Geological Resources of Texas 488
The Mineral Resources of Texas... 493
The Coal-Bed of Texas... 498
Climatology of Texas 502
The Migratory Locust in Texas.. 511
The Mesquit Tree.......................................'........................ 512
Constitutional Government in Texas 515
Extract from the Address of Honorable Ashbel Smith to the Veteran Association 553

PART IV.
STATISTICAL.

Austin's Original Three Hundred............................. 557
List of all the Men in the Texas Army at the Battle of San Jacinto................. 562
List of the Officers and Men under Command of Colonel J. W. Fannin.............. 569
Constitution of the Texas Veteran Association 574
Texas Necrology 578
List of Old Texans who have died and been killed by Mexicans and Indians from 1828
    to 1874.. 580
Names of Veterans—First Class... 585
    "   "   Second Class... 620
The General Consultation 633
Houston's First Administration.. 636
Lamar's Administration 636
Houston's Second Administration.. 637
Anson Jones' Administration.. 637
Prominent Officials of the Republic—
    Judges of the District Court 638
    District-Attorneys.. 638
    Speakers of the House of Representatives................................ 639
    Chief Clerks of the House... 639
    Presidents, *pro tem.*, of the Senate.................................... 639
    Secretaries of the Senate 639

APPENDIX.

James W. Fannin—Commission, Orders, and Correspondence..................... ... 643

LIST OF ILLUSTRATIONS.

STEPHEN H. AUSTIN ....Frontispiece
MISSION OF SAN JOSÉ 18
INDIAN CHARGE 35
FIRST SUNDAY SCHOOL IN TEXAS....................................... 75
PLAN OF BATTLE OF SAN JACINTO 94
HOUSTON AND SANTA ANNA 96
STORMING OF THE ALAMO... 109
MONUMENT TO THE HEROES OF THE ALAMO............................... 112
GROUND PLAN OF THE ALAMO.. 115
HOUSE IN WHICH FIRST CONGRESS MET................................. 119
THE CAPITOL AT AUSTIN... 120
TEXAS INDIANS 132
MRS. EBERLY FIRING OFF CANNON..................................... 143
THOMAS J. RUSK... 155
SANTA ANNA 189
THOMAS F. McKINNEY... 206
MIRABEAU B. LAMAR... 226
HOUSTON PIERCED BY AN ARROW 255
THOMAS WILLIAM WARD.. 272
STERLING C. ROBERTSON 288
ELLIS P. BEAN 322
ANSON JONES.. 339
DUVAL DRAWING A PIG THROUGH THE FLOOR 371
GENERAL SAM HOUSTON 397
DAVID CROCKETT 419
DAVID G. BURNETT 441
HOUSTON ISSUING ORDERS... 464
CATHEDRAL AT MEXICO.. 500
R. M. WILLIAMSON 524
EDWARD BURLESON.. 565
TOM GREEN.. 584
SIDNEY SHERMAN... 600
COLONEL JOHN CALDWELL 630

PART I.

HISTORICAL.

TEXAS SCRAP-BOOK.

I.

EARLY SPANISH MISSIONS IN TEXAS.

(Compiled principally from Yoakum's Texas.)

THESE were established by Franciscan monks, under the auspices of the Spanish government, and were called Presidios. These missions, (*los missiones*) consisted of the chapel for worship, the cells for the monks, the dwellings for the inhabitants, and a fort for defence. The mission was under the control of the ecclesiastical power, and the military force was under an officer of the army, who, in most matters, was under the control of the priest.

In 1690, the mission of San Francisco was established on the Lavaca River at Fort St. Louis, by the Spanish under Captain Alonzo De Leon.

In the same year, the mission of San Juan Batista was founded on the Rio Grande River.

In 1714, Captain Ramon established the mission of San Bernard, also the mission of Adaes, among the Indians of that name, fifteen miles west of Natchitoches.

In 1715 was established the mission of Dolores, west of the Sabine, among the Orquisaco Indians.

In the same year a mission was founded among the Nacogdoches Indians, near the site of the present town of that name ; also another among the Aes Indians, near the site of the present town of San Augustine.

The mission and fortress of San Antonio de Valero was, soon after this, established on the San Pedro River, near the site of the present city of San Antonio.

Captain Don Ramon, who was the most efficient and active in building up these missions, was a great favorite among the Indians, who adopted him as a son, and assisted him in his labors.

In the year 1721, a post and mission was located at the crossing of the Neches, and another on the bay of San Bernard, called "Our Lady of

Loretto." In the same year the mission of La Bahia (the bay) was established at the lower crossing of the San Antonio River.

In 1730, the church of San Fernando, in the present city of San Antonio, was founded.

In 1731 was established, not far from the same place, the mission of La Purissima Concepcion de Acuna.

The mission of San José alluded to above, under another name, and an excellent picture of which we give, deserves a more extended notice.

It was first founded on the Rio Grande in 1703. Five years afterward it was moved to a place called San Ildephonso. In 1710 it was taken back to the Rio Grande, where it continued under the charge of good Father José de Soto until 1718, when it was removed to the west bank of the San Pedro, about a mile from the main plaza of the present city of San Antonio. From this time it was called San Antonio de Valero. Here it continued until 1722, when, for better protection against the Indians, it was removed with the post to the San Antonio River. It remained here, and in 1744, the walls of the church of the Alamo,* which were never finished, were erected. This chapel was used in connection with the mission of San Antonio de Valero, called by some, San José del Alamo, until the latter part of the eighteenth century, when all the missions in Texas were secularized, or subordinated to the Spanish civil authorities.

The missions of Texas yet stand, and will for many centuries continue to speak from their crumbling ruins, in trumpet tongues, of the self-sacrificing labors and devotion of the Franciscan missionaries, whose efforts to convert the native Indians to Christianity challenge the highest admiration.

HISTORICAL NOTES

Collected from the Registers of the old Mission of San Antonio Valero,† now called the Alamo, by F. Geraud, Esq., San Antonio.

(From Yoakum's Texas.)

From the heading of the register of baptisms delivered over by Fra. José Francisco Lopez (the last of the Franciscans remaining at the Alamo, and entitled *parroes* or parish priests of the pueblo or village de San Antonio de Valero,) to Gavino Valdez, curate of the Villa de San Fernando y Presidio de San Antonio de Bexar—which delivery was made by an order of the Bishop

* Alamo means Poplar tree.

† This mission was founded in the year 1703, in the Cienega of the Rio Grande, under the invocation of San Francisco Solano. From this place it was removed to the neighborhood called San Ildephonso, having that invocation. Thence it was moved once more to the Rio Grande, where it had the name San José. Finally it was transplanted to the river San Antonio, where it now is under the name of San Antonio de Valero.

MISSION OF SAN JOSE.

To face p. 18.

of Monterey, dated January 2, 1793—we learn that the mission located finally where the Alamo now stands was several times removed before it was settled on the San Antonio River.

The following is the translation of the heading referred to : " Book in which are set down the Baptisms of the Indians of this Mission of San Antonio de Valero, situated on the bank of the river of San Antonio, in the government of this province of Texas, and New Philippines, belonging to the Apostolic College of Propaganda Fidei, of the most Holy Cross of the City of Santiago de Queretaro."

II.

THE NAME TEXAS.

(Texas Almanac, 1872.)

IN the correspondence between John Quincy Adams, Secretary of State, and Don Onis, the Spanish minister, on the question of the boundary line between Louisiana and the Spanish provinces, Don Onis, in order to prove the prior possession of Spain, gives the official report of a Spanish officer who took possession of the country (west, I believe,) on Matagorda Bay. He stated that he met a tribe of Indians soon after his arrival, who saluted him with " Tehas," which in their language meant friendly. This is doubtless the true meaning of the word. The correspondence is to be found in the state papers published by Congress.

(From "A Brief History of Texas.")

How and when Texas received its present name, has been a subject of controversy and speculation. Some writers assert that it was so called because its supposed discoverer found the dwellings of the inhabitants to have roofs, which in the Spanish language are called *tejas* or *texas*, and hence the name ; but if this be the true reason, then Mexico should also have been called Texas, because Jean de Grijalva, who discovered it, found these houses not only with roofs, but otherwise in point of construction and comfort compared so favorably with those in Spain at the time, that he called the newly discovered country New Spain. Others seem to find a solution of the difficulty in the assumption that the word *tecas*, in the language of the aborigines meant friends, with which expression they are said to have hailed La Salle and his companions ; but he and those of his followers who perished at their hands had rather a rough demonstration of the fact. There is another hypothesis, which is probably the true one, and that is, that *tecas* was used as an affix to the names of many Indian provinces or countries, to denote their inhabitants ; as, for instance, those of Tlaxcalla were called Tlax-caltecas ; those of Cholula, Cholutecas ; those of Cuitlahuac, Cuitlachtecas. The territory now called Texas was known to the Spanish missionaries in 1524, as Mixtecapan, and its inhabitants as Mixtecas: these were the descendants of Mixtecatl, the fifth of the six sons of Iztac Mixtecatl, the reputed progenitor of the inhabitants of Mexico at the time of its conquest by Cortes. By a slight mistake in copying the word Mixtecas, and using a small instead of a capital M, by the Spaniards, in the beginning of the seventeenth century (who it is well known paid but little attention to the use of capital letters in their writings), it was probably written tastecas in the old manuscript in San Antonio, by which expression some tribes of Texas Indians were then known, and thus Texas acquired its name, (See Torquemada's Monarquia Indiana, Madrid, 1723.)

Teja (Spanish) means Roof-tile ; Tejas, plural, would be Roof-tiles ; and this is the way Spanish writers spell the word Texas. Whether the name Texas has any reference to this is a question for the reader to investigate.

III.

GEOGRAPHY OF TEXAS.

AREA.—Texas contains about 274,366 * square miles of territory.

LOCATION.—Texas is bounded on the north and west by the Indian Territory, New Mexico, and Mexico ; and on the south and east by the Gulf of Mexico and Louisiana.

TOPOGRAPHY.—Texas is naturally divided into three parts, each differing from the other.

First—The sea-board extending from the Sabine to the Rio Grande, and running inland sixty to one hundred miles.

Second—The uplands, or Middle Texas. This constitutes the great part of the State. It is from three to six hundred feet above the level of the sea, and is well diversified with hills and valleys, prairies and forests.

Third—The great plains or table-lands stretching away to the northwest. The plains are occasionally broken with lofty mountains upon the upper waters of the Pecos, the Brazos, and Red rivers.

* From data obtained at the General Land Office. It is impossible to be exact in this particular, but the area of Texas is not far from these figures.

The first and second of these divisions of Texas cannot be excelled for fertility of soil, and scarcely for salubrity of climate.

The third is still the abode of the Indian and the buffalo.

PRINCIPAL PRODUCTS.—The chief products of the soil in Texas are cotton and the cereals. Sugar and tobacco are also raised to considerable extent.

CATTLE AND HORSES.—In Western Texas, the raising of cattle and horses, for the Northern markets, constitutes a very important and lucrative branch of industry. Scores of thousands of beef cattle are annually driven from Texas to Kansas and Missouri ; and while the mighty prairies continue to supply such cheap and abundant pasturage, this trade is not likely to diminish.

MINERALS AND METALS.—Recent examinations have proved, beyond a doubt, the fact that Texas is rich in several of the most valuable ores. Iron abounds in Eastern Texas, and iron, lead, and silver is found in Llano, Burnet, and other counties. Copper of a rich quality exists abundantly in the northwest, and coal-fields of considerable extent have lately been opened.

MINERAL WATERS.—A number of mineral springs possessing valuable medicinal properties have long since been found in Texas. Among the most noted of these are the Sour Lake and wells in Hardin County, and the Sulphur Springs in Lampasas County.

The following is an analysis of the Lampasas Springs, made by the author of this book, in 1855 :

There are two principal springs—Hancock's, or the Great Boiling Spring, and Burleson's, or the Lower Spring.

The former contains in one wine-pint : sulphuretted hydrogen, $2\frac{1}{2}$ cubic inches ; carbonic acid, amount undetermined ; common salt, 7 grains ; carbonate of lime, 2 grains ; carbonate of magnesia, 1 grain. The latter, or Burleson's contains in one wine-pint : sulphuretted hydrogen, 4 cubic inches ; carbonic acid, amount undetermined ; common salt, 32 grains ; carbonate of lime, 3 grains ; carbonate magnesia, $1\frac{1}{2}$ grains. The temperature of the water is 70 degrees Fahrenheit.

PRINCIPAL TOWNS.—The largest towns in Texas are Galveston (upon the eastern part of the island of that name), Houston (at the head of Buffalo Bayou), Jefferson (in Marion Co.), San Antonio (in Bexar Co.), and Austin (in Travis Co.).

OLDEST TOWNS.—The oldest towns in Texas are San Antonio, first settled in 1692 by the Spanish Catholics ; Goliad, or La Bahia, as it was first called ; and Nacogdoches.

OLDEST AMERICAN TOWNS.—Among the oldest American towns in Texas are San Felipe, Liberty, Brazoria, Columbia, and Washington.

POPULATION.—The population of Texas was—

In 1820,	about	20,000.	In 1850, census	212,592.
" 1830,	"	25,000.	" 1860, "	601,039.
" 1836,	"	52,000.	" 1870, "	818,579.
" 1840,	"	60,000.	" 1873, estimated *over one million.*

CLIMATE.—The climate of Texas is generally uniform, pleasant, and healthy. A meteorological record kept at Austin for about seventeen years, by Professor J. Van Nostrand, shows an average of about 88° in summer, and 46° in winter ; and an annual rain-fall of 33 inches during same time.

PRINCIPAL RIVERS.—The principal rivers of Texas are, the Sabine, on the east; the Trinity,* the Brazos,† the Colorado,‡ the Guadaloupe,§ the San Antonio, and the Rio Grande,‖ on the west.

The three first flow in a southerly course, and empty into the Gulf of Mexico. They are partially navigable. The Colorado takes its rise from springs in the northwestern part of the State, flows for about four hundred miles through the central portion, and empties into Matagorda Bay. The Guadaloupe is a clear and rapid stream similar to the Colorado, but smaller. The San Antonio takes its rise from springs four or five miles above the city of San Antonio, and flows in a limpid current toward the Gulf, receiving in its course the Medina, and then uniting with the Guadaloupe above its mouth. The Rio Grande is the western boundary of Texas. The rivers of western Texas on account of their rapid currents are not navigable, except the Rio Grande, which is navigable for light-draft boats for about 250 miles.

RAILROADS.—Texas has now in operation about 1000 miles of railway. The following grand trunk railways are now being, or will soon be, constructed, and when completed will open Texas to free communication with all parts of the continent. Several other roads have also been chartered and are now being built. The railroads of Texas have generally been munificiently endowed by the State, which has given liberally of its public domain and loaned its money to create these great arteries of commerce and travel. The Houston and Great Northern Railroad ; the Houston and Texas Central

---

* *Trinity* means *three in one*, so called from the three forks of this river, which unite to form the main stream.

† *Brazos* means *arms ;* on the old map called Brazos de Dios, *arms of God.*

‡ *Colorado* means *red*, and is so named from the color which the water of this stream assumes during a freshet. The color is imparted by the soil through which it flows.

§ *Guadaloupe* means *Wolf River*, from *Guada* (Arabic) *river*, and *Lupus* (Latin) *wolf.*

‖ *Rio Grande,* meaning *Grand River.* This stream had much more appropriately been called long river, than grand river.

Railroad; the Southern Pacific Railroad; the International Railroad; The Missouri, Kansas and Texas Railroad.

Texas has granted to railroads in all more than 8,000,000 acres of land.*

UNAPPROPRIATED DOMAIN.—Texas has still about 89,000,000 acres of vacant and unappropriated land.

————▸◂————

IV.

A COMPEND OF TEXAS HISTORY.]

BEFORE ANNEXATION.

THE first organization in Texas, in opposition to Santa Anna, was the *General Consultation,* which met at San Felipe de Austin on the 3d day of November, 1835. Of this body, Dr. Branch T. Archer was elected president, and P. B. Dexter, secretary. This consultation established a provisional government, and elected the following officers, viz: Henry Smith, governor, James W. Robinson, lieutenant-governor, Sam Houston, commander-in-chief, and Branch T. Archer, Stephen F. Austin, and W. H. Wharton, commissioners to the United States. This consultation adjourned on the 14th of November, 1835, on which day the provisional government went into operation. On the 2d day of March, 1836, a convention met at Washington on the Brazos, for the purpose of declaring the independence of Texas, and establishing a permanent government. Of this convention, Richard Ellis was elected president, and H. S. Kimble, secretary. A declaration of independence was adopted, and the Republic of Texas established. A constitution was framed, and a government ad interim established, until an election could take place under the constitution. David G. Burnett was president, and Lorenzo de Zavalla, vice-president of the government ad interim. The first congress assembled on the 3d day of October, 1836, and on the 22d day of October, 1836, a constitutional government for Texas was established, by the inauguration of General Sam Houston, president, and M. B. Lamar, vice-president. Houston's first administration continued until December 10, 1838, when M. B. Lamar was inaugurated president, and David G. Burnett, vice-president. On the 13th day of December, 1841, Houston's second administration commenced, Gen. Ed. Burleson being vice-president. On the 9th day of December, 1844, Dr. Anson Jones was inaugurated president, and K. L. Anderson, vice-president of Texas.

* From the last report of the Commission of the General Land Office.

On the 23d day of June, 1845, the Congress of Texas approved the joint resolution of annexation which had passed the Congress of the United States ; and on the 4th of July following, a convention met at Austin, Texas, which framed and adopted· a state constitution, which being ratified by the people, the state government went into operation a few months later.

AFTER ANNEXATION.

First Governor of Texas.	J. P. Henderson.	Inaugurated Feb. 19, 1846.
Second " "	George T. Wood.	1847 to 1849
Third " "	P. Hansboro Bell.	1849 " 1853, two terms.
Fourth " "	E. M. Pease.	1853 " 1857, two terms.
Fifth " "	H. R. Runnels.	1857 " 1859
Sixth " "	Sam Houston.	1859 " 1861
Seventh " "	Edward Clark.	A few months in 1861.
Eighth " "	F. R. Lubbock.	1861 to 1863
Ninth " "	P. Murrah.	1863 " 1865
Tenth " ."	A. J. Hamilton.	1865 " 1866
Eleventh " "	J. W. Throckmorton.	1866 " 1867
Twelfth " "	E. M. Pease.	1867 " 1870
Thirteenth " "	E. J. Davis.	1870 " 1874
Fourteenth " "	Richard Coke.	1874 —

V.

THE ANAHUAC OR OPENING CAMPAIGN OF THE TEXAS REVOLUTION.

BY COL. F. W. JOHNSON.

(Texas Almanac, 1859.)

I HAVE read with much care and interest Dr. N. D. Labadie's manuscript in relation to the causes which led to open resistance in 1832, and fully concur in his statement of facts and circumstances leading to the first outbreak of hostilities. The usurpation of civil power and the arbitrary conduct of Colonel Bradburn in deposing the Alcalde (Hugh B. Johnson) and the members of the Ayuntamiento of the municipality of Liberty, and substituting in their stead, creatures of his own, seizing, and appropriating to his own use, private property, arresting and imprisoning, without cause, citizens who claimed a trial before the civil authorities of the Jurisdiction, if guilty of any offense, are a few of many causes which might be enumerated, and led to resistance. Among the most prominent citizens arrested and held in prison by Bradburn, were William B. Travis, Patrick C. Jack, Monroe Edwards, and Samuel T. Allen.

William H. Jack, of San Felipe de Austin, on learning that his brother Patrick C., together with others, had been arrested and imprisoned by order of Colonel Bradburn, commandant at the post of Anahuac, proceeded to that place and waited on Colonel Bradburn for the purpose of ascertaining what, if any, offence had been committed by his brother and the other prisoners and to obtain for them a trial before the civil authorities, or their release. In vain did he urge the necessity and justice of their immediate release or a trial before the proper authorities of the Jurisdiction. No argument that Jack was master of, had the least effect upon this petty tyrant, who with great effrontery informed Jack that the prisoners would be sent to Vera Cruz and tried by à military court. Mortified and pained to think that he could not release, nor get a trial for the prisoners, nor in any way better their painful situation, he returned to his home in San Felipe, determined to make an appeal to the people of Austin's Colony. On his arrival at home he called together a few friends, and informed them of the result of his visit to Bradburn, and his determination to appeal to the people. In this his friends agreed with him. The most prominent citizens of the place were consulted, and a plan of operations soon agreed upon: Colonel William Pettus and William H. Jack were to proceed to the settlements of Fort Bend, Brazoria, etc. Robert M. Williamson was to visit the settlements of Mill Creek, Coles on the Goliad road and Washington, and give notice to the people of the wrongs and outrages committed by Bradburn, and solicit them to aid in subjecting the military tyrant to the civil authorities of the country. Benjamin Tennell and Francis W. Johnson were to visit the settlements on Spring Creek, Buffalo Bayou, San Jacinto and Trinity, as high up as Liberty. These arrangements being completed, Horatio Chrisman, Esq., first constitutional Alcalde of the Jurisdiction of Austin, was informed of what had been done. Each one who had volunteered to rally the people proceeded on their routes. Wherever they went they were greeted, and the people responded to the call. Tennell and Johnson were the first to arrive at Liberty and communicate what was being done in Austin's Colony and to solicit their coöperation. They joyously joined us, and made common cause. After consulting the Alcalde—Hugh B. Johnson—and other citizens of Liberty, it was determined to meet at Minchey's, a few miles below Liberty, and there organize and concert such measures as the occasion required. As fast as the men from Austin's Colony arrived, they were directed to Minchey's, where all were abundantly supplied by the citizens.

Some two or three days after the arrival of Tennell and Johnson at Liberty, a respectable number of men assembled at Minchey's, where it was resolved that an armed force, composed of the citizens of Austin's Colony, and the Jurisdiction of Liberty, should march upon Anahuac, take up a position, appoint a committe to wait on Colonel Bradburn, and inform him of the object of the assemblage of the citizens before that place. We organized by electing Francis W. Johnson 1st, Warren D. C. Hall 2d, and Thomas H. Bradley 3d, in command. This over, and necessary measures for subsisting the force, the troops were formed and took up the line of march for Anahuac. Sergeant Blackman with sixteen men under the direction of Robert M. Williamson, formed the advance. Flankers were thrown out on each side. Thus we moved forward. We had not marched more than half the distance to Turtle Bayou when the advance came upon a party of Mexican cavalry. So completely were they surprised that not a gun was fired. We halted and encamped on the west side of Turtle Bayou—White's crossing. While posting the guard, a miscreant by the name of Haden—a creature of John M. Smith—shot and instantly killed Sergeant Blackman, and escaped under cover of night.

The next morning we resumed our march, and entered Anahuac at or before noon. As soon, thereafter, as our little force was properly posted, a committee, composed of Alcaldes Austin and Johnson, G. B. McKinstry, H. K. Lewis, and Francis W. Johnson, was appointed, and proceeded to the Fort. They were conducted, through the guard, to the quarters of Colonel Bradburn, and made known to him the object of their visit. The committee enforced their demand by every argument they were masters of. Bradburn, after being driven to the wall by argument, finally informed the committee that Colonel Souverin was the commander of the garrison. This gentleman, who had taken part in the conference, now for the first time is pointed out as the commanding officer. Not being able to effect any thing peaceably, we informed Colonels Bradburn and Souverin that we would try what virtue there was in force, made our bows and returned to our camp, where we reported the result of our mission.

Thus matters remained until the following day, when some skirmishing took place, but resulted in no loss or injury. Several attempts were made to draw the enemy out, but without success. On the third day it was determined to send a detachment to take a position opposite and within rifle-shot of the fort. For this purpose the ground was examined and found practicable. By marching under the river bank, the detachment would be covered, and reach the position assigned. The bank at that point being high, completely covered the detachment from the fire of the fort. While arrangements were being made with this view, John A. Williams solicited an interview, which was granted. After expressing his regret at the turn things had taken, he stated that he had accompanied Colonel Souverin from Matamoras ; that he had had frequent conversations with him ; and that he was devoted to the cause espoused by Santa Anna, and was using his influence with the garrison at Anahuac to declare for Santa Anna ; that he had been assured by Colonel Souverin that he was disposed to accommodate the citizens, and that present difficulties could be amicably and satisfactorily arranged through commissioners. Williams, although strongly suspected of being favorable to Bradburn, manifested such zeal and honesty that the Texans agreed to appoint commissioners to meet those of the Fort at a time and place agreed upon (Wm. Hardin's). The commissioners on our part were Captains John Austin, Hugh B. Johnson, and Wyly Martin. Terms having been agreed upon, they were made known to the command. They were not such as had been expected, and gave a good deal of dissatisfaction on account of the want of confidence in Mexican faith. Captain Martin assured the command that he had the utmost confidence in their good faith ; that no one wearing an epaulet would be base enough to forfeit his plighted honor. This reconciled most of the men. The command was then ordered to march to Taylor White's, on Turtle Bayou, and there await the arrival of the commissioners and the Texan prisoners. A small party—from fifteen to thirty—remained with the commissioners. At an early hour the next day, firing was heard in the direction of Anahuac, and very soon after, an express arrived and informed us that the Mexicans had refused to comply with the terms agreed upon, and were marching out to attack the small party in Anahuac. The command was immediately put under marching order, and had advanced within some two miles when they were met by the commissioners and their small party retreating in good order.

The enemy being in position, and occupying a piece of woodland, and with artillery to cover their lines, it was deemed prudent not to attack them under such disadvantageous circumstances. The command was faced about and marched back to Turtle Bayou. After consulation, a meeting was called and its object stated, whereupon a committee was appointed to draw up a preamble and resolutions declaratory of the wrongs and abuses committed by the chief magistrate of the nation and his minions, the military ; and also of the determination of Texas to repel further aggressions by the military, and to maintain their rights under the constitution of 1824. The committee having performed this duty, the preamble and resolutions were unanimously adopted by the meeting. Thus this little band boldly proclaimed their rights, and a determination to defend them, and called upon all Texas to join them.

In the evening of the same day we marched up to Dunman's. Here it was determined that Captain John Austin, Geo. B. McKinstry, and others, should proceed to Brazoria, for the purpose of raising men and getting artillery and munitions, all of which were to be transported by water, and landed at some suitable point near Anahuac. Colonel William Pettus and Robert M. Williamson were sent to San Felipe, for the purpose of raising and forwarding men. In the meantime, the small force left in the field, were to occupy such positions as would enable us to watch the movements of the enemy, and, if occasion offered, to strike a blow. From Dunman's we took a position at Mosses Spring, where, in a few days after, we were joined by Captain Abner Kuykendall and his company, of from forty to sixty men from Austin's Colony. Small parties were daily arriving. Thus reinforced, we marched forward again, and took up a position at Dunman's, where we were further reënforced by parties from Austin's Colony, and from Bevil's Settlement, on the Neches. Thus again we were enabled to resume offensive measures, and only awaited the arrival of artillery to march upon Anahuac. Under this state of things, and at this point, we were visited by commissioners from the camp of Colonel Piedras, who had marched with a part of his forces, from Nacogdoches, on a call from Colonel Bradburn. The conference with the commissioners resulted in nothing more than the information that Colonel Piedras was encamped some twenty miles north of Liberty. The commissioners were informed of our objects and wishes, and an agreement to meet again, on a day named, at James Martin's, near Liberty.

With the enemy in our front and rear, it was determined to take up a stronger position, and, accordingly, we were marched to Mosses Spring. On the day appointed, the commissioners of Piedras were met at Martin's. Not being able to agree upon anything satisfactory and definite, the commissioners were directed to say to Colonel Piedras that we would meet him at or near his camp on a certain day, but that, in the meantime, he was not to move forward or backward, as in either event it would be held hostile, and and put an end to further negotiation.

With a view to prevent a junction of the two forces, it was determined to take up a position near Martin's, where we could more effectually prevent such a union, and, if need be, fight them in detail. Before leaving Mosses we received news, by express, of the battle of Velasco.

On the day appointed, Francis W. Johnson, Captain Randal Jones, and James Lindsay, as commissioners, and Captain Francis Adams, as interpreter, met Colonel Piedras and his commissioners near their camp. The conference was conducted with all that politeness and courtesy characteristic of the Mexican gentleman. We were not long in agreeing on terms, which were, that the prisoners should at once be released and delivered over to the Alcalde of Liberty ; that Bradburn should be put under arrest, and the command given to the next senior officer. Colonel Piedras accompanied us, that evening, to Captain George Orr's, where he spent the night.

The next morning, Colonel Piedras, accompanied by the Alcalde, Hugh B. Johnson, passed our encampment. Being notified of their approach, the troops were drawn up in line and saluted them. In the evening of that day, they arrived at Anahuac, where, the next morning, he was to release and turn over the Texan prisoners to the Alcalde. Bradburn was put under arrest soon after the arrival of Colonel Piedras. During the night an attempt, it is believed, was made on the life of the Alcalde and William Hardin by some of Bradburn's creatures. Johnson escaped with no clothing or covering but pants, shirt, and socks, and arrived at our camp at an early hour in the morning. Hardin arrived later on the same day. The arrival of these two men and under the circumstances, created great excitement and distrust. A company, under Captain Peyton R. Splane, was ordered out on the road to Anahuac, to watch the movements of the enemy, and another detachment in the direction of Piedras' camp, with orders to report at the camp to be established on the west side of Trinity, near Duncan's Ferry. The reports, made the following day, show how groundless were the excitement and fears of the preceding day. Colonel Piedras complied, to the letter, with his agreement, and the Texan prisoners, once more admitted to enjoy the free air and light of heaven, were greeted by their countrymen as they wended their way to Martin's.

Thus ended the Anahuac campaign, and the citizen soldiers returned to their respective homes.   Yours respectfully,   F. W. JOHNSON.

[We should here remark, that, at Colonel Johnson's request, we have submitted the above account, given by him, to several of those who participated in that first campaign, that subsequently led to the Texas revolution, and have received the fullest assurance that the facts are all correctly stated. We take pleasure in adding that we have the promise of Colonel Johnson that he will furnish us, for a subsequent number of our Almanac, a more full and detailed account, not only of all the events of the Anahuac campaign, but of other subsequent campaigns in which he participated.—*Ed. Texas Almanac.*]

VI.

BATTLE OF VELASCO IN 1832.—FULL PARTICULARS.

BY A PARTICIPANT.

(From the Texas Almanac, 1872.)

FOR over two years previous to the battle of Velasco, the Mexican authorities had been engaged in surrounding the colonists with a cordon of military posts, but in so secret and cautious a manner as not to arouse suspicion
or lead the colonists to suspect their real intention.

In addition to the old forts at Bexar and La Bahia, they had erected one
on the Brazos, above the settlements, called Tenoxtitlan, and at Nacogdoches ; one at Anahuac, and one at Velasco. To each of these were sent,
alternately, reinforcements in small numbers. Early in 1832, Colonel Bradburn, in command at Anahuac, openly developed the object of these military
posts by the arrest and imprisonment of W. B. Travis, Patrick C. Jack, and
Munroe Edwards, and that too upon the most frivolous pretexts. The news
of this act of tyranny soon spread through the settlements on the Trinity
and Brazos, producing great excitement. Meetings were held at San Felipe,
Brazoria, and at other points on the Trinity.

In the meeting at Brazoria it was thought to be unsafe for the men to
leave their families in a defenseless condition, with the avowed intention of
attacking Bradburn, at Anahuac, while Ugartichea was strongly fortified at
Velasco, with a garrison of about one hundred and fifty soldiers, who might
at any moment, in order to save Bradburn, fall upon the defenseless settlements, and destroy them. Under such circumstances, prudence dictated the
necessity of an understanding with Ugartichea, and to obtain from him a
pledge that he would neither interrupt the settlements, nor send reinforcements to Bradburn to assist him to repel the intended attack upon him ; but
if a satisfactory pledge could not be obtained from him, to attack him at
once and drive him from Velasco, and then unite in the attack on Anahuac.
He gave the pledge, and so for the time was not interrupted.

This arrangement being satisfactory, a company was soon raised to proceed, with all possible despatch, for Anahuac. The names still remembered
of that small band are—John Austin, W. D. C. Hall, William S. Hall,
Thomas Chadowin, and William J. Russell, the latter the only survivor.

By the time this company reached the Trinity, they were joined by others.
Of these were Wyley Martin, F. W. Johnson, and R. M. Williamson ; soon
after this, and upon reaching the immediate vicinity of Anahuac, an organi-

zation was had, and F. W. Johnson was elected captain, and W. D. C. Hall first lieutenant. Captain Johnson took possession of an old barrack, which Bradburn occupied before moving into his new brick fort, and at once began to operate, and that too in a manner that he was not prepared for. On one occasion two of Captain Johnson's men, William J. Russell and a man by the name of Morrison, crawled over an open prairie for some two hundred yards to a point very near the fort, where they discovered two Mexican soldiers standing together under a lone tree very near the fort. These two men approached to about forty yards of the soldiers, and, after taking a careful aim, both fired—Russell with a long, heavy musket, charged with fifteen heavy buckshot, and Morrison with a rifle—and then and there, in the month of May, 1832, the germ of liberty for Texas was planted; then and there the first blood was spilt, and as it is a historical fact, it may not be improper to state that William J. Russell and —— Morrison are entitled to whatever credit may attach to this act. Captain Johnson having no means of a direct assault, or an assault on the fort, moved his command up to Turtle Bayou, about six miles from Anahuac, and there it was that the meeting was had, not on the 13th of June, 1831, as per Yoakum, but in the month of May, 1832. In this meeting it was decided to send to Brazoria for reinforcements, and to get some cannon, not from Velasco, as per Yoakum, but a few small pieces that were known to be at Brazoria. John Austin and William J. Russell were selected for that purpose, and started immediately.

On arriving at Brazoria, they found that Ugartichea had broken his pledge by sending assistance to Bradburn, and in addition had created fears of violence among the citizens. A meeting was called immediately, when it was determined to attack Velasco, and a call for volunteers was made for that purpose, intending, so soon as Velasco was disposed of, to raise recruits and return to Anahuac, if necessary; but by the time this was accomplished, Bradburn had given up his prisoners and abandoned the fort. Colonel Piedras had been compelled to abandon Nacogdoches, and retired toward Bexar; and the garrison at Tenoxtitlan left for the same point, and so all these matters were out of the way for the time being. Volunteers for the attack on Velasco soon reached an amount believed to be sufficient, but not one of whom had ever been in a battle. An organization was effected, placing John Austin in command, and William J. Russell second in command, and to the immediate command, of a fine large schooner, then lying at mooring (Yoakum says, a schooner lying aground above the post was dislodged and set afloat, and from whence he derived this information it would be difficult to tell), which belonged to Captain John G. Rowland. This gentlemen had engaged in the trade to Texas, and built this vessel for that purpose, and named her Brazoria.

At this juncture of time, Captain Rowland was absent on a trip to San Felipe, and the vessel was pressed for the attack on Velasco and used for that purpose. Volunteers were called for to man the vessel, and a sufficient number was soon obtained ; but of them all there were but two besides the captain who knew one rope from another. The mate of the vessel under Captain Rowland, a Northern man, offered his services to Captain Russell, so far as to assist in "working" her down to a point near the post, with the understanding that he was not to be called on to take any part in the battle, giving as a reason that he was a poor man with a large family dependent on him for support.

This was agreed to, and his services were very valuable. There were three small pieces of cannon at Brazoria, which were put on board the vessel, and one on board belonging to her, and with these a move was made down the river for the fort, some twenty-five or thirty miles distant. Captain Austin proceeded by land with the main force. The two divisions met at what was known as Calvert's Labor, on the river about two miles above the fort, where final preparations were made for the attack.

The plan and structure of the fort were well understood, of circular form, built of logs and sand, with strong stakes, sharpened, and placed close together, all around the embankment ; in the center stood a bastion, in height considerably above the outer wall, on the top of which was mounted a long nine-pounder, worked on a pivot, and around which, on the top of the bastion, was a parapet wall made of wood, about two feet in height. This parapet, while affording protection to the men working the gun, prevented the depression of the gun so as to operate on any object in close proximity to the fort. All this was well known to the attacking party, and corresponding arrangements were made to save them from the destructive effects of this bastion gun. In order to do this, a lot of thick, heavy plank was procured from William H. Wharton, which were strongly battened together, in width about four feet, and which, it was believed, would afford protection against any arms in the fort except the bastion gun. These, together with such tools as were necessary for ditching and forming embankments, etc., were carried by hand.

Finally, just at night, 25th of June, 1832, a general move was made, with the understanding between the principal officers that, at a point just below the mouth of East-Union Bayou, a final interview was to be had. To this end, after bringing the vessel to anchor at the point proposed, the captain went on shore for the contemplated interview. The plan of attack was : The vessel should take position as near as possible to the fort, and open and keep up a fire on it, so as to direct the attention of the garrison from the point where the main attack was to be made ; this was accomplished after great labor and risk, owing to a strong south-easterly wind and rapid current, against both of which she had to contend. Auxiliary to this, and for a like purpose, Captain Henry Brown, with his company, took a position on the south-east side of the fort, and, concealed among the drift-wood, opened fire on the fort. From these two points—the schooner, and Captain Brown—so constant a fire was poured into the fort that they seemed to have no idea that anything else was in store for them. At the proper time, Captain Austin moved with his division, carrying the breastworks as above described, with tools, etc. Strict orders had been issued for every man to empty his gun during the march, and performing all necessary labor, all of which was carefully explained to the men, and that the most perfect silence should be observed.

He reached the point proposed, thirty-one yards from the fort, at which it was well known the bastion gun could not be made to bear upon them.

The breastworks were placed as desired, which formed a line of about sixty feet, and all went cheerfully to work making a ditch, and throwing up an embankment behind and against the wooden works, feeling perfectly confident that before daylight they would be strongly fortified, at which time— daylight—and not before, the fire was to open on the fort.

The work progressed with entire satisfaction, and was well-nigh completed, with no suspicion in the fort of the danger that awaited them from this point, until just about midnight, when a man, by name Edward Robinson, who had contrary to orders kept the charge in his gun, caught it up and fired at the fort. In a moment a blaze of fire opened upon that position. It was well known by the attacking party that there was mounted on the wall of the fort a small piece of artillery facing the point of their approach, but it was believed that the wooden breastwork was of sufficient thickness to protect those behind them. This proved quite a mistake. Very much damage was done by this small gun, the balls often passing through the planks, inflicting death or wounds. The man Robinson, who gave the alarm, was the first man killed.

There was but little firing from the attacking party until after daylight. So soon, however, as it was light enough to use the rifle, the fire was so destructive that but little return was made from the fort. The contest continued until about eight o'clock A. M., 26th June, when a very heavy fall of rain at once put a stop to all operations from that point, and nothing but a retreat could save them, leaving the dead, seven in number, where they fell. All the wounded succeeded in getting off, and, surprising to tell, not one of the retreating party was touched by the grape and canister shot that fell thick and fast among them, so soon as the bastion gun could bear upon them.

A number of the retreating party, responding to the call of Captain Russell, who had climbed nearly to the mast-head that he might be the better heard, came on board the vessel; among whom were Captain Austin and Henry Smith, the latter having an ugly but not dangerous wound in the head. These were all properly cared for, there being a physician and stores on board the vessel.

Very little use was made of the artillery after daylight, as by that time the ammunition for them was well-nigh exhausted; enough was reserved to protect her from an assault should this be attempted from the fort, it being impossible to moor her, as during the night her moorings had been shot away, and she had drifted on the bank at full tide, where she lay hard upon the ground. A brisk and, no doubt, fatal fire was kept up, however, with rifles—the distance being only one hundred and sixty-nine yards from the schooner to the bastion gun in the fort—to assure the enemy that the contest was not yielded, notwithstanding the retreat, in a shattered condition, of the forces from the principal point of attack. The only serious damage done on board the vessel by the post was, that during the night a nine-pound shot passed through her side, striking the mate (who, as per agreement, had retired, as was supposed, to a place of safety) just between his shoulders, passing entirely through him. His death was instantaneous.

The rifle fire was continued from the vessel until ten A. M., when a white flag was hoisted in the fort. This was a welcome sight to those on board the vessel, and was readily responded to. Captain Austin, who was in the cabin enjoying a refreshing and much-needed sleep, was called to the deck. At this time two officers were seen approaching the vessel under a white flag.

Captain Austin dispatched William H. Wharton and William J. Russell to meet them, to communicate the terms of capitulation which had been agreed upon, if this was the desire or object of the flag of truce. Terms of capitulation were soon settled, ond the garrison allowed to return, and thus this initial movement against tyranny was rewarded by a most signal triumph, and that too at a comparatively small sacrifice. Not a soldier was left east of the San Antonio River, and the colonists were left to enjoy peace until the more important movements of 1835, which led to the independence of Texas.

NOTE.—A subscription was immediately circulated and a respectable amount of money was raised—the amount not remembered—and given to Captain Rowland, to be handed by him to the family of his mate, who was unfortunately killed on board the vessel.

INDIAN CHARGE.

To face p. 35.

VII.

THE CELEBRATED INDIAN FIGHT OF 1831.

(Compiled from Mrs. Holly's Texas.)

ON the 2d day of November, 1831, Rezin P. Bowie, James Bowie, David Buchanan, Robert Armstrong, Jesse Wallace, Mathew Doyle, Cephas Hamm, James Coriell, Thomas McCaslin, and two servant boys, Charles and Gonzales, set out from San Antonio to search for the old silver mines at the San Saba Mission. "On the nineteenth," says Rezin P. Bowie, whose narration we quote, "we fell in with two Comanche Indians, and a Mexican, who informed us that we were followed by one hundred and twenty-four Twowokana and Waco Indians, and forty Caddoes, who were determined to have our scalps. We were at this time within thirty miles of the old San Saba fort, to which place we determined to press forward the same day. Our horses' feet being sore, we did not reach the fort, and made choice of a cluster of live-oak, thirty or forty in number, as a camping place for the night. To the north of these trees was a thicket of oak bushes, and near by was a stream of water. The surrounding country was an open prairie. We were at this time six miles distant from the San Saba fort. We prepared ourselves for defense as well as we could, by clearing away the inside of the thicket, and going in there with our horses, thereby concealing ourselves, as well as having the protection of the dense undergrowth in case of sudden attack. Nothing occurred during the night, and early in the morning we were about resuming our journey, when we discovered the Indians following us, about two hundred yards distant. Instantly the cry was "All hands to arms!" We dismounted, and tied our horses to the trees. The Indians gave the war-whoop, and commenced stripping for the fight. The disparity in numbers was so enormous, one hundred and sixty to eleven, that I was deputed to go toward them and try to compromise rather than fight. Accordingly I, with Buchanan, proceeded to within forty yards of them, and in their own tongue asked them to send out their own chief to talk. They replied, "How de do," "How de do," and at once fired a volley of buckshot at us, which broke Buchanan's leg. This salutation I answered by a discharge from my double-barrel gun, and taking my companion's arm started back. They now opened a heavy fire upon us, and eight of their number pursued us to cut us off. When they were close upon us, our friends rushed forward and gave them a volley which killed four of their number, and sent the others howling back. We now discovered on a hill behind us, and within sixty yards, a large body of Indians, who with loud yells, opened a heavy fire upon us, their chief urging them to the charge in a loud voice. Our guns were at this moment all empty, except Mr. Hamm's. James Bowie cried out, "Who is loaded?" "I am," responded Mr. Hamm, and he fired at the chief, breaking his leg and killing his horse. He fell and was immediately picked up and borne off by his warriors. The whole body then retreated behind the hill out of sight. Again they approached, under the leadership of another chief, and opened upon us with bows and arrows, as well as bullets. This time, James Bowie's rifle brought their leader from his horse, and he was at once picked up and borne off by six or eight warriors. While defending ourselves from these attacks, a party of Caddoes had, by creeping along under the bank of the stream, succeeded in getting within forty yards of us, and poured a volley from their rifles, which severely wounded Doyle. As he cried out, McCaslin rushed to the spot, shouting "Where is the Indian that shot Doyle?" and at the same instant, while raising his gun, he fell mortally wounded. Armstrong cried out, "Where is the Indian that shot McCaslin?" and on the instant a bullet cut away a part of his gun-stock. Our enemies had now surrounded us, and the firing was general from behind rocks, trees, and bushes. We made a rush from the trees, and gained the thicket before spoken of. This afforded us partial shelter, as we could see our enemies through the undergrowth, while they could not see us. They now suffered severely from our rifles, losing four or five men at every discharge, while they could only fire at us at random, not seeing us. Finding they could not dislodge us from the thicket, they resorted to the alternative of burning us out. They set fire to the dry grass of the prairie to the windward of us. At this fearful moment we saw no chance of escape. The fire was coming toward us, impelled by a high wind, and leaping high in the air. What could we do? We must either be burned up alive, or rush into the prairie to be killed by the savages. At the same time their yells rent the air, and they fired volley after volley into our covert. We held a hurried consultation. Would they charge us under the smoke? The sparks were flying so thick that we could not open our powder-horns to load our pieces without being blown up. Should they charge upon us, we agreed to give them one volley, then, standing together, to fight them with our knives to the death. Our thicket was now so much scorched and thinned that it afforded little shelter; and getting together into the center of it, we hurriedly threw up around us our baggage, consisting of buffalo robes, blankets, saddles, loose rocks, brush, etc., and stood ready to sell our lives as dearly as possible. Meantime the fire had pretty much spent itself, and the Indians, seeing us alive and still ready for fight, drew off without range of our rifles, and held a council of war. During the respite thus afforded us, we busied ourselves in piling up every thing movable we could find, behind which to shelter ourselves. It was now night, and our enemies did not seem inclined to renew the engagement that day. During the night we heard them wailing over their dead, and at daylight, they shot a mortally wounded chief, which is a custom of theirs. Their dead and wounded they carried to a cave in a mountain a mile distant, and there deposited them. After this, though they hovered around us several days, they did not renew the battle. Our loss was one man killed and three wounded; theirs, as we afterwards ascertained, was eighty-two killed and wounded.

We remained in our fortification eight days, and then, the coast being clear, started for San Antonio, which we reached safely in twelve days.

VIII.

STORMING OF SAN ANTONIO DE BEXAR IN 1835.

(From the State Gazette, 1849.)

In December 1835, the Texan forces under General Burleson invested San Antonio, then held by General Cos, with twelve or fifteen hundred regular troops. It had been determined by the officers, after consultation, not to attempt carrying the place by storm against the great odds, but to go into winter quarters. At this juncture, a deserter from the town gave information that the place was not as strong as had been represented, and he advised an immediate attack. Colonel Ben Milam at once made a call for volunteers, in these words: "Who will go with old Ben Milam into San Antonio?" Officers and men, to the number of about four hundred, responded with a shout. General Burleson was requested to hold his position with the rest of the army until the result of the attack should be known, which he promised to do. The attacking force was divided into two companies, the first under command of Colonel Milam, assisted by Colonel Frank and Major Morris: the second under the command of Colonel F. W. Johnson, assisted by Dr. Grant and Colonel Austin. Arnold, Cook, and Maverick, and Deaf and John W. Smith acted as guides. Colonel Neil was sent to make a feint on the Alamo, which he did in good style, and then joined Milam in town. The attack was made early on the morning of the 5th of December, the signal being the discharge of a cannon near the Alamo. The enemy were unprepared. Their bugle sounded a wild alarm, and their drums beat hastily to arms. Silently cutting down the sentinels at their posts, the Texans entered the town amid the roar of artillery. Grape-shot and musket fell thick around them, doing but little execution, as they had got near enough to be sheltered by the walls of the houses. Having effected an entrance, the desperate fight was waged from house to house, by making holes through the soft adobe walls, and dislodging the enemy, driving him before them step by step, and street after street. We proceed in the language of the narrator.

"The order was given for fifteen or twenty men to take possession of the roofs of some houses ; ten succeeded in gaining the roof, but it was a hot berth, for the enemy poured a deadly fire upon us, killing and wounding several. In the main plaza, or public square, was a large church, in the cupola of which was a party of the enemy's sharp-shooters, who were picking us off. The weather being very cold, and a stiff norther blowing, we had great difficulty in loading our rifles, as the wind blew the powder away. At this moment, Deaf Smith, the spy of the army, the Harvey Birch of Texas, appeared upon the roof of the house where we were, but as he raised himself up and shouted to us the order to come on, he received a ball in the shoulder which disabled him. There were now but five men remaining of the ten who had mounted the roof, and finding that it was certain death to remain in that position, we attempted to return to the ground. We soon cut a hole through the roof large enough to admit of a man's body, and placing myself in my blanket, I requested my comrades to lower me through the opening into the house. Down I went, holding on tight, as I did not know how far it was to the bottom. It was an uncomfortable position to be in, but my friends did not leave me long to my apprehensions, for the blanket slipping through their grasp, down I went ten or twelve feet into the middle of a fire which was burning on a dirt floor, scattering embers and ashes in all directions. Jumping up, the first thing that met my gaze was a Mexican officer about to make an attack upon me, but jerking a pistol from my belt, I fired at him before my somewhat disordered faculties assured me that my foe was not an officer, but an officer's uniform hanging in such a position as to resemble one. My friends hearing the report, supposed it to be a gone case with me, but their fears being relieved, they joined me in the room below, from which the late occupant had evidently beat a hasty and undressed retreat." Then the fight continued from house to house, and from street to street, for five days, the loss of the assaulting party being comparatively small. On the 7th, the brave Milam, while leading a charge, was instantly killed by a rifle ball in the head, from a sharp-shooter. The impetuous Captain Thomas Wm. Ward, also, lost a leg in the fight. On the night of the 9th, a combined attack was made upon the priest's house and other buildings upon the public square, and after a determined resistance, the enemy retreated and fled precipitately across the river to the Alamo, where they afterward capitulated.

By this affair General Cos and twelve hundred Mexican troops, together with a large quantity of army stores and munitions of war, fell into our hands.

IX.

HISTORICAL REMINISCENCES.

MEMORIAL FROM THE TEXAS CONVENTION OF APRIL, 1833.

To the General Congress of the United Mexican States:

The inhabitants of Texas, by their representatives elect, in convention assembled, would respectfully approach the National Congress, and present this their Memorial, praying that the union which was established between Coahuila and Texas, whereby the two ancient provinces were incorporated into one free and independent State, under the name of Coahuila and Texas, may be dissolved, abrogated, and perpetually cease ; and that the inhabitants of Texas may be authorized to institute and establish a separate State govern-ment, which shall be in accordance with the Federal Constitution, and the Constitutive Act : and that the State so constituted shall be received and incorporated into the great Confederation of Mexico, on terms of equality with the other States of the Union.

To explain the grounds of this application, your memorialists would respectfully invite the attention of the General Congress to the following considerations :

The consolidation of the late Provinces of Coahuila and Texas was, in its nature, provisional, and in its intention, temporary.

The decree of the Sovereign Constituent Congress, bearing date May 7th, 1824, contemplates a separation, and guarantees to Texas the right of having a State government whenever she may be in a condition to ask for the same. That decree provides that " so soon as Texas shall be in a condition to figure as a State of itself, it shall inform Congress thereof for its resolution." The implication conveyed by this clause is plain and imperative, and vests in Texas as perfect a right as language can convey ; unless it can be presumed that the Sovereign Constituent Congress, composed of the venerable fathers of the Republic, designed to amuse the good people of Texas by an illusory and disingenuous promise, clothed in all the solemnity of a legislative enactment. Your memorialists have too high a veneration for the memory of that illustrious body to entertain any apprehensions that such a construction will be given to their acts by their patriotic successors, the present Congress of Mexico. The decree is dated anterior to the adoption of the Federal Constitution, and therefore, by a clear and fundamental principle of law and of justice, it obviates the necessity of recurring to the correspondent provision in the 50th article of that instrument, which requires " the ratification of three-fourths

of the other States" in order "to form a new State out of the limits of those
that already exist." And it assures to Texas, by all the sanctity of a legislative promise, in which the good faith of the Mexican nation is pledged, an
exemption from the delays and uncertainties that must result from such multiplied legislative discussion and resolution. To give to the Federal Constitution, which is the paramount law of the land, a retrospective operation, would
establish a precedent that might prove disastrous to the whole system of the
nation's jurisprudence, and subversive of the very foundations of the government.

The authority of precedent is decidedly in favor of the position which your
memorialists would respectfully sustain before the General Congress. By the
Constitutive Act, adopted 31st of January, 1824, Coahuila, New Leon, and
Texas were joined together, and denominated "the Internal Eastern State."
By a law passed by the Constituent Congress on the 7th of May, 1824, that
union was dissolved, and the province of New Leon was admitted into the
confederacy as an independent State. It is on the second article of this law
that the people of Texas now predicate their right to a similar admission.
The Constitutive Act above mentioned consolidated the late provinces of Chihuahua, Durango, and Mew Mexico, under the style of "the Internal Northern
State ;" and on the 22d day of May, 1824, a summary law decreed, that "Durango should form a state of the Mexican federation," and she was admitted
accordingly. The same privilege was extended to Chihuahua, by a decree of
the 6th of July of the same year. ·These conjunct provinces stood, at the
period of their separation, in precisely the same relation to the Federal government that Texas and Coahuila occupy now. They have been separated
and erected into free and independent States in a summary manner, and the
same right was guaranteed to Texas "whenever she should be in a condition
to accept it." The other case of Sonora and Sinaloa is materially variant in
matter of fact. Those provinces were originally incorporated into the confederation as one State, without any antecedent condition or guarantee ; and, at
the adoption of the present constitution, they justly became liable to all the
forms and restrictions prescribed in that national pact.

We would further suggest to the honorable Congress, that the present
juncture is peculiarly felicitous for dispensing with interminable and vexa-
tious forms. The Federal government is wisely employed in adopting important organic improvements, and aiming at a salutary renovation of the political system. The disasters of an eventful civil convulsion are yielding to the
regenerating influences of domestic concord and improved experience ; and
every department of the confederacy is open to such needful modifications as
the wisdom of the renewed Congress may designate. Texas solicits, as her
portion in the general reformation, to be disenthralled from her unhappy con-

nection with Coahuila ; and she avails herself of this opportunity, by means of her chosen delegates, who are the authorized organs of the people, to.communicate " to the General Congress " that she is now "in a situation to figure as a State of herself," and is profoundly solicitous that she may be permitted to do so.

The General Congress may possibly consider the mode of this communication as informal. To this suggestion, we would, with great deference, reply, that the events of the past year have not only violated the established forms and etiquette of the government, but have suspended, at least, its vital functions ; and it would appear exceedingly rigorous to exact from the inhabitants of Texas, living on a remote frontier of the republic, a minute conformity to unimportant punctilios. The ardent desire of the people is made known to the Congress through their select representatives, the most direct and unequivocal medium by which they can possibly be conveyed. And surely, the enlightened Congress will readily concur with us in the sentiment, that the wishes and the wants of the people form the best rule for legislative guidance. The people of Texas consider it not only an absolute right, but a most sacred and imperative duty to themselves and to the Mexican nation to represent their wants in a respectful manner to the general government; and to solicit the best remedy of which the nature of their grievances will admit. Should they utterly fail in this duty, and great and irremediable evils ensue, the people would have reason to reproach themselves alone ; and the General Congress, in whom the remedial power resides, would also have reason to censure their supineness and want of fidelity to the nation. Under this view, we trust the Congress will not regard with excessive severity any slight departure which the good people of Texas may, in this instance, have made from the ordinary formalities of the government.

And we would further suggest to the equitable consideration of the Federal Congress that, independent of and anterior to the express guarantee contained in the decree of the 7th of May, 1824, the right of having a separate State government was vested in and belonged to Texas, by the fact that she participated as a distinct province in the toils and sufferings by which the glorious emancipation of Mexico was achieved, and the present happy form of government was established. The subsequent union with Coahuila was a temporary compact, induced by a supposed expediency, arising from the want of an adequate population on the part of Texas " to figure as a State of itself." This inducement was transient in its nature, and the compact, like all similar agreements, is subject to abrogation at the will of either party, whenever the design of its creation is accomplished, or is ascertained to be impracticable. The obvious design of the union between Coahuila and Texas was, on one part at least, the more effectually to secure the peace, safety, and happiness of Texas.

That design has not been accomplished; and facts piled upon facts afford a melancholy surplusage of evidence that it is utterly impracticable. Texas never has, and never can, derive from the connection benefits in any wise commensurate with the evils she has sustained, and which are daily increasing in number and in magnitude.

But our reasons for desiring the proposed separation are more explicitly set forth in the subjoined remarks.

The history of Texas, from its earliest settlement to the present time, exhibits a series of practical neglect and indifference to all her peculiar interests on the part of each successive government which has had the control of her political destinies. The recollection of these things is calculated to excite the most pungent regrets for the past, and the most painful forebodings for the future. Under the several regal dominations, Texas presented the spectacle of a province profusely endowed by nature, abandoned and consigned to desolation by the profligate avariciousness of a distant despot. The tyrants of Spain regarded her only as a convenient barrier to the mines of the adjacent provinces; and the more waste and depopulated she was, the more effectually she answered their selfish and unprincipled purpose. Her agricultural resources were either unknown or esteemed of no value to a government anxious only to sustain its wasting magnificence by the silver and gold wrung from the prolific bosom of Mexico. To foster the agricultural interests of any portion of her splendid viceroyalty, or of her circumjacent conquests, was never the favorite policy of Spain. To have done so, would have nurtured in her remote dominions a hardy and industrious population of yeomanry— the peculiar dread of tyrants and the best assurance of a nation's independence.

It was natural, then, that the royal miscreants of Spain should regard Texas with indifference, if not with a decided and malignant aversion to her improvement. But it would be both unnatural and erroneous to attribute similar motives to the paternal government of independent, confederate, republican Mexico. She can have no interest adverse to the common weal, can feel no desire to depress the agricultural facilities of any portion of her common territory, and can entertain no disquieting jealousies that should prompt her to dread the increase or to mar the prosperity of any portion of her agricultural population. These are the best, the broadest, and the most durable basis of free institutions.

We must look to other causes, therefore, for the lamentable negligence that has hitherto been manifested toward the prosperity of Texas. The fact of such negligence is beyond controversy. The melancholy effects of it are apparent, both in her past and present condition. The cause must exist somewhere. We believe it is principally to be found in her political annexation to Coahuila. That conjunction was, in its origin, unnatural and constrained, and the longer it is continued the more disastrous it will prove. The two territories are disjunct in all their prominent respective relations. In point of locality, they approximate by a strip of sterile and useless territory, which must long remain a comparative wilderness, and present many serious embarrassments to that facility of intercourse which should always exist between the seat of government and its remote population. In respect to commerce, and its various and intricate relations, there is no communion of interests between them. The one is altogether *interior*—is consequently abstracted from all direct participation in maritime concerns, and is naturally indifferent, if not adverse, to any system of polity that is calculated to promote the diversified and momentous interests of commerce. The other is blest with many natural advantages for extensive commercial operations, which, if properly cultivated, would render valuable accessions to the national marine and a large increase to the national revenues. The importance of an efficient national marine is evinced not only by the history of other and older governments, but by the rich halo of glory which encircles the brief annals of the Mexican navy. In point of climate and of natural productions, the two territories are equally dissimilar. Coahuila is a pastoral and a mining country. Texas is characteristically an agricultural district. The occupations incident to these various intrinsic properties are equally various and distinct ; and a course of legislation that may be adapted to the encouragement of the habitual industry of the one district might present embarrassment and perplexity, and prove fatally deleterious to the prosperity of the other.

It is not needful, therefore, neither do we desire to attribute any sinister or invidious design to the legislative enactments or to the domestic economical policy of Coahuila, (whose ascendency in the joint councils of the State gives her an uncontrolled and exclusive power of legislation,) in order to ascertain the origin of the evils that afflict Texas, and which, if longer permitted to exist, must protract her feeble and dependent pupilage to a period coeval with such existence. Neither is it important to Texas, whether those evils have proceeded from a sinister policy in the predominant influences of Coahuila, or whether they are the certain results of a union that is naturally adverse to her interests. The effects are equally repugnant and injurious, whether emanating from the one or the other.

Bexar, the ancient capital of Texas, presents a faithful but gloomy portrait of her general want of protection and encouragement. Situated in a fertile, picturesque, and beautiful region, and established a century and a half ago, (within which period populous and magnificent cities have sprung into existence,) she exhibits only the decrepitude of age, the sad testimonials of the absence of that political guardianship which a wise government should always bestow upon the feebleness of its exposed frontier settlements. A hundred and seventeen years have elapsed since Goliad and Nacogdoches assumed the distinctive names of towns, and they are still entitled to the diminutive appellations of villages only. Other military and missionary establishments have been attempted, but, from the same defect of protection and encouragement, they have been swept away, and scarce a vestige remains to rescue their localities from oblivion.

We do not mean to attribute these specific disasters to the union with Coahuila ; for we know they transpired long anterior to the consummation of that union. But we do maintain that the same political causes, the same want of protection and encouragement, the same mal-organization and impotence of the local and minor faculties of the government, the same improvident indifference to the peculiar and vital interests of Texas, exist *now*, that operated then : and like causes will produce like effects, *ad infinitum.* Bexar is still exposed to the depredations of her ancient enemies, the insolent, vindictive, and faithless Comanches. Her citizens are still massacred, their cattle destroyed or driven away, and their very habitations threatened, by a tribe of erratic and undisciplined Indians, whose audacity has derived confidence from success, and whose long continued aggressions have invested them with a fictitious and excessive terror. Her schools are neglected, her churches desolate ; the sounds of human industry are almost hushed, and the voice of gladness and festivity is converted into wailing and lamentations, by the disheartening and multiplied evils which surround her defenseless population. Goliad is still kept in constant trepidation ; is paralyzed in all her efforts for improvement ; and is harassed on all her borders by the predatory incursions of the Wacoes, and other insignificant bands of savages, whom a well-organized local government would soon subdue or exterminate.

These are facts not of history merely, on which the imagination must dwell with an unavailing melancholy ; they are events of the present day, which the present generation feel in all their dreadful reality. And these facts, revolting as they are, are as a fraction only in the stupendous aggregate of our calamities. Our misfortunes do not proceed from Indian depredations alone ; neither are they confined to a few isolated, impoverished, and almost tenantless towns. They pervade the whole territory—operate upon the whole population ; and are as diversified in character as our public interests and necessities are various. Texas, at large, feels and deplores an utter destitution of the common benefits which have usually accrued from the worst system of internal government that the patience of mankind ever tolerated. She is virtually without a *government*—and if she is not precipitated into all the unspeakable horrors of anarchy, it is only because there is a redeeming spirit among the people which still infuses a moral energy into the miserable fragments of authority that exists among us. We are perfectly sensible that a large portion of our population, usually denominated "the colonists," and composed of Anglo-Americans, have been greatly calumniated before the Mexican government. But could the honorable Congress scrutinize strictly into our real condition ; could they see and understand the wretched confusion in all the elements of government which we daily feel and deplore, our ears would no longer be insulted, nor our feelings mortified, by the artful fictions of hireling emissaries from abroad, nor by the malignant aspersions of disappointed military commandants at home.

Our grievances do not so much result from any positive misfeasance on the part of the present State authorities, as from the total absence, or the very feeble and inutile dispensation of those restrictive influences which it is the appropriate design of the social compact to exercise upon the people, and which are necessary to fulfil the ends of civil society. We complain more of the *want* of *all* the important attributes of government, than of the abuses of any. We are sensible that all human institutions are essentially imperfect. But there are relative degrees of perfection in modes of government, as in other matters, and it is both natural and right to aspire to that mode which is most likely to acccomplish its legitimate purpose. This is wisely declared in our present State constitution, to be "the happiness of the individuals who compose it." It is equally obvious that the happiness of the people is more likely to be secured by a local than by a remote government. In the one case, the governors are partakers in common with the governed, in all the political evils which result to the community, and have therefore a personal interest in so discharging their respective functions, as will best secure the common welfare. In the other supposition, those vested with authority are measurably exempt from the calamities that ensue an abuse of power, and may very conveniently subserve their own interests and ambition, while they neglect or destroy "the welfare of the associated."

But independent of these general truths, there are some impressive reasons why the peace and happiness of Texas demand a local government. Constituting a remote frontier of the republic, and bordering on a powerful nation, a portion of whose population, in juxtaposition to hers, is notoriously profligate and lawless, she requires, in a peculiar and emphatic sense, the vigorous application of such laws as are necessary, not only to the preservation of good order, the protection of property, and the redress of personal wrongs, but such, also, as are essential to the prevention of illicit commerce, to the security of the public revenues, and to the avoidance of serious collision with the authorities of the neighboring republic. That such a judicial administration is impracticable under the present arrangement, is too forcibly illustrated by the past to admit of any rational hope for the future.

It is an acknowledged principle in the science of jurisprudence, that the prompt and certain infliction of mild and humane punishment is more efficacious for the prevention of crime than a tardy and precarious administration of the most sanguinary penal code. Texas is virtually denied the benefit of this benevolent rule, by the locality and the character of her present government. Crimes of the greatest atrocity may go unpunished, and hardened criminals triumph in their iniquity, because of the difficulties and delays which encumber her judicial system, and necessarily intervene between a trial and a conviction, and the sentence and the execution of the law. Our "supreme tribunal of justice" holds its sessions upwards of seven hundred miles distant from our central population; and that distance is greatly enlarged, and sometimes made impassable, by the casualties incident to a mail conducted by a single horseman through a wilderness often infested by vagrant and murderous Indians. Before sentence can be pronounced by the local courts on persons charged with the most atrocious crimes, the copy of the process must be transmitted to an assessor, resident at Leona Vicario, who is too far removed from the scene of guilt to appreciate the importance of a speedy decision, and is too much estranged from our civil and domestic concerns to feel the miseries that result from a total want of legal protection in person and property. But our difficulties do not terminate here. After the assessor shall have found leisure to render his opinion, and final judgment is pronounced, it again becomes necessary to resort to the capital, to submit the tardy sentence to the supreme tribunal for "approbation, revocation, or modification," before the judgment of the law can be executed. Here we have again to encounter the vexations and delays incident to all governments, where those who exercise its most interesting functions are removed by distance from the people on whom they operate, and for whose benefit the social compact is created.

These repeated delays, resulting from the remoteness of our courts of judicature, are pernicious in many respects. They involve heavy expenses, which, in civil suits, are excessively onerous to litigants, and give to the rich and influential such manifold advantages over the poor as operate to an absolute exclusion of the latter from the remedial and protective benefits of the law. They offer seductive opportunities and incitements to bribery and corruption, and endanger the sacred purity of the judiciary, which, of all the branches of government, is most intimately associated with the domestic and social happiness of man, and should therefore be, not only sound and pure, but unsuspected of the venal infection. They present insuperable difficulties to the exercise of the corrective right of recusation, and virtually nullify the constitutional power of impeachment. In criminal actions they are no less injurious. They are equivalent to a license to iniquity, and exert a dangerous influence on the moral feelings at large. Before the tedious process of the law can be complied with, and the criminal, whose hands are perhaps imbrued in a brother's blood, be made to feel its retributive justice, the remembrance of his crime is partially effaced from the public mind, and the righteous arbitrament of the law, which, if promptly executed, would have received universal approbation, and been a salutary warning to evil-doers, is impugned as vindictive and cruel. The popular feeling is changed from a just indignation of the crime into an amiable but mistaken sympathy for the criminal; and by an easy and natural transition, is converted into disgust and disaffection toward the government and its laws.

These are some of the evils that result from the annexation of Texas to Coahuila, and the exercise of legislative and judicial powers by the citizens of Coahuila over the citizens of Texas. The catalogue might be greatly enlarged; but we forbear to trespass on the time of the honorable Congress, confiding to the worthy citizens who shall be charged with the high duty of presenting this memorial, and the protocol of a constitution which the people of Texas have framed, as the basis of their future government, the more explicit enunciation of them. Those evils are not likely to be diminished, but they may be exceedingly aggravated by the fact that that political connection was formed without the cordial approbation of the people of Texas, and is daily becoming more odious to them. Although it may have received their reluctant acquiescence in its inception, before its evil consequences were developed or foreseen, the arbitrary continuance of it now, after the experience of nine years has demonstrated its ruinous tendencies, would invest it with some of the most offensive features of usurpation. Your memorialists entertain an assured confidence that the enlightened Congress of Mexico will never give their high sanction to anything that wears the semblance of usurpation or of arbitrary coercion.

The idea may possibly occur in the deliberations of the honorable Congress, that a territorial organization would cure our political maladies, and effectuate the great purposes which induce this application; and plausible reasons may be advanced in favor of it. But the wisdom of Congress will readily detect the fallacy of these reasons, and the mischief consequent to such vain sophistry. In this remote section of the republic a territorial government must, of necessity, be divested of one essential and radical principle in all popular institutions — the immediate responsibility of public agents to the people whom they serve. The appointments to office would, in such case, be vested in the general government. And although such appointments should be made with the utmost circumspection, the persons appointed, when once arrayed in the habiliments of office, would be too far removed from the appointing power to feel the restraints of a vigilant super-

vision and a direct accountability.   The dearest rights of the people might
be violated, the public treasures squandered, and every variety of imposition
and iniquity practised, under the specious pretext of political necessity, which
the far distant government could neither detect nor control.

And we would further present, with great deference, that the institution
of a territorial government would confer upon us neither the form nor the
substance of our high guarantee.   It would, indeed, diversify our miseries,
by opening new avenues to peculation and abuse of power ; but it would
neither remove our difficulties nor place us in the enjoyment of our equal
and vested rights.   The only adequate remedy that ˌour memorialists can
devise, and which they ardently hope the collective wisdom of the nation will
approve, is to be found in the establishment of a *local State government.*   We
believe that if Texas were endowed with the facilities of a State government,
she would be competent to remedy the many evils that now depress her
energies and frustrate every effort to develop and bring into usefulness the
natural resources which a beneficent Providence has conferred upon her.
We believe that a local legislature, composed of citizens who feel and participate in all the calamities which encompass us, would be enabled to enact
such conservative, remedial, and punitive laws, and so to organize and put
into operation the municipal and inferior authorities of the country, as would
inspire universal confidence ; would encourage the immigration of virtuous
foreigners ; prevent the ingress of fugitives from justice of other countries ;
check the alarming accumulation of ferocious Indians, whom the domestic
policy of the United States of the North is rapidly translating to our borders ;
would give impulse and vigor to the industry of the people ; secure a cheerful subordination and a faithful adhesion to the State and general governments ; and would render Texas, what she ought to be, a strong arm of the
republic, a terror to foreign invaders, and an example of peace and prosperity,
of advancement in the arts and sciences, and of devotion to the Union, to
her sister States.   We believe that an executive chosen from among ourselves
would feel a more intense interest in our political welfare, would watch with
more vigilance over our social concerns, and would contribute more effectually to the purposes of his appointment.   We believe that a local judiciary,
drawn from the bosom of our own peculiar society, would be enabled to
administer the laws with more energy and promptitude ; to punish the dis-
obedient and refractory ; to restrain the viciousness of the wicked ; to impart
confidence and security, both of person and property, to peaceable citizens ;
to conserve and perpetuate the general tranquillity of the State, and to render
a more efficient aid to the coördinate powers of the Government in carrying
into effect the great objects of its institution.   We believe that if Texas were
admitted to the Union as a separate State, she would soon "figure" as a

brilliant star in the Mexican constellation, and would shed a new splendor around the illustrious city of Montezuma. We believe she would contribute largely to the national wealth and aggrandizement, would furnish new staples for commerce and new materials for manufactures. The cotton of Texas would give employment to the artisans of Mexico, and the precious metals, which are now flowing into the coffers of England, would be retained at home, to reward the industry and remunerate the ingenuity of native citizens.

The honorable Congress need not be informed that a large proportion of the population of Texas is of foreign origin. They have been invited here by the munificent liberality and plighted faith of the Mexican government; and they stand pledged by every moral and religious principle, and by every sentiment of honor, to requite that liberality, and to reciprocate the faithful performance of the guarantee to "*protect their liberties, property, and civil rights*," by a cheerful dedication of their moral and physical energies to the advancement of their adopted country. But it is also apparent to the intelligence of the honorable Congress that the best mode of securing the permanent attachment of such a population is to incorporate them into the federal system on such equitable terms as will redress every grievance, remove every cause of complaint, and insure not only an identity of interests, but an eventual blending and assimilation of all that is now foreign and incongruous. The infancy of imperial Rome was carried to an early adolescence by the free and unrestricted admission of foreigners to her social compact. England never aspired to "the dominion of the seas" until she had united the hardiness of Scotland and the gallantry of Ireland to her native prowess. France derives her greatness from the early combination of the Salii, the Frank, and the Burgundian. And Mexico may yet realize the period when the descendants of Montezuma will rejoice that their coalition with the successors of Fernando Cortes has been strengthened and embellished by the adoption into their national family of a people drawn by their own gratuitous hospitality from the land of Washington and of freedom.

For these and other considerations, your memorialists would solemnly invoke the magnanimous spirit of the Mexican nation, concentrated in the wisdom and patriotism of the Federal Congress. And they would respectfully and ardently pray, that the honorable Congress would extend their remedial power to this obscure section of the republic; would cast around it "the sovereign mantle of the nation," and adopt it into a free and plenary participation of that "constitutional regime" of equal sisterhood, which alone can rescue it from the miseries of an ill-organized, inefficient internal government, and can reclaim this fair and fertile region from the worthlessness of an untenanted waste, or the more fearful horrors of barbarian inundation. Your memorialists, in behalf of their constituents, would, in conclusion,

3

avail themselves of this opportunity to tender to the honorable Congress their cordial adhesion to the plan of Zavaleta, and to express their felicitations on the happy issue of the late unhappy conflict. They would also declare their gratitude to the patriot chief and his illustrious associates, whose propitious conquests have saved from profanation "the august temple in which we have deposited the holy ark of our federal constitution," and have secured the ultimate triumph of the liberal and enlightened principles of genuine republicanism. And they would unite their fervent aspirations with the prayers that must ascend from the hearts of all good Mexicans, that the Supreme Ruler of the universe, "who doeth his will in the army of heaven, and among the inhabitants of the earth," would vouchsafe to this glorious land the blessings of peace and tranquillity; would preserve it, in all future time, from the horrors of civil discord, and shed down upon its extended population the increased and increasing effulgence of light and liberty, which is fast irradiating the European continent, and extirpating the relics of feudal despotism, the antiquated errors of a barbarous age, from the civilized world.

DAVID G. BURNETT, *Chairman of Committee.*
THOMAS HASTINGS, *Secretary of the Convention.*
WILLIAM H. WHARTON, *President of the Convention.*

TO THE FEDERAL CONGRESS OF MEXICO:

The people of Texas, by their chosen representatives, in General Convention met, for the purpose of making known their wants and grievances to the Congress of the Confederation, respectfully represent:

That they view with emotions of regret the existence and operation of the 11th article of the law of 6th of April, 1830. A retrospective view of the kind partiality manifested toward the citizens of the republic from which we emigrated, furnishes some apprehension that a suspicion of our fidelity was the cause of its enactment. Relying, however, upon the justice of the nation, and the purity of intention by which we are and ever have been actuated, as well as upon the identity of interest existing between the States of Mexico and the colonies in Texas, your memorialists confidently anticipated its speedy repeal. In respect of our claims to the indulgent and confiding consideration of the Congress of the republic, we submit the following statement of facts:

The products of agriculture and of manufactures are worth nearly a hundred per cent. more in the markets of Mexico than they are in those of the United States of the North. Our interest, therefore, as an agricultural and commercial people, the strongest cement of society, is diametrically opposed to any convulsion or change of situation that might deprive us of that preference in the Mexican market, to which, as colonists, we are clearly entitled.

This law, if permitted to operate, must defeat the original design of the Mexican republic, in relation to the settlement of Texas. In 1823, the Congress of the nation invited citizens of the United States of the North to settle on this frontier; and, as an inducement, offered a liberal donation of land to each family. The supposed object of the government was to reclaim a wilderness, and make the country subservient to the best interests of the nation. It was then unexplored by civilized man. It was the abode of prowling and hostile Indians. They had long obstructed the extension of the Mexican settlements, had harassed the frontier establishments, and excluded them from any participation in the commerce of the North, and, at times, threatened their depopulation. Thus situated, Texas was not only a useless but a dangerous appendage of the republic. It presented an uncovered flank to the invader, and was dependent on the mercy of a foreign enemy. Without any adequate means of defense against the depredations of hostile Indians, the attention of your statesmen was invited to the adoption of measures for its future protection and repose. Had the liberal policy of 1823 been steadily pursued — had no blighting restrictions been imposed by future legislatures — Texas would, ere this, have exhibited the proud achievement of legislative wisdom, and the government have realized the glorious meed of its munificence and bounty.

Colonies were granted, and North Americans were the first to brave the dangers and privations attending an acceptance of the liberality of the government. The native citizens of Mexico, unwilling to dispute with the savage the occupancy of an unsubdued wilderness, declined its participation. Spain had not, as yet, ceased her hostilities; the cabinets of Europe, shocked at the threatened establishment of republican institutions, denounced your glorious struggle for independence as treasonable and rebellious. But the republic of the North boldly defended your declaration, recognized your independence, and gave you admission into the community of nations. Many of her sons espoused your cause, heroically aided in the expulsion of your ancient tyrants, and joyfully celebrated, with the friends of freedom throughout the earth, the final consummation of Mexican emancipation. The doors of immigration were then open. Confiding in the honor, the proffered liberality, and the plighted faith of the Mexican government, many who had fought in the ranks of your armies settled, under the provisions of your laws, on a wild frontier of the land which they had volunteered to defend. They had acquired an unrivaled character for daring enterprise, and they contended, face to face, with the barbarian for the forests of Texas. They succeeded. The savage has been driven back. Extensive improvements, cultivated fields, and an enterprising population are the fruits of *your* bounty, and of *their* untiring perseverance.

What have *we* done to tarnish this faithful picture of the past and invite the blasting restrictions of the government for the future ? To what event in our past history can we refer, meriting either the want of confidence or the unfriendly feeling so emphatically proclaimed to the world by the 11th article of the law of the 6th of April, 1830 ? In what point of view does it place the settlers of Texas ? Does it not present us in the most suspicious and odious light ? Does it not brand our countrymen as undeserving the confidence of any government ? Have our acts provoked it as a just punishment for *supposed* aberrations from the path of duty heretofore, or is it feared or suspected that we *may* become dangerous hereafter ? Of the *past*, at least we are in no danger ; *it* is the property of history now ; and the fair fame of Americans can not be soiled by the historic details of the part which they have borne in the redemption of Texas from a savage to a civilized state. For the FUTURE, the past is the best guarantee that we can offer. The *interest* of Texas is the *interest* of Mexico. Each is necessary to the other. And unless we are foolish and unwise enough to wage a war with our own best and dearest interests, any *other* change than a repeal of the above article, accompanied with such other advantages as are guaranteed by the laws of Congress, would be deprecated as the heaviest misfortune that could fall upon her infant society.

We feel and we vow every attachment to the government of our adoption which the one can merit or the other can cherish. With these remarks we rest our cause, relying on a returning sense of magnanimity in the delegated authorities of the nation to remove *all* the causes which impede our prosperity, to relieve us, particularly, from the pernicious and disheartening influence of the above-named law, and to restore us to all the promised enjoyments of the laws of colonization.

WYLY MARTIN, *Chairman of Committee.*

We here close our compendium of Texan early history as taken from the files of *The Constitutional Advocate.* We find nothing more worthy of notice.

D. W. Anthony, editor and proprietor of *The Advocate*, died of the cholera in July, 1833, at which time, Colonel William T. Austin informs us, that paper was suspended. The foregoing shows that the cholera commenced in the preceding February in a family just arrived from New Orleans, where it was then epidemic. In the month of May of that year (1833), the Brazos River overflowed fully four feet higher in Brazoria than has ever been known since that time. As the water receded, the cholera made its appearance ; and from Velasco to Columbia it scourged and decimated that section of the country, taking off entire families. The water disappeared about the 23d of June, having entirely destroyed all the planted crops. Some cotton and corn were replanted, but even these second-planted crops were destroyed by an early frost, and the consequence was an entire destitution of breadstuffs, so that the people had to live on jerked beef as their principal sustenance, until the crop of 1834 was made.

[We have been indebted to Colonel William T. Austin, one of the early pioneers of Texas, for some of the foregoing reminiscences.]

THE CONVENTION OF 1836—THE DECLARATION OF TEXAN INDEPENDENCE.

BY JOHN HENRY BROWN.

By authority of a resolution adopted December 10th, 1835, by the provisional government of Texas, which existed from November, 1835, to March, 1836, delegates, clothed with plenary powers, were elected on the first day of February, 1836, to meet in convention at Washington, on the Brazos, on the first day of March. The provisional government was composed of Henry Smith, Governor, James W. Robinson, Vice-Governor, and a Council of —— members. At the period of the meeting of the Convention, the Council had quarreled with and deposed the Governor, and Mr. Robinson was occupying the gubernatorial chair.

The Convention assembled accordingly on the first day of March, 1836. Its official journal opens thus : " *Convention of all the People of Texas, through their Delegates elect.*"

On motion of Mr. George C. Childress, of Milam (the counties being then called municipalities), Mr. James Collingsworth, of Brazoria, was called to the chair, and Willis A. Farris appointed Secretary *pro tem.*

After the roll of members was completed, on motion of Mr. Robert Potter, the Convention proceeded to the election of a President, when Mr. Stephen H. Everitt, of Jasper, nominated Mr. Richard Ellis, of Red River (then called Pecan Point), who was unanimously elected.

For Secretary of the Convention, Messrs. H. S. Kimble, E. M. Pease, and Willis A. Farris were nominated. The vote stood: Kimble, 24 ; Farris, 10 ; Pease, 7. E. M. Pease was then elected assistant secretary ; Iram Palmer, sergeant-at-arms ; John A. Hizer, door-keeper ; Mr. Saul, engrossing clerk.

On the afternoon of the first day, Mr. George C. Childress offered the following :

Resolved, That the president appoint a committee, to consist of five delegates, to draft a *Declaration of Independence.*

Mr. Martin Palmer offered the following as a substitute:

Resolved, That the president appoint one delegate from each municipality, as a committee to draft a *Declaration of Independence.*

Dr. Palmer's resolution was negatived, and that of Mr. Childress adopted; whereupon the president appointed as the committee Messrs. George C. Childress, of Milam; James Gaines, of Sabine; Edward Conrad, of Refugio; Collin McKinney, of Red River; and Bailey Hardeman, of Matagorda.

On the second day, March 2d, Mr. Robert Potter moved the appointment of a committee of one from each municipality to draft a constitution for the (contemplated) Republic of Texas, which was carried, and Messrs. Martin Parmer, chairman, Robert Potter, Charles B. Stewart, Edwin Waller, Jesse Grimes, Robert M. Coleman, John Fisher, John W. Bunton, James Gaines, Lorenzo de Zavala, Stephen H. Everitt, Bailey Hardeman, Elijah Stapp, William C. Crawford, Claiborne West, James Power, Jose Antonio Navarro, Collin McKinney, William Menefee, William Motley, and Michael B. Menard were appointed the committee.

On the same day, March 2d, Mr. Childress, chairman of the committee, reported the draft of a Declaration of Independence, and " asked that the same be received by the Convention as their report."

Here I quote from the journals:

" Mr. Houston moved that the report be received by the Convention, which, on being seconded, was done.

" On Mr. Collingsworth's motion, seconded, the House resolved into a committee of the whole, upon the report of the Committee on Independence.

Mr. Collingsworth was called to the chair, whereupon Mr. Houston introduced the following resolution:

" *Resolved,* That the Declaration of Independence, reported by the committee, be adopted; that the same be engrossed and signed by the delegates of this Convention.

" And the question being put, the resolution was unanimously adopted."

The Declaration of Independence was thus unanimously adopted, enrolled, and signed on the second day of the session—being March 2d— as follows:

THE DECLARATION OF INDEPENDENCE

Made by the Delegates of the People of Texas, in General Convention, at
Washington, on March 2d, 1836.

WHEN a government has ceased to protect the lives, liberty, and property of the people from whom its legitimate powers are derived, and for the advancement of whose happiness it was instituted ; and, so far from being a guarantee for their inestimable and inalienable rights, becomes an instrument in the hands of evil rulers for their oppression ; when the federal republican constitution of their country, which they have sworn to support, no longer has a substantial existence, and the whole nature of their government has been forcibly changed, without their consent, from a restricted federative republic, composed of sovereign states, to a consolidated central military despotism, in which every interest is disregarded but that of the army and the priesthood, both the eternal enemies of civil liberty, the ever-ready minions of power and the usual instruments of tyrants ; when, long after the spirit of the constitution has departed, moderation is at length so far lost by those in power, that even the semblance of freedom is removed, and the forms themselves of the constitution discontinued, and, so far from the petitions and remonstrances being disregarded, the agents who bear them are thrown into dungeons, and mercenary armies sent forth to enforce a new government upon them at the point of the bayonet.

When, in consequence of such acts of malfeasance and abduction on the part of the government, anarchy prevails, and civil society is dissolved into its original elements, in such a crisis, the first law of nature, the right of self-preservation, the inherent and inalienable right of the people to appeal to first principles, and take their political affairs into their own hands, in extreme cases, enjoins it as a right toward themselves, and a sacred obligation to their posterity, to abolish such government and create another in its stead, calculated to rescue them from impending dangers, and to secure their welfare and happiness.

Nations, as well as individuals, are amenable for their acts to the public opinion of mankind. A statement of a part of our grievances is therefore submitted to an impartial world in justification of the hazardous but unavoidable step now taken, of severing our political connection with the Mexican people, and assuming an independent attitude among the nations of the earth.

The Mexican government, by its colonization laws, invited and induced the Anglo-American population of Texas to colonize its wilderness under the pledged faith of a written constitution, that they should continue to enjoy that constitutional liberty and republican government to which they had been habituated in the land of their birth, the United States of America.

In this expectation they have been cruelly disappointed, inasmuch as the Mexican nation has acquiesced in the late changes made in the government by General Antonio Lopez de Santa Anna, who, having overturned the constitution of his country, now offers us the cruel alternative, either to abandon our homes, acquired by so many privations, or submit to the most intolerable of all tyranny, the combined despotism of the sword and the priesthood.

It hath sacrificed our welfare to the State of Coahuila by which our interests have been continually depressed, through a jealous and partial course of legislation, carried on at a far-distant seat of government, by a hostile majority, in an unknown tongue ; and this, too, notwithstanding we have petitioned in the humblest terms for the establishment of a separate state government, and have, in accordance with the provisions of the national constitution, presented to the general congress a republican constitution, which was, without a just cause, contemptuously rejected.

It incarcerated in a dungeon, for a long time, one of our citizens, for no other cause but a zealous endeavor to procure the acceptance of our constitution and the establishment of a state government.

It has failed and refused to secure, on a firm basis, the right of trial by jury, the palladium of civil liberty, and only safe guarantee for the life, liberty, and property of the citizen.

It has failed to establish any public system of education, although possessed of almost boundless resources (the public domains), and although it is an axiom in political science that, unless a people are educated and enlightened, it is idle to expect the continuance of civil liberty or the capacity for self-government.

It has suffered the military commandants, stationed among us, to exercise arbitrary acts of oppression and tyranny, thus trampling upon the most sacred rights of the citizen, and rendering the military superior to the civil power.

It has dissolved, by force of arms, the State Congress of Coahuila and Texas, and obliged our representatives to fly for their lives from the seat of government, thus depriving us of the fundamental political right of representation.

It has demanded the surrender of a number of our citizens, and ordered military detachments to seize and carry them into the interior for trial, in contempt of the civil authorities, and in defiance of the laws and the constitution.

It has made piratical attacks on our commerce, by commissioning foreign desperadoes, and authorizing them to seize our vessels, and convey the property of our citizens to far distant parts for confiscation.

It denies us the right of worshipping the Almighty according to the dictates of our own conscience, by the support of a national religion, calculated to promote the temporal interests of its human functionaries, rather than the glory of the true and living God.

It has demanded us to deliver up our arms, which are essential to our defense—the rightful property of freemen, and formidable only to tyrannical governments.

It has invaded our country both by sea and by land, with the intent to lay waste our territory, and drive us from our homes, and has now a large mercenary army advancing to carry on against us a war of extermination.

It has, through its emissaries, incited the merciless savage, with the tomahawk and scalping-knife, to massacre the inhabitants of our defenseless frontiers.

It has been, during the whole time of our connection with it, the contemptible sport and victim of successive military revolutions, and hath continually exhibited every characteristic of a weak, corrupt, and tyrannical government.

These and other grievances were patiently borne by the people of Texas, until they reached that point at which forbearance ceases to be a virtue. We then took up arms in defense of the national constitution. We appealed to our Mexican brethren for assistance ; our appeal has been made in vain ; though months have elapsed, no sympathetic response has yet been made from the interior. We are therefore forced to the melancholy conclusion that the Mexican people have acquiesced in the destruction of their liberty, and the substitution therefor of a military government ; that they are unfit to be free, and incapable of self-government.

The necessity of self-preservation, therefore, now decrees our eternal political separation.

We, therefore, the delegates, with plenary powers, of the people of Texas, in solemn convention assembled, appealing to a candid world for the necessities of our condition, do hereby resolve and declare, that our political connection with the Mexican nation has forever ended, and that the people of Texas do now constitute a *free, sovereign, and independent republic,* and are fully invested with all the rights and attributes which properly belong to independent nations ; and, conscious of the rectitude of our intentions, we fearlessly and confidently commit the issue to the Supreme Arbiter of the destinies of nations.

In witness whereof we have hereunto subscribed our names.

RICHARD ELLIS, *President and Delegate from Red River.*
H. S. KIMBLE, *Secretary.*

NAMES, AGE, PLACE OF BIRTH, AND FORMER RESIDENCE OF THE SIGNERS OF THE TEXAN DECLARATION OF INDEPENDENCE, MARCH 2, 1836.

NAMES.	AGE.	PLACE OF BIRTH.	FORMER RESIDENCE.
Richard Ellis...........	54	Virginia..................	Alabama.
C. B. Stewart...........	30	South Carolina...........	Louisiana.
James Collingsworth.....	30	Tennessee................	Tennessee.
Edwin Waller...........	35	Virginia..................	Missouri.
Asa Brigham.............	46	Massachusetts	Louisiana.
J. S. D. Byrom..........	38	Georgia..................	Florida.
Fras. Ruis..............	54	Bexar, Texas.............	———
J. Anto. Navarro........	41	Bexar, Texas.............	
J. B. Badgett...........	29	North Carolina...........	Arkansas Territory.
W. D. Lacy..............	28	Kentucky.................	Tennessee.
William Menifee........	40	Tennessee	Alabama.
John Fisher.............	36	Virginia..................	Virginia.
M. Coldwell.............	38	Kentucky.................	Missouri.
W. Motley..............	24	Virginia..................	Kentucky.
L. D. Zavala............	47	Yucatan..................	Mexico.
George W. Smyth........	33	North Carolina...........	Alabama.
S. H. Everitt...........	29	New York................	New York.
E. Stapp................	53	Virginia..................	Missouri.
Clae. West.............	36	Tennessee	Louisiana.
W. B. Scates...........	30	Virginia.............. ...	Kentucky.
M. B. Menard...........	31	Canada	Illinois.
A. B. Hardin...........	38	Georgia..................	Tennessee.
J. W. Bunton...........	28	Tennessee	Tennessee.
Thomas G. Gazeley......	35	New York................	Louisiana.
R. M. Coleman.........	37	Kentucky.................	Kentucky.
S. C. Robertson*.......	50	North Carolina...........	Tennessee.
George C. Childress*....	32	Tennessee	Tennessee.
B. Hardiman.............	41	Tennessee	Tennessee.
R. Potter	36	North Carolina...........	North Carolina.
Thomas J. Rusk.........	29	South Carolina...........	Georgia.
Charles S. Taylor.......	28	England..................	New York.
John S. Roberts	40	Virginia..................	Louisiana.
R. Hamilton............	53	Scotland.................	North Carolina.
C. McKinney............	70	New Jersey..............	Kentucky.
A. H. Lattimer	27	Tennessee	Tennessee.
James Power............	48	Ireland..................	Louisiana.
Sam Houston...........	43	Virginia..................	Tennessee.
David Thomas..........	35	Tennessee	Tennessee.
E. Conrad..............	26	Pennsylvania............	Pennsylvania.
Martin Parmer..........	58	Virginia..................	Missouri.
E. O. Legrand	33	North Carolina	Alabama.
S. W. Blount...........	28	Georgia..................	Georgia.
James Gaines...........	60	Virginia.................	Louisiana.
W. Clark, Jr............	37	North Carolina	Georgia.
S. O. Pennington	27	Kentucky................	Arkansas Territory.
W. C. Crawford.........	31	North Carolina	Alabama.
John Turner............	34	North Carolina	Tennessee.
B. B. Goodrich.........	37	Virginia..................	Alabama.
G. W. Barnett	43	South Carolina...........	Mississippi.
J. G. Swisher......	41	Tennessee	Tennessee.
Jesse Grimes...........	48	North Carolina	Alabama.
S. Rhoads Fisher*......	41	Pennsylvania	Pennsylvania.
Samuel A. Maverick*....	29	South Carolina...........	South Carolina.
John White Bower*......	27	Georgia..................	Arkansas Territory.
James B. Woods*.......	34	Kentucky.................	Kentucky.
Andrew Briscoe*	—	———...............	———
John W. Moore*.........	—		
Thomas Barnett	—	———...............	———

Members who failed to reach the Convention in time : James Kerr, from Jackson, born in Kentucky, September 24, 1790; came to Texas in 1825. John J. Linn, from Victoria, born in Ireland, in 1802 ; came to Texas in 1830. Juan Antonio Padilla, from Victoria, a Mexican.

The above is from a statement furnished in the Convention to Dr. B. B. Goodrich by the members themselves.

* Not present at the signing.

On the 16th of March, the Convention adopted the Executive Ordinance by which was constituted the government *ad interim* of the Republic of Texas.

The Constitution of the Republic of Texas was adopted at a late hour on the night of the 17th of March, but was neither engrossed nor enrolled for the signature of the members prior to the adjournment next day. The secretary was instructed to enroll it for presentation. As I learn from the Hon. Jesse Grimes, Mr. Kimble, the secretary, took it to Nashville, Tennessee, where it was published in one of the papers, from which it was republished in a Cincinnati paper, and from the latter copied into the Texas *Telegraph* of August 2d of the same year, being its first publication in Texas. No enrolled copy having been preserved, this printed copy was recognized and adopted as authentic, and became *the Constitution;* thus adding another striking evidence of the wonderful capacity of our people for self-government, of their ability to establish order out of chaos, and of their power to enforce law and order even in the turmoils of revolution.

During the sitting of the Convention, General Sam Houston took leave of the body in order to take command of the army, then concentrating at Gonzales.

At eight o'clock, on the 18th of March, the convention assembled for the last time, and elected David G. Burnett, president, *ad interim*, of the republic, and Lorenzo de Zavala, a patriot Mexican exile, vice-president. They also elected the members of the cabinet, to wit: Samuel P. Carson, secretary of state; Bailey Hardeman, secretary of the treasury; Thomas J. Rusk, secretary of war; Robert Potter, secretary of the navy; and David Thomas, attorney-general. Having closed its business, the Convention adjourned *sine die* at eleven o'clock of the same day.

The Convention adjourned somewhat hastily, in consequence of the rapid advance of the enemy, reported on the evening previous. Some members repaired to the army, and some to their respective homes.

President Burnet, with two members of the cabinet—Mr. Hardeman and Mr. Rusk—remained in Washington for three days after the adjournment of the Convention. Late in the afternoon of the third day they left, and stayed a night and part of the ensuing day at the house of Colonel Croce, and from thence proceeded to Harrisburg. Before leaving Washington, the president issued a proclamation that the government would assemble at Harrisburg, on Buffalo Bayou, alleging that the movement was not made merely in consequence of the advance of the enemy. He had, previous to the election, suggested Harrisburgh as in all respects a more eligible position for administrative purposes than the more interior town of Washington. At the time he left Washington, there was but one family (Mr. Lott's, who kept the hotel) remaining in town, and the entire population west of the Brazos had broken up and fled eastward, such as were not in the army.

The names of the delegates in attendance appear to the Declaration and the Constitution ; but several western members were unable to be present, on account of the advance of the Mexican army. Of this number were Major James Kerr, of Jackson, John J. Linn and Juan Antonio Padilla, of Victoria.

X.

A DECLARATION ADOPTED BY THE GENERAL CONSULTATION OF TEXAS, NOVEMBER, 1835.

" WHEREAS General Antonio Lopez de Santa Anna, and other military chieftains, have by force of arms overthrown the federal institutions of Mexico and dissolved the social compact which existed between Texas and other members of the Mexican Confederacy, now the good people of Texas, availing themselves of their natural rights,

" DO SOLEMNLY DECLARE

" 1. That they have taken up arms in defense of their rights and liberties, which are threatened by the encroachment of military despots, and in defense of the republican principles of the Federal Constitution of Mexico, of 1824.

" 2. That Texas is no longer morally or civilly bound by the compact of Union, yet, stimulated by the generosity and sympathy common to a free people, they offer their support and assistance to such members of the Mexican Confederacy as will take up arms against military despotism.

" 3. They do not acknowledge that the present authorities of the nominal Mexican Republic have the right to govern within the limits of Texas.

" 4. They will not cease to carry on war against the said authorities while their troops are within the limits of Texas.

" 5. They hold it to be their right, during the disorganization of the Federal system and the reign of despotism, to withdraw from the Union, and establish an independent government, or adopt such measures as they may deem best calculated to protect their rights and liberties, but they will continue faithful to the Mexican Government so long as that nation is governed by the constitution and laws that were formed for the government of the political association.

" 6. That Texas is responsible for the expenses of her armies now in the field.

" 7. That the public faith of Texas is pledged for the payment of all debts contracted by her agents.

"8. That she will reward by donations in land all who volunteer their services in her present struggle, and receive them as citizens.

"9. These declarations we solemnly avow to the world, and call God to witness their truth and sincerity; and invoke defeat and disgrace upon our heads, should we prove guilty of duplicity."

————————

XI.

DECLARATION OF INDEPENDENCE.

MADE AT GOLIAD, DEC. 20, 1835.

(Texas Almanac, 1860.)

[WE take the following interesting document from the *State Gazette*, in 1852, as copied from the *Texas Republican*, published at Brazoria, and dated January 13th, 1836. It is said to have been the only copy in existence.]

Solemnly impressed with a sense of the danger of the crisis to which recent and remote events have conducted the public affairs of their country, the undersigned prefer this method of laying before their fellow-citizens, a brief retrospect of the light in which they regard both the present and the past, and of frankly declaring *for themselves*, the policy and the uncompromising course which they have resolved to pursue for the future.

They have seen the enthusiasm and the heroic toils of an army bartered for a capitulation, humiliating in itself, and repugnant in the extreme to the pride and honor of the most lenient, and no sooner framed than evaded or insultingly violated.

They have seen their camp thronged, but too frequently, with those who were more anxious to be served by, than to serve their country—with men more desirous of being honored with command than capable of commanding.

They have seen the energies, the prowess, and the achievements of a band worthy to have stood by Washington and receive command, and worthy to participate of the inheritance of the sons of such a Father, frittered, dissipated, and evaporated away for the want of that energy, union, and decision in council, which, though it must emanate from the many, can only be exercised efficiently when concentrated in a single arm.

They have seen the busy aspirants for office running from the field to the council hall, and from this back to the camp, seeking emolument and not service, and swarming like hungry flies around the body politic.

They have seen the deliberations of the council and the volition of the

camp distracted and paralyzed, by the interference of an influence anti-patri-
otic in itself, and too intimately interwoven with the paralyzing policy of the
past, to admit the hope of relief from its incorporation with that which can
alone avert the evils of the present crisis, and place the affairs of the country
beyond the reach of an immediate reaction.

They have witnessed these evils with bitter regrets, with swollen hearts,
and indignant bosoms.

A revulsion is at hand.   An army, recently powerless and literally imprisoned, is now emancipated.   From a comparatively harmless, passive, and
inactive attitude, they have been transferred to one pre-eminently commanding, active, and imposing.   The North and East of Mexico will now become
the stronghold of centralism.   Thence it can sally in whatever direction its
arch deviser may prefer to employ its weapons.   The counter-revolution in
the interior once smothered, the whole fury of the contest will be poured on
Texas.   She is principally populated with North-Americans.   To expel these
from its territory, and parcel it out among the instruments of its wrath, will
combine the motive and the means for consummating the scheme of the President Dictator.   Already, we are denounced, proscribed, outlawed, and exiled
from the country.   Our lands, peaceably and lawfully acquired, are solemnly
pronounced the proper subject of indiscriminate forfeiture, and our estates of
confiscation.   The laws and guarantees under which we entered the country
as colonists, tempted the unbroken silence, sought the dangers of the wilderness, braved the prowling Indian, erected our numerous improvements, and
opened and subdued the earth to cultivation, are either abrogated or repealed,
and now trampled under the hoofs of the usurper's cavalry.

Why, then, should we longer contend for charters, which, we are again and
again told in the annals of the past, were never intended for *our* benefit?
Even a willingness on our part to defend them, has provoked the calamities
of exterminating warfare.   Why contend for the shadow, when the substance
courts our acceptance?   The price of each is the same.   War—exterminating
war—is waged ; and we have either to fight or flee.

We have indulged sympathy, too, for the condition of many whom, we
vainly flattered ourselves, were opposed, in common with their adopted
brethren, to the extension of military domination over the domain of Texas.
But the siege of Bexar has dissolved the illusion.   Nearly all their physical
force was in the line of the enemy and armed with rifles.   Seventy days' occupation of the fortress of Goliad, has also abundantly demonstrated the
general diffusion among the Creole population of a like attachment to the
institutions of their ancient tyrants.   Intellectually enthralled, and strangers
to the blessings of regulated liberty, the only philanthropic service which we
can ever force on their acceptance, is that of example.   In doing this, we

need not expect or even hope for their co-operation. When made the reluctant, but greatly benefited recipients of a new, invigorating, and cherishing policy—a policy tendering equal, impartial, and indiscriminate protection to all ; to the low and the high, the humble and the well-born, the poor and the rich, the ignorant and the educated, the simple and the shrewd—then, and not before, will they become even useful auxiliaries in the work of political or moral renovation.

It belongs to the North-Americans of Texas to set this bright, this cheering, this all-subduing example. Let them call together their wise men. Let them be jealous of the experienced, of the speculator, of every one anxious to serve as a delegate, of every one hungry for power, or soliciting office ; and of all too who have thus far manifested a willingness to entertain or encourage those who have already tired the patience of the existing Council with their solicitations and attendance. Those who *seek* are seldom ever the best qualified to *fill* an office. Let them discard, too, the use of *names* calculated only to deceive and bewilder, and return like men to the use of words whose signification is settled and universally acknowledged. Let them call their assembly, thus made up, *a Convention;* and let this convention, instead of declaring for " the principles " of a constitution, for " the principles " of Independence, or for those of Freedom and Sovereignty, boldly, and with one voice, proclaim *the Independence of Texas.* Let the convention frame a constitution for the future government of this favored land. Let them guard the instrument securely, by the introduction of a full, clear, and comprehensive bill of rights. Let all this be done as speedily as possible. Much useful labor has already been performed ; but much is yet required to complete the work.

The foregoing, we are fully aware, is a blunt, and in some respects, a humiliating, but a faithful picture. However much we may wish, or however much we may be interested, or feel disposed to deceive our enemy, let us carefully guard against deceiving *ourselves.* We are in more danger from this —from his insinuating, secret, silent, and unseen *influence* in our councils, both in the field and in the cabinet, and from the use of his silver and gold, than from his numbers, his organization, or the concentration of his power in a single arm. The *gold* of Philip purchased what his *arms* could not subdue —*the liberties* of Greece. *Our* enemy, too, holds this weapon. Look well to this, people of Texas, in the exercise of suffrage. Look to it, Counselors, your appointments to office. Integrity is a precious jewel.

Men of Texas ! nothing short of independence can place us on solid ground. This step will. This step, too, will entitle us to confidence, and will procure us credit abroad. Without it, every aid we receive must emanate from the enthusiasm of the moment, and with the moment, will be liable to pass away or die forever. Unless we take this step, no foreign power can either respect or even know us. None will hazard a rupture with Mexico, impotent as she is, or incur censure from other powers for interference with the internal affairs of a friendly State, to aid us in any way whatever. Our letters of marque and reprisal must float at the mercy of every nation on the ocean. And whatever courtesy or kindred feeling may do, or forbear to do, in aid of our struggle, prosecuted on the present basis, it would be idle and worse than child-like to flatter ourselves with the hope of any permanent benefit from this branch of the service, without frankly declaring to the world, *as a people*, our *independence* of military Mexico. Let us then take the tyrant and his hirelings at their word. *They* will not know *us* but as enemies. Let us, then, know them hereafter, as other independent States know each other —as " enemies in war, in peace, friends." Therefore,

1. *Be it Resolved*, That the former province and department of Texas is, and of right ought to be, *a free, sovereign, and independent State.*

2. That as such, it has, and of right ought to have, all the powers, faculties, attributes, and immunities of other independent nations.

3. That we, who hereto set our names, pledge to each other our lives, our fortunes, and our sacred honor, to sustain this declaration—relying with entire confidence upon the co-operation of our fellow-citizens, and the approving smiles of the God of the living, to aid and conduct us victoriously through the struggle, to the enjoyment of peace, union, and good government; and invoking His malediction if we should either equivocate, or, in any manner whatever, prove ourselves unworthy of the high destiny at which we aim.

Done in the town of Goliad, on Sunday, the 20th day of December, in the year of our Lord one thousand eight hundred and thirty-five.

Wm. G. Hill,	John Shelly,	Thomas Todd,
Joseph Bowman,	Patrick O'Leary,	Jeremiah Day,
Geo. W. Welsh,	Timothy Hart,	Wm. S. Brown,
J. D. Kilpatrick,	James St. John,	Benjamin Noble,
Wm. E. Howth,	John Bowen,	M. Carbajal,
Albert Pratt,	Michael O'Donnell,	T. Hanson,
Alvin Woodward,	Nathaniel Holbrook,	John Johnson,
D. M. Jones,	Alexander Lynch,	Edmund Quirk,
J. C. Hutchins,	J. W. Baylor,	Robert McClure,
E. B. W. Fitzgerald,	H. George,	Andrew Devereau,
Hugh McMinn,	Benj. J. White,	Charles Shingle,
Wm. Robertson,	R. L. Redding,	J. B. Dale,
Horace Stamans,	James W. Scott,	Ira Ingram,
Peter Hynes,	Lewis Powell,	John Dunn,

Dugald McFarlane,	John Pollan,	Walter Lambert,
H. F. Davis,	James Duncan,	Miguel Aldrete,
Francis Jones,	David George,	William Quinn,
G. W. Pain,	Gustavus Cholwell,	B. H. Perkins,
Allen White,	John James,	Benj. J. White, Jr.,
Joseph Cadle,	Morgan Bryan,	Edward St. John,
W. H. Living,	Thomas O'Connor,	D. H. Peeks,
Victor Loupy,	Henry J. Moris,	Philip Dimitt,
Sayle Antoine,	James O'Connor,	Francis P. Smith,
Michael Kelly,	Spirse Dooley,	T. Mason Dennis,
Geo. W. Cash,	E. Brush,	C. A. Parker,
Charles Malone,	W. Redfield,	C. M. Despallier,
C. J. O'Connor,	Albert Silsbe,	Jefferson Ware,
Edward McDonough,	Wm. Haddon,	David Wilson,
Wm. Gould,	James Elder,	William Newland,
Charles Messer,	John J. Bowman,	J. T. Bell.
Isaac Robinson,		

I hereby certify the foregoing to be a true copy of the original in my possession. IRA INGRAM, *Secretary.*

TOWN OF GOLIAD, December 22, 1835.

———◦◦◦———

XII.

BATTLE OF CONCEPCION.

(Texas Almanac, 1859.)

THE assemblage of volunteers at Gonzales increased rapidly, insomuch that Colonel Ugartechea, having made a demonstration with five hundred troops, of all arms, including two field-pieces, to expunge the blot which the affair with Castonado had flung upon his own military reputation and on his nation's escutcheon, was constrained to return to his quarters and relinquish his commendable purpose. Soon after the institution of the general Council, Colonel Austin proceeded to Gonzales, and was elected Commander-in-Chief of all the forces of Texas. The western settlements, sparse and few, had from the' beginning, been foremost in every military operation. The East now sent forth some volunteers and gallant men, such as Thomas J. Rusk, our late distinguished Senator, Colonel Frank W. Johnson and others, who repaired to the camps to participate in the conquest of San Antonio, the little Malakoff of Texas. The Municipality of Liberty also contributed its quota of brave men.

General Austin became impatient of delay, and on the 20th of October, 1835, advanced to the Salado, a tributary of the San Antonio, and took a strong position about five miles from the town. Cos was busily occupied in strengthening his fortifications, barricading the streets, and preparing for the assault. He had about one thousand men, and was looking for re-enforcements. Austin's force was about six hundred, recruits occasionally arriving. He dispatched a flag of truce to the enemy; but Cos in the fullness of his military hauteur, refused to recognize General Austin, and peaceful interchanges became impracticable; the sword must do its work. Occasional skirmishes took place, but of slight effect. On the 27th of October, Austin directed Colonel James Bowie and Captain J. W. Fannin, both eventually victims in the strife, to proceed with ninety men to make recognizances about the old Missions, and select an eligible and more proximate position for the army. Passing the Missions of San Juan and San José, now in ruins, they reached that of La Purissima Concepcion,* about one and a half miles from San Antonio. They encamped for the night and reposed in peace. The morning of the 28th revealed the startling fact that they were surrounded on three sides by the enemy; the river making a sharp bend, forming an obtuse triangle, and fordable at several points, being on the other side. To cross it and retreat through an open prairie, in face of the town, was worse than forlorn. A desperate fight in their position presented a better and more genial hope of relief. They descended to the river bottom, an irregular depression of six to ten feet along the margin of the stream, and about one hundred yards wide, interspersed with timber. The prairie in front, occupied by the enemy, was a level plain, running into the bend. From their natural covert, the riflemen could fire and reload without being fully exposed.

The enemy's infantry advanced imposingly, with trailed arms, but halted about two hundred yards from the bluff, and opened a general fire. While the air was illumined by their rapid and random discharges, the rifles coolly, deliberately, and fatally sent forth their deadly missiles. They then pushed forward their brass six-pounder, escorted by a corps of cavalry, within about eighty yards, and sounded a charge. The rifles soon swept away the gunners and halted the charging column. The cannon had been fired five times without effect, and three times cleared of men, and the charge as often repulsed; when the Texans, coveting the gun, resolved to take it. The resolution had scarcely assumed an active form, when the enemy hastily retreated, leaving the gun with its munitions, to the victors. The Mexicans

* The Immaculate Conception.

numbered about four hundred ; the Texans precisely ninety-two men, including officers. The enemy's loss was about sixty killed and forty wounded. Sixteen lifeless bodies were strewed around the useless cannon. The Texans lost one brave man (Robert Andrews), killed. Thus ended the battle of Concepcion, presenting another instance of the disparity in military prowess of the two contending races.

XIII.

EARLY HISTORY OF TEXAS.

THE CAMPAIGN OF 1835.

(From the Austin Record.)

As a contribution to the history of the country, and for the use of the future historian of Texas, as well as for the interest of our columns, we continue this week the publication of a series of letters connected with the campaign of 1835, at Goliad and Bexar. These letters are produced from the originals that have been placed at our disposal ; from which it will be seen that the current of events did not run smoothly at that early day.

CAMP BELOW BEXAR, Nov. 2d, 1835.

To GENERAL S. F. AUSTIN.

SIR: I take the liberty to tender to you my resignation of the nominal command I hold in the army. I hope you will appoint some other person to occupy the post, more capable than myself.

Very respectfully,

JAS. BOWIE.

N.B. I deem it of the utmost importance for you to effect a union of the two divisions of the army as soon as practicable. Great dissatisfaction now exists in this division, and unless counteracted by the measure suggested, I seriously apprehend a dissolution of it. The causes which have produced this state of things will be explained when I see you; when I will also explain my motives for taking the step I have taken in reference to myself. Very respectfully,

JAS. BOWIE.

A true copy.

W. RICHARDSON.

HEADQUARTERS, Nov. 2d, 1835.

To COLONEL BOWIE AND CAPTAIN FANNIN :

In accordance with the decision of a majority of your officers and my own views, you will march the detachment under your command to this encampment, either to-night or in the morning, as you may choose. It may be inconvenient to march to-night after receiving this dispatch. Of this you will however be able to judge, and can use your own discretion. I send you a good guide. The mill is at present occupied by a detachment under Colonel Burleson.

S. F. AUSTIN.

W. D. C. HALL, Adj.-Gen.

HEADQUARTERS, Nov. 2d, 1835.

At a council of war called on this morning, consisting of General S. F. Austin, commander-in-chief, Colonel Warren D. C. Hall, adjutant-general, Colonel John H. Moore, Lieutenant-Colonel Burleson, Major William H. Jack, Colonel Patrick Jack, quartermaster-general, Major' Somerville, Major Benjamin W. Smith, Captain Caldwell Captain Ebberly, Captain Bennett, Captain Swisher, Captain Bird, Captain ———, Captain John Alley, Captain Nail, Lieutenant Aldridge, Lieutenant Spear, Lieutenant Hallsell, Lieutenant Barnett, Lieutenant Money, Lieutenant Hunt, Lieutenant Pivey, Lieutenant Stapp, Lieutenant Hensley, Lieutenant Richardson. The object of the call of the council being explained by the commander-in-chief to be to have the opinion and determination of the officers in regard to the best measures of immediate operation on the enemy, whether by close investment simply, or by storm. After much conversation and discussion, it was proposed by Major William H. Jack, that the question be directly put to the council whether a storm would or would not be expedient at the present moment. All the information in possession of the commander-in-chief in regard to the state of fortifications in Bexar, being submitted, the question was submitted by the commander-in-chief, and the same was decided in the negative by all the officers present, with the exception of Major Benjamin W. Smith, who voted substantially in the affirmative, saying, that in his opinion the town ought to be taken immediately. It was then decided unanimously by the council that such positions should be taken for the army at present as would best secure it from the cannon shot of the enemy, and enable it at the same time to carry on offensive operations, whilst we are waiting for the large cannon (18-pounders) and additional re-enforcements.

S. F. AUSTIN.

XIV.

FIRST SUNDAY SCHOOL IN TEXAS.

IN the Fall of 1828, I started from the western part of the State of New York for Texas, in company with sixty others, men, women and children, under the leadership of Elias R. Wightman, who had resided about three years in the country, and whose intelligence, energy, and enterprise well fitted him to be the leader of a colony. We traveled in wagons to Olean Point, on the head waters of the Alleghany River; then constructed a craft in two pieces, turning up at one end, the other square, and the square ends being lashed together formed a scow with two apartments; in these we placed our baggage and pushed off to drift down the stream at the mercy of the current. Our voyage the first day was prosperous, but night at length coming on cold and wet, we sought shelter in an Indian village on the north bank of the stream. The old chief seemed moved with pity at our forlorn condition, for the weather was very inclement, and pointed out to us a cabin about twenty feet square, with a good floor and fire-place; the floor was covered with peas and beans in the shuck, which he showed us could be scraped up in one corner and a fire made in the fire-place; truly grateful for his kindness, we soon had a good fire and a plain but comfortable meal, and all slept soundly. The next day being Sunday, we lay by and spent it in such devotional exercises as the surrounding circumstances would permit. The next morning we started on our voyage, having taken on board a pilot to accompany us as far as Pittsburg. About noon we heard a roaring ahead resembling a waterfall, and soon found it proceeded from a dam constructed across the stream. On one side was a mill, on the other a narrow space was left, through which a gentle current flowed, and where boats or rafts could pass with safety; but our pilot, through either ignorance or obstinacy, kept the center of the current, and we were soon passing over a fall about four feet high, and now was evident the advantage of our mode of construction, for the lashing giving way, the scow parted, which enabled the forepart to rise, but both apartments were nearly full of water, and all completely drenched. We all fell to bailing with such vessels as we could seize, and were again on our way in fair trim, but overtaking a raft of pine plank before night, we exchanged our rude craft for still ruder accommodations, though much more ample, on board the raft. Soon we reached Pittsburg, where we discharged our pilot, feeling that he had been the cause of our greatest calamity, without rendering us any valuable service. Here it had been intended to take a steamer, but finding none ready to leave, we continued on our raft to Cincinnati. Here we remained for several days, and I purchased a set of Spanish books and commenced to study the language. Soon we took passage on a steamer's deck for Orleans, and in due time arrived at the Crescent City. Cincinnati was at this time a small town of about 10,000 inhabitants. St. Louis was just coming into notice, and between that and the Pacific was an unbroken wilderness. In Orleans we remained about a fortnight, waiting for a conveyance, as there was little trade between Orleans and Texas, and vessels seldom passed from one to the other. At length we found a little vessel from Maine, of twenty-two tons burden, manned by only three hands, and only one of these very efficient. The captain offered to sell us the vessel for 500 dollars, or to take us to Texas for that amount; we bargained for the latter, and having provided ourselves with a suitable outfit for the voyage, we all embarked, and were soon drifting down the Mississippi in a perfect calm, at the mercy of the current. This calm continued for many days, until we were far out of sight of land, on the bosom of the Gulf, drifting about we knew not whither, as there was not sufficient breeze to steer the vessel. At length the wind rose and blew a gale, but directly ahead, and soon all on board except myself and crew were suffering severely from sea-sickness, and perfectly helpless; and then might have been heard many a regret expressed at ever having undertaken the journey, and many a wish to once more step foot on land. For two days the gale continued, and then again a perfect calm, and thus gale and calm succeeded each other, until we found ourselves off the entrance to Matagorda Bay; but the wind blowing directly out of the pass, there was little prospect of being able to enter, yet we resolved to make the effort. Of all on board, I was the only one who knew how to work a vessel, and the only one who was not liable to sea-sickness; and, as the captain and one hand were frequently intoxicated, the labor devolving on me was necessarily very great; besides, we were nearly out of provisions, and had been for several days allowanced to one half pint of water each daily, and for several days I drank none, giving mine to the children, and subsisting only on pilot bread and raw whiskey. Everything seemed to indicate that, if within the reach of human skill, we must make harbor.

For twenty-four hours we beat against wind and current, every one doing his duty and sparing no effort which might promise success; but all in vain, for we fell to leeward about three miles. It was now evident we must make some harbor, as we could not longer continue at sea, and as the wind would permit and was still blowing fresh, we ran down to Aransas and soon entered the bay in safety. Soon all were landed, and having made fires and procured water, the women proceeded to do some washing, which was greatly needed, and the men, with their rifles, twelve in number, proceeded in search of game, leav.ng on board only three men, the captain, mate, and myself. The vessel was anchored about 200 yards from shore, and we had remained about one hour when we saw several canoes coming down the bay with Indians. These we knew to be Carankawans, who were said to be cannibals, and as the men were gone and only one old musket on board, no little fear was felt for the safety of the women and children; but we could only watch their movements and act according to circumstances. Soon they were seen to halt and turn toward the shore, and shortly landed and were proceeding in the direction of the women. The mate and myself jumped into our little skiff, or bateau; he took the oars and I the old musket and stood in the bow; we proceeded in the direction of the Indians, but keeping between them and the women, and when near I drew the musket and presented it toward the chief, who beckoned not to fire and made signs of friendship. This position we both maintained for some time, we seeking to detain them, hoping the men would soon appear. Soon we raised our eyes and beheld the men all running toward the boat and not far from us. We then felt safe. The women were taken on board first, then the men, and lastly a few Indians were allowed to come. They manifested no hostility, for they evidently saw that all hostility would be unavailing. Their canoes were well stored with fish, all neatly dressed, which they bartered to us in such quantities as we needed, and then left us, truly glad that we had escaped so well. After remaining here for several days, and supplying ourselves with water and such provisions as we could obtain, which consisted only of wild meats, and an article of greens resembling purslane, and the wind becoming fair, we again crossed the bar, and shaped our course for Pass Caballo. The captain gave me the helm, and retired to his berth for sleep. In a few moments the wind subsided and a dead calm ensued; the current tended toward the shore, and a gentle swell was rolling in. I now felt quite disheartened, and thought our chance of reaching our destination by water was small. I went to Mr. Wightman, whom we considered our leader, and informed him of our condition and danger, and told him I had charge of the vessel, and if he consented I would beach her, and we would make our way as best we could by land.

He said that would never do, we were more than one hundred miles from any white settlement, there was no means of conveyance, and the country was infested with hostile Indians. Our only safety consisted in clinging to our vessel. I went to the captain, awoke him, and informed him of our danger; he at once saw and recognized it. I told him there were four sweeps on board, and, if he approved, I would rig them, and we would try to sweep her up to the pass. He consented, and by night the vessel was swept up opposite the pass; but no one knew the channel. The mate and myself went in our skiff, and sounded till we found it, then taking a long rope, we carried it on shore, and soon conducted our little vessel into the bay. A gentle breeze and fair wind sprang up, and soon we were off the mouth of the Colorado, and within about two miles of Matagorda, which then contained two families, who had lately moved down and commenced a settlement. The next day Mr. Wightman and another went to the settlement, and returned with the present of a Christmas dinner, which consisted of some hominy, beat in a wooden mortar, and fresh milk, which were gratefully received and promptly dispatched. The people of the new settlement, anxious to have it said that a vessel had arrived at Matagorda, came down to assist us; the women and chattels were taken on shore, the little vessel was careened over on one side, and by main strength dragged over the bar, and soon lay alongside of Matagorda. Our Christmas dinner, as stated, was taken on board, and the next day we landed, having been twenty-two days from New Orleans.

Some went to work immediately to prepare a home on the spot, and five young men started to go up the country, in search of some conveyance. We were told it was twenty-two miles to a settlement, and as we had been confined so long on board a vessel, we thought to walk this distance would be a mere recreation. In the morning we started fresh and vigorous, without a blanket or overgarment, and with no other provision than three little biscuits, which one of our number was so fortunate as to procure. This was the last of December, and the whole face of the country was nearly covered with water, and the only road was a dim trail made through the high grass by the passage of a single-horse carryall. Many of the little streams had to be swum; sometimes we traveled with the water to our waists, and all our shoes were worn through at the toes, by striking them against the high sedge grass. About noon the rain began to fall in torrents, the wind blew strong from the north, the depth of water increased, and night was approaching, with no appearance of settlement, when three of our number, and those apparently the strongest, fell to the ground, declaring they could go no farther. I remonstrated with them, and told them that to remain there was certain death, that our only hope was to keep moving, and thereby promote circulation; but in vain, they stated that if life depended upon it, they could go no farther. Near us was a venerable looking live-oak, which had fallen and perhaps lain there for ages; on the under side of its trunk, we contrived to kindle a fire, which we kept burning during the night, and having gathered sufficient of the tall grass to raise us above the water, we laid down and rested quite well, notwithstanding the falling rain and whistling blast. In the morning we arose quite refreshed, and started forward, the rain still falling, the wind increasing in coldness, and the water deepening. We had proceeded only about a mile, when we heard the crowing of chickens, when all jumped up, clapped their hands, and said they must be on the borders of civilization. Soon we struck a plain path, and were shortly at the hospitable residence of Daniel Rawls, where Captain John Duncan now resides. Here we found plenty of good country fare, which was provided without money or price. The rain continued to fall, and in the evening of the second day, looking out we saw a miserable looking object approaching, and as he neared us, we discovered it was one of our number who had been left behind. He had left with another, from whom he had become separated on the way, and could give no further account of him. Mr. Rawls remarked that we must go in search of him, as it would not do to leave him to perish; two horses were soon ready, and he taking one and I the other, we soon started; darkness soon overtook us, and unable to follow the trail longer, we entered a thicket, staked out our horses, and by breaking off limbs of bushes, which we covered with the long moss, and raising a bed above the water, contrived to rest very comfortably until morning, when we continued our course to Matagorda; but finding the lost one had not returned, and hearing nothing of him, we returned, and found that during our absence he had come in. Here we all remained, until the weather cleared up, when we separated and left, the others going east toward the Brazos, and I on foot and alone, wending my way north in the direction of San Felipe de Austin, about sixty miles distant. On the Bernard I was hospitably entertained by a Mr. Huff, where I met Josiah H. Bell on his way to his home in Columbia, and from him I received a cordial invitation to accompany him home. I cheerfully accepted, and the next night was spent with his estimable family. Mr. Bell was an estimable gentleman, a pure patriot, of stern, unyielding integrity; he had endured the privations, toils, and hardships incident to the settlement of a new country, and knew well how to sympathize with others in like circumstances. He told me had gone thirty miles and packed corn horseback to feed his family, had taken his rifle in the morning and gone in search of a deer, knowing if successful, they would have meat, if not, they must all do without; but seldom did his trusty rifle fail him or his family suffer. They were now living in comparative affluence, with an interesting family of children. Mrs. Bell was one of the noblest women I ever knew in any country; though living in the wilds of Texas, her intelligence, good taste, and polished manners, would have graced the most refined circles of New York or Philadelphia. Her house was a welcome home to every stranger, where the hungry were fed, the naked clad, the sick nursed with that tenderness and sympathy which removed many a dark cloud from the brow of sorrow, and caused the lonely wanderers to feel less acutely the absence of home and relatives. Texans now know very little how much the country owes to the early efforts of this pure woman, how much suffering she was instrumental in relieving, and when the dark clouds of war lowered, what confidence and courage she inspired in the bosoms of the timorous and desponding; for she was a stranger to fear, and of our final success she never doubted.

While here I became acquainted with Stephen F. Richardson, on his way to his home in San Felipe de Austin, and as that was my destination, I cheerfully accepted an invitation to accompany him; and on the night of the second day I was at the capital of the little colony. The following day I was introduced to the empresario, Stephen F. Austin, whom I found an intelligent and affable gentleman, and whom, so long as he lived, I was proud to number among my warmest and most devoted friends. To speak here of his many virtues would be superfluous, as his fame is world-wide and his works follow him; and when Texas shall become the wealthiest and most populous State in the Union, as, from her size and natural advantages she must soon be, her intelligent millions, looking back to his early efforts, will do justice to the memory of this great and good man.

I soon engaged in teaching, and succeeded in a short time in raising a school of about forty scholars, mostly boys, with expressive and intelligent countenances who were easily controlled, and some of whom gave indications of future greatness and usefulness. Contemplating, in imagination, what Texas, from its great natural advantages, must soon become, I felt the necessity of moral and religious, as well as intellectual culture, and resolved to make an effort to found a Sunday-school. Notice was given through the school, that on the following Sunday an address would be delivered on the subject, and I was gratified to see at the time appointed, a large and respectable audience assembled. An address was delivered; they seemed to feel interested, and on the following Sunday a school was organized of thirty-two scholars. There were not lacking intelligent gentlemen and ladies to act as teachers, but of the other appurtenances of a well-regulated Sunday-school we had none. This lack was supplied, as best it could be, by contributions of the citizens of such books as they had, and by the oral instructions of superintendents and teachers.

The next Sunday found the school under way, and giving promise of great success. A lecture was delivered each Sunday morning, intended for both old and young; and to hear these lectures, people came from the distance of ten miles; and as this town was the capital of the colony, many people were sometimes in attendance from different parts of the country, who carried the good seed here sown all over the colony. This school, and these morning lectures, were continued regularly, and well attended, until a difficulty occurring between some intelligent Mexicans visiting the place from the interior and some citizens, growing out of a law-suit which was decided against the Mexicans, the empresario deemed it prudent to discontinue them for a time, as these Mexicans could not be deceived in relation to the character of our

FIRST SUNDAY-SCHOOL IN TEXAS.

To face p. 75.

exercises, and it was well known that we were acting in violation of the colonization law, which strictly prohibited Protestant worship and prohibited Austin from introducing any but Catholics as colonists.

Now let us for a moment contemplate this little Sunday-school. In a black-jack and post-oak grove near the center of the town is a rude log-cabin about eighteen by twenty-two feet, the roof covered with boards held down by weight-poles, the logs unhewn, and the cracks neither chinked or battened, a dirt floor, and across it are placed several logs hewn on one side for seats. At one end stands the superintendent, a mere stripling, and before him are about half a dozen gentlemen and ladies as teachers, and thirty-two children, without any of those appendages which are now considered necessary to a well conducted Sunday-school. Forty-five years have passed since the organization of that little Sunday-school, and now on a Sunday morning of a pleasant day 60,900 children are assembled in our beloved State, under the guidance of 10,000 intelligent and, for the most part, pious young gentlemen and ladies, with a good supply of papers and libraries written by the ablest divines of our age, and containing interesting biographies, and the very pith and marrow of Christian theology. Surely we may exclaim, What hath God wrought? That same superintendent still lives and still labors in the delightful task of training the young in the Sunday-school, and as he contemplates, in imagination, the five and a half millions of children now being trained in the Sunday-schools of the United States, and then looks forward down the long corridors of time when these children shall be the actors in the great drama of life, he sees the dawn of that happy day foretold by seers and prophets when the knowledge of God shall cover the whole earth, the lion shall lie down with the lamb, and "the wilderness and the solitary place shall be glad for them ; and the desert shall rejoice and blossom as the rose."

I would here correct one erroneous impression in relation to the character of the early settlers of Texas. Many believe they were rude and ignorant, with many vices and very few virtues, and for the most part refugees from justice and enemies to law and order. That there were some rude and illiterate people among them is no more than may be said of almost any society, and that some were vicious and depraved is equally true, but what there was of evil you saw on the surface, for there was no effort at concealment and no reason to act a borrowed part. Assassins, if there were any, appeared as such ; now they often appear in the guise of gentlemen, that they may conceal their true characters and accomplish their object. No one estimates more highly than the writer, the intelligence, enterprise, and virtue of the present population, and yet he fully believes there were in the early history of Texas more college-bred men, in proportion to the population, than now, and as much intelligence, good common sense, and moral and religious culture among the females as among the ladies of the present day. Many had moved in the higher circles of our large cities, and some had filled stations of honor and responsibility. Some, were incited to emigrate by a spirit of enterprise and romance, and some, having been unfortunate in their pecuniary enterprises, sought to improve their circumstances in a new country, and not a few were the votaries of health who, unable to endure longer the rigors of a cold climate, sought relief in the sunny climes of the South.

If they had failings, let us throw the mantle of charity over them, and let their acts proclaim their noble virtues. When Texans took up arms against Mexico, it was in the maintenance of rights guaranteed to them by the constitution under which they had been invited to settle, and their population did not exceed 35,000; and does it not argue great energy, enterprise, and courage in their small numbers to take up arms against 8,000,000, and, with few resources except their own courage and power of endurance, to win the day?

A kinder and more hospitable people, perhaps, never lived. Their houses were welcome homes to each other; and never was the stranger rudely repulsed or sent empty away. When one was seen approaching, the inference was that he had come a considerable distance and was hungry and tired: preparations were immediately made to give him as comfortable a meal as their plain larder would permit, and without money or price, and although they could not boast then of the luxuries we now enjoy, their fare was nevertheless far from being meager. Bears, deer, turkeys, geese, ducks, and squirrels were plenty and easily obtained, and chickens, eggs, sweet potatoes, milk, butter, and honey were found in abundance on every table. The traveler always carried with him a blanket laid over his Spanish saddle-tree on which he rode, and a pair of saddle-bags; the former always furnished him wherever he stopped, a bed, and the latter a pillow, and, if he slept out of doors, which many preferred, the canopy of heaven was his covering.

New-Englanders have always been proud of their Christian ancestors who bequeathed to them so rich an inheritance, and well may the present generation of Texans look back with gratitude and pride to those noble-souled heroes who by their toils, energy, self-sacrifice and daring, won and bequeathed to them the fairest land on which the sun ever shone. A few of these old heroes still survive and move among us as mementoes of the past, their heads whitened with the frosts of many winters, and their steps tottering with the weight of years. God forbid that they should ever feel want where plenty abounds, and that the sun of their brighter days should set behind the dark clouds of sorrow.

T. J. P

XV.

THE TEXAS NAVY.

COMPILED BY SWANTE PALM.

DURING the busy period of the Revolution which began in 1835, the "Authorities" managed, through the kindness of good friends, in the early part of the year 1836, to pick up a small navy of three vessels, viz., the *Invincible*, Captain L. Brown; the *Brutus*, Captain Hurd; and the *Independence*, Captain Hawkins. These vessels were not idle, but were of infinite service to Texas in preventing the enemy from receiving supplies. In the first days of April the *Invincible* sailed on a cruise off Brazos Santiago, and fell in with the *Montezuma*, Captain Thompson. After a fight of two hours, the Mexican vessel was driven on shore, and left in a sinking condition. After repairing his rigging (the only injury he received), Captain Brown stood out from the harbor, and fell in with the brig *Pocket*, from New Orleans to Matamoras, freighted with flour, lard, rice, and biscuits for the Mexican army, under contract with a house from the former city. The *Pocket* was brought into Galveston. In August following, the Texan Navy consisted of the *Invincible*, carrying eight port-guns and one pivot nine-pounder; the *Brutus*, of like force; the *Independence*, of eight guns; and the *Liberty* of three guns, undergoing repairs.

The appearance of the Mexican fleet in the gulf was followed by some damage to Texas. The *Champion*, freighted with provisions, etc., for the army, was taken by the enemy; and also, on the 12th of April, 1837, the *Julius Cæsar*, whose cargo was valued at thirty thousand dollars. President Houston had previously issued an order for the release of the Mexican prisoners taken at the battle of San Jacinto and at other fights; but, learning that those on board the captured vessels had been taken into Matamoras and confined, he revoked the order of release.

The blockading navy of the enemy necessarily came in contact with the commerce of the United States; and the Mexican brig-of-war *Urrea*, having captured some American vessels and property, was taken by the United States sloop-of-war *Natchez*, and sent into Pensacola as a pirate. On the 17th of April, the Texan schooner *Independence*, having a crew of thirty-one men, besides several passengers, among whom was William H. Wharton, on his return from his mission to the United States—was met, about thirty miles from Velasco, by two Mexican brigs-of-war, the *Libertador*, having sixteen eighteen-pounders and one hundred and forty men, and the *Vincedor del Alamo*, carrying six twelves and one long eighteen-pounder, and one hundred men. After a severe fight, in which the Texans behaved most gallantly, the *Independence* was overpowered and taken into Brazos Santiago, where the crew and passengers were transferred to Matamoras and confined. In this engagement, Captain Wheelwright, of the *Independence*, was severely wounded.

The Texan navy, on leaving Galveston in May, proceeded to the mouth of the Mississippi, but, failing to find any of the enemy there, after a cruise of seven or eight days, turned to the coast of Mexico. The Texans made some small prizes about the island of Mugere, and thence proceeded to Yucatan, where they cannonaded the town of Sizal for some three hours, but with little effect. The Texan schooner *Invincible* took, and sent into port as a prize, the Mexican schooner *Alispa*, of eighty tons; and the *Brutus* captured and sent in the schooner *Telegraph*. The Texans also made repeated landings along the coast, and burnt eight or nine towns. Another vessel, the *Eliza Russell*, of one hundred and eighty tons, belonging to English subjects, which was taken by the *Invincible* off the Alicranes, and brought into Galveston, not being freighted with a contraband cargo, was afterward restored, with damages, by the Republic.

Colonel John H. Wharton, desirous of making an effort to release his brother from the prison in Matamoras, obtained permission and a flag, and proceeded with thirty Mexican prisoners to that town, to make an exchange. But on landing, he was made a prisoner, and confined in a dungeon. After an imprisonment of six days, he made his escape and returned to Texas. In the meantime, his brother, William H. Wharton, through the aid of the well-known Captain Thompson, of the Mexican navy, also escaped and reached home. It was intended that Thompson should desert the enemy's service, and leave with him; but Thompson's departure was precipitated by some information given to the Mexican authorities, and he arrived in Texas before either of the Whartons.

On the 25th of August, the *Brutus* and the *Invincible* arrived off the bar at Galveston, having in tow a Mexican armed schooner, which they had captured near the banks of Campeachy. On the same evening, the *Brutus* and the prize entered the harbor, but the *Invincible* could not get in. On the following morning the latter was attacked by two of the enemy's armed brigs. The *Brutus*, in attempting to go out to her aid, ran aground; so the *Invincible* was obliged to continue the *unequal* contest alone during the day. Toward evening she attempted a retreat, but struck on the breakers near the southeast channel. The crew landed in safety, but during the night the vessel went to pieces. The *Invincible* was a favorite craft in the Texan navy, and her loss much regretted.

In pursuance of an act for augmenting the navy, November 4, 1837, Samuel M. Williams was appointed by the President to contract for the vessels required by the law. Accordingly, on the 13th of November, 1838, he contracted with Frederick Dawson, of Baltimore, for one ship, two brigs, and three schooners, to be fully armed, furnished with provisions and munitions, and delivered in the port of Galveston. In accordance with this contract the Texan government received, on the 27th of June, 1839, the schooner *San Jacinto;* on the 7th of August, the schooner *San Antonio;* on the 31st of August, the schooner *San Bernard;* and, on the 18th of October the brig *Colorado.* A corvette and a brig were yet wanting to complete the contract. On the 23d of March following, was also delivered the steam ship-of-war *Zavala,* purchased by General James Hamilton, agent of James Holford. These vessels, with the *Charleston,* undergoing repairs, and the receiving-brig *Potomac,* constituted the navy of Texas, and with which the Secretary of the Navy said "it was confidently believed that, in a very short time after the navy should have received orders for capture and reprisal, it would be enabled to afford a source of revenue to the government, *equal* to the amount which had been expended for its creation."

In 1841 the fifth Congress digested and passed an act, January 18th, greatly reducing the number of officers of the government; placed all the public vessels in ordinary, except a schooner. On the subject of the navy, etc., the president, on the 22d of December, 1842, sent a secret message to Congress. He had not referred to it in his annual message, not wishing the world to know the deplorable condition of that arm of the public service. The vessels of the navy had returned from Yucatan early in May previous, and were ordered to repair to New Orleans and Mobile to refit, preparatory to the enforcement of the blockade of the ports of Mexico. This blockade had been proclaimed by Texas in the confident belief as expressed by Commodore Moore, that, with the aid of the friends of the republic in the United States, the squadron would be ready for sea in a few weeks. In July the navy was ordered to report at Galveston for further instructions; and Commodore Moore was directed on the day the secret message was sent to Congress, he having disobeyed repeated orders, to turn over the command to the senior officer present and report in person. The *San Antonio* had been dispatched to Yucatan in August, 1842, without the knowledge of the Texan government, and was lost in a storm. The president recommended the sale of the vessels, and he believed that the person from whom they had been purchased could be induced to take them again; and owing to the impoverished treasury and this representation, the Texas Congress passed a secret act authorizing the president to sell the war vessels. Through the Commissioners appointed to do so Commodore Moore was informed of this act. One of them reported that Commodore Moore had large claims against the navy for money expended for its use, that he was inclined to hold on to the vessels, and that he considered himself not bound to obey orders from the navy department, under a law not promulgated. It was also stated that Colonel Zavala, of Yucatan, was at New Orleans, urging Commodore Moore to sail down the Gulf coast and capture the Mexican fleet. Commodore Moore, after corresponding on the subject, at last declared himself without authority to enter into any arrangement with Yucatan, and Commodore Moore sailed for Galveston ; one of the commissioners, Colonel Morgan, being on board. Arriving at the mouth of the Mississippi, they learned that the Mexican war-steamship *Montezuma* was at Telchak, and that it could probably be taken. Sailing to that point, the steamship had on their arrival left. Commodore Moore, proceeding down the coast with the *Austin* and *Wharton*, had two important engagements with several of the enemy's vessels, in which the Texans fought gallantly and gained much advantage. At last Commodore Moore, in command of the navy, arrived in Galveston in July. After the return of the vessels of the navy to Galveston, they were placed in ordinary, and, for want of funds to equip and man them, they so remained until the annexation of the Republic to the United States.

The above sketch is principally from Yoakum's History of Texas and the archives of the Republic.

——▸•◂——

XVI.

EXPEDITION WEST, UNDER JOHNSON, GRANT, AND MORRIS.

BY COL. F. W. JOHNSON.

THIS expedition had for its object the taking and holding of Matamoras, an important commercial post, which yielded a large revenue to the government of Mexico. As a military point it is of but little value except as a depot.

After the capitulation of General Cos, and the surrender of San Antonio de Bexar and the Alamo, December, 1835, most of the Texans, then in the volunteer army, returned to their homes, leaving the place to be garrisoned by United States volunteers, who had joined previously, and were still arriving almost daily. All were anxious for active service. An expedition against Matamoras was soon organized, consisting of the major part of the troops at that place. Under this state of things it only remained to obtain the consent of the Provisional Government. For this purpose Colonel Johnson, then in command of the post, turned the command over to Colonel Niel, and repaired to San Felipe de Austin, made known his object, which was readily approved by the Government, and the necessary order was made for the expedition, which he communicated to his friends, who left San Antonio de Bexar the latter part of December and proceeded to Goliad, and thence to Mission Refugio, where Colonel Johnson joined them. While at Goliad, General Houston arrived, and followed them to Refugio. At first the general favored the expedition, but on his arrival at Refugio, declared the expedition both unwise and unauthorized. This caused a division of opinion, which ended in most of the men joining Houston's forces, which, at the time, consisted of a single company at Goliad.

A considerable number of volunteers from the United States, at the time spoken of, were at Velasco, mouth of the Brazos, and had tendered their services to the government and were accepted. Colonel I. W. Fannin was authorized to transport them to Copano, thence by land to Refugio, and join Colonel Johnson, with whom they were to co-operate. The difficulty of procuring vessels delayed Fannin. In the meantime Colonels Johnson and Grant, and Major R. C. Morris, formerly of the New Orleans Grays, marched to San Patricio, with a force of less than 100 men. Here they remained until Colonel Fannin arrived at Refugio. In the meantime learning that there was a small detachment of Mexican soldiers west and below San Patricio, Colonel Grant, with a small force, marched down, surprised and made them prisoners.

After conferring with Colonel Fannin, Colonel Johnson determined to proceed west for the purpose of getting horses. They pursued their way within some twenty or twenty-five miles of Sal Colorado, and had horses sufficient to mount 100 men. Here the command divided, and Grant and Morris with the largest half of the men, went in pursuit of more horses. This was contrary to Johnson's judgment ; however, Grant and Morris insisted on visiting a rancho where it was said there was a large number of horses belonging to the Mexican government.

About this time they had received intelligence of the advance of General Santa Anna with a well appointed army, for the purpose of invading Texas. General Urrea, in the meantime, was collecting a force at Matamoras, intending to enter Texas from that point.

Grant and his party were successful, and obtained a large number of horses. In the meantime, Johnson and his band had returned with the horses they had, to San Patricio, where Grant was to join them and proceed together to Goliad, where Fannin had established his headquarters. While waiting at San Patricio for Grant, Johnson and his party were surprised, and most of the men killed. In this connection it is proper to remark that there were no sentinels posted ; first, for the reason that Grant's force was in the rear, and, sec-

6

ond, the men were thinly clad, and the weather very cold. Johnson and four others—Dan. J. Toler, John, H. Love, James M. Miller, and a Frenchman, escaped in the following manner. The attack was simultaneous. The house occupied by Johnson and his companions was surrounded, and being hailed they were ordered to make a light. Toler, who spoke Spanish well, kept them in conversation, but was in no hurry to make a light. But a few minutes had elapsed when there was a discharge of arms in front of the house, which caused those in rear to move to the front. Johnson took advantage of this propitious moment, and ordered his companions to open the back door and try to escape. They acted promptly, and Johnson followed. The Frenchman secreted himself until morning, when he surrendered. Having resided in Matamoras, and being acquainted with many of the officers, he was kindly treated.

Toler, Love, and Miller kept together, and made their way as best they could for Refugio. The night was very dark, and greatly favored their escape. The next morning Johnson overtook them, and they proceeded together, keeping the brush, and halting and secreting themselves in clumps of bushes as long as they could for the coldness of the weather. In this way they traveled until night, when they struck out for the road to Refugio, and, after getting to it, kept it to within some two miles of Refugio, deeming it unsafe to enter it at night. Here they were joined by another companion who had made good his escape.

After resting, refreshing themselves, and giving notice to the few families at that place, they proceeded to Goliad, where they arrived the second day. From thence, Johnson, Toler, and Love proceeded to San Felipe de Austin. On their way thither, at Victoria, they learned the sad fate of Grant's party, all of whom were butchered, except Plaude, who brought the information to Goliad and Victoria, and William Innlock. Colonel R. R. Brown was made prisoner and held for months before he effected his escape from Matamoras.

Miller who joined Fannin, was butchered with his command. Innlock escaped death by being retained as a nurse.

XVII.

FIRST BREAKING OUT OF THE TEXAS REVOLUTION AT GONZALES.

(Texas Almanac, 1861.)

THE writer of this has not yet seen any full and correct account of the first breaking out of the Texas revolution at Gonzales in 1835, and having been personally present, he gives the following details of facts from his own knowledge.

The usurper, Santa Anna, having prostrated the constitution of 1824, which the Texans had subscribed to and sworn to support, and having reduced some of the Mexican states, to the most humiliating subjection, by forcing upon them a *Central Military Despotism*, his ire was then turned toward Texas, as a part of the State of Coahuila. Knowing what kind of men he had to contend with, his first object was *to disarm*, and then to *coerce*.

For the consummation of these tyrannical objects, the usurper sent an armed force from San Antonio of some three hundred cavalry to take a cannon from the citizens of Gonzales, which had been furnished them by the Mexican government to defend themselves against the incursions of the Indians.

The Mexican commander demanded the cannon. The citizens replied that their Alcalde was absent, and that they would give him an answer on the Alcalde's return. This produced a suspense of some three days. No time was lost in sending an express to the Guadaloupe, the Colorado, and the Brazos, for aid. Volunteers from each of these points turned out and hastened to the rescue.

On the arrival of Captain Goheen from the Guadaloupe, Captains Moore and Coleman from the Colorado, and Captain Smith from the Brazos, with their companies, the citizens then informed the Mexican commander that Mr. Williams, their Alcalde, had returned, and that he had determined not to give up the cannon. The Mexican officer said: "*I have come for the cannon, and will not return without it.*" He was then informed that he would not get the cannon without a fight.

The Mexican force occupied the west and the Texans the east bank of the Guadaloupe river, for some two days. In this time of suspense, Major R. M. Williamson and others drew the cannon in open view of the Mexican army, and elevated upon it in large and glaring letters: "COME AND TAKE IT !" The Mexican officer, thinking prudence the better part of valor, declined making the effort ; but moved his encampment about six miles on the direction to San Antonio. The Texans completed their organization by electing Colonel John H. Moore and Lieutenant-Colonel J. W. E. Wallace to the command. There were seven physicians in the army—they formed themselves into a medical board by electing Rev. W. P. Smith, M.D., President, and Thomas J. Gazley, M.D., Secretary.

On the 1st of October, 1835, Colonel Moore called a council of war, consisting of the field, staff, and company officers. It determined that it was too much to bear their own expenses and to ride the distance that they had done to meet the enemy, and then to return home without a fight. Hence the unanimous voice of the council was : *" We will hoist the flag of liberty and attack the Mexicans in their encampment on to-morrow morning at daybreak."* Orders were issued on the evening of the same day, that the army take up the line of march, cross the Guadaloupe River, form on the west bank, and await further orders. The army having crossed, and at about the hour of eleven at night, being formed into a hollow square, Colonels Moore and Wallace, with the Rev. W. P. Smith, rode into the square, when the latter, being seated on his favorite mule, addressed the army as follows :

" FELLOW-SOLDIERS : To cap the climax of a long catalogue of injuries and grievances attempted to be heaped upon us, the government of Mexico, in the person of Santa Anna, has sent an army to commence the disarming system. Give up the cannon, and we may surrender our small-arms also, and at once be the vassals of the most imbecile and unstable government upon earth.

" But will Texas give up the cannon ? will she surrender her small-arms ? Every response is *No, never !* never will she submit to a degradation of that character !

" Fellow-soldiers, the cause for which we are contending is just, honorable, and glorious—our liberty ! The same blood that animated the hearts of our ancestors of '76 still flows warm in our veins.

" Having waited several days for the Mexican army to make an attack upon us, we have now determined to attack them on to-morrow morning at the dawn of day. Some of us may fall, but if we do, let us be sure to fall with our faces toward the enemy. Your humble speaker has had the pleasure of examining the contemplated plan of attack. It is judiciously arranged ; and to show you that he has had some opportunity of judging, he would simply say that he was with Generals Jackson, Carroll, and Coffee in the great battles at New Orleans in 1814–15.

" Fellow-soldiers, let us march silently, obey the commands of our superior officers, and united as one man, present a bold front to the enemy. *Victory will be ours !* We have passed the Rubicon, and we have borne the insults and indignities of Mexico until forbearance has ceased to be a virtue. A resort to arms is our only alternative; *we must fight and we will fight.* In numerical strength, the nation against whom we contend is our superior; but so just and so noble is the cause for which we contend that the strong arm of Jehovah will lead us on to victory, to glory, and to empire.

"With us, every thing is at stake—our firesides, our wives, our children, our country, our all! Great will be the influence over the colonies resulting from the effort we are about to make. We *must sustain ourselves in the contest.* This will inspire confidence in the minds of our countrymen.

"Fellow-soldiers, march with bold hearts and steady steps to meet the enemy, and let every arm be nerved, while our minds are exercised with the happy reflection that the guardian angels are directing our course.

"Let us all go into battle with the words of the immortal Patrick Henry, before the Virginia House of Burgesses, deeply impressed upon our hearts, when, with arms extended toward heaven, and with a voice of thunder, he exclaimed in the most patriotic manner, ' *Give me liberty, or give me death!* ' "

The address being concluded, the army took up the line of march silently and in good order. As soon as daylight had fairly dawned, Colonel Moore demanded of the Mexican officer to surrender. On his refusal to do so, the order passed rapidly along the line—"Fire." Immediately the Mexicans were saluted by a volley of grape thrown into their camp from that very cannon which had been the bone of contention. Being quickly seconded by a general discharge of small-arms, the Mexicans retreated precipitately toward San Antonio, and in accordance with their usage, took their killed and wounded with them. The Texans then returned to Gonzales, where all hearts were made glad at the arrival of the Father of his Country, Colonel Stephen F. Austin, from the prisons of Mexico.

Several other companies of volunteers having arrived, so as to make a more extensive organization of the army necessary, Colonel S. F. Austin by acclamation was announced the commanding General of the army, and he appointed Colonel William T. Austin his aid, and Rev. W. P. Smith, Surgeon-General. While drilling and preparing for the march to San Antonio, the Sabbath day arrived, on the evening of which Rev. W. P. Smith, acting in the joint capacity of surgeon and chaplain to the army, preached to a large and promiscuous assembly of officers, soldiers, and citizens on these words: "If ye be willing and obedient ye shall eat the good of the land; but if ye refuse and rebel, ye shall be devoured by the sword, for the mouth of the Lord hath spoken it." (Isaiah i. 19, 20.) This text was appropriate at the commencement of a revolution. Other battles had previously been fought in defense of the Constitution of 1824, but the attack as above narrated may justly be considered the one which put in motion the great ball of the Texan Revolution.

A few days having been spent in preparations, the line of march was taken up for San Antonio. While *en route* for that point, General Austin received an appointment from the Provisional Government as one of the financial commissioners to the United States, and as war can not be successfully carried on without money, duty compelled him to accept.

His vacancy being filled by the election of General Edward Burleson, the army continued its march to San Antonio, where by a bold and patriotic effort, in which the lamented Colonel Benj. R. Milam, with other noble spirits, fell, the Texan army were successful·in gaining a signal victory over General Cos and his numerous army. The country being cleared of its enemies, the sunshine of peace again shone brightly in all her borders during the little remainder of 1835.

AN OLD SOLDIER.

XVIII.

TEXAS.

(From the New York Times.)

TEXAS was a name to conjure with, some thirty or forty years ago, and it will always be remembered as the origin of these exasperations, which, in 1848, left the United States in possession of nearly half the Republic of Mexico. The area of Texas is 274,000 square miles, about six times as large as the State of New York; and nature seems to have formed it to be, like Arabia and Poland, a broad field of warlike enterprise and liberty—though the Polish part of the parallel must be assumed to represent the Sobieski days of the *Liberum Veto* and the equestrian parliaments with drawn swords.

The name Texas is Celtiberian or Spanish. Some tell us it has the meaning of " Paradise,"—the suggestion no doubt, of a Carankawa buffalo-hunter; and others—our author among them—seem to' think it meant *Friend*, a much feebler sort of guess. But, as in all original cases of the kind, nature herself has vindicated the sense of the nomenclature. *Tehas* meant and means *Plain*, in the Celtic—the great plain near Spanish Seville being named *Dehesa*. Texas and Poland were named in the same way, and for the same reason, meaning level or plain countries. There was a *Texas*, or raised platform for the noble family, in the hall of every prince and baron of the mediæval ages, and it was spelled *Dais*—a term curiously mistaken for a canopy.

Texas was always a "hard" ground for the march of civilization. The Indians loved "horse to ride and weapon wear," better than they loved the Catholic missionaries, and the latter were by degrees exterminated. In 1758, the last lingering priests were massacred at La Saba, and the station broken up. France had a claim on Texas as touching on Louisiana ; but in 1763 she gave it up. In 1806, Aaron Burr planned an expedition for the invasion of that derelict and debatable ground, but it was arrested by the Government while on its way, and Burr tried for the offense.

In 1814, Magee, Kemper, Gutierez, Perry, and others, whose names suggest the very mixed quality of the enterprise, made a more resolute attempt on that territory, and fought battles with the Mexican forces for three or four years before they were overpowered. Others made similar attempts ; and in 1819 Dr. Long of Tennessee went in and established a provisional government at Nacogdoches. But he, too, failed, and was put to death in the city of Mexico. Then came the daring corsair, Jean Lafitte of Bordeaux, who raised his flag at Galveston, in the Gulf, and had an idea of establishing a Texan Carthage in that place. He offered a reward of $5,000 for the head of Governor Claiborne of Louisiana, who had begun the quarrel by offering the same amount for his ; and when he had captured the whole expedition sent against him by Claiborne, he feasted them with a piratical magnanimity, and sent them back to his enemy with a sarcastic message. Lafitte also failed ; and then, in 1821, came Stephen F. Austin, of Missouri, armed with a grant of territory on the Brazos River, conceded by the Republican Congress of Mexico. From the ground of that advance there was no more retreating. The modern growth of Texas is sufficiently remembered. In 1830 it held 20,000 Americans. It has now about 1,000,000, and holds 90,000,000 of acres to dispose of as public lands. In his "Brief History of Texas," Mr. Baker gives a concise and authentic record of all its early troubles, and the subsequent administrations, acts of legislature, remarkable events, and domestic progress of the territory, both as "Lone Star" and State of the Union. It is very well fitted to be a book of instruction in schools.

XIX.

AUSTIN'S FIRST COLONY.

(Texas Planter.)

PEACH POINT, BRAZORIA CO., July 1st, 1852

MR. EDITOR:

. In the last number of the " Planter," I noticed an article under caption of Austin's First Colony, in which I detected several errors which I respectfully beg leave to correct. You say that Austin arrived on the banks of the Brazos River on the first day of January, 1822. He arrived on the banks of the Brazos on the first day of August, 1821, with Edward Lovelace, Neil Gaspar, —— Bellew, H. Holstein, William Little, Joseph Polly,* James Beard, —— Beard, —— Marple, William Wilson, Dr. Hewitson, —— Irwine, W. Smithers, and —— Barre. These were the hardy men with whom Austin first blazed his way through the Brazos bottom. They were the first pioneers of the old "three hundred." None preceded them. Austin arrived at San Antonio with his little party, in company with the commissioner Don Erasnio Seguin, on the 12th day of August, 1821, and not in January, 1822, as stated by you. In justice to the name of Seguin, let me add that no Mexican ever did more for Texas and the colonists, than did that true-hearted man. In the infancy of Texas, in the days of her weakness and his strength, he was the faithful friend of the Americans. (Would I could say the same of the Americans toward him.) A man of intelligence and position, having the confidence of his government, through him Austin obtained many favors for the colonists.

In San Antonio, whenever an American got into difficulty, Seguin was the first and best friend he had, and those who lived here in early times, when the Mexican was strong, know how valuable such a friend could prove. Austin, through the representations of Seguin and Beumende, was received with great kindness by General Martinez.

He obtained permission of the Governor to explore the country on the Colorado and Brazos, and to sound the entrances, harbors, etc., of those rivers. With nine of his men he made these explorations sufficiently to satisfy him of the great fertility of the land along these streams. He then returned to Louisiana, preparatory to carrying out the colonization plan.

In December, 1821, he arrived on the Brazos, where the La Bahia road crosses it, with his settlers, the first families of the old " three hundred."

* Recently of this county.

On New Year's eve, he encamped on New Year's creek. Andy Robinson * was the first permanent settler on the Brazos, near where the town of Washington now stands. In March following, Austin went to San Antonio to report to the Governor, when he was informed that it would be necessary for him to proceed to Mexico, to procure from Congress, then in session, confirmation of the grant to his father, Moses Austin, and to receive special instructions as to the distribution of land, issuance of titles, etc. This trip to Mexico was totally unexpected and very embarrassing; for, not anticipating anything of the kind, he was entirely unprepared.

There was no time for hesitation. Arrangements were at once made for Mr. Josiah H. Bell to take charge of the settlement, and Austin departed for Mexico, a distance of twelve hundred miles by land. The greater part of this journey he performed on foot, dressed like a mendicant soldier to avoid robbers. Mrs. Mary Bell, widow of Josiah H. Bell, now lives in this county; and a purer, nobler-minded woman never breathed its air. Not an old Texan lives who does not love and revere this admirable lady—this good Samaritan of Austin's Colony.

GUY M. BRYAN.

XX.

MOMENTOUS INCIDENT OF THE TEXAS REVOLUTION

RECONCILIATION OF AUSTIN AND WHARTON.

(Galveston News.)

AUSTIN, May, 1874.

EDITORS NEWS:

Believing as I do, that incidents often indicate the character of men, I propose to relate one connected with the undisputed and practical commencement of the revolution which separated Texas from Mexico.

Early in the month of October, 1835, and but a day or two previous to the organization of the volunteer army of Texas, at Gonzales, the writer, in company with Wm. H. Wharton, and Wm. G. Hill, arrived at that place a short time after dark, and seeing a glimmering light in an old-fashioned double-logged cabin, we rode to it. At the suggestion of Mr. Wharton, the writer dismounted and entered the house, and much to our gratification, found Pleasant D. McNeil of Brazoria county. I at once asked him the news. He replied, "I fear we are to have trouble: there are several gentlemen here (and he named them), each of whom has been, and is, aspiring to the chief command of the army; each one has his squad of friends, but neither

* Now living in this county.

seems able to harmonize a majority ; so that a few days ago it was agreed to send an express to San Felipe for Colonel S. F. Austin, with the hope that, sooner than abandon the contemplated and cherished object of driving the garrison from San Antonio, all would unite on him : and," said he, in conclusion, " Colonel Austin reached here a short time since, very much fatigued, and is in the next room lying down." I asked for nothing more, but without ceremony entered the room where Colonel Austin was, and found him lying on his blanket, with, an " inch " of candle stuck on a chip by his side, evidently in feeble health. He greeted me very cordially, and prepared a seat for me on the side of his blanket. I accepted, and he related to me in a few words what he understood to be the condition of matters, and with much feeling expressed fears that he would not be able to reconcile existing difficulties ; that it was well known by all that he knew nothing practically about military matters ; that there were men of influence whose feelings, he regretted to say, were so bitter toward him that he greatly feared that they would never consent to abandon their ambitious views for the purpose of harmonizing any difficulty by uniting on him.

Just then he recognized the voice, as he thought, of Mr. Wharton in the next room, and asked me if he was there. I told him he was ; that we came together. He then spoke of Mr. Wharton as one of the men of ability and influence, whose feelings toward him were very bitter—than whom there was not a man who would use greater exertions to defeat any effort to unite on him, without reference to the object to be accomplished thereby. He then came to a pause, evidently desiring to have my opinion as to what he had expressed, for he well knew that the personal relations between Mr. Wharton and myself were of the most cordial nature. I said to him, " Colonel Austin, both Mr. Wharton and yourself are sensible and patriotic men, and it will not do for the feelings to which you refer, and which I understand, to militate against the public good ; we have too much at stake ; this must be settled, at least for the present." He sprang from off his blanket and, deeply excited, grasped me by the hand and asked if I thought Mr. Wharton would listen to an advance of that nature coming from him. I told him I had no doubt of it ; if he did not, I should tell him plainly he was not the man I had believed him to be. With a lip quivering with emotion, still holding my hand, he said, " Captain Russell, all I am and all I have, except my personal honor, which, at all hazards, must be saved, belongs to Texas, my own dear Texas. Go, then, as a messenger of peace, and with the solitary reservation of my personal honor, make any pledge in my name that may be necessary to secure the object, and I will indorse." I left him, passed to the room where I had left Mr. McNeil, and found that both Wharton and Hill had entered the room. I asked Mr. Wharton out in the yard, and told him I had a message for him, and enjoined silence on his part until the message was delivered in full. When I had concluded the message, to which, in brief, I appended my own views, the first words uttered by Mr. Wharton, were, " Great God ! is it possible for that man to entertain sentiments so elevated ? From my heart I honor him. Return to him ; tell him any thing for me you may deem necessary. We all have the same great object in view, and no man shall excel me in the performance of any duty deemed necessary to accomplish our purpose." I understood the impulsive nature of Mr. Wharton well, and before leaving him said, " Mr. Wharton, perhaps no man knows better than yourself that occasionally there are feelings entertained, or lurking in the heart of man, which silence best, and it may be which silence only, can express. I, therefore, deem it proper to stipulate that you return to the room, from whence you came—I will go for Colonel Austin, take him to the room— that you meet, take each other by the right hand, and not a word to be uttered by any person until the silence be broken by others present." I proceeded for Colonel Austin, told him how they were to meet, and con- ducted him to the room, where they met as stated, with a silent grasp of the hand, encircled by William G. Hill, Pleasant D. McNeil, and Wm. J. Russell, with the servants of Colonel Austin, Wharton, and Russell, named respect- ively Isam, Abram, and John, as lookers-on. Here indeed was exhibited a tableau upon which, I have often thought, an angel might have looked with approval. Of the eight persons above named, the writer is the only survivor : and although he has often thought of giving the incident to the public, it is quite likely that it would be delayed until he, too, had passed away, but for the suggestion of some friends, who, being apprised of it, insisted that it be given to the public. There are those still living of that comparatively small band of patriot brothers, some of whom have said to the writer within the past week, that but for the personal reconciliation above described, there would have been no organization of the army at that time ; and had that happened, no one could say what disastrous consequences might have followed. If this opinion be correct, it furnishes but another in the long and interesting catalogue of incidents with which the true history of Texas is full, and which, though of but apparent trifling import at the time, have developed into results. I may be permitted to add, that my acquaintance with General Stephen F. Austin dates back to 1828, and I am clearly of the opinion that his true character has never, in general, been fully understood, nor properly appreciated ; and hence, not only his memory, but the true history of Texas, have suffered and will continue to suffer to a greater or less degree.

WM. J. RUSSELL.

XXI.

THE GRASS FIGHT.

(Texas Almanac.)

THIS fight took place November 28th, 1835. I was then in the army at San Antonio, and most of the facts stated were known to me personally. Several days previously to this fight it was currently reported in camp, that there was a quantity of silver coming from Mexico, upon pack mules, to pay off the soldiers of General Cos. Our scouts kept a close watch, to give the news as soon as the convoy should be espied, so that we might intercept the treasure. On the morning of the 28th, Colonel Bowie was out in the direction of the Medina, with a company, and discovered some mules with packs approaching; and supposing this to be the expected train, he sent a messenger for re-enforcements. The camp was then above town at the old mill on the San Antonio River. Colonel Burleson immediately started with additional troops to join Bowie, but before reaching him, the latter, fearing the train would escape, made the attack with what forces he had. When Burleson arrived, Bowie had fallen back to a ditch or ravine near by, as affording a better position. As soon as they effected a union of their companions, they made an attack upon the Mexicans, who fell back, but being followed, they soon broke and fled. Thus ended the celebrated grass fight. The enemy left their packs, as they fled; which upon examination were found to be filled with grass, which they had gone out for and cut the night before, and were bringing into the fort for their horses. This circumstance was of course quite a disappointment to men whose heads were filled with visions of gold and silver; and the encounter was denominated the "Grass Fight." We lost one man and two wounded. The loss of the enemy is unknown.

WILLIAM S. TAYLOR.

———➤◄———

XXII.

MILITARY EVENTS OF TEXAS.

(From an old newspaper.)

BATTLE of Nacogdoches, August 2, 1827; Texans under Colonel Hayden E. Edwards, with a force of 250 defeated the Mexicans under Colonel Don Je de las Piedras, with 350.

Fort of Velasco, commanded by Colonel Don Domingo Ugartechea, with 175 men, taken by the Texans, under John Austin, with 130 men, June 26th, 1832.

In June, 1835, the Texans, under Colonel Travis, took the garrison of Anahuac, under Captain Tenora.

Rout at Gonzales, of a detachment of cavalry from the Mexican garrison, at Bexar, October 1st, 1835.

Capture of Goliad, under Sandoval, by Captain Collingsworth, with 50 men, October 9th, 1835.

Battle of Conception, near Bexar: 450 Mexicans defeated by Bowie and Fannin, with only 92 men.

Capture of Lipantitlan, on the river Nueces, by Adjutant Westover, November 3d, 1835.

The Grass Fight, near Bexar—400 Mexicans retreated from 200 Texans, November 8th, 1835.

Attack upon San Antonio de Bexar,—1,400 Mexicans, under General Cos, surrendered to the Texans, December 10th, 1835.

Retreat of General Houston from Gonzales, March 10th, 1836.

Assault of the Alamo, by Santa Anna—garrison put to the sword, March 6, 1836.

Mexicans defeated in the first fight of the " Mission del Refugio," by the Texans, under Captain King, March 9th, 1836.

Expedition against Matamoros, by the Texans, under Johnson, Grant, etc., proved an entire failure, January, 1836.

The town of Bexar taken by the Mexicans and the Texans retired into the Alamo, February 21st, 1836.

Second fight of " Mission del Refugio." Colonel Ward attacked and drove back a large body of Mexicans, March 10th, 1836.

Ward's retreat from the Refugio, March 11th, 1836—surrendered 24th—massacred on the 28th.

Defeat of Fannin, with 415 men, and all massacred by the Mexicans, March 19th, 1836.

San Felipe de Austin burned by the Texans, March 31st, 1836.

Harrisburg burned by the Mexicans, April 16th, 1836.

New Washington burned by the Mexicans, April 20th, 1836.

Battle of San Jacinto—750 Texans, under General Houston, defeated the Mexicans under Santa Anna, with about 1,600 men, killing upward of 750, and taking the remainder, with Santa Anna himself, April 21st, 1836.

Retreat of the Mexicans beyond the frontier of Texas, April 24th, 1836.

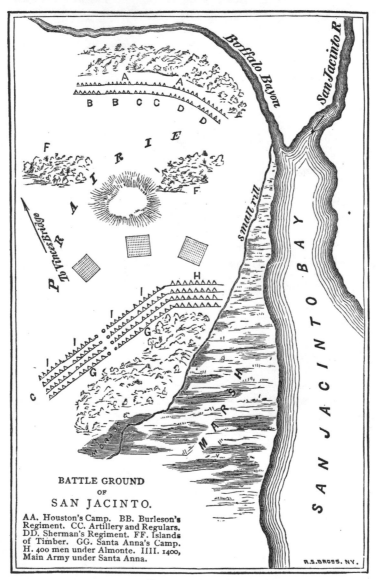

BATTLE GROUND
OF
SAN JACINTO.

AA. Houston's Camp. BB. Burleson's
Regiment. CC. Artillery and Regulars.
DD. Sherman's Regiment. FF. Islands
of Timber. GG. Santa Anna's Camp.
H. 400 men under Almonte. IIII. 1400,
Main Army under Santa Anna.

R.S.BROSS. NY.

PLAN OF BATTLE

XXIII.

THE BATTLE OF SAN JACINTO.

(From A Brief History of Texas.)

ON the morning of the 19th of April, the Texan army crossed over and marched down the right bank of the Buffalo Bayou to within half a mile of its junction with the San Jacinto River. Here they formed in line of battle on the edge of a grove of trees, their rear protected by the timber, while before them was the open prairie.

A few days before this, the army of the young Republic had received two pieces of artillery as a gift from some of the citizens of Cincinnati, Ohio. These were named the " Twin Sisters," and were placed in position. On the morning of the 20th of April, and soon after General Houston had dispersed his forces, Santa Anna came marching up in battle array. A volley from the " Twin Sisters" brought him to a sudden halt, and falling back to a clump of trees a quarter of a mile distant, he formed in line of battle. In return for the *feint* of the evening, Colonel Sherman, at the head of his mounted men, made a gallant charge upon the Mexican army, which, although it did not accomplish any decisive result, seemed to inspire our men with fresh enthusiasm.

The 21st of April dawned bright and beautiful. It was felt by those who were to participate in its stirring scenes, to be the day upon which the conflict for Texas was to be decided.

On this side was arrayed the whole available army of Texas, embracing 750 * men. On that, were the best troops of Mexico, to the number of 1,800, and commanded by an able and wily general. The men of Texas were aware that every thing for them depended upon the issue of the fight, and every heart was beating quick and every nerve well strung.

The men of Mexico were flushed with pride at recent successes, and felt secure of the result.

Early in the morning General Houston sent Deaf Smith, the celebrated Texas spy, with two or three men, to destroy Vince's bridge across the bayou over which the Mexican army had passed, thus cutting off their only available avenue of escape. The daring exploit was executed almost in the presence of the foe. It was now decided to be the moment to attack Santa Anna in his intrenchments. With the stillness of death the patriot army moved, in three divisions, to the charge. No music heralded the advance. No sound but the quiet tread of determined men broke the stillness of that

* See General Rusk's Report.

spring morning.   When within two hundred yards they received the volley of the enemy's advanced column without quailing, and then increased their pace to a "double quick."

When within seventy yards the word "FIRE" was given, and six hundred Texas rifles belched forth their deadly contents.   Then the shout, "ALAMO" and "GOLIAD," rang along the entire line, and they rushed forward to a hand to hand encounter.   But Mexican valor had already given way before the impetuosity of that charge, and in a few minutes more the boastful legions of the "Napoleon of the West" were in full retreat.   The rout soon became general.   Finding the bridge destroyed, the Mexicans plunged into the bayou,

HOUSTON AND SANTA ANNA.

where many were drowned or slain by their pursuers.   Seven hundred dead Mexicans upon that day atoned for the butchery at the Alamo and Goliad; and seven hundred and thirty prisoners were in the hands of the victorious army.

Santa Anna in vain tried to escape.   He was discovered, on the morning of the 22d, hiding in the long grass with a blanket thrown over his head, and was taken to the quarters of General Houston.

At the time Santa Anna was brought before him, Houston, who had been severely wounded in the battle, was lying on a mattrass under a tree which constituted his headquarters.   The President of Mexico, bowing low before him, said, "I am General Antonio Lopez de Santa Anna, a prisoner of war at your disposal." General Houston requested him to sit down, which he did, at the same time asking for opium. A piece of this drug was brought him, which he eagerly swallowed. He then at once proposed to purchase his freedom, but was answered, "that was a matter to be negotiated with the government of Texas." He however persisted saying to Houston, "You can afford to be generous, you have conquered the Napoleon of the West."

General Houston asked him "how he could expect mercy after showing none at the Alamo?"

He replied, that "by the rules of war, when a fort refused to surrender, and was taken by assault, the prisoners were doomed to death." General Houston answered him that "such a rule was a disgrace to the civilization of the nineteenth century." He was then asked "by what rule he justified the massacre of Goliad?" He replied that "he had orders from his government to execute all that were taken with arms in their hands."

General Houston told him that "*he* was the government—a Dictator had no superior, and that he must at once write an order for all his troops to abandon Texas and return home." This he did, and the dispatch was sent by a trusty messenger to his subordinates.

How to dispose of Santa Anna was a troublesome question. Among the soldiers the feeling existed that his life only could atone for the cruelties perpetrated by his order. But prudence as well as humanity dictated another course, and his life was spared. The following agreement was entered into between him and the President of Texas:

First. That he would never again take up arms against Texas.

Second. That he should order all Mexican troops in Texas to return home.

Third. That he should cause to be restored all captured property.

In consideration of the fulfillment of these conditions he was to be set free. When the time came for his release, the storm of popular indignation was so great, that President Burnet thought best to order his longer detention as a prisoner of war.

Santa Anna was liberated by President Houston, in January, 1837, and sent to Washington, D. C., whence he returned to Mexico.

7

XXIV.

REVOLUTIONARY INCIDENTS.

BURNING OF VINCE'S BRIDGE.

(Texas Almanac, 1861.)

SAN ANTONIO, January 14, 1858.

HON. JESSE GRIMES.

DEAR SIR: In compliance with the promise I made you when at Austin the other day, I shall endeavor to perform a task, to me extremely delicate, if not difficult. Delicate, because of the great diversity of opinion respecting the incident of burning the bridge over Vince's Bayou, on the morning of the 21st of April, 1836, the day of the memorable victory of San Jacinto.

Although many years have rolled by since that event, the leading circumstances attending the incident are still fresh in my memory; and if I err in giving its details, I feel assured that the error springs from the deficiency of recollection, but not from design.

On the morning of the 21st of April, 1836, Captain Carnes' cavalry company, commonly called Deaf Smith's Spy Company, were drawn up in line on the edge of General Houston's position. As well as I recollect, we were between thirty and forty strong. The Mexican cavalry, whom we fought the evening before, at that moment were drawn up in line, on the south of our position, about six hundred yards distant. I think they were from sixty to to eighty strong. They seemed to invite us again to combat; but prudence, in my humble opinion, dictated to our leaders a different course than to engage them at that moment. While sitting in our saddles, John Coker, my left file-leader, made the following remark, and the suggestions following:

"Boys, before many hours, we will have one of the damnedest, bloodiest fights that ever was fought, and I believe it would be a good plan to go and burn that bridge so as not only to impede the advance of re-enforcements of the enemy, but it will cut off all chance of retreat of either party."

The proposition was seconded by the whole company, when Deaf Smith proposed to go and see the General, and get his approval to the enterprise. Word for word of what passed between our leaders, I am not able to repeat, except that Smith told us Houston asked him:

"Can you do it without being cut to pieces by the Mexican cavalry?"

Smith said that he replied to Houston:

"Give me six men, and I will try."

On Smith's return to our little party, he stopped about the center, facing us, and in the saddle, some questions were asked him, as:

"What did the General say?" He made no answer then; but, after surveying us from right to left with an iron-like countenance, he said:

"I want six men. I am going to burn the bridge. I want six men who
are willing to follow me through, or perish in the attempt."

There was silence for several moments, as six of us dropped out of the
little line and volunteered to follow our favorite chief. But let me here do
justice to the remainder of our companions-in-arms, by saying, and believing
what I say, that there were scarcely a man of our spy company who would
not have volunteered to follow Deaf Smith, had each and all been well-mounted.
I will here mention the names of all who joined Deaf Smith in the enterprise;
yet, before doing so, beg leave to state, that I differ from the opinion of my old
friend, "Uncle Jack Coker," as we called him, as to the name of one of the
party, but, having the most implicit confidence in "Uncle Jack's" honesty I
am willing to risk his statement, and give the names as he has set them down:
Deaf Smith, Denmore Rives, John Coker, Y. P. Alsbury, —— Rainwater, John
Garner, —— Lapham; seven in all. We were compelled to pass within gun-
shot of the extreme left of the Mexican cavalry, who were drawn out, as
stated, with their left reaching within gun-shot of Buffalo Bayou, up which we
had to go to reach the bridge, situated some eight or nine miles on the road
leading to the Brazos.

It being understood that we would maneuver so as to pass the Mexican
horse, if possible, without a fight, the remainder of our company followed
slowly, under a soldier's pledge, that, were we attacked by the cavalry, they
would come to our assistance. Our main body maneuvered, with the feint of
an engagement, so that we passed to the rear unmolested, some distance;
when our comrades regained the camp, leaving the enemy to enjoy the belief
that we were too cowardly to fight.

We moved rapidly, till reaching the mouth of the lane, on the north side
of which was situated the double log-house before occupied by Mr. Vince, we
filed off to the left, so as to avoid an ambuscade, should the enemy be concealed within the dwelling. We threw down the fence where it joined Vince's
Bayou, over which the bridge was built. One hundred and fifty yards more,
and we were at the bridge, over which Deaf Smith and myself passed, with
the view of reconnoitering, leaving the remainder of our party to "strike fire,"
and make the necessary preparations for burning the bridge on our return.

We had gone about half a mile, when we noticed, in the sandy soil, the
track of a carriage-wheel. Smith, with a countenance of mixed rage and
disappointment, exclaimed:

"Santa Anna has made his escape! Here is his carriage-track, going
back, pulled by mules in a great hurry!"

I proposed to him that we should gallop on, about one mile, to a difficult
crossing of another bayou, where we might get the honor of helping him to

cross. He replied: "My orders are to burn the bridge, and return as quick as possible."

In a few minutes we were at the bridge, where we found our comrades, prepared with fire, and plenty of dry rails and wood. In a few minutes the bridge was in flames. If I recollect aright, it was built of cedar.

Nothing of interest occurred till we reached the first deep, dry hollow, half or three-quarters of a mile above our camp, when an incident happened, which goes to illustrate strongly the extraordinary sagacity of that masterly man, Deaf Smith. After ordering a halt, he observed:

"I will ride up the high ground, next to camp, far enough to see whether any of the Mexican horsemen are near, so that we may avoid them."

Our eyes were bent on our leader, as we suddenly saw him drop down on the mane of his horse, and turn toward us. When up to us, the question was asked:

"What news?"

When, with an eye and a countenance I shall never forget, he said:

"The prairie is filled with Mexican horse. I can not see how, or where, they got their re-enforcements from."

Eyeing every man with the eye of a tiger, he asked: "What shall we do?" We told him:

"You are our leader, and we shall follow you, let your course be forward or back."

"My orders are, to return to camp: I will do it or die; but," eyeing every one of us with a scrutiny even painful, he said, "If there is one or more of you prefers making your escape, I now give you leave." We loved our leader almost as we did our country, and replied to him again:

"Lead on, we follow!" A change, I thought, then came over his countenance as I discovered his terrible eye moisten with a tear. He asked:

"Are your arms all right?" He then added, "We will go down the dry hollow to where it joins the bayou, and then, in Indian file, run to the level above, which will bring us in about one hundred yards of the enemy's extreme left. When discovered by them we will raise the Texan yell, and charge, at full speed, through their line. They will, no doubt, kill me, my boys! but, by God! I will make an opening for the rest of you to pass!"

Such was the plan understood; and, sir, I have heard men say, that they could meet such scenes with cool indifference; but, sir, they are braver than I profess to be. Although I must say, and when I say it, do so with candor and truth, that not one of Smith's men but would have preferred the risk of death, rather than an ignominious, disgraceful desertion of the leader we all loved. But to conclude:

When fairly on the level which commanded a partial view of both armies, we saw no Mexican cavalry; but knew, from the hearty laugh of our leader that he had, as he boastingly said, put our fidelity to the test. For my part, I felt well satisfied that I had saved my credit for courage without having the work to do ; and doubt not but my companions felt as I did.

I have thus, in obedience to your wish, and in accordance with my promise, given you a plain, candid and continuous narrative of the facts, and leading incidents attending the enterprise of burning the bridge ; also, the testimony of Mr. John Coker, of Bexar county, authenticating the correctness of my account of the chief incident herein narrated. Mr. Coker is a man who, in the estimation of his acquaintances, is second to none in honesty of purpose, valor, and patriotism.

As what I have repeated to you, concerning this affair, is dictated at least by a clear conscience, if not a clear mind, I feel no reluctance in letting the world see it, if it suits your pleasure.

If I have committed an error, or made a blunder in my detail of the chief incident that is believed to have insured the capture of Santa Anna, it will afford me great pleasure to correct either one or the other. Lest the belief just expressed may appear presumptuous, I may state that the undersigned was one of thirteen who followed the distinguished Santa Anna and the remnant of his staff and cavalry back to the site of the bridge I had left in flames some three hours before. Respectfully and truly yours,

Y. P. ALSBURY.

I, John Coker, of the county of Bexar, State of Texas, have no hesitation in stating, that the material facts in the preceding narrative are correct. Signed this seventeenth day of January, 1858.

JOHN COKER.

XXV.

EARLY HISTORY OF TEXAS.

(Texas Almanac, 1873.)

FROM the *Life and Times of David G. Burnet*, by Colonel A. M. Hobby, of Galveston :

From the first settlement of Texas, in 1691 to 1821, Texas and Coahuila constituted a province of Mexico, under the domination of Spanish authority. After the achievement of Mexican independence, and by the Constitution of the Mexican United States, adopted in 1824, this territory constituted the State of Coahuila and Texas in the Republic of Mexico. The constituent Congress of the combined States decreed its installation, agreeably to the constitutive act of the Mexican Confederation, in 1824, but the State Constitution was not framed and sanctioned until 1827. Public officers were appointed provisionally, and derived their authority from the constituent Congress.

This union, alike between the States and the Republic, proved to be an unhappy one. There was little in common between the inhabitants of Coahuila and the intrepid Anglo-Americans of Texas. So great was the national dissimilarity that not even judicious compromises, early and graciously made, nor reciprocal forbearance generously practiced, would long have preserved the hollow truce between these divided States. No line of policy could have been pursued that would have been acceptable to both, nor long have maintained amicable relations between the liberty-loving colonists and those whe had inherited the prejudices and intolerance of a European parent. As early as 1826 an attempt was made in the Department of Nacogdoches to establish a Texan Republic, under the name of 'Fredonia. Though unsuccessful, it attracted the jealous eye of the Supreme Government, who believed that a modified system of terror was essential to the welfare of the country, and under the ostensible pretext of securing the revenues, gradually introduced troops and garrisoned posts, whose real object was to overawe the Anglo-American colonists, whose increasing power and prosperity inspired envy and alarm.

The violent decree of Bustamente, in 1830, created profound dissatisfaction and fired the colonists with the sentiment of resistance. It resulted in the first military collision, which, under fresh causes were periodically renewed, until 1835, when a deep sense of the necessity of a permanent separation from the National Government seems to have penetrated alike all classes and conditions of society. The chances of war offered a sad alternative to those who could be so illy spared from their families and farms, yet it afforded the only means of escape from the exactions of an intolerant government. In truth, the time had arrived when it was no longer a question of the forms of government, but of life or death.

Notwithstanding the general feeling of the necessity of separation from Mexico, some wise and able men were to be found in the ranks of the opposition, who opposed the movement as impolitic and dangerous at the time, success being regarded as almost impossible, and a resort to arms to redress these wrongs would only result in speedy and universal ruin. We copy as a matter of interest (historical information on the subject being meager,) part of an address to the people, written after the election of Delegates, and before the assembling of the Convention which declared the independence of the Republic. It gives us not only an insight into the character of the times, and the views and spirit of the opposition, but reveals the comparative resources of Mexico and Texas ; and while it discloses the paucity of numbers and feeble resources of the latter, it serves to enhance our admiration of the bold men who assumed the perilous responsibility of the act, in full view of the consequences of failure :

"A declaration of independence imports a final and forcible separation from Mexico, and a claim to be received and acknowledged as a sovereign power, entitled to rank among the nations of the earth. The smallest member of this great family numbers about 1,500,000 inhabitants; the largest numbers, etc. * * * *

"We state these plain statistical facts in order to show by numerical indications what an independent nation is, and to exhibit by the same simple means some of the things necessary to constitute a nation. But population and territory are not all that are requisite for this purpose. Every nation has its government, and governments are costly institutions. That of the United States expends about $25,000,000 per annum, and that frugal people, as we know, are famed for administering their public affairs on the strictest principles of economy. With these few simple data before us, let us inquire if Texas be in a condition to assume forcibly and maintain respectably, an independent government. * * * *

"And is the population of Texas sufficient? We presume it may be stated with tolerable accuracy at 50,000 souls, inclusive of Indians. Ten hundred thousand make one million; and the smallest nation that sustains its relations with the powers of Christendom numbers, we believe, one million and a half of souls. Texas, then, contains one-twentieth of the population of of the most insignificant among the nations of the earth. The population of Mexico is over 7,000,000. The disparity, therefore, is 140 to 1. We are proud to claim for the citizens of Texas much gallantry, and much greater aptitude for war than can be accredited to their antagonists, but 140 to 1 is fearful odds. The towering form of Thermopylæ, which stands pre-eminent among the monuments of ancient glory, was achieved against mighty odds, but not such odds as this. The hosts of voluptuous Persia greatly outnumbered the hardy and heroic bands of Greece, but not in the ratio of one hundred and forty to one; and the heroes of Thermopylæ perished in one common slaughter under the weight of the odds against them. But between Texas and Mexico there is greater disparity in other facts than in mere numerical population. Texas is without finances or financial resources. The whole amount of circulating medium within her limits would scarcely be sufficient for a decent outfit to her first mendicant mission to a foreign court. We assert with confidence that if all the property, real and personal, of all the colonists of Texas were exposed to public sale, with twelve months' advertisement throughout the world, it would not yield enough to maintain a respectable independent Government, and a vigorous war with Mexico for the space of five years, and without pretending to a spirit of prophecy, we venture to assert that Mexico will not relinquish the contest and acknowledge the independence of Texas within twenty years from the day the impotent Declaration shall be promulgated." (Here follows an estimate of the annual expenses of the war and necessary tax to sustain it.) "Therefore it is obvious that Texas could not support herself and sustain a war with so powerful an antagonist. Even the estimate we have made would not be sufficient for her purposes, for she is without an army, or a navy, or fortifications, and is almost totally destitute of the common munitions of war, or means of procuring them ; it will cost, with the most rigid economy, at least one million of dollars to place her on a respectable and efficient war establishment. Vain will it be to expect sympathy from other nations. The ancient heroic and oppressed Poland lifted up the voice of four millions of people to invoke the sympathy of other governments, and their unavailing supplications died away in despair amidst the triumphant shouts of Cossack barbarity. And Poland had many weighty 'reasons of state' to give energy to her appeals for help. Texas has none such to offer, for no nation dreads the gigantic growing power of Mexico, and none can desire the diminution of that power."

"Among the many delusions that seem to have obscured the intellects, and perverted the feelings of some who assume to be your political advisers, there is none more dangerous in its tendencies, than the notion that the Americans of Texas could conciliate the friendship of the Indians, and secure their entire neutrality or their auxiliary services. The most formidable Indians of Texans are ignorant bands from the nations of the North ; and, surely, no *American*, who is acquainted with the hornbooks of his country's history, can fail to know that the northern Indians entertain a deep and inveterate hatred to the very name of an American. The scattered relics of those tribes, once numerous and powerful, have not forgotten the localities of their fathers' sepulchres and of their ancient dominion. They remember well who have desecrated the one, and usurped the other. Their recollections are as vivid and abiding as their resentments are implacable ; and their cherished hopes of vengeance are transmitted from parent to child in the same impassioned traditionary tale, that recites the history of their fathers' wrongs. Toward the native Mexicans these beings, of fierce and untempered passion, entertain no hostile feelings, no lingering recollections of wrongs sustained or injuries unavenged. They may, indeed, regard them as less warlike than the destroyers of their nations, but *they* know, and *we* know, that they themselves *are not so ;* that they have been driven from mountain to mountain, and beyond river after river, but they have yielded to numbers and not to courage ; to physical power and not to skill in arms.

"But we will not dilate upon this branch of our subject. It is delicate ; it may be dangerous, or we could present to you other suggestions, that ought to be sufficient to flash conviction on every mind that Mexico has a better chance and ampler means to secure the alliance of "the tomahawk and the scalping-knife " than the colonists can have. That she will employ every device and exert every means to do so, should the present unhappy contest become national, no sensible man can doubt. The consequences of such an alliance many of you may experience in the conflagration of your dwellings and the massacre of your families ; but no pen, however graphic, can adequately depict them. Let the dispersed families of Texas and the responsible *heads* thereof, think of it, ere it be too late."

The address closes thus : " Fellow-citizens, and you especially members of the Convention—the select of the land—we leave the subject with you. We have discharged a solemn duty, and if Texas is doomed to destruction, our hands are clean. When we say Texas doomed to destruction, we do not mean the country itself, for Texas will remain a delightful portion of the earth when the folly of its present inhabitants has passed beyond the recollection of man."—[*February*, 1836.]

These predictions were speedily falsified by events.

A few intrepid spirits. sounded the tocsin of alarm, and from hill-top to seaboard, the great-hearted patriots gathered at the call. No people ever undertook an enterprise so hazardous and important with such slender assurances of success, or achieved their independence with such inadequate resources against an opposition so formidable and disproportioned. The absence of an exchequer caused little embarrassment to a race of men who held their services in such a cause above price.

They did not miscalculate their strength ; their frontier life had familiarized them with hardships in every form ; their hardihood and endurance proved equal to the utmost demands of an unequal contest ; and history will justly pronounce the patriotism and courage, which bore such burdens and wrought such results, exalted and sublime. The plowshare was withdrawn from the golden glebe and beaten into the bayonet. The little army of the struggling colonists marched to the most exposed points, and illustrated the art of defense by the stubborn valor inspired by the danger and responsibility of the situation. The campaign, after many trials and disasters, closed with a signal and splendid triumph. The Texans, closely pursued, had fallen back across the Colorado and Brazos, and made a last stand on a field which lights the historic page of the infant republic with the blaze of victory. The morning sun of the 21st of April, 1836, shone on the comparatively powerful forces of Santa Anna as they descended the right bank of Buffalo Bayou to conquest and victory ; but his evening beam beheld the Mexican army beaten and flying, and the President himself a prisoner in the hands of the Anglo-Texans. The battle of San Jacinto was fierce and short, and may be regarded as one of the decisive battles of the world. It determined forever the independence of the Republic.

XXVI.

THE FALL OF THE ALAMO.

BY R. M. POTTER.

(From the Texas Almanac of 1868.)

THE fall of the Alamo, the tragic results of which are so well known, so far as the final assault is concerned, have not been fully or correctly given in any of the current histories of Texas. The reason is obvious when it is remembered that not a single combatant from within survived to tell the tale, while the official reports of the enemy were neither circumstantial nor reliable. A trustworthy account of the assault could only be compiled by comparing and combining the verbal accounts of such of the assailants as could be relied on for veracity, and adding to this, such light on the matter as may be gathered from the military documents of the day. As I was a resident of Matamoras when the event happened, and for several months after the invading army returned thither, I had opportunities for obtaining the kind of information referred to which few persons if any, still living in Texas, have possessed; and I have been urged to publish what I have gathered on the subject that an interesting fragment of history may be saved. Among the facts which have been perverted is the number of Mexican troops engaged in the campaign and in the assault. The whole force with which Santa Anna invaded Texas in 1836 probably amounted to seven thousand five hundred men. It consisted of two regiments of horse and thirteen battalions of foot. It may here be remarked that the Mexicans apply the term regiment only to cavalry corps; those of infantry of the same size are always called battalions, and the latter terms, as used by them, designate the whole of a colonel s command of fcot instead of a subdivision of it. The nominal complement of a regiment or battalion is one thousand five hundred men; but I have never known one to be full, or much exceed one-third of that number. I saw all the corps which returned, of 1836, and from the size of those which had not been in action, as well as from the remaining bulk of those which had suffered, after allowing for probable loss, I am convinced that their average strength, when they entered Texas, did not differ much from five hundred men, which would make the agregate above surmised.

That the estimate will apply to the third of it engaged on storming the Alamo, I consider very likely, for I paid more attention to the strength of these corps than of the others. At the beginning of the invasion the Mexican officers spoke of their armies as ten thousand strong. After its failure, Santa Anna, in his letter to General Jackson, referred to his invading force as numbering six thousand. 'The truth may be found midway between the figures.* The main army, under Santa Anna in person, moved from Laredo upon San Antonio in four successive detachments.

This was on account of the scarcity of grass and water on portions of the route. The lower division, under Brigadier-General Urrea, moved from Matamoras upon Goliad in one body. It consisted of the cavalry regiment of Cuatla, the infantry battalion of Yucatan, and some companions of militia. The aforesaid battalion, which I counted, numbered three hundred and fifty men. The regiment of dragoons was about the same, and the whole command about one thousand. This, reinforced by two battalions, was the force which vanquished Fannin at the Coleta. The advance detachment from Laredo, consisting of the dragoon regiment of Dolores, and one or two battalions, arrived at San Antonio about the 21st day of February, 1836. The Alamo was at that time garrisoned by one hundred and fifty-six men, under command of Lieutenant-Colonel W. B. Travis. James Bowie was second in command. David Crockett of Tennessee had also joined the garrison a few weeks before, but whether he had any command I do not know. One of the most estimable and chivalrous men attached to the garrison was J. B. Bonham óf South Carolina, who had recently volunteered in the service of Texas. What was his position, I am unable to say. Travis had been commissioned by the Provisional Government of Texas, lieutenant-colonel of cavalry; but his corps had not been raised, and the men under him were volunteers. Some of them had been engaged in the recent siege of San Antonio when Cos capitulated, and others had lately arrived from United States.

No regular scouting service seems to have been kept up by Travis; for, though the enemy was expected, his near approach was not known until his advance was seen descending the slope west of the San Pedro. The guard in the town seems to have retired in good order to the fort: yet so complete was the surprise of the place, that one or more American residents engaged in mercantile business, fled to the Alamo, leaving their stores open. After the enemy entered, a cannon shot from the Alamo was answered by a shell from the invaders; but little more was done that day. The fortress was not at once invested, and the few citizens who had taken refuge in it, succeeded in leaving it that night. On the 23d, Santa Anna with the second

---

* When Santa Anna summoned General Taylor to surrender at Buena Vista, he announced his army as twenty thousand strong. After his repulse he reported it sixteen thousand. The truth was eighteen thousand.

division arrived, and the same day a regular siege was commenced. Its operations, which lasted eleven days, are pretty correctly detailed in Yoakum's Texas.

Several batteries were opened on successive days. The enemy had, however, no siege train, but only light field-pieces and howitzers. No assault was attempted, as has been asserted, until the final storming of the place. Neither was the investment so close as to prevent the passage of couriers and the entrance of one reenforcement; for on the night of March 1st a company of thirty-two men from Gonzales made its way into the fort, never again to leave it. This raised the number of the garrison to one hundred and eighty-eight men. In a letter from Travis, March 3d, he says:

"With one hundred and forty-five men I have held this place ten days against a force variously estimated at from one thousand five hundred to six thousand men, and I shall continue to hold it until I get relief from my countrymen, or perish. We have had a shower of bombs and cannon-balls continually falling among us, yet none of us are injured. We have been miraculously preserved." Thus it appears there could have been no loss on our side until the final assault. Santa Anna, after calling a council of war on the 4th of March, fixed upon the morning of March 6th for the assault. Before narrating the particulars I will try to describe the Alamo as it then was.* It had been founded soon after the settlement of that vicinity, and was first built as a place of safety for the settlers and their property in case of Indian hostility; but it was large enough for that purpose, it had neither the strength compactness nor arrangement which belong to a regular fortification. The front of the Alamo Chapel bears date 1757. The other works must have been built earlier. The chapel of the fortress is seventy-five feet long, sixty-two feet wide, and twenty-two and a half feet high, surrounded by walls of solid masonry four feet thick.* It was built in one story, with upper windows under which platforms were built for mounting cannon. The long barrack which was connected with the church is one hundred and eighty-six feet long, eighteen feet wide, eighteen feet high, and of two stories. There was another barrack one hundred and fourteen feet long, and seventeen feet wide These barracks, like the church, were of solid rock, and their walls are still standing.† The fortifications were manned by fourteen guns; but these proved of little use in the defence, as the enemy either kept out of their range, or approached from a quarter which they could not be made to bear upon.

It was resolved by Santa Anna that the assaults should take place at

---

* See Diagram on page 113.

† The church and fortress of the Alamo, or Poplar Grove (so called from the trees of this kind then there), were built and occupied for many years by Roman Catholic Missionaries from Spain.

early dawn. The order for it, which I have read, but have not a copy of, was full in its details, and was signed by Brigadier-General Amador, chief-of-staff. The besieging force consisted of the battalion of Toluca, Ximenes, Matamoras, Los Zapadores (or sappers), and the regiment of Dolores. The infantry were directed, at a certain hour between midnight and day, to form at a convenient distance from the fort in four columns of attack and reserve. This disposition was not made by battalions; for the light companies of all were incorporated with the Zapadores to form the reserve, and other changes may have been made for the occasion. A certain number of scaling ladders and axes were to be borne with particular columns. The

STORMING OF THE ALAMO.

cavalry were to be stationed at different points around the fortress, to cut off fugitives. The immediate command of the assault was intrusted to General Castrillo, a Spaniard by birth, and a brilliant soldier.* Santa Anna took his station, with a part of his staff and all the regimental bands, at a battery south of the Alamo and near the old bridge, from which the signal was to be given by a bugle note for the columns to move at a double quick simultaneously against different points of the citidel. The battalion of Toluca was to enter the north breach, the other two to move against the south side, one to attack the large gate, the other to storm the chapel. It was so arranged that the columns should reach the foot of the wall at daybreak.

* It seems that upon the eve of the attack, the plan was so modified, as to combine the infantry into three columns, instead of five.

When the hour came the batteries and the music were alike silent, and the single blast of the bugle was followed by no sound save the rushing tramp of soldiers. The guns of the fort soon opened upon them and then the band at the south battery struck up the assassin notes of *dequello !* * But few and not very effective discharges from the works could be made before the enemy was under them, and it is thought that the worn and wearied garrison was not till then fully mustered. The Tolucan column was first at the base of the wall, but was not the first to enter the area. A large piece of cannon at the northwest angle commanded the breach. Either this, or the deadly fire of the riflemen at that point, where Travis in person commanded, brought the columns to a disordered halt, and its leader, Colonel Duque, fell dangerously wounded. But at this time another column arrived and entered the gate, or by escalade near it. The defense of the outer wall had now to to be abandoned, and the garrison took refuge in the buildings already described. It was probably while the enemy were pouring through the breach that Travis fell at his post, for his body was found beside the gun just referred to. All this passed within a few minutes after the bugle sounded.

The early loss of the outer wall so thinly manned was inevitable ; and it was not until the garrison became more concentrated that the main struggle began. They were more compact as to space, but not as to unity, for there was no communicating between buildings, nor always between rooms. There was now no retreat from point to point. Each group of defenders had to fight and die in the den in which it was brought to bay. From the doors, windows, and loop-holes of the several rooms around the area, the crack of the rifle and the hiss of the bullet came thick and fast ; and the enemy fell like grass before the scythe, and recoiled in his first attempts to charge.

The gun beside which Travis lay was now by the Mexicans brought to bear upon the buildings, and shot after shot, in quick succession, was sent crashing through the doors and barricades of the several rooms. Each discharge of cannon was followed by a storm of musketry and a charge ; and thus room after room was gradually carried at the point of the bayonet, while all within them died fighting to the last. The struggle was made up of a series of separate and desperate combats, often hand to hand, between squads of the garrison and bodies of the invaders. The bloodiest spot about the fortress was the long barrack and the ground in front of it, where the Mexicans fell in heaps.

Meantime the turning of Travis's gun had been imitated by the garrison. A small field-piece on the roof of the chapel was turned against the area

* A Spanish martial air, which signifies to the soldier, *No quarter.*

while the rooms were being stormed.   It did more execution than any other cannon of the fortress ; but after a few effective discharges, all who manned it fell under the enemy's fire.   Crockett had taken refuge in a room of the low barrack near the gate.   He either garrisoned it alone, or was left alone by the fall of his comrades.   Alone he gallantly charged in the face of the foe, and fell.   Bowie had been severely hurt by a fall from the platform, and at the time of the attack was confined to his bed in an upper part of the barrack.   He was there killed on his couch, but not until he had shot down with his pistols several of the foe as they entered his chamber.   The church was the last point taken.   The column which moved against it, consisting of the battalion of Ximenes and other troops, was at first repulsed, and took refuge among some old houses outside of the barrier, near the south-west angle, but it was rallied and led on by General Amador.   It was soon joined by the rest of the force, and the church was carried by a *coup de main*.   Its inmates, like the others, fought to the last, and continued to fire from the upper platform after the Mexicans had occupied the floor.

A Mexican officer told me of a man shot in the top of the head during this mêlée.   During the closing struggle Lieutenant Dickenson, with one of his children in his arms, or as some say, tied to his back, leaped from an upper window.   Both were killed.   Of those he left behind him, the bayonet soon gleaned what the bullet missed ; and in the upper part of the church, the last defenders must have fallen.   The morning breeze, which received his parting breath, probably still fanned his flag above him ere it was pulled down by the victors.

The Alamo had fallen.

MONUMENT ERECTED

TO

THE HEROES OF THE ALAMO,

AND NOW STANDING AT THE ENTRANCE TO THE STATE HOUSE AT AUSTIN, TEXAS.

INSCRIPTION
ON THE SHAFT.
NORTH FRONT.

TO THE
GOD
OF THE
FEARLESS
AND **FREE**
IS
DEDICATED
THIS
ALTAR
MADE FROM
THE RUINS
OF THE
ALAMO

MARCH
6TH
1836
A. D.

Crockett

INSCRIPTION
ON THE
WEST FRONT.

BLOOD OF
HEROES
HATH
STAINED ME
LET THE
STONES
OF THE
ALAMO
SPEAK
THAT THEIR
IMMOLATION
BE NOT
FORGOTTEN.

MARCH
6TH
1836
A. D.

Bonham.

INSCRIPTION
ON THE
SOUTH FRONT.

BE THEY
ENROLLED
WITH
LEONIDAS
IN THE
HOST
OF THE
MIGHTY
DEAD.

MARCH
6TH
1836
A. D.

Travis.

INSCRIPTION
ON THE
EAST FRONT.

Thermopylæ
HAD HER
MESSENGER
OF
DEFEAT
BUT THE
ALAMO
HAD NONE.

MARCH
6TH
1836
A. D.

Bowie.

THE FOLLOWING NAMES ARE INSCRIBED UPON THE NORTH AND SOUTH FRONTS.

M. AUTRY,	W. DEARDUFF,	LEWIS,	ROBBINS,
R. ALLEN,	J. EWING,	W. LINN,	W. SMITH,
M. ANDRESS,	T. R. EVANS,	WM. LIGHTFOOT,	SEARS,
AYRES,	D. FLOYD,	J. LONLY,	C. SMITH,
ANDERSON,	J. FLANDERS,	LANIO,	STOCKTON,
W. BLAZEBY,	W. FISHBAUGH,	W. LIGHTFOOT,	STEWART,
J. B. BOWMAN,	FORSYTH,	G. W. LYNN,	A. SMITH,
BAKER,	G. FUGA,	LEWIS,	J. C. SMITH,
S. C. BLAIR,	J. C. GOODRICH,	W. MILLS,	SEWALL,
BLAIR,	J. GEORGE,	MICHESON,	A. SMITH,
BROWN,	J. GASTON,	E. T. MITCHELL,	SIMPSON,
BOWIN,	J. C. GARRETT,	E. MELTON,	R. STAR,
BALENTINE,	C. GRIMES,	McGREGOR,	STARN,
J. J. BAUGH,	GWYN,	T. MILLER,	N. SUTHERLAND,
BURNELL,	J. E. GARWIN,	J. McCOY,	W. SUMMERS,
BUTLER,	GILLMORE,	E. MORTON	J. SUMERLINE,
J. BAKER,	HUTCHASON,	R. MUSSULMAN,	THOMPSON,
BURNS,	S. HOLLAWAY,	MILLSOP,	TOMLINSON,
BAILEY,	HARRISON,	R. B. MOORE,	E. TAYLOR,
J. BEARD,	HIESKELL,	W. MARSHALL,	G. TAYLOR, } Bros.
BAILESS,	J. HAYES,	MOORE,	J. TAYLOR,
BOURN,	HORRELL,	R. McKENNY,	W. TAYLOR,
R. CUNNINGHAM,	HARRIS,	McCAFERTY,	THORNTON,
J. CLARK,	HAWKINS,	J. McGEE,	THOMAS,
J. CANE,	J. HOLLAND,	G. W. MAIN,	J. M. THRUSTON,
CLOUD,	W. HERSIE,	M. QUERRY,	VALENTINE,
S. CRAWFORD,	INGRAM,	G. NELSON,	WILLIAMSON,
CARY,	JOHN,	NELSON,	D. WILSON,
W. CUMMINGS,	J. JONES,	J. NOLAND,	WALSH,
R. CROSSAN,	L. JOHNSON,	NELSON,	WASHINGTON,
COCKRAN,	C. B. JAMISON,	WM. G. NELSON,	W. WELLS,
G. W. COTTLE,	W. JOHNSON,	C. OSTINER,	C. WRIGHT,
J. DUST,	T. JACKSON,	PELONE,	R. WHITE,
J. DILLARD,	D. JACKSON,	C. PARKER,	J. WASHINGTON,
A. DICKINSON,	JACKSON,	N. POLLARD,	T. WATERS,
C. DESPALIER,	G. KEMBLE,	G. PAGGAN,	WARNALL,
L. DAVELL,	A. KENT,	S. ROBINSON,	J. WHITE,
J. C. DAY,	W. KING,	REDDENSON,	D. WILSON,
J. DICKENS,	KENNEY,	N. ROUGH,	J. WILSON,
DEVAULT,	J. KENNY,	RUSK,	A. WOLF,

L. J. WILSON,

WARNER.

8

DESCRIPTION OF THE MONUMENT.

THIS monument is ten feet high, and made from stones taken from the ruins of the Alamo. The style of architecture is the Composite, and is divided into ten sections. The 1st section, or base of the monument, is one solid piece, bearing the whole structure. The 2d section is a square plinth, neatly impaneled. The 3d section is a sub-plinth, with Gothic molding and roped bead, symbolical of binding the whole structure firmly. The 4th section is the *die*, or main body of the monument, consisting of four panels in recess, supported by rude fluted pilasters at each corner. On two of these panels are raised shields, on which are inscribed, in raised letters, the names of every man who fell at the ever-memorable battle of Alamo. Each shield is suspended from a beautiful wreath, in the center of which is a bouquet of flowers. The shields and wreaths sustaining them are encircled by honeysuckles and vines. On the other panels of section 4th is represented the skull and bones crossed. Above the skull are two angels facing each other, blowing trumpets. Below the cross bones are the symbols of Time—the hour-glass, scythe, and wings. Section 5 is a solid cap resting on the main body, projecting with Gothic moldings handsomely carved, representing oak leaves at the corners. On the top of the cap is a square *facia* forming recesses in which is inscribed, in large raised Gothic letters, the names of the gallant spirits who fell at the head of the heroes of the Alamo. Each name—that of CROCKETT, BONHAM, TRAVIS, and BOWIE—stands out singly in bold relief, on each of the four fronts. From the center of this cap springs the main shaft or spire, and upper structure.

Section 6 is a Corinthian base, forming four square angles. At each angle is a dolphin, in solid carved work. On each side, in the center, is a bomb-shell of full size, and made of solid stone. Section 7 is the base of the shaft, with raised fluted corners, and rests upon the Corinthian base, supported at the corners by the tails of the dolphins, and at each side by the bomb-shells. In the panels on the base and over the bomb-shells, are raised hands in the grasp of friendship. Section 8 is the 1st division of the shaft, with raised fluted corners and panels in recess. At the base of each panel are cannon crossed in bold relief. Above these cannon, on each panel, is the Cap of Liberty, surrounded by branches of oak and laurel. Immediately above these, in raised letters, is inscribed, on each of the four fronts, MARCH 6th, 1836, the date of the memorable battle. On top of this section of the shaft is a cap, with raised fluted corners and recess panels. In two of these panels stand in relief the heads of angels with wings. On one of the other panels is, in relief, a heart pierced with two crossed daggers; and on the other panel is a skull with twigs crossed underneath. Section 9 is the second division of the shaft, with the devices in raised Gothic letters, as printed on each side of the wood-cut of the monument above. Section 10 is a cap on top of section 9, forming four Gothic points; and in each, in a recess panel, stands in bold relief THE LONE STAR OF TEXAS. Underneath the stars are raised daggers. In the center of the cap above the stars stands an urn with flame issuing from it; and at each corner of the cap on which the large urn rests, are four smaller urns, out of which also issues flame.

This monument was made in the Republic of Texas by American artists. Viewing the work as a whole, both as to boldness and appropriateness of design and beauty of execution, it would reflect credit on any artist of ancient or modern times.

XXVII.

GROUND PLAN AND DESCRIPTION OF THE ALAMO.

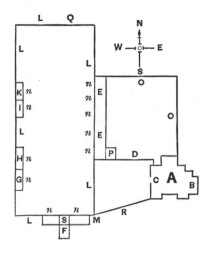

(A) rep. .sents the chapel of the fortress, which is 75 feet long, 62 wide, and 22½ high, the wall of solid masonry being four feet thick. It was originally in one story, but had upper windows, under which platforms were erected for mounting cannon in those openings. (B) designates one of those upper windows which I will have occasion to mention, and (C) the front door of the church. (D) is a wall 50 feet long, connecting this church with the long barrack, (E E.) The latter is a stone house, 186 feet long, 18 wide, and 18 high, being of two stories. (F) is a low stone barrack, 114 feet long, and 17 wide. Those houses, or at least their original walls, which (except those of the church) are about thirty inches thick, are still standing. They had at the time flat terrace roofs of beams and plank, covered with a thick coat of cement. The present roofs and the adjoining sheds and other woodwork, have been added since the place was converted into a quartermaster's depot. (G, H, I and K) were rooms built against the west barrier, and were demolished with it. The (L^s) designate a barrier wall, from 6 to 8 feet high and 2¾ thick, inclosing an area 154 yards long and 54 wide, which the long barrack fronted on the east, and the low barrack (F) on the south. (M) designates the gate of the area, and the (n^s) locate the doors of the several houses which opened upon it. Most of those doors had within each a semi-circular barricade or parapet, composed of a double curtain of hides upheld

S represents a *porte cochere*, or wide passage through the center of the house F, with but one room on each side. The dotted lines represent a projecting stockade which covered a four-gun battery in front of the outer door.

by stakes and filled in with earth.   From behind these the garrison could
fire front or oblique through the doors.   Some of the rooms were also loop-
holed.   (o o) describes a wall from 5 to 6 feet high, and 2¾ thick, which
inclosed a smaller area east of the long barrack and north of the church,
63 yards by 34.   (P) locates an upper room in the south-east angle of said
barrack, (Q) a breach in the north barrier, and (R) an intrenchment running
from the south-west angle of the chapel to the gate.   This work was not
manned against the assault.   According to Santa Anna's report, 21 guns of
various calibers were planted in different parts of the works.   Yoakum,
in his description of the armament, mentions but 14.   Whichever number
be correct, however, has but little bearing upon the merits of the final defense,
in which the cannon had little to do.   They were in the hands of men unskilled in their use, and, owing to the construction of the fort, each had a
limited range, which the enemy in moving up seem in a measure to have
avoided.

———— ◆ ◆ ◄ ————

XXVIII.

THE BABE OF THE ALAMO.

(From Field's Scrap-Book.)

THE beautiful remarks which follow are extracted from speeches delivered in the House of Representatives of Texas, on a bill proposing a donation to the daughter of Almiram Dickenson, one of the martyrs who fell
at the Alamo in the beginning of the Texas revolution.   History will never
record a nobler deed, a more daring stand, a purer, self-sacrificing devotion
to the interests and liberties of their adopted country, than the fight and
fall of Travis, Bowie, Crockett, and their gallant compatriots.   One hundred and fifty men were arrayed against thousands of Mexicans under Santa
Anna, the then President of Mexico, who styled himself the second Napoleon ; and heroically did they wield the battle blade, till the last man of that
devoted band measured his length upon the earth.   No quarter was asked
or given, none were left to tell the tale, but the wife of Dickenson and her
infant daughter.   How heart-sickening to this woman must have been that
conflict, that massacre !

Hon. GUY BRYAN said : " .   .   .   .   I intended, Mr. Speaker, to be
silent on this occasion, but silence would now be a reproach, when to speak is
a duty.   No one has raised a voice in behalf of this orphan child ; several have
spoken against her claim.   I rise, sir, in behalf of no common cause.   Lib-

erty was its foundation, heroism and martyrdom consecrated it. I speak for the orphan child of the Alamo. No orphan children of fallen patriots can send a similar petition to this House—none save her can say, 'I am the Child of the Alamo.' Well do I remember the consternation which spread throughout the land, when the sad tidings reached our ears that the Alamo had fallen ! It was here that a gallant few, the bravest of the brave, threw themselves betwixt the enemy and the settlements, determined not to surrender nor retreat. They redeemed their pledge with the forfeit of their lives—they fell, the chosen sacrifice to Texan freedom ! Texas, unapprised of the approach of the invader, was sleeping in fancied security, when the gun of the Alamo first announced that the Atilla of the South was near. Infuriated at the resistance of Travis and his noble band, he marshaled his whole army beneath the walls, and rolled wave after wave of his hosts against those battlements of freedom. In vain he strove—the flag of liberty—the Lone Star of Texas, still streamed out upon the breeze, and floated proudly from the outer wall. Maddened and persistent, he reared his batteries, and after days of furious bombardment, and repeated assaults, he took a blackened and ruined mass—the blood-stained walls of the Alamo. The noble, the martyred spirits of all its gallant defenders, had taken their flight to another fortress, not made with hands. . . . But for this stand at the Alamo, Texas would have been desolated to the Sabine. Sir, I ask this pittance, and for whom? For the only living witness, save the mother, of this awful tragedy—'this bloodiest picture in the book of time,' the bravest act that ever swelled the annals of any country. Grant the boon ! She claims it as the Christian child of the Alamo—baptized in the blood of a Travis, a Bowie, a Crockett, and a Bonham. To turn her away would be a shame ! Give her what she asks, that she may be educated, and become a worthy child of the State !—that she may take that position in society to which she is entitled by the illustrious name of her martyred father—illustrious because he fell in the Alamo."

Hon. J. C. WILSON said : " . . . . The student of Grecian history, in every age, in every land, has felt his bosom glow with a noble fire, while reading of Leonidas and the three hundred who fell with him at Thermopylæ ; but when the Alamo fell, a nobler than Leonidas, a more devoted band than the Spartans, sank amid its ruins. They shed their blood for us—they poured out their lives as water for the liberties of Texas ! and they have left us, of that bloody, yet glorious conflict, one sole memento—one frail, perishable keepsake—the child whose petition for assistance is now before us. Shall we turn her away ? Shall we say—"Though your father served the State in his life ; though he fell in the ranks of those men whose names history shall chronicle and nations shall delight to honor ; though you, alone, of all the children of Texas, witnessed that direful scene, whose bare contemplation makes the stout heart quail ; though the credit and honor of Texas are alike concerned in taking care of your childhood and watching over your youth, in providing for your happiness and respectability ; though you, the *Babe of the Alamo*, will be an object of interest to all who may visit our State in after years, when the pen of the historian shall have recorded your connection with the early glories and sufferings of our now happy land—yet for all this, we will suffer you to grow up in uncultured wildness, in baneful ignorance, perchance in vice, rather than make this pitiful appropriation to enable you to render yourself capable of occupying that position in society to which you are in a peculiar degree entitled by the strange and thrilling circumstances surrounding your life.   Sir, I trust such an act may not mar the history of Texas.   Sure am I, by my vote it never shall.   It is related of Napoleon, that when an officer whom he loved was wounded, and, from the narrowness of the defile in which the conflict raged, was in imminent danger of being crushed to death by the feet of contending friends and foes, while the emperor looked on in deep anxiety for his fate, a female, an humble follwer of the army, with a babe on one arm, pressed through the mêlée to the wounded man, and passing her other arm around him, conveyed him to a place of comparative safety near the emperor ; but just as she turned away from the object of her daring and benevolent solicitude, a ball struck her dead at the feet of Napoleon.   He, taking the motherless babe in his arms, called a grenadier, saying, ' Bear this child to the rear, and see that it is well attended to, for henceforth it is the Child of the Empire.'   Mr. Speaker, the Child of the Alamo is *the Child of the State*, and we can not treat her with neglect without entailing lasting disgrace upon Texas."

XXIX.

SEAT OF GOVERNMENT.

(From A Brief History of Texas).

THE Congress of Texas, January, 1838, appointed five commissioners to select a site for the Capital of the Republic.   The commissioners, consisting of Albert C. Horton, Lewis P. Cook, Isaac W. Burton, William Menifee, and J. Campbell, after careful examination, made choice of the present location on the Colorado River.   At the time of its selection it was on the extreme frontier, Bastrop being the nearest town, thirty-five miles lower down on the river.   To this place—temporary buildings having been erected—the government offices were moved in October, 1839, and in the November following, the Congress met at the new city of Austin.

CHANGES.—Before that time the councils of the young Republic had been held by Executive appointment at different places, for convenience and safety.

First at San Felipe, November, 1835.

Next at Washington, March, 1836.

Next at Harrisburg, same month.

Next at Galveston, April 16, 1836.

Next at Velasco, May, 1836. At this place the treaties with Santa Anna were signed.

HOUSE IN WHICH FIRST CONGRESS MET.

Next, by order of Congress, at Columbia, in October, 1836.

Next at Houston, in May, 1837.

Next at Austin, in October, 1839.

Austin City was incorporated in 1840.

MORE CHANGES.—In this connection we will follow the removals of the seat of government of Texas up to the present time. In 1842, during an invasion of the Mexicans under General Vasquez, into Western Texas President Houston, thinking the national records in danger, ordered their removal to Houston.

ARCHIVE WAR.—This caused the disturbance which is known as the archive war. The citizens of Austin, thinking the removal ill-judged and unnecessary, held a mass meeting, organized a company, and pursued and captured the wagons containing the records of the General Land Office, which they took back in triumph to Austin.

CAPITAL AT HOUSTON.—The government offices remained at Houston until November, 1842, when by Executive proclamation Congress met at Washington. Here the capital remained until it was again established at Austin in 1845. In 1850 an election was held to locate the seat of government of Texas, and Austin City was chosen by the people to be the capital for twenty years, or until the next general election after the year 1870. This election was held in obedience to Sec. 37, Art. 3, new State Constitution, November 5 to 9, 1872, and resulted in the re-election of Austin by a majority of 15,355, votes over both Houston and Waco, its competitors. This finally settles the question of a seat of government for Texas while the State remains undivided.

XXX.

HISTORICAL STATISTICS CONCERNING TEXAS.

(Texas New Yorker, 1874.)

THE distinguished French explorer, La Salle, landed in Texas in 1680.

La Salle was murdered by one of his followers, March 30, 1687, near the Neches River.

The first attempt at Spanish settlement in Texas was made under Captain De Leon, who was sent, 1689, to hunt out the French. On the 22d of April, he arrived at Fort St. Louis, previously erected by the French near the mouth of the Lavaca River. Here he subsequently established the Spanish Mission of San Francisco.

In 1691, Spain appointed a Governor and sent soldiers to enforce his authority.

Prior to the Texas revolution of 1835 and '36, Texas and Coahuila constituted a Mexican State, with the capital at Saltillo, in Coahuila.

San Antonio, in Bexar county, is the oldest city in the State—it was founded in 1693.

Goliad, in Goliad county, and Nacogdoches, the county seat of the same named county, were founded in 1717.

The Declaration of Texan Independence was adopted March 2, 1836.

The Constitution of the Republic of Texas was adopted March 17, 1836.

The first Government of the Republic of Texas was represented in the persons of—

THE CAPITOL AT AUSTIN.

To face p. 120.

David G. Burnet, President.
Lorenzo de Zavala, Vice-President.
Samuel P. Carson, Secretary of State.
B. Hardeman, Secretary of the Treasury.
Thos. J. Rusk, Secretary of War.
Robt. Potter, Secretary of the Navy.
David Thomas, Attorney-General.

General Sam Houston was first Commander-in-Chief of the Texan army, and achieved the complete overthrow of the Mexican forces sent to subjugate Texas, at the memorable battle of San Jacinto, fought on the banks of the river of the same name, April 21, 1836. To him, General Antonio Lopez de Santa Anna, the Mexican Commander-in-Chief, and President of the Republic of Mexico, surrendered himself and entire army.

Texas was annexed to the United States, in 1845.

The population of Texas, in 1835, was estimated at 50,000. In 1845, 150,000. In 1850, by United States census, 212,592. In 1860, census returns 601,039, and by the census of 1870, 818,579. Now it is believed to be about one million two hundred thousand, so great has been the immigration during the last year.

The population of Galveston, the principal seaport of Texas, is about 25,000.

The population of Houston, the present railroad center, is about 20,000.

The population of San Antonio, the present Military Headquarters of the District of Texas, is about 16,000.

The population of Jefferson is about 10,000.

The population of Austin, the State Capital, is about 12,000.

The first President of the Republic of Texas, regularly elected by the people, was General Sam Houston.

The second President thus chosen, was Mirabeau B. Lamar.

The third President thus chosen, was General Sam Houston, for a second term.

The fourth and last President thus chosen, was Anson Jones.

The first Governor of the State of Texas, chosen by the people, was J. Pinckney Henderson, elected November, 1845.

The second Governor was George T. Wood, elected November, 1847.

The third Governor was P. Hansborough Bell, elected November, 1849.

The fourth Governor was P. Hansborough Bell, re-elected November, 1851.

The fifth Governor was Elisha M. Pease, elected November, 1853.

The sixth Governor was Elisha M. Pease, re-elected November, 1855.

The seventh Governor was Hardin R. Runnels, elected November, 1857.

The eighth Governor was General Sam Houston, elected November, 1859.

The first merchant who traded at Houston, was Colonel Wm. T. Austin, in 1833.

Houston was laid out as a town in 1836.

The first steamboat which visited Houston, was the *Laura*, Captain T. W. Grayson, January 22, 1837.

XXXI.

EARLY HISTORY OF TEXAS.

THE humorous description given below of a Christmas frolic which took place at the time and place mentioned below, will be appreciated by some, still living, who took part in the fun.

It is taken from the *Daily Bulletin*, a paper printed in Austin in 1841, and published and edited by S. Whiting. This paper was printed here during a session of Congress of the republic:

The congress extraordinary of the rounders of the republic of Texas, will convene at the grand hall above the Bexar Exchange, on Saturday the 25th inst. All distinguished rounders of the republic are invited to attend. Several members have already arrived; among them are the members from Screw-Auger Creek, Screamersville, Schubatansville, Squizzlejig County, Toe Nail, Kamchatka, Epidemic, Hyena's Hollow, and Racoon's Ford. The dictator-general of the rounders of the republic is hourly expected. The message of his excellency is expected to combine originality, vigor, philosophy, and sage advice to the members of the fraternity. We are requested to publish the two subjoined rules, and call the particular attention of members to their provisions prior to the commencement of business. "If any member is too drunk to rise from his seat to speak, the chair shall appoint a committee of three to hold him up; but provided the member shall be dead drunk, and unable to speak, the chair shall appoint an additional committee of two to speak for him: provided, however, that if the member is able to hold up by tables, chairs, etc., then, and in that case, one of the committee shall gesticulate for him." "No member shall absent himself from the house, unless he have leave to be sick."

Christmas passed with but one memorable event in Austin, which was the meeting of the congress extraordinary of the rounders of the republic. The day was chill and damp, and all without was uninviting, but the merry congress we have mentioned met in high spirits, in their grand hall, and the acts of the day, and extraordinary deliberations and oratorical efforts prior to their passage are without parallel. The great congress of sovereigns at Vienna was not more magniloquent, nor half so jovial. The republic of Texas, the civil and judicial officers and the congress that convened on the hill, were abolished without ceremony, and in little more time than it takes to relate it. This effected, and the country placed under new and more efficient government, bills were introduced and passed with a celerity that would have done credit to more practiced legislators ; and one of the standing rules being that no member should be required to speak with any relevancy to the subject under consideration there was a diffusion of humor and and a latitude of figure and simile, beyond any previous example. Bills were introduced and passed, corrective of the general ills of society, the troubles and difficulties of Austin, and the pecuniary embarrassment of the members in particular. Valuable reports on finance and other important subjects were made, and ingenious projects for gulling the world were adopted. The general tendency of legislation was to benefit the people a great deal, and the congress much more, a course for which there is plenty of precedent. The congress was liberally supplied with plenty of the source of hilarious vitality, and never, we venture to say, has a more intelligent, witty, or business-like body convened in the world. The message of the dictator was a document which dealt less in the sophistications of government and diplomacy, than such documents generally do ; and there was a plain directness in its advice and recommendations worthy of imitation by other higher dignitaries. During the day, various members of the Senate and House of Representatives of the republic of Texas were introduced to the congress as a matter of courtesy to the bodies they represented, and by them, and other persons of distinction, appropriate addresses were made, and thanks returned for the honor conferred upon them. Wit and eloquence flashed upon and lighted up the assemblage from morning till night, and grace of posture and gesture date an epoch from the day that the first congress of the rounders of this republic assembled.

XXXII.

DEATH OF BIG FOOT.

(Houston Telegraph.)

In August, 1842, some horses were stolen from the farm of Captain Monroe, on Little River. Next morning the settlers collected, and found an Indian trail, in which was the well-known track of Big Foot the chief. They pursued the trail through a heavy rain, about thirty miles up the river, when they suddenly came upon four Indians with the stolen horses. When discovered, the Indians were skinning a buffalo, and before they knew it, the whites were so near them, there was no chance for escape. The Indians dropped their knives, and seized their guns. The colonists instantly leveled their pieces, and tried to fire, but owing to the wet, they would not go off. The savages now took deliberate aim, and snapped their guns, but their powder also proved to be wet. Both parties then clubbed their guns, and a hand-to-hand fight of a desperate character followed. In the end the settlers were victorous, and not a redskin escaped. The warlike Captain Big Foot was killed after a manful resistance. He had been for months the scourge of the frontier.

The names of the white men who were in the fight, were Captain Monroe, Mr. Ross, Mr. Bryant, and Mr. Woolfalk.

XXXIII.

DAWSON'S DEFEAT.

BY J. C. ROBINSON.

(From the Texas Almanac, 1868.)

In September, 1842, General Adrian Woll led about twelve hundred Mexicans to the city of San Antonio, Texas. The expedition was conducted with such rapidity and secrecy, that they reached the town before any intimation was had of their approach. The place was taken, the American inhabitants dispersed, and the district court, then in session, was captured. The indignation and excitement caused by these proceedings need not be described here. Honest patriots required no other appeal, and a simultaneous rush of volunteers toward San Antonio commenced. A company from Fayette county, of which the writer was one, participated in the tragic scenes which followed ; and what follows is intended as a faithful narration of them, and an honest tribute to the memory of his companions.   Our company organized by electing Nicholas Dawson, of La Grange, to the command.   We numbered fifty-three, including officers.   It was the 17th day of September.   The distance to the Salado was about forty-five miles.   Toward this point we rapidly hastened, expecting there to join Colonel Caldwell, and anxious to participate in the expected engagement.   A scout was sent forward to reconnoiter. He soon returned with the intelligence that Caldwell was in battle with the Mexicans, on this side the Salado, and that he himself had narrowly escaped with this intelligence.   Captain Dawson now addressed himself to the company, and asked if we should go on.   All said " Yes."   We advanced rapidly, and ascending a hill, saw the glitter of arms in the timber skirting the Salado. Our approach did not remain long unobserved, and about one hundred and fifty dragoons came out toward us.   The enemy continued to advance, while we hastily took possession of a small mesquit grove, dismounted, and prepared to give them a warm reception.   They halted at some distance from us, while their leader, Colonel Corasco, advanced and summoned us to surrender.

Captain Dawson made no reply.   He returned and led his men rapidly to the right of our position, as if to attack us there, or pass around us ; then suddenly wheeling, they deployed across our front.   Dawson embraced the chance thus offered to bring on the battle.

We saluted them with a volley of rifle balls, which tumbled several of them from their horses.   They quickly halted on our left, and returned the fire, but almost without effect.   This continued several minutes, during which time a re-enforcement of three hundred men came up with a field-piece.   We were now nearly surrounded, while the cowardly distance at which they kept themselves, rendered our fire of but little effect.   Our position was fully exposed to their cannon, of which they were aware.   A cannon-ball soon clipped the tops of mesquits, quickly succeeded by another, which wounded some of the horses, and then a swarm of grape-shot swept along and leveled several of our brave fellows in the agonies of death.   We sustained this unequal contest about half an hour, during which time the incessant discharges of grape-shot had mowed down nearly two-thirds of our number, and the fate of all seemed inevitable.   Among our dead was the aged veteran, Zadoc Woods, nearly eighty years of age.   By the side of this old soldier lay his son, Norman, faint from loss of blood, who, handing his pistol to his brother, told him to make his escape if possible.   The scenes around us were well calculated to fill the breast with horror and pity.   Hand to hand and shoulder to shoulder, there is little doubt but that even at this juncture, we might have cut our way through them, and reached the position of Caldwell.   The cannon of the enemy almost alone gained the day for them. Dawson, who with a few men still remained uninjured, conducted himself with unflinching intrepidity, but at length, seeing the hopeless nature of the contest, he asked those around him if he should hoist a white flag. He was told to do so, and upon displaying it, the firing of the enemy ceased. They now had us upon their own terms. The surrender became a scene of confusion and cruelty. Expecting nothing but butchery, some of our men fled into the prairie, and being overtaken by the cavalry, were lanced or shot. Dawson walked out toward three who were coming toward us. He handed his pistol to one of them, but no sooner had he done this, than another began to cut him on the head with a sword. Dawson sprang forward and caught him, but was instantly killed. Several others who surrendered were massacred. A few of their officers attempted to stay the carnage, and but for their efforts, none of us would have survived the dreadful day. Fifteen were made prisoners, five of whom were wounded. Two only escaped ,one of these, Gonzales Woods, son of the old man above alluded to, at first gave up his arms and surrendered, but the inhuman wretch whose mercy he thus claimed, struck him on the head. Another on horseback darted at him with his lance. Quick as thought, Woods seized this lance and jerked this valiant warrior from his horse sprawling on the ground, then mounting, made his escape. Thus terminated another tragic conflict with the same ungenerous enemy whose hands had been before reddened with the carnage of the Alamo and Goliad. We were now tied and led to General Woll, who promised us that we should be treated as prisoners of war, which promise (to his credit be it said) so far as he was concerned, was kept. Our dead were stripped and left upon the field, a prey for wolves and vultures, until their friends from Fayette county gathered their bones for sepulture. The Mexicans stated their loss in killed to have been twenty-nine, and their wounded still more ; but then these figures were below the truth.

XXXIV.

THE SANTA FE EXPEDITION OF 1841.

In 1841 an expedition was set on foot in Texas for the occupation of New Mexico. The object was a peaceful occupation of that country, and to prevail upon its people to submit quietly to the laws of Texas. The enterprise was encouraged by a spirit of adventure always prevalent among the young men of a new country, and also by many who expected to reap a golden harvest from a trade to be opened with the Santa Fé country. It was also sanctioned by President Lamar, then the Executive of Texas, who gave it his active aid. He also appointed three commissioners to accompany the expedition as the accredited agents of the Texas government. This project did not receive the sanction of the Congress of Texas, which adjourned without having made any appropriation for it.

The volunteers for this expedition collected together and mustered at Brushy Creek, Williamson county, to the number of about two hundred and seventy men, under command of General H. D. McLeod. There were also accompanying the command about fifty traders, servants, and others.

President Lamar issued the necessary order to the secretary of the treasury to furnish means for equipping the expedition, and gave the commander special orders for his guidance. All things being in readiness, the line of march was taken up on the 20th day of June, 1841. The President spent the night of the 19th in camp.

This expedition proved to be very unfortunate. After experiencing many vicissitudes, being lost among the Wichita Mountains, and suffering much from hunger and thirst, it finally arrived within seventy miles of San Miguel.

Here they sent forward a party under command of Captain W. P. Lewis, who was prevailed upon by Armijo, Governor of New Mexico, to betray the whole body of the Texans into his hands. This was accomplished by specious promises, and the Texans were induced to surrender, and were afterward searched, plundered, bound, and marched of to San Miguel.

They were afterward separated and thrown into the prisons of Santiago, Puebla, and Peroti, where they remained until their release in April, 1842. The commissioners appointed by President Lamar to accompany this expedition, were W. G. Cooke, R. F. Brenham, and José Antonio Navarro.

XXXV.

THE BATTLE OF MIER.

(Houston Telegraph.)

On the 15th of December, 1842, news was received by General Ampudia, in Matamoras, by an extra courier from Generals Woll and Canales, that the Texans, one thousand strong, had captured Laredo, and that their own force was not large enough to attack them, in consequence of which they had fallen back. Meantime the Texans had advanced toward Matamoras. General Ampudia at once prepared to march up the south bank of the Rio Grande, and the next day set out with two battalions, known as the sappers and miners, and Yucatan regiment. They proceeded by forced marches, and reached Mier on the 22d December. News had already reached there, that the Texans had crossed the river three leagues from the town, and the Mexican forces were stationed with a battery of artillery, ready to receive them. On the morning of the 23d, the town was attacked by a force of two hundred and fifty Texans, under command of Colonels Fisher and Green. By daylight the attacking party had cut their way through the Mexican ranks, and taken their artillery, driving them for shelter to the houses. The fight continued from house to house, and street to street, the Mexican dead being piled in heaps wherever they attempted to make a stand. Owing to their greatly superior numbers, however, they were afterward enabled to detach a part of their army, and recapture and hold their artillery. The hand-to-hand fight in the town continued all day, the Mexicans retreating before our men, when late in the afternoon, one of our captains hoisted, without orders, a flag of truce. The Mexican general seeing this, sent a prisoner to inquire if this meant surrender. After some time and much conflict of opinion among the Texan officers and soldiers, the reply was returned that our men would discontinue the fight, if allowed to retire without being molested or disarmed. General Ampudia replied that he had ample forces at his command, but would receive a surrender upon honorable terms. Colonel Fisher asked for two hours to consider the matter, which was granted, hostilities meantime ceasing. At the end of the time, articles of capitulation were drawn up and signed by General Ampudia on the one part, and Colonels Green and Fisher, on the other part. The battle of Mier lasted seventeen hours, with a loss to the Mexicans, of about a thousand killed and wounded, and on the side of Texas, of eleven killed and nineteen wounded. The following were the terms of capitulation:

1st. All who give up their arms will be treated with the consideration which is in accordance with the character of the magnanimous Mexican nation.

2d. Conformably with the petition that General Fisher has made, all persons belonging to the Santa Fé expedition will be treated in the same manner as the rest.

3d. All who desire to avail themselves of these terms, will enter the square, and deliver up their arms.

SEQUEL TO THE MIER EXPEDITION.

The following letter of General T. J. Green gives the conclusion of this unfortunate expedition:

CASTLE OF PEROTE, MEXICO, April 15th, 1843.

DEAR FRIENDS: You will learn by this letter, that I am one of the prisoners confined in this filthy dungeon, and loaded with chains. General Fisher,

I, and four others, were in advance of the other Mier prisoners, when they broke from their guard at Salado, Feb. 11th last. We were about one mile in advance of the others, under charge of an escort of cavalry, when the firing commenced. The officer in charge of us immediately put us off in a gallop at the point of the lance, and rushed us seventy miles that day. Eighteen of those who overpowered the guards refused to escape with the others. Four of these eighteen were badly wounded, namely, Captains Fitzgerald and Baker, John Sansberg, and Higginson. Fitzgerald and Higginson died soon after. Captain Reese, Stephen Clark, and twelve others are here. Sixty-two are here ; I will tell you what I know of the rest. At the charge at Salado three were killed, Brenham, Lyons, and Wright. The other one hundred and ninety-three started for Texas. One hundred and sixty-seven were retaken, after being pursued two hundred and fifty miles. Six died of fatigue or were killed, and it is hoped that the remaining twenty arrived at home. An order was received to shoot every tenth man of the one hundred and sixty-seven. The report was that this order was countermanded, but yesterday, to our unspeakable sorrow, we learned that the following brave men were lotteried for and shot, to wit: Major J. D. Cocke, Major R. H. Dunham, J. M. Ogden, Captain Eastland, T. L. Jones, J. M. Thompson, H. Whaling, W. N. Cowan, C. H. Roberts, E. Esty, J. Trumbull, R. H. Harris, M. C. Wing, P. Mahan, J. L. Cash, J. Torry. These, together with the noble Cameron, made up the costly sacrifice. Of the others a fearful apprehension prevails, that they will have or will share the same fate. This is the history of the two hundred and sixty-one heroes who fought the battle of Mier against odds of ten to one, save the eleven killed in battle and twenty-two wounded and left in Mier, and eight left in Matamoras with W. Reese now on his way home.

THOMAS J. GREEN.

The lottery spoken of was drawn in the following manner : White and black beans were drawn from an earthen mug or crock, 159 white and 17 black beans, the whole corresponding to the number of prisoners. The white beans signified exemption, and the black, death. It was evidently determined that Captain Cameron and the other officers should die, and the black beans were placed on top with this design. The mug was first presented to Cameron ; next to the other officers, and lastly to the men. All acted with manly dignity and firmness. Some jested over the solemn ceremony. One said, "Boys, this is the tallest gambling I ever did." Another, "Raffling is nothing to this." As the black beans one after another were drawn, scarcely a change of countenance could be seen, while those who drew the white exhibited no joy. The doomed seventeen were placed in separate confinement, and were shot about sundown.

9

Previous to execution, they were bound with cords, their eyes bandaged and they were placed in line and shot.

The following thrilling description of the decimation of the Mier prisoners, is from the Houston *Telegraph and Register*, May, 1845 :

Who can describe the thrill of horror and consternation that electrified every heart, when the interpreter, in broken and tremulous tones, announced it as the order from the supreme government that every tenth man among us should be shot, the lots to be decided on the instant, and the execution to follow immediately. So entirely unexpected was this murderous announcement, so atrocious in its character, so inhuman and indecent in the haste of its consummation, that a stupor seemed to pervade the whole assembly, not a word escaping the lips of any for more than a minute. The silence was at length interrupted by the interpreter, who, in obedience to his orders, proceeded to inform us further, that *all* had been sentenced to the same fate, but the *humane* government had been graciously pleased to commute the just claim to this decimal execution. A low clatter of handcuffs was now heard, as some of the most desperate of our fellows essayed to free themselves from their shackles. This had been foreseen and provided against. An order was promptly given to fall back within the shed, and the doorway, and top of the low walls bristled with the muzzles of muskets presented to enforce it. We were helpless as the bound victims under the sacrificial knife. While we were marshaled in an extended line, a Mexican subaltern and soldier entered the yard together, bearing a bench, and an earthen crock. The bench was placed before the officer who had communicated the order, and the crock set upon it, containing one hundred and seventy-five beans (the number of prisoners), among which were seventeen black ones. A handkerchief was folded so as to hide the color of the beans, and was thrown over the crock, and a list of our names, taken down when we were recaptured, placed in the hands of the interpreter. When these funereal preliminaries had been completed, the name of our dauntless leader was first called, who, with a step as stately and brow as serene as he had ever previously worn, stepped forward and drew.

Each man in his order on the list continued to be called, and the individual compelled to draw, until the seventeen black beans had been taken from the crock. When a bean was drawn it was handed to the officer, and the jar well shaken before the dread lottery proceeded. As they drew, each person's name was entered upon another memorandum, with the color of his bean. In many instances the doomed victim was forced to revisit the fatal urn to allow the comrade to whom he was chained to try the issue of life and death. Appalling as had been the first effect of the order, and as rapidly and voraciously as our self-dug graves yawned around us—not a step faltered, not a nerve shook, as the sickening ceremony went on. Several of the Mexican officers seemed deeply affected, shedding tears profusely, and turning their backs upon the murderous spectacle. Others again leaned forward over the crock to catch a first glimpse of the decree it uttered, as though they had heavy wagers on the result. Three-fourths of the beans were exhausted before the fatal seventeen had been drawn. When the sacrifice was made up, the victims' names were read, their persons scrutinized, and being removed outside, their irons were knocked off. A few of us were permitted to go out and take a hasty leave of them. A priest had accompanied the march from Saltillo, who was now present to administer extreme absolution, but only two could be prevailed upon to accept his intercession. Major Robert Dunham, being importuned to confess him to the holy father, repelled the proposition with warmth, preferring like a good Protestant to shrive himself, which he knelt down and did mutely and earnestly. This brave and honest man was then solicited by the rest to offer up a prayer in their behalf, but as he was about to comply, he was rudely stopped by the officer on duty, who sternly and profanely forbade it. As twilight advanced, two files of infantry of twenty men each, with the whole body of cavalry, escorted the doomed men to the eastern wall, selected as the place of execution. Here being made to kneel down with their faces to their butchers, they were blindfolded, and shot in two parties successively, nine first, and eight afterward. Huddled together in the stalls of the corral, the surviving prisoners were forced to sit down, and a heavy body of sentinels placed over them with their firelocks cocked, and at present, ordered to shoot the first man who should speak or move while the execution was progressing. Tears forced their way down many a rugged cheek- as silent and manacled we listened to the mournful notes of the dead march, swelling and sinking on the ear, as the procession rounded our prison to the eastern flank. The wall against which the doomed men were placed was so near us that we could distinctly hear every order given in halting and arranging for the work of death. The murmured prayers of the kneeling men stole faintly to us—then came the silence more eloquent than sound, then the signal taps of the drum—the clank of muskets brought up to the aim— the sharp burst of the discharge, mingled with shrill cries of anguish and heavy groans, as body and soul took their sudden and bloody leave.

XXXVI.

TEXAS INDIANS.

(From the Texas Almanac, 1869.)

OF the numerous Indian tribes that once inhabited the territory of Texas, some have become entirely extinct, others are almost so, and those which are still respectable in numbers are rapidly passing away. The Alabamas, Coshatties, and Caddos, were once inhabitants of Louisiana, but have been for many years sojourners in Texas. The first two tribes live in the south-

INDIANS.

eastern part of the State, and are engaged in cultivating the soil, and in raising stock. The State has granted them a small amount of land, and has made a limited provision for an agent to act as a friend and protector to them. They are regarded as truthful and honest, and have the good-will of the whites living around them. It is understood that they number less than five hundred of all ages.

Several years since, the Caddos were settled upon lands granted to them on the Brazos River. They were afterward moved to a new reservation on the Wichita River in the Chickasaw nation. These Indians have made considerable progress in civilization. They cultivate the soil, and raise horses hogs, and cattle. They entered into treaty stipulations with the Cònfederate Government, and with other bands remained during the civil war of 1861–5 in the Indian territory near Fort Arbuckle. They now, with other tribes, reside on the reservation known as the Wichita Indian Agency. The Wichitas were once a powerful tribe, inhabiting the country on the Red River, above and contiguous to the Upper Cross Timbers. They are a warlike and athletic people, once the greatest scourge of Northern Texas ; but are now nearly extinct.

The Wacoes, Anadarkos, and Kechis have but few if any representatives. If any numbers of these tribes still survive, they have become incorporated with other tribes. The Tonkawas once inhabited the country on the Lower Colorado and its tributaries. They have receded toward the plains as the white settlements have advanced. It is said of this tribe, and it is believed with truth, that they have always remained steadfast in their friendship to the people of Texas. They were moved with the Caddos and others to the Wichita, and entered into treaty stipulations, with the other bands and tribes of that agency, with the Confederate authorities, as above stated. Shortly after these relations were established, disaffected Indians attempted to frustrate the alliance, at which time the Tonkawas seemed to be especially singled out for destruction. In the attack made upon them, many of their warriors, and children as well as women, were killed. Among the victims was the gallant old chief, Placido, who has enjoyed the confidence of General Ed. Burleson during the life-time of the latter ; and had also been regarded with friendship by General Sam Houston, as well as by other eminent men of Texas. After the attack upon the Tonkawas, the survivors fled for refuge to Texas. They assisted the frontier troops during the war against the hostile Indians. They were subsisted by the people and the State authorities until 1867, when they were taken in charge by the officers of the United States Army, and are now on the frontier near Fort Richardson, They number about one hundred and sixty souls. The Lipans were once quite numerous, inhabiting Western Texas. The tribe is now divided, one part living on the Mexican side of the Rio Grande. These Indians, in connection with a band of Kickapoos, commit most of the depredations on the western frontier.

The remainder of this tribe live upon the Staked Plains, and in the *panhandle* region of Texas. They are, and have generally been hostile to the people of our State. The Comanches, so long the terror of our frontier countries, are the most numerous of the Texas Indians. They roam over the whole extent of the Staked Plains, between the Canadian and the Rio Grande. During the summer they follow the buffalo still farther north, and some of the bands claim the valley of the Arkansas River as their home.

The western limit of the territory occupied by them extends to the regions inhabited by the Navajos, Utes, and Apaches. Frequent efforts have been made by the government to reclaim them from their wandering mode of life. Through the efforts of the late Major R. S. Neighbors, the legislature of Texas made ample donations of lands for Indian reservations. Four leagues were to be selected on the Pecos for Southern Comanches and Lipans ; four leagues on the clear fork of the Brazos, where a portion of the Northern Comanches were induced to settle ; and an equal quantity on the main Brazos below Fort Belknap, where were located the Caddos, Kechis, and Tonkawas. But the constant invasion of Kiowas, and other wild bands, and the jealousy of the frontier settlers toward these Reserve Indians, frustrated this well intended policy, and previous to 1860, the Indians were moved to a new reservation on the Wichita, near old Fort Cobb.

The Comanche nation is composed of eight distinct bands, each having its own chief and head men. It is not supposed that any one chief ever exercised authority over the whole, although some prominent ones have exerted great influence. The Pennatethca band was settled by Major Neighbors, on one of the Reserves, and moved with other tribes to the Wichita agency. This band has made some progress in husbandry. It is thought that as a body, they have proved faithful to their treaty obligations. All these unlettered children of the prairies are reared in the belief that the Great Spirit will reward the successful warrior and robber, after death, with pleasant hunting grounds. It would, therefore, be strange if they should prove an exception to the rule, that depravity exists to some extent among all classes of people. The Yamparekah, Cochatethca, Noconu, Tenawah, Moochakah, Pohobis, and Quahadechaco, still roam the plains, and prey upon the borders of Texas. These several bands constitute the Comanche nation. The Kiowas are a numerous, warlike, and treacherous tribe. They are not perhaps, strictly speaking, Texas Indians. Inhabiting a portion of country frequented by the Comanches, and partaking of their habits and customs, they are sometimes confounded with them. They are nevertheless a distinct tribe, and differ widely from the Comanches. The latter are usually of a stouter build, lower stature, and more agreeable appearance. The Kiowas are sullen, dogged, and reserved. They roam from the upper waters of the Arkansas River to Red River, and down that stream to the Cross Timbers, and when on the war-path, far into Texas. Their home is properly the territory between New Mexico and Kansas. They have always been at war with our people. They have never kept their treaties with the whites.

The wild tribes of Indians still continue their depredations upon the frontiers of Texas. From official sources it appears that between May, 1865, and August, 1867, no less than one 162 persons were murdered, 24 wounded, and 43 carried into captivity from Texas by the Indians. Many thousand dollars' worth of property was also stolen or destroyed.

These outrages still continue, and many victims are yearly added to the bloody catalogue. It is not easy to estimate the number of the wild tribes.

The Comanches, Kiowas, and Lipans could probably put into the field 5,000 warriors.

XXXVII.

DESCRIPTION OF OLD GOLIAD, OR LA BAHIA.

(From an old newspaper.)

IT was founded soon after the arrival of the Spaniards in Texas. The town is on the west bank of the San Antonio River. It once contained near two thousand inhabitants. During the war between Spain and Mexico, Gutierrez was besieged in the Mission * by a large Spanish force, but repulsed by them.

The missionary priests had in charge a large number of Indians. These were under overseers, and were compelled to work. Many of them acquired considerable property in cattle and horses. By frequent intermarriages with Mexicans, and by casualties of various kinds, these Indians have almost disappeared. Goliad was at one time a place of some business importance. The trade between it and the Rio Grande was by no means inconsiderable. There was a custom-house near the old Mission, the ruins of which remain. The church proper consisted of an oblong room about 20 by 80. It is still used for worship. The church adornments are few and simple. The officiating priest is now a Frenchman. The roof of the church is arched, and of solid masonry. It is surrounded by a stone wall, three hundred and fifty feet square. At each corner is a bastion. The fort commands the river and the town. It is at this point that Fannin could have made his best defense against the Mexicans in 1836. He is said to have had an abundance of provisions, arms, and ammunition. When he decided to retreat, he burned his supplies in the church. The marks of the flames are still visible on the wall. These works have been constructed many years. In the soil which has accumulated on the roof of the church, two trees are growing. Colonel Fannin at first prepared for a vigorous defense. When he received the order from General Houston to fall back, he delayed to concentrate his forces. Ward and King were thirty miles distant, at Refugio. Grant on the Agua Dulce,† eighty miles away; and Pierce at San Patricio. These detachments were all

* A church and fortress.   † Sweet water

attacked in detail, and captured by the enemy. Near the fort are spots where Fannin's men were butchered. He was shot within the walls. The old town of Goliad is classic, venerated ground. It is dear to the heart of every Texan. Here a bloody sacrifice was made upon the altar of liberty, an offering of men who were battling in a holy cause. Perfidy here completed a work which oppression had begun. The funeral wail which here ascended to heaven from many a woe-stricken heart was a prelude to the song of triumph which arose soon afterward from the field of San Jacinto, where a crimson field was piled with dead, and where the war-cry of vengeance called back the minds of the victors and the vanquished to the Alamo and Goliad. The old town is still principally inhabited by Mexicans, some sixty or seventy families. The new town is on the north side of the river, and is inhabited by Americans. It has been built for the most part within twenty years, and is a handsome town.

The above was written about the year 1850, and is a truthful account.

XXXVIII.

SCENE ON THE BATTLE-FIELD OF SALADO.

(From the Texas Almanac, 1860.)

OUR camp was on the banks of the lovely San Antonio River. As the sun came peering above the prairie hills east of us, the loud command, "Saddle up" came ringing down the line. Soon, all was in motion. Some leading forth their horses from the prairie ; some busy loading their guns ; some looking for missing articles ;—all bustle and confusion.

At length every one being in readiness, the order was given, "Mount, and form in line." Up to the time of marching, our destination was unknown save to a few of the officers ; and when the command, "Right face— march," was given, and the head of our long column filed away to the east, all was conjecture. Nor was our suspense relieved till, after a march of four miles, our troops wound up a long prairie slope toward a beautiful mesquit grove on its summit. As we neared the grove all was hushed. The object of our march was soon evident. It was the battle-field of the Salado, where the sound of fierce strife had scarcely ceased. Soon we dismounted and turned to view the scene. I have beheld many a sad scene. I have stood upon many a battle-field, I have seen companion after companion fall by my side, and as they lay weltering in their gore, witnessed their dying agony. But oh ! compared with the scene now before us, it was nothing. Many of those present had lost relatives, all had lost friends. It had been my fortune to lose no relatives. Yet as I stood there, and saw the grief-stricken father, as he discovered the unburied corpse of his son; as I marked the brother with dry and burning eyes fixed upon the gaping wound which laid his only brother low; as I saw the son weeping over the inanimate form of his gray-haired sire, I felt as though I had better have fallen with them, than live to look on such a scene.

Friend after friend of mine lay upon that deadly field. There the gallant Dawson, by whose side I had stood upon the field of San Saba. He whose fearless and noble bearing had cheered my youthful courage through that dark and doubtful conflict. Yes, there he lay,—slain in a contest where his brave arm was powerless. Near him lay the gallant Woods, brave old man! he had often wished to die on the battle-field. His wish, alas! was gratified. I had known him when I was a prattling child; he was an old man then. From him I had received many acts of kindness. And as I stood over him, on that field of death, and looked upon the manly form from which the wind swept back the long, silvered hair, I wept—yes, for him—as a father. It is called weakness in the soldier to shed a tear, yet the man who could stand and gaze upon that scene, unmoved, might boast a heart harder than granite. Not far off, sleeping his last sleep, was old David Berry. Who, in the early struggles of Texas, did not know brave old David Berry? When was the alarm sounded that he was not the first to shoulder his gun and hasten to the scene of danger, where he was ever to be found in the van. That heart, one of the noblest that ever beat in the breast of man, was still.

His battles were all fought, even the last, the great fight of death. Sleep on, good soldier. Thy laurels encircle thy brow; long will thy countrymen remember thee. There, too, was lion-hearted Pendleton. His country was in danger. Scarce waiting to bid his weeping wife farewell, with eager haste he sped to the fatal field. There, battling in the sacred cause of freedom, he fell. Brave friend—nobly hast thou done thy duty. Freely was thy blood poured out to water the tree of liberty in the Lone Star Republic. Faithful soldier! thou art not forgotten. A few steps farther on might be seen the daring Alexander. When the note of war first echoed along our western border he tore himself away to meet his country's foes on that bloody field. There he offered upon his country's altar the sacrifice of his life. All these fell not alone. Around them lay many a gallant soldier, to whom war's wild alarm shall come no more. War-worn soldiers! your trials, your hardships, are over. Your long sleep shall be unbroken until the last trump shall sound to call your slumbering spirits to meet again those friends from whose embrace ye were so rudely torn.

Long will Texas mourn her gallant dead.

XXXIX.

TEXAS—INDIAN WARS.

SCALPING OF WILBARGER IN 1833.

BY JOHN HENRY BROWN.

(Texas Almanac, 1861.)

SMALL and individual incidents, transpiring in the infancy of frontier set-tlements, are often clothed with vivid interest and long remembered by the contemporary settlers as part and parcel of their own or their neighborhood's history. To perpetuate the record of such events in the pioneer days of Western Texas, has long been the desire of him who pens these sketches—the truth of history being strictly observed in their relation.

Josiah Wilbarger, a man of plain, practical sense and strong nerve, was a native of Bourbon county, Kentucky, and in 1823, when just arrived at man-hood, removed with his parents to Pike county, Missouri, where the writer, then a child, knew him and his family, the farms of our respective fathers adjoining. Having married, he removed to Texas in 1826–7, somewhat at the instance of the writer's father, who had already spent three years in Texas, and about 1830, settled at or near Bastrop on the Colorado, then the extreme outpost of our settlements in that direction. The event we are about to relate occurred in the autumn of 1833.

Wilbarger, in company with two other men, whose names we can not recall, had gone on an exploring or hunting excursion in the mountains near and above the present city of Austin. After a trip of several days, they encamped for the night, on their homeward march, on a little stream, perhaps Walnut Creek, at the foot of one of the numerous mountain spurs in that vicinity, feeling quite secure, as they had seen no indication of the presence of Indians on their route ; but they were doomed to a sad disappointment.

While quietly dispatching their morning repast, after a pleasant night's repose under the star-lit canopy of heaven, they were surprised by the sudden roar of horses' feet on the mountain-side above them, and, on looking up, beheld a large body of mounted warriors, dashing at full speed, with wild and savage shouts, upon them. Ere a second thought could enter their excited minds, the barbarian horde were throwing their balls and arrows among them. One of the men instantly fell with a death-shriek ; and Wilbarger, receiving a ball through the neck and several arrows elsewhere on his person, sank sense-less to the ground. Seeing this, and terrified to wildness, the survivor, a visitor to the country, mounted his fine steed without saddle or bridle, with nothing but a rope around his neck hastily thrown over the nose, and gave the noble animal full opportunity to do, or—*let his rider die!* The horse, whether from fright or instinctive affection for his master we know not, performed what his rider considered a noble part, and soon left the whooping pursuers far behind. He was left to pursue his course in safety, but so excited and terrified was the poor fellow (who was on his first frontier expedition), that it was said he arrived in Bastrop, thirty-five miles distant, with the piece of buffalo-meat he was masticating when the assault was made, firmly clenched in his teeth. He, of course, reported both Wilbarger and the other person as slain. The settlement was then very feeble, and it required some little time for the necessary number of men to prepare for going out to bury the dead.

They did not reach the spot till about sunset on the following day, when, to their surprise, they espied a bloody, hideous-looking mass, in the shape of a man, reclining at the base of a tree, near a small pool. So shocked were they that they involuntarily hesitated whether to advance or retire. But a voice was heard—" 'Tis I—Willbarger, come on, friends!" faintly spoke the object of their gaze. And so it was—poor Wilbarger had not only been shot three times, but the surface of his head had been scalped, while he was yet unconscious, and left for dead. He was indeed a horrid, piteous-looking object; the burning sun had literally parched his naked skull, and but for returning consciousness and the ability to drag his enfeebled body to the edge of the pool, he must have died ere succor came. He was totally unable to rise.

The remains of the deceased were speedily interred, and a litter constructed on which Wilbarger was borne into Bastrop, where kind nursing in a few weeks restored him to ordinary health. But his head—that tender organ—had too long been bleached in the sun ever to heal up. For twelve years it remained an incurable wound, tormenting and agonizing the unfortunate man, until his death, which occurred at his home near Bastrop, in 1845.

An interesting and curious incident connected with the scalping of Wilbarger, and his recovery the subsequent day by his friends, may be here briefly and appropriately mentioned. The night before he was found in his wounded and helpless condition, the late Mrs. Reuben Hornsby thrice woke her husband, to tell him that in a dream she had seen their friend in the hands of the Indians, and that they were scalping him. Twice he succeeded in allaying her apprehensions, by assuring her that dreams are always airy and unreal, and that it is unwise to allow them to disturb our quiet. The third time, however, she refused to be pacified, insisting that he should immediately quit his couch, arouse his neighbors and go to the rescue of Wilbarger. She furthermore told her husband where the wounded man

would be found, describing with the utmost particularity the spot and its surroundings.   Mr. Hornsby, in compliance with his wife's wishes, and to
relieve her intense anxiety, left his bed, roused from their slumbers a few
friends who were at hand, and went forth with them in the direction of the
place indicated.   They reached the spot late in the afternoon, and there
found Wilbarger weltering in his blood, just as Mrs. Hornsby had seen him
in her dreams.   The foregoing facts are authentic and reliable.   To say the
least of them, they exhibit a marvelous coincidence of circumstances.

J. H. H.

XL.

INDIAN WARS IN TEXAS.

THE MORGAN MASSACRE, AND BRYANT'S DEFEAT.

BY JOHN HENRY BROWN.

(From the Texas Almanac, 1868.)

On Sunday night, January 1st, 1839, a part of the families of James
Marlin, Mrs. Jones, and Jackson Morgan, were together at the house of
George Morgan, at Morgan's Point, six miles above the town of Marlin on
the Brazos River.   The remainder of the families were at the house of John
Marlin, seven miles lower down the river.   A little after dark the house of
John Marlin was suddenly surrounded by Indians, who rushed in, giving the
inmates no time for defense.   Old George Morgan and wife, their grandson
Jackson Jones, Jackson Morgan's wife, and Miss Adelaide Marlin, a young
lady of sixteen, were all tomahawked and scalped within a few minutes after
the first alarm.   William Morgan's wife was severely wounded and left for
dead.   Three children were in the yard when the onslaught was made; one
of these, a child of ten years, secreted himself under the fence, and there
remained until the tragedy was over.   Another ran into the house, but seeing
the Indians entering and tomahawking the family, ran out again unobserved,
and was followed by Mary Marlin, another child.   They both escaped.   The
wounded lady, retaining consciousness, feigned death, and was not scalped,
though all the others were.   The Indians robbed the house of such things as
they could take away, and left.   When they had gone, and silence reigned,
the heroic child first mentioned, Isaac Marlin, crept from his hiding place,
and entering the house, examined the bodies to find which were dead.   His
wounded sister, supposing him to be an Indian, remained motionless until he

had gone, when she crawled out of the house. Isaac then took the trail for John Marlin's, and ran the whole distance, seven miles, to convey the dreadful intelligence to his kindred. The other children and Mrs. Morgan were found the next day. Ten days later, the Indians, seventy in number, attacked the house of John and Benjamin Marlin, who, in company with Jarrett Menifee and his son Thomas, made a stout and gallant fight, killing seven Indians and wounding others, without receiving any injury. The savages, not relishing that kind of reception, withdrew. When the attack was made, Menifee's negro man Hinchey, was at work a short distance from the house, and not being able to get into it, he left at a double quick for the settlements below, some twenty-five miles. Hinchey's news soon brought together a company, who at once repaired to the scene of action, but the redskins had departed.

BRYANT'S FIGHT AND DEFEAT.

Next morning, Bryant took the trail of the enemy, and pursued it, crossed the Brazos near Morgan's Point; on the west side found a deserted camp with fresh signs. About a mile further found a fresh trail, and followed it to the river. At the river he counted fifty-four fresh horse tracks, and a large trail of Indians on foot, all of whom seemed to have crossed. Seeing the prairie on fire below, they supposed it to be Marlin's house, hastened back without finding the enemy, and halted for the night. Next morning, January 16th, they started again, and found the Indians had been at the deserted homes, and had plundered them.

They then traveled six miles up to Morgan's Point, and suddenly came upon the Indians in the open post oak near a dry branch. The noted chief, José Maria, who was coolly riding in front, dismounted, slipped off his gloves, and taking deliberate aim, fired at Boren, cutting his coat sleeve. José Maria gave the signal to his men, and the action commenced. Bryant ordered a charge, which was gallantly made, though the captain received a wound at the same instant, which accident called Ethan Stroud to the command.

The Indians fired, and fell back into the ravine. At the moment of the charge, David Campbell fired at José Maria, hitting him on the breast-bone, but failing to dismount him. Albert Gholson then shot the chief's horse, which died in the ravine. Our men then charged to the bank of the ravine and fired, at which the Indians commenced retreating down its sides. Seeing this, several of our sharp-shooters rushed below them to cut them off. This brought the enemy back to his first position, and our men, supposing the day to be won, became scattered. The Indians suddenly renewing their fire, some disorder ensued, to remedy which our men were ordered to fall back, to draw the Indians from their ambush. This unfortunate order, being in the confusion understood by some to be an order to retreat, became a cause of panic, which being discovered at once by the wily José Maria, he gave the command, and charged with his whole force, at the same time making the air resound with hideous yells. A rout, commencing in a causeless panic, ensued, and our men were pursued four miles, their pursuers dealing death among them. In the retreat, some acts of daring were performed which deserve notice. David Campbell, not at first observing the retreat, was about being surrounded by the savages, when the brave Captain Chandler, already mounted, rushed to his relief, and took him up behind him. Young Jackson Powers whose arm was broken, missing his own horse, mounted a pony behind William McGrew. His brother came by, mounted on a larger horse, and told him to leave the pony and get up behind him; this he tried to do, but from the broken arm and the restlessness of the horse, he was unable to mount, till the Indians rushed up and tomahawked him, his brother barely escaping. William Marlin during the action was severely wounded in the hip, so that he could not mount his horse, and was about to be left, when David Cobb ran to him and threw him on his horse. Wilson Reed, a daring fellow, in the retreat was knocked from his horse by a tree, the enemy being close at hand, when he called out in a jocular tone, " O Lord, boys, Mary Ann's a widow." But a brave comrade picked him him up and bore him off. The loss of the Indians was about the same as that of our party, but they were greatly elated by their success, and became more daring than ever, until checked by that decisive engagement known as Bird's Victory near Little River. José Maria has always acknowledged that he was whipped, and retreating, until he saw the sudden confusion among the Texans.

XLI.

THE ARCHIVE WAR.

A LEAF FROM THE HISTORY OF AUSTIN.

BY GEORGE H. GRAY.

EARLY in March, 1842, the Mexican forces under General Vasquez made an incursion into Texas, which was promptly met by the people, and the invaders driven back. President Houston, deeming the national archives in danger from the enemy, felt it his duty to order their removal, as well as the removal of the government offices. to a place of safety. Accordingly he ordered their prompt removal to Houston. This gave rise to what is known as the Archive war, the result of which has been the location of the seat of

MRS. EBERLEY FIRING OFF CANNON.

To face p. 143.

government at Austin up to this time. The gallant citizens of Travis county had, a short time before, gone to meet the invaders of their country, leaving behind them a growing and prosperous city, and on their return found a deserted village. They were exasperated, and had good cause to be. They thought the president had acted in bad faith toward Austin. They had expended for city lots half a million dollars, had built houses on them, and had felt secure under the strong arm of the government. This was now suddenly removed from them. The president was urged to come back, but without avail. The citizens then determined to take the matter in their own hands. The records of the General Land Office had not yet been taken away. These the citizens of Austin determined at all hazards to keep, that one branch at least should remain. The president insisted that these archives should also be taken to Houston; and sent up for them, but without success. The young men of the city, in order to show their contempt for the executive, went so far as to shave the manes and tails of the horses of two of the messengers sent up, who did not relish the joke at the time, but afterward became reconciled to it, and became permanent citizens of Austin. The president, seeing that he could not obtain the records of the Land Office peaceably, determined to take them by force. Accordingly, he sent an armed force of thirty men, with instructions to take them at all hazards.

This company arrived on the morning of the 29th of December, 1842, drove their wagons to the Land Office building, and at once commenced loading. The citizens, finding out what was going on, at once armed, and assembled in force. Great excitement prevailed. Cannon charged with grape and canister were brought out and planted, so as to bear on the wagons; and the signal for action was impatiently waited for. The wagons were by this time loaded, and were about starting, when the word "Fire" was given, and the cannon were discharged, taking effect on the building but hurting no one. As to who touched off the guns, it is not definitely settled, but it is generally conceded that it was done by Mrs. Eberly, a worthy and respected lady, and at the time proprietress of the Eberly House, now owned by Mrs. Beale. The wagons, with their load and escort, now left town in double-quick time. The citizens at once formed themselves into a company under command of Captain M. B. Lewis, and pursued them, overtaking them during the night at Brushy Creek, eighteen miles north-east of Austin. The wagons and escort were surrounded, and negotiations were opened. The citizens demanded that the archives should be taken back to Austin, which, after some parley, was agreed to. Next morning early, the train went back in triumph to Austin, and arriving there the records were deposited in the house of Mrs. Eberly, until the Land Office was reopened. No further attempt was made to remove them. Thus ended the "Archive War," decisive though bloodless.

XLII.

FANNIN'S MASSACRE.

BY ONE WHO ESCAPED.

IN March, 1836, Colonel J. W. Fannin, with between five and six hundred men, occupied the town of Goliad on the San Antonio River. While there, he detached Captain King, with a small company of men, to occupy the old Mission of Refugio, about twenty-five miles distant. King, after taking possession of the fortress, found himself threatened by a large force of Mexicans, and sent an express to Fannin for aid. Accordingly, Colonel Ward, with one hundred and twenty-five men, were sent to his relief. Having arrived at Refugio, King insisted upon taking command of the whole force, but the men declared themselves in favor of serving under Colonel Ward, who was lieutenant-colonel of the regiment. Captain King then withdrew, with his original company of twenty-eight men, and they were almost immediately afterward surprised and killed. The Mexican forces then attacked Colonel Ward and his men in the Mission, and after a sanguinary fight, which lasted nearly all day, were repulsed with heavy loss. Meantime, orders were received from Colonel Fannin to join him and his command at Victoria, and the line of march for that place was taken up at night. But Fannin and his men, having set out for Victoria, were intercepted, and after a bloody battle were captured and taken back to Goliad. Ward and his detachments, when they arrived at Victoria, instead of finding their countrymen, found the place occupied by a large force of Mexicans, and retreated, but next day were surrounded and taken prisoners by the enemy under command of General Urrea. They were then taken to Goliad, where they found their brave fellow-captives, numbering in all four hundred and eighty men. On the morning of the 27th of March, in defiance of the terms of surrender, which were, that they should be held honorably as prisoners of war until exchanged, the whole company of Texans were marshaled in line and counted into four divisions of one hundred and twenty men each. Each division was then placed in charge of a strong guard, and ordered to march in different directions from the fort, for what purpose, the prisoners could only guess. "When about half a mile from the fort," says our informant, "we were ordered to halt; the guard was then halted, and ordered by the captain to face to the right, and then, almost instantly, to *fire*. The horrible order was promptly complied with, and nearly all of our brave boys fell in death. A few, myself among the number, made a desperate run for life, and by concealing ourselves in the grass and weeds, finally got away. The men having been shot, the officers, who had been reserved until the last, met the same tragic fate. Colonel Ward, having refused to kneel, was shot as he stood, and Colonel Fannin, having left his effects, together with his dying request, with the officer in command, calmly seated himself in a chair, and awaited his death. Of the whole number who were marched out for slaughter on that memorable Sunday, fifty-five only escaped."

XLIII.

THE CARANKAWA INDIANS.

BY J. H. KUYKENDALL.

(Texas Almanac, 1872.)

BOTH history and tradition preserve the names of several tribes of Indians, which had become extinct, or blended with other tribes, before the State was colonized by Anglo-Americans in 1821, at which time the tribes with which the settlers came in contact were the Comanches, Wacoes, Towacannies, Ionies, Kechis, Lipans, Tonkawas, and Carankawas. The last named were the most remarkable. The men were of large stature, six feet high, and the bow of every warrior was as long as his body, and as useless in the hands of a man of ordinary strength as was the bow of Ulysses in the hands of the suitors of Penelope, but when bent by one of these sons of Anak, it sped the "cloth yard" arrow with deadly force two hundred yards These Indians navigated the bays and inlets with canoes, and subsisted, to a considerable extent, on fishes.

They were believed by many of the early settlers to be cannibals! but it is probable, that the only cannibalism to which they were addicted, was that occasionally practised by the Tonkawas, if not all the Texas Indians. This consisted in eating bits of an enemy's flesh at a war dance, to inspire them with courage. A dance and feast of this kind I once witnessed on the Colorado, where the Tonkawa tribe was encamped. A party of its braves on a war tramp slew a Comanche, and upon their return to their tribe, brought with them a portion of the dried flesh of their slain foe. This human *tasajo*, after being boiled, was partaken of by the warriors, with cries of exultation. It is remarkable that this anthropophagous rite is practiced by some of the black savages in Africa. An English missionary, speaking of a negro tribe on the Zambezi, called the Ajawa, says, "Under some circumstances they eat man as other tribes eat lion, to make them brave." They told us of a certain chief called Neria, against whom the Ajawans fought for a long time

10

without success, and who sustained his cause almost single-handed. When at last he was overpowered and slain, his body was cut into minute portions and eaten by the Ajawa warriors, that they might be valiant as he. To return to the Carankawas.

Their thievish and murderous propensities early involved them in war with Austin's colony, by whom they were repeatedly defeated with heavy loss, in consequence of which, in 1825, they fled west of the San Antonio River, whither they were pursued by Austin at the head of a strong party. When Austin arrived at the Waanahuila Creek, six miles east of Goliad, then called La Bahia, he was met by a Catholic priest with a message from the Indians, that if he would desist from the pursuit, they would never after that time range east of the San Antonio River. The colonists agreed to this and returned home. The Carankawas did not long keep their promise; but in a short time returned to the Colorado, and again committed depredations, for which they were again scourged by the colonists. Efforts were made by the Catholic missionaries to christianize these Indians, and the Mission of Refugio, thirty miles south of Goliad, was built for that purpose. But the Carankawas were proof against all civilizing influences. At length, about the year 1843, forty or fifty men, women, and children, the sole remnant of this tribe, which twenty-one years before had numbered more than one thousand, emigrated to Mexico and were permitted to settle in the State of Tamaulipas. At this time, it is probable that the Carankawa Indians are entirely extinct. I am not positive whether any of the other tribes mentioned at the beginning of this chapter are verging on extinction, but it is well-known that they have all rapidly diminished in number, and the conclusion is inevitable that in a score or two of years, all the smaller tribes and bands will become as extinct as the mammoth and the mastodon which preceded them. The Comanches being still a large tribe, with extensive hunting grounds, will last somewhat longer; but they, too, are fast approaching the termination of their tribal existence; and the child is now born who will live to say, "The Comanches are no more."

XLIV.

TEXAS HISTORY.

I HAVE been permitted to copy the following letter, written January 8th, 1837, by Governor E. M. Pease to his father, from Columbia, Texas. It contains a brief but comprehensive glance at Texas affairs from the beginning of the campaign of 1835 to the inauguration of the Constitutional Government in 1836.—COMPILER.

In the month of May, 1835, our State legislature was dispersed by the military of the general government. Some of its members, the governor, and Colonel Milam who was at the seat of government (Monclora), were arrested and thrown into prison. This proceeding aroused public feeling in Texas. Hitherto the revolutions in the interior had disturbed them very little more than if they had been a different nation. They feared they were to become the sport of the different chieftains who were struggling for power. We remained during the summer in that feverish and excited state which usually precedes some great convulsion.

Frequent public meetings were held, and committees of safety appointed in every part of Texas. Little that was satisfactory could be learned of the doings of the general government, and still less of their intentions toward Texas. The military officers of the general government who were near us, constantly said to us, "Peace," and protested that there was no intention to change the government. The central government had always kept a small garrison at Goliad, sometimes called La Dahia and also at San Antonio de Bexar, sometimes called San Antonio and sometimes Bexar or Bejar. I am thus particular that you may identify these places by their different names. At the former place, 30 or 40 men, and at the latter about 60. During the summer they increased the garrisons, and collected large quantities of military stores at these places, until about the close of August there were about 600 men at Bexar, and Cos, a general of division, had been ordered, and was on his way, to take command of them. These warlike signs awakened our attention.

Meetings were held more frequently, and a meeting in the county of Brazoria recommended a "General Consultation," to be composed of members from all the counties, to meet on the 15th of October, and consult and adopt such measures as might be necessary to insure peace, if it could be had without a sacrifice of our dearest rights; and to devise some remedy for the evils under which we had labored since the overthrow of our State government. Most of the counties concurred, and elected delegates. Previous to the time fixed for the meeting of the Consultation, I think about the 20th of September, the commandant of the forces at Bejar sent an order to the authorities of Gonzales, to return to that post a piece of ordnance (4-pounder) that had been furnished them some years since, by the government, as a defense against the Indians, threatening, in case they refused to comply with the order, to send a force to take it. This was considered a signal for the commencement of hostilities. The authorities refused to deliver it, and immediately dispatched couriers to all parts of the country, advising their fellow-citizens of their refusal, and determination to resist, and calling upon them for assistance. As we expected, when the refusal reached Bejar, a detachment of cavalry, about 150 men, were sent to enforce the order.

This detachment reached the west bank of the Rio Guadaloupe, opposite Gonzales, on the evening of the 28th of September.

The appeal to the citizens had been promptly responded to, and on the same morning there had collected about 100 Texans in the town, ready for a fight. The Mexicans, seeing that a force was ready to repel them, made no attempt to cross the river. Several conferences were held with the Mexican commander. He was told that if he wanted the cannon, he must take it. Both parties remained in their positions for three days. On the evening of the third day, the Texans resolved to cross the river and compel them to fight, surrender, or run away. Accordingly the Texans, to the number of 120, crossed. The Mexicans on our approach, after receiving a few shots from our cannon, retreated to Bejar. The war was now fairly commenced, and our only course was to fight it out. Our forces remained at this place until the 12th of October, re-enforcing daily, when it was resolved to march and attack the town and garrison of Bejar before any more troops were introduced into the country.

Accordingly our forces, now numbering about 500 men, under command of General Austin (who had a few weeks before returned to this country, after his long imprisonment in Mexico), took up the line of march, and in about a week, encamped in the neighborhood of the town. There were slight skirmishes almost daily, until on the evening of the 27th of October, a detachment of about 95 men, under command of Colonels Fannin and Bowie, were sent up to the old Mission Concepcion, situated one mile below the town, and in plain sight, to select a more commodious camping ground. The rest of our forces remained about eight miles below. The Mexicans had discovered them the same evening, and learned very accurately their number. Early on the morning of the 28th of October, which was very foggy, our men discovered that they were nearly surrounded by the enemy, who at a considerable distance were advancing upon them. A courier was at once dispatched to the main body and preparations were made for battle. A position was selected on the bank of the river, in a bend behind a small bluff which served our men as a breastwork. The force of the enemy was about 170 infantry and artillery, and about 300 cavalry, with two pieces of ordnance. They continued to advance, bringing up a 4-pounder. Very few guns were fired by our men, until the enemy came within about forty yards, when a brisk and deadly fire was poured upon them from our rifles. They faltered and retreated, leaving their cannon. Rallying, they again came up to the cannon, but our fire was so destructive, that they again retreated, leaving the cannon on the ground. A man was killed in the act of spiking it. Our main body now came up, and the enemy retired to the town. This is called the Battle of Conception, from the place where it was fought. Our loss was one man killed, none wounded. The enemy left 17 dead on the field, and it is supposed that not less than 100 were disabled and killed. A part of our forces now encamped at this place, and a part about the same distance above the town, watching the enemy closely. On the 27th day of November there was a severe action called the " Grass Fight," between a portion of our men and a body of the enemy, in which several of them were killed and a few of our men wounded. Our troops now became weary of this mode of warfare. Many were very uneasy, and resolved upon storming the town. On the evening of the 4th of December, about 300 volunteers under command of Colonel B. R. Milam, were ordered to storm the town next morning. The town was strongly fortified, the streets barricaded, and it was considered by the enemy as impregnable. About daylight on the 5th, our men in two divisions marched into town under a severe fire from the enemy's cannon at the Alamo, which is a large stone fortress surrounded by a yard and stone wall. They succeeded in getting possession of two houses near the public square, which served as a cover from the shot. The enemy kept up a constant firing of small arms and artillery for five days and nights. Our men fought their way from house to house until, on the morning of the 9th, the enemy were entirely driven from the town into the Alamo.

A flag of truce was now sent out from the Alamo, a capitulation was agreed upon, and about 1300 men surrendered, with a large number of arms, and a quantity of munitions. The prisoners were permitted to return to the interior with their arms, under parole not to " oppose the re-establishment of the Constitution of 1824."

Thus closed the campaign against Bejar.

Now let us glance at the war in other quarters.

About the 1st of October, a party was hastily collected in the neighborhood of Matagorda, consisting of fifty or sixty men under command of Major Collingsworth, who marched and surprised the garrison at Goliad without losing a man. The garrison consisted of about 50 men. A large quantity of provisions, munitions, and arms were here taken. These were destined to be transported to the garrison at Bejar. They were transported to Bejar, but for a different purpose than that originally intended. They were served out to our troops instead of theirs. About November 1st, 40 men under command of Adjutant Westover left Goliad to attack the garrison at Lipantitlan on the west bank of the river Nueces, near San Patricio. On the evening of the 3d of November, they surprised and made the garrison prisoners. Here they captured two small pieces of ordnance. The prisoners were released on parole and the fort destroyed. In recrossing the river, our party were attacked by 70 of the enemy, who had gone out from the fort the day before, and returned to find it destroyed. A severe fight ensued, and the Mexicans were repulsed with the loss of 28 killed and wounded. We had one man wounded. This brings down our military operations to the close of the first campaign. It had lasted about two and a half months, and the enemy had been driven from the country.

I will now resume civil affairs. On the 15th day of October, the day for the assembling of the Consultation, few were there. The war had commenced since the election, and most of the delegates were in the field. The meeting was adjourned until the 1st of November, at which time a sufficient number assembled to form a quorum at San Felipe. The condition of the country had changed since the election. They were at war, and something must be done to defend the country. They very properly at that time made a declaration in favor of the Constitution of 1824, and called on the " Liberals " of the nation to support them. They organized a provisional government, consisting of a governor, lieutenant-governor, and general council, composed of one member from each county. This government was to continue until the 1st day of March next following, by which time we should know whether the nation responded to our declaration, if not, a new convention was to be held to decide upon our future course. This provisional government commenced operation on the 14th day of November, 1835.

They immediately prepared for organizing a regular army. General Houston was made commander-in-chief; commissioners were dispatched to the United States to make loans, and purchase arms, munitions of war, and provisions. They did all that men could do without funds or credit. Texas was now cleared of its enemies, and had something like a government. Volunteers from the United States now came in rapidly, all anxious for fight. After the close of the first campaign, most of the Texans returned to their homes, and Goliad and Bejar were mainly garrisoned by the volunteers coming in. The people of Texas having been so fortunate thus far, imagined their independence already achieved, and trusted for security to the weakness and disorder of their enemies. To this apathy is to be attributed the reverses to our arms in the spring of 1836, which came well-nigh ruining the country. All volunteers who came in were concentrated at Goliad and Bejar. During the month of January, a party of about 100 men, under command of Colonels Grant and Johnson, made an expedition toward the Rio Grande. Meeting no opposition, they became careless, and were, about the last of February, surprised near San Patricio and nearly all destroyed. The few that escaped brought us the first news of the large force that was already upon us, and we entirely unprepared. 500 men at Goliad, and 150 at the Alamo, were all the forces Texas then had in the field to oppose the progress of 8,000. The militia were called out. They collected, but slowly, at Gonzales, which was the place of rendezvous. Meantime one division of the enemy, three or four thousand strong, arrived at Bejar on the 23d of February. They summoned our garrison of 150 men, under Colonel W. B. Travis to surrender, or to be put to the sword. They answered the summons by the thunder of their artillery. This intelligence aroused the people to a true sense of their danger. They began to rally. Thirty-two men from Gonzales succeeded in getting into the Alamo, notwithstanding it was closely invested. This made the number in the Alamo 182. The enemy made frequent attempts to storm the place between the 23d of February and the 6th of March, but were as frequently repulsed with great loss. Our men were occupied night and day in watching the foe and strengthening the works. The works were large, and required at least 500 hundred men to man them well. On the night of the 5th they had worked nearly all night upon the walls until nearly exhausted, when they retired to rest. About two hours before day on the 6th, the enemy had resolved to attack them. The infantry were drawn out around the fort at a distance, and the cavalry outside of them, with orders to shoot every man that turned back, thus driving their own forces to the attack. About one hour before daylight the attack commenced. It is supposed that our sentinels, worn out with fatigue, had fallen asleep and were killed at their post. Simultaneously with the first alarm within the fort, the Mexicans were on and within the walls in large numbers. Our men were soon rallied, and cleared the yard and the walls in a few minutes.

> " They fought like brave men long and well,
> They filled the ground with foe they'd slain ; "

but, overpowered by numbers, they sank with weariness and loss of blood. You have probably heard many accounts of that scene. They are all more or less fancy sketches. But one male escaped to tell the news. He was a servant boy belonging to Colonel Travis. There was also a Mrs. Dickinson, wife of a Lieutenant Dickinson of the garrison. They however saw nothing, being shut up in the fort during the fight. The boy says there was one man found alive when the enemy had full possession of the place, and he was shot by order of Santa Anna. Travis had said, " If they took the fort it should be a defeat to them," and truly it was. From the first attack to the fatal morning of the 6th, they had not less than one thousand killed. The bodies of our men were burned the same day. I blame not the enemy for the fate of the Alamo. Our friends died nobly ; one only survived to ask for quarter, and he was refused.

While these events were passing at Bejar, Colonel Fannin was hourly expecting them at Goliad. The vanguard of the division destined for that place, as stated before, had surprised Colonels Grant and Johnson, and were advancing along the coast. Fannin dispatched Captain King, with twenty-five men, down to the Mission Refugio, twenty-five miles south-west of Goliad, to bring off some families there. While there, the advance of the enemy came upon him and drove him into the Mission, where he defended himself, and sent a courier back to Goliad to inform them of his situation. Fannin dispatched Colonel Ward, with one hundred men, to his relief. This was probably on the 13th of March. They arrived at the Mission toward night, and drove off the enemy. The next morning Captain King went out scouting with his men. The enemy were re-enforced that morning, and numbered six or eight hundred. They succeeded in cutting off King, and attacked Ward in the Mission. A severe fight was kept up during the day. A large number of the enemy were killed. We had three men wounded. That night Colonel Ward succeeded in getting out of the way of the enemy without being noticed. The turned their course direct toward Victoria, about twenty-five miles east of Goliad, but being unacquainted with the country they wandered about and did not, with the exception of a few who separated from the main-body and were fortunate enough to get into the settlements, arrive at Victoria until after Fannin's capitulation. Here they were surrounded ; and learning of Fannin's surrender they capitulated upon the same terms, and most of them shared the same fate. General Houston, who was now in the field at Gonzales, on the fall of the Alamo, ordered Colonel Fannin to abandon Goliad and fall back to Victoria. This order arrived at Goliad after Ward had left for the Mission. Fannin delayed to give Ward time to return, until the 19th of March, when, presuming that Ward was cut off, he blew up Goliad and retreated toward Victoria. After marching a short distance they were overtaken by the enemy. A severe battle ensued, which lasted all night. A large number of the enemy were killed and a few of our men. They remained on the ground all night. In the morning they found themselves surrounded by the enemy, who proposed to them to capitulate to prevent the effusion of more blood. A capitulation was entered into : our men were to return to Goliad and be sent by water to New Orleans, on parole not to fight unless exchanged. They were sent back to Goliad ; and after being kept eight days were, together with Ward's men, marched out and shot.

General Houston, who was at Gonzales with about 400 men when the Alamo fell, prudently burned Gonzales, and fell back to the Colorado River to await re-enforcements. There he remained until about the 25th of March, when, learning of Fannin's defeat and the large force of the enemy approaching, he fell back to the Brazos, and encamped twenty miles above San Felipe. One company was stationed at San Felipe, who, on the approach of the invading army burned the town and crossed the river. The enemy did not attempt to cross the river here, but marched down to Fort Bend, about thirty miles below San Felipe, where they succeeded in crossing.

The whole country west of the Trinity River was now occupied alone by the two armies. Eight or nine hundred of the enemy, under Santa Anna in person, pushed on from Fort Bend to Harrisburg, then the seat of government. The officers of government, knowing of their approach, went down the bay in a steamboat. The enemy burned Harrisburg, and marched down the bayou as far as New Washington, about ten miles below a place called, on the maps of Texas, Lynchburg. They also burned New Washington. Houston, learning of the advance of this division, crossed the Brazos and marched down to Harrisburg to find the enemy. At this place they intercepted a courier, from whom they learned that Santa Anna was with that division, and also the number.

The Texans pushed on down the bayou, and at Lynchburg, or very near that place, the opposing armies came in sight of each other.

On the evening of the 20th April, there was a severe skirmish between our cavalry and the enemy. On the same evening the enemy was re enforced by 600 men under General Cos. On the 21st April, our forces, about 800 strong, attacked and completely routed the Mexican army. I can give you no better account of this battle than you have seen. A short armistice was concluded, and the enemy hurried from the country. Thus much for the war on land. On the water, our armed schooner the *Liberty*, four guns, succeeded in cutting out and bringing off from the Port of Sisal, from under the guns of the fort, the Mexican merchant schooner *Pelican*, with a valuable cargo. Our armed schooner *Invincible*, seven guns, had an action off the Brazos Santiago with the Mexican armed schooner, of the same force, *Bravo*, disabled her, and she ran on the bar and was lost in attempting to go in. Our privateers have also made several valuable prizes.

I now return to the affairs of government.

A new convention assembled at the town of Washington, on the 1st of March, and declared our independence. They framed a constitution, and organized a government *ad interim*, until the new constitution should be approved and an election held. The first Monday in September, an election was held and the constitution approved. General Sam Houston was elected president, M. B. Lamar, vice-president. On the 1st of October, Congress assembled, and soon afterward the new officers were installed. Congress passed the necessary laws for organizing the different branches of the government, and all went into immediate and harmonious operation.

XLV.

COMANCHE FIGHT AT SAN ANTONIO.

(From the official report of General H. D. McLeod.)

On the 19th day of March, 1840, sixty-five Comanches, including warriors, women, and children, came by previous appointment to San Antonio to treat for peace. The meeting had been agreed upon a month before, and the Indians had promised to bring in thirteen white persons, whom they held as hostages. They however brought but one, a daughter of Mr. Lockhart. Twelve chiefs, leaders of the deputation, were met by our commissioners, Colonel W. G. Cooke, and General H. D. McLeod, in the Government House, as it was called, and the question was at once put to them, "Where are the prisoners you were to bring?" Mukwarrah, the chief who had made the promise at the former talk, replied, "We have brought the only one we had." This was known to be false, from the girl's statement. She said that she had seen several prisoners at the camp a few days before, and that the intention was to get a high ransom for her, and then for each of the others, bringing them one by one. A pause ensued, after which the chief asked, "How do you like the answer?" No replied was made, but an order was sent to a company of soldiers, to advance into the room. Meantime the terms were explained to the chief, which should have been agreed to in case they had complied with their engagements.

The soldiers under Captain Howard entered the room, and the chiefs were told they were prisoners until they sent for and brought in the rest of the white captives. As the commissioners were retiring from the room, one of the chiefs attempted to escape by leaping past the sentinel, who in attempting to prevent him, was stabbed by the Indian, Captain Howard was also severely wounded in a similar manner. The rest of the braves drew their bows and arrows and knives, and made a general attack. The soldiers fired and killed the twelve chiefs. The warriors in the yard fought with

THOMAS J. RUSK.

See p. 264.

desperation, but were soon repulsed by Captain Redd's company. A portion of them retreated across the river, but were pursued, and finally all killed. The Indian women fought desperately, and several of them were killed. The loss of the Indians was thirty-two chiefs and warriors, three women, and two children. Twenty-seven women and children, and two old men were made prisoners. Our loss was seven killed and eight wounded.

XLVI.

ANOTHER CHAPTER OF OUR EARLY HISTORY.

(Galveston News.)

[WE are indebted to an old friend, and an earlier pioneer of Texas, for the following documents, the authenticity of which can not be questioned. Our readers abroad should bear in mind that La Bahia is the Spanish name for old Goliad. The date of the letter shows that it was written but a short time after the massacre of Fannin's troops:]

LA BAHIA, June 4, 1836.

On our arrival at this place we found no difficulty in discovering the ground where Fannin and his gallant band were shot by order of Santa Anna. Most of their bodies were burned, while there were many bones and some entire skeletons scattered over the plains for some distance. It had long been determined that as soon as practicable after the arrival of the army here, these remains should be collected, and a day set apart for their burial with all the honors of war. Accordingly, on Wednesday, the 1st inst, General Rusk issued the following order:

"As a token of respect as well to the men who fell a sacrifice to the treachery and bad faith of our enemy, as a duty which we owe to the relations of the unfortunate deceased and ourselves, it is ordered that the skeletons and bones of our murdered countrymen be collected into one place, in front of the fort, and buried with all the honors of war.

"THOMAS J. RUSK,
"*Brigadier-General Commanding.*"

On the evening of the ensuing day, the bones having been collected, the following order was given:

"A general parade of the army will take place to-morrow morning at half-past eight o'clock. The funeral will take place at nine o'clock A. M. Colonel Sidney Sherman will take command, and conduct the procession in the following order:

" 1. Artillery.

" 2. Music.

" 3. Major Morehouse's command.

" 4. Six commissioned officers [Corpse] Six commissioned officers.

" 5. Mourners.

" Those of Fannin's command who are in the army, and who have so miraculously escaped, will attend as mourners.

" 6. Commanding General and staff.

" 7. Medical staff.

" 8. Second regiment.

" 9. First regiment.

" 10. Regulars.

" Major Poe will order a minute gun fired from the fort, commencing at the time the procession moves, and until it arrives at the grave.

"THOMAS J. RUSK,
" *Brigadier-General Commanding.*"

The following morning being Friday, June 3d, the army was paraded within the walls of the fort, at the hour appointed ; and at nine o'clock, with arms reversed, moved slowly toward the place of burial. On reaching the grave General Rusk delivered a short, but feeling and eloquent address.

" FELLOW SOLDIERS : In the order of Providence we are this day called upon to pay the last sad offices of respect to the remains of the noble and heroic band, who, battling for our sacred rights, have fallen beneath the ruthless hand of a tyrant. Their chivalrous conduct entitles them to the heart-felt gratitude of the people of Texas. Without any further interest in the country than that which all noble hearts feel at the bare mention of liberty, they rallied to our standard. Relinquishing the ease, peace, and comforts of their homes, leaving behind them all they held dear, their mothers, sisters, daughters, and wives, they subjected themselves to fatigue and privation, and nobly threw themselves between the people of Texas and the legions of Santa Anna. There, unaided by re-enforcements and far from help and hope, they battled bravely with the minions of a tyrant, ten to one. Surrounded in the open prairie by this fearful odds, cut off from provisions and even water, they were induced, under the sacred promise of receiving the treatment usual to prisoners of war, to surrender. They were marched back, and for a week treated with the utmost inhumanity and barbarity. They were marched out of yonder fort under the pretense of getting provisions, and it was not until the firing of musketry and the shrieks of the dying, that they were satisfied of their approaching fate. Some endeavored to make their escape, but they were pursued by the ruthless cavalry and most of them cut down with their swords. A small number of them now stand by the grave—a bare remnant of that noble band. Our tribute of respect is due to them ; it is due to the mothers, sisters, and wives who weep their untimely end, that we should mingle our tears with theirs. In that mass of remains and fragments of bones, many a mother might see her son, many a sister her brother, and many a wife her own beloved and affectionate husband. But we have a consolation yet to offer them: their murderers sank in death on the prairies of San Jacinto, under the appalling words, " Remember La Bahia." Many a tender and affectionate woman will remember, with tearful eye, " La Bahia." But we have a another consolation to offer. It is, that while liberty has a habitation and a name, their chivalrous deeds will be handed down upon the bright pages of history. We can still offer another consolation : Santa Anna, the mock hero, the black-hearted murderer, is within our grasp. Yea, and there he must remain, tortured with the keen pain of a corroding conscience. He must oft remember La Bahia, and while the names of those whom he murdered shall soar to the highest pinnacle of fame, his shall sink down into the lowest depths of infamy and disgrace."

During the delivery of this address the general had the undivided attention of the whole army. When he spoke of the sufferings of these martyrs in the cause of liberty, I observed the tear-drop fall from the eye of more than one brave man. In its conclusion I observed several compress their lips and involuntarily grasp their weapons more firmly, as if the scenes of San Jacinto had not compensated the brutal murder of their friends at La Bahia. The army then marched back to their quarters.

SAMUEL DEXTER,
Aid-de-camp.

XLVII.

INCIDENTS OF TEXAS HISTORY.

(From the Brownsville Sentinel.)

DURING the month of January, 1851, Lieutenant Ed. Burleson, since Major Burleson, was ordered to San Antonio, to deliver to an officer of the United States a Comanche prisoner taken in a fight at Amargosa, May 29, 1850. The captive was returned to his people.

Burleson was on his return to Camp Los Ojuelos. On the 27th of January, when just this side of the Nueces, on the road from San Antonio to Laredo, he saw three Indians on horseback. He took eight men and pursued them—directing the balance of his party to keep the road, and move on.

After a vigorous pursuit for two or three miles, the Indians halted, and prepared for battle. In addition to three mounted there were eleven red devils on foot. The Rangers promptly opened the fight—moving up to within fifty or sixty yards of the Comanche line. By some mistake the men dismounted, and as they improperly thought by order of Burleson. The Indians charged them immediately, and a terrible hand-to-hand fight ensued. Shots were delivered at the distance of a foot or two.

They fought under the bellies of the horses, over the saddles—there was a general mêlée of red men and white. Colt's six-shooting carbines and bows and arrows—repeating pistols and lances—were blent in a confused and struggling mass. There was no time for shouting—for maneuver—each man fought for life, and taxed his energies to the utmost. The field was an open prairie, devoid of even bushes. There could be no cover. It was a trial of skill, strength, and courage. A few minutes decided it. Victory trembled in the balance. Baker Barton, a gallant soldier, received three mortal wounds and died on his feet, holding to the horn of his saddle. He knew not how to yield. He was killed, but his indomitable spirit was not conquered. William Lackey received two or three wounds—one of them mortal. Jem Carr, brave and cool, received three or four severe wounds. He said, " It was like clock-work—every time I raised my Colt's carbine, they stuck an arrow in me." He did good service. A warrior singled him out—charged at him with bow and lance. Jem sent a ball through him—then another. The brave still advanced, discharging arrows—they came with less and less force, until at last they scarcely left the bow. Jem, however, had ceased to fire at him— knowing there were others demanding his attention.

Jem's last wound was inflicted when he had his carbine at his face, and ready to fire—an arrow passed through the last joint of his right fore finger, and penetrated the breech of his gun—luckily the wood splintered, and his hand was released.

William Lackey lived eight or ten days. He was wounded in the lung.

The other wounded recovered without any unpleasant symptoms having been developed. The fight summed up : Comanches, four killed, eight wounded. Rangers, two killed, eight wounded.

This was one of the most closely contested Indian fights that ever occurred in Texas.

Thirty days after it came off the writer was on the ground. It was literally covered with arrows. Over two hundred were picked up on a space of less than one-fourth of an acre.

All the evidences of a desperate struggle were apparent. Both parties were exhausted. The wounded Rangers were unable to pursue the discomfited and flying Comanches.

The bodies of the Comanche dead had been removed, otherwise things remained in *statu quo*.

A number of Mexican carts were traveling the road to San Antonio. The Comanche gentlemen were so busy watching them, that they failed to discover the near approach of the Rangers. They had set a trap and were caught themselves.

What a difference there was between murdering and scalping unarmed cartmen, and meeting Rangers in deadly conflict. There was no plunder for them to divide no captives for them to beat and drag through prickly pears at the end of a rope. There were death, and wounds, and escape from danger, to contemplate instead.

It was an escape to the cartmen savoring of a providential interposition. They expressed their gratitude to the victors.

Major Burleson has been for many years a peaceful and thrifty farmer. He lives near the town of San Marcos, Hays county.

He left Brownsville for home a few days since.

Burleson himself had an encounter, across his horse, with a stalwart savage. He received an arrow wound in the head, before he sent his antagonist to "kingdom come."

Alf Tom was wounded, but fought nobly

Jem Wilkinson was wounded severely, and continued fighting.

Warren Lyons, the interpreter, had been raised among the Comanches. He came at his old *companeros* in true Indian style—jumping—stooping down and changing position in various ways. He wished his "boots off"— they were too heavy. He told Burleson what the Indians were saying.

Leach did his duty well. He was perfectly self-posssesed. Burleson saw an Indian aiming at him with a pistol. He immediately presented his six-shooter. Leach called out, "Don't shoot at him, Lieutenant, he's only bluffing. I've been watching him, there is no load in that pistol."

Jack Spencer had two or three Indians to deal with at one time. He was wounded, yet there was no time for surgery. He was using his horse for a cover, and fighting as best he could. The chances were rather against him. At other points the charge of the savages had been repulsed. Spencer received help, and the Comanches left the field. They had been consulting in a hurried manner about retreating. They did not see their way clear. They had gotten into a tight place, and feared they could not make their way out without great damage. Lyons told Burleson this, and said they were whipped.

They finally stood not "upon the order of their going." They left four dead on the field, and had eight wounded. The defeat was complete, else they would have carried off their dead in defiance of the Rangers.

About the time the fight closed Sam Duncan came upon the field. He was sent by Burleson to a water-hole twenty miles to the front.

Barton was packed on a mule and buried on a hill some miles from where he fell. The wounded were cared for as well as circumstances permitted. The water gourds had been exhausted, and they were suffering terribly from thirst.

Burleson made a forward movement about nine o'clock A. M. At one o'clock P. M. they met Duncan returning with water.

The water-hole was reached that evening, and a courier dispatched to Laredo for ambulances to carry in the wounded. Several of them were unable to ride on horseback. They reached Fort McIntosh the next day. Captain Sidney Burbank was in command. He saw that the wounded had proper care and attention.

XLVIII.

ADVENTURES OF A VOLUNTEER.

(Galveston News.)

MACON, June 6th, 1836.

DR. ROBERT COLLINS.

SIR: As you were principally instrumental in sending out the company of volunteers to Texas, under the command of Colonel Ward, and furnishing the means of the expedition, and as there is no officer remaining of the company to tell their fate, and being myself the last man of the original company who made an escape previous to the capture and massacre of the Georgia battalion, I think proper to give you a plain history of the expedition, as far as I am able.

It is known to you that we marched from here in the latter part of last year, and proceeded to New Orleans. By the usual route from there, we embarked on the schooner *Pennsylvania*, and after being out eleven days, were landed at Velasco, a port in Texas, on the Gulf of Mexico, about four or five hundred miles from New Orleans. Here we remained about a month, nothing extraordinary occurring beyond the usual camp duty, there being at that time but few Mexicans in the country. From here we sailed to Copano, which is another port still further on the coast toward Matamoras. There we landed and marched up to the Mission, as it is commonly called, twelve or fifteen miles from the coast. Here we remained about three weeks, and then went up to Goliad, about twenty-seven miles further into the interior.

Here we took possession of the fort, and remained in it until the 13th of March, when Colonel Ward and the Georgia battalion were ordered to march in haste to the Mission to relieve Captain King, who, with about thirty men, was down there endeavoring to protect some families, but who had been surrounded by the enemy, and his situation become desperate. We marched at 3 o'clock in the morning and arrived at the Mission about 2 P. M. the same day, and, as we expected, found Captain King and his company in the church and a large company of Mexicans in sight, across the river. We succeeded in getting to the church, where we remained until night, when we crossed the river by fording it at a shallow place, and made an attack on them and completely routed them, killing about twenty-five, with no loss on our side. We then returned to the church, and early next morning again went out to the Mexican camp, where we saw a few Mexicans endeavoring to carry off their dead, but they made their escape on our approach. From here we went about two miles to a ranch, and burned the houses and provisions. By this time the enemy began to re-enforce so fast, in our sight, that we retreated forthwith to the church, and were attacked at once by their whole force. We immediately blocked all the entrances with the images, benches, pews, etc. We had greatly the advantage in position. They came up bravely for awhile, received our rifle balls, fell, and were carried off, and others took their place. But after awhile we could see that it was with great difficulty the officers could whip up their soldiers with their swords to make a charge. This continued until near evening, when they retired a short distance, but not out of sight. We then started an express to Colonel Fannin, to let him know we were nearly out of ammunition—having only taken thirty-six rounds from Goliad—and were still surrounded by a large Mexican force. A Mr. Murphy and a Mr. Rogers, both of Captain Wadworth's company, were to carry the express, both of whom were pursued by the enemy's cavalry and taken. In this battle we had three wounded— none killed. The loss of the enemy was variously stated, but believed to be not less than 200, though it was reported more.

Captain King's company, which we went down to relieve, had gone out early in the morning before the battle commenced, to a branch a few miles distant. They were taken by the enemy, and all shot but two, who made their escape. That night we made our escape from the church, and after traveling through the woods and swamps, where their cavalry could not well pursue us, on the third day we reached the San Antonio River. On the second day after leaving the Mission, David I. Holt, of Macon, and a few others, left the company in search of water, and we never saw them again ; but now understand they succeeded in getting in safe. That night we lay in the swamp ; next morning crossed the river and made our way toward Victoria,

11

and in the evening heard the firing between Colonel Fannin and the Mexicans, apparently distant about ten miles. We attempted to get near them, but night came on and the guns ceased to fire, and we could not proceed, but got into the Guadaloupe swamps, where we remained all night ; and on leaving it and entering a prairie, next morning, we were attacked by a force of 600 cavalry. We fired about three rounds at them, when our powder gave out, and we had not a load left. We then retreated back to the swamp ; every man was told to take care of himself. We then got scattered and I never saw Colonel Ward or the company again, but understood that at night, while I was asleep in the cane, he rallied all the men he could and made his way toward Dimmit's Landing, but was next day overtaken by the Mexican cavalry, and, having no ammunition, surrendered as prisoners of war and was carried back to Goliad, and all his men shot, as has been heretofore published. In this battle Wm. L. Wilkinson of this city was supposed to be killed. On awakening the next morning, I found myself alone in a swamp, in a country full of Mexicans, near two hundred and forty miles from the main army of Texans, and thirteen or fourteen hundred miles from my home, then without a mouthful of provisions for five or six days ; nor was there a prospect of any, except a few wild onions which I could get in the swamp. I remained in this swamp all day and all night ; next morning went out and took a small path and kept it for about two miles, and came to a Mexican house, where I saw several Mexicans in and about the house ; but being forced by hunger, I determined to go in and ask for something to eat, let the consequences be what they might. On entering the house one of the men arose and offered me his chair. I asked a woman who was in the house for something to eat. She readily gave me some milk, cheese, and dried beef. The men, with their guns, all looked astonished, and in a few moments all left the house, and appeared to be looking over the country in every direction, I presume expecting an attack from a large force, of which they thought I was the spy. As soon as they all left the house, the woman told me in broken English that they were all Mexican soldiers, and I had better leave as soon as possible. In a few minutes we saw them returning toward the house, and the woman urged me to start. I did so, and ran toward a swamp which I saw two or three hundred yards distant. As I ran they fired twelve or fifteen guns at me, but without effect.

They pursued me to the swamp, but I escaped them. I kept in the swamp all day, and that night I heard the drums beat in Victoria. Next morning I went near enough to see the Mexican cavalry. I then returned to the swamp, and kept in it all day. That night I went out and made my way up the river until I reached a crossing place. Here I overtook three men that had made their escape from the enemy in the swamp at the same time I did, but whom I had not seen before since we retreated and scattered in the swamp. Their names were Andrews, Moses, and Trevesan. We here got some meal from a house which had been left by the enemy. We remained here all night, and the next day made our way through the woods toward the Colorado River, and that night got to a place where the Mexican army had camped a night or two before. Here we remained all night, and the next morning we reached the river, and crossed it on a bale of cotton, which we found on the bank of the river, about two miles above where the enemy were crossing at the same time. We lay in the swamp that day. At night we heard the drum, but supposing it was the enemy, would not go to it. Next morning Moses and myself ventured to go in sight of the camp to see who they were, and soon discovered they were Mexicans. We retreated, and in short a distance saw six horsemen charging toward us. We discovered they were Americans, and did not run. They came up, and much to our relief, we found they were spies from General Houston's camp. Their names were Cawmack and Johnson, from Tennessee. Shipman and Laplam, of Texas, and two others I did not know. They were astonished to see us at that place, and when I say we were glad to see them, I but feebly express the feelings of my heart. I was then without hat and shoes, and had only a few rags of clothing.

While we were here narrating our adventure, and waiting for one of the company, who had got to go back a short distance after Andrew, we were attacked and fired upon by a small scouting party of Mexicans, but at such a distance as to do us no injury. But upon their seeing that we had got among some trees, and were prepared to give them a fire, they retreated and left that place, and the spies carried us on to General Houston's army, where we arrived, I think, on the 2d day of April, our appearance being such as to excite the sympathy of every soldier ; and on our meeting some gentlemen who had known us in this country, the noble tear of compassion was seen to trickle on their cheeks. We here received all the kindness we required, or desired, and remained with the army, and fought under General Houston in Captain Baker's company, in the memorable battle of the 21st of April, in which Santa Anna was captured, half his men slain, and the other half taken prisoners. Incredible as it may appear, this battle was fought with only about 700 effective men, while the enemy had double that number. The loss on our side was only six or seven killed, and about twenty wounded. Among the latter was our captain and General Houston. The fight commenced in the afternoon, about three or four o'clock, by two six-pounders on our side, and a long twelve-pound brass piece by the enemy ; but by some fortunate shot at the very beginning, we silenced their big gun and pressed down upon them, continuing the fire from our artillery, and receiving the fire from their small-arms, which was doing us no harm, as they seemed to shoot above us. When we reached within fifty yards of them, we fired two or three rounds from our deadly rifles, which seemed to produce a tremendous effect, and, at this moment, a charge from all quarters was ordered, and our men rushed upon them with fury and desperation, and with pistols, guns, and cutlasses, the destruction of human life was speedy and immense. As soon as we had time to look, we saw the white flag was hoisted, and the Mexicans had thrown down their arms, and were running in every direction. As soon, however, as the call for quarters was heard, and the white flag was seen by the commanders, the work of death was stopped, and the balance taken prisoners. Santa Anna himself made his escape that evening, but was taken next morning in a common citizen's dress, about ten miles from camp. He was not recognized until he was brought in, but when the prisoners saw him they tipped their hats, and exclaimed in their own language, "Santa Anna's alive."

The appearance of the ground may be better imagined than described. Piles and clusters of dead and dying lay in every direction, indeed the ground was literally covered. But the recollection of the dreadful massacre of our brave companions at Alamo and Goliad in a great manner relieved our feelings from the horrors of the scene.

On the 30th of April I left the camp, under a furlough from General Houston, for four months, and proceeded overland to Natchitoches, where I arrived after eight days traveling on foot. From there I took the usual route via New Orleans and Mobile to Montgomery, Alabama. There I understood that a war had broke out with the Creek Indians, and that it would be extremely dangerous to attempt to pass on the stage route through the Nation to Columbus; but being anxious to reach home, and finding there a party of about fifteen others who wished to come through, we determined to make the attempt. On Sunday evening, 15th of May, we left there in two mail stages, passed on that night, and early next day reached Tuskeegee. There we got breakfast, and learned there was great trouble with the Indians. We then passed on to the next stand, and found it had been plundered. As we continued on we found every house and place plundered or burned, and some burning, until we reached Thorn's stand, about twenty miles from Columbus. There we saw the house in flames, and after we had got a short distance by the place, we were fired upon by a party of Indians which we had not seen, but they being some distance off no injury was done.

Our drivers then put whip to their horses and ran them near half a mile, when we came to the stages that had been taken the day before, so piled up across the road with the dead horses and one dead white man, that we could not pass, and the stages were therefore stopped, and we saw the Indians in close pursuit. The drivers and passengers loosed the horses from the stage, and as soon as possible all who could get on them mounted and made a start;

but in a few minutes they were fired upon by a considerable party of Indians, who seemed to be coming in on all sides. Not having been so fortunate as to get a horse myself, a Mr. Haltete of New York, a Mr. Williams, Hamil, and Lackey were on foot running after the horses. The two latter were killed, and the moment after they were shot, I ran directly through where the Indians were who had fired at me, but without effect. I made the best of my way toward a swamp which I saw distant some three or four hundred yards, and discovered I was pursued by two Indians. Just before I entered the swamp, I turned and discharged my musket at the foremost, who was within forty or fifty yards of me. I saw him fall, but before I entered the swamp I saw him rise again. The other Indian ran up to him and stopped a few minutes, during which time I got in the swamp and reloaded my gun. He then came down to the swamp and appeared to be searching for me, and while he was parting the cane, not more than fifteen or twenty yards distant, I shot him in the body and he fell dead. I remained in the swamp three days, living on green whortleberries. I went out every night, but could not find my road until Thursday night. I got into the road near where the stages were left, and traveled all night back toward Tuskeegee, and arrived there on Friday morning about sunrise. Here I was received by General Woodard, and treated kindly. I remained here two days and then went back to Montgomery, and from there, in company with two gentlemen, took the upper route through the Nation, on horseback, and on the third day crossed the Chattahoochee and again set my foot on the soil of Georgia.

Very respectfully, your ob't serv't,

(Signed)   SAMUEL G. HARDAWAY.

XLIX.

A RELIC OF THE TEXAS REVOLUTION.

THE following is from the Austin *Statesman* of December 18, 1874:

The heroic deeds of the Texans under General Sam Houston and other kindred spirits, for the independence of Texas, were heralded throughout the civilized world, and the victory of San Jacinto immediately induced a more rapid influx of adventurous young men from all parts of the country into Texas. Organized companies, armed and equipped to help sustain the independence of Texas, were raised in many of the old States, and made rapid marches to Texas to offer themselves as recruits to the tried and wasted Texan army. Among these companies was one from Zanesville, Ohio, commanded by Captain Burroughs, and organized in the summer of 1836. Captains Burroughs,

Morgan, of Pennsylvania, and Colerick, of Ohio, all with companies, reached Matagorda Bay in September, and at once reported to General Felix Huston, then in command of the Texas army.

It was not long after this that Albert Sydney Johnson was assigned command of the Texas army, giving rise to the personal quarrel between Huston and Johnson, which resulted in a duel on Lavaca River, in which the latter was seriously wounded.

The Mexicans had again commenced to make strong demonstrations on the Rio Grande, but, owing to the increasing strength of the Texas army, they never dared to make another united march upon the settlements.

A son of Captain Burroughs has placed us in possession of an interesting relic of these days. It consists of a flag, presented to his company upon the eve of its departure from Ohio by the ladies of Zanesville. It is badly worn by age, but except where the paint was put upon it, the material is quite well preserved. The field is of light blue silk, with a border of white silk and fringe. In the center, upon a dark blue ground, is a golden Texas star, with the usual letters between the five points. Above this stands the American bird of liberty in shaded gilt, holding a streamer gracefully encircling the star, upon which is inscribed, "Hero of San Jacinto." In the lower staff corner of the flag is printed "Zanesville, Ohio." The flag-staff is gone, but the figure-head remains. It is of solid brass, the device a battle-axe and spear combined. Upon one side of the point is engraved, "To the Texan Volunteers of Muskingum County, Ohio," and on the other is, "From the Ladies of Zanesville. September, 1836."

The Zanesville *Gazette*, of 1836, gives the following account of the presentation of this flag. It showed the interest felt in Texan independence:

TEXAN EMIGRANTS.

The company of Texan emigrants raised at this place by Colonel George H. Burroughs, together with Captain Colerick's company, embarked for Texas on Monday last, amidst the cheers of hundreds collected upon the adjacent shores to witness their departure.

On Saturday last, the company under the command of Captain Burroughs was presented by the ladies of Zanesville with a splendid flag, handsomely finished, and bearing the motto, "The Hero of San Jacinto."

The companies marched out to receive the flag, which was presented, in the presence of the assembled multitude, by Miss Mary Love, who, at the same time delivered the following neat and appropriate address:

"SIR: In the name and in behalf of the ladies of Zanesville, we present you the standard we hold, as an evidence of our respect personally, and as a pledge of our unchanging devotion to that truly glorious cause in whose defense you have so nobly determined to embark.

"If prosperity attend you, let the deeds of San Jacinto's blood-stained field cheer you onward.

"If adverse clouds o'ershadow your path, let the deathless fame of Freedom's Martyrs instill into your minds a determination that you will never lower this banner until you have achieved for Texas her liberty, or for yourselves a glorious grave.

"Above all (and we present it as our united requests), we ask you to let no deed of yours cast a shadow upon the reputation of him whose honored name your standard bears—

"'THE HERO OF SAN JACINTO.'

"The inscription it bears is worthy of you; may you prove worthy of it!

"Receive it, soldiers, in the spirit in which it is given."

To which Captain Burroughs replied with much feeling—

"MADAM: In accepting this standard at your hands, I feel it difficult to express the feelings which predominate in my own heart, as well as those of the company, whose organ I am.

"We receive it as one of the repeated proofs of the chivalry of the American ladies—that spirit which shone so brightly in the dark and trying hour of the Revolution.

"To the ladies of Zanesville, for this token of patriotism, we can only return our sincere and heartfelt thanks; and permit me to assure them, that this banner shall never be unfurled in a bad cause, and never relinquished in a good one, unless it be in the agonies of death.

"We are about to bid adieu to our native country, and assist a brave, but unfortunate people—people speaking our own language—blood of our own blood. Perhaps some of you now present may have near and dear relatives there, that are at this moment imploring our aid, and who are lavishing their blood to regain their sacred and inalienable rights—rights which they derived from the God of nature, but which have been wrested from them by a bloodthirsty usurper.

"It is a glorious cause! and we believe we go with the warmest wishes and purest prayers of the American people.

"When for the first time, the folds of this banner shall float upon the plains of Texas, the recollections of this day, as well as the justness of the cause in which we battle, shall nerve us on to deeds of noble daring.

"These sentiments will animate us in the hour of trial, and sustain us in the van of conflict.

"And if it be our lot to fall, the folds of this sacred banner, as it waves triumphantly, shall be the last object of earth on which to rest the dying eye.

Then, turning to the company, he said:

"Soldiers! will you receive this banner, and pledge yourselves to defend it?"

A low bow marked their assent.   Then, turning again to the young lady who presented the banner, he said:

"MADAM: Allow me once more to assure you that the ladies of Zanesville shall never have cause to blush for the conduct of their Texan Emigrants. So long as I have nerve sufficient in my arm to wield a sword, this splendid banner, emblem of hope to the world, shall never go into the hands of the enemies of Texas."

The emigrants then returned to their camp, and the citizens dispersed; but no doubt the feelings of that hour will be remembered by the former when far away from the hills of old Muskingum.   The pledge then given may nerve their arm in battle, and cheer their way on the weary march. May success attend them.

Captain Burroughs, and Thompson, the first lieutenant, both resigned their commissions in about four months after they came to Texas, and Anthony Deffenbaugh, the second lieutenant, remained in command until the company was disbanded early in the summer of 1837.   Mr. Deffenbaugh took the flag back to Ohio in August of that year, and gave it to Captain Burroughs, in whose family the relic has remained up to this time.   Mr. Deffenbaugh returned to Texas and is now well known in this city.   His profession is that of a printer.   He has been engaged in various newspaper enterprises, which of course have kept him poor.   He merchandized a number of years in San Antonio, and took up his residence in Austin some six years since.   He was one of the original proprietors of the *Statesman,* and worked zealously with the writer and others in building it up and giving it stability.   Mr. Deffenbaugh is now fifty-eight years old, and during and since the sale of his proprietorship in the *Statesman* has been one of the most constant workers in the composing room of the office.   He seems still as active and energetic as when, a youth of nineteen, he took his sword in hand to struggle for liberty in the land we all love so much.

L.

MORE OF THE TEXAS REVOLUTION.

(Galveston News.)

INDEPENDENCE, Aug. 24, 1873.

EDITORS NEWS : I saw, in my tri-weekly of the 20th inst., a letter written by Major Samuel Dexter, who was one of General Thomas J. Rusk's aids, giving some of the incidents and facts upon the arrival of the army at old Goliad (La Bahia). I, with others, was engaged in gathering up the remains (ashes mainly), bones, chunks of human flesh, parts of bones and whole skeletons, to be placed in a large hole that was prepared near the church. Fannin and his men (except a few who escaped, I think about twenty-five,) were shot in *four divisions*. They were formed with their backs to brush fences, and the brush was used to consume the bodies. At one of the places where the bodies were burned I picked up a good sized chunk, which I supposed might be a knot of wood, but on scraping off the charred part with my pocket-knife, I found it to be human flesh. When the remains were deposited in the pit or large hole, the army, as Major Samuel Dexter says, was collected, and General T. J. Rusk commenced the address, and gave utterance to the sentiments mentioned. But, in truth, General Rusk did not finish what he intended to say, for he was overpowered by his feelings, and the tears rolled down his cheeks, and he had to stop speaking. There were but few dry eyes on that occasion.

The skeletons were placed upon the top of ashes, bones, and charred human flesh. General Rusk had many personal friends and acquaintances who belonged to Ward's batalion from Georgia. General M. B. Lamar, also, had many friends who gave their lives to save Texas from being overrun by Santa Anna and his *eight thousand men*, as did, also, the gallant Colonel W. B. Travis and his comrades at the Alamo.

The day after the burial of the ashes, bones, and charred human flesh and skeletons of Colonel Fannin and his men, General Andrade sent a letter to General Rusk, asking permission to pass on the main road through Goliad on to San Patricio, where General Filisola was at the time. General Rusk wrote to General Andrade that it would not be safe for him to come in sight of his men, for he did not believe he could control them after witnessing what had been done with Colonel Fannin and his men, in violation of a treaty made with General Urrea.

General Rusk sent Major Wells, six men, and myself, as interpreter, with a letter to General Andrade, demanding the release of any prisoners he might have, and the surrender of any property, belonging to Texans, in his possession, in accordance with the terms agreed upon by General Houston and General Santa Anna, and for a cessation of hostilities. Andrade commanded the reserve corps, which had been in San Antonio all the time—principally cavalry. Major Wells found Andrade's command about six or seven miles above Goliad. Nearly the whole of Andrade's force was on guard, and they evidently expected an attack. Major Wells demanded to see General Andrade, to deliver in person the letter from General Rusk, and after Colonel Maro had passed to and from General Andrade two or three times, Major Wells finally yielded to the position taken by General Andrade, that there was no need of any of Major Wells' party entering his lines, except the one who spoke Spanish. Major Wells then gave me the letter to Andrade, and told me to go with the Mexican colonel and deliver it to General Andrade. I found the general surrounded by his staff and other officers, and they were preparing to cross their artillery and baggage over the San Antonio River. They had to make a crossing and cut a road some seven or eight miles through a chaparral thicket to intersect the road from Goliad to San Patricio. General Andrade invited me to one side, out of hearing of his officers, and asked me to translate General Rusk's letter. Andrade said he never had but two Texan prisoners, Doctor Bernard and Doctor Shackelford, whom he had released before he had left Bexar, and had given them horses, money, arms and ammunition to defend themselves against Indians. This was true. And that he had not been in conflict with any Texans, consequently had no property in his possession belonging to Texans. On the return of Major Wells and party to our camp, we found that the whole army was in hopes that Major Wells and party would be seized and kept as prisoners, so as to furnish an excuse to attack Andrade and his finely dressed and equipped officers and men, and capture the large amount of horses, mules, wagons, cannon, etc., etc. Part of the cannon being carried off belonged to the Alamo, where Travis and his men fell to the last man.

On the arrival of the Texan army at Goliad I picked up, among other printed documents, some copies of the law of the Mexican Congress prescribing what should be done with the prisoners taken under different circumstances. It required those taken with arms in their hands fighting against the government to be shot. But the last article of the law left the whole matter to the superior judgment and discretion of "the president and commander-in-chief of the army of operations," which made General Santa Anna responsible for the base violation of a treaty made between Colonel Fannin and General Urrea. Santa Anna had to issue three distinct, separate orders before he could have Fannin and his men shot, and it was said that the colonel in command refused, and finally tore the epaulets from his shoulders and said he would not serve a government that would perpetrate such a barbarous act. I think it was Colonel Garrie who put in execution the cold-blooded order. I was present when General Santa Anna was brought up to General Houston, and heard all the conversation between Santa Anna and Houston, and between Santa Anna and Colonel Rusk, the secretary of war, for some two hours. Colonel Almonte was sent for, who was Santa Anna's right-hand man, and who spoke English with as much facility as he spoke his own language. Santa Anna proposed to stop the war and order General Filisola out of Texas. General Rusk told him that Filisola would not obey any order that he, Santa Anna, would issue, as he was a prisoner, etc. Santa Anna said such was the attachment of officers and men to him that they would obey any order he would issue. General Rusk then required Santa Anna to issue an order to his second in command, Filisola, to surrender himself and his army as prisoners of war. Santa Anna promptly replied that " he would do nothing that would be disgraceful to himself or his nation ; he was but a single Mexican and they could do with him as they pleased." Colonel Almonte modified this spirited reply of Santa Anna, and said that while he was willing to order General Filisola to march out of Texas, he could not consent to order him to surrender ; that the Mexican force was far superior to the Texan, etc.

General Rusk asked what excuse Santa Anna had to make for the massacre of Colonel Travis and his men. Santa Anna said it was usual in war to put all to the sword when a small force refused to surrender, and compelled the superior force to sacrifice so many men in storming a fort.

General Rusk then asked what apology Santa Anna had to make for shooting Colonel Fannin and his men, after one of his generals, Urrea, had entered into a capitulation with Fannin by which they were all to be sent to New Orleans in a week. Santa Anna denied that there had been any capitulation that he knew of, and that there was a law of Congress which required him to have all prisoners shot, taken with arms in their hands fighting against the government.

General Rusk said, " Colonel Almonte, you can say to General Santa Anna that if he has no better excuse or apology to make than this, the less he says about the matter the better for him, for we all know that General Santa Anna was Dictator of Mexico and did as he pleased."

General Rusk was right, for I, at Goliad, translated the law referred to by Santa Anna, for General Rusk, and he sent the translation to President Burnet, and the last clause of the law, as previously mentioned, left every thing to the discretion of the president and commander-in-chief of the army of operations.

I was sergeant of the guard around the tent the second night Colonel Almonte, Colonel Nunes, Santa Anna's brother-in-law, and Corre, Santa Anna's secretary, occupied the tent with Santa Anna. They talked all night about the condition of the army, the navy, and what would be the result in the City of Mexico on hearing of the disastrous defeat and their capture, etc., etc.

I would be glad to know if Major Samuel Dexter and Major Bula Hoxie are living. They were General Rusk's aides. Major Hoxie was a nephew of my old friend and neighbor, Dr. Asa Hoxie, who died at his old homestead near me, in 1863, and where he first settled in 1833.

I could go on writing for many days about what I have seen and heard since January, 1831, in Texas, under eight different governments, as I find my memory is still good. I would be glad to hear from all old Texans, and to receive from them their recollections of events in the history of Texas from 1820 up to annexation in 1845. Material might be collected in this way to preserve the true history of Texas, and might be made useful by the Texas Veteran Association in creating a fund from which the oldest, the most infirm and needy old veterans could receive relief and assistance. All communications sent to me will be filed and recorded in a bound book, and will be held subject to the direction of the Texas Veteran Association.

Now, Messrs. Editors, if I have written any thing worthy of being printed in your widely circulated paper, you have my permission to publish any portion, or the whole, as you please.

Your old friend and obedient servant,
MOSES AUSTIN BRYAN.

LI.

A REMINISCENCE OF THE MEXICAN WAR OF 1846.

BY J. A G.

BEFORE the movement of General Taylor on Monterey, he ordered Colonel Jack Hays, with his regiment, to make a long détour from Matamoras to the south, to ascertain the strength of the enemy in that quarter, passing through San Fernando and up the Rio Tigre, across to China on the San Juan.

Upon the movement of General Taylor from Camergo, the Texan troops under Hays were required to join the main body on their march. This they effected at Marin, near Monterey.

Hays' regiment then occupied the advance till they reached the city.

Arriving there, General Worth was ordered to make a circuit to the north, so as to attack the city in the rear on the Saltillo road. Captain Tom Green went with his regiment, and was in the battle with the Mexican cavalry and the storming of forts across the river, and in that of the next morning, of the hill above, and the same day, of the bishop's palace itself, all of which were gallantly carried. Two days after, the regiment was ordered into the city to aid in the attack upon the place.

Arriving, they were divided into two parts : five companies commanded by Colonel Hays, took the block of buildings to the right, and the other five, under Lieutenant-Colonel Walker, who was afterwards killed at Huamentla, took the block of buildings to the left.

With this party was Green and his company—and all the evening and until night the fight was waged from the housetops, the Texans advancing, and the Mexicans retiring.

This little party now found themselves in the heart of the city, within two squares of the main plaza.

All night they remained in this position, the sentinels of each party being so close to each other that occasional firing between them was kept up during the night. Here they were, surrounded on all sides except in their rear, by the enemy, which was unknown to themselves, because they supposed the party on their right, under Colonel Hays, and the party of regulars on their left, under Captain Miles, had kept pace with them ; but this was not the case, for General Worth had, the evening before, ordered out all the troops preparatory to a bombardment of the plaza by him from the cemetery, but the messenger failed to reach the party of Walker, and they were allowed to remain, and witness during the livelong night, the flight of the shells over them into the plaza.

The next morning, before full daylight, the party was on the move, and occupied the post-office in front of them, at the corner of the street, which afterward become the quarters of General Worth.

Occupying this large building, they opened the fight at close quarters with the surrounding enemy. This was continued with unabated spirit, till about nine o'clock, when an officer with a white flag and a bugle approached from a side street.

After some time, by the exertion of the officers, the firing ceased, and the officer was allowed to approach the house occupied by the Texans. He said that General Ampudia had sent him to ask the officer in command down to the plaza, that they might treat concerning a capitulation. He was asked if General Ampudia desired to see the commander of the American army, or the commander of the forces here engaged, and said in reply that it was the commander of the forces engaged. With that he was introduced to Lieutenant-Colonel Walker.

Walker, and in fact all, suspecting Mexican treachery, hesitated what to do. At last he turned to Captain Green, who was really the soul of the party, and said to him he would go down with the officer to see General Ampudia, if he, Green, would go with him.

Green hesitated ; but, not to be outdone in anything that required courage, he consented, and the two, with the flag of truce, went down to the plaza. Arriving, they found the place filled with troops. They had not long to stay till an officer came to them, when Green again introduced Walker as the Lieutenant-Colonel of the Texan Rangers, Walker being a rather bashful man. Thereupon the officer, who spoke English, told them that they were mistaken, that General Ampudia desired to see the commander of the army. Walker replied that they were not mistaken as to the message delivered by the truce officer. The officer politely waived a discussion of the question ; and, asking permission to send a flag by the position of the Texans, which was granted, he had Walker and Green again conducted back to their position through the Mexican lines.

And well that the truce officer was with them, for a negro Mexican soldier, on the way back, leveled his musket to shoot them, which was knocked aside by the sabre of the officer.

In a few moments a Mexican officer, bearing a flag of truce, passed the position of the Texans to General Worth's headquarters, and in a little while after, an officer of General Worth's, the writer thinks Lieutenant Pemberton, passed down into the plaza, and negotiation for an armistice began.

Shortly after General Worth sent a large body of regular infantry to occupy the place of the Texans, who were permitted to go back to their camp and obtain food and refreshment.

After the capitulation of Monterey the Texans were disbanded and returned home ; first having formed in line before General Worth's quarters, and giving him three cheers, and on the special invitation of General Worth, partaking of his cheer, and each one personally shaking hands and bidding him adieu.

LII.

JUDICIAL ORGANIZATION OF AUSTIN'S COLONY.

(Texas Almanac, 1858.)

BELOW we give a brief outline of the criminal and civil regulations for the administration of the laws of the colony, adopted by Mr. Austin, with the approval of the government.

Histories of Texas furnish little or no information on this subject, and yet the omission of all that concerns the civil polity of Austin's colony must be considered a radical defect. These regulations for the civil government of the colony will strike the reader as admirably adapted to the condition of the country, and show that Mr. Austin possessed the qualifications of a practical lawgiver in an eminent degree. We have been at the trouble of making this synopsis, because we think it should constitute a part of Texas history.

CIVIL REGULATIONS.

The alguazil, or sheriff of the colony, was appointed by the Supreme Judge (Austin), to serve process and execute decrees issued by himself. He also appointed a constable for each district, to act in the same capacity for the alcalde. The alcaldes were required to keep dockets or registers of all their official acts, which, when certified, had to be delivered to their successors in office. Any person having cause of complaint against another, was required to present a written petition to the alcalde of the district, stating the cause fully. Whereupon, the alcalde issued a summons, which, with the petition, was served upon the defendant by the constable.

The return day was fixed, according to distance and other circumstances, at the discretion of the alcalde, allowing a reasonable time. Service had to be made at least five days before the return day, adding one more day for every fifteen miles of travel.

The constable was required to read the complaint and summons to the defendant.

In case the defendant was absent from the district, the service was made by leaving a certified copy with some white person at his residence.

In case the defendant did not appear at the trial, judgment was given against him by default, at the discretion of the alcalde. And then notice of this judgment was served on the defendant, and a time given him to show cause, why it should not be made final. When the parties appeared, it was the duty of the alcalde, in the first place, to try and bring them to an amicable settlement. But if this could not be done, the parties were next required to choose one arbitrator each, if the sum in dispute was over ten dollars. The arbitrators were required to be men of unexceptionable character, and free from any interest. A day was then fixed for the arbitration, all the parties and the witnesses being duly summoned. After a full and fair trial, the alcalde enforced the award of the arbitrators, as the final judgment.

The jurisdiction of the alcade extended to all sums under two hundred dollars. Sums over that amount could only be acted upon by the judge of the colony.

Sums under ten dollars were decided upon by the alcalde alone. And also on sums from $10 to $25, unless the parties preferred arbitrators. On sums from $25 to $200, abitrators were required.

The judgment was in all cases required to conform, as nearly as possible, to the contract, whether in money or any kind of property. Stay of execution was at the discretion of the alcalde, security being required. Appeal to the judge of the colony was allowed on sums over $25, two good securities being required.

When there was no stay or appeal, an execution was issued returnable in sixty days ; and in case no property could be found, the constable was required to take the body of the defendant.

When property was levied on, thirty days' notice of sale was given, if it was real estate, negroes, etc., or ten days' notice, if perishable property.

In case the body of the defendant was taken, in the absence of property, it was then the duty of the alcalde to examine into his circumstances, and if he was satisfied that he had taken no steps to elude payment, fraudulently, he then discharged him ; but if he found he had conveyed away or concealed his property, then the alcalde could, at his discretion, hire out the defendant to the highest bidder, until his wages paid the debt.

In case any person apprehended his debtor was about to abscond, or leave the colony, taking his property away, so as to cause him to lose his debt, he could get an attachment by making oath to that effect, and have the property and person of the debtor seized forthwith, until a judgment and execution could issue. The property and person were, however, released, if good appearance bail was given. The person suing out the attachment was also required to give an indemnity bond.

In case the alcalde had reason to believe that any security was about to leave, taking away his property, he was authorized to detain said person and his property, until further security was given.

Should any person make oath to an alcalde that a person in legal possession of property belonging to some one else was about to remove it, so as to cause the owner to lose it, the alcalde could then compel him to give up such property, or give security for it.

Cases, wherein the cause of action arose out of the colony, were tried before the judge of the colony.

The alcalde could, at his discretion, appoint regular days to hold his court monthly.

FEES.

The fees prescribed were as follows:

Issuing a Criminal Warrant	$	.50
" Forthwith Summons		.37½
" Subpœna		.05
" Summons		.05
" Judgment		.37½
Entering Stay of Execution		.25
Entering appeal and writing bond		1.00
Issuing Execution		.25
Entering special bail and taking bond		.37½
Recording 100 words		.06¼
Serving criminal warrant		1.00
" forthwith warrant		.50
" summons		.25
Mileage per mile, going and returning		.05

Selling property and collecting money, 4 per cent. on sums under $200, and 1 per cent. on every $100 over.

CRIMINAL REGULATIONS.

The first five articles under this head related to Indians, who were treated in the most kind and considerate manner. In all cases it was enjoined upon the officer, or other person apprehending Indians, when behaving improperly or committing depredations, not to resort to the use of arms, unless absolutely necessary. In case of bad behavior or ill-treatment toward the colonists, the Indians were liable to receive, not exceeding twenty-five lashes, and to be sent under guard beyond the limits of the settlements, or delivered to the chiefs of their nation. Any person guilty of ill-treating or abusing any Indian was subject to a penalty of $100, for the first, and $200 for every subsequent, offense.

In cases of theft, murder, or robbery, any person was authorized to use arms in apprehending the guilty party, and taking him or them before the alcalde. In case the guilty parties should attempt to escape, the nearest militia officer or alcalde was required to raise men and make pursuit ; in case of resistance when overtaken, the pursuers were authorized to fire on them, being held responsible, however, for injuring or killing an innocent person.   When stolen property was thus recovered, the alcalde, upon proof of ownership, delivered it to the proper owners.

All gambling was strictly prohibited.   Any person guilty of this offense was liable to a fine of not less than $20, nor over $200, and every person allowing gambling in his house was liable to the same fine.   Horse-racing was not prohibited, as it was considered as having a tendency to improve the breed of horses ; bets on races were not, however, recoverable at law.

Profane swearing and drunkenness were offenses finable, not less than one, or more than ten dollars.   The habitual drunkard was liable to imprisonment forty-eight hours.

For a man and woman to live together as man and wife without being married, was a gross misdemeanor, and the parties, when convicted, were liable to a fine, not less than $100, nor more than $500, in addition to being condemned to hard labor on the public works.

Harboring or protecting runaway slaves was an offense punishable by a fine of $500, and damages sufficient to compensate the owner for the loss of the slave's labor.   In addition to which, the party convicted was condemned to labor on the public works.

Any person convicted of stealing or enticing away a slave, or inducing him to run away, was fined $1,000, and condemned to hard labor on the public works.

Any slave convicted of stealing was liable to receive fourteen to one hundred lashes, the owner being notified to attend his trial, with the privilege of saving his slave from the whipping, by paying the costs and then twice the amount of the property stolen, the person whose property was stolen receiving one-third, two-thirds being for the use of the public.

Every slave found absent from his owner's premises, without a written permit, was liable to be taken up, and to receive ten lashes ; and should the person finding him have reason to believe he had run away, it was made his duty to deliver him to his master or the nearest alcalde, and the owner was required to pay all reasonable expenses.

A fine of not less than $25 nor more than $100 was imposed on any person for trading with a slave, without written authority from his owner, and should he purchase stolen property from the slave, he was condemned to return threefold its value to the owner.

Any person buying stolen property of any kind, was condemned to pay three times its value to the owner, and to labor on the public works.

Any person guilty of assault, of abusing, maiming, or ill-treating another willfully and maliciously, was fined not exceeding $100, imprisoned not over three months, and required to give security for good behavior.   He was also liable in a suit for damages to the party injured.

False and malicious slander was punished by a fine of from $10 to $100 the party guilty being liable also in a suit for damages.

Any person guilty of passing counterfeit money, knowing it to be such, was liable to a fine of double the amount, and condemned to labor on the public works.

An alcalde knowing any person to be guilty of a crime, gross immorality, breach of the peace, etc., was required to bring such person before him, to summon witnesses, and make a record of the testimony, upon which the verdict of six disinterested men was required to be rendered, and a transcript of the whole was then required to be sent up to the superior judge for final judgment, the prisoner having the privilege also of sending up his written defense, but to be kept in confinement, or released on bail, according to the degree of the offense charged, until final judgment was rendered.

It was also made the duty of the alcalde to take up any person of bad character, vagrant, or fugitive from justice ; to examine the evidence for and against him, and to send up to the superior judge a record of the same, together with his own opinion in writing, keeping the prisoner in his custody till final judgment should be rendered.

Any person attempting to resist the administration of justice, or to prevent the execution of legal process, or order, or decree, or abuse an alcalde, or other officer, in the discharge of his duty, was liable to a fine not to exceed $50, and imprisonment not longer than one month ; besides which, he was also liable to criminal prosecution and to be condemned to hard labor.

In all cases when a person was unable to pay the fine adjudged against him, he was condemned to labor, until his wages, at the usual rates, should amount to the fine.

All fines were required to be applied by the alcalde, under direction of the superior judge, to the support of schools, or other public purposes.

LIII.

LA SALLE.

(From A Brief History of Texas.)

ROBERT CAVALIER DE LA SALLE was a native of Rouen, in Normandy, date not known. His early years were spent in a nunnery of the Jesuits, where he acquired an accomplished education. He was intended for the church, but his restless disposition led him in another direction. He early evinced a desire to travel. In 1667 he came to Canada, and spent many years in exploring the St. Lawrence and other rivers, and in traveling among the great lakes. He acquired an intimate acquaintance with, and influence over the various Indian tribes with whom his travels brought him in contact. In 1683, he made a voyage of exploration down the Mississippi River, and returned to France. In 1685, having obtained royal letters patent, and provided with four vessels, he set sail to discover the mouth of the Mississippi, but drifting too far west, he landed in Texas, supposing Matagorda Bay to be the object of his search. After exploring the country, La Salle conceived the bold project of traversing the country northward a distance of two thousand miles, to the Illinois River. Selecting a few of his friends, and leaving his colony in charge of his sub-officers, he started northward through the unexplored wilds of Texas, but on the 20th of March, 1687, he fell a victim to the treachery of his own men. Dr. Sparks says of him (" American Biography") : " He was saturnine in temperament, reserved in his communications ; he asked counsel of none. There was a certain hardness in his manners, a tone of lofty self-reliance, which though it commanded the obedience of his followers, did not gain their good-will. On the other hand, his capacity for huge designs has few parallels. He has been called the Columbus of his age : and had his success been equal to his ability, this distinction might justly have been awarded to him. Cool and intrepid, never for a moment yielding to despair, he bore the burden of his calamities manfully, and his hopes expired only with his latest breath."

According to the narrative of Father Anastase, who accompanied La Salle's expedition, the ill-fated explorer was slain by a musket-ball fired by Duhaut, one of his men, who had become jealous and dissatisfied with him and others in the party. "Thus perished," says he, "our wise conductor, constant in adversity, intrepid, generous, engaging, adroit, skillful, and capable of anything. The spot where La Salle was murdered has not been precisely ascertained. It was several days' journey west of the Cenis Indians, whose dwellings were on the Trinity River. The place was probably on one of the streams flowing into the Brazos from the east, and not far from the river ; perhaps forty or fifty miles north of the present town of Washington."

LIV.

SPEECH OF HON. GUY M. BRYAN

BEFORE THE TEXAS VETERANS,

DELIVERED IN THE CITY OF HOUSTON, MAY 14, 1873.

PIONEERS, VETERANS OF THE TEXAN REVOLUTION :

I greet you with a heart that always has been, and always will be *yours*. I greet you gladly, as with full hearts you joyously clasp hands in reunion. Historic occasion ! the past mingling with the present ! Old Texans, veterans of the Republic of Texas, rejoice, be proud, for you can well indulge a manly, patriotic pride in the thought that, in looking around, all about you are the results of what you were a part.

Look on these moving throngs of people ; this prosperous, solid city ; these telegraph wires, railroads, steamboats, warehouses, manufactories ; and down yonder, a little way off on the Gulf, that beautiful pearl of the sea, the growing metropolis of your State.

Turn your eyes east, west, north—on and on over what once was the wide range of the mustang and wilder Indian, and number there the ten hundred thousands of your countrymen, of whom you were the advance.

This is your monument—the monument of your co-laborers and compatriots. Grander and more lasting than pyramids of granite, marble, or brass ; vast as the surface that rolls out in plains, hills, valleys, and mountains, from the Sabine to the Rio Grande and from the blue waters of the Gulf to the endless plains of the North. Thus it stands—beautiful, majestic, sublime, enduring as time. God's work and your work, redeemed from the wilderness, disenthralled from Mexico by forecast, energy, and industry ; by blood, valor, and wisdom, for the benefit of millions born and unborn. What eulogy can I pronounce on her—so beautiful, so wonderfully formed—her blue skies, green pastures, and healthful winds? What eulogy on those heroic men who sleep in her sod ?

" As sleep the brave who sink to rest
By all their country's wishes blest."

On you, who now look on this growing work, who hear the tread of the advancing millions, to take peaceful possession of the places prepared by those who blazed and traced the way through forests and prairies wild, and planted for them the tree of law and liberty ! Eulogy itself stands silent before the picture.

No matter what the mutations of time and the passions of men may bring, *your monument is complete*, and will stand as long as civilization shall last. Wonderful work! Benefactors of your race! Fathers of the state you reared in your strength, now, in your weakness and old age your child will revere and love you, and smooth your passage to the grave.

It is true your labors have been severe, and your sacrifices many for Texas, but like all parents, you must watch until the end. Fathers of Texas, you and all of her children have a sacred duty to perform, that must not be forgotten, that must be continuous and unceasingly cherished—to preserve, in its *unity, our beloved Texas.*

Texas, Texas !—sound it, think of it, to where does it lead the mind? Between the Colorado and Trinity? Between the Trinity and Sabine? Between the Colorado and Rio Grande? Between a tier of counties on the south, and Red River and Staked Plain on the north? No, Texans. The Texan heart leaps over all these narrow spaces, and everywhere within its broad *united limits*, worships at the same Texan altar of patriotism. The soil of Rio Grande has drunk the blood of the sons of Sabine ; Red River has made her offerings on the coast, and the coast has her bleached skeletons on the arid plains of the north—Texas has but one second of March, but one Alamo, but one Goliad, but one San Jacinto. She has but one Lone Star. Every point of that star must remain, for when you take them away the star is gone. Who will put out this glorious luminary? What mercenary, with soul so dead, would barter it away? We plead for *unity* of Texas, as Camillus pleaded for *one* Rome !

United ! Where is the state that ultimately can compete with Texas ! How vast will be her resources, how light her taxes. Where we count dollars levied as tax now, we will count mills then, and yet how ample will be our revenues ! How potent will be our efforts ; when we stretch forth our arm it will be mighty ! When we raise our voice in council, all will be hushed to listen.

Our seaboard will have its coronet clustering around a queen of pearls. Our interior will have her Lowells, and Manchesters, and Pittsburgs ; our railroads, subordinated to just laws and the interests of the public—the servants, and not the masters of the people—will bind our extended parts together in social and mercantile intercourse, preserving confidence, community of interest, and patriotic affection. Our institutions of learning, benevolence, and religion, will all rise higher and tower loftier, because of the ample resources and great name of our mighty State. Nothing little will live here— ideas, thoughts, feelings, all will be great, because of the association of greatness.

On the other hand, *divide*, and the fragments, with their contracted limits, will be common. Each State, with its burden of taxes, and its comparative insignificance of position and influence at home and abroad, because partaking of mediocrity, will be *small*. And more (grievous the thought) Texas will be Texas no longer. Our glorious past will be left to history only, and no longer exist in the hearts of a *living people*. Then raise your voice with mine, that Texas a unit shall be forever—*forever* shall be united!

And to you, all of you Texans, who have immigrated since the imposing events that founded this great State were enacted, we hail, we welcome you as brothers and countrymen, and we implore you, by the sad recollections and wise experiences of the past, to affiliate with us in love and devotion to our great State. We invoke you for your own, and your children's good, to act and teach the union of Texas as our Texas—our whole Texas!

Veterans, you have done your work for progress. You are now conservative. Age brings wisdom. We have witnessed so many changes of government that all our experiences strongly incline us to love peace and oppose intestine commotion or violent governmental changes. War is the worst and least reliable method of righting wrongs within the body politic. Especially has this been the result, legitimately or not, of the recent civil war. It has not only changed the characteristics of a noble people of a great section, in which was the highest type of civilized man I have ever seen, and is creating of the surviving people and their descendants *a new people*, but it has occasioned the change of the practical working of the general government, and the relation of that government to the States as we have heretofore understood them. Whether these changes are to endure, or are for the better, time and experience will tell. We shall not quarrel about it here, and only refer to it in passing as an historical truth for reflection. We should recognize the facts as they exist, and try to make the most and the best of our situation ; and in a right spirit, with intelligence and truth, support the governments, State and federal, and patriotically work under them for our good and the well-being of the people, and zealously endeavor to so shape their destiny that it may be great in spite of adverse fortune and unjust legislation ; and avoid in Texas what I fear is the fate of some of her sister States—that their *descent* is and will be in proportion to their *former elevation*. One fact we should realize and be governed by : it is, that on *ourselves*—on the prudence and wisdom of the people of Texas—depend our improvement in government, as well as in material prosperity. For if our own experience has not taught us, Louisiana, South Carolina, and I may add, Alabama and other States, tell us in unmistakable language that the masses of the North, engaged in their own affairs, are *too* remote from us to understand properly the condition of the conquered States. They think these States are reconstructed with departments of government like their States, and hence suppose that all things

will work as with them ; and if they do not, the local governments or people
of the State must repair the wrongs.   *They do not, and will never realize the
influences that operate on us.*

This condition of mind in the masses of the North gives the strongest
practical reason in favor of State rights, or local government, resting in the
hands of the intelligent people affected by it, as the surest means to secure
the enactment and execution of wise and just laws, and thereby perpetuate the
Union.   And that it may be *thus perpetuated*, and be perpetual, is your prayer
and my prayer.   You want, we all want, to leave our children a safe, beneficent and enduring government ; a government that commands their love,
and for which they will cheerfully battle.   And when they march to the tented
field, they will go as soldiers against a *foreign* enemy, and never more against
their own countrymen.   I most devoutly pray that civil war never again
visit our land ; but Texas will climb to such a lofty height of influence that
she will overtop all such storms, and still them in their brewing.   And, that
she may be able to do this most effectually, and all else that is for her good
and the good of the country, her vast resources must be developed by
population.   The prospect for this is most encouraging ; by the increased
facilities of transportation, through the railroad connections already completed, and others that soon will be made, which will open up to her that vast
tide of immigration that annually flows westward ; and largely increase
that which has steadily flowed in from those Southern States where freedmen's rule prevails and will predominate ; also, by the line of steamers that run
direct to Europe ; and with the increasing number of sail vessels to the same
quarter, will bring to our State what is so much needed : many and willing hands
to cultivate our fertile lands.   *For her influence* depends upon her material prosperity and power, and both of these rest upon her *union.*

Texas is twice as large as Prussia, more than twice as large as England,
Scotland, and Ireland combined, and larger than Austria.

Should the vicissitudes of human governments bring disruption upon
ours, as they have brought it upon all large empires, sooner or later, then
Texas *united*, can stand alone and raise her head proudly among the nations
of the earth.

Originally, the western boundary of Texas was the Nueces ; when the
convention met that separated Texas from Mexico, it is a most significant
and memorable fact that Stephen F. Austin, then a commissioner in the
United States, urged by letters upon members not to fix the boundary westward, but to leave it open to the Sierra del Madre and Chihuahua.

When President Burnet formed his secret treaty with the captive Santa
Anna, he thought the good of Texas required the establishment of her west
ern boundary, and the Rio Grande was named in the treaty.

When the first Congress of the Republic met at Columbia, in the fall of 1836, General Thomas Jefferson Green, of the House, introduced a bill that became a law, declaring the Rio Grande as the western boundary. Settlements were then made west of the Nueces, and our troops, under the hero, Jack Hays, Ben. McCullough, and others, gave them sufficient protection to enable them to hold possession until annexation.

The United States admitted Texas with her boundaries defined, stipulating to treat with *Mexico* only in regard to them. No Congressional act can change or divide Texas without her own consent; and the consent of her people can never be obtained for dismemberment. No representative in Congress will dare to favor division in opposition to the will of her people, for no Credit Mobilier or political Dugald Dalgetty, it is to be hoped, will ever be found among her members. All of Texas not surrendered to the general government belongs to her people, for they have emphatically made her what she is. The fear of Indians and jealousy of Americans on the part of Spaniards, kept her almost an unknown land, except on the San Antonio road, before the Anglo-American settlement began. The small towns of San Antonio and Goliad were the only settlements within this vast wild, when in 1820, it was traversed to San Antonio by Moses Austin, on his mission of colonization. From the 16th of July, 1821, the day that Stephen Austin entered into the wilderness of Texas, "to lay the foundation on which our present magnificent edifice is constructed," she has, under *Texan* energy and enterprise, advanced to what she was when she entered the American Union.

Let us turn now and contemplate some of those historical events appropriate to be recalled, and of which you were a part, before annexation. Moses Austin's application to colonize was confirmed on the 17th of January, 1821, and we have seen that on the 16th of July, of the same year, his son Stephen, who succeeded him, entered Texas with the first pioneers, viz., Edward Lovelace and Henry Holstein, both from Louisiana; James Beard and William Little, both from St. Louis, Mo.; W. Smithers, from Indiana; Doc. Hewitson, Irwin, Burnum, Polly, Marple, Gasper, Bellew; William Wilson, D. C., late lieutenant U. S. A.—thirteen in all. I get these names from the diary kept by Austin on his first trip, I think there were four others, but their names are not in the diary. Some of these we know as among our most respectable and useful citizens. I believe each one of them, except Burnum, has gone to the great unknown land, but some have left descendants behind to enjoy the rewards of their toils. With these, Austin reported at Bexar—was kindly received by Governor Martinez, recognized as the successor of his father, and secured his commission as civil commandant of his colony. He then left for the lower San Antonio—explored the lower Guadaloupe, Lavacca, Colorado, and Brazos, and then returned to Louisiana, and brought out at the close of the year his first body of settlers with families and established them on the Brazos, which was the beginning of his settlement.

The difficulties, sufferings, and dangers of settlement were all heroically surmounted by the first settlers without great loss of life ; they made the way easier for those who followed. The colonists of Austin as a class, from first to last, for general intelligence, social worth, probity of character and high manly virtues—and the women, many of them refined and accomplished, possessing the best domestic virtues, with fortitude and courage cheering their husbands, fathers, and brothers in the wilderness, and strengthening them in the field of battle—were the equals of any people.

Mexico, with her revolutions and changing governments, and the absence of Austin at the City of Mexico, gave uneasiness to immigrants and retarded settlement. But Austin skillfully and bravely overcame every impediment, gained the confidence of the changing Mexican officials, and worked into form what would have been a hopeless puzzle to most minds.

Clothed with executive, legislative, and judicial powers, without laws or guide, but his own good sense and love of right, under his judicious and prudent adminstration as lawgiver, judge, military commander and empresario, the colony grew and prospered until it became a well-organized community, when, February 1, 1828, the State laws of Coahuila and Texas were extended over it.

During Austin's absence for a year (parts of '22–'23) immigrants coming to his colony, discouraged by his absence, stopped on the Ayish Bayou and Trinity, and thus recommenced the settlement of Eastern Texas. This settlement steadily increased in numbers, until the Fredonian war, in 1827, threatened to destroy it. But on the approach of the political chief, Sancedo, with a strong force, the disaffected leaders crossed over the Sabine and, through the influence of Colonel Austin and Colonel Ahuamada with Sancedo, the people were permitted to remain in undisturbed possession of their homes.

President Burnet says : " At the time of this unhappy outbreak, Austin's colony was receiving large accessions. Several persons had succeeded in procuring empresario grants, but in truth Stephen F. Austin was the only empresario who fully carried out his contracts, and he labored sedulously in doing so." Texas continued to grow, and immigration flowed steadily in, and formed scattered settlements over her large surface, and the people were prosperous and happy. Indians were peaceful, and Mexican officials occupied with their own affairs, and having confidence in Austin, permitted remote Texas to enjoy her quiet improvement. But this was not to continue long ; it might have been protracted for several years longer than the time of rupture, if the wise and prudent councils of Austin had been observed.

This was, perhaps, more than could be expected under the circumstances. But we shall not here discuss politics and questions that are not suitable to our space or the occasion. We will recur to some of those historical events that were obnoxious to the Texans, and precipitated revolution.

On the expiration of the term of Guadalupe Victoria, the first and best of the Mexican presidents, Guerro and Pedraza were candidates for the presidency. Guerro had the popular majority, but Pedraza obtained the highest electoral vote, and was declared president in September, 1828. Santa Anna pronounced against him, and, after some fighting, Guerro was installed into office. Vice-president Bustamente deposed Guerro and assumed the reins of government. On the 6th of April, 1830, he issued a decree prohibiting any further immigration from the United States to Texas, and directed regulations to be made for the introduction of Mexican convicts into Texas, and the opening of custom houses and collection of onerous duties. General Teran came to Texas, 1831, established Colonel Bradburn at the mouth of the Trinity (Anahuac) with one hundred and fifty men, Colonel Ugartacha at the mouth of the Brazos with one hundred and twenty-five men, and sent Colonel Piedras to Nacogdoches with three hundred and fifty men. Troops were also stationed at San Antonio and Goliad.

Although an American, Bradburn appears to have been weak and vain, and made himself obnoxious by his arrogance and petty tyranny. Piedras and Ugartacha were soldiers and gentlemen, and much respected by the settlers. Bradburn imprisoned Francisco de Madero, a commissioner sent to the Lower Trinity to issue to the settlers titles to their lands; he abolished the ayuntamiento of liberty and appointed one of his own at Anahuac; he imprisoned Travis, Patrick C. Jack, S. T. Allen, and other citizens, and in conjunction with Ugartacha, issued an order closing all the ports of Texas except Galveston, and making Anahuac the only place of entry and collection of customs dues. This latter arbitrary order he afterward rescinded, upon the representations of the citizens of the Brazos, backed by the countenance of his junior, Ugartacha.

William H. Jack visited his brother Patrick and endeavored to prevail upon Bradburn to deliver him and the other prisoners to the civil authorities. He was told that they should be sent to Vera Cruz for trial. Jack returned to San Felipe, stated the facts and aroused the friends of the prisoners. Steps were immediately taken that resulted in the collection of a respectable force in the vicinity of Anahuac, from the Brazos, Lower Trinity, and Bevil's settlement on the Neches, under the command of F. W. Johnston, first; W. D. C. Hall, second, and Thomas H. Bradly, third.

Bradburn, after being interviewed by a deputation from the settlers, determined to resist.

John Austin, George B. McKinstry, and William J. Russell were sent to Brazoria for cannon, munitions of war, and men. Colonel William Pettus and R. M. Williamson were sent to San Felipe, to raise more men there and in the adjacent settlements. Johnston was soon after re-enforced by Captain A. Kuykendall with fifty or sixty men from the Brazos, and small parties daily coming in. He felt sufficiently strong, when he was informed that Colonel Piedras was near by, with a strong force of Mexicans and Indians from Nacogdoches, to say to him, "You must halt, and not move backward or forward, for either movement will be regarded as hostile."

By agreement, F. W. Johnston, Captain Randal Jones, and James Lindsay, as commissioners, met Colonel Piedras, and after a free interchange of opinions, it was agreed the prisoners should be delivered to the Alcalde of Liberty; that Bradburn should be put under arrest and the command given to the officer next in rank—all of which was done, and Colonel Piedras returned to Nacogdoches and the settlers to their homes.

In the meantime, Ugartacha had refused to declare for Santa Anna, and the settlers on the Brazos and lower Colorado, under John Austin, on the 26th of June, 1832 (one hundred and twenty in number), attacked the fort at the mouth of the Brazos, and after eleven hours of fighting it capitulated. Captain William J. Russell commanded the schooner Brazoria, and, co-operating with the land forces, did most efficient service in this action. I must here say a few words about John Austin, brother of that old veteran and gallant soldier, Colonel William T. Austin, of ·Galveston. At an early age, without the knowledge of his parents, he left his native Connecticut for the sea. One of his voyages brought him to a port of Mexico, and he made his way to the capital. Stephen F. Austin was there making his final arrangements regarding his first colony—the name attracted their notice, and they became acquainted, and John Austin returned with Stephen F. Austin to Texas. An intimacy ensued, which friendship ended only with the life of John, who died in 1833 in Braoria, of cholera. Mrs. Holley, in her history of Texas, says: "John Austin was a valuable man to Texas; he had great strength of character, was foremost in every important crisis, and ready at every post of danger. His name appears at the head of many interesting documents; he was a faithful friend, and a good citizen." And as my mind runs over the names of others who were prominent in the capture of Velasco, I cannot, in passing, refrain to pause on that of the distingushed Captain John Henry Brown, one of the leaders of "the Brazoria boys." Although his body for more than thirty years has rested in the soil of that "Texan cradle of liberty," yet his voice, through his son bearing his full name, is still heard in our councils.

SANTA ANNA.

To face p. 189.

General Mexia, a friend of Santa Anna's, shortly after these events arrived at the mouth of the Brazos with five armed vessels and 400 men, accompanied by Colonel S F. Austin, who hastened back from Saltillo, where he was attending the legislature, when he heard of these revolutionary events. Mexia invited Colonel Piedras to declare for Santa Anna, and on his refusal the settlers of eastern Texas assembled and respectfully invited him to declare for the Constitution of "'24." He declined. They attacked him at once and fought him all day. At night, Piedras silently withdrew from Nacogdoches and retreated rapidly toward the west. He was pursued, and the whole force surrendered. Texas was relieved of Mexican troops east of San Antonio, and the colonists were the avowed adherents of Santa Anna, and supporters of the Constitution of 1824. Mexia sailed back to Tampico and reported to Santa Anna the loyalty of Texas.

The civil war between Santa Anna and Bustamenta was hushed by compromise on the 23d of December, 1832, by recall of Pedaza to the presidency, who was succeeded by Santa Anna, March, '33, with Gomez Ferias as vice-president.

Santa Anna at this time was the favorite of the nation. Now, whether from purely selfish ambition, or from a nobler motive—to give to his country a permanent government—he commenced his plans for changing the form of government. After some military operations, he retired to Mango de Clavo, his hacienda, and left the government in the hands of Gomez Ferias, who seems to have been a fierce and earnest Republican.

Texas was now quiet, and rapidly increasing in population and resources of every kind. But there were those who thought her condition could be bettered, and that her local government should be improved. The legislature of Coahuila and Texas consisted of ten deputies from Coahuila and two from Texas. The address of Austin, and the confidence with which he was regarded by Mexican officials, had so far prevented any oppressive laws from being enacted against the colonists by the legislature. But now, the State colonization law of 1835 was repealed, and another enacted embodying the spirit of the odious law of the 6th of April, 1830. This law, to be enacted by the State government, caused discussion which ultimately grew into discontent that resulted in a convention, which met at San Felipe on the 1st of April, 1833, of which William H. Wharton was president, David G. Burnet, Sam Houston, and Stephen F. Austin were members.

The convention adopted a constitution, also a memorial to Congress setting forth the reasons why Texas should be separated from Coahuila, and have a State government of her own. Stephen F. Austin was selected to bear these documents to the Mexican capital, and urge upon the government the admission of Texas into the Mexican Confederacy. You all know how faithfully he performed his mission, and what were the consequences to himself.

After a long delay, having obtained the repeal of the 6th of April decree, that forbade the immigration of North Americans to Texas, becoming satisfied that in the distracted condition of Mexican politics, Texas had better bide her time for a more favorable opportunity for action on her memorial, and, in the meantime, organize a home local government under that clause of the organic law that united her to Coahuila, to wit : " Until Texas possessed the necessary elements to prove a separate State of herself." And writing to this effect to the Ayuntamiento of Bexar, on the 10th of December he left for Texas. He was arrested at Saltillo, carried back to Mexico and incarcerated in a cell of seven by twelve feet of the dungeon of the Inquisition of Ocadordo, without books or writing materials, or solar or artificial light.

There were now two legislatures in Coahuila, one sitting at Monclova and one at Saltillo, each with their State officers claiming to be the rightful government. Santa Anna acted as umpire, and decided there should be a new election for State officers.

Santa Anna now repaired to the capital, resumed his authority and banished Ferias, and released Austin from his dungeon, but not confinement, in the prison of Ocadordo. On the 5th of October, 1834, he called a meeting of his principal functionaries, and with Austin discussed the affairs of Texas. He decided that an immediate separation of Coahuila and Texas was not advisable, but assured Austin then, and afterward, that Texas should have a government suited to her peculiar people, and that he recognized the difference between them and his own countrymen and their capacity for self-government. Had events been different, this truly able man might have been the real friend of Texas, as perhaps he tried to be to his own country.

In April, 1834, a law was passed forming Texas into one judicial circuit and three districts—Bexar, Brazos, and Nacogdoches. T. J. Chambers was appointed circuit judge, and David G. Burnet was appointed for the district of Brazos. The Superior Court was not organized, but Judge Burnet held his court at San Felipe for several terms, and disposed of many cases. On the 9th of February, 1835, Augustin Viesca was chosen governor, and Ramon Musquiz, lieutenant-governor, and a new legislature was elected. Expectations were now entertained that affairs would improve at the capital of the State, but it was not long before such hopes where shown to be fallacious. Santa Anna now exercised dictatorial powers, with a partisan Congress at his beck. It decreed that the militia of the States should be reduced to one in five hundred, and the remainder should be disarmed. It united the Senate with the House of Representatives, and declared itself invested with full powers as a national convention. It annulled the federal constitution and system, and established a central, or consolidated government, by decree of October 3d, 1835. In relation to this decree, Austin subsequently said, in his report to the provisional government, on the 30th of November, 1835, "However necessary, then, the basis established by the decree of the 3d of October may be to prevent civil wars and anarchy, in other parts of Mexico, it is attempted to be effected by force and unconstitutional means. However beneficial it may be to some parts of Mexico, it would be ruinous to Texas. . . .

The decree of the 3d of October, therefore, if carried into effect, evidently leaves no remedy for Texas but resistance, secession from Mexico, and a direct resort to natural rights."

Santa Anna deposed Governor Viesca and appointed General Cos in his stead. He subjected all of the States to his authority, and increased the military at San Antonio. Colonel Ugartacha, commanding at this place, by orders of General Cos, demanded of Wiley Martin, political chief, *pro tem.*, of the Brazos, Lorenzo de Zavala ; also the arrest of Travis, Johnson, Baker, Williams, J. H. Moore, and Williamson, as agitators and disturbers of the peace. The demand was met with refusal, and by none more firmly than the "peace party." Meetings were held and committees appointed, and resolutions passed, but the peace party was firm, resolute, and determined in opposition to precipitate and rash actions. At this juncture, on the last day of August, Stephen F. Austin arrived from Mexico. He was met by a large concourse of his colonists at Brazoria on September 8, 1835. He had been absent from Texas since the spring of 1833, two years of that time a prisoner, and part of it in a loathsome dungeon. His health was gone, but his heart was full of love, and his mind strong and clear for his beloved Texas. He counseled union and resistance ; favored a consultation, but opposed extreme measures. You know, old Texans, with what delight his return was hailed, and how all hearts and hands were united in one and the same cause. *Now*, there was no peace party, no war party ; they were one and same with the masses. Immediately he was installed as chairman of the Committee of Safety at San Felipe, to which all Texas now looked for orders and advice. Preparation for organization and war was seen and heard everywhere. Like fire spreading over the prairies ran the news that Mexican forces were concentrating at San Antonio, and that there had been a fight at Gonzales, the Lexington of Texas. Volunteers flocked to the latter place, and soon a force assembled there that required organization. Austin had succeeded in establishing a temporary government at San Felipe, composed of one member from each of the committees of safety. He was sent for from Gonzales and urged to come there to reconcile the troops. He went, and was elected by acclamation to the chief command on October 11, 1835. The enemy were beaten in every engagement, and finally driven into San Antonio and closely besieged. Our troops were thus being trained and instructed, which gave confidence that told on other fields.

The consultation met at San Felipe on November 3, and established a provisional government, consisting of a governor, lieutenant-governor, and council. On the 13th of November it appointed Stephen F. Austin, William H. Wharton, and Branch T. Archer, commissioners to the United States, to obtain aid from the people and government of our native land. It called a convention with plenary powers ; provided for a regular army, and appointed Sam Houston to the command. Austin resigned the command of the army of the people to accept that of commissioner. Before leaving the army, Burleson was chosen to succeed him in the command. Milam and Johnson led a storming party into Bexar ; Milam fell and Johnson conquered. General Cos surrendered and marched out his forces, and left for the Rio Grande. Burleson dismissed the army, leaving a few Texans, and the gallant volunteers from the United States, in charge of San Antonio and Goliad. Matamoros then being the objective point for the next move, questions of authority, and who should command, now arose. Houston's appointment was for the *regular* army, and the troops in the field were volunteers. We will leave for a more critical student to amplify this interesting portion of Texan history, and determine on whom rests the responsibility for the fate of Fannin and Travis, and the noble men who were sacrificed with them. Those with Fannin were volunteers from the United States, comparatively ignorant of the locality, and of Mexican character. Even at this remote period, our hearts are stirred afresh when we are reminded of their untimely and tragical fate. Texas still weeps for those chivalrous spirits who left their peaceful homes to water the Texan tree of liberty with their blood. Survivors of those bloody scenes, come, enroll your names with ours, that we may honor and revere you.

The convention met on the 1st of March, and on the 2d declared Texas free and independent of Mexico. It elected the virtuous and cultivated David G. Burnet, president of the Republic, and selected his cabinet, and appointed Sam Houston, one of the body, commander-in-chief of all the forces in the field.

Houston left for Gonzales on the 6th. On the night of that day the last wail of the Alamo ascended on high. When he reached Gonzales, he found the streets of that little town crowded with the weather-beaten faces of old Texans, most of them soldiers of the campaign of the previous year. Also, the gallant Sherman, with his company of Newport volunteers, who had just arrived. These formed the nucleus of that little army which was to decide the fate of Texas.

Houston and the Texans in the field knew but little of each other. He stopped in eastern Texas a few weeks before the meeting of the convention of April 1, 1833. He was elected to that body from San Augustine, and at the outbreak of hostilities in the previous fall, he was chosen at a meeting in San Augustine, and by the Committee of Safety of Nacogdoches, to command the "Redlanders," but they did not take the field.

He was a member of the consultation from Nacogdoches, and of the convention from Refugio. He had had experience from having served when a young man in the United States army, and with General Jackson at the battle of the Horse Shoe, where he was wounded, and promoted for gallant conduct. He was one of the finest looking men of his day ; his martial appearance and military reputation gave hope to those gallant men who now composed the little army at Gonzales. He very properly decided to fall back until he could be re-enforced. He left Gonzales on the night of the 13th of March, and reached Burnam's, on the Colorado, on the 17th ; crossed over and marched down the east bank to Beason's, where he remained until the 25th. General Sesma arrived opposite Beason's on the 18th, with a force eight hundred strong, with two pieces of artillery and sixty or seventy cavalry. Houston's force has been variously stated from 1300 to 1600. He crossed the Brazos at Groce's, where he fortunately met the steamboat Yellow Stone, which, loading with cotton for McKinney and Williams, transported his army. The Brazos was very high from heavy rains. It was the belief of many that he would continue his march eastwardly, but at Donohue's he turned down towards Harrisburg, and reached Buffalo Bayou, opposite that place, on the 18th of April.

It was generally thought that the enemy would now be met, and on the evening of the 18th, Deaf Smith, the more than Harvey Birch of Texas, brought in a courier of the enemy he had captured, from whom it was ascertained that Santa Anna had marched in the direction of Lynche's Ferry on the San Jacinto.

The facts were these : The enemy had advanced under Santa Anna to San Felipe, and thence down to Fort Bend, where Richmond now stands, where they were temporarily held in check by a company of the citizens of that locality, under the command of Captain Wyley Martin, who was stationed at Moreton's, on the east bank. The other division under Urrea had proceeded to Brazoria and Columbia. Santa Anna, leaving Filasola in command of the army at Fort Bend, dashed on across the country with a force between 600 and 800 strong with the *élite* of his army and one brass twelve-pounder, to Harrisburg, where he arived on the 15th; but Burnet and his cabinet had left. He burned Harrisburg, and hastened down to New Washington, or Morgan's Point; and his advance under Colonel Almonte had the mortification to see President Burnet standing amidst the shower of balls

13

sent after him, on a flat boat, as it was pushed off into deep water. He retraced his steps up to the fatal field of San Jacinto, where Houston, having
crossed Buffalo Bayou, confronted him on the 20th. That night he was re-enforced by Cos. On the afternoon of that day a brilliant engagement ensued
on the part of our cavalry under the lead of the dashing Sherman, to capture
the enemy's artillery, which whetted the appetite of our men for the battle of
the morrow.

I need not tell you of that glorious onset and rout of the enemy. Texans
would have won that battle had the whole Mexican army been there, instead
of the sixteen hundred they killed, wounded and captured. Under the thrilling cries of "Remember the Alamo! Remember Goliad!" with the conviction of success, with the high-souled determination and enthusiastic energy
inspired by the past, a full knowledge of the awful responsibility of the present; with the cries of their fleeing wives and children sounding in their ears,
with bated breath and pallid cheeks, they sprang forward on their foe. No
Mexican army could have stopped that onward moving mass of resistless
Texans on that day! What Waterloo was to Napoleon, was San Jacinto to
Santa Anna! What Bannockburn was to Scotland, was San Jacinto to
Texas!

Houston was wounded in the ankle, which always caused a perceptible
halt in his walk, reminding one of the "hero of San Jacinto."

He formed an armistice with Santa Anna that included the immediate retreat of Filasola, which really amounted to a flight. He asked the president
to relieve him from the command, in consequence of his wound, and was
succeeded by the secretary of war, General Thomas J. Rusk. General
Houston's military career here closed. He left for the United States, and
shortly after his return to Texas was elected president of the Republic.
He continued in public civil life from that time to the outbreak of the late
civil war.

He was a remarkable man, and a politician of eminent ability, and in the
days of the Republic always exercised great influence in shaping her destiny.
In speaking to me, as he also did to Santa Anna, and to the country in
his place in the United States Senate, he spoke of Stephen F. Austin, as the
FATHER OF TEXAS.

Though Austin never professed to have had experience in military affairs,
yet his conduct, with the knowledge of facts, we believe, will stand the test of
military criticism. His position at the head of the army in "35" came to
him; he did not seek it, and only accepted it for the good of Texas, as he
often did, when accepting the numerous positions he filled in her times of
trouble and danger, generally defraying his own expenses, when many times
he was illy able to do so. He justly felt that Texas was a child of his crea-

tion, and he loved her with more than eastern adoration, and for her he sacrificed his life. The moral grandeur of his character grows brighter with time and comparison. Epaminondas-like, he regarded it a virtue not to resent injuries received in public life, when his country was in danger. His generosity, mildness, and prudence were proverbial. His devotion to his colonists, and his love for Texas, his pure and unselfish character, his admirable judgment and knowledge of men, his love of justice and of his race, and stern adherence to high principles under all circumstances, give him a character worthy the admiration of the good of succeeding generations. An admiration freely accorded by Burnet, Lamar, Jones, Rusk, Burleson, Archer, and others of his associates, as well as by the historians Kennedy, Foote, Yoakum, Holley, Edwards, Stiff, and every one who has written on Texas that I have read.

Simple in his habits, straightforward, truthful and faithful in character, free from all those arts that are so often used to beguile and flatter the people, yet easy and persuasive in manners toward all, he had the affection and confidence of his colonists; and with patience, forbearance, and fortitude, he achieved success in the great object of his life, where all others failed except De Witt, whom he assisted. I have said this much of Austin, whose life and history so largely enter into that of Texas, from a sense of duty : for, possessing his private papers, I question whether any one living understands his character so well, or who has studied it so closely to arrive at the truth, as myself.

I could refresh your minds by recurring to the historical events, civil and military, of later date, when Rusk, Felix Huston, and Sidney Johnston were in command of our army, and when, in 1842, Somerville marched to the Rio Grande, and the men of Mier were captured ; but the field is too large even to your willing minds ; I fear I might become tedious. We have the satisfaction of knowing that our flag, high advanced, moved onward, and waved proudly until the Stars and Stripes were raised above it.

As an interesting reminder, I will briefly give some facts in relation to the history of that flag so dear to the heart of every old Texan—the flag of the Lone Star.

The first Lone Star flag that I can find account of was made at Harrisburg in this county, and presented to the company of Captain Andrew Robinson in 1835. The Lone Star was white, five pointed, and set in ground of red.

The Georgia battalion flag was azure, lone star, five points, in white field. This flag was raised as a national flag on the walls of Goliad by Fannin when he heard of the declaration of independence. The National flag adopted by President Burnet, at Harrisburg 9th of April, 1836, for naval service was—union blue, star central, and thirteen stripes alternate red and white.   December 10, 1836, Congress adopted a national flag—azure ground, with large golden star central, combined with flag adopted by President Burnet.   This was amended by act, January 25, 1839, that made the permanent flag, blue perpendicular stripe, width one-third of the whole, white star, five points in the center, and two horizontal stripes of equal breadth, upper white and lower red.

Veterans! because you have just cause to be proud of your works; have lived for a good purpose and been successful; have planted that others may reap, making your lives nobly useful, and that the ending of your days may be peaceful and pleasant in the enjoyments of reunion, it has been proposed that these events of the past, so dear to you, shall be commemorated by *annual meetings*, and in manner as you may determine.   We are not singular in this desire; it belongs to people, ancient and modern.   Jews and Christians have celebrated, and do celebrate, their illustrious days.   History tells us that the great festivals of the ancient Greeks promoted a spirit of union among the various branches of the Greek race, and that the only prize given at the games, to the conqueror, was a simple garland of wild olive, "but that this was valued as one of the dearest distinctions in life; to have his name proclaimed as victor was an object of ambition with the noblest and the wealthiest of the Greeks."   New England and other portions of our country have organizations to celebrate their early settlement and achievements. And why should not we?   We have met here, then, that we may effect this by organization.   We organize that we may know each other, perpetuate our names and services and those of our buried companions, recount deeds and events of early times, and keep them and their actors alive in mind, and thus hand them down to posterity, fresh and green, by tradition, song, and story, from the living actors of those days.   We organize for no *party political purposes*, but that we may have annual meetings, and there renew our pledges·of affection for each other, and devotion to our great *united* State.   We desire to deserve the good-will, respect, and approval of all Texans, young as well as old, and to cultivate the feeling that we are all Texans, having a common destiny, a common interest, and a common object—the prosperity and UNITY of Texas.

These are the objects of our association, nobler ones we could not have. The enjoyment of them will tend to soften our hearts, and drive away for the time all the asperities of life.   We mean to be a respected and devoted band, cultivating the associations of the past—endearing them to ourselves and to others; cherishing emotions akin to those felt by friends of early days, when, meeting in after life, turning from the busy world, they joyfully go over in heart and mind the scenes of the old school-house and college, drink from the cool running spring—" the moss-covered bucket that hung in the well,"—sit in the old arm chair, and sing, "Woodman, spare that tree." These are our holy desires and motives. Let none asperse them.

Veterans ! we have dwelt on colonization, settlement, and revolution, of that extraordinary battle that settled the liberty and fixed the destiny of Texas. Of your conduct and courage during these perilous times when your mission was to *found and create*. The mission of the present generation and those who come after you is, and will be, to *preserve and improve* what you have contributed to make of *united* Texas.

The associate of Milam, the leader of the conquerors of San Antonio in '35, is here—Colonel Frank W. Johnston ! Rise, veterano, and do him honor ! That old Caranquaha Indian-fighter, Captain Randal Jones, 87 years old, though blind, is here ! That Nestor of the Texan press, the founder, editor, and publisher of the only newspaper in the campaigns of '35, and '36, the time-honored *Telegraph*—of whom Stephen F. Austin, when looking around for the proper man to compile the land papers of his colonies, said, he was essentially an honest man : that young old man, Gail Borden, is here ! One of the veterans of San Jacinto and first judge of the Republic, Ben Franklin, and first marshal of Texas, Judge Calder, are here ! The only survivor of the aides of Austin, Burleson, and Johnson, in '35, Colonel William T. Austin, is here ! That old veteran of the civil government of '35–'36, Judge Waller, is here ! One of the heroes of the Lexington of Texas, the associate of Moore, Colonel Wallace, is here ! Walter P. Lane is here, whom Lamar, at San Jacinto, rescued from a Mexican lancer, when wounded, knocked from his horse and down, and who would have been killed but for his placing him behind a comrade and killing the Mexican, and then carrying him off the field. Captain Horatio Chriesman, the first surveyor of Austin's colony, and Colonel John Forbes, commissary-general of the army of '36, are here ! Old veterans !—Companions of the founders and fathers of Texas, there are so many of you I see before me who have performed important services in the past, I would love to mention and embrace you all. May God smile on and spare the old veterans for many reunions. May you live long, and enjoy the prosperity of imperial Texas, which you aided to found, and feel the consolation in your last hour that Texas has done to you *honor* and *gratitude*.

LV.

OLD FORT PARKER.

ITS HISTORY—INDIAN MASSACRE—TEXAS VETERANS—ABRAM ANGLIN.

BY R. F. MATTINSON, SENIOR EDITOR OF GROESBECK ARGUS.

THE following biographical sketch has been kindly furnished us by Mr. Anglin, with the privilege of using it as we choose.   We give it almost in his own language, and no one who knows him will doubt his statements:

Abram Anglin was born in Kentucky, December 28, 1817.   His father moved to Illinois when he was one year old, and came to Texas in 1833. They settled on the frontier, now Limestone county, many miles from any white habitation.   The little colony with which they came consisted of about eight families.   In 1835 he enlisted in the service as a Texas Ranger.   As the Indians and Mexicans were, at that time, becoming troublesome, they built Fort Parker, near the present site of Groesbeck.   These families were the advance-guard of civilization.   Fort Houston, in Anderson county, was the nearest protection, except their own trusty rifles.

In 1835, the hostility of the Indians and Mexicans compelled this little band of brave men and women to abandon Fort Parker.   Among those who were compelled to flee before the invading army of Mexicans, was the father of Mr. Anglin.   His son Abram accompanied him to the Trinity River, intending to see them safe over, and return for the purpose of joining our forces.   They were delayed at the river in consequence of an overflow.

Before they could cross the river, the joyful news reached them that the Mexicans had been defeated at Jacinto.   Going on to Fort Houston, and remaining there a few days, he returned to Fort Parker, in company with Seth Bates, his son Silas, David Faulkenbury and his son Evans, to look after the crops and stock.   These hardy sons of toil spent their nights sometimes in the fort and sometimes on their farms.

On the night of May 19, 1830, they slept at the fort, and left early next morning to work on their farms, as was their custom.   About eleven o'clock, the 19th, a lady brought them news that a force of six hundred Indians had attacked the fort, murdered the few men left, and had taken the women and children prisoners, except those who had escaped by hiding in the brush. Mr. Anglin gathered up his comrades, David Faulkenbury, his son, and Plummer, and picking the flints of their trusty weapons, started to the scene of conflict, resolved to rescue the women and children, even against such fearful odds. On their way they encountered several Indians, who had a Mr. Nixon, Mrs. Silas Parker and two of her children, prisoners. They followed them to the fort and there recaptured the prisoners. Seeing the fort had been destroyed, and finding such a large force of Indians, the brave little band retreated ; Mr. Anglin carrying a child in his arms, and another one of the company another. Nixon fled the field as soon as he was released. The Indians from whom they had taken the prisoners, returned to the main body which was collected about two hundred yards from the fort containing the hapless women and children, whipping them and maltreating them in every conceivable way. About thirty mounted Indians, armed with bows and arrows strung and drawn, would charge them, uttering the most unearthly yells, but on the presentation of their guns they would halt, right-about wheel, and retire to a safe distance. This continued until they had passed through a forty-acre field and entered the woods, when they ceased to pursue, supposing that they were being led into an ambuscade. They carried Mrs. Parker and her children about five miles, stopping several times for the exhausted mother to rest. Mr. Anglin was compelled to dip water in his shoe to give her drink. On the way to a place of safety, the party met with old man Bates, his son Silas, and old man Lunn. They carried Mrs. Parker and her children into the Navisota bottom ; left them with Mr. Bates, agreeing upon a signal—the hooting of an owl—on their return.

Mr. Anglin, David and Evans Faulkenbury, and Silas Bates started back to the fort to succor the wounded and those who might have escaped. The party had to pass by the farm of Mr. Anglin's father. Being himself in front of the little company, he saw the first and only ghost he ever saw. It was dressed in white, with long white hair streaming down its back. He admits that he was scared worse then than when the Indians were yelling and charging. Seeing him hesitate, his ghost beckoned him to come on. Approaching the house, it proved to be old Granny Parker, whom the Indians had abused, stabbed, and left for dead, because of her age and infirmity. She had made her way to this house from the fort by walking and crawling. Mr. Anglin took some bed clothing, carried her some distance from the house, made her a bed, covered her up and left her until the party should return from the fort. On their arrival at the fort they could not see or hear a single human sound. But the dogs were barking, the cattle bellowing, the horses neighing and the hogs squealing, making hideous medley of sounds. Mrs. Parker had told Mr. Anglin where she had thrown some silver, one hundred and six dollars and a half. This he found under a hickory bush, by moonlight. Finding no one at the fort, they returned to where they had hidden Granny Parker. One taking her up behind him, they went to where they had left the other parties rescued, and giving the signal, it was answered by the man Nixon, whom they had not seen since his inglorious flight from the fort. In the book published by Jas. W. Parker, on pages 10 and 11, he states that Nixon liberated Mrs. Parker from the Indians and rescued old Granny Parker. Mr. Anglin asserts that this is a mistake. He is willing to be qualified to the statements he here makes, and can prove the same by Silas H. Bates, now living near Groesbeck.

The party remained in the bottom the balance of the night, and in the morning, leaving the men of the party with the women, the younger portion went back to the fort to get provisions and horses.

On the return of the young men to the fort, they found about five horses, a few old saddles and some bacon and honey. They were forced to leave the dead unburied. They then returned to the party in the bottom, concealed themselves until dark, when they started through the woods to Fort Houston. It took them three days to reach the fort. They raised a company of about twelve men, came back to Fort Parker, buried the dead, and drove off the stock. Mr. Anglin remained in Anderson county until the 28th of January, 1837. He then set out, accompanied by David and Evans Faulkenbury, Douthet, Hunter, and Anderson, to gather up some hogs that had strayed. Finding some on the east side of the Trinity, they sent them back by Douthet and Hunter, who promised to return next day and bring a canoe for the purpose of crossing the river. Being impatient to accomplish their mission, they constructed a raft of logs and crossed over, and searching all the forenoon for the hogs, they repaired to the place where they were to meet the parties with the canoe.

The remainder of the story details facts of an interesting nature, and we prefer giving them in Mr. Anglin's own language.

" Arriving at the river we found no canoe, but plenty of Indian sign ; and supposing the tracks to have been made by friendly Indians, went near the river where the bank shielded us from the wind, and lay down to await the canoe. We all fell asleep, and were awakened by the war-whoop and firing of Indians. About thirty of the dastardly red-skins had crept up within fifteen feet of us, some armed with bows and arrows and some with guns, and the first we knew they opened fire on us. David Faulkenbury was the first to rise, handed me my gun and picked up his own. I noticed that he was wounded, as was Anderson also. Just as I arose a ball struck me in the thigh, inflicting a terrible wound. David Faulkenbury said, " Come on, boys, it is time to go ; " and throwing his gun into the water, plunged into the river himself. Anderson also jumped into the river. Evans Faulkenbury and myself sprang behind an ash tree, intending to shoot at the Indians, but they had concealed themselves behind a bluff, and knowing it to be useless for two of us to fight so many when they had every advantage, I threw my gun in, jumped into the river and swam to the opposite side. As I was swimming, the Indians were discharging their arrows, and while climbing out on the opposite bank I received several other slight wounds. Weak and exhausted, however, as I was, I reached the bank, where I found David Faulkenbury too badly wounded to travel. He told me to make my way to the fort as best I could. I had gone about four hundred yards when I met Hunter coming to carry us in the canoe. He took me up behind him and traveled as fast as he could toward the fort. We soon met the other men, and by their assistance I reached Fort Houston, greatly exhausted and suffering from the wounds. A company of men went back the same night to look for the rest of our party, but did not find them until the next day. They found the corpse of David Faulkenbury near a hole of water. He had cut the long grass and made him a bed on which to die. About two miles further on they found the remains of Anderson, with two arrows sticking through his back. He had run that distance after swimming the river, and fell dead. Evans Faulkenbury was never seen or heard from. We could see his tracks some distance down the edge of the water, and we supposed he was mortally wounded. We searched for his body in the river, but never found it. All my comrades with me on that occasion perished, and I alone was left to tell the tale of our suffering."

Mr. Anglin remained at Fort Houston until March, when he again entered the service as a Texas Ranger; came to the frontier, and served six months. In the fall of 1837, he and his father and a few others brought their families to the neighborhood of old Fort Parker. The Indians became troublesome again in the spring of 1838; they had to leave their farms and fall back to Whelock. Here he remained, now following agricultural pursuits, and then shouldering his rifle as his country needed his services. In 1844, he served as a volunteer, and met the wily Indian on these same broad prairies that are now being rapidly filled with peaceable and peace-loving citizens. Mr. Anglin has helped to drive out the Indian, and now lives to enjoy the fruits of his toil and privation. All honor to the veterans of Texas.

At the time of the massacre spoken of above, there were only six men in the fort, viz., Elder John Parker, Benjamin and Silas Parker, Samuel and Robert Frost, and J. E. Dwight. These had been left in the fort while the others had gone out for the purpose of working on their farms. Including the men whose names are mentioned, there were thirty-four in the fort eighteen of whom were children. Mr. Dwight was the only man who escaped from the fort; all the rest were killed. Several of the women escaped, and some were subsequently rescued from the Indians, as related above. Mrs. Plummer and her son James Pratt, only about eighteen months of age, Mrs. Kellogg, and the two oldest children of Silas Parker, were captured and carried into captivity. By almost a miracle, old Granny Parker, as she was familiarly known, being left for dead, was rescued by Mr. Anglin and his intrepid party. The Indians plundered the fort, killed all the cattle they could find, fled immediately to the mountains, leaving the dead, and those whom they thought were dead, exposed to the wild beasts of the prairie, until they were buried by the returning party, as narrated above. Their remains now repose near Old Fort Parker. Mrs. Plummer, her child, and others, were carried into captivity, where they remained for eighteen months.

LVI.

LETTER FROM STEPHEN F. AUSTIN TO THE SENATE OF TEXAS.

(Texas Almanac, 1857.)

A HIGHLY interesting letter was addressed to the Senate of Texas by Stephen F. Austin, dated Columbia, December 5, 1836, which throws much light on some important matters connected with his labors in colonizing Texas, and the breaking out of the revolution. General Austin fully explains, in this letter, the difficulties attending the colonization contract at first given to R. Leftwich and afterwards transferred by him to the Nashville (Tennesee) Company. It seems, however, that this transfer to foreigners was considered illegal by the Governor of Texas, on the ground that the contract gave no such right to empresarios without the consent of the government ; but General Austin procured the sanction of the transfer at Saltillo by a decree dated October 15, 1827. The Nashville Company, however, did nothing to settle the country, for six years, to 1830, except to make locations for persons not in the country. But they adopted the plan of selling land scrip, in the United States, by advertisements and publications, which example was followed by other companies and empresarios, and caused *the first great alarm in Mexico as to Texas,* leading to the prohibition of emigrants from the United States, and all the restriction measures against Texas.

Major Sterling C. Robertson and Mr. Alexander Thompson arrived in Austin's colony in November, 1830, about five months before the expiration of the above contract, with a few families. But having had some difficulty with Piedras, the military commandant of Nacogdoches, as they passed through that place. orders were issued by General Teran, Governor of Texas, to expel them from the country. General Austin afterward procured a counter order from Teran, with permission to receive him himself as colonist. General Austin says this caused him a great deal of trouble, and jeopardized the interests of his own colony. Afterward, while attending the legislature at Saltillo, in January, 1831, General Austin applied for an extension of time to the Nashville Company, or a new contract to Robertson ; but this application produced great offense, as the governor (Viesca) said it would be in direct violation of the law of 1830, forbidding all contracts with citizens of the United States, and would involve him in trouble with both State and General Governments especially as Robertson had made himself so obnoxious. General Austin says that by thus interfering in behalf of Robertson, he lost sight of his duty to his own colonists, inasmuch as this application tended to destroy his influence with the government, at a time when that influence was essential to secure the best interests of his colonists. He says, applications to colonize that section of country had been made by several foreigners, and that Governor Viesca expressed a preference for them, and would not interfere with the prohibiting law of 1830. General Austin says he was alarmed at the ruinous consequences that would ensue to Texas, should the contracts be granted, as these foreign contractors had uniformly made their contracts a matter of speculation, by selling land scrip and imposing upon the ignorant and credulous, and thereby bringing great discredit upon Texas, and deterring instead of promoting immigration. It was under these circumstances that he applied for a contract in the name of himself and Sam'l M. Williams, who had both become Mexican citizens, and were not under the prohibition of the law of 1830, against citizens of the United States. This contract was granted with some difficulty, and embraced all the vacant land of his former colony (except the coast), and extended over the country above the San Antonio road. General Austin considers that the obtaining of this contract, and thereby keeping out foreign companies, was among the most valuable services he had rendered Texas. Instead of having done anything to the injury of the Nashville Company or Roberston, he says he did all he could to serve them. He says he foresaw, in 1830, that a *break* with Mexico was inevitable, but that it was of the greatest importance to keep it off as long as possible, to gain time and strength for the contest.

He says the contract of Austin and Williams was essentially necessary to the best interests of his colonies below, as by settling the upper colony, the lower ones would be protected. General Austin alludes to the grants he had made in the upper colony, which he considers valid, though disputed, and it appears that the same land was often claimed by others as having been granted under Robertson. General Austin concludes by saying that this exposition is made to elucidate a question then before Congress, as to what should be done with Robertson's colony.

LVII.

SPEECH OF COLONEL CHARLES DE MORSE,

DELIVERED BEFORE THE TEXAS VETERAN ASSOCIATION IN HOUSTON,

MAY 20, 1874.

MY BRETHREN : When I say that such a meeting as this is a real pleasure to me, suggestive of the loftiest emotions, I say what proves itself in each of your hearts, for the pleasure is mutual—it is the long-deferred meeting of a family circle annually contracting, whose members have been separated for years by the pressing necessities of life, after the cessation of war. We come together now, and look into each other's faces, who may never all meet again in this world.

I see around me, in the presence of its founders, the remains of the ever-glorious little Republic of Texas, in whose era every citizen of intelligence knew something of every other citizen of average respectability, from the Sabine to the Rio Grande, because the progenitors of the Republic were so few in number, that individuality, which was the element of success in founding the Republic, stood out in bold relief, like a lone oak in a wide prairie. There sit around me men whom I have not seen before ere this since the fall of 1836—near thirty-eight years. I meet again the remains of that little army, which knew Thomas J. Rusk, Sam Houston, Albert Sidney Johnston and Mirabeau B. Lamar, as its prominent members, and William G. Cooke, George W. Hockley, Edward Burleson, and Sidney Sherman, as its secondary but not less gallant leaders.

I look upon those who shared in the dangers and privations of the first settlement with Austin and the orignal three hundred ; and there come with me from the Red River border, men who were within the limits of Texas in 1818, prior to the settlement by Austin, and who, in those days, ranged the Red River country, to repel and punish Indian aggression. And we have with us a few specimens of the generous old Texan planter of the coast counties, noble specimens of human nature, who in other days, illustrated the genial hospitality of the pioneer period.

Is there not an involuntary swelling of the heart when such men as these come together after years of severance ? and when the well-remembered forms of the departed pioneers, still dearly cherished, pass in the review of memory, and we feel again their genial presence, and have impressed upon us vividly, their civic and military, and social virtues ? Are we not necessarily carried back again into that era when 25,000 men, women, and children constituted all the white population of Texas, and the largest forces it ever banded were 1200 men at Beason's Ferry, and 1800 when Rusk's call to resist invasion, brought that number to the Colette for a short period in the fall of 1836? Was not San Jacinto fought by about 750 patriots? Was not San Antonio captured by 301 daring men driving out of a fortified city a force of 1400? Did not Bowie and Fannin at Concepcion, with ninety men, drive off 400 assailants, and capture their cannon? When we look upon the face of the President of this Association, who received the capitulation of San Antonio, do we not look into the glorious past?

With us now, is the second in command at Gonzales, the Lexington of Texas, who came with Ned Burleson and Tom Dennis, the first to succor the eighteen who had thrown up temporary breastworks, and were determined to resist the removal of their single piece of artillery, which the Mexican commander had sent to take from them. Re-enforced by squads until they outnumbered the assailants, they organized under Moore and Wallace, crossed the river and drove the enemy into an ignominious flight after a short skirmish. With us also is Amasa Turner, who commanded one of the three companies which came first to re-enforce Houston, as he fell back from the Colorado, coming in with Colonel John Forbes, Houston's aid, who is also with us. From another one of these captains, Richard Roman, dated San Francisco, April 25th, I have a letter evincing the deepest interest in our meeting to-day, and soliciting a copy of the proceedings, which, he says, "several of us veterans living here will be pleased to read." He says, "I, of course, cannot be with you, except in sentiment and feeling. I regret this, because of the pleasure I should enjoy in personally meeting with our old companions in the early days of trouble." The third of this gallant trio, William S. Fisher, participating at San Jacinto, acting as Secretary of War under Houston's first administration, and subsequently commanding the ill-fated Mier expedition, has gone to his reward. All these came out again in the fall of 1836, when Rusk called for men to repel Urrea. When we think of these men we pass back into the chivalric period of our history, when patriotism in Texas was an intuition, and as the committee of San Felipe said, "it required more patriotism to keep men at home than to get them into service." Is not this expression descriptive of the revolutionary period of our history?

We have also with us Alexander Horton, a representative of the force which pursued Piedras to the Angelina in 1832, and Edwin Waller and Robert H. Williams, who were at the capture of Velasco, and who participated in the earliest civil councils of Texas, and E. M. Pease, who was Secretary of the Council of the Provisional Government before the Declaration of Independence; and William J. Russell, whose name appears in the earliest movements for liberty. We have also Duncan and Reed, who were at the capture of Goliad, and Hunter, Cooper and Scurlock, nearly all who remain of the few who escaped the general massacre of Fannin's men. We have with us, too, McKneely and Brown, who were with Grant's forces when captured at Goliad, and were carried captives to Matamoras. We have with us also, six signers of the Declaration of Independence, Charles B. Stewart, S. W. Blount, J. W. Bunton, William Menifee, Edwin Waller, and William B. Scates, whose action changed the flag under which we rallied, from the white, red, and green of the Republican party of Mexico, to the azure field and the golden star of the Republic of Texas. These men carry us back to the incipiency of the Texas Revolution.

In those days, my friends, patriotism was the animating impulse. There were no peculations upon the public funds—there were no public funds. We had no speculative army contractors, because the only contractor we had—Tom McKinney, had no means but his own money and credit, and the basis of his authorized purchases was first to solicit assistance, and endeavor to negotiate a small loan. That army contractor, full of zeal, and not looking to profit, did not enrich himself, as army contractors do in this day, but impoverished himself, and sacrificed his personal prosperity upon the altar of his country, dying in poverty, with the debt that Texas justly owed him unpaid. Texas, I fear, is not likely to disprove the old maxim which describes republics as ungrateful.

In the past, which I am attempting feebly to describe, when the citizen heard of Indian aggression or Mexican invasion, he caught up his rifle, molded a pouchful of balls, saddled his horse, arrayed his pack-mule, supplied himself with provisions, met the other male members of his settlement at an agreed place, and in squads or small companies, all available men went out to fight for the general good, with a will which always insured success. Armed mainly with rifles, they attacked forts bristling with artillery, and captured them by picking off the defenders at the guns, or wherever a head was presented. Where else in the world has this been done, except in Texas?

My friends, though Texas was to us, in those days, a new country, and though little of her virgin sod had ever been pressed by the foot of the white man prior to the settlement by Austin and the contemporary empresarios, except on two military roads or trails, from east to west, and at the localities of a few military posts, yet it had a history running back to 1685—a history commencing with religious colonization, and occupancy for the extension of territory, by ambitious European sovereigns—and its native loveliness had impressed the senses of discoverers and pioneers of colonization a century and a half before our time, as they did ours. Yet their foot-prints were mere tracks in the vast wilderness, effaced as fast as made, and the legendary relations that we heard, and the slight visible remains, made impression upon us

THOS. F. MCKINNEY.

See p. 279.

as the Toltec ruins of the Casa Grande do upon the traveler of to-day. We saw the missions of Goliad and San Antonio, evidences of the secondary occupation, and heard something about a long-abandoned mission, and the open shaft of an abandoned silver mine in the San Saba region, and we see yet, in a bend of Red River, traces of an old fortification in Montague county, known by tradition as the old Spanish fort. Yet, these were at our coming the remains of a forgotten past, of which scarcely a memorial was then accessible, and they came to us as dim traditions, like the poetry of the Scottish border, which relates incidents not verified by later chronicles. The settlements we found, were mere oases in the surrounding wilderness, and to us, and in the aspect of nature, Texas was a new country, rich in primeval beauty, without sign of prior occupation, except at the four or five localities to which I have referred, remote from each other, and connected by narrow trails for travel in single or double file.

The only route of travel from the South-west to the North, as late as 1842, was by the old military road to Nacogdoches, passing the Bradshaw place and the Mound Prairie, which had once been the central seat of the Nassonis, the pioneer Indian tribes of the earliest known occupation of Texas. Those mounds are there now, silent memorials of a people who lived before our time, but have left no other evidences of their occupation save these mounds, and record that La Salle, the first white man to penetrate the wilderness, found their builders there. Not a descendant exists to bear witness of their personal peculiarities. On the margin of Red River, in my own county, in three separate places, and in Bowie county in one, the same silent evidences attest prior occupation ; how many centuries ago we do not know. In them may be found flint arrow-heads, bones, and potter's ware.

Beginning, then, with her earliest recorded history, the landing of La Salle, nearly two hundred years ago, then seeking the mouth of the Mississippi, which he had discovered three years before, and which he had taken formal possession of in the name of Louis le Grand, as the territory of France, we note his wanderings to the Colorado, the Brazos, the Trinity, and Neches, reminding the reader of the earlier explorations by De Soto, of Florida, and the discovery of the great father of waters at the Natchez Bluff. From the first, Texas has seemed to each explorer a land of strange beauty, and its successive historic periods, including the expeditions of McGee, Long, Perry, Kemper, and Ross, to the settlement by Austin, De Leon and Edwards, terminating at San Jacinto, have been full of a rare interest which clings to them yet. Do we not all remember *our* first sensations, and can we not realize from them how La Salle and his companions must have felt, when passing through the beautiful Bay of St. Bernard, now recognized as Matagorda, they looked upon the flower-gemmed prairies of the Navidad and La Vaca, to which La Salle gave its name?

We all know how, at our first view, the strange wild beauty of the land aroused emotions of wonder ; how the undulating formation impressed us ; how the exuberance of verdure impressed us ; how the wide prairies and clear-running, narrow streams, fringed with trees to the water's edge, excited our sense of the beautiful.   We saw the herds of wild horses, moving a little away, and facing about and scanning our movements.   We saw great herds of deer feeding in the open prairie within two or three hundred yards, and heedless of our presence.   We saw the sleek cattle nearly everywhere.   But most attractive of all, and differing from all elsewhere, the latch-string to every cabin door literally, not metaphorically, hung upon the outside, and there were no locks to dwelling, or meat-house, or corn-crib ; but every comer was welcome to the primitive hospitality—a cordial, not passive hospitality.   Then no man feared robbery or wayside danger, but singly camped out anywhere that fuel could be found ; turned his horse upon the abundant grass, cooked his meat upon a stick, and his hoe-cake in the ashes, and the little camp coffee-pot from behind his saddle furnished him the facility for an invigorating beverage.   The ease with which life could be sustained was wonderful—when the deer were everywhere, the cattle were everywhere, when salt marshes bordering the bays were covered with myriads of wild fowl, when the plover, the killdee and the prairie chickens would hardly keep ten steps away ; when small fish might be drawn from the bays and bayous almost as fast as one would drop a line and leisurely withdraw it ; when the great red fish might be stranded at Galveston by circling around them in shallow water, as the Mexican prisoners from San Jacinto procured them ; when the islands of the bays furnished gulls' eggs by the bucketful, and the margins of the creeks abounded with the pecan and the grape.   The land was a land of plenty and a paradise of beauty.   All who saw it in those days can understand the effect produced upon La Salle and his companions, when coming through the sheltered bay of Matagorda, after a tedious voyage, not without dangers, they landed upon the bluff upon the Lavaca River, where they constructed Fort St. Louis, and where the outlines of breastworks and ditches attest to this day the presence of the first European explorer and his colonists.   Note the record of these first white settlers, and observe how identical were the impressions made upon them and upon us.   The historian of that expedition says : " The colony was greatly refreshed by the abundance of game and fish, and charmed with the country, and the herds of buffalo and deer that were seen grazing upon the prairies, they began to think they would soon realize the paradise they had come so far to find."   This, my friends, was written in 1685. - How identical with our own experience ; save that the buffalo had receded from the coast, and the cattle we found were, in part at least, the successors of those which La Salle introduced from St. Domingo, by his ships, and the wild horses we saw were the successors of those they found the Indians then in possession of, or which, perhaps, the Spaniards had brought when they established the missions.

Does not the mind of every one of you turn back to those days of primeval beauty, of hearty sincerity, of undying and devoted friendship, of patriotism never surpassed ; and contrasting that remembrance with this day of progress, this hard, grinding, money-loving, struggling day, when show is everything, and pretense in many instances takes the place of reality, does not the past seem a picture of beauty in a framing of gold ? Compare it with the present ! Certainly nature is not now more beautiful than then, for the natural beauty is already marred by the marks of more dense settlement. How is it with your own hearts ? Are your impulses as elevated? Do you feel the same proud intensity of individuality as in the old Texas—the proud, glorious, and indomitable ?

Comparing the intercourse and bearing of men, we had antagonisms then, as acrid as now, but we had friendships that were warmer and purer ; more devoted than now; and we did not idolize money. It must be confessed, that with the habit of the Anglo-Saxon race, we dreamed of enterprise and development in the future ; but was not the dream more enchanting than the reality ? *Then*, we diversified life and avoided monotony, by plunging into the surrounding wilds, in which there was always novelty of scene and freshness of sensation. We lived in a land of hope, with a thought of enlargement of capacities and general wealth to ·result from development at some time ; but among *real* men, who illustrated in the present the nobility of manhood, and were not wholly absorbed by thoughts of gain or any immediate expectation of it.

Did we appreciate fully how beautiful it was? how near to the Utopia of the dreamers ? The hopes of youth ever run to the future, as did ours; but most of you have trodden both ends of the happy valley, and I think you have found the entrance most enchanting ; and now, as you stand and look back at the setting sun, you regret that its bright gleams are disappearing, although another and brighter day is promised.

Another such land of beauty and fertility, of health, pleasant temperature, and natural conveniencies, settled by a primitive American people, can no more be found again, than can there be a renewal of Lexington and Bunker Hill, of Trenton, or King's Mountain, or of Yorktown. The new land, and the simple but powerful elements of character are wanting. Henceforth, life is artificial, and elementary grandeur of character is secondary to the control of organized systems, and the power of money.

14

In the early days we had leisure—now all is haste, anxiety, and wearing cares; and yet we all longed for the change. Human nature is ever the same, discontent with the present. All situations have their drawbacks, but the natural is more satisfying than any work of art. The primeval beauty and the prospective hopes of the early settlement have passed away; the patriotic excitements, with their glorious blending of self-confidence, indomitable will, and uncalculating zeal for the general good, are of the memory only, and you can only refresh your impulses by looking back; the glowing illusions upon which you constructed your day-dreams are gone forever. We shall find no more Austins, Milams, Travises; no more Rusks, Houstons, nor Sidney Johnstons; no more Tom McKinneys; no more Deaf Smiths. We may find many others as. intelligent, as brave and as honest, but not of that type of manhood. The men were suited to the era. Their character grew out of the surroundings.

And when I refer to these men of the old Texas, let it not be said that it is an exhibition of mere local pride, or pride of the past; an overestimate of men who figured on a narrow field of action.

Were not the unselfishness, the resolution, the patient perseverance of Stephen F. Austin, during serious difficulties and long imprisonment in a distant land, where he was representing the interests of his colonists : his calm statesmanship at home during the incipiency of the Revolution, impressing itself upon Houston, who justly termed him the Father of Texas; the marked effect he produced in the United States as a commissioner from Texas, seeking sympathy and assistance; and his modest proposition to surrender his command of the army to Houston before the appointment of the latter to the chief command, upon the ground of his own inexperience in military affairs; were not these all evidence of rare personal qualities, self-denial, and exalted patriotism ?

Did not Daniel Webster, and William H. Seward, and Charles Sumner, all estimate the mental capacity of Thomas J. Rusk as of a very high order, though not illuminated by any oratorical power? They have placed that estimate upon record. I know myself, being personally present, and having an inside view, that in the crisis of 1850, when the Union of the States was seriously endangered and the power of the Great Pacificator had failed with his own party, that the influence of Thomas J. Rusk was relied upon by Millard Filmore to secure the passage of the compromise resolutions, still needing a few votes to make the result certain, and save the country from immediate discord; and that the earnest management and direct influence of Rusk, through others in the House of Representatives, did procure their passage. In the Senate they were safe. What a power he was at home—though always retiring and diffident of his own merits—all old Texans know.

And what was Albert Sidney Johnston? First our adjutant-general under Rusk, in '36, and subsequently commander-in-chief of the army, then secretary of war. He abandoned the army of the United States to come to us ; and when Texas had no pressing use for him sought employment again in the old service, and at once rose to position. He was assigned to the chief command in Utah, when that service was deemed critical and superior ability was needed. He was considered by the then secretary of war the first soldier in the service of the United Sates. I have heard him say so. There is no call to eulogize him now. His character and fame are above that necessity. We, who personally knew him, loved him for his social qualities and his elevated tone, before he had ascended the eminence upon which fame now builds his monument.

The character of Sam Houston was coupled with a romantic interest long before he came to Texas, and as the friend and favorite of Jackson, and with his popularity as a young Governor of Tennessee, he sought Texas with a prestige which commanded confidence and popularity. Inspection of his acts and his correspondence at the commencement of the struggle in Texas, will establish at once his character for great judgment of men and circumspection, and his final action at San Jacinto, and his joint appeal with Rusk, to the people, two days before, manifest a calm comprehension of the crisis and the surroundings, and a confidence of a favorable result, while his reply to the taunts of the acting secretary of war, and his certificate of the benefits to the army of the presence and counsels of Rusk, evince at the same time the magnanimity of Houston's character, and the brotherly unity between these two. His military policy, however it may have been questioned—and there was at the time much variance of opinion, and a disposition to charge him with a want of nerve in retreating from the Colorado, and permitting the breaking up of the settlements west of the Trinity—resulted in the greatest little victory ever achieved by a people struggling against overwhelming preponderance of numbers and resources. San Jacinto did not equal Marathon in grandeur of proportions, but was identical in objects and results.

Of Mirabeau B. Lamar, another of our heroes, it is proper to say, that in conduct, in manner, in presence, he illustrated the courtly chivalry of Sir Philip Sidney, with a similar poetic temperament and more mental ability. His gallantry and modesty enforced the warmest eulogiums from Rusk and Houston, and by general acclamation of the army, to which he was a new comer, he won his spurs in one day, the action of the 20th, and on the final day, the 21st, by common approval, was placed in command of the cavalry. Coming to Texas, a Knight Paladin, offering his sword and person in the cause of liberty, as Lafayette did, by a vote almost unanimous, he rose to the highest position in the country. I doubt if he was a strictly prudent executive, but he was a noble and chivalrous man, whose actions were prompted by the most generous impulses which govern humanity.

David G. Burnet, our first president, was a devotee of liberty in his boyhood, and signalized his tendencies by joining Miranda's expedition to relieve a South American Republic from the oppression of Spain. The same free idealistic views led him to Texas, where his talent and purity of character were appreciated by making him first president, and afterward vice-president, under Lamar. He was a writer of great force and perspicuity, and a pure and fearless man. No profits inured to him from public service. No profits inured to any of the men of that day. They did not work for public plunder. They all died poor, and this is an element of their pure fame.

Has there ever in the world's history been gallantry more conspicuous than that of Travis and his companions? and was not his defense of the Alamo in all respects equal to that of Thermopylæ? And the declaration upon which he stood and by which he died, sword in hand, it is a memorial to be emblazoned always upon the historic pages of Texas ; to be impressed upon the minds of her youth ; to be cut deep into her historic monuments of bronze and marble, to challenge comparison with the proudest evidences of patriotic valor which the world has ever afforded. Let me read :

COMMANDANCY OF THE ALAMO, BEXAR, February 24, 1836.
FELLOW-CITIZENS AND COMPATRIOTS :

I am besieged by a thousand or more Mexicans under Santa Anna. I have sustained a continued bombardment for twenty-four hours, and have not lost a man. The enemy have demanded a surrender at discretion ; otherwise the garrison is to be put to the sword, if the place is taken. I have answered the summons with a cannon shot, and our flag still waves proudly from the walls. I shall never surrender or retreat ! Then I call upon you, in the name of liberty, of patriotism, and of everything dear to the American character, to come to our aid with all dispatch. They enemy are receiving re-enforcements daily, and will no doubt increase to three or four thousand in four or five days. Though this call may be neglected, I am determined to sustain myself as long as possible, and die like a soldier, who never forgets his own honor and that of his country. Victory or death !

" W. BARRETT TRAVIS, *Lieutenant-Colonel commanding.*

" P.S.—The Lord is on our side. When the enemy appeared in sight we had not three bushels of corn. We have since found in deserted houses eighty or ninety bushels, and got into the walls twenty or thirty head of beeves.—T."

Then in his private letter dated 3d of March, he says: "I am still here, in fine spirits and well to do. With one hundred and forty-five men, I have held this place ten days against a force variously estimated from fifteen hundred to six thousand, and I shall continue to hold it till I get relief from my countrymen, or I will perish in its defense. We have had a shower of bombs and cannon balls continually falling among us the whole time, yet none of us have fallen. We have been miraculously preserved."

Still the same heroic spirit unfaltering. But re-enforcements did not come in any considerable number. Assistance was delayed too long, and at the final struggle there were only 183, weary with endless watching, to resist 4,000. At a little after midnight, on Sunday, the 6th of March, the final effort of the surrounding host commenced. Urged on by promises and threats, though terribly thinned out by the Texan fire, they kept up the attack until daylight, and then advanced with scaling ladders. Twice the host was repulsed by the little band of worn defenders, but physical capacity was unequal to the requirement, and the tremendous disproportion of force carried the walls at the third assault, and every hero within sold his life as dearly as possible. When pressed upon, and no time for reloading, they clubbed their guns, and fell fighting. Around the bodies of Travis and Crockett were piles of slain. Bowie, sick in bed, was butchered and mutilated. In the attempt to perform the last agreed duty of patriotism, by firing the magazine, and hurling masses of the assailants to destruction, the ordnance officer, the faithful Evans, was slain, and the glorious immolation of a servile horde upon the altar of liberty was prevented. The record of the historian reads:

"Thus fell the Alamo and its heroic defenders; but before them lay the bodies of five hundred and twenty-one of the enemy, with a like number wounded. At an hour by sun, on that Sabbath morning, all was still: yet the crimson waters of the aqueduct around the fort resembled the red flag on the church of Bexar! The defenders of Texas did not retreat, but lay there in obedience to the command of their country: and in that obedience the world has witnessed among men no greater moral sublimity."

Little did the victor in that day's fight understand its effect upon the men he had to contend with. He counted upon intimidation and repression. There could not have been lighted a more brilliant beacon fire to rally the free spirits of Texas, and their sympathizing brethren of the South-west of the Union, and from that day of butchery the merciless despot marched in his narrow pathway to a certain defeat, and the destruction of his power and his prestige as a conqueror. In the words of President Burnet's proclamation, of the 18th of March:

"The fall of the Alamo is the surest guarantee of our success. The Spartan band who so nobly perished there, have bequeathed to us an example which ought to be, and will be, imitated; and have inflicted on the enemy a terror and a loss that are equivalent to a defeat."

The heroic Milam gave his life as Warren did at Bunker Hill. The examples are identical. Travis, Bowie, Crockett, Bonham, and their fellows in the Alamo, invested San Antonio with more than the patriotic interest of the opening battle of the American revolution. The gallantry was much more signal, persistent, and self-sacrificing. The Alamo, as a field of heroism, has but one rival in the world's history, and that is Thermopylæ.

It has been said that "it is sweet to die for our country." Compared with the ignoble survival of the victor of the hour, the self-vaunted " Napoleon of the West," for years a wretched outcast from his country, devoting the remainder of a misspent and dishonored life to low gratifications, was it not a glorious departure that Travis and his heroic band made on that bright Sabbath morning in March, when all nature was growing into beauty, and men feel least like bidding farewell to the surrounding attractions of the world?

Look at the submission of Fannin to his fate after being received as a prisoner of war. It is well known that his bearing elicited the admiration of his captor, who certified it both before and after the brutal massacre. Wounded and unable to stand, he sat down, calmly tied the bandage required over his own eyes, bared his bosom to the balls, meeting death as a hero and a patriot may do, without the quivering of a muscle. It was fitting that this act of sacrifice of Fannin and his three hundred and thirty men, like that of the Alamo was consummated on the blessed Sabbath day. Our blood offerings were all sanctified, and God accepted them; and upon the glorious field of Jacinto came the redemption which they purchased for us; came in the fire and smoke of battle; came to the appalled wretches who had obeyed the behests of their tyrant leader, with the ominous cries of " Remember the Alamo and La Bahia," ringing in their ears like trumpets braying retributive vengeance. And indeed it was appalling. Though double the number of our little army, they made but ten or fifteen minutes' resistance, and, shot down by hundreds and fleeing under the impulse of an indescribable terror, the proud array of the Napoleon of the West shrunk away like the dry grass of the prairie before a raging fire; and its Dictator-General, but an hour before a mighty potentate, the head of eight millions of people, was pursued and caught, a disguised and crest-fallen fugitive; and blanched by terror, and conscious of crime, sought to retain his justly forfeited life by imploration and abject flattery. What a change within a day! How soon the despot became the supplicant! Vividly the scene of that day of retribution brings to mind the lines of Macaulay detailing the incidents of another field centuries ago, in which vengeance claimed payment for unhallowed slaughter:

"Their ranks are breaking like thin clouds before a Biscay gale;
  The field is heaped with bleeding steeds, and flags and cloven mail,
  And then we thought on vengeance, and all along our van,
'Remember St. Bartholomew,' was passed from man to man.
.   .   .   .
For our God hath crushed the tyrant, our God hath raised the slave,
  And mocked the council of the wise, and the valor of the brave—
.   .   .   .
Then glory to His holy name from whom all glories are."

Certainly, in the almost instantaneous results of this battle, there is something to indicate the fiat of a just God, who rules the destinies of nations, and who strengthened that little band of ragged patriots, without the usual appliances of warfare, to overcome the well appointed and intrenched army opposed to them, the choicest troops and the bravest generals of the Mexican army.

Rusk said of it in his official dispatch, "This glorious achievement is attributed to the valor of our soldiers and the sanctity of our cause. . . The officers and men seemed to be actuated by a like enthusiasm. There was a general cry which pervaded our ranks, 'Remember the Alamo—remember La Bahia.' These words electrified all. 'Onward' was the cry. The unerring aim and irresistible energy of the Texan army could not be withstood. It was freemen fighting against the minions of tryanny, and the result proved the inequality of such a contest. . . . The sun was sinking in the horizon as the battle commenced; but at the close of the conflict, the sun of liberty and independence rose in Texas, never, it is to be hoped, to be obscured by the clouds of despotism. . . A volume would not contain the deeds of individual daring and bravery."

This is the testimony of the not over-declamatory secretary of war.

In this commemorative reference to the participators in our early history, our little navy should not be forgotten, for it had gallant material in Hawkins, Hurd, Brown and George Wheelwright, and later under the gallant Moore, who carried our flag boldly into the enemy's waters, and drove them before him. The little *Independence* was captured by superior force, and one side of the gallant *Wheelwright* carried away by a cannon shot. She was attacked by four times her weight of metal, and perhaps ten times her number of men. As evincing the spirit of those who carried the flag upon the waters, your speaker is able to testify that when Hawkins sailed down the coast to the Brazos Santiago, prior to San Jacinto, fifteen men, including officers, seamen, and marines, comprised the entire force to sail the vessel and man the six side guns and the nine-pounder pivot amidship. But with always an insignificant force in number, we defied the enemy upon the waters of the Gulf, and kept our coasts clear; and at Copano, Burton's cavalry—horse marines—captured three of the enemy's vessels freighted with supplies for their army.   The navy was always a favorite with the people, though it never had brilliant opportunities, and from the field of San Jacinto the army divided Santa Anna's treasure with it.

Passing from the military to the legislative, do you remember what congresses the little republic assembled, first at Columbia, then at Houston, and then at Austin, in the old wooden capitol, stockaded as a gathering place for women and children, in the case of a sudden irruption by Indians?

Do you recollect of the first congress William H. and John A. Wharton, Mosely Baker, Anson Jones, Branch D. Archer, Bill Williamson; and after that Sam Houston, Cornelius Van Ness, Robert Potter, James H. Mayfield, David S. Kaufman, Kenneth L. Anderson, James B. Miller, James Shaw, William B. Ochiltree, William H. Jack, James Webb, William Henry Daingerfield, John B. Jones, John Caldwell, Antonio Navarro? These were solid men in any legislative body.   I shall not invite special comparison, but men of this grade do not abound in our legislatures now.   Probably a reason is that State legislatures are seldom so attractive of talent as national legislative bodies, and in those days all public councils had loftier repute than at the present.   We, who have been the associates of these men, and had the felicity to know them personally, and feel that our lives have in some degree been hallowed thereby; who have, in our humble sphere, had a part in the formation of an empire; whose thoughts have been elevated and purified in the past, by a consciousness that we were ministering to a great future— we experience only the common fate of all pioneers of progress, in finding that our ships of venture do not come home laden with attar of roses, and fragrant spices, and gold and gems of the Indies, but only with the common merchandise which serves the ordinary use of life, and that our ventures have not materially enriched us; yet if they have secured homes and national enjoyment of life to others; if they have populated a fair land, and conduced to the good of great masses, may we not console ourselves that we have not lived in vain; but that doing this good for others, even though those others were in great part strangers, we have wrought out a great work, perhaps, hardly appreciating the full magnitude of what we did?   And so doing, with consciences unseared, and remembrances of good intent, can we not feel that our lives have been useful if not pecuniarily profitable; and can we not, when the indicator halts upon the dial, wrap the drapery of our couches around us and quietly lie down, to be passed through the portals of the future, content, trustful, satisfied? Life is at best, until we pass the meridian, but a continued longing for the happy days beyond our view—the bright to-morrow which never comes.   Are those who struggle for a little more gain, and who handle much, and are responsible for much, constantly apprehensive of loss, though they have to leave it all, without reserve—are these happier than we who have not much but quiet homes and quiet minds?

My friends, happiness is in the heart, in the memory, in the fixed purpose to do good, and the consciousness of having done good. Standing upon the verge of the great future of the Empire of Texas; looking into the glorious past of which we have been a humble part; treasuring our old friendships; pleading for the preservation of the entirety of the old Texas and the continued fealty of all to its perpetuation and prosperity; let us annually all meet who may continue in this life, and do honor to those who annually depart. Let us offer up daily prayers for the perpetuity of the great confederacy of which we are a part, and its purification from political harlotry and jobbery. Let us give calm counsel and hopeful to those who are following us upon the tide of Time, and whom we are to recognize as our legitimate successors, and we shall have played our parts faithfully, and may confide in the appreciation of the Power that overwhelms armies and creates States; and yet notices the least act of the least conspicuous of us all.

I may trespass upon your patience if I attempt to forecast the future of the empire, of which you were substantially the founders; and yet I will indulge in a glance at the future, as compared with the past. San Felipe de Austin, its once noted seat of government, has about the same relation to the present of Texas as Jamestown has to that of Virginia. The traveler who has a taste for antiquities, and desires to see the first capital of Texas, may find it difficult to ascertain its precise locality, even from the people of a county adjoining that in which its deserted site is to be found. And Washington, the first seat of government of the independent Republic of Texas, is in a state of dilapidation, and its name rarely mentioned. Events are rapid in succession in this day. The city of Campeche, but sixty years ago, was the naval station of the army, and subsequently the headquarters of the brilliant, courteous, and gallant Buccaneer of the Gulf, who assisted in the defense of New Orleans, and at his red house in Campeche, surrounded by a flourishing town, dispensed profuse hospitalities to official agents and other visitors, and diplomatically foiled naval commanders ordered to dispossess him. Thence, for years, he sent out squadrons which destroyed the commerce of one of the proudest monarchies of Europe. After its abandonment by him in 1822, it became again a waste, and when your speaker first saw it 1836, was a desolate sand-bank, with but two descriptive marks—the rough board custom-house of the government of Mexico, comprising one room with a ground floor, and the bushes known as the Three Trees, where Lafitte defeated the Curanchuas; and by which the navigator sailing along the low line of coast recognized the locality. Into that harbor the Texan schooner of war, *Independence*, under the command of Charles Edward

Hawkins, a gallant gentleman, sailed on the 21st of March, 1836, and found an uninhabited island, and at a little distance from the shore, the schooner *Dart*, with Monroe Edwards' cargo of Africans. On that locality now rises, from the low lands surrounding, a city like Venice, ardent and ambitious, and with commercial prospects nearly as brilliant as its archetype. So located as to command the trade of an immense area, and to become perhaps the natural marine outlet for the wares, silks, and teas of the Indies, on their route from the Pacific coast to the Atlantic shore; drawing from her direct tributaries the fruits of an empire; growing in population and commerce now with great rapidity; her prospects under enterprising management are boundless. And as the commercial metropolis of the Union has run on from the swampy pastures of the Collect, and spread itself all over the island of Manhattan, and over the contiguous shores of Long Island and New Jersey, some of us may live to see the city of Galveston embracing Bolivar and Virginia Points and Pelican Island, destined as it is to commercial supremacy on the southern boundary of the great Republic.

LVIII.

OFFICIAL ACCOUNT OF THE FALL OF BEXAR AND SURRENDER OF GENERAL COS.

HEADQUARTERS VOLUNTEER ARMY, BEXAR, December 14, 1835.

TO HIS EXCELLENCY, THE PROVISIONAL GOVERNOR OF TEXAS.

SIR: I have the satisfaction to inclose a copy of Colonel Johnson's account of the storming and surrender of San Antonio de Bexar, to which I have little to add that can in any way increase the luster of this brilliant achievement to the federal arms of the volunteer army under my command; and which will, I trust, prove the downfall of the last position of military despotism on our soil of freedom.

At three o'clock in the morning of the 5th instant, Colonel Neil, with a piece of artillery, protected by Captain Roberts and his company, was sent across the river to attack, at five o'clock, the Alamo, on the north side, to draw the attention of the enemy from the advance of the divisions which had to attack the suburbs of the town, under Colonels Milam and Johnson. This service was effected to my entire satisfaction; and the party returned to camp at nine o'clock A.M.

On the advance of the attacking divisions, I formed all the reserve, with the exception of the guard necessary to protect the camp, at the old mill position, and held myself in readiness to advance, in case of necessity, to assist when required ; and shortly afterward passed into the suburbs to reconnoiter, where I found all going on prosperously, and retired with the reserve to the camp. Several parties were sent out mounted, under Captains Cheshire, Coleman, and Roberts, to scour the country, and endeavor to intercept Ugartechea, who was expected, and ultimately forced an entry with re-enforcements for General Cos. Captains Cheshire, Sutherland, and Lewis, with their companies, were sent in as re-enforcements to Colonel Johnson, during the period of attack ; and Captains Splann and Ruth and Lieutenant Borden, with their companies, together with Lieutenant-Colonels Somerville and Sublett, were kept in readiness for further assistance, if required. On the evening of the 8th, a party from the Alamo, of about fifty men, passed up in front of our camp and opened a brisk fire, but without effect. They were soon obliged to retire precipitately, by opening a six-pounder on them, commanded by Captain Hunnings, by sending a party across the river, and by the advance of Captain Bradley's company, who were stationed above.

On the morning of the 9th, in consequence of advice from Colonel Johnson, of a flag of truce having been sent in, to intimate a desire to capitulate, I proceeded to town, and by two o'clock A. M., of the 10th, a treaty was finally concluded by the commissioners appointed, to which I acceded immediately, deeming the terms highly favorable, considering the strong position and large force of the enemy, which could not be less than thirteen hundred effective men—one thousand one hundred and five having left this morning with General Cos, besides three companies and several small parties which separated from him in consequence of the fourth article of the treaty.

In addition to a copy of the treaty (marked No. 1) I inclose a list (No. 2) of all the valuable property ceded to us by virtue of the capitulation.

General Cos left this morning for the mission of San José, and to-morrow commences his march to the Rio Grande, after complying with all that had been stipulated.

I can not conclude this dispatch without expressing in the warmest terms, my entire approbation of every officer and soldier in the army, and particularly those who so gallantly volunteered to storm the town, which I have the honor to command, and to say that their bravery and zeal on the present occasion merit the warmest eulogies which I can confer, and the gratitude of their country. The gallant leader of the storming party, Colonel Benjamin R. Milam, fell gloriously on the third day, and his memory will be dear to Texas as long as there exists a grateful heart to feel, or a friend of liberty to lament his worth. His place was most ably filled by Colonel F. W. Johnson, adjutant-general of the army, whose coolness and prudence, united to daring bravery, could alone have brought matters to so successful an end, with so very small a loss, against so superior a force, and such strong fortifications. To his shining merits on this occasion I bore ocular testimony during the five days' action.

I have also to contribute my praise to Major Bennet, quartermaster-general, for the diligence and success with which he supplied both armies during the siege and storm.

These dispatches, with a list of killed and wounded, will be handed to your Excellency by my first aid-de-camp, Colonel William T. Austin, who was present as a volunteer during the five days' storm, and whose conduct on this and every other occasion merits my warmest praise.

To-morrow I leave the garrison and town under command of Colonel Johnson, with a sufficient number of men and officers to sustain the same, in case of attack, until assisted from the colonies; so that your Excellency may consider our conquest as sufficiently secured against every attempt of the enemy. The rest of the army will retire to their homes.

I have the honor to be your Excellency's obedient servant,

EDWARD BURLESON,
Commander-in-Chief of the Volunteer Army.

GENERAL BURLESON, COMMANDER-IN-CHIEF OF THE FEDERAL VOLUNTEER ARMY OF TEXAS.

SIR : I have the honor to acquaint you, that on the morning of the 5th instant the volunteers for storming the city of Bexar, possessed by the troops of General Cos, entered the suburbs in two divisions under the command of Colonel Benjamin R. Milam. The first division, under his immediate command, aided by Major R. C. Morris, and the second, under my command, aided by Colonels Grant and Austin, and Adjutant Brister.

The first divison, consisting of the companies of Captains York, Patton, Llewellyn, Crane, English, and Landrum, with two pieces and fifteen artillerymen, commanded by Lieutenant-Colonel Franks, took possession of the house of Don Antonio de la Garza. The second division, composed of the companies of Captains Cooke, Swisher, Edwards, Alley, Duncan, Peacock, Breece, and Placido Venavides, took possession of the house of Berrimendi. The last division was exposed for a short time to a very heavy fire of grape and musketry from the whole of the enemy's line of fortification, until the guns of the first division opened their fire, when the enemy's attention was directed to both divisions. At 7 o'clock, a heavy cannonading from the town was seconded by a well-directed fire from the Alamo, which for a time prevented the possibility of covering our lines, or effecting a safe communication between the two divisions. In consequence of the twelve-pounder having been dismounted, and the want of proper cover for the other gun, little execution was done by our artillery during the day. We were, therefore, reduced to a close and well-directed fire from our rifles, which, notwithstanding the advantageous position of the enemy, obliged them to slacken their fire, and several times to abandon their artillery within the range of our shot. Our loss during this day was one private killed, one colonel and one first-lieutenant severely wounded; one colonel slightly, three privates dangerously, six severely, and three slightly. During the whole of the night the two divisions were occupied in strengthening their positions, opening trenches, and effecting a safe communication, although exposed to a heavy cross-fire from the enemy, which slackened toward morning. I may remark that the want of proper tools rendered this undertaking doubly arduous. At daylight of the 6th, the enemy were observed to have occupied the tops of the houses in our front, where, under the cover of breastworks, they opened through loop-holes a very brisk fire of small-arms on our whole line, followed by a steady cannonading from the town, in front, and the Alamo on the left flank, with few interruptions during the day. A detachment of Captain Crane's company, under Lieutenant W. McDonald, followed by others, gallantly possessed themselves, under a severe fire, of the house to the right, and in advance of the first division, which considerably extended our line; while the rest of the army was occupied in returning the enemy's fire and strengthening our trenches, which enabled our artillery to do some execution, and completed a safe communication from right to left.

Our loss this day amounted to three privates severely wounded, and two slightly. During the night the fire from the enemy was inconsiderable, and our people were occupied in making and filling sand-bags, and otherwise strengthening our lines. At daylight on the 7th it was discovered that the enemy had, during the night previous, opened a trench on the Alamo side of the river, and on the left flank, as well as strengthening their battery on the cross-street leading to the Alamo. From the first they opened a brisk fire of small-arms; from the last a heavy cannonade, as well as small-arms, which was kept up until eleven o'clock, when they were silenced by our superior fire. About twelve o'clock Henry Carns, of Captain York's company, exposed to a heavy fire from the enemy, gallantly advanced to a house in front of the first division, and with a crowbar forced an entrance, into which the whole of the company immediately followed him, and made a secure lodgment. In the evening the enemy renewed a heavy fire from all the positions which could bear upon us, and at half-past three o'clock, as our gallant commander, Colonel Milam, was passing into the yard of my position, he received a rifle shot in the head, which caused his instant death; an irreparable loss at so critical a moment. Our casualties, otherwise, during this day, were only two privates slightly wounded.

At a meeting of officers, held at seven o'clock, I was invested with the chief command, and Major Morris as my second. At ten o'clock P. M., Captains Llewellyn, English, Crane, and Landrum, with their respective companies, forced their way into and took possession of the house of Don J. Antonio Navarro, an advanced and important position close to the square. The fire of the enemy was interrupted and slack during the night, and the weather exceedingly cold and wet.

The morning of the 8th continued cold and wet, and but little firing on either side. At nine o'clock the same companies who took possession of Don J. Antonio Navarro's house, aided by a detachment of the Grays, advanced and occupied Zambrano's Row, leading to the square, without any accident. The brave conduct, on this occasion, of William Graham, of Cooke's company of Grays, merits mention. A heavy fire of artillery and small-arms was opened on this position by the enemy, who disputed every inch of ground, and, after suffering a severe loss in officers and men, were obliged to retire from room to room, until at last they evacuated the whole house. During this time our men were re-enforced by a detachment from York's company, under command of Lieutenant Gill.

The cannonading from the camp was exceedingly heavy from all quarters during the day, but did no essential damage.

Our loss consisted of one captain seriously wounded, and two privates severely. At seven o'clock P. M., the party in Zambrano's Row were re-enforced by Captains Swisher, Alley, Edwards, and Duncan, and their respective companies.

This evening we had undoubted information of the arrival of a strong re-enforcement to the enemy, under Colonel Ugartechea. At 10½ o'clock P. M., Captains Cooke and Patton, with the company of New Orleans Grays and a company of Brazoria volunteers, forced their way into the priest's house in the square, although exposed to the fire of a battery of three guns and a large body of musketeers.

Before this, however, the division was re-enforced from the reserve by Captains Cheshire, Lewis, and Sutherland, with their companies.

Immediately after we got possession of the priest's house, the enemy opened a furious cannonade from all their batteries, accompanied by incessant volleys of small-arms against every house in our possession and every part of our lines, which continued unceasingly until 6½ o'clock A. M., of the 9th, when they sent a flag of truce, with an intimation that they desired to capitulate. Commissioners were immediately named by both parties, and herewith I accompany you a copy of the terms agreed upon.

Our loss in this night-attack consisted of one man only—Belden, of the Grays, dangerously wounded while in-the act of spiking a cannon.

To attempt to give you a faint idea of the intrepid conduct of the gallant citizens who formed the division under my command, during the whole period of attack, would be a task of no common nature, and far above the power of my pen. All behaved with the bravery peculiar to freemen, and with a decision becoming the sacred cause of Liberty.

To signalize every individual act of gallantry, where no individual was found wanting to himself or to his country, would be a useless and endless effort. Every man has merited my warmest approbation, and deserves his country's gratitude.

The memory of Colonel B. R. Milam, the leader of this daring and successful attack, deserves to be cherished by every patriotic bosom in Texas.

I feel indebted to the able assistance of Colonel Grant (severely wounded the first day), Colonel Austin, Majors Morris and Moore, Adjutant Bristow, Lieutenant-Colonel Franks, of the artillery, and every captain—names already given—who entered with either division, from the morning of the 5th until the day of capitulation.

Doctors Levy and Pollard also deserve my warmest praise, from their unremitted attention and assiduity.

Dr. Cameron's conduct, during the siege and treaty of capitulation, merits particular mention. The guides, Erastus Smith, Norwich, Arnold and John W. Smith, performed important service; and I can not conclude without expressing my thanks to the reserve under your command for such assistance as could be afforded me during our most critical movements.

The period put to our present war by the fall of San Antonio de Bexar will, I trust be attended with all the happy results to Texas which her warmest friends could desire.

I have the honor to subscribe myself your most obedient servant,

F. W. JOHNSTON, *Colonel Commanding.*

A true copy from the original.

WILLIAM T. AUSTIN, *Aid-de-camp.*

LIX.

REVOLUTION OF TEXAS IN 1812.

(From notes furnished by Col. W. D. C. Hall.)

In 1811 and 1812 Colonel W. D. C. Hall was residing at Nachitoches, and engaged in the study of law under the late distinguished Judge William Murray, who was then a practicing lawyer in the parishes of Nachitoches and Rapides. General Overton was then captain commanding the post at Nacogdoches, and Lieutenant Magee, as first lieutenant of artillery, was sent to aid the civil authorities in arresting a band of robbers who were making their headquarters on the east side of the Sabine. He succeeded in making prisoners of ten or twelve of them, who were sent to the penitentiary, and also twelve or fifteen others, who were sent for trial to Alexandria. He caused some of them to be whipped, to make them tell where the others were, by which he incurred the bitter ill-will of the whole party, and though nearly all of them afterward joined him in his expedition for revolutionizing Texas and throwing off the government of Spain, yet they always sought every opportunity to do him all the injury they could.

About this time, Magee had a quarrel with a Frenchman, and a duel with swords was the result; Judge Murray acting as the second of Magee. Magee had his little finger cut off, but, at the same time, he cut the Frenchman down with a heavy blow of his sword.

It was soon after this event that Magee conceived the plan of attempting to revolutionize this country, when he resigned his office in the army, and finally matured his measures in July, 1812, when his first step was to take possession of Nacogdoches with the small force he had been able to collect, composed in part of the very outlaws whom he had been sent to arrest. On his entrance into Nacogdoches, the royal troops evacuated the town, leaving him in undisputed possession. He remained there till the following September, during which time he recruited his troops till they numbered about three hundred. In September he set out on his expedition, taking the road to the La Bahia crossing of the Trinity below Robbin's Ferry. Here he remained, endeavoring to obtain re-enforcements, till some time in October, when he took up his line of march for La Bahia or Goliad. On crossing the Colorado where Columbus now is, the advanced guard met a Mexican with a led horse, and believing him to be a spy, they took him prisoner. He denied being a spy, and subsequent events proved that he told the truth. He said he was from La Bahia, and that Governor Salcedo and General

Herrera were at San Antonio with all their forces. After their arrival at La Bahia, all these statements proving true, the Mexican was released, and he subsequently fought bravely with the Americans.*

Proceeding from the Colorado crossing, the expedition arrived at Goliad on November 1st or 2d, 1812, and at once took possession of the town, as there was not a single soldier in the place. They could find but one old cannon, a nine-pounder, which they managed to mount on one of the bastions.† They immediately proceeded to fortify the place as well as they could, and prepare for its defense. On the 7th of November, they found themselves suddenly surrounded by the royal troops, 2,000 in number, commanded by Governor Salcedo in person, and General Herrera. These troops had left Goliad some time before and proceeded to San Antonio, and thence they had taken the old San Antonio road to the St. Mark's, expecting there to meet Magee's expedition. But finding that Magee had taken the lower or La Bahia road to Goliad, he then immediately struck across the country toward Goliad, which place he invested, as above stated, on the 7th. The royal troops were posted in three divisions around the fort, one on the east, one on the west, and another at the Mission on the north or opposite of the San Antonio River. On the evening of the 7th, Magee marched out and attacked the division at the Mission. After a short skirmish, night coming on, both parties retired without any decisive result.

The royal troops, finding they could effect nothing without heavier ordnance, waited till about the 15th or 20th, when they received nine splendid brass cannon which would throw shot a distance of three miles. But after trial, finding they could effect nothing against the strong walls of Goliad, from so great a distance, they began to approach nearer; finally, even coming into the town. Magee's force was just 365 men, with the one nine-pounder above named, and three or four carronades. It was about the 20th of November that the severe fight occurred that took place within the town and under the

---

* Yoakum says several spies were taken at the crossing of the Colorado, who gave information that Salcedo was in command at Goliad, while the truth is, he had not been there at all, nor was any such information given, the above-named Mexican being the only one taken, and the information he gave was quite the reverse.

† Colonel Hall here notices other errors in Yoakum's History, far Yoakum says Magee found 160 Spanish troops there and 16 pieces of ordnance, while Colonel Hall says the facts are as above stated. It is proper we should here remark, that our first compendium of the early history of Texas was chiefly compiled from Yoakum (see Texas Almanac for 1857). It is proper also to remark that Mr. Yoakum says he obtained his information of the events of this campaign from one McKim. Colonel Hall states that he knew this man perfectly well, and that he was a fit associate of the robbers with whom he had been connected at the Sabine, and that he was unworthy of credit. Colonel H. does not find a word of truth in Yoakum's account of this expedition, except what he obtained from the records.

15

walls of the fort, and lasted from eight or nine o'clock in the morning till two
P. M., when the royal troops hastily retreated from the town after suffering a
heavy loss in killed and wounded.   The actual number of the enemy's killed
was not known, as, according to their custom, they carried off their dead with
them when they retreated.   The Americans had seven wounded, but not
one killed.   Finding they could not take the town by assault, the enemy now
determined to invest the place closely and starve the Americans out.   The
investment continued till the 16th of February, during which time skirmishes
took place nearly every day, but there were only two general engagements.
One of these was on the 24th of January, and it was brought on in this way:
The main force of the enemy were posted on the opposite side of the river at
the Mission ; and while attempting to kill a white cow for beef, she made her
escape, running toward the river and in the direction of the fort on the opposite side, when one of Magee's companies attempted to capture the cow
from her pursuers, and crossed the river for that purpose.   This company
speedily came in conflict with the enemy, and soon after, the engagement
became general, and lasted some two hours, or until night came on, when
Magee's men retired, fording the river back again to the fort.   This engagement was afterward known as "The battle of the white cow."   The enemy's
loss was nearly 200, while the Americans lost but one killed, and had six
wounded.

The attempt to starve out the Americans was quite as ineffectual as the
attempt to take the place by storm.   For when Magee first took the town, he
found an abundant supply of corn, and several houses nearly filled with salt ;
so that by procuring beeves from time to time, during the siege, they were
amply supplied with food.   They obtained the beeves by sending out foraging parties at night, who proceeded a considerable distance, sometimes as
far as the Nueces, and having collected their cattle, they would then seize
their opportunity to drive them in between the divisions of the investing troops,
sometimes having to fight or kill the enemy's sentinels.   The cattle were
then in the greatest abundance and of the finest quality.

The last general engagement took place on the 10th of February, which
was brought about by a party from the fort attacking a picket of the enemy just
before day.   This attack soon brought on a general engagement, which lasted
till 4 P. M., during which time the enemy got possession of the town three
different times, and were as often compelled to retire, suffering severe loss in
each instance.   Having been driven, after the third assault, to the opposite
side of the river, they made no further demonstration, but continued in their
quarters there till the 16th, and then raised the siege, and commenced their
retreat toward San Antonio.

It was about the 1st of February that Magee died of consumption, having

MIRABEAU B. LAMAR.

See p. 258.

been suffering from that disease for a long time, and in consequence of his rapidly declining health, Colonel Kemper, the second in command, had, during most of the siege, directed the operations.* Colonel Hall knew Magee intimately. He was a native of Massachusetts, had been a regular graduate from West Point, and from the time he graduated was an officer in the United States army till he embarked in this expedition, at which time he was first lieutenant of artillery, and was universally esteemed as a chivalrous, high-minded, and strictly honorable man, of undoubted courage and intrepidity of character, possessing talents that eminently fitted him for a commander. On the death of Magee, the chief command devolved on Colonel Samuel Kemper, who had, in fact, been occupying that position for some weeks previously during Magee's sickness.

Soon after Magee's arrival at Goliad, information reached him that a report was in circulation to the effect that he and his men had been captured, and that, in consequence, several parties who were on their way to join him had returned home. This information induced him to send Major Reuben Ross, early in January, to contradict the report, and to bring all the re-enforcements he could. Ross proceeded as far as Nacogdoches, but as the men who intended to join Magee had generally dispersed, in consequence of the report referred to above, he could only get about twenty-five Americans and thirty Cooshatta Indians to return with him. These Indians were from the Trinity, and were commanded by their chief, Charles Rollins, a half-breed, whose father was then in Magee's army. The twenty-five Americans were commanded by James Gaines, who had been sheriff of one of the eastern parishes of Louisiana, and had just arrived in Texas.†

The small re-enforcement brought by Ross arrived a day or two after Salcedo commenced his retreat, when preparations were at once made to go in pursuit of the enemy. Kemper, having organized his whole force, set out on the 21st or 22d of February. It was not long after Salcedo's arrival in San Antonio before he heard of the approach of the Americans, when General Herrera

---

* Those who have read our first compend of the early history of Texas, will remember that it is there stated on Yoakum's authority, that Magee had, in private correspondence, agreed to capitulate to Salcedo : that Salcedo's letter to him referring to that agreement was read by Bernardo to the troops, who unanimously refused to assent to such an arrangement ; that Magee soon after died, either from mortification or by his own hands, etc. Colonel Hall states that there is not a word of truth in all this. He says that no such agreement was heard of in the army, nor was any such letter from Salcedo read to the troops.

† Here again Yoakum is in error, as he states that Gaines had joined Magee before he set out from the Trinity. Yoakum also says that the force of Magee amounted to about 800 men, whereas Colonel Hall asserts positively that it only amounted to 365, until after the accession of the 50 or 60 Americans and Indians brought out by Ross, and that even then, Americans and Indians all counted, the entire force was considerably short of 500.

immediately marched out the royal army to meet them, and took a position below the Salado, on the road leading directly from La Bahia to San Antonio. The American army however took the left-hand road by the way of the Missions of Espada and Concepcion. The enemy were posted not far above the forks of the two roads, and the first information the Americans had of the enemy was given by their right flank being fired on by a picket from the royal army. This soon brought on a general engagement ; the Americans forming in order of battle without a moment's delay. An order was given that, at the tap of the drum, a general charge should be made. The Indians being stationed on the extreme right, under the command of Major Ross, not understanding the order, made the charge sooner than they should have done, in consequence of which they suffered greatly, losing some of their principal men in a hand-to-hand fight ; but they fought with the most desperate courage, killing large numbers of the Mexicans. Meantime the Americans came up from the center and left, and made a general charge, after which it was not more than fifteen or twenty minutes before the enemy were routed and fled, in spite of every effort of their officers to rally them, leaving 330 men dead on the field, and 60 taken prisoners, together with six pieces of artillery and all their baggage. In this battle the enemy were commanded by Herrera in person, and his army, having received a re-enforcement after its arrival in San Antonio, numbered 2,500 strong. In this engagement, the officers of the enemy behaved with the utmost gallantry. Some of them, seeing they could not bring their men to fight, rushed forward sword in hand, determined to sell their lives as dearly as possible in single combat, and in consequence, a disproportionate number of officers was found among the dead. The Americans lost but six men killed and twenty-six wounded. This battle was on the 2d of March.

The royal army having retreated to San Antonio, the Americans, having taken possession of the Mission of the Concepcion, on the 3d proceeded to invest San Antonio. On the 4th, Salcedo sent a flag of truce and requested a parley. Colonel Kemper refused all terms except a surrender of his army as prisoners of war, and a delivery of the city into his possession. These terms were finally accepted, and on the 6th the Americans marched into the city, the Mexicans at the same time marching out, leaving their arms stacked. On the 7th, one of the most horrible and cold-blooded murders on record was perpetrated by the nominal commander-in-chief of the Americans, Bernardo Guterrés. This Mexican gave an order that Salcedo, Herrera, and ten of the other principal royalist officers, should be delivered up to a company of Mexicans commanded by Juan Delgado. At first the officers of the guard under whom these royalist officers were placed, refused to deliver them up, whereupon Bernardo got Colonel Kemper to sign the order, giving some reason or other to allay any apprehension of foul treatment. The order being signed by Kemper, the officers were accordingly delivered up to Delgado, who then immediately took them to the battle-ground of Salado, where he had their throats cut in the most horrible manner ; and their bodies, it was said, were thrown into the river. There was but one exception to this savage butchery, and this one was shot in compliance with his earnest entreaties. The reason assigned for this infamous atrocity by Delgado on his subsequent trial, was, that his father had been executed by Salcedo after been taken prisoner while fighting under Hidalgo, and that, besides, he had the order of Bernardo to perpetrate the act. Bernardo was then tried and deposed from office ; but many of the American officers became so disgusted with such brutality in the service that they soon after left, and among others, Colonel Hall, who then held a captaincy, to whom we are indebted for the foregoing narrative.

LX.

PHILIP NOLAN.

(Texas Almanac, 1868.)

PHILIP NOLAN, of Irish origin, and a citizen of the United States residing in Natchez, Mississippi, obtained a passport from the Baron de Carondelet, governor of Louisiana, July 17, 1797, to go to Texas, for the purpose of buying horses for the Louisiana regiment then being organized at New Orleans. He repaired to San Antonio de Bexar, where he made the acquaintance of the Governor of Texas, Don Manual Muñoz, and, through the kind offices of the latter, entered into a correspondence with General Pedro de Nava, then commanding the Spanish provinces, with headquarters at the city of Chihuahua.

A permit was granted Nolan to obtain the horses desired, both in the province of Texas and that of New Santander (now Tamaulipas, Mexico), and about the end of July, 1798, he took with him 1297 head, which he kept for awhile on the pasture grounds of the Trinity River. Soon after, he returned to Natchez.

The Viceroy of Mexico, Marquis de Branciforte, on the 12th of February, 1798, transmitted a communication from the Governor of Louisiana, Don Manuel Gayoso de Lemos, successor of the Baron Carondelet, to General Nava, requesting him, as of great importance to the service, to arrest any foreigners that might go into the Spanish provinces, because he was aware that some Americans intended to visit the country for the purpose of becoming friendly with the Indians and making a revolution. He desired Nolan to be closely watched. At that time, the movements of the English and Americans had created some suspicions, and it was thought that even the French designed to invade Louisiana.

On the 1st of June, 1799, the Governor of Louisiana, Gayoso de Lemos, addressed an official communication to the commanding general, Don Pedro Nava, recommending that no American should be permitted to reconnoiter the territory ; that he knew that some strangers had gone into Texas, and that the most dangerous was Philip Nolan, who, through deception, had obtained a passport from his predecessor, the Baron de Carondelet ; that Nolan was a hypocrite and a sacrilegious man ; that he professed to be a Catholic among Spaniards, and laughed at this religion when he was among Americans ; that it would be important to secure him, and dispose of him in such a manner that he might never be heard of ; that Nolan was commissioned by General Wilkerson—who had raised and educated him—to reconnoiter the country, draw maps, and make offers to the friendly Indians to rebel against the Spaniards.

On the 8th of August, 1800, the commanding general ordered the Governor of Texas to arrest Nolan, in case he returned to the province.

On the 6th of October, 1800, the commander of the post at Concordia, Louisiana, addressed an official communication to the military commander at Nacogdoches, informing him that Philip Nolan was (under the pretext of chasing wild horses) organizing an expedition of thirty or forty armed men to enter the territory of Texas ; that he had remonstrated with the authorities at Natchez, Mississippi, but he was satisfied that they would not discountenance the plans of Nolan. The above communication was forwarded from Nacogdoches to the commanding general at Chihuahua, who transmitted it to the viceroy.

The commander at Concordia, under date of December 13, 1800, forwarded a copy of the voluntary statement of Mordecai Richards, in which the latter declared, before the above-mentioned military authority, that he had left Natchez with Nolan and about thirty-four armed Americans and six or seven Spaniards ; that at Nogales (walnuts) they crossed the Mississippi, and Nolan told him (Richards) that he relied on him to guide them—he being well acquainted with the territory of Texas—which he promised, on account of the advantageous offers made by Nolan to him ; that thence they veered north-west ; that during their march he was obliged to hunt for the party ; that about six miles from the Wachita post, Nolan was detained by a party of militia-men, and Nolan sent a letter to the commander of the said post by the officer in command of the party ; that after the militia-men left, Mordecai Richards asked Nolan the reason why they had been stopped, when he (Nolan) had assured them that he had a permit to go into Texas ; that Nolan then called him aside and said to him : " You are a man on whom I rely to carry out my plans, and for that reason I have appointed you third in command. If we succeed, you will make your fortune. My plan is to travel north-west, and, passing the settlements of Caddo Indians, at a certain distance therefrom to build a fort, to protect us from any attack. Then we will sally forth to explore the country and its mines, and, after obtaining a sufficient number of horses, we will proceed to Islas Negras and Kentucky without finding any obstacles. There we will find many friends awaiting our arrival, and by that time I will receive authority to conquer the province of Texas. I will be the General, Mr. Fero the second, and yourself the third in command." That Richards became alarmed, and, soon after this conversation occurred, began to consider the dangers of the expedition, and determined to desert Nolan's party, although he had a son and a nephew in it.

Richards finally escaped, with two others, and, on his return to Natchez, made the foregoing statement to the military authority of Concordia.

After the events which we have briefly mentioned, Lieutenant M. Muzquiz was ordered to start in pursuit of Nolan, and he left Nacogdoches with that object on the 4th of March, 1801. The following is a diary of his march. (Force, 100 men : 68 regular army and 32 volunteers.)

"*March 4th.*—Left Nacogdoches early in the morning. Took the road leading to San Antonio, and camped at the Rancho de la Botija.

" *5th.*—Continued my march on the same road. Camped on La Rais creek.

" *6th.*—Arrived at the Terroros creek.

" *7th.*—Continued my march on the same road. About nine o'clock in the morning arrived at the Angelina River, which, having risen, I ordered some rafts to be made to cross it. Camped on its banks.

" *8th.*—At daybreak sent a corporal and six men to repair a wooden bridge on the Neches river, so as to facilitate our march. Left with the troops at eight o'clock in the morning. At one in the afternoon reached the Neches, and, the bridge being repaired, I crossed.

" *9th.*—Left the Neches at seven in the morning. About nine o'clock I quitted the San Antonio road, and, taking a course between north and west I arrived at San Pedro creek, where I camped for the night.

" *10th.*—Started early in the morning, and camped for the night at La Laguna.

" *11th.*—Left at seven in the morning, traveling west. About ten A. M. arrived at Trinity River, which, having risen, I ordered ten rafts to be made, to cross it. At sundown six Texas Indians joined us.

" *12th.*—At daybreak I sent four volunteers to the settlement of the Tahuacan Indians, on the Brazos River, in order that they might bring with them a captain of the Texas Indians called El Blanco, to show me the spot where Nolan was. The warrior refused to furnish me with the information desired. Continued traveling west. About noon passed a lagoon, and between it and the Kechi settlement I camped for the night.

"13th.—Continued traveling west. Passed, about nine in the morning, an abandoned settlement of Kechi Indians. About three P.M. arrived at Santa Maria de Gracia creek.

"14th.—Traveled from morning until one o'clock P. M., when I arrived at Los Piedros creek, and camped.

"15th.—Traveled north until about twelve o'clock M., when I turned west. About 4 P. M. I arrived at La Vibora creek, where I spent the night.

"16th.—Started at sunrise, course south. Passed through an abandoned settlement of Tahuacan Indians, whence I wended my way west. About three o'clock P. M. I arrived at the head of the Navasoto.

"17th.—At daybreak I started, course west. About eight A. M., I was informed by the sergeant commanding the vanguard that two persons on horseback had been seen, and that they had suddenly hid themselves in the thicket. I sent after them, and they were soon after found and brought before me. They proved to be two Indians. After some questions I asked them, they informed me that there were in that region about twenty-five men, with Nolan ; that all of them had long beards ; that, if I traveled fast, course west, I would get to the place where they were about sundown. The Indians told me that they would guide me on a route between north and west, so that I could get, without being seen, to the place where Nolan was. They said that the place was between the Monte Grande and the Brazos River. I camped for the night at the Arroyo del Atole.

"18th.—Started at daybreak, course between north and south. Traveled until two o'clock P. M., when I camped close to a spring.

"19th.—Traveled, course north, until about six o'clock P. M. Then I took course west, and stopped on the banks of the Blanco River. I sent seventeen men with the interpreter, Mr. Barr, to explore the place where Nolan was. They returned before daybreak, and informed me that they had found a wooden intrenchment and a pasture-ground, with some horses, on the banks of the Blanco. I immediately started, wending my way between west and south.

"20th.—At daybreak I arrived at the wooden intrenchment. Detained two Indians, who informed me that Nolan and his men were at a place between a creek and some hills, and that they had a house without roof. As soon as night closed, I started, guided by the Tahuaya Indians ; and, traveling all night, I arrived before daylight at the place where Nolan was, and, concealing our men behind a hill, awaited for the morning to act.

"21st.—At sunrise, having divided my force into three bodies—one commanded by me, and carrying a four-pounder, I marched on Nolan's intrench-ment. When I was at a distance of about thirty paces from it, ten men sallied from the intrenchment, unarmed. Among them was Nolan, who said, in a loud voice : 'No lleguen porque seremos muertos unos ú otros' ('Do not approach, because either one or the other will be killed'). Noticing that the men who accompanied Nolan were foreigners, I ordered Mr. William Barr, an Irishman, who had joined my command as interpreter, to speak to them in English, and say to them that I had come for the purpose of arresting them, and that I expected them to surrender in the name of the King. Nolan had a brief conversation with Barr, and the latter informed me that Nolan and his men were determined to fight. Nolan immediately entered his intrenchment, followed by his men, and I observed that two Mexicans (Juan José Martinez and Vicente Lara) escaped from the rear of said intrenchment. Soon after, they joined us, stating that they had brought with them Nolan's carbine, which was handed to me. At daybreak Nolan and his men commenced firing. The fight lasted until nine o'clock A. M., when, Nolan being killed by a cannon-ball, his men surrendered. They were out of ammunition. His force at the time of the engagement was composed of 14 Americans, 1 Creole of Louisi-ana, 7 Spaniards or Mexicans, and 2 negro slaves. Nolan had three men wounded and several horses killed. His men had long beards. After the surrender I learned that they had left Natchez with supplies for two months, and had been in the woods and prairies of Texas over seven months, living on horse meat. Nolan's negroes asked permission to bury their master, which I granted, after causing his ears to be cut off, in order to send them to the Governor of Texas.

"22d.—Remained at the same·place.

"23d.—Started for Nacogdoches."

Here ends the diary of Lieutenant Muzquiz.

Judging from the route taken by the Spanish commander, we are led to believe that Nolan and his men were camped between Limestone and McLennan counties, probably in the neighborhood of Springfield or Waco.

From the Mississippi River, whence Nolan started, to the place where he had his intrenchment, is an immense distance. He was in the desert, near the Chactas, Guazas, Tahuacan, Candacho, Taguayan, and Comanche tribes. There is no doubt that one of his plans was to gain the friendship of the Indians, to turn them against the Spanish government.

The following is the list of the men who followed Nolan :

Stephen Richards, from Pennsylvania, aged 20 years ; Simon McCoy, Pennsylvania, 25 ; Jonah Walters, Virginia, 26 ; Solomon Cooley, Kentucky, 25 ; Ellis Bean, North Carolina, 22 ; Joseph Reed, Pennsylvania, 26 ; Wil-liam Danlin, Pennsylvania, 27 ; Charles King, Maryland, 27 ; Joel J. Pierce,

North Carolina, 22 ; Thomas House, Virginia, 27 ; Ephraim Blackburn, Maryland, 35 ; David Fero, New York, 24 ; Vicente Lara, Mexico, 38 ; Refugio de la Garza, Mexico, 30 ; Juan José Martinez, Mexico, 31 ; José Jesus Santos, Mexico, 21 ; Lorenzo Hinojosa, Mexico, 34 ; Jose Berban, Mexico, 20 ; Luciano Garcia, 42 ; Juan Bautista and Robert, negro slaves.

The following, although belonging to Nolan's command, escaped, soon after the surrender, from the prison at Nacogdoches, to wit :

Robert Ashley, of South Carolina, aged 38 years ; John House, Virginia, 21 ; Michael Moore, Ireland, 25.

Joel J. Pierce died in prison.

Nolan's men were tried by the Spanish authorities as invaders of the country. The prosecuting attorney was Don Juan José Ruiz de Bustamante. The counsel for the defense was Don Pedro Ramos de Verea. The judge, Don Pedro Galindo de Navarro, on the 23d day of January, 1804, ordered their release ; but as General Nemesis Salcedo, commanding the provinces, objected to it, the proceedings were sent to the King of Spain, who, by a royal decree, dated at El Pardo, February 23d, 1807, ordered one out of five of Nolan's men to be hung, and the balance to suffer ten years of hard labor.

Simon McCoy, Stephen Richards, and Thomas House, who were out of the intrenchment at the time of the attack, were not to draw lots, but only those who fought the Spanish troops, to wit, Luciano Garcia, Jonah Walters, Solomon Cooley, Ellis Bean, Joseph Reed, William Danlin, Charles King, Joseph Pierce, Ephriam Blackburn, and David Fero.

Judge Galindo was ordered to be removed from his office ; but, when the royal decree was received, he had already died.

Here it is necessary to state that, when the king issued his decree to have one out of every five of Nolan's men executed, he was under the impression that the ten prisoners above alluded to were alive ; but as one of them (Joseph Pierce) had died, the new judge decided that only one out of the nine remaining was to suffer the penalty of death, which legal opinion was approved by General Salcedo.

DRAWING OF LOTS.

" In the town of Chihuahua, on the 9th day of the month of November, 1807, in compliance with a decree of His Majesty the King of Spain, transmitted to the commanding general of these provinces with a royal order of the 23d of February of said year, I, Don Antonio Garcia de Tejada, adjutant-inspector of the Internal Provinces of New Spain, proceeded to the barracks of said town, together with Don Pedro Ramos de Verea, counsel for the foreigners who invaded the country under Philip Nolan, and Don Juan José Diaz de Bustamante, prosecuting attorney ; and having caused the nine prisoners confined in said barracks to assemble in a room in order to draw lots so that one of them may be executed, after they knelt, I read the decree of His Majesty the King.

"The prisoners, having heard the same, agreed to throw dice ; that the oldest of them should throw first, and he who threw the smallest number should be hung.

"This agreement being made, a drum, a crystal tumbler, and two dice were brought, and I ordered the prisoners to kneel before the drum and be blindfolded.

"Ephraim Blackburn, being the oldest among the prisoners, took first the glass.

"The throwing was as follows :

"Ephraim Blackburn, 3 and 1, making 4 ; Luciano Garcia, 3 and 4, making 7 ; Joseph Reed, 6 and 5, making 11 ; David Fero, 5 and 3, making 8 ; Solomon Cooley, 6 and 5, making 11 ; Jonah Walters, 6 and 1, making 7 ; Charles King, 4 and 3, making 7 ; Ellis Bean, 4 and 1, making 5 ; William Danlin, 5 and 2, making 7."

Ephraim Blackburn, having thrown the smallest number, was hung at the Plaza de los Urangas, in the town of Chihuahua, on the 11th of November, 1807. Blackburn was a Quaker, and, before the execution, was converted to the Catholic religion, and baptized.

The balance of Nolan's men were sent to the different penal settlements of the provinces, the furthest from Louisiana, where they remained until 1818. It is believed that only Ellis Bean returned to the United States, the others having died after an imprisonment of eighteen years !

The diary kept by Nolan, and many of his letters, which are in my possession, show conclusively that he was not only a gallant and intelligent gentleman, but an accomplished scholar. He was thoroughly acquainted with astronomy and geography. He made the first map of Texas, which he presented to the Baron de Carondelet on returning from his first trip to Texas. Had he lived to see his plans carried out, Texas, the land he loved, would have been proud of him.

Nolan is buried in a spot between Springfield and Waco, where his fight with the Spaniards took place. If that spot could be found, it might not be inappropriate to mark it with a slab and the following inscription :

"SISTE, VIATOR, HEROEM CALCAS."

LXI.

THE LAST OF THE ALABAMAS.

(Telegraph, May, 1869.)

IT may not be generally known that remnants of the aborigines of Eastern Texas are still to be found in the middle section of the Trinity region; and, though surrounded by all the power and influence of civilization, they still retain the dress and the habits of the savage. One of these remnants at present inhabits a small and straggling village, some miles to the east of the county town, Livingston, on the Trinity. This little colony of aborigines numbers some two or three hundred souls; the members of it belong to the tribe of the Alabamas, and their number appears to be stationary. These red men live in rude huts without chimneys, the fire being built in the center of the dirt floor, and an opening in the roof serving as an exit for the smoke. All their instruments and utensils are of the rudest character; all their domestic arrangements are unlike those of their Anglo-Saxon neighbors; and these, as well as their daily habits and manners, smack of savage peculiarity and instinct. The men are usually dressed in buckskin trowsers, terminating in nicely sewed leggings, and the famous " moccasin." None of the tribe wear shoes. Along with their attire these Indians also retain that fine proportion of form, full development of muscle, that athletic beauty of figure and elastic ease of movement, which might be said to distinguish them from their puny white brethren.

The females of this " Indian village," as it is called, dress more in conformity to the Paris fashions than the men; being commonly habited in well-cut calico skirts, which show their tall and graceful shapes to advantage. A tasteful hood, of the same material as their dresses, usually surmounts the head, whence black clouds of hair are allowed to fall over the shoulders.

The women, like the men, are able to speak English even fluently; but the former, probably owing to some regulation of the tribe, never speak to strangers. But the full orbs of their dark and expressive eyes often convey to the pleased visitor a language as plainly as words could do.

These Indians have so far adopted civilized life as to depend for subsistence, not upon the chase like their ancestors, but upon the products of the farm, tilled in a rude way, and one peculiarly their own. Each of their huts is surrounded by a small field, in which corn is chiefly cultivated.

While they evidently desire no social commingling with the whites, the conduct of the Alabamas is extremely peaceable, even inoffensive, toward that race which, in its march to power, has despoiled them of their possessions, driven them from their romantic hunting grounds given them by the Great Spirit, and which is now pursuing the poor Indian to the precipice of his doom.

LXII.

WACO—A LEAF FROM ITS HISTORY.

(Waco Register).

WHEN or in what year the present city of Waco first became an Indian village, we are not informed. History has not recorded the year, and tradition is silent. But certain it is that the town itself is not wanting in some evidences of its great antiquity. Those old fortifications or earth-banks north of Austin street, in the neighborhood of Dr. McDonald's, and extending up-hill as far as Mr. George Barnard's, and which time has long since nearly leveled down to the surface of the earth, are mute witnesses which inform us of inhabitants or villagers who once dwelt here, and of dangers which begirt them. That oldest inhabitant, Mr. George Barnard, who came to Waco a little in advance of the on-coming tide of civilization, once informed us that Wacoes, Kechis, and Wichitas, all of whom probably passed under one general appellation of Wacoes, founded Waco.

An incident in the history of the Wacoes, occurring about the year 1824, may be here related :

" For be it remembered that these children of the forest were not destitute of those savage instincts of the red man, whose prominent characteristics were inextinguishable love of adventure, of danger, and of possessing themselves of their neighbors' ponies. They have from time immemorial kept up their raids upon their nearest (though remote) white or Mexican neighbors.

" While returning from one of their ill-starred expeditions to the Red River, the unhappy, because it proved to be fatal, idea occurred to them of bringing away the Cherokees' ponies, and probably some red captive Helen, which they did, and returned to their village with ' booty and beauty.' This feat they effected in true Indian style, a circumstance which so enraged the warlike Cherokees that they soon presented themselves, all painted for war, at the Wacoes' village. The Wacoes now defended themselves in their fortifications with probably true Trojan valor ; but the incensed Cherokees, led on by their Agamemnons and Nestors, so furiously assaulted the besieged in their intrenchments, that they compelled them to flee to the mountains, leaving their dead and wounded behind. The village was then plundered and burned—and the history of this beautiful village became that of ancient Troy—*Troja fuit.*"

LXIII.

ABORIGINAL ANTIQUITIES OF TEXAS

BY J. H. KUYKENDALL, ROCKPORT.

THE authentic history of the western hemisphere only reaches back between three and four centuries ; hence the term " prehistoric," when applied to American antiquities, does not always imply that they correspond in age with the prehistoric remains of the old world, whose history embraces thousands of years. But writers on American archæology do not, I believe, designate as prehistoric any memorials that are referable to the existing race of aborigines, but only such as are believed to have belonged to races that have passed away, and which may be supposed to correspond in antiquity with many of the prehistoric relics of the other hemisphere.

The prehistoric remains of man and his arts found in the *tumuli* of the Mississippi valley indicate that that country was once inhabited by a more civilized people than the red men ; yet the former may not have preceded the latter in the occupation of this continent, for the flint arrow-heads found in innumerable localities throughout this State (and indeed throughout this continent), buried in some instances several feet beneath the surface in alluvium, attest the presence here of the red race untold ages before the advent of the " pale-faces." These tiny monuments of the American aborigines are, in fact, more enduring than the pyramids of Egypt, and thousands of years hence they will continue to be turned up by the plow of the farmer, looking almost as fresh and untarnished as when they were first wrought from the pebbles in the early ages of human existence.

Though the prehistoric people of America—or, at any rate, those of the Mississippi valley—do not seem to have emerged from the stone cycle, and, therefore, in common with our aborigines, probably pointed their weapons with stone, yet, as we find no traces of their abodes in Texas, we may reasonably attribute the fabrication of the flint arrow-heads, which are so abundant here, to the Indian race.

In my frequent walks, some years since, along the beaches of the bays and inlets, a few miles south of the Guadaloupe River, I rarely failed to find a number of these aboriginal relics—especially immediately after the ebb of a very high tide. I have also found many about the bases of the sandy hillocks, or " dunes," which have been heaped up by the winds in many places along the coast. I have occasionally found one large enough for the arrow of a Titan; but these were probably used for harpoons. Some of these arrow-heads are very rudely wrought, while others, particularly a very small kind, are of exquisite finish, with a point as sharp as a lancet, and the cutting edges finely and beautifully serrated. One can not but wonder how they were wrought with the imperfect tools of the Indians. Most of the specimens collected by me had necks or shanks by which they were fitted into the shaft; a few, however, were without this appendage, but were either grooved or beveled on both sides of the base of the tongue.

It is not improbable that other tribes occupied the littoral hunting-grounds, before the Carankawas, or, at any rate, at some period shared them conjointly with the latter. The various tribes probably possessed various degrees of skill in the manufacture of flint weapons; hence the marked differences in design and finish among them. The earlier or later age in which they were wrought may also have had its influence.

The flint pebbles from which these arrow-heads were chipped were probably obtained from thirty to forty miles inland, where they abound in several localities.

All the Indian tribes of Texas, when it was first colonized by Americans, used metallic arrow-heads, which they had probably substituted for flint ones nearly a century before, or not long after the establishment of the missions and military posts of San Antonio and La Bahia, where they doubtless obtained copper, brass, and iron, all of which metals they used for pointing their missiles. Fragments of earthen pottery are co-extensive with the flint relics. But they bear evidence that our aborigines were never much skilled in the ceramic art.

The Indian dead usually receive very shallow sepulture. Often the Texas tribes do not bury their dead at all, but merely pile logs or stones upon the bodies, which are soon extricated and the flesh devoured by beasts of prey. The bones being thus left to the action of the elements, rapidly decay. Hence the osseous remains of the aborigines are rarely found far inland; but in various places along the coast the winds have performed the rites of sepulture by blowing the sand upon the dead. At Ingleside, in 1861, human bones were disinterred at two localities more than a hundred yards apart, from a depth of eight feet; and recently (in October, 1867), a little Golgotha was discovered in a sand-hill, or " dune," near what is locally known as the " False Live-Oak " in Refugio county. About a month after the discovery, I went to the house of Mr. C——, who resides within a hundred paces of the place of skulls, and upon inquiring of Mrs. C——

(her husband not being at home), she informed me that a large quantity of human bones, including several skulls, had been exposed by the caving of the "dune"; but being much decayed, they broke to pieces in falling, and quickly dissolved in the tide at the base of the "dune." Mrs. C—— added that the bones had all caved in and disappeared, but bade her little son Tommy, about eight years of age, go with me and point out the spot where they had been found. When we had got near the hill, Tommy exclaimed, "Oh! how the sand has caved since I was here before." When we arrived at the spot, I looked up and beheld for forty feet along the face of the steep slope, from which the sand had slidden, a number of human bones projecting at various angles. The skulls, of which three were exposed, looked like brown cobble-stones. Tommy's squirrel-like agility enabled him to reach the skulls sooner than I, and in his eagerness to extract them from the sand-bank, he broke two of the rotten ones in pieces, but the third one, being in a better state of preservation, received no damage from his rather violent handling. This skull was of medium size, and remarkably round. The others seemed of similar size and type. The teeth of all were well preserved, and did not exhibit any appearance of having been faulty during the life-time of the owners. None of the bones semed to have belonged to persons above the average size, with the exception of one *femur*. Neither the vertebral nor pelvic bones, the ribs, the omoplates, nor the bones of the hands and feet, were preserved. These human remains were from five to seven and a half feet beneath the surface of the ground, and ten or twelve feet above the level of the bay.

After an interval of six weeks, I again visited the spot. About two feet of the hill had caved away since my first visit; but the bone deposit was still unexhausted, for I found three more skulls and several limb bones, all of which broke into fragments in extracting them from the compact sand.

Aware of a custom among many Indian tribes to bury the arms of the dead with them, I was disappointed in not finding stone arrow-heads in the caved sand. But my search for them was not thorough. There is no reason, however, to doubt that these are aboriginal remains, and very ancient ones too. Their imperfect state of preservation in a kind of earth very conservative of organic substances alone warrants this conclusion, which is reënforced by an argument which I will here state. These remains are found at the southern extremity of a sand-ridge, or dune, about two miles in length from north to south, and varying in height from twenty to forty or fifty feet, and which was evidently formed while the gulf beat directly upon the shore of the mainland. But ever since the long, sandy islands extending parallel with our coast were heaped up by the action of the waves and currents of the sea, the only communication between the interior bays or lagoons has been through a few narrow channels called "bayous." The consequence is, that the sandy materials of which the "dunes" are formed, instead of reaching the shore of the mainland as in former ages, are now deposited on the gulf side of the islands and blown up by the east and south-east winds into hillocks similar to, but generally less elevated than, those which were formerly heaped by the same agency upon the mainland.

Now, on the assumption that these human remains, in accordance with the univeral custom of North American savages, were only interred to the depth of two feet at most, several feet of sand must subsequently have been blown over them to account for the depth at which they were found, and the sand for this purpose must have been transported to the adjacent beach by the currents of the gulf. Hence I conclude that these remains were deposited in the dune before the gulf was cut off from the mainland by the formation of the chain of island barriers above-mentioned. The length of time that has elapsed since that event occurred can only be conjectured, but it doubtless amounts to centuries. The sand-ridge containing the osseous relics has been preserved from the wasting effects of the winds by the thickets of dwarf oak and sweet bay with which it is overgrown. Some of the live-oaks at its eastern base are of sufficient girth to indicate an age of two centuries. Other oaks of the same species, a short distance south of the "dunes" and very near the bay, are of much greater antiquity. All these trees must have grown up since the gulf retreated behind Matagorda Island, which, at this point, is about eight miles distant from the mainland. From all of which it follows as highly probable that the human remains which I have described were inhumed at a period when the broad waves of the sea resounded along the shore of the mainland, and before the sail of a ship had gleamed on the Gulf of Mexico or the foot of a civilized man had pressed the soil of the American continent.

16

LXIV.

FANNIN'S MASSACRE.—ACCOUNT OF THE GEORGIA BATTALION.

THE following letter from Captain Kennymore, who was among the few survivors of the Massacre of the Georgia Battalion at Goliad, in 1836, gives assurance that the accompanying account of that massacre is correct, and we have additional authority for giving the subjoined list of the killed, and survivors, as entirely correct.

CITY OF GALVESTON, TEXAS, February 5, 1836.

EDITORS OF TEXAS ALMANAC.

GENTLEMEN: Accompanying this note you will please find a roll of Colonel Fannin's command, which I look upon as correct. It has been in my possession years, and deeming it an act of justice to the lamented dead, hope you will publish it in your next issue. Also, in giving a description of the battle of the Mission del Refugio, Lieutenant-Colonel William Ward (of Georgia), commanding, I inclose a letter of Mr. Samuel T. Brown, a nephew of Colonel Ward, giving a narrative of the battle, etc.

It appears to me that the world at large, and the people of Texas in particular, should know something that would throw light upon the movement of Colonel Fannin. Mr. Brown's description of the battle of the Mission del Refugio is correct, also in regard to the order for Colonel Fannin to abandon Goliad, of which so much has been said.

I fully corroborate the statements of Mr. Samuel T. Brown as to the time the order reached Colonel Fannin at Goliad. It was on the night of the 12th March, 1836, the Georgia Battalion was ordered to go to the relief of Captain King, who had been sent out for the purpose of protecting the women and children at the Mission. A good number of us were on camp-guard the night of the 12th, and our officer of guard was Captain Jack Shackelford, who had us relieved by details from other companies, and told us to hurry off and be back soon, as General Sam Houston had ordered Colonel Fannin to abandon and blow up the Fort at Goliad and join him at Victoria.

These are all the facts pertaining to that transaction that I know of. I can refer you to the only survivors that I now know to be living. General Samuel G. Hardaway, of Bullock's Cove, now living in Montgomery City Alabama; Thomas I. Smith, Richmond, Texas; A. J. Hitchcock, of Shreveport, Louisiana; and L. P. Tresvant, of Carroll Parish, Louisiana; these are the survivors.

Such as it is, is at your service, and I can bear testimony as to the skill and ability of Colonels Fannin and Ward as military men, and at all times subordinate to their superiors. Misfortune befell them; bloody scenes followed: and I hope their memory will be spared and held sacred by the patriotic people of Texas. Respectfully,

J. C. P. KENNYMORE,

Late Captain 1st Reg. Texas Inf. in the days of the Republic.

The following letter was addressed by Mr. S. T. Brown, to his uncle, Thomas Ward, Esq., brother of the late Colonel Ward of the Texas Army, and appeared first in the *Voice of Sumpter* (an Alabama newspaper), of November 28, 1839. It was written at the suggestion of a friend, who gives the following summary of the various companies, showing what disposition was made of each:

Company.	Detained.	Escaped.	Killed.
1. Duval's	1	5	38
2. King's	2	0	20
3. Pettus'	2	5	32
4. Bullock's	9	2	26
5. Winn's	1	0	37
6. Wadsworth's	4	1	20
7. Ticknor's	3	0	36
8. Wyatte's	1	1	26
9. Westoover's	2	0	42
10. Burke's	3	3	28
11. Shackleford's	0	3	52
12. Horton's	2	6	21
Field officers	3	0	7
Total,	35	55	385

Speaking of Mr. Brown, the writer says:

"Having formed his acquaintance soon after his return from Mexico, I suggested to him the propriety of publishing a narrative of his adventures in the form of a letter to Thomas Ward, Esq., brother of the late Colonel Ward of the Texan Army. Viewing it as a piece of history to be relied on, I desire you to give it circulation in your columns. Mr. Brown was a young gentleman of intelligence and veracity. He is now dead. I always attributed the kindness with which he was treated by the Mexican general, to his rare personal beauty—his dark, piercing eyes, his bronze complexion and graceful figure giving him the appearance of a Spanish cavalier. He was a native of Georgia and a nephew of Colonel Ward."

25

Mr. Brown's letter is as follows:

LIVINGSTON, ALABAMA, November 1, 1837.

DEAR SIR: Having been among the first who volunteered from Georgia in the service of Texas, under the command of your brother, the late Colonel William Ward, whose name is destined to occupy a place in history, I have thought that a communication of my adventures in a form you might preserve, would not be unacceptable or improper. All I have in view is to give the facts which came within my own observation and knowledge; and if they can be deemed of interest as occurring to one of my years (twenty at the present time), I shall feel perfectly satisfied in having related them.

About the 20th November, 1835, I left Macon in the stage for Columbus, where I joined Captain Ward's company, which had rendezvoused at that place, from whence we marched to Montgomery, Alabama, and took passage for Mobile on the steamer *Ben Franklin*. Remaining in Mobile five or six days, near which a public dinner was given us, we embarked on the steamer *Convoy* for New Orleans, where we halted about a week, and received some addition to our number, making the company about a hundred and fifty strong. Here Captain Ward laid in supplies for his men, and chartered' the schooner *Pennsylvania* to take them to Velasco, where we arrived on the 20th of December, 1835, and found Captain Wadsworth's company, fifty strong; and the two companies were organized into a battalion, of which Captain Ward was elected major, called the Georgia Battalion. Captain Ward's original company was divided into two equal parts, as near as practicable the command of one of which was given to Captain Uriah J. Bullock, of Macon, and that of the other to Captain James C. Wynne, of Gwinette county. Major Ward lost no time in reporting in person his battalion to Governor Smith at San Felipe de Austin. Our troops encamped about two miles from Velasco, on the Brazos River, where they subsisted on the two months' provision laid in at New Orleans. After a week's absence to the seat of government, Major Ward returned with commissions for the several officers. We remained in the camp near Velasco, until 1st February, 1836, when the battalion was ordered by the then acting Governor Robinson, to repair to Goliad on the San Antonio River, and it was forthwith transported by the schooner *Columbus*, United States vessel, to Copano, on Aransas Bay, after five days' passage. There we were furnished with supplies by the government and four pieces of artillery, two six and two four-pounders. From Copano to Goliad the distance is forty-five miles, and about half-way the battalion halted at the Mission, where we were joined by Captain Ticknor's company, of Montgomery, Alabama, making our ranks about two hundred and fifty strong. From there we marched to Goliad, took possession, and repaired the fort, and were joined by the Lafayette Battalion, made up from North Alabama, Tennessee, and

Kentucky. Previous to this, the lamented Colonel Fannin had not taken any part in service, but was actively engaged in collecting and diffusing information highly useful to the cause of Texas. At Goliad the two battalions were formed into a regiment, between five and six hundred strong, of which Fannin was elected colonel and Ward lieutenant-colonel; Dr. Mitchell, of Columbus, commanded the battalion in the place of Major Ward, promoted.

For some purpose Captain King, of the Lafayette Battalion, had been dispatched by Colonel Fannin to occupy the Mission, about twenty-two miles off, who found himself annoyed in his new position by a party of Mexican cavalry and sent an express to Goliad for a re-enforcement. Lieutenant-Colonel Ward, with one hundred and twenty men, of which I was one of the number, was directed by Colonel Fannin to support Captain King at the Mission. This was on the 12th March, and the next day Lieutenant-Colonel Ward's command reached the Mission, at which a large Catholic church built of stone, made a very good fort, in which we took protection. The Mexican cavalry that reconnoitered the Mission and tried to attack it was estimated at two hundred, and on the night of the 19th, a party of fourteen men under Captain Micknor, surprised their camp, a mile from the Mission, killing eight of them and putting the rest to flight. Among the slain was recognized a Mexican lieutenant who had been with Colonel Fannin at Goliad, pretending to have joined the Texans with eighteen men. On the morning of the 16th, Lieutenant-Colonel Ward and Captain King differed as to who should command at the Mission, the latter claiming it by being there first. A large majority of the troops declared they would serve under Lieutenant-Colonel Ward only, which induced Captain King, with his original company of twenty-eight men, to withdraw, and he was followed by eighteen of Lieutenant-Colonel Ward's command, who had been detailed from Captain Bradford's company at Goliad, leaving Colonel Ward one hundred and seven men. About ten o'clock in the morning, a party of fifteen, with myself, was sent to a river about two hundred yards off, with oxen and cart, to bring two barrels of water into the fort. We had just filled the vessels and were leaving the river when we were fired upon from an open prairie on the other side by General Urrea's army of eleven hundred men, about half a mile distant. We made all possible speed for the fort, holding on to the water, except about half a barrel, which was let out by one of the bullets piercing the head. The enemy kept firing as they crossed the river, and marched within fifty paces of the church, when Colonel Ward ordered his men to fire, which drove the Mexicans back and left the ground pretty well spotted with their dead and wounded. They made four regular charges both cavalry and infantry, about half of each, and were as often repulsed with great slaughter.

At four o'clock in the afternoon they retreated, leaving between four and five hundred of their dead upon the field. Colonel Ward had only three of his men wounded, one of them an Irishman who resided at the Mission. When the attack was made in the morning, Colonel Ward sent an express (James Humphrey, of Columbus, Georgia) to Colonel Fannin at Goliad ; and orders were received at ten o'clock at night, to abandon the church, take a northeast course for Victoria, on the Guadaloupe, twenty-five miles beyond Goliad, where Colonel Fannin would join him. About twelve o'clock at night we left the fort silently, formed five deep, marched without a guide in the open prairie, and were only eight miles from the Mission at day-light. For two days we had nothing to eat, and on the third we killed some cattle near the San Antonio, which revived us a good deal. On the 21st of March we reached Victoria, and had advanced within one hundred yards of the town, expecting to find Colonel Fannin and his men there, when to our utter dismay it was in possession of the enemy, who fired upon and caused us to retreat to the swamp. Colonel Fannin had set out to meet us in due time, but his whole command was taken prisoners by a large force within six miles of Goliad, and carried back to the fort. We had expended all our ammunition at the battle of the Mission, and very few of our men had a single cartridge ! In this dilemma we marched a night for Dimmit's Point on the La Bacca River, near Matagorda Bay, where supplies were landed for the Texan troops.

Next day, 22d March, we halted to rest and conceal ourselves within two miles of our destination, sent two men to the Point to see who was in possession and await their return. The remnant of the Mexican army that attacked the Mission, which was hovering over this quarter under General Urrea, took the two men prisoners and surrounded us. The two men came within speaking distance of us, stated our situation and the power of the enemy, and desired Colonel Ward to see General Urrea upon the terms of surrender : upon which Colonel Ward, Major Mitchell, and Captain Ticknor, had an interview with General Urrea and returned, making known to us the offer of the enemy, if we surrendered prisoners of war, that we should be marched to Copano without delay, and from thence to New Orleans, or detained as prisoners of war and be exchanged. Colonel Ward addressed his men and said he was opposed to surrendering ; that it was the same enemy we had beaten at the Mission, only much reduced in numbers, and that he thought our chance of escape equally practicable as it was then. He proposed that the attack on us might be evaded until night, when he might *possibly* pass the enemy's lines and get out of danger. At all events, he thought it best to resist every inch, as many of us as could save ourselves, and if we surrendered, he had doubts of the faith and humanity of the Mexicans ; that he feared we should all be *butchered*. The vote of the company was taken, and a large majority were in favor of surrendering upon the terms proposed ; Colonel Ward informed them that their wishes should govern, but if they were destroyed, no blame could rest on him.

The same officers as before, to wit : Colonel Ward, Major Mitchell, and Captain Ticknor, again saw General Urrea, and I understood a paper was signed by the Mexican general, to dispose of us as above stated, on condition that we should never serve Texas any more ; one copy in Spanish, and another in English. Then came the hour for us to see all our hopes entirely blasted. We marched out in order and grounded arms, cartouch-boxes, and weapons of every kind. Our guns were fired off, the flints taken out, and returned to us to carry. When we left the Mission, on the night of the 14th of March, we had about a hundred men ; at the time of the surrender we had only eighty-five, the others having left us on the route from the Mission to Victoria—a most fortunate thing for them. We were put under a strong guard, and the next morning, 23d March, proceeded to Victoria, where we were engaged the next day in bringing the baggage of the Mexican army across the Guadaloupe, about four hundred yards from the town, and hauling it up. On the morning of the 22d, we were marched toward Goliad, where we arrived next day late in the evening. There we found Colonel Fannin and his regiment prisoners in the fort. All the Texan troops then in the fort as prisoners, belonging to Fannin's command, after we were brought in, amounted to four hundred and eighty men. Early on the morning of the 27th, we were all marched into line and counted, and divided into four equal parts of one hundred and twenty each. The nearest to the door of the fort marched out first, and were received by a strong guard and placed in double file, going we knew not whither nor for what purpose. I was in this division, in the right-hand file, and about half a mile from the fort we were ordered to halt ; the guard on the right then passed to the left, and instantly fired upon the prisoners, nearly all of whom fell, and the few survivors tried to escape by flight in the prairie and concealing in the weeds. The firing continued, and about the same time I heard other firing toward the fort and the cries of distress.

At the time our division of prisoners was shot, Drury H. Minor, of Houston county, Georgia, immediately on my left, was killed; and just before me, next in file, Thomas S. Freeman, of Macon, was killed. As I ran off, several poor fellows, who had been wounded, tried to hide in the clump of weeds and grass, but were pursued, and I presume killed. Soon after I made my escape, I was joined by John Duval and —— Holliday, of the Kentucky volunteers, both of whom were with me at the massacre, but not until I had swum across the San Antonio, about half a mile from the butchery.

For five days we had nothing to eat except wild onions, which abound in the country ; when reaching the Guadaloupe found a nest of young pigs, and these lasted us several days. In the course of a few days, wandering at random in the open country, often wide of our supposed direction, we saw fresh signs of cavalry, and withdrew to the swamp, but had been perceived going there, and were taken by two Mexicans armed with guns and swords; that is, Duval and myself were captured; Holliday lay close and was not discovered. One of the men seized me and held on; Duval was placed between them, to follow on. He sprang off and one man threw down his gun and ran after him in vain. Duval made his escape, and I have not seen him since. I was taken to their camp close by, when they saddled their horses in a hurry and rode off without me. From their actions I judged they were of opinion a party of Texans was near, and so made off. I then went to the swamp where I was taken, and found Holliday in his old position. Next day we came to a deserted house on the La Bacca River, apparently that of an American settler, where we found plenty of provisions, such as meat, corn, lard, chickens, and eggs, upon which we feasted there two days, camping at night a little way off. Taking with us a good stock of provisions, we traveled quite refreshed, and in four days reached the Colorado. From almost constant rain and exposure, I had lost the use of my right arm and shoulder, and could not swim the river. Holliday swam across with the provisions, and promised to return and help me; but he was so weak and exhausted from the cold and rapid current, that he was not able to do so. Thus we parted, and I never saw him afterward.

I went up the river, and next day found a canoe, in which I crossed, and then wandered till I got sight of the Brazos, on the 20th April, where I was taken by a party of twenty Mexican cavalry, who carried me to the main army at Ford Bend, under General Sesma, and put me under guard with other prisoners they had picked up. I recollect the names of but three of them, and they had resided several years in Texas: Johnson, from New York, Leach, an Englishman, and Simpson. Fort Bend was about thirty miles from San Jacinto, where the battle was fought the next day, 21st April. The night after the battle a Mexican officer, who escaped from San Jacinto, brought the news into camp, and the army instantly retreated. When I was brought to the camp, I pulled off my boots to dry, and relieve my swollen feet; my boots were stolen, and I had to march barefoot through the mud and water, nearly knee-deep all over the prairies, the rain falling in torrents pretty much all the time. The army returned to Victoria, where I saw four of the Macon company, who had been detained there after the surrender, on account of their being mechanics : William Wilkinson, John C. P. Kinnymore, —— Barnwell, and Callahan.

I was then taken to Goliad, where I remained five days, and saw the places where the four divisions of prisoners had been butchered; some of the carcasses remained, many burnt, and others mangled; all so disfigured that I could recognize no particular person. A company of eighty-two men, from Tennessee, under Captain Miller of Texas, who had been taken prisoners the moment they landed at Copano, and whom we left in the fort at Goliad at the massacre, still remained there on my return. One of its members, Mr. Coy, told me the particulars of Ward and Fannin's death, as he said he was an eye-witness. After all the men had been shot, the time of the officers came. Colonel Ward was ordered to kneel, which he refused to do ; he was told, if he would kneel his life might be spared. He replied, they had killed his men in cold blood, and that he had no desire to live ; death would be welcome. He was then shot dead. Colonel Fannin made an address to the Mexican officer in command, through an interpreter; handed him his gold watch, to be sent to Colonel Fannin's wife, also a purse to the officer to have him decently buried. He sat on a chair, tied a handkerchief over his eyes and requested that he might not be shot in the head, and that the marksmen should stand far enough off for the powder not to burn him. He was shot in the head and expired.

Leaving Goliad in the month of May, with a dozen other Texan prisoners, under a guard of cavalry attached to the main army, then about three thousand strong, we marched to San Patricio on the Nueces River, where Colonels Teale and Carnes, of the Texan service, came under a flag of truce, and obtained passports from General Felisola to go to Matamoras, where Colonel Teale informed me I should be discharged. I was kept with the main army, until General Felisola received orders from Mexico to hasten there. He took with him a body-guard through the Indian country, about fifty cavalry, who had charge of me ever since leaving Goliad, and they still held on to me. Generl Felisola left his guard at Saltillo, and took the stage to the City of Mexico, where the cavalry arrived with me, their only prisoner, in August, 1836. I was then confined in the Quartede, or barracks, until the 1st of February, 1837, and about that time General Felisola expected to leave the city to take command of the army at Mata- moras. His interpreter, an Italian named Quarri, often visited the barracks and treated me with great humanity. He said he would get my release, and took me to General Felisola's house to accompany him to Matamoras. From some delay he did not start until the 28th of March, during which time I was a member of the family and treated with perfect kindness, under orders, however (for my own safety, it was said), not to leave the guard alone.

I may be allowed to say a few words about the City of Mexico and the manner of my detention. I was put in the barracks among a number of Mexican prisoners, who were confined for various offenses ; and from the time I entered, in August, 1836, until I went to General Felisola's house, in February, I had no other food than boiled beef.

The water in the barracks was fresh and pure, brought there by an aqueduct which supplies the whole city twelve miles from the mountains. The city itself is quite pleasant, clean, and the buildings durable, if not elegant. What I viewed as a great blemish to the houses (which were nearly all of stone and rock), were the images of saints and idols carved in endless variety.

On the 25th March last I left the City of Mexico in company with General F., his staff, and a small guard, and arrived at Matamoras the 1st of June, a distance of nine hundred miles from one place to the other. General F., it was said, declined the invasion of Texas with his army, on hearing of the death of General Montezuma at San Luis, and sent a large portion of it to quell the insurgents. On the 17th June, General F. gave me a passport, and on the 1st of July I embarked for New Orleans on the schooner *Comanche*, Captain Briddle, where I arrived in due time.

This unpretending narrative is at your service, and you have my permission to make what use of it you think proper.

I am, very respectfully, your obedient servant,

S. T. BROWN.

THOMAS WARD, Esq., Sumter Co., Ala.

PART II.

BIOGRAPHY.

NOTE.

THE biographical part of this book is as complete as the author has been able to make it. Special notices of other early Texans would have been inserted, had the undersigned been able to procure the necessary information. And he takes this occasion to ask all who are interested in the collection and preservation of material for Texas history, to send him, for future use, such unpublished facts as may be known to them.

D. W. C. BAKER.

DISTINGUISHED TEXANS.

STEPHEN F. AUSTIN.*

THIS distinguished man, who was the first successful American colonist to Texas, was a native of Austinville, Virginia, 1793.

When only eleven years old he went to Connecticut to pursue his academical studies.

Entering Transylvania University in 1808 he advanced with rapidity and graduated with distinction. Previous to this time, his family had removed to Missouri.

In 1813, Austin being twenty years old, he was elected to the territorial Legislature of Missouri, and was annually reëlected to that position until 1819, when he removed to Arkansas.

His father, Moses Austin, having received a grant of land in Texas from the Mexican authorities for colonization purposes, went to that country to prosecute his undertaking ; but, dying soon after, he bequeathed his darling scheme to his son Stephen, with instructions to carry it to a successful termination.

Accordingly, Colonel Austin, having obtained, after many delays and difficulties, all the guarantees possible from the treacherous and ever-fickle Mexican government, introduced at different times a large number of substantial colonists from the United States.

To these settlers were given, at a mere nominal price, grants of land for their permanent homes. During all the years of Austin's intercourse with his people, to whom he was a protector and a father, he was beloved and respected by them all.

Honesty and straightforward and conscientious dealing were the qualities which secured to him their esteem and confidence.

* See Frontispiece.

Says one who knew him well, and by whose pen a well-written sketch of Austin has been indited, " He was known and beloved by all. Every child of every colonist was known to him, was eager to welcome him, and to be permitted to play upon his knee."

When Austin entered Texas in 1821, there was but one settlement from the Sabine to San Antonio. This was at Nacogdoches.

No sound of the settler's axe had ever waked the echoes from the forests of the Brazos to the hills of the Colorado. Austin first planted upon the banks of these rivers the cabins of the Anglo-Saxon, and opened the vast wilderness to the plough of the husbandman.

When Austin counseled peace, the voice of discord was hushed throughout his colony. When his voice was raised for resistance every rifle within its borders was taken from its rest to do his bidding.

After devoting the best years of his life to the consummation of the great plan to which he had devoted himself with untiring assiduity, he was seized with a violent disease at Columbia, Brazoria Co., and there died December 25, 1836, in the forty-fifth year of his age.

Much that is interesting in his life must necessarily be omitted here. His long and perilous pilgrimages to Mexico in the interest of his people ; his exertions to obtain for them the fulfilment of the pledges made to him ; his unwarrantable detention and imprisonment in Mexico ; his unwillingness to counsel his people to take up arms against that government, while a vestige of hope for peace remained ; his firm and decided voice, speaking words of encouragement and hope during the dark hours of war ; his laborious travels in the United States to obtain needed succor for his struggling countrymen—all these afford ample material for a volume of absorbing interest.

But let this suffice. His name and his fame belong to Texas ; and no blot ever rested upon either. To him justly belongs the name " The Father of Texas."

HOUSTON PIERCED WITH AN ARROW.

To face p. 255.

SAM HOUSTON.

THE subject of this sketch was born in Rockbridge county, Virginia. When yet a child, his parents moved to the mountains of Tennessee, where he was reared. His ancestors were of Scotch origin. His mother is said to have been a lady of much beauty, and high degree of intellectual culture. She was also noble and benevolent, and ever ready to sacrifice her own comfort to those whose wants or sufferings excited her sympathy.

Houston was a sad truant when a school-boy. The schools amid his native hills were not numerous, nor of a first-class character, and his delight was rather in the chase of the deer than in the haunts of knowledge. When thirteen years old his father died, and his mother moved, with her large family, to Tennessee.

Here the boy Sam became acquainted with the Cherokee Indians, who lived near by his home, and much of his time was spent with them in the chase.

This was much more to his liking, than studying, or working on the farm. Much of Houston's early life, indeed, till he was eighteen years old, was spent in this manner, living alternately with the Indians, with whom he became a favorite, and at his home.

In 1813, the second war with England having broken out, Houston enlisted as a private soldier, and was made sergeant of a company. He soon became the best drill-officer in the regiment.

During the war with the Creek Indians, Houston served under General Jackson. He participated in the sharp conflict with that enemy which took place at To-ho-ne-ka, or Horseshoe Bend of the Tallapoosa River, Alabama.

The breastworks of the enemy were gallantly stormed by the 31st regiment, and he was the second to scale the works, the major (Major Montgomery) being the first, and instantly killed. Here he received a painful wound from an arrow which remained sticking in his thigh.

After trying in vain to extract the arrow, he called upon a comrade to do it. The comrade, a lieutenant, tried and failed. "Try again," said Houston, raising his sword; "and pull it out or I strike you down." With this incentive, the next effort to withdraw the barbed point succeeded, tearing away the flesh, and leaving an ugly wound which never completely healed.

General Jackson ordered Houston to the rear; but, regardless of the order, he was soon in the thickest of the fight.

Just before the conclusion of this decisive action, when volunteers were called to make a charge upon the only part of the fortification from which the Indians had not been dislodged, Houston instantly leaped to the front, calling upon the men to follow him; dashed across the precipitous ravine, and up to the breastworks, from which came deadly volleys of musketry and arrows.

Here the gallant young officer received two balls in his right shoulder, which at once disabled him, and he was carried from the field just before complete victory crowned the arms of his comrades.

Houston's recovery was for a long time doubtful, but at length he recovered sufficiently to join his regiment just before peace was declared.

In November, 1817, Houston was appointed to an agency for the Cherokee Indians, and during the winter went with a delegation of that tribe to Washington, to represent their interests to the Federal authorities.

When Houston was twenty-five years old, he went to Nashville, and engaged in the study of law. He was soon admitted to the bar, and was, even from the first, a successful advocate. He was about this time made Adjutant-General of Tennessee.

He was, in 1823, elected to Congress, and afterward re-elected by an almost unanimous vote.

In 1827, he was elected Governor of Tennessee, by a large majority.

While Houston was Governor of Tennessee, he married a lady of respectable connections; but in little more than two months a sudden and inexplicable separation between the parties took place. This sudden sundering of the marriage tie, about which many conjectures were afloat but nothing definite was known, gave rise at the time to great excitement, and the friends of the lady made many serious charges against the governor. To none of these did he reply, and quietly resigning his office he left the State of Tennessee. Houston now returned to his friends, the Cherokees, with whom he remained, occasionally visiting Washington City in their behalf, until December, 1832, when with a few friends he came to Texas. He was elected a delegate from Nacogdoches to the convention which met at San Felipe in 1833, for the purpose of framing a State constitution. From this time General Houston appears as a prominent actor in the affairs of Texas.

In 1835, he was appointed general of the military district east of the Trinity. He was a member of the Consultation of 1835, also of the Convention which declared the independence of Texas, in March 1836. Immediately after the Declaration of Independence, the convention elected Houston commander-in-chief of the armies of Texas.

He at once took the field, and after the fall of the Alamo and Goliad, he conducted the retreat of the army to San Jacinto, where, on the 21st of April, 1836, he administered to the Mexican forces under Santa Anna the crushing defeat which secured the independence of Texas.

In the action he suffered a painful wound in the ankle, from which he never fully recovered. In the fall of 1836 he was elected First President of the Republic of Texas. In 1839 and '40, after his time of office expired, he served in the Congress of the Republic. In 1841 he was again, almost by acclamation, elevated to the head of the Texas government.

After annexation, Houston was elected Senator from Texas to the Congress of the United States.

This position he filled with marked ability until March, 1859. After his return to Texas Houston was elected Governor in the fall of 1859.

At the breaking out of the civil war in 1861–5, General Houston opposed the secession of Texas, and favored separate State action. This course not agreeing with the views of the advocates of unconditional secession, he was deposed from the office of Governor, March, 1861.

On the 18th day of that month Governor Houston left his official chair. This was the end of his public career. He retired to the privacy of his home in Walker county, where he died in July, 1863.

His well-earned fame, and the remembrance of his virtues, are alike the property of his countrymen. The praise of the historian is not needed to magnify the one, nor could his silence or censure detract from the other.

DAVID G. BURNET.

THIS distinguished citizen of Texas was the son of William Burnet of Newark, New Jersey, where he was born in 1789. He received a liberal education, and in 1805 entered the counting-house of Robinson & Hartshorne, New York.

His tastes were not in accord with the dull routine of a clerk's life, and in 1806 he entered under General Miranda, in the expedition for the independence of Spanish America. After the failure of this he returned home, where he remained until 1817, when he went to Natchitoches, Louisiana.

At this time his lungs were threatened with disease, and by advice of his physician he went among the Indians, with whom he remained, following their mode of life for more than a year, when he went to Cincinnati, Ohio.

Mr. Burnet came to Texas in 1826, and at once became an active participant in her affairs.

Going to Saltillo, he entered into a contract with the Government of Coahuila and Texas, for the colonization of the latter State.

This contract, through the bad management of the company to whom he intrusted it, amounted to nothing.

In 1831 Mr. Burnet, having married in New York, came again to

17

Texas. The vessel in which he was, in approaching Galveston, was partially disabled, and he and Mrs. Burnet barely escaped being swallowed up in the waters of the Gulf.

In 1833, he was elected a delegate to the Convention at San Felipe, and was a leading member in its deliberations. In 1834 he was appointed Judge of the Municipality of Austin, which position he filled with marked ability.

When the oppressive acts of Santa Anna drove the people of Texas into resistance, Judge Burnet took an early and decided stand in favor of the independence of that State.

He was, in 1836, elected President *ad interim* of the Republic of Texas. In 1838, Judge Burnet was elected Vice-President of Texas, Lamar being President. After the termination of his vice-presidency, he for many years lived in the quiet seclusion of his home near the San Jacinto River.

Judge Burnet was made Secretary of State in 1846, and held that office until the close of Henderson's administration.

In 1866 Burnet was elected Senator to Congress by the Legislature of Texas, but was not admitted to a seat.

In 1868 he visited the place of his nativity, Newark, New Jersey, and after a few months' absence returned to Texas. His death occurred in 1870.

Judge Burnet was a man of culture and refinement. He was a ready and fluent writer, and an eloquent orator.

His oration upon the death of John A. Wharton was a masterpiece of its kind.

MIRABEAU B. LAMAR.

(From Baker's History of Texas.)

MIRABEAU B. LAMAR was born in Georgia in 1798. He came to Texas in 1835. He served with distinction in the Texas revolution, and afterward in the Mexican war. He was the first Vice-President and the second President of the Republic of Texas. He died in 1859. General Lamar possessed fine literary taste. He was the author of a book of poems called "Verses, Memoriales." The following poem from his pen is appended to this notice:

"THE STAR AND THE CUP.

"I love the bright *lone star* that gems
The banner of the brave :
I love the light that guideth men
To freedom or the grave

But oh! there is a fairer star
 Of pure and holy ray,
That lights to glory's higher crown,
 And freedom's brighter day.
It is the star before whose beams
 All earth should bow the knee—
The star that rose o'er Bethlehem
 And set on Calvary.

"Let others round the festive board
 The maddening wine-cup drain;
Let others court its guilty joys,
 And reap repentant pain.
But oh! there is a sweeter cup,
 And be its raptures mine,
Whose fragrance is the breath of life,
 Whose spirit is divine.
It is the cup that Jesus filled:
 He kissed its sacred brim:
And left the world to do the same
 In memory of Him."

ANSON JONES.

ANSON JONES was born in Massachusetts in 1798. He studied medicine, and commenced its practice in Philadelphia in 1826. He came to Texas in 1833. During the struggle for independence he entered in the army as a private soldier. He was elected to the second Congress of Texas in 1837. In 1838 he was appointed Texas minister to the United States. After his return he was elected Senator from Brazoria county, and was Secretary of State under Houston's second administration. In 1844 he was elected president of Texas which position he held until after annexation, when he surrendered the executive office to Governor Henderson, who had been elected first Governor of the State of Texas. He put an end to his life in a fit of mental aberration in 1858.

LORENZO DE ZAVALLA.

(From Baker's History of Texas.)

LORENZO DE ZAVALLA was a native of Yucatan. While quite young he was elected to represent his State in the Cortes of Spain. He was afterward a member of the Mexican Congress and Governor of Mexico.

After the overthrow of the Republic in Mexico, he came to Texas, where he took an active part in the struggle for liberty. He was elected vice-president of Texas in 1836.

He died shortly afterward.

BARON DE BASTROP.

THIS distinguished foreigner and friend to Texas came from Prussia to our shores at a very early day. He was the first commissioner of Austin's colony. He died in 1828. A county in Texas bears his name.

DON ERASMO SEGUIN

was a Mexican. He lived in Bexar, Texas. He was a member of the Congress of Coahuila and Texas. He was a stanch friend of Texas and of Stephen F. Austin. He died in 1836.

BENJAMIN R. MILAM.

HE was born in Kentucky, in 1791. He came to Texas in 1816. He afterward went to Mexico where he espoused the republican cause, and while there experienced many hardships. At the breaking out of the Texas Revolution, he returned to that State. He assisted in the capture of Goliad, or La Bahia, in the fall of 1835. He led one of the divisions at the storming of San Antonio, and was there killed, December 10, 1835.

The following incident in the life of Colonel Milam, is extracted from Pease's History of Texas :

" While in Mexico, Colonel Milam was imprisoned in Monterey. His winning manners soon made him a favorite with the jailer, who occasionally allowed him a walk to the river to bathe. He profited by the indulgence, and made arrangements with a friend to have a fleet horse ready for him at an appointed place. The colonel passed the sentinel, as he was wont to go to the river, walked quietly on, mounted and fled. A few days' hard riding brought him to Texas. When he reached there, he found the war of independence begun. With a few choice spirits it was determined to attack the fort at Goliad, or La Bahia, then in the hands of the Mexicans." The account of the attack is thus given :

" Their axes hewed down the door of the room where the colonel commanding slept, and he was taken prisoner in his bed. A sentinel fired. A rifle-ball laid him dead on the spot. The discharge of fire-arms and the shout of voices now became commingled. The Mexican soldiers fired from their quarters, and the blaze of their guns served as a target for the colonists. The garrison were summoned to surrender. They asked for terms. The reply was, No terms, come out and surrender, and come quick, or you will be killed every one of you. I can not keep the men back much longer." "Oh!" shouted the Mexicans, "keep the men back, for God's sake; and we will come out at once." And they rushed out with all possible speed, and laid down their arms. Thus by a handful of men was this fortress of Goliad taken, a fort which with a garrison of 350 men in the war of 1812–13, had withstood a siege of more than 2,000 Spanish troops, and forced them to retire discomfited. The colonists in this affair were led by Captain Collingsworth, assisted by Colonel Milam. Of the garrison three were killed and seven wounded, and many prisoners taken. Of the Texans, one was wounded.

WILLIAM B. TRAVIS.

(From Baker's History of Texas.)

WILLIAM B. TRAVIS was a native of Georgia. He came to Texas in 1830, and established himself in the practice of law, first in the town of Liberty, and afterwards in San Filipe. He was one of the first who entered in the army for her independence. He commanded the garrison of the Alamo, at the storming of that fortress, and was killed after a defense unparalleled for heroism, March 6th, 1836. A monument commemorating the defense of the Alamo stands in the rotunda of the capitol at Austin.

On the 24th of February Colonel Travis issued this stirring appeal, which was sent by a trusty messenger through the Mexican lines:

" TO THE PEOPLE OF TEXAS AND ALL AMERICANS IN THE WORLD.

" FELLOW-CITIZENS AND COMPATRIOTS :

"I am besieged by a thousand or more Mexicans under Santa Anna. I have sustained a continual bombardment and cannonade for twenty-four hours, and have not yet lost a man. The enemy have demanded a " surrender at discretion," or the garrison is to be put to the sword when taken. I have answered the summons with cannon-shot, and our flag still waves proudly from the walls.

I shall never surrender or retreat.

Then I call upon you, in the name of liberty, patriotism, and everything dear to the American character, to come to our aid with dispatch. The enemy are receiving re-enforcements daily, and will doubtless in a few days be increased to three or four thousand. Though this call may be neglected,

I am determined to sustain myself as long as possible, and die like a soldier who never forgets what is due to his own honor and that of his country.

Victory or death.

WILLIAM BARRETT TRAVIS, *Lieutenant-Colonel Commanding.*

J. W. FANNIN.

(Baker's History of Texas).

J. W. FANNIN was a native of North Carolina. He came early to Texas, and took an active part in the stirring events of 1835 and 1836.

In January, 1836, he was appointed by the provisional government of Texas, an agent to raise troops and money for the republic. He, with his regiment, was captured at the Coleto by the Mexican forces under General Urrea, after a hard-fought battle; and was shot in violation of the terms of surrender, at Goliad, Texas, on the 27th day of March, 1836.

DAVID CROCKETT.

THE remarkable subject of this sketch was born in what is now the State of Tennessee, on the Nolachucky River, on the 17th day of August, 1786.

His father was an Irishman, and his mother a native of Maryland. He was one of a large family of children, was born in a rugged locality in a rough community, and was possessed in an eminent degree of the strong and inflexible will which characterized the early settlers of a wild and unbroken country.

He enjoyed no opportunities for the cultivation of a naturally vigorous intellect, and until the age of eighteen could neither read nor write.

When he was seven years old, his parents moved to Jefferson county, Tennessee, where our hero's time was spent in alternately hunting and working at home under the supervision of a stern but kind-hearted father.

When about eighteen years of age he fell desperately in love with a young Quaker girl ; or, as he says himself, "I fell head over heels in love, and I thought that if all the hills around her house were pure gold, and were mine, I would give them all to talk to her as I wanted to, but when I tried to say anything to her, my heart would begin to flutter like a duck in a puddle, and if I tried harder, my heart would get up in my throat and choke me like a cold potato." He however found voice to plead his cause with success, and soon afterward married and settled in Franklin county, Tennessee.

At the breaking out of the Creek war, Crockett volunteered and served with gallantry until its close, when he again settled down quietly at home, where he seems to have lived in great happiness with his wife who bore him several children ; and to her death, which took place in 1821, he alludes in the most touching manner.

He married a second time, and for the second partner of his adventurous life he seems to have cherished a strong affection. During those early days, the settlers in the backwoods were but little troubled with law or government, and for mutual protection they organized in Crockett's neighborhood a sort of *de facto* government, and elected him magistrate.

This position he seems to have filled with justice and impartiality ; and, to quote his words, " although my warrants for arrest were never written, my word was enough, and the offender was taken dead or alive ; nor were my judgments ever appealed from, but stuck like wax."

In 1821, he was first, and against his own inclination, elected to the State Legislature. At that time he first met in Nashville, Colonel, afterward President Polk.

The following incident is told, illustrating the ignorance of Crockett then. In a company Colonel Polk addressed him thus, " I suppose, Colonel Crockett, the legislature will make a change in the judiciary." " I suppose so," said Crockett, and got out of the way as soon as possible, "for," says he, " I at that time did not know what in thunder the judiciary was."

Guided by his sound sense and acute observation, and assisted by a wonderful quickness of perception, he soon mastered all the necessary problems in the theory of his State government, and served his constituents with such fidelity that he was returned to the legislature in 1823, although in the meantime he had removed his home to a distant part of his district.

In 1827, and again in 1829 and 1831, Crockett was elected to the Congress of the United States. He afterward made a tour through the principal cities of note in the North and East ; and was received with much attention as a genuine representative man of the hardy frontiersman of the South-west.

In the canvass of 1834–35, Crockett having taken strong ground against the Jackson and Van Buren democracy, was defeated for Congress by a small majority.

Soon afterward and as he says, chagrined at his defeat and disgusted at the political condition of his State, Crockett bade farewell to his family and came to Texas, where in a short time he enrolled among the 150 brave spirits in defense of the fortress of the Alamo in Bexar.

Here he fought, the bravest of the brave, until on the memorable 6th of March, 1836, he yielded up his noble life to the resistless weapons of the blood-thirsty foe.

He died as he had lived. He was slain, but dauntless to the last.

David Crockett was a man of wonderful native eloquence, and during the last five years of his life, made many speeches to his countrymen, and wielded a sharp and trenchant pen.

His life of Martin Van Buren, published in 1835, abounds in keen satire, unstudied humor, and bitter invective. We give one or two extracts from its preface, to show the straightforward way in which he used the English language. He says, "Van Buren is as opposite to Jackson as dung is to diamond. Jackson is open, bold, warm-hearted, confiding, and passionate to a fault. Van Buren is secret, sly, selfish, cold, calculating, distrustful, treacherous." Again he says, "There are some who will read this book with such strong prejudice against its author, and such idolatrous worship (not for the subject of these pages, but for the *man* who makes him, Jackson), that if every letter was bible light, every word gospel truth, every sentiment inspiration, read out by the Angel Gabriel with a tongue of thunder from the top of the reddest streak of lightning that ever split the blackest cloud of heaven, they would not believe a syllable of it."

David Crockett was a wonderful man. What culture might have made him, no one can tell. What he *was*, all Texans know, and to them his memory will be ever dear.

THOMAS J. RUSK.

(From Baker's History of Texas.)

THOMAS JEFFERSON RUSK was one of the noblest sons of Texas. He was born in South Carolina in 1803. He was educated for the law, and having removed to Georgia, he became distinguished at the early age of twenty-nine as one of the first lawyers in that State.

In 1835 he came to Texas and settled in Nacogdoches. In 1836 he was elected a delegate to the convention at Washington, and by that body was chosen secretary of war.

In the battles which followed, General Rusk took an active and distinguished part, and General Houston being disabled by his wounds received at San Jacinto, he was made commander-in-chief of the Army.

In November, 1836, he was appointed to a seat in the cabinet. The congress of 1838 elected him chief-justice of the supreme court, which position had been vacated by the death of James Collingsworth.

In 1843, Rusk was elected major-general of State militia. In 1845, he was made president of the convention which assembled at Austin to frame a State constitution.

In 1846, the first legislature of Texas elected him United States senator, which position he filled with marked ability and satisfaction to the people of Texas until his death in 1857.

Thomas J. Rusk was one of those men whose death was the signal of mourning to a host of friends all over the State he had faithfully served. Modest in manners and disposition, social and domestic in his habits ; and with a warm and generous heart, he was indeed one of nature's noblemen.

DR. BRANCH T. ARCHER.

THE subject of this sketch was a native of Virginia. At an early age he went to Philadelphia to pursue the study of medicine.

In 1831 he emigrated from Virginia to Texas.

Immediately upon his arrival he declared his intention to take part and lot with the people in the struggle which he believed to be inevitable.

He soon informed himself of the past history of Texas, and of the differences between them and the general government of Mexico, and took an active part in the discussion of all public questions.

It was in the latter part of 1831 that the first movement was made by the inhabitants of the jurisdiction of the Brazos, to oppose the execution of orders issued by the military commanders at Anahuac and Velasco, closing all the ports in Texas except the port of Anahuac (Galveston). This step was taken to facilitate the collection of taxes for the payment of troops sent by the general government for the regulation of the civil administration of the province.

The offensive order had been issued by Colonel Bradburn, commandant at Anahuac, and had only been repeated by Lieutenant-Colonel Ugartechea, commanding at Velasco.

A public meeting was held at Brazoria on the 16th day of December, 1831, and it was resolved to demand the revocation of the obnoxious order. The meeting appointed Dr. Archer and G. B. McKinstry to act as commissioners to make the demand. They accordingly proceeded to Anahuac.

The conference concerning the matter in hand was between Archer and Bradburn.

They walked together from the site of the old fort to the shore of the bay. Bradburn attempted to gain time by suggesting why he could not give a definite answer at once. Archer pressed the subject with warmth. He declared that the act in question was a usurpation of power on the part of Bradburn ; that it was wholly unauthorized. Bradburn replied that it did not become him to listen to such language, and that he should take no action in the matter until he could communicate with his superior, General Teran.

Archer rejoined as follows, "I once more appeal to you to rescind this decree; if you refuse it the flames of war will be kindled in this country at once, and, as the immediate author of that war, you will be held accountable."

The eagle glance and bold bearing of the deputy shook the nerves of Bradburn.

His countenance fell, and he consented to revoke the obnoxious decree.

During the year 1835 Archer attended at the public meetings of the colonists, and declared himself in favor of separation from Mexico at any hazard.

When the consultation of all Texas met at San Felipe in November, 1835, Dr. Archer was chosen President of that body, and in that capacity distinguished himself by firmness and ability.

By the consultation, Dr. Archer, W. H. Wharton, and Stephen F. Austin were chosen agents to proceed to the United States, and solicit aid and comfort for Texas.

He was a member of the first congress of the republic from Brazoria county, and was made speaker at the second or adjourned session held at Houston, in June, 1837, and he was secretary of war for some time under Lamar's administration. Through all the trials of Texas, he was her stanch and able friend.

In 1845, when the people of Brazoria assembled in mass meeting, to express their views on the question of annexation, Dr. Archer was sent for to preside at the meeting. The messenger found him in feeble health, and in profound distress at the death of a favorite daughter. The wishes of the people were made known to him. He replied that he could not preside over the meeting. His heart, he said, was torn by affliction, his firmness was gone.

The messenger urged him to attend the meeting of so much moment to the people of Texas, and added, "We do not forget, sir, that you helped to rock the cradle of our revolution, and we now ask your aid in a moment as vital as any in the past." The old gentleman's eye kindled, and rising with dignity he said, "Tell the people I will comply with their wishes. I will bury my griefs."

In private life Dr. Archer was above all praise. His name was never coupled with reproach; he was polite, patriotic, brave, and humane. His name is written where it will be read in coming ages.

He sleeps in the same earth with his friends and co-laborers in the cause of independence, W. H. Wharton, and John A. Wharton, the latter of whom has been finely named by Burnet, "the keenest blade on the field of San Jacinto."

Dr. Archer died at Brazoria, in September, 1856.

WILLIAM H WHARTON.

HE was a native of Tennessee ; came to Texas in 1829. Returned, and came again in 1831. Was a member of the convention of 1833 ; and also of the general consultation of 1835 ; and was one of the three commissioners appointed by that consultation to the United States. He was a member of the first senate of the republic, was first minister to the United States. After his return, he was again elected senator, which position he held until his death, in 1839.

JOHN A. WHARTON,

a brother of the former, was one of the most gallant of the early defenders of Texas. He came to Texas in 1829, and died in 1838. He was adjutant-general of the Texas army ; and was a member of the house in the first and second congress. Of him David G. Burnet eloquently said in his funeral oration, pronounced in December 1838, that " the keenest blade on the field of San Jacinto is broken."

PATRICK C. JACK

was a native of Alabama. He came to Texas prior to the year 1832. During that year he participated, under the command of Colonel F. W. Johnson, in the capture of the port of Anahuac, which was commanded by Colonel Bradburn. He died at Houston in 1844, at which time he held the position of judge of that district.

WILLIAM H. JACK,

brother of Patrick, came to Texas at the same time. He served in the Texas army in the battle of San Jacinto. He was secretary of state of the government *ad interim* under President Burnet, was also a member of the congress of the republic. He was a lawyer of distinction. He died in Brazoria county, in 1844.

DR. JAMES B. MILLER,

a native of Kentucky, came to Texas in 1829. He soon afterward associated himself in the practice of medicine with Dr. R. Peebles at San Felipe de Austin, where he continued to reside and practice his profession until 1834, when he engaged in the mercantile business with A. Sommerville. In the winter of 1834, he was appointed political chief of the department of the Brazos. In 1835 when the black cloud of war was about to burst upon Texas, he at first favored conciliatory measures. As soon, however, as he became satisfied that Texas had to choose between submission to the worst of tyrannies, or resistance, he joined the party who had determined to defend their rights, and gave the war his hearty support. He was appointed by General Houston secretary of the treasury; subsequently, after annexation, he became a candidate for the office of governor, and though not elected received a large vote.

SIDNEY SHERMAN.

HE was born in March, 1805. 1831 he moved west and settled in Cincinnati, Ohio. Early in 1836, fired with zeal to aid in the struggle of Texas against Mexican misrule, he raised a company of fifty men and departed for that territory. Arrived at Washington on the Brazos, he found everything in confusion, the enemy in large numbers were occupying the country, and Travis was besieged in San Antonio by a vastly superior force. The Alamo fell, and Travis and his brave fellows were butchered, and the whole available Texas force, under the command of General Houston, fell back to the Brazos and made a stand at the memorable field of San Jacinto. Upon this bloody and decisive field General Sherman behaved with distinguished gallantry. He led a charge of cavalry with great coolness and intrepidity, on the 20th, the day preceding the battle. He is said first to have sounded the battle cry, "Goliad and the Alamo," and he participated in all the stirring scenes of that decisive day. His rank at San Jacinto was Colonel of the second regiment of Texas Volunteers. In 1842 General Sherman was elected representative to the congress of the republic from Harris county, and afterwards major-general of State militia. Since annexation he has pursued a quiet life at his residence by Harrisburg, Texas. The last years of his life were spent in energetic efforts to build up the railroad interests, of Texas, and especially of his own section.

He died at Galveston in August, 1873.

EDWARD BURLESON.

(From Baker's Texas.)

EDWARD BURLESON was born in North Carolina in 1789. In 1815 he moved to Virginia. In 1824 he moved thence to Tennessee. In 1831 he came to Texas and settled on the Colorado River, a short distance below

Bastrop. When the Texas revolution broke out, General Burleson was made second in command to Stephen F. Austin. He was in command when the gallant Johnson and Milam assaulted and took the city of San Antonio, and captured the Mexican army under General Cos. He commanded the first regiment of volunteers at San Jacinto. After the war he was appointed Brigadier-general of State troops. From 1838 to 1841 he was unremitting in his exertion to protect the frontier from Mexican and Indian depredations. Under his command the Cherokees were expelled from Texas. In 1841 General Burleson was elected vice-president of Texas. In 1842 he was again in the field to repel the invasions of Valasquez and Woll. During the Mexican war with the United States, Burleson enlisted as a private soldier and fought at Monterey, and at the other hard contested fights. He was afterward elected to the State senate, and while in that position died at Austin, 1851.

FRANK W. JOHNSON.

(From Baker's Texas.)

THE subject of this sketch was born in Virginia, October, 1799. He came to Texas in 1824, and engaged in land-surveying until 1831. He was then elected alcalde of the jurisdiction of Austin. In 1832 he led an expedition against the Mexican post of Anahuac. He was, the same year, appointed surveyor-general of Austin's colony. In 1835 he volunteered in the army, and was appointed adjutant and inspector-general by Generals Austin and Burleson. In December, 1835, he led one of the columns which so gallantly stormed and took the post and city of San Antonio de Bexar. In 1836 he made a raid through the country between the Nueces River and the Rio Grande ; but was surprised, and most of his command lost. After the war Colonel Johnson was for the most part engaged in land-matters for several years. He is now, and has for some time been collecting and compiling notes in reference to a history of Texas. He is now in Austin, Texas.

JAMES BOWIE

was born in Georgia. Moved with his family to Louisiana in 1802. Was early remarkable for his bold and fearless disposition. In 1827 he participated in a bloody fight in Mississippi, where several men were killed and he was wounded. He came to Texas in 1828. He encountered many remarkable adventures in Texas, among which was his great fight with the Indians near the San Saba. He enlisted in the patriot army, and was killed at the Alamo in March, 1836.

J. B. BONHAM

was a native of South Carolina ; was one of those noble spirits who early volunteered in defense of the cause of Texas. He fought bravely under Travis at the Alamo, when, with the rest of that heroic band, he was slain March, 1836.

JAMES HAMILTON

was born in South Carolina, May 8, 1786. He was educated for the law, but entered the army and served with credit in the war of 1812. General Hamilton was representative from South Carolina and Governor of that State in 1830. He declined the secretary-ship of war, in 1828. In 1841, having become ardently devoted to Texas, he accepted the position of envoy extraordinary to the courts of England, France, and Belgium, and did much to secure for Texas credit and standing abroad. He spent his large fortune in behalf of his adopted country, and at last lost his life at sea in a voyage to her shores in 1857.

E. W. MOORE

was a native of Virginia ; was in early life a lieutenant in the United States navy. He came to Texas in 1839. He was commodore of the Texas navy, and while in that capacity fought several brilliant naval battles in the service of his State. Commodore Moore died in 1863.

THOMAS GREEN

was born in Amelia county, Virginia, June 8th, 1814. In 1817 his father Nathan Green removed to Tennessee, and was for many years one of the supreme court judges of that State. The subject of this sketch received a liberal education at Princetown College, Kentucky, and afterward at ' ..e University of Tennessee at Nashville. In 1834 he studied law. In the fall of 1835 he, in company with Gillispie, Finch and others, came to Texas, and enlisted in the army of the revolted colonists. He was with the Texan army in its retreat from Gonzales to the Brazos. For gallant service on the field of San Jacinto he was promoted to a lieutenancy. He then received a furlough and returned to Tennessee, whence he came again to Texas, in the spring of 1837. He was one of the clerks of congress of Texas in 1838. In that year he was by congress elected surveyor of Fayette county. In 1840, he was elected to Congress from that county. In 1841, he was appointed clerk of the supreme court, which position he filled with great fidelity and clerk of the supreme court, which position he filled with great fidelity and satisfaction to that tribunal until he laid it down in 1861, to join the army of the Confederate States. In the performance of the duties of clerk of the supreme court, Green acquired a personal popularity throughout the State which few men could boast of. In 1841, he commanded a company in the expedition against the Indians up the Colorado River under Major M. B. Lewis. In 1842 he was inspector-general under General Sommerville, and pursued the retreating Mexican invaders under Woll to the Rio Grande. Green served through the Mexican war as captain in Jack Hays' regiment of rangers. In 1847, he married Mary, eldest daughter of Dr. J. G. Chalmers, former secretary of the treasury under Lamar. When the war of the States broke out in 1861, Green, who at first strongly disapproved of secession, stood with his State and accepted a colonelcy in the Arizona expedition under General Sibley.

Returning from New Mexico, his command went to Louisiana, and in that State and in Texas he gallantly did his duty as a soldier until his death, which was caused by a grape-shot from one of the federal gunboats at Bayou de Pierre, Louisiana, on the twelfth day of April, 1864. For his gallantry and efficiency he was during the war promoted successively to the rank of colonel, brigadier-general, and major-general.

Thomas Green was a man who was almost universally beloved. He was a man without fear and without reproach. Brave, courteous, and generous, he was always approachable, always sympathetic, and always ready to help those who needed his assistance.

ALBERT SIDNEY JOHNSTON

was a native of Kentucky. He was educated at West Point. He served with distinction in the Black Hawk war. He came to Texas in 1830, and was for a time in command of the army of the republic in 1836. He was secretary of war, under President Lamar's administration. He participated in the Cherokee war in 1839. He commanded the second Texas regiment in the Mexican war. He was afterward appointed paymaster in the United States army. He was appointed colonel of one of the new cavalry regiments of the United States army, during President Pierce's administration, and was afterward made brevet brigadier-general. He was killed at Shiloh in 1862.

BEN McCULLOCH.

THIS gallant man came from Tennessee to Texas in 1836. He served in the Texas army at San Jacinto. He was member of Congress of the republic, and a member of the legislature of the State of Texas. He served with distinction in the Mexican war of 1846, and was major-general in the

Confederate army, in the war of 1861–5. He was killed at the battle of Elk Horn, in Arkansas, in 1863.

MOSELY BAKER

came from Alabama to Texas was for several years a member of congress of the republic ; served in the Texas army during the revolution, and commanded a company in the battle of San Jacinto. He died in 1848.

G. W. HOCKLEY

came to Texas in 1835, or early in 1836. He was adjutant and inspector-general at the battle of San Jacinto. He died in 1851.

MEMUCAN HUNT

was from North Carolina. He came to Texas in 1836. He was appointed by General Houston minister to the United States. He died in 1854.

THOMAS WILLIAM WARD

was a native of Ireland. He was one of those gallant spirits who came to Texas at the breaking out of hostilities in 1835. He was a member of the first company of " New Orleans Greys." He was captain of an artillery company at the storming and taking of San Antonio, under the gallant Colonels Johnson and Milam. In this action he distinguished himself for gallantry, but suffered the loss of a leg, which was shot off by a cannon-ball. Colonel Ward was nearly all his remaining life in Texas in one way or another occupied in public affairs. He was commissioner of the general land office under the Republic of Texas, and some four years after it became a State. In firing a salute at Austin on the anniversary of Texan independence in March, 1841, he lost his right arm. Thus maimed, he still continued in active life, and occupied several positions of honor and trust. His conduct as a public officer was marked by promptness and fidelity. He was United States consul at Panama in Buchanan's administration. Colonel Ward was a generous and warm-hearted man, and a true and unswerving friend to those who possessed his confidence. He died at Austin on the 25th day of November, 1872.

JOSEPH BAKER

was a native of Maine. He came to Texas in 1834. He was second judge of the municipality of Austin, was chief-justice of Bexar District, was

THOS. WM. WARD.

To face p. 272.

representative in the congress of the republic from Bexar, in 1837. He was first sergeant of Captain Mosely Baker's company in the battle of San Jacinto, and was familiarly known among his friends as "Don José." In 1835, he, with Gail and Thomas H. Borden, established at San Felipe de Austin the first permanent newspaper in Texas, the *Telegraph*. Joseph Baker was for many years Spanish translator in the General Land Office. He died at Austin in 1846.

Gail, Thomas H., and J. P. Borden, came from Indiana to Texas. The two former, with Joseph Baker, were the founders of the *Telegraph* first published at San Felipe de Austin. Gail Borden was the first collector of customs at Galveston. He is famous as the inventor of condensed milk. John P. Borden was commissioner of the general land office during the Republic. Gail Borden died in 1874.

DR. FRANCIS MOORE

came to Texas from Ohio in June, 1836. He was a native of New York State. He come to Texas as a volunteer in the "Buckeye Rangers." In company with J. W. Creuger, he published the *Telegraph* newspaper early in 1837, and was connected with it until 1856. He was an energetic mayor of the city of Houston, and all who rode on "Dr. Moore's mud road" through the prairies from Houston, through the bottom to the Brazos River, will recollect this first harbinger of the railroad system which now spreads out from Houston in every direction. Dr. Moore was afterward appointed State Geologist, which office he held about two years until his death in 1864.

GEORGE W. SMYTH

came to Texas as early as 1832. Was commissioner of one of the colonies, was a member of the consultation and constitutional convention. He was for years commissioner of the general land office of Texas. He was elected a member of congress from Texas. He died in 1866, while a member of the constitutional convention.

ALBERT C. HORTON

was a native of Georgia. He came to Texas from Alabama in 1835. He had previously been a member of the Alabama Legislature. He commanded the advance guard of Fannin's regiment, when he retreated from Goliad, and being cut off from the main body, he made his escape with his command. He was a member of the first congress of the republic, and was also a member of the constitutional convention in 1845. He was the first lieutenant-governor of

18

the State of Texas, and acting governor while Governor Henderson was in Mexico, in 1846. He died in 1865.

R. M. WILLIAMSON.

THIS gentleman was born in Georgia in 1806. In his fifteenth year he was attacked with a disease known as the white-swelling, which made him a permanent cripple and rendered it necessary for him to wear a wooden leg, which gave him his common sobriquet " Three-legged Willie." He came to Texas in 1826, was judge of the third district of the Republic of Texas ; was member of congress from 1840 to 1850. He died in Wharton county, 1859. Judge Williamson was an able lawyer and a man of noble and generous impulses.

WYLIE MARTIN

came to Texas prior to the year 1830. He was formerly a captain in the United States army. He was a member of the ayuntamiento * of the munici-pality of Austin. He commanded a company in the campaign of 1836. He served several years in the congress of the republic. He died, in the year 1842, in Fort Bend county.

BENJAMIN C. FRANKLIN

was a native of Georgia. He came to Texas in April, 1835. He served in the battle of San Jacinto ; was appointed by President Burnet, under the government *ad interim*, judge of the district of the Brazos. He was elected by the first congress judge of the third judicial district of the Republic; was often in the legislature of Texas, from Galveston county. He was senator elect at the time of his death, which occurred in the year 1873, at which time he was 68 years of age.

HENRY SMITH

(From Baker's Texas.)

HENRY SMITH was a native of Kentucky. He emigrated thence to Mis-souri and afterward to Texas. He was the first political chief of the department of the Brazos, and afterward was first secretary of the treasury of of the Republic of Texas. He was elected by the consultation in November, 1835, first provisional governor of Texas. After annexation he removed to California, where he died in 1853. He was a gentleman of agreeable manners, well informed and having social qualities.

* Corporation of judges. A court.

BAILEY HARDEMAN

came from Tennessee to Texas in 1835 and died in 1836. He was a member of the convention of 1836 and secretary of the treasury under the government *ad interim.*

DAVID THOMAS

came from Tennessee to Texas in 1835, and died April, 1836. He was a member of the convention of 1836, and was attorney-general of Texas under the government *ad interim.*

ROBERT POTTER

came from North Carolina to Texas in 1835. Had been a member of United States Congress from that State; was a member of the convention which declared the independence of Texas in 1836. Was secretary of the navy under the government *ad interim*, and was afterward senator in the congress of the Republic of Texas. Was killed in 1841, in Eastern Texas.

JOSHUA FLETCHER

was a native of New Hampshire. Went thence to St. Louis, and for many years was engaged in the Santa Fé trade. He came to Texas in 1832. Was first treasurer of the provisional government. He afterward left Texas; and the writer has been unable to ascertain the time and place of his death.

JOHN RICE JONES

came from Missouri to Texas about the year 1831. He was postmaster-general under the first provisional government. He was for years a merchant, and he died in 1845.

JAMES W. ROBINSON

was a native of Ohio. He came to Texas in 1834, was a member of the consultation from Nacogdoches. Was lieutenant-governor of the provisional government under Henry Smith. He served in the battle of San Jacinto. Was first judge of the fourth judicial district of the Republic. He was captured by the Mexicans while attending court at San Antonio in 1842, and carried to the castle of Perote in Mexico. He removed to California in 1850, and settled at San Diego. He died in California in 1857 or 1858.

SAMUEL P. CARSON

came from North Carolina to Texas in 1835. He had been for several years member of the United States Congress from North Carolina. He was a member of the convention which declared the independence of Texas in 1836. He was appointed secretary of state under the Burnet government *ad interim.* He left Texas in bad health, in 1836, and soon afterward died in North Carolina.

THOMAS J. CHAMBERS.

(From Baker's Texas.)

HE was a native of Virginia, was a lawyer by profession, and emigrated to Mexico at an early day. He was licensed to practice law in the Mexican courts, and was appointed surveyor-general of Coahuila and Texas, and afterward, in 1834, superior judge of the District of Texas. In 1836, by authority of the provisional government, he went to Kentucky, and raised for the service of Texas, a division of men. General Chambers was a gentleman of quiet deportment, and easy, dignified manners. He was largely engaged in land matters, and was well and prominently known in Texas until his death, which took place in 1863.

THOMAS JEFFERSON GREEN

was a native of North Carolina ; came to Texas with a regiment of volunteers in April, 1836, just after the battle of San Jacinto. He served in the first congress of the republic ; was with Colonel Fisher in the Mier expedition, about which he wrote and published a history. After being released from the captivity in Mexico, he returned to Texas and was elected to congress from Brazoria county. He died in North Carolina, in 1864.

HUGH McLEOD

came to Texas from Georgia in 1837. He was a graduate of West Point. He served in the campaign of 1839 against the Cherokees. General McLeod commanded the Santa Fé expedition of 1841, served in the congress of the Republic of Texas. His death occurred in Virginia in 1862, while commanding a regiment in the Confederate army.

ALEXANDER SOMMERVILLE

was a native of Maryland. In 1817 he went to Louisiana. In 1824 he went thence to Missouri and engaged in mercantile business. In 1833 he removed to San Felipe, Texas, and established himself in the same occupation. He took an active part in the Texas revolution, and served as major in the army in the campaign in and around Bexar in 1835.

In 1836 he was made lieutenant-colonel. He was in the battle of San Jacinto, where he acted a gallant part. He was in the congress of the republic in 1836 and 1837. Served in the Indian war of 1839, under Colonel J. C. Neill. He was afterward elected general of the first brigade of Texas militia.

When General Woll, with twelve hundred Mexicans, invaded Texas in September, 1842, and then retreated, General Sommerville led a force of Texans in pursuit of the invaders far as Laredo, on the Rio Grande, where the command separated, and he, with a portion of it, returned. He was drowned accidentally, in January, 1854.

LIEUTENANT-COLONEL WARD

came from Georgia to Texas in 1835, in company with the volunteers from his State. He entered with his whole heart into the defense of the cause of Texas, and was captured and afterward killed with Fannin at Goliad.

FELIX HUSTON

was from Mississippi, whence 'he came to Texas in 1836. General Felix Huston was for a short time commander of the army of the republic, succeeding Rusk in that position. After the war, he went back to Mississippi. He came again to Texas, and led the Texans in the memorable Plum Creek fight with the Indians. After this he returned again to his home, where he died in 1857.

DOCTOR JAMES GRANT

was a Scotchman by birth. Being of an adventurous disposition, he came to Mexico and Texas at an early day. He was a man of education, and was a member of the congress of the States of Coahuila and Texas. Colonel Grant entered heartily into the cause of Texas, and joined the expedition against Matamoras in company with Colonel F. W. Johnson, in which he was killed by the Mexicans.

PETER W. GRAYSON

came to Texas in 1832. He was sent as a commissioner to Washington by the Burnet government *ad interim*. He was subject at times to fits of deep gloom and despondency, and during one of these attacks took his own life.

ROBERT MORRIS.

THIS gallant soldier of Texas was first captain of the first company of New Orleans Greys. He came to Texas and participated in the storming of Bexar in 1835, and afterward joined the expedition of Colonels Johnson and Grant, and was killed with Grant on the Agua Dulce.

"DEAF SMITH."

ERASTUS, or Deaf Smith, as he was called, was born in New York in 1787. He went to Mississippi in 1798. He came to Texas in 1817, and having returned home, came again to Texas in 1821. Being hard of hearing, he became silent and fond of solitude. He was a most efficient and indefatigible observer of the movements of the Mexican army during the war, and his perfect knowledge of the country, and an astonishing coolness and bravery, made him an invaluable scout for the patriot army. He married a Mexican lady in San Antonio, by whom he had several children. He died at Fort Bend, in 1839, and is buried at Richmond.

ASA BRIGHAM

came to Texas from Massachusetts in 1832. He was alcalde of the municipality of Brazoria, was a member of the constitutional convention of March, 1836. Was first treasurer of the Republic of Texas under the constitutional government. He died in 1844.

JAMES COLLINGSWORTH

came from Tennessee to Texas in 1834. He was a member of the convention at Washington which declared the independence of Texas. Before coming to Texas he held the position of district attorney in Tennessee. He was the first chief-justice of the Republic of Texas. He died in 1838.

PHILIP DIMMITT

was an early emigrant to Texas, and was for some time a merchant. Captain Dimmitt commanded the post of Goliad for some time after its capture in 1835. He was killed in Mexico in 1841.

W. S. FISHER

was a native of Virginia, came to Texas in 1833. He was in command of a company at the battle of San Jacinto. Colonel Fisher was appointed by General Houston, secretary of war during his first administration. He commanded the Mier expedition, was captured and a prisoner at the Castle of Perote. He died in 1845.

S. RHOADS FISHER

was from Philadelphia, Pennsylvania. Came to Texas in 1830, or '31. He was a member of the constitutional convention of March 1836. He was secretary of the navy under the first constitutional government. He died in 1839.

RICHARD ELLIS

came to Texas from Alabama in 1833. Was president of the constitutional convention. Was senator in the first Texas Congress, and he died soon afterward.

SAMUEL M. WILLIAMS

was from Baltimore, Maryland; came to Texas as early as 1823. Was for several years secretary of Austin's Colony. He served in the congress of the republic, from Galveston, was for years president of the Agricultural Bank at Galveston. He died in September, 1858.

Mr. Williams was always an active business man. He was for years in partnership with Thomas F. McKinney, and furnished material aid to Texas during her early struggle.

THOMAS F. McKINNEY

was born in Kentucky, in 1801. He went to Missouri in 1818. Engaging in mercantile speculations he went to Sante Fé, and Chihuahua, in Mexico. In 1829 he came to Texas, and in company with Samuel M. Williams, did a large business at Quintana, opposite to Velasco. The firm of McKinney & Williams furnished both money and supplies to Texas in the day of her need. After annexation, he served in the State legislature, both in the house and senate. He died in 1873.

MICHAEL B. MENARD.

THIS man, who may with propriety be called the founder of Galveston, was a Canadian. He moved from Illinois to Texas. Was a member of the Texas Congress from Galveston county. He died in 1854.

OLIVER JONES

was a native of Massachusetts. Was in Texas as early as 1823 or 1824. Was sheriff of the municipality of Austin. In 1835, was a member from Texas to the congress of Coahuila and Texas. He was member of congress of the Republic of Texas for several years. He died in 1868.

JESSE GRIMES

was from North Carolina; was one of the Austin original "three hundred." Came to Texas in 1824. He settled in Grimes county, which is called by his name. He was a member of the consultation of 1835, and of the convention of 1836. He was senator in the first congress of the republic, and served afterward in both senate and house. After annexation he was a member of the State legislature. He died at his home in Grimes county, in 18—.

KENNETH LEWIS ANDERSON

was born at Hillsboro', North Carolina, September 11, 1805; emigrated from Shelbyville, Tennessee, to Texas, in 1837; subsequently represented San. Augustine county in the congress of the republic; filled the office of speaker for one or two terms; elected vice-president in 1844; died while on his way home from the session of Congress at Washington, July 3, 1845; was buried at "Fanthorps," Grimes county, since named, in his honor, Anderson.

MARTIN PARMER.
(From Yoakum's Texas.)

He was born in Virginia, in 1775. At twenty years of age he emigrated to Tennessee, where he married Miss Sarah Hardwick. He was engaged for some time in superintending the works of Montgomery Bell, of Dickson county. But his ambition was not satisfied. In 1818, he emigrated to Missouri, and settled fifty miles above the highest county formed in the then territory, surrounded by the Sioux, Iowa, and Osage Indians. He gave fifty dollars for a bear dog, and by the chase kept such supplies of meat as drew the Indians around him. One of them, called Two Heart (from the fact that he had killed a white man, and eaten his heart), came to partake of his bounty, when he spread before him a large quantity of meat, and, standing over him with a drawn knife, forced him to eat it till it ultimately killed him. Parmer had numerous and fearful fights with the savages, but at last acquired an influence over them, which induced the government at Washington to appoint him an Indian agent. He was elected a colonel of the militia, and then a member of the convention to form a State constitution. It was shortly after taking his seat in this body, that two of the members getting into a fight, he interfered in behalf of one of the parties, announcing himself as the "Ringtailed Panther," by which name he was afterward known in the west. After serving two or three terms in the Missouri legislature, Parmer emigrated to Texas and settled near the Mound prairie. It is said he fired the first gun in the Fredonian war. Among the numerous stories told of him, it is related, upon good authority, that when his bear dog died, he sent fifty miles for a clergyman to attend the funeral, which he actually did, supposing it to be one of Colonel Parmer's family! His son, from whom the above account is obtained, says he heard the sermon.

Parmer was a member of the convention of 1836, which declared the independence of Texas.

(From Yoakum's Texas.)

HENRY KARNES

is another of those remarkable characters whose true history is a romance. He was raised in Tennessee. At an early age he joined a company of Arkansas trappers, who turned their attention to attacks on the Pawnee villages on the head branches of Red River; but having disagreed they separated. Karnes, with three or four others, proceeded across to the head of the Trinity. Here having their horses stolen, they obtained a canoe and floated down the river to Robbin's Ferry. Karnes procured employment at Groce's Retreat, where the war found him. He entered the Texas service, and fought with a hearty good-will.

One who was often with him, and by his side at Concepcion, says he never knew him to swear before or since that day. But when he came into the lines, after being shot at so often, and began to load his rifle, he exclaimed, with some wrath, the " d——d rascals have shot out the bottom of my powder horn." Karnes rose to the rank of colonel in Texas. He was of low stature, and weighed about a hundred and sixty pounds ; was quite sober and temperate, and had an effeminate voice. He was wholly illiterate, yet he had remarkable gentleness and delicacy of feeling, and was otherwise amiable in private life. He died at San Antonio, in August, 1840, surrounded by his numerous friends.

REMINISCENCES OF EARLY TEXANS.

(Texas Almanac, 1873.)

CAPTAIN HENRY S. BROWN,

an early and well known pioneer of Texas, was born in Madison county, Kentucky, March 8, 1793, and remained there till 1810, when the spirit of adventure, characteristic of him through life, led him, friendless and alone, to the wilds of Missouri, in which territory he took up his abode in St. Charles county. His immediate parents and ancestors for several generations had been respectable citizens of Baltimore and Carroll counties, Maryland. They were, without an exception, sterling patriots in the revolution of 1776, both his paternal and maternal grandfathers having been officers in that struggle. In the war of 1812–15, being but twenty years of age, he volunteered and served in the extreme west against the Indians till its close. At Fort Clark (now Peoria), on the Illinois River, under the immediate eye of his colonel (Musick), and Governor Howard, of Missouri, he performed an act of gallantry, during the siege by a large Indian force, which caused those officers to compliment him by name in their reports to the secretary of war. Having married, about the close of the war, he began and for nine years continued a trade in flat and keel boats from Missouri to New Orleans, a life then checkered with many thrilling incidents of danger and adventure unknown of late years.

In December, 1824, he landed at the mouth of the Brazos River, Texas, having an outfit of goods for the Indian and Mexican trade. He was accompanied by a younger brother, John, afterward known as Waco Brown. Captain Brown in person fitted out a caravan and proceeded to Monterey, Mexico, at the same time sending his brother, with three men and a supply of goods, to trade with the wild Indians for horses, and mules, buffalo robes, etc. Mr. John Brown proceeded to the Clear Fork of the Brazos, traded off his merchandise to the Indians for over a thousand head of horses and mules and a large number of robes. He had safely returned as far as the Bosque, when his camp was attacked at night and everything captured. His three companions, Thomas Jameson, James Musick, and Andrew Scott, escaped on foot and finally reached the lower Brazos. Mr. Brown, who was a confirmed cripple in one leg, secreted himself for the moment, supposing his companions would do the same, but when daylight came he found himself alone. After traveling as best he could for a day or two, he was taken prisoner by a party of Waco Indians, and by them kept for about fifteen months in their then favorite region, of which the present town site of Waco was one of the chief villages. He was captured in July or August, 1825, and by his stay among the Indians acquired a vast amount of information about the Waco and other tribes which proved to be of great value to General Austin and the early settlers.

On reaching the settlements, Mr. Brown's comrades expressed the confident belief that he was killed at the time the camp was attacked, from the fact that he fell over them as they were awakened, an incident explained by him after his escape.

On returning from Monterey and learning these facts, Captain Henry T. Brown determined to learn the fate of his brother, and fitted out a company of forty-two men who volunteered to follow his lead. He penetrated far up the country, found the Indians hostile at the intrusion, and had several encounters with them, the principal of which was at the Waco village, where he drove the whole force into and across the river, killing a considerable number. At that time his brother was in another village only two miles above, but on the opposite bank. The expedition returned convinced that Mr. John Brown was dead.

About a year later, in the autumn of 1826, Mr. Brown made his escape from a war party of seventeen Wacos on Cumming's Creek, now in Fayette county, the party having come down to kill and rob the settlers. He hastened to San Felipe, on the Brazos, where he found his brother, just returned from a second trip to Mexico, having a well-armed party with him. With these and some volunteer citizens Captain Brown hastened in search of the Indians, completely surprised them at daylight on the following morning, and killed all but one.

From that time till 1832 Captain Brown continued in the Mexican trade, making his headquarters at Brazoria, Gonzales, and San Antonio. His life was one akin to the legends of romance, and won for him among those early pioneers of Texas the character of a brave, chivalrous, and sagacious border chief.

His heart was warm and generous to a fault, but throughout those years of danger, as previously on the Mississippi River, his habits were sober, his intercourse with others honorable, and he rarely ever had a difficulty with his fellow man. Misfortune often attended him, and he several times lost heavily by the Indians.

Having located at Columbia in 1832, he was called to the command of the largest company (about eighty men and boys,) in the bloody battle of Velasco on the twenty-sixth of June, 1832. His gallantry on that occasion has been for nearly forty years the theme of praise by his surviving comrades. Soon afterward he was on the field as next friend to Colonel Wm. T. Austin, in the issue between that gentleman and the chivalrous Colonel John A. Wharton, on the Brazos, an event in which both of the distinguished contestants bore themselves as men of courage and honor, and one always remembered with regret by their many mutual friends.

In 1833 Captain Brown was again in the West, and had several adventures with both Indians and border Mexicans. It was often said by old citizens that he had more contests with the Indians, and was more generally successful, than any of the brave pioneer chiefs of that day.

He died in Columbia on the twenty-sixth of July, 1834, and sleeps his last sleep within a few a feet of Josiah H. Bell and the once famous Captain Bird Lockhart. His memory is honorably perpetuated in the name of the beautiful county of Brown, which was named in his honor.

Mr. Rufus E. Brown, of Kendall county, and John Henry Brown, of Dallas, are his only surviving children.

CAPTAIN RANDAL JONES.

(Texas Almanac, 1857.)

CAPTAIN RANDAL JONES was born in Columbia county, Georgia, on the 19th of August, 1786. In 1810, he went to Wilkinson county, in Mississippi Territory. In 1812, he entered the United States army as a volunteer, and continued in that service until 1814; was a captain during almost the entire term of his service. It will be seen in Pickett's History of Alabama, that the celebrated "Canoe Fight," is said to have been fought by Jere Austill, and that Dale and Smith were principal actors in it. No mention is made by Pickett of Captain Jones. The true version of this fight is this: Captain Randal Jones was the commander, and gave every order on that occasion. The following is from the *Washington Republican*, printed by Marschalk & Etin, in Washington, Mississippi Territory, on the 23d of December, 1813:

Extract of a letter from the Volunteer Army, dated East Bank of the Alabama, November 25th, 1813.

"On the 11th inst., Captain Jones, of the twelve months' volunteers, with a detachment of sixty volunteers and militia, marched from Fort Madison, for the Alabama, and on the 12th fell in with two parties of Creeks, which he entirely routed, and killed nine warriors, without sustaining any loss on his part. Captain Jones and his party deserve the greatest praise and honor for the handsome manner in which the enterprise was conducted."

This is but the beginning of his eventful career. In the fall of 1814, he came to the Sabine, and at Gaine's Ferry met with General Toledo, just after his defeat at the Medina. The General was then recruiting for another effort. Captain Jones thought his followers (about 200 in all, Mexicans and Americans) rather too ragged and motley a set to join. He therefore turned merchant, went to Natchez, and procured about $600 worth of goods, and spent the winter of 1814-15 trading with the Comanches in Texas.

In 1816, he established a store in Nacogdoches, and traded with the Indians and Mexicans until 1818. In the spring of this year he visited Lafitte, at Galveston, for the purpose of buying some necessaries of him. Prior to this time, Lafitte had been in the habit of selling negroes at this place, at the *convenient price of one dollar per pound!* Captain Jones spent two days and nights with Lafitte. He found him anything else than the rough, uncouth, savage pirate, popular opinion had made him. The captain says a more gentlemanly and courteous host he never met. 1819, Captain Jones joined the forces of General James Long, at Nacogdoches, where the general was maintaining an independent government, and was acting as governor and commander of the northern forces of Mexico. Here Captain Jones received the title of " Brigade Major." He was sent with a party of 21 men to go to " *Galveston at the mouth of the Brazos.*" He struck the Brazos River opposite where the town of Washington now is, commenced building boats to descend with, was set upon by about 60 Mexicans, broke up and made his way back to Louisiana. Early in the year 1822, he slept opposite to the town of San Felipe, as one of Austin's colonists. From that time forth he participated actively in all the vicissitudes of the early times of Texas, much of the time acting as captain of parties. As such he fought the Indians in September, 1824, in Brazoria county, at a creek which took its name from the fight, and is now known as " Jones' Creek." He was elected to the consultation, served in the ayuntamiento, and was at the Bradburn affair in 1835. He died in 1873.

SKETCH OF THE LIFE OF HENRY CASTRO.

(Texas Almanac, 1870).

HENRY CASTRO, the pioneer of that portion of Western Texas situated west of the city of San Antonio, was born in France, in July, 1786, of rich parents, and descended from one of the oldest Portuguese families, one of his ancestors, Zoao of Castro, having been fourth viceroy of the Indies for the King of Portugal. In 1805, at the age of nineteen, he was selected by the prefect of his department (Landes) to welcome the Emperor Napoleon, on the occasion of his visit to that department. In 1806, he was one of the guard of honor that accompanied Napoleon to Spain. In 1814, being an officer in the first legion of the National Guards of Paris, he fought, with Marshal Moncey, at the gate of Clichy. Having emigrated to the United States, after the fall of Napoleon, in May, 1827, he was consul at the port of Providence for the King of Naples, having become an American citizen, by choice, the same year. He returned to France in 1838 ; was the partner of Mr. Lafitte, and took an active part in trying to negotiate a loan for the Republic of Texas. In 1842 he was appointed, in consideration of the services he had rendered to the Republic of Texas, consul-general of Texas at Paris. Having received large grants of lands under certain conditions of colonization, he immediately proceeded to comply with his contract, and after great expense and labor, succeeded in bringing to this State four hundred and eighty-five families and four hundred and fifty-seven single men, in twenty-seven ships, from the year 1843 to 1846. He encountered much opposition from the French government, which was trying to procure emigrants for the colony of Algiers, and much expense on account of the Mexican war. His first settlement was established on the Medina, in September, 1844, and was called Castroville, now a flourishing little town, situated in one of the most beautiful and healthy portions of Texas. In 1845, he settled the town of Quihi ; in 1846, that of Vandenberg ; in 1847, that of Dhanis, all of which settlements are now in a prosperous condition. The colony lands, which were all in Bexar county formerly, now form the counties of Medina, Frio, part of McMullen, Lasalle, and Uvalde. He published many memoirs on Texas, both in the French and German languages, and also maps, which were principally circulated in the Rhine provinces, and greatly aided in procuring emigration to this country.

He was a man of great energy and of rare aptitude for labor. He developed the country, and received the most flattering testimonials from the most prominent persons of the United States. He was a corresponding member of the Washington Institute ; and a great friend and admirer of General Houston. He was on his way to visit the graves of his family, in France, when death overtook him, at Monterey, Mexico.

JOHN AUSTIN

was a native of Connecticut; came to Texas in 1829. He was in command of the Texas forces at the gallant attack upon Velasco, in 1832. He died at Brazoria in 1833.

W. T. AUSTIN,

brother of the former, came from Connecticut to Texas in 1831. He was aid to General Burleson at the storming of Bexar in 1835. Was for many years clerk of the county court of Brazoria county. Died in 1874.

COLLIN McKINNEY,

from whom Collin county and its county seat are named, came to Texas at an early day. He was the oldest member of the convention of 1836, and of the first congress of the republic, being at that time seventy years of age. He died in 1860.

JAMES G. SWISHER

came from Tennessee. He was in command of a company at the storming of Bexar in 1835. He was a member of the convention of 1836. He died at Austin in 1862.

SAM. ·MAVERICK

was a native of South Carolina, came to Texas in 1835. Participated in the storming of Bexar in that year. He was a member of the convention of 1836. Was also a member of the congress of the republic and of the legislature after annexation. He died at San Antonio in 1870.

ANDREW BRISCOE

came from Mississippi to Texas prior to 1836. He was for some time a merchant at Harrisburg, Texas. He commanded a company in the army of the revolution ; was at the battle of Concepcion in 1835, but was prevented by sickness from participating in the battle of April 21, 1836. He was afterward chief-justice of Harris county. He died in 1839.

IRA INGRAM

came from Vermont to Texas. He was for some time surveyor of Austin's colony. Was a member of the first congress of the republic, and was speaker of the House of Representatives. He died in 1839.

STERLING C. ROBERTSON

was born in Nashville, Tennessee, in 1785. He served in the war of 1812–14. He came to Texas in 1823. Having determined to raise a colony for Texas, Robertson returned to Tennesee, to carry out that design.

In 1825, Robert Leftwick made a contract with the Mexican government, to introduce 800 families into Texas, but abandoning the design, he sold out the contract to Robertson, who thereupon revisited Saltillo, Monclova, and the city of Mexico, and was recognized as the legal successor of Leftwick in the colony contract.

In April, 1830, a law was passed for the expulsion of all foreigners from Texas, who had not been introduced into the country in accordance with the colonization laws of March, 1825. This resulted in the expulsion of Robertson's first colonists, and necessitated several laborious trips on his part to the Mexican capital to secure the rights guaranteed to him under his contract.

This he at last, in 1834, succeeded in doing, and during that year he founded the town of Sarahville de Viesca on the heights overlooking the falls of the Brazos River.

In 1835, Colonel Robertson visited the States of Louisiana, Mississippi, Tennessee, and Kentucky, and prior to the breaking out of the revolution of 1835, he had introduced into Texas more than 600 families of settlers. He was a member of the convention of 1836, and was one of the signers of the declaration of independence. He commanded a company in the spring of 1836, and participated in the battle of San Jacinto. He was a member of the senate of the republic of Texas.

Colonel Robertson died, at his home in Robertson county, Texas, on the 4th of March, 1842.

STERLING C. ROBERTSON.

To face p. 288.

WARREN D. C. HALL

came from Louisiana to Texas in 1828. He had been in Texas in 1812-13, and was present at the defeat of Toledo. He was in the army, and was adjutant-general in 1835. He died in 1867.

GEORGE C. CHILDRESS

came to Texas from Tennessee in 1834. He was a member of the convention of 1836, and had the honor of drawing up the "declaration of independence" adopted by that body. He was appointed by the Burnet government *ad interim* one of the commissioners to Washington. He died in 1841.

JOSE ANTONIO NAVARRO

was one of those noble men of Mexican parentage whose heart beat in accord with the patriots of Texas. He was born in Bexar. He was a true friend of Texas during the revolution. Was one of the commissioners sent out by President Lamar with the Santa Fé expedition, and was for a long time a prisoner in Mexico. He served in the first and second legislature of Texas after annexation. Died in 1870.

ROBERT WILSON.

"*Honest Bob*" came to Texas in 1833. He was for some time a partner in the sawmill business with John R. Harris at Harrisburg (named for the latter). He served in the congress of the republic. Died in 1856.

THOMAS J. HARDEMAN,

brother of Bailey Hardeman, came from Tennessee in 1835. He served in the congress of the republic and the legislature of the State of Texas. He had the distinction of proposing the name of Austin for the capital of Texas in 1836. He died in 1854.

COLONEL BARNARD E. BEE

came from South Carolina to Texas in 1836. Was secretary of war of the republic under Houston's first administration. Died in 1853.

19

R. R. ROYAL

was from Alabama. Came to Texas before the year 1835. Was a member of the consultation of that year. He died in 1840. Royal was chosen temporary chairman of the consultation when it first met on the 16th day of October, at which time Sam. Whiting was made temporary secretary.

BENJAMIN FORT SMITH

was a native of Kentucky. Moved thence to Mississippi, where he was for a while in the legislature. Was for some time agent with the Chickasaws. He served under General Jackson in the campaigns of 1814–15. He came to Texas in 1830 or '31. Served as a captain in the Bexar campaign of 1835. Was afterward a member of the congress of the republic. Died in 1841.

JAMES KERR.

AMONG the very early pioneers of Texas, valued for wisdom in council and long and faithful services, few deserve more honorable remembrance than James Kerr, the first permanent American settler west of the Colorado River.

The son of Elder James Kerr, an estimable Baptist preacher, the subject of this sketch was born two miles from Danville, Kentucky, on the 24th of September, 1790.

With his father, brothers, and sisters, he removed to the territory of Missouri in 1808, and settled in St. Charles county. He was an active and daring soldier in the war of 1812–15, and accounted the most popular young man of his day in that region. He was the lieutenant and companion in arms of Captain Nathan Boone, and a great favorite of the latter's father, the famed Colonel Daniel Boone. He studied law under one of the ablest men of the territory, but never practiced, having no talent in that line. He was long sheriff of St. Charles county, when it was immense in territory. In 1819 he married the only child and daughter of General James Caldwell, of Ste. Geneviève, long speaker of the Territorial House of Representatives, as he had been of that of Kentucky. Colonel Kerr then located in Ste. Geneviève and was soon elected twice to the legislature, and in 1824 to the State senate. In that body he established a reputation for prudence, wisdom, and honor ; but having long been intimate with Stephen F. Austin, then colonizing Texas, he resolved to cast his lot with him. At the close of the session he resigned his seat, and in February, 1825, landed at Brazoria.

Before May, death claimed his young wife and two of his children, leaving him an infant daughter (Mrs. J. C. Sheldon, of Galveston), and his colored servants.

By Green De Witt, the empresario, he was appointed surveyor of the projected colony and, by the governor of the State, authorized to lay out and name the future capital of the same. He arrived where Gonzales now stands in June, 1825, with his servants, the celebrated Deaf Smith, Basil Durbin, and several other young men ; pitched his camp and erected cabins, and thereby became, as before stated, the first permanent American settler west of the Colorado. He laid out and named the town Gonzales, in honor of the then first governor of Coahuila and Texas, and proceeded with the survey of the lands. But, during his absence, on the 3d of July, 1826, his house was attacked by Indians, two of the young men killed and the settlement, for the time being, broken up. He then located on the lower La Vaca, and, being joined by a few others, built a log fort. This was in the fall of 1826. He at once selected his headright league, in the vicinity, on the east side of the La Vaca, and in 1827 made the first crop ever raised in that part of the country, sending into Louisiana for milch cows and peach scions and seeds, which were planted the same year, the stumps of which are yet visible on the same farm on which still resides his only surviving son—child of a second wife.

For several years he continued as surveyor of De Witt's colony, and also of De Leon's. In 1827 he was one of the peace commissioners sent from Austin's colony to secure an amicable adjustment of the Fredonian outbreak at Nacogdoches, which resulted auspiciously. He was a member of the conventions of 1832 and 1833 ; was elected to the consultation of 1835, but being in the army west of the Goliad, did not take his seat. He, however, rendered valuable service in the general council of the provisional government, and was the author of the wise and timely decree appointing Sam Houston, John Forbes, and John Cameron, commissioners to treat with the Cherokee Indians and their twelve associate bands.

On the 1st of February, 1836, he was elected to the convention which declared our independence, but the advance of the Mexican army forbade his taking his seat. He was compelled to flee from his frontier home with his family, and before he could place them in safety and reach the assemblage the convention had closed its brief but portentous session.

He served in the congress of 1838-9, and was the author of the first law in Texas to prevent duelling. To him and his friend William Menefee the west was more indebted than to any other two members, for frontier protection, and for the removal of the seat of government from Houston to Austin, essentially a western frontier measure.

The necessities of frontier life, diligent study, and great practical experience, made him an excellent physician. He finally made it a profession and enjoyed a large and successful practice.

He was a man of splendid intellect, well cultivated, of winning address, unostentatious habits, kind, genial, of great prudence mingled with marked firmness. As a citizen his example and counsels were invaluable through all the twenty-six eventful years in which he aided in fostering Texas. He was greatly esteemed by the Austins, Whartons, Jacks, Dr. Archer, President Burnet, and that bright constellation of early patriots and statesmen. His memory was wonderful. He was a living history of the Great West and Texas, thoroughly versed in Mexican character, and was ever ready to impart information. It was with him that his nephew, John Henry Brown, resided, on first coming to Texas, and through him had his instinctive admiration of pioneer history and life cultivated almost into a passion. To Colonel Kerr, his loved maternal uncle, that gentleman has ever ascribed the credit of directing his mind in that direction, and exalting patriotism above selfishness and intrigue.

Colonel Kerr died at his old home in Jackson county, December 23, 1850, in his sixty-first year, and was interred amid the sorrows of the whole county. The county of Kerr (pronounced Kar), named in his honor, perpetuates his name ; but his virtues are embalmed in thousands of yet surviving hearts.

JOHN CALDWELL

came from Alabama to Texas in 1831. He was born in Kentucky in 1802, but moved thence to Alabama. He served several sessions in the congress of the Republic of Texas, and also was, in the State senate after annexation. He was a member of the constitutional convention of 1845. He died in 1870.

MATT CALDWELL

came from Tennessee to Texas. He took an active part in the war against Mexico. He is well known as the hero of the battle of Salado in 1842. He participated in the battle of Plum Creek under Generals Huston and Burleson. He was in the Santa Fé expedition under General McLeod, and was captured and afterward released. He was commonly known as " *Old Paint.*" Died in 1842. His impetuous disposition is well expressed in the following report of the battle of Salado, written by himself at the time :

" September 17, 1842.

" At the Salado, two miles above the old crossing, we commenced fighting at eleven o'clock to-day. A hot fire was kept up until about an hour, by sun,

when the enemy retreated, bearing off their dead and wounded, which were many. We have a glorious band of Texas patriots, among whom only ten were wounded, and not one killed. The enemy are around me on every side, but I fear them not. I will hold my position until I receive re-enforcements. Come and help us. It is the most favorable opportunity I have seen. There are eleven hundred of the enemy. I can whip them on any ground, without help, but can not take any prisoners. Why don't you come? Hurra for Texas! "MATTHEW CALDWELL,
"*Colonel Commanding.*"

BIOGRAPHIES OF THE GOVERNORS OF TEXAS.

(From Baker's History of Texas.)

JAMES PINCKNEY HENDERSON

was born in North Carolina, in 1809. He studied law, and was admitted to the bar at the age of twenty-one. In 1836, he raised a company of volunteers in Mississippi, and came to Texas. In November, 1836, he was appointed attorney-general of Texas. In 1837, he was appointed minister plenipotentiary from Texas, to England and France, to secure the recognition of Texas by these powers. Returning to Texas in 1840, he resumed the practice of law. In 1844, he was appointed one of the envoys to Washington, to negotiate a treaty of annexation. In 1845, he was elected a delegate to the convention, to frame a State constitution. In November, of same year, he was elected first governor of Texas. The war with Mexico breaking out, General Henderson took command of the Texas troops, and served with ability and distinction until the close. In 1857, he was elected by the legislature to the senate of the United States, in place of the lamented Rusk. In spite of feeble health, he repaired to the national capital, but had scarcely entered upon his duties when he was stricken down by the hand of death.

GEORGE T. WOOD

was a native of Georgia. He came to Texas in 1836. He was a senator in the first legislature; was in the Mexican war, in command of a regiment of Texas volunteers, and was elected governor in 1847. He died in Polk county, Texas.

P. HANSBORO BELL

is a native of Virginia. He came to Texas in 1836. He took part in the battle of San Jacinto, and was for some time in command of the Texas troops upon the Indian frontier. He was elected governor of Texas in 1849, and again in 1851. He was elected representative to United States Congress in 1853, and again in 1855. After his marriage, which took place while he was representative in Congress, he removed from Texas to North Carolina, where he now resides.

ELISHA M. PEASE

was born in Connecticut, in 1812. He was educated to the profession of law. He came to Texas in 1835. He was secretary of the general consultation at San Felipe, in 1835. He was chief clerk in the navy, and also in the treasury department under the government *ad interim*, holding the later post until the adjournment of the first congress. In June, 1837, he was appointed comptroller of public accounts, by General Houston. This he resigned in December, 1837. After annexation, Governor Pease was elected successively to the house in the first and second legislature of Texas, and senator in the third legislature. In 1853, and again in 1855, he was elected governor. In 1867 he was, by General Sheridan, appointed provisional governor, which post he resigned in 1869. In 1874, he was tendered the appointment of collector of the port at Galveston, which he declined. He is now vice-president of the First National Bank at Austin, Texas.

HARDIN R. RUNNELS

was born in Mississippi. He came to Texas about the year 1842 ; was speaker of the House of Representatives in 1853 ; was lieutenant-governor of Texas during Pease's second term of office ; was elected governor in 1857. He died in Bowie county, Texas, 1873.

EDWARD CLARK

is a native of Georgia. He was a member of the constitutional convention in 1845. He was a member of the house in the first legislature of Texas, and senator in the second. He was secretary of state under Governor Pease. He was elected lieutenant-governor in 1859, and became governor on the retirement of General Houston in 1861. He now resides in Marshall, Harrison county, Texas.

FRANK R. LUBBOCK

is a native of South Carolina. He came to Texas in 1836. He was for a short time comptroller of public accounts, during the existence of the Republic of Texas. He was for many years clerk of the district court of Harris county, which position he filled with marked ability and fidelity. He was elected Governor of Texas in 1861. He now resides in Houston, Harris county, Texas, where he conducts a large commercial business.

PENDLETON MURRAH

was a native of Alabama. He came to Texas and settled in Harrison county, where he devoted himself to the practice of law. He was a member of the State legislature in 1857. He was elected governor of the State in 1863. He went to Mexico after the close of the war, in June, 1865, where he shortly afterward died.

A. J. HAMILTON

was born in Madison county, Alabama, January 28, 1815 ; was admitted to the bar in 1841 ; was married in 1843. He came to Texas in 1846 ; located first in Lagrange, and moved to Austin in 1849. In 1843 he was appointed by Governor Bell, attorney-general of Texas. In 1851 was elected representative to the State legislature from Travis county, and served in the same capacity in 1852. In 1856 was chosen elector on the Buchanan ticket. In 1859 was elected, as an independent candidate, representative to congress from the western district of Texas, defeating General T. N. Ward, the democratic nominee. General Hamilton was one of the few from the South who stood at their posts in congress until after secession was accomplished. He returned to Austin in March, 1861, to find himself the Union candidate for the State senate, from the counties of Travis, Hays, and Bastrop. To this post he was elected, but did not take the requisite oath, or appear in the senate chamber. In 1862 General Hamilton left his home in Texas, and went by way of Mexico to Washington city. In November, 1862, and again in September, 1863, he was appointed brigadier-general of volunteers and military governor of Texas. In June, 1865, he was appointed by President Johnson, provisional governor of Texas, which post he held until May, 1866. In 1866, he was appointed associate justice of the supreme court, which post he held until September, 1869. General Hamilton was elected a delegate to the second reconstruction convention, which assembled at Austin, in June, 1868, and was acknowledged leader in that body. He died at Austin in 1875.

J. W. THROCKMORTON

is a native of Sparta, Tennessee. Born February 1, 1825. He came to Texas in 1841, and settled in what is now Collin county, then part of Fannin. In 1851, was elected representative to the State legislature. Served in that capacity until 1856, when he was elected State senator, which position he held until 1861. He was elected delegate from Collin county to the secession convention in 1861 ; was one of the six who voted against the ordinance of secession, and did not sign it. After secession was accomplished, Governor Throckmorton, having raised a company, entered in the army, and was in active service in the States of Arkansas, Mississippi, and Louisiana, until the fall of 1863, when he was disabled by severe illness. At this time he was elected to the State senate, where he served during the sessions of 1863 and 1864. In 1864, he was appointed brigadier-general of the State troops. In 1865, was appointed by General E. Kirby Smith a commissioner to negotiate treaties with the different wild Indian tribes on the Texas border. He returned in June, 1865, having made treaties, in conjunction with the agents of the friendly tribes, with the Comanches, Kiowas, Lipans, Arrapahoes, Cheyennes, and others. He was elected a delegate to the constitutional convention of 1866, and was president of that body. In June, 1866, was elected governor of Texas ; was inaugurated August 8, 1866, and was removed by military order, August 9, 1867. In 1874, he was elected representative to the United States Congress from his district of Texas. He resides in Collin county, Texas.

EDMUND J. DAVIS

is a native of San Augustine, Florida. He came to Texas in 1848. While yet in his minority, he was admitted to the bar in 1849, and went to the Rio Grande. He resided in Webb and Cameron counties until the breaking out of the war for secession. He was deputy collector of customs at Laredo from 1850 until 1853. In the latter year he was elected district-attorney of that district ; and in 1855 was elected judge of the same (12th) district. To this position he was re-elected, and continued in its occupation until secession was accomplished in 1861, when, refusing to take the oath of allegiance to the Confederate States, he left the office. In 1862 he went to the Northern States, and in October was commissioned colonel of the 1st Texas cavalry, United States volunteers, which regiment was raised from refugees from Texas. In March, 1867, while at the mouth of the Rio Grande in Mexico, for the purpose of embarking his family, he was captured by a party of Confederate soldiers, who crossed the river in the night and surrounded the house of the Mexican commandant where he with his family was. After three days he was released, upon demand of the Mexican authorities. He returned to New Orleans, and was employed in various military services until the close of the war. He was appointed brigadier-general of United States volunteers in November, 1864, and was finally mustered out of service in September, 1865. Having returned to his home in Corpus Christi, he was elected a delegate to the convention which met at Austin in February, 1866. In September, 1867, he was tendered by General Griffin the appointment of chief-justice of the State, but declined. In January, 1868, he was elected a delegate to the second reconstruction convention, which assembled at Austin in June of that year, and was president of that body. Was by it chosen one of the six commissioners to lay before the authorities at Washington the new constitution of the State. In November, 1869, he was elected governor of Texas. He resides in Austin, now practicing law.

RICHARD COKE

was born in Williamsburg, Virginia, on March 13, 1829 ; was educated at William and Mary College, and studied law under Judge Beverly Tucker, professor of law in that institution. He came to Texas in October, 1850 ; located at Waco, and has lived there ever since. In September, 1865, he was appointed by Provisional Governor A. J. Hamilton, judge of the 19th judicial district. After the constitution of 1866 was framed, he was nominated by the democratic party on the ticket headed by Throckmorton for governor, for one of the positions of associate justice of supreme court of the State, and was elected. He went on the supreme court bench in September, 1866 ; and just one year from that time, with his associates in the supreme court bench, was removed by Brigadier-General Griffin, then commanding in Texas, as " an impediment to reconstruction." He returned to the practice of law in Waco, and continued in professional practice until he was elected governor of Texas, which office he now holds.

W. B. OCHILTREE.

(From a Sketch of his Life by C. S. West.)

THE long connection of Judge Ochiltree with the public service of Texas, as well as his high position at the bar, held for so long a period, render it proper that, in a publication of this character, a sketch of his career should be preserved, although he came to Texas subsequent to 1836.

He was born in North Carolina in 1811, and after moving first to Florida and then to Alabama, he emigrated from that State to Texas in 1839. Here he settled at Nacogdoches and engaged in the practice of law. From 1842 to 1844 he held the position of judge of the fifth ·district of the Republic, and was then, *ex officio*, a member of the Supreme Court of Texas. In December, 1844, Judge Ochiltree was by President Jones appointed secretary of the treasury.

In 1845 he was appointed attorney-general.

He was a member of the convention of 1845.

In 1855 and '6 he was a member of the legislature of Texas. In 1861, he was a member of the secession convention and was one of the signers of the ordinance of secession. He was afterward elected a delegate to the Provisional Congress of the Confederate States, then in session at Montgomery, Alabama. During the war he raised an infantry regiment for General Walker's division, but in 1863, on account of ill health he resigned his command and returned home. From this time until his death, which occurred in December, 1867, he was in feeble and gradually failing health. At the time of his death he was fifty-six years of age.

MAJOR VALENTINE BENNET,

migrated to Texas about 1830. He was with the Brazoria and Columbia boys in the battle of Velasco, where he was shot down, receiving severe wounds in the hip and face. He joined De Witt's Colony and located his head-right on the Gaudaloupe River, having his citizenship at Gonzales, introducing his family there in 1838. He was one of the notable " Eighteen" who at that place stood for he defense of the cannon when the Mexicans came on to remove them in 1835. He thus was one of the first to enroll in the army of Texas, and became of considerable service to General Stephen F. Austin in drilling the citizen soldiers who gathered to the defense of Texas, and were organized into an army by that statesman, at that Lexington of Texas. He soon received from General Austin a commission in the army, and continued with energetic constancy in public service, participating in the siege of San Antonio de Bexar ; and, ranking as major in the quarter-master and commissary department, remaining in the army until after the battle of San Jacinto. He was also major in the same department in the Santa Fé expedition, and chain-mate to George W. Kendall in one of the dungeons of Mexico. Returning from that imprisonment late in 1842 to his home at Gonzales, he again took a prominent part in the defense of that frontier, by co-operating with his old companion-in-arms, Captain Caldwell, in hurrying forward volunteers to meet the Mexican forces under General Woll, who was advancing upon San Antonio. He was, by his well-known devotion to Texas, able to raise immediate supplies of sub-sistence from voluntary contributions of the citizens ; and thus furnished many squads of poorly provisioned volunteers with jerked beef, and such small stores of corn as could upon the instant be collected. Finding from the dispatches of Colonel Caldwell that the Mexican advance was likely to be formidable, he in person hurried to the assistance of that officer at the well-known battle-field of the Salado, and joined in the pursuit of the de-feated enemy, continuing until the Texans returned to their homes. He then assisted in organizing the Somerville expedition and remained in the service of the Republic until his death, which occurred at Gonzales in July, 1843. The following notice of him was at the time published in the *New Orleans Picayune:*

"ANOTHER SANTA FE PRISONER DEAD."—Major Valentine Bennet, one of the members of the unfortunate Santa Fé expedition, died at Gonzales, Texas, on the 24th of July, of the cramp colic. Major Bennet was one of the companions of Mr. Kendall in his dreary march to the city of Mexico, and was imprisoned in the same quarters. He was a man far advanced in life, and was one of the earliest and bravest defenders of Texas, and bore an honorable part in the most sanguinary conflicts of the young Republic. He was a man of sterling integrity and honest deportment."

The following incident showing Major Bennet's ready humor, as told by some of those who were present at its occurrence, will perhaps bear men-tion : General Sam Houston and some of the members of the cabinet were one day discussing the adoption of a Texas uniform for the army ; Major Bennet passing hurriedly by was thus good- humoredly accosted by the Gen-eral, "Well, major, what uniform do you recommend for our boys ? " "Oh ! rags, rags ! they are the only uniform which we can procure at present," said the major, as he passed on amid loud bursts of laughter from the General and all who were near.

BIOGRAPHICAL NOTICES OF DECEASED JUDGES
OF THE SUPREME COURT OF THE STATE OF TEXAS.

BY C. S. W.

THE first supreme court of Texas, organized immediately after annexation, was composed of Chief-Justice John Hemphill and Associate Justices Abner S. Lipscomb and Royal T. Wheeler.

JOHN HEMPHILL

was born in Chester District, South Carolina, about the year 1804, and graduated at Jefferson College, Carmonsburg, Tennessee. He emigrated to Texas in 1838. He was judge of the 4th judicial district of the Republic of Texas, in 1840. In 1841 hc was made chief-justice of the republic, which office he held until annexation. He was a member of the convention of 1845. At the organization of the supreme court of the State of Texas, in 1846, he was appointed chief-justice, and after the change in the constitution requiring the election of judges, he was, in 1851, and again in 1856, elected to that high position. In 1857, Judge Hemphill was elected United States senator. He was afterward, in 1861, elected to the congress of the Confederate States, and while holding that position died at Richmond, Virginia, on the 7th day of January, 1862.

ABNER S. LIPSCOMB

was born in Edgefield District, South Carolina, on the 10th day of February, 1789. His father Joel, and his mother whose maiden name was Elizabeth Chiles, were both natives of Virginia. He studied law with John C. Calhoun. He came to the bar in 1810, and practiced in the now deserted town of St. Stephens, on the Tombigbee River, Alabama. On the 17th day of December, 1819, he was appointed one of the circuit judges of Alabama. The circuit judges sitting in *banco*, then constituted the supreme court of that State. From 1823 to 1835 he held the position of chief-justice of the supreme court of Alabama. In 1839 he came to Texas and became secretary of state under General Lamar's presidency. In 1845 he was a member of the convention that framed the constitution of 1845. In 1846 he was appointed one of the associate justices of the supreme court by Governor J. P. Henderson. In August, 1851, and again in 1856, he was elected to that position, and continued to hold it until his death, which occurred at Austin on the 8th day of December, 1856, he being then in the 68th year of his age.

ROYAL T. WHEELER

was born in Vermont, in 1810. He was reared in the State of Ohio, and after being admitted to the bar in that State in 1837, he emigrated to Arkansas, and settled at Fayetteville, where he practiced his profession. In 1839, he married Miss Emily Walker, and then removed to the republic of Texas and settled at Nacogdoches. Here he practiced law successfully, as the partner of the distinguished Kenneth L. Anderson, who was cut off in the flower of his fame while holding the office of vice-president of the Republic of Texas.

In 1846, he was appointed one of the associate justices of the supreme court. In 1851, he was elected to the same office, and re-elected in 1856. In December, 1857, when Chief-Justice Hemphill was elected to the United States senate, he became chief-justice of Texas. He died in April, 1864, while holding that office. He was the survivor of those who constituted the first supreme court of Texas. In a short sketch of Judge Wheeler occurs the following allusion to his two distinguished associates, which it is deemed appropriate to insert here : "Judges Hemphill, Lipscomb, and Wheeler have now passed away from among us. The subject of this imperfect sketch was the last of that illustrious trio, who constituted the original supreme court of the State of Texas. Their names are imperishably connected with the judicial history of our State. They constitute the *dii majores* of Texas jurisprudence. That the subject of this notice was deemed a fit colleague of Hemphill and Lipscomb is in itself no mean tribute to his worth. He was the youngest of the three, and while he did not perhaps possess the deep, varied, and almost exhaustless learning both in civil and common law that so eminently distinguished his illustrious predecessor as chief-justice, nor was he so largely endowed by nature as was Judge Lipscomb, with that keen-sighted every day practical sense and that strong iron logic that so abundantly supplied in him the want of mere book-learning : yet Chief-Justice Wheeler possessed other mental faculties of a high order, by the exercise of which he elevated himself to the full level of his great compeers.

" His conscientiousness, his calm, profound, and patient industry, his deep love of truth for its own sake, his familiarity with our statute law and reports, his accurate common law knowledge, especially in the great department of criminal jurisprudence (in which he surpassed both his associates), served him in the place of genius, and eminently fitted him for the successful discharge of the delicate and exacting functions of the high office to which he was called."

PART III.

MISCELLANY.

MISCELLANY.

I.

HOUSTON'S FIRST INAUGURAL ADDRESS.

On the third of October, 1836, the delegates assembled at Columbia, and the first congress of the Republic of Texas was organized. On the morning of the 22d of the same month, the President *ad interim* tendered his resignation, and a resolution was immediately introduced, " that the inauguration take place at four o'clock this day." A committee from both houses waited upon the president elect, and at four o'clock, he was introduced within the bar of the house of representatives. The speaker administered to him the oath of office, and then proclaimed Sam Houston, President of the Republic of Texas.

The following is his inaugural address—delivered on this occasion.

MR. SPEAKER AND GENTLEMEN:

Deeply impressed with a sense of the responsibility devolving on me, I can not, in justice to myself, repress the emotion of my heart, or restrain the feelings which my sense of obligation to my fellow-citizens has inspired— their suffrage was gratuitously bestowed. Preferred to others, not unlikely superior in merit to myself, called to the most important station among mankind, by the voice of a free people, it is utterly impossible not to feel impressed with the deepest sensations of delicacy, in my present position before the world. It is not here alone, but our present attitude before all nations, has rendered my position, and that of my country, one of peculiar interest.

A spot of earth almost unknown to the geography of the age, destitute of all available resources, few in numbers, we remonstrated against oppression ; and when invaded by a numerous host, we dared to proclaim our independence and to strike for freedom on the breast of the oppressor. As yet our course is onward. We are only in the outset of the campaign of liberty.

20

Futurity has locked up the destiny which awaits our people. Who can contemplate with apathy a situation so imposing in the moral and physical world !

The relations among ourselves are peculiarly delicate and important ; for no matter what zeal or fidelity I may possess in the discharge of my official duties, if I do not obtain co-operation and an honest support from the co-ordinate departments of the government, wreck and ruin must be the inevitable consequences of my administration. If then, in the discharge of my duty, my competency should fail in the attainment of the great objects in view, it would become your sacred duty to correct my errors and sustain me by your superior wisdom. This much I anticipate—this much I demand.

I am perfectly aware of the difficulties that surround me, and the convulsive throes through which our country must pass. I have never been emulous of the civic wreath—when merited it crowns a happy destiny. A country, situated like ours, is environed with difficulties, its administration is fraught with perplexities. Had it been my destiny, I would infinitely have preferred the toils, privations, and perils of a soldier, to the duties of my present station. Nothing but zeal, stimulated by the holy spirit of patriotism, and guided by philosophy and reason, can give that impetus to our energies necessary to surmount the difficulties that obstruct our political progress. By the aid of your intelligence, I trust all impediments to our advancement will be removed ; that all wounds in the body politic will be healed, and the constitution of the republic derive strength and vigor equal to any emergency. I shall confidently anticipate the consolidation of constitutional liberty. In the attainment of this object, we must regard our relative situation to other countries.

A subject of no small importance is the situation of an extensive frontier, bordered by Indians, and open to their depredations. Treaties of peace and amity and the maintenance of good faith with the Indians, seem to me the most rational means for winning their friendship. Let us abstain from aggression, establish commerce with the different tribes, supply their useful and necessary wants, maintain even-handed justice with them, and natural reason will teach them the utility of our friendship.

Admonished by the past, we can not, in justice, disregard our national enemies. Vigilance will apprise us of their approach, a disciplined and valiant army will insure their discomfiture. Without discrimination and system, how unavailing would all the resources of an old and overflowing treasury prove to us. It would be as unprofitable to us in our present situation, as the rich diamond locked in the bosom of the adamant. We can not hope that the bosom of our beautiful prairies will soon be visited by the healing breezes of peace. We may again look for the day when their verdure will be converted into dyes of crimson. We must keep all our energies alive, our army organized, disciplined, and increased to our present emergencies. With these preparations we can meet and vanquish despotic thousands. This is the attitude we at present must regard as our own. We are battling for human liberty ; reason and firmness must characterize our acts.

The course our enemies have pursued has been opposed to every principle of civilized warfare—bad faith, inhumanity, and devastation marked their path of invasion. We were a little band, contending for liberty ; they were thousands, well-appointed, munitioned, and provisioned, seeking to rivet chains upon us, or to extirpate us from the earth. Their cruelties have incurred the universal denunciation of Christendom. They will not pass from their nation during the present generation. The contrast of our conduct is manifest ; we were hunted down as the felon wolf, our little band driven from fastness to fastness, exasperated to the last extreme ; while the blood of our kindred and our friends, invoking the vengeance of an offended God, was smoking to high heaven, we met our enemy and vanquished them. They fell in battle, or suppliantly kneeled and were spared. We offered up our vengeance at the shrine of humanity, while Christianity rejoiced at the act and looked with pride at the sacrifice. The civilized world contemplated, with proud emotions, conduct which reflected so much glory on the Anglo-Saxon race. The moral effect has done more toward our liberation than the defeat of the army of veterans. Where our cause has been presented to our friends in the land of our origin, they have embraced it with their warmest sympathies. They have rendered us manly and efficient aids. They have rallied to our standard, they have fought side by side with our warriors. They have bled, and their dust is mingling with the ashes of our heroes. At this moment I discern numbers around me who battled in the field of San Jacinto, and whose chivalry and valor have identified them with the glory of the country, its name, its soil, and its liberty. There sits a gentleman within my view, whose personal and political services to Texas have been invaluable. He was the first in the United States to respond to our cause. His purse was ever open to our necessities. His hand was extended in our aid. His presence among us, and his return to the embraces of our friends, will inspire new efforts in behalf of our cause.

[The attention of the speaker and that of congress was directed to Wm, Christy, Esq., of New Orleans, who sat by invitation within the bar.]

A circumstance of the highest import will claim the attention of the court at Washington. In our recent election, the important subject of annexation to the United States of America was submitted to the consideration of the people. They have expressed their feelings and their wishes on that momentous subject. They have, with a unanimity unparalleled, declared that they will be reunited to the Great Republican family of the North. The appeal is made by a willing people. Will our friends disregard it? They have already bestowed upon us their warmest sympathies. Their manly and generous feelings have been enlisted on our behalf. We are cheered by the hope that they will receive us to participate in their civil, political, and religious rights, and hail us welcome into the great family of freemen. Our misfortunes have been their misfortunes—our sorrows, too, have been theirs, and their joy at our success has been irrepressible.

A thousand considerations press upon me; each claims my attention. But the shortness of the notice of this emergency (for the speaker had only four hours' notice of the inauguration, and all this time was spent in conversation) will not enable me to do justice to those subjects, and will necessarily induce their postponment for the present.

[Here the president, says the reporter, paused for a few seconds and disengaged his sword.]

It now, sir, becomes my duty to make a presentation of this sword—this emblem of my past office. [The president was unable to proceed further; but having firmly clenched it with both hands, as if with a farewell grasp, a tide of varied associations rushed upon him in a moment, his countenance bespoke the workings of the strongest emotions, his soul seemed to dwell momentarily on the glistening blade, and the greater part of the auditory gave outward proof of their congeniality of feeling. It was, in reality, a moment of deep and painful interest. After this pause, more eloquently impressive than the deepest pathos conveyed in language, the president proceeded.] I have worn it with some humble pretensions in defense of my country—and should the danger of my country again call for my services, I expect to resume it, and respond to that call, if needful, with my blood and my life.

II.

SUDDEN FLOODS IN TEXAS.

(From State Journal.)

COLONEL MERRIAM, of the 24th infantry United States army, with his family and an escort, encamped on the Concho River on Sunday, the 24th day of April, 1870. This river is formed by the junction of the rills of water from several large springs. The stream at its head is so small that a man can step across it anywhere. The tops of the banks are usually about twenty-five feet above the water. Fatigued with their journey, the party were pleasantly resting, when early in the evening Colonel Merriam saw signs of the coming storm. The tent was fastened, and made as secure as possible, and about nine o'clock a hail storm burst upon them-accompanied with some rain and a strong wind. The fall of hail was unprecedented, lasting until eleven o'clock, the stones being of the size of hen's eggs, and striking the tent with a noise like that of incessant musketry. The colonel, who was not ignorant of the sudden and extreme overflows to which the mountain streams of Texas are liable, went out into the darkness as soon as the storm had ceased, to see what effect had been produced on the rivulet. To his amazement he found, in the formerly almost dry bed of the creek, a resistless torrent, loaded and filled with hail, rolling nearly bank full, white like milk, and silent as a river of oil. He at once saw the danger, and rushed back to the tent, shouting at the same time to the soldiers and servant to "turn out." He placed Mrs. Merriam, and their child and nurse, in the ambulance, and with the aid of three men started to run with it to the higher ground, a distance of not more than sixty yards. Scarcely a minute had elapsed from the time the alarm had been given, but the water had already surged over the banks in waves of such volume and force, as to sweep the party from their feet before they had traversed thirty yards. The colonel called for assistance upon some cavalry soldiers, who had just escaped from the United States mail station near by, but they were too terror-stricken to heed. Colonel Merriam then gave up the hope of saving his family in the carriage, and tried to spring into it, intending to swim out with them; but the icy torrent instantly swept him away. Being an expert swimmer, he succeeded in reaching the bank two hundred yards below, and ran back to renew the attempt to save his dear ones, when he received the awful tidings, that the moment he was borne away by the stream, the carriage, with all its precious freight, turned over and went rolling down the flood ; his wife saying, as she disappeared, " My darling husband, good-by." The little rill of a few hours before, which a child might step across, had become a raging river near a mile in width, from thirty to forty feet deep, and covered with masses of drift-wood. The bereaved husband procured a horse from one of the cavalry, and rode far down the river, but could see nothing distinctly in the darkness, while nothing could be heard but the wild roar of the waters. Thus passed the long, wretched night. Before day, the momentary flood had passed by, and the stream had shrunk within its accustomed limits. The search began. The drowned soldiers and servants, four in number, were soon found, and the body of the wife was taken from the water three-fourths of a mile below. The body of the child was not found until three days after, four miles down the stream, and a long distance from its channel. The carriage was drifted by the current about a mile, and lodged in a thicket.

The storm had been frightful beyond description. The beaver ponds at the head of the Concho were so filled with hail, that the fish were killed, and were washed out and deposited on the surface of the surrounding country in loads. Three days after the storm, when the searching party left the Concho, the hail still lay in drifts to the depth of six feet.

Heavy indeed was the heart of the bereaved husband and father when he commenced his melancholy march to the post of the Concho, fifty-three miles distant.

III.

M. DE SALIGNY.

(From A Brief History of Texas.)

AN amusing incident is said to have occurred at the French court, pending the acknowledgment of the independence of Texas. General Henderson, who was minister from Texas, and urging the measure upon the French government, was asked in the presence of M. de Saligny, who had just returned from Texas, " What was the population of that country ? "

Henderson, desirous of making the number as large as possible, and almost ashamed to say what he really thought the figures to be, artfully referred the question to Saligny, who, with French promptness, instantly replied, " About a million."

The court was too polite to doubt the statement, and of course the question of population did not stand in the way any longer. At the time, the population of Texas could not have exceeded fifty thousand souls.

IV.

ANECDOTE OF DAVID G. BURNET.

IN 1829, a young Mexican officer came to San Felipe with dispatches to Stephen F. Austin. While waiting a few days for his replies, he went often to the room of Mr. P., who was teaching a school there, and had a library, which was a rare thing in those days. His attention was arrested by a Spanish Testament, which he read with deep and absorbed attention. After reading it for hours he turned to Mr. P. and abruptly said, " Will you sell me this ? " Mr. P. replied, " I don't see how I can replace it, and therefore I don't like to part with it, as I am now studying your language."

Next day the young Mexican returned and pored over the pages of the

Gospels with increased interest. Again he said to the teacher, "Will you *give* me this book?" Mr. P., who was a pious man and was pleased with the interest displayed by the young man, said, "Why are you so anxious to have that book?" "Oh, my friend, he replied, it is a good book. God gave us this book to show us the way to heaven. It shows me how to be happy. I have three sisters. I want to take it to them that they may read it and be happy too." "Take it, my friend," said Mr. P. "Take it and welcome."

Sometime afterward, while on a visit to President Burnet, Mr. P. related the above incident, and instantly when he had concluded, Mr. Burnet arose, and walking to his book-case he took therefrom a handsomely bound edition of the complete Bible in Spanish, and presented it to Mr. P. saying, "Here, dear sir, allow me to replace the book you gave in such a cause."

V.

ANECDOTE OF STEPHEN F. AUSTIN.

In the days of the early settlement of Texas, General Austin sent Mr. —— from San Felipe to the Colorado, to take the census of the families in that part of his colony. The duty being performed, the messenger returned, and the following conversation occurred:

Austin.—"Well, Mr. —— how do you like that part of the country?"

Mr. —— (who had recently come to Texas and was somewhat unused to the rougher type of frontiersman).—"I like the country much, but would'nt live in such a community if you would give it all to me."

Austin.—"Why? Did'nt they treat you well?"

Mr. ——.—"Yes indeed, never was better treated."

Austin.—"Tell me about it."

Mr. ——.—"Well, General, to give you a sample of the people living up there. I went to a log-cabin where I found only a lady at home. I asked her who lived there. She said, 'I and the old man.' I told her I had come to take the census. She told me to take it. I said to her, 'Have you any children?' She replied. 'Yes, lots on em.' 'Please give me their names, madam.' 'Well, thar's Isaiah, and Bill, and Tom, and Jake, and Ed, and John, and Bud, and—oh yes, I'd like to forgot Joe, he's gone so much.' These being duly noted, with ages, 'Have you no girls?' "No, sir," emphatically, 'boys is trouble enough, but arter awhile they can take care of themselves, but gals is allers trouble, and never can take care of themselves.' General, those people are too rough to live with."

Austin. "Well, Mr. ——, those are exactly the people we want for the pioneers on our frontier. They are hardy, honest, and brave. They are not your kid-glove·sort. As the settlement becomes denser they will strike farther out upon the borders. I wish we had more of them."

VI.

FRED DAWSON.

APROPOS of Fred Dawson, the following verses, written by one who will recognize them, are inserted here. They were designed to cheer him up when desponding in regard to getting his claim against Texas paid:

FRIEND DAWSON!

> Has fortune frowned, my honest friend?
> Don't hang your head so low.
> 'This is no time to falter now.
> Up! Strike another blow.'

> Don't sit and groan and grunt, and tell
> What you have tried to do;
> But place your shoulder to the wheel,
> Strain nerve and put her through.

A. SOVEREIGN.

VII.

GOVERNOR BELL AND CAPTAIN S——.

IN November, 1850, the writer was in Collin county, Texas. P. Hansboro Bell was then governor, and his personal popularity with those men who as soldiers had served under him was unbounded.

Among his warm friends was Captain Jesse S——, a resident of Collin county, and this gentleman invited the writer to accompany him to his home for a deer hunt. Captain S—— lived about six miles from McKinney, the county seat, and during the ride out the following colloquy took place. In explanation it may be said that the Congress of the United States had just passed the bill offering Texas ten millions for a slice of her New Mexican boundary. The bill was known as the Pearce boundary bill, and the question of the acceptance or the rejection of the measure was to be submitted to the people of Texas on the following Monday.

Writer.—" Well, captain, how will you vote next Monday ? "

Captain.—" Don't know. What's the question.'

Writer.—" The ten million boundary bill."

Captain.—" Oh ! I haven't thought much about it, but I'll vote for Bell."

Writer.—" Oh, yes."

VIII.

ANOTHER UNPUBLISHED ANECDOTE OF GENERAL SAM HOUSTON.

It was the custom of General Houston, while governor, to mingle and talk with the people a good deal.

In 1860, he might have been seen almost daily on Congress avenue, Austin, Texas, standing at some corner with a crowd around him. Upon one occasion, and while in the center of a knot of men with whom he was conversing in an animated manner, an individual, whom we will call Mr. K——, being determined to get his ear, elbowed his way through the crowd and suddenly confronting General Houston addressed him thus : " Governor, I am told you have devoted considerable attention to the culture of shrubbery. What do you consider the best time for setting out shade trees, and how ? "

The General, being thus suddenly interrupted in the middle of a sentence, lowered his shaggy eyebrows, and quietly regarding his interlocutor a moment slowly replied, " The best time, Mr. K——, is perhaps in the winter, and the way in which I have succeeded best is to set the roots down."

A shout went up, and K—— went off.

IX.

A BEAR FIGHT.

(From T. N. Morrill's book, " Thirty-six Years in Texas.")

Returning home from one of my monthly tours under the burning sun of August, I found myself greatly exhausted in consequence of a ride of one hundred miles from Providence Church, Navarro county, north of Chambers Creek. After a little rest, I mounted my horse, gun in hand, with a view first to look after the farm, and secondly, if possible, to get a deer or turkey ; as fresh meat was called for. The farm was in the Brazos bottom, and at this season of the year, the weeds were from four to six feet high. Passing around the field, I watched every motion of the weeds, expecting to see a deer or turkey. Presently my attention was called to my right, and about thirty steps from my path my eyes rested upon the head of an old she-bear, standing upon her hind feet and looking at me. My horse was wild, and I dared not shoot from the saddle. Leaping to the ground as quickly as possible, my rifle was leveled, and the mark at which I aimed was as " black as the tents of Kedar." As I was in the act of pulling the trigger, my game disappeared behind the weeds. Just then the weeds shook nearer by, and two cubs, not more than ten feet from me, ran up a hackberry tree.

Resting among the limbs, they turned their anxious eyes upon me. The old bear was gone ; and very deliberately I tied up my horse, and with a smile on my face and none but the bears and the God of the Universe in hearing, I said, " I am good for you, certain ! " As I was about pulling the second time, the case of old Davy Crockett flashed into my mind, when he shot the cub, and the old bear came upon him with his gun empty.

With this distinguished hunter, I had gone on the bear chase in Tennessee. Well was it that I thought of him at this moment, for I had not even a knife or a dog to help me in extremity, and as, unlike the king of Israel, I did not feel able to take a bear by the beard, I lowered my gun and unsprung the trigger. Just then, an angry snarl fell upon my ears, a short distance away. The old bear was after me. The weeds cracked and shook, and she stood upon her hind feet, walking toward me, swaying her body first to one side then the other. Her hair was all standing on end and her ears laid back, presenting a frightful appearance. Life was pending on the contest. Either T. N. Morrill or that bear had to die. The only chance was to make a good shot. The bear was not now more than forty feet from me, and steadily advancing. The days of flint and steel had passed away, and, remembering that my caps were too small and sometimes failed to fire, I kept my eye on the bear and pressed my hammer firmly on the cap. By this time I had what the old Texans call buck ague. My nerves were all unstrung, and for my life I could not hold my gun steady, as I pointed it toward the bear. I had faced the cannon before, but never did I feel as when facing that bear. I gripped the gun, but the tighter I gripped, the worse I trembled. The bear was now less than twenty feet away, walking straight on its hind legs.

By moving the gun up and down, I finally succeeded in getting the range of the body, but not until the animal was within ten feet of me, did I get an aim upon which I was willing to risk a shot. The bear was in the act of springing when I fired. At the crack of the gun, the bear sprang convulsively to one side, and fell. I then reloaded, and killed the cubs.

X.

A PIG MEDDLES IN DIPLOMACY.

IN February 1841 a funny affair occurred, which well-nigh caused a rupture of the friendly relation which existed between France and Texas. One of the pigs of Mr. Bullock, an Austin landlord, found his way into the stable of M. De Saligny, the French chargé, and proceeded to appropriate a portion of the corn of the minister's horses. For this offense a servant slew the swinish invader, whereupon the irate landlord horsewhipped the dependent of the French ambassador.

Saligny thereupon complained, and Bullock was arrested and bound over to next term of court. Afterward the landlord ordered the envoy off his premises. These indignities to French honor were not to be put up with, and the Texas government, failing to give satisfaction, the French minister abandoned his post. A conciliatory letter from President Houston afterward healed the breach and brought the testy Frenchman back.

XI.

JUDGE BURNET'S ORATION AT THE FUNERAL OF JOHN A. WHARTON.

FRIENDS AND FELLOW-CITIZENS :

The keenest blade on the field of San Jacinto is broken?—the brave, the generous, the talented John A. Wharton is no more! His poor remains lie cold and senseless before you, wrapped in the habiliments of the grave, and awaiting your kind offices to convey them to the charnel-house appointed to all the living. A braver heart never died. A nobler soul, more deeply imbued with the pure and fervent spirit of patriotism, never passed its tenement of clay to the more genial realms of immortality. He was young in years, and, as it were, at the very threshold of his fame ; and still it is a melancholy truth, to which every heart in this assembly will respond in painful accordance, that a mighty man has fallen among us. Many princes of the earth have perished in their prime, surrounded with all the gorgeous splendors of wealth and power, and their country has suffered no damage. But surely it will be engraven on the tablets of our history, that Texas wept when Wharton died !

Colonel Wharton was among the early emigrants to Texas. Young, active, enterprising, intelligent, and endowed with an indomitable spirit of persever-ance, he was peculiarly fitted to figure conspicuously in the new, and to ordi-nary minds, the difficult circumstances in which Providence and his own adventurous energies had placed him. In his early sojourn among us, when Texas was but the feeble and neglected nursling of an unkind foster parent, he devoted his time and very precious talents to the practice of the law. Zealously devoted to his profession, he soon attained an eminence beyond his years, and a character for candor, integrity, an exemption from the little-ness of practical quirks and quibbles, that endeared him to all his liberal associates of the bar. His mind was constructed for the highest acquisitions of human knowledge ; and in choosing the profession of the law, he followed the natural propensity of his great intellect ; for there is no business of man that is better adapted to the almost illimitable range of genius, or to the severe exercises of judgment, than that comprehensive and useful science. I have said his talents were precocious ; but I intend a relative precocity ; for the ripeness of his mind was just beginning to adorn his adopted country by its rich developments, when the precious fruit was nipped by the frost of death ; and the majestic plant, whose fragrance had shed a sweet savor of prom-ised blessings on all around, was translated to a more propitious clime, where, I trust in God it will flourish in immortal bloom.

In the fall of '35, when the alienation of feeling between Texas and Mexico was first manifested by deliberate overt acts of aggression on the part of the central usurpers, Colonel Wharton was selected by a numerous and intelligent constituency to represent the county of Brazoria in the general Consultation. His active mind had been intently observant of the rapid and apparently fortuitous fluctuations that marked the political career of that distracted and unhappy republic ; and in his deep forethought, acting upon feelings of unwonted sensibility, and on a spirit which the brightest hero in the romance of chivalry might have coveted, he early and warmly advocated the separation of Texas from the perverse politics, the bigoted misrule, and the retrogressive destinies of Mexico. The impetuous ardor of his mind seized the first indication of a design to subvert the constitutional franchise-ments of his adopted country ; and his gallant spirit could brook no delay in asserting her sacred and unalienated rights. He was among the first to pro-pose the independence of Texas ; and true to the frankness of his nature, he was foremost with those who nobly bared their bosoms to the storm, when that declaration, which gave assurance to the world that a man child was born into the family of nations, was pronounced.

The brief time permitted us to linger about his waste and attenuated form, is insufficient to recite the testimonials of his gallantry. It is enough to ·say that he was distinguished on the field of San Jacinto—for there were no recreants there. All had strung their chafed and dauntless spirits to the high resolve of Liberty or Death ; and he who could make himself conspicuous on such a battle-field, was something more than hero : a hero among heroes !—for never in the annals of war did braver hearts or stouter hands contend for Liberty.

Colonel Wharton was not only a brave man and a patriot : he was a kind, affectionate, confiding friend. Having no guile himself, he had an instinctive aversion to a suspicion of deception in others. Frank, open, honorable, and without fear, he never entertained a thought of men or things which his lips could hesitate to utter. If he had an enemy, it was the uncalculating frankness of his nature that made him so; for it is a truth to be deplored, that the ingenuous are often misunderstood, and give undesigned offense when they ought to excite admiration.

With you, gentlemen of the house of representatives, the lamented deceased was associated by an intimate political connection. You have observed his assiduity, his untiring zeal, his singleness of heart, and his profound and accurate judgment in all the exalted duties of a legislator. To you he furnished ample evidence that his great professional attainments were only inductive to the still more enlarged capacities of his intellect, and that when his mind was turned to politics, it seemed as if nature had fashioned him for a statesman. You are bereaved of a valuable and much valued member—whose vacant seat it will be difficult to fill with equal endowments. That eloquent tongue is hushed in death, and the grave worm will shortly fatten upon it. Those lips that never quivered except under the gush of " words that breathe and thoughts that burn," are closed forever, and no more shall these walls reverberate their thrilling enunciations. To you, soldiers ! he was endeared by many ties. You have shared with him the toils and privations of an arduous and protracted campaign. You have witnessed and have participated in his devotion to his country, and his patient endurance of fatigue and suffering in the tented field : his agonized indignation at every successive retreat before the invading foe. Many of you retain, in vivid recollection, his burning impatience for the conflict when on the great day of San Jacinto, his buoyant spirit gratulated his companions in arms on the near prospect of a battle ; and you have marked his gallant bearing when the shock of arms first sounded on the plain, and the war-cry of Alamo ! carried terror and dismay into the camp of the bloody homicides of Goliad. Behold your brother in arms ! A cold, silent, prostrate corse. No more shall the din of war arouse his martial spirit to deeds of high enterprise. That lifeless clay would heed it not ; for the bright spirit which lately animated and adorned it, has passed triumphantly beyond the narrow bourn of mortal strifes, to that blessed region where " wars and rumors of wars are never heard."

To you, members of the benevolent Fraternity! he was an object of peculiar regard. He exemplified, in an eminent degree, all the cardinal virtues which your order proclaims and inculcates. His benevolence was not merely masonic, it was catholic; universal; and comprehended all classes of the distressed. To the poor he was kind, generous, and open "as day in melting charity." To the weak and friendless, he was a ready refuge and defense. Of him, it may be said with great propriety, in the language of the poet—

> That all the oppressed who wanted strength,
> Had his at their command.

And to you, mourning friends! kindred of the dear deceased, oh! how precious was he. You knew his virtues: his kind and gentle benevolence, which dispensed its benefactions like the dew of heaven, unheard, unseen, except in the substantial blessings on the objects of his charity. The splendor of his forensic talents, the high blazonry of his military fame, are subordinate to the mild and amiable qualities that beautified his social and domestic relations. To you he was a devoted brother in the full, free, unreserved practical sense of the fraternal tie. But he is gone! No more will he grace your social circle: no more give the blandness of his cheerful presence to your hospitality. But despond not, I beseech you, nor weep as those who have no hope. Your friend and our friend died not as the fool dieth. He calmly contemplated his approaching dissolution; and in the pure spirit of christian philosophy he avowed his forgiveness of all his enemies, and professed a hope of receiving a full and free pardon through the meritorious intercession of the blessed Redeemer.

While we indulge this pious confidence that a merciful God has sealed that hope with the signet of his favor, be it our deep concernment to apply this inscrutable Providence to our own hearts, and to educe from it the only advantage it confers, by taking heed to our own ways.

XII.

AARON BURR.

THE following interesting account of the arrest of Aaron Burr, although not directly relating to the subject matter of our volume, still deserves a place here, when we consider that the daring subject of the sketch was at the time planning an expedition for the occupation of Texas and Mexico. It is from "Pickett's History of Alabama."

It was a cold night in February 1807. Nicholas Perkins, a lawyer, and Thomas Malone, clerk of the court, were sitting in their cabin in Wakefield,

Alabama, playing chess. It was ten o'clock. The sound of horses' feet arrested their attention. Two travelers rode up to the door, and calling, inquired for the tavern. It was pointed out to them, and one of them inquired the road to Colonel Hinson's. Perkins told him that it was seven miles distant, that the road was in places indistinct, and that a dangerous creek intervened.

The fire being replenished threw a light upon the face of the one who propounded the question. His countenance was remarkable. His eyes sparkled like diamonds. He was splendidly mounted, and his fine horse was richly caparisoned. No sooner had the strangers rode off than Perkins said to Malone, "That is Aaron Burr, I can not be mistaken. We must arrest him." He instantly aroused the sheriff. The strange travelers made their way to Hinson's, arriving there at eleven o'clock. The moon was just up, and enabled the lady of the house, whose husband was absent, to see that they were travelers by their saddle-bags and tin cups. The travelers alighted and went into the kitchen, where a cheerful fire was blazing. Perkins and the sheriff soon reached the house, when the former, as he had been seen, thought it politic to remain behind while the sheriff went to the house to make discovery. Mrs. Hinson, being a relation of the sheriff (Brightwell), was greatly relieved when he made his appearance. Brightwell went to the kitchen, where he found the two men sitting by the fire, one of them with his head bent forward, while a handkerchief partly concealed his face. They soon were invited into the dining-room, where the hostess had hastily prepared supper.

While eating, the elder of the travelers engaged in conversation with the lady, and thanked her for her kindness, apologizing for the intrusion at that hour. At the same time he cast keen glances at the sheriff, who stood near the fire. Mrs. Hinson, who had been prompted by Brightwell, after supper was over inquired of the younger of the travelers, " Is not your companion Colonel Burr?" The gentleman made no response, and in a few minutes both travelers went out. Next morning after breakfast the two travelers, again and again thanking the lady for her hospitality, inquired the road to Pensacola and rode away.

We now return to Perkins, who remained at his post in the woods, shivering with cold and wondering why Brightwell did not return. His patience at length being exhausted, he mounted his horse and made the best of his way to Fort Stoddard, where he arrived at daylight, and notified Captain E. P. Gaines of his suspicions. That officer instantly called a file of mounted men and, with Perkins, started for Hinson's. At about nine o'clock they met the two travelers descending the hill two miles from Hinson's.

The following conversation ensued:

Gaines.—" I presume I have the honor of addressing Colonel Burr?"

Stranger.—" I am a stranger traveling in this State, and do not recognize your right to ask that question."

Gaines.—" I arrest you at the instance of the Federal government."

Stranger.—" By what authority do you arrest a traveler who is about his own private business ? "

Gaines.—" I am an officer of the army, and hold in my hand, the proclamation of the president and governor, ordering your arrest."

Stranger.—" You are a young man and may not be fully aware of the responsibility you assume."

Gaines.—" I am aware of the responsibility and know my duty."

The stranger then in an animated manner denounced the proceedings as illegal, and attempted to intimidate the officer; but the latter sternly replied, " You must accompany me to Fort Stoddard, where, if you make no attempt to escape, you shall be treated with the respect due to the ex-vice-president of the United States."

The stranger gazed at the young officer a moment with earnestness, evidently surprised at his cool firmness, and then at once wheeled his horse and signified his readiness to accompany him.*

The party reached the fort in the evening; and Colonel Burr was conducted to his room, where he dined alone. Next day he appeared at the dinner table, and was introduced to the wife of Captain Gaines, the company of which lady he frequently sought while a prisoner at the post, and was often her competitor in the game of chess, of which he was fond. He was also very attentive to George S. Gaines, brother of the captain, who was sick, and the good heart of that gentleman went out in sympathy for the trials and reverses of the remarkable man. In all their conversations, the imperturbable Burr never once alluded to the designs he had failed to carry out, to his present arrest, or to his future plans.

Meantime Captain Gaines, having made his arrangements to carry his distinguished prisoners to Washington, placed Colonel Burr in a boat with a file of soldiers, and he was rowed up the Alabama. During their journey the ladies often showed their sympathy for the ill-fated and brilliant man. Not only the ladies, but many prominent men in the southwest, favored Burr's enterprise, and sympathized with him in his misfortunes. Arrived at the boat-landing, Burr was placed in charge of Colonel Nicholas Perkins, Thomas Malone, Henry B. Slade, John Mills, John Henry, two brothers McCormick, and two soldiers.

Perkins, who was in command, obtained from each man before starting, a

* It has never been known why Brightwell did not keep his promise with Perkins. It is accounted for by supposing that he became so fascinated with the wonderfully captivating manner of the man, that he was conducting him on the road he wished to go.

solemn pledge that he would not suffer the prisoner to influence them in his behalf, and to this end he cautioned each not to converse with him when it could be avoided. When the prisoner was captured he was attired in a disguise, consisting of coarse homespun pantaloons, a roundabout of drab color, and a flapping wide-brimmed hat. He was permitted to ride the same elegant horse upon which he was arrested. He bestrode him gracefully, and flashing his dark eyes upon the bystanders, bade them farewell, and departed. The guard were well armed with pistols, and the soldiers had muskets.

The only tent taken along was for Burr, and under it he lay the first night, while his ears were all night saluted with the fierce howling of wolves. Thus in the wilds of Alabama reposed this man, surrounded by a guard and without a friend or congenial spirit. He was a prisoner of the United States, for whose liberties he had fought ; an exile from his own State, New York, whose laws bore in part the impress of his mind. Death had taken his wife, his only child was on the distant coast of Carolina, his profession was abandoned, his fortune gone, his great scheme of the conquest of Mexico defeated, and he was harassed from one end of the country to the other. Such things were quite enough to weigh down a common man. But Burr was not a common man. The next morning he arose, and with a cheerful face fell into traveling order with his taciturn companions. Though guarded with vigilance he was treated with respect, and his few wants were gratified. The route was a trail running eight miles south of Montgomery, and across several large creeks, all of which they were forced to swim. It was a perilous and exhausting march, and for days the rain descended in torrents upon the unsheltered horsemen. Hundred of Indians thronged the trail, and they might at any moment have been killed.

But the fearless Perkins pressed onward despite all obstacles. Burr sat firmly in the saddle, always on the alert, although drenched with rain, and at night lying on the damp ground, and marching forty miles a day ; yet he never for a moment complained. They crossed the Chattahoochee, Flint, and Ockmulgee, in canoes, swimming their horses. At Fort Williamson, they were first sheltered by a roof—that of a Mr. Bevin.

At this place and while at breakfast, the publican, in the hearing of the prisoner, questioned the guard, " If Burr had not been arrested, and if he was not a very bad man ? " The guard made no reply; but Burr majestically raised his head and said, " I am Aaron Burr, what do you want ? " The man stood aghast, and asked no more questions. Reaching South Carolina, the prisoner was guarded even more closely, for here lived Colonel Alston, a man of influence who was the husband of Burr's only daughter.

Before reaching Chester court-house, Perkins made a halt, and placed two men in front of, and two behind his prisoner ; the other two on either side.

21

In this manner they were passing the tavern where many men were standing, when Burr suddenly threw himself from his horse, and exclaimed in a loud voice:

"I am Aaron Burr, under military arrest, and I claim protection of the civil authority."

Perkins ordered the prisoner to remount; but he said, "I will not." Perkins instantly threw down his pistol, and seizing him around the waist with the grasp of a giant, he lifted him into his saddle.

Malone caught the reins of the horse, and rapidly led him through the town. The astonished citizens thus saw a party enter their village with a prisoner, heard him appeal for protection, saw him again thrust into his saddle, and the whole party vanish, before they recovered from their confusion. The least hesitation of Perkins would have lost him his prisoner. Burr burst into a flood of tears. The attempt to escape, and its failure, unmanned him. Without further incident worthy of note, they reached Fredericksburg, and thence, by way of Richmond, arrived at Washington.

XIII.

ELLIS P. BEAN.

THE following account of the adventures of this bold pioneer will be found interesting. In the year 1800, Ellis P. Bean, then a boy of eighteen, possessed with a spirit of adventure, left his father's home at Bean's station, Tennessee, and reaching Natchez on the Mississippi, enlisted in the trading company of Philip Nolan, then en route for Texas. The company consisted of twenty-two men, having in charge a large amount of goods.

Reaching Texas, and while at a point between the Trinity and Brazos rivers, they were attacked by a body of Spanish troops. Nolan and his men made a desperate resistance, but were finally overpowered. Thirteen, including Nolan, were killed, and the remaining nine, with Bean, made prisoners. The prisoners were taken to San Antonio, and there confined several months. Thence they were sent to Chihuahua, by way of Monclova, and there chained and imprisoned. Thus they were kept three years, when they were allowed the privilege of the city limits, and to labor for themselves. Bean had learned the hatting business, and he followed it for a year in Chihuahua, when his longing to see his native land induced him, with two comrades, to run away, and endeavor to reach the United States. The three were arrested near El Paso, severely lashed, and again ironed and imprisoned.

ELLIS P. BEAN.

To face p 322.

Bean's many friends in Chihuahua soon obtained for him again the freedom of the city, and he made a second effort to escape, but was again taken. He was now sent under a strong guard to the south of Mexico. On their way they came to the city of Guanajuato, where they remained several days. While there, Bean's noble and manly bearing won the heart of a beautiful Mexican senorita of rank, who wrote a letter to him avowing her passion, and promising her influence to obtain his liberation ; when she would bestow upon him her hand and fortune. But he was hurried away, and never permitted to see her. Poor Bean was next conveyed to Acapulco, one of the most sickly places on the Pacific, and thrown into a filthy dungeon, where no ray of the light of heaven penetrated, and the only air admitted was through an aperture in the base of the massive wall, which was six feet thick. In this foul abode his body was covered with vermin ; no one was allowed to see him, and his food was of the coarsest and most unhealthy kind. In his confinement his only companion was a white lizard, which he succeeded in taming, and which become very fond of him.

The only air-hole had to be closed at night to prevent the ingress of serpents. One night, having neglected to close it, he was awakened by the crawling of a monstrous serpent over his body. His presence of mind enabled him to lie perfectly still until, getting hold of a pocket knife which he had been able to keep concealed on his person, he pierced the monster in the head and escaped his fangs. This exploit so astonished the keeper of the prison that by his influence a petition was sent to the governor for a mitigation of his confinement. That dignitary graciously decreed that he might work in chains, and under a guard of soldiers. Even this was a relief. Bean's noble desire for freedom again overcame his prudence. He succeeded in freeing himself from his shackles, and with a piece of iron killed three of the guard, and fled to the mountains. Again he was hunted down and recaptured, nearly starved. His cell now became his only abode, and flogging and other indignities were heaped upon him. Another year passed, and he was again allowed the liberty of the prison yard under strict surveillance.

Once more he made a desperate attempt to escape, killing several soldiers, and taking the road to California. This time he had traveled three hundred miles, when he was once more recaptured and carried back. He was now confined upon his back, and for weeks was almost devoured by vermin. His appeals for mercy were treated with mockery. But his freedom drew nigh. The Mexican revolution of 1810 broke out. The royalists became alarmed. They had learned to look upon Bean as a chained lion, and now in the hour of their trouble they offered him liberty if he would join their standard. He promised, secretly determining that he would desert them the first opportunity.   He was in a few days sent out with a scout to reconnoitre the position of General Morelos, the chief of the republicans. When near the camp of that officer, Bean proposed to his comrades that they should all join the patriots.   His persuasive eloquence was so successful that they all agreed, and at once reported to Morelos.

Upon the information Bean was able to give, an attack was planned and executed against the royalists, resulting in a complete victory.

For this, Bean received a captain's commission, and his fame spread like wild-fire through Mexico.   For three years he was the chief reliance of Morelos, and when he fought, victory followed.   He was soon conducted, with flying banners, into the town of Acapulco, the scene of his sufferings. The wretches who had persecuted him, now on bended knees begged for mercy, expecting nothing but instant death.

But Bean scorned to avenge his wrongs upon them, and dismissed them with warnings as to their future conduct.   Three years later it was agreed that Bean should go to New Orleans and obtain aid for the republicans of Mexico.   With two companions, he made his way across the country.   On the route, while stopping a few days at Jalapa, Mexico, he became suddenly and violently enamored of a beautiful lady, and married her, promising that, after having accomplished his mission, he would return to her.   After various adventures he reached New Orleans two days before the memorable battle of January 8, 1815.

He at once volunteered as aid to General Jackson, whom he had known when a boy; and fought bravely in that decisive action.   He afterward returned to Mexico, and joined his wife, with whom he lived happily many years. In 1827, when the Fredonian war broke out at Nacogdoches, Texas, he was colonel commanding the Mexican garrison at that place.   In 1835, he returned to Jalapa, Mexico.   In 1843, he was still living in Mexico as an officer on the retired list of the army of that nation.   A volume containing an account of his almost fabulous adventures was written by Bean in 1817, and published soon afterward.

XIV.

TEXAS SPORTS.

THE following extracts are from the graphic pen of our fellow-townsman, Major C. S. West, who, under the *nom de plume* Mark Boyd, has delighted the readers of the *Turf, Field, and Farm.*

"On the 27th of Febuary, Dr. J. and your humble servant concluded to pay a visit to the quail in this region. We did so, with three dogs and two breech-loaders, and in about six hours, steady work knocked down fifty-six birds. We hunted over inclosed land within three or four miles of the city, and would have done much better but for the quantity of birds that had been destroyed by traps and nets. We found one of these machines (traps) in nearly every thicket, and whenever we came across them we performed a piroutte, varied occasionally with a Virginia breakdown. My very soul abhors those trappers and netters: creatures—for all are not men who wear the human form—who delight in driving a whole covey of innocent birds into a net, and bagging and destroying them all at one fell swoop, or inveigling them all at once into some infernal trap, without giving the poor little things one manly chance for their lives, as we wing shooters do. Is there no law that will reach such cold-blooded murder? Are these babes of the wood to be thus ruthlessly taken off?

"I have no toleration for those men with their traps and nets. There is not space for both of us in this breathing world. As Owen Meredith hath it,

"' There is no room beneath the all-circling sun
For me and him."

"Fair play is a jewel. Give the game little bird a chance; and if you can cut him down while he is going at the rate of sixty miles an hour, do it. Another similar nuisance we encountered near a dog-wood thicket, where we came upon four or five men prowling mysteriously near the spot. At first we took them for a party of *francs-tireurs*, and were at once transported in imagination to the scenes of the Franco-Prussian war. But a nearer inspection proved them to be nothing more formidable than a party of pot-hunters from the city. They are fit companions for the heroes of the net and trap. They were shooting with long, cheap single guns, the barrels of which were apparently made from refuse gas-pipes. Each had his pants deeply stuffed into a pair of heavy pot-metal boots, and each had an enormous game-bag slung across his shoulders, bell-crowned hats on their heads, and were carrying havoc, death, and destruction among doves, robins, field-larks, sap-suckers, yellowhammers, blackbirds, and killdee. They were accompanied by a mangy, woolly, bench-legged cur, and were shooting that peculiar quality of shot that the lamented De Los Llanos used to call high brister. This shot is composed of all sizes, from No. 7 up to buckshot. Thus armed and equipped, they are ready at a moment's notice to discharge their shooting-irons at anything, from a tomtit up to a five-point buck with branching antlers.

"They occasionally vary the monotony of the scene by shooting a load into one of their *compadres.*"

The following, from the same pen, well describes the scenery in the neighborhood of Austin, and a few miles south of that place.

"Though, like many ardent sportsmen, a devoted lover of the beauties of nature animate and inanimate, yet it so happened, that shooting over the ground only in the autumn and winter, it had never occurred to me to imagine how lonely it looked in the pleasant spring time. In approaching the spot where we intended to try our luck, you gradually ascend from the valley until at the end of two or three miles you attain a considerable elevation, probably five hundred feet or more above the level of the gulf, and reach the summit of a bold prairie ridge, extending, with occasional broken spurs, three or four miles to his right and left. From this point, looking toward the north, the spires and domes of the lovely capital of Texas, twelve miles distant, shimmer in the sunlight ; immediately beyond them Mount Bonnell, with its summit wreathed in a light mist, looks down upon the city ; while at the mountain's base, the crystal waters of the Colorado leap over the Mormon Falls and hurry on to Matagorda Bay. Immediately in front, in all its quiet pastoral beauty, lies the valley of Onion Creek. The blue sky above is flecked with masses of light gulf clouds, driven northward by the wind. Such a breath of air nothing can surpass, and as I felt it playing upon my cheek I almost fancied I could hear the roar of the Mexican gulf from whence it had come, and could not help thinking it was the very breezes that Bryant must have felt, in all the pulses of his blood, when he wrote :

> "'. . . . Breezes of the South
> Who toss the golden and the flame-like flowers,
> And fan the prairie hawk that, poised on high,
> Flaps his broad wings yet moves not :
> Ye have played
> Among the plains of Mexico and vines of Texas.
> . . . . tell us,
> Have you fanned a lovelier scene than this?'"

XV.

FLOODS IN THE COLORADO.

THE most notable floods in the Colorado since the settlement of Austin have occurred as follows.

February, 1843, river rose about 36 feet,
March, 1852, " " " 36 "
July, 1869, " " " 43 "
October, 1870, " " " 36 "

The following account of the flood of 1869 is from the diary of the compiler of this volume.

"The period between the 3d and 7th days of July, 1869, will long be remembered by the inhabitants of the Colorado valley, in Texas. On the 3d of July began the longest and most uninterrupted rain ever known in this locality. It rained without any cessation for about sixty-four hours. The usual amount of rain had fallen during the previous months of the year, and dry weather might naturally have been expected. But this year the usual summer drought did not come.

"Austin City, the capital of the State, is, as our readers are aware, situated on the Colorado River. Its location is upon the east bank of that stream. The bank on the Austin side of the river is from forty to fifty feet high above the usual water level, and presents a perpendicular bluff.

"On the opposite side is a sand beach, varying in width from one quarter to one mile. The Colorado takes its rise from springs three hundred miles north-west of Austin, and several streams of considerable size empty into it during its course. Among these are the Concho, the San Saba, the Llano, the Pedernales, and others. After two days of rain the river, which had been running full, commenced rising rapidly, showing that the rain had been general, and that the tributaries were pouring down their contents. Tuesday morning the river was unusually high. But it continued steadily to rise, and Wednesday afternoon serious apprehensions began to be felt by those who lived upon the lower banks. Their fears were fully realized. During Tuesday night and on Wednesday the river rose to the fearful and unprecedented height of forty-five feet above the usual level. This of course could not take place without producing terrible results. On Wednesday the confusion and panic were indescribable. It did not show itself however by noisy demonstrations. People went to work with a will, to help their neighbors; and during Wednesday all who lived in the immediate vicinity of the river moved their families, and such of their chattels as they could, to a place of safety. All day the foaming torrent continued to rise higher and higher, bearing down upon its bosom houses, trees, fences, cattle, and every thing that came in its way.

"Several persons were drowned, but how many the writer is unable to say. On Wednesday night few eyes were closed. All were anxiously watching and waiting for news from the great torrent which was passing by their dwellings, threatening to ingulf them. At ten o'clock the river came to a stand, and after continuing so for an hour or two, began very slowly to fall. During these days of terror and excitement many interesting incidents occurred which would well bear recording had we room. The damage done at this place was not so great as below on the river, where the banks are not so high.

"A few houses were washed away and others were invaded by the flood, being in some cases nearly filled with water, and great damage was done to furniture by hasty and careless moving. But the most of our beautiful city is above high-water mark.

"The town of Webberville, sixteen miles below Austin, was overflowed and partially destroyed. Bastrop, sixteen miles still lower down, was partly inundated and seriously injured. Lagrange, thirty-five miles below Bastrop, was from two to ten feet under water, and the inhabitants were compelled to fly to the hills near by and remain without shelter until the flood receded. The latter town, which is small, suffered immense loss in property of various kinds. After the freshet everybody went to work heartily and cheerfully to repair damages.

"The crops of corn and cotton were very large that year, notwithstanding the flood.

"The mails throughout Western Texas were stopped for about two weeks, as the rain prevailed throughout all that portion of the State, and the Blanco, Comal, Guadaloupe, and all the other rivers and creeks, overflowed their banks."

XVI.

From the Proclamation of General Sam Houston, Commander-in-Chief, December 12, 1835.

"CITIZENS OF TEXAS: Your rights must be defended. The oppressors must be driven from our soil. Submission to the laws and union among ourselves will render us invincible ; subordination and discipline in our army will guarantee to us victory and renown.

"Our invader has sworn to exterminate us or to sweep us from the soil of Texas. He is vigilant in his work of oppression, and has ordered to Texas ten thousand men to enforce the unhallowed purposes of his ambition. His letters to his subaltern in Texas have been intercepted, and his plans for our destruction are disclosed. Departing from the chivalric principles of civilized warfare, he has ordered arms to be distributed to a portion of our population for the purpose of creating in our midst a servile war. The hopes of the usurper were inspired by a belief that the citizens of Texas were disunited and divided in opinion : that alone has been the cause of the present invasion of our rights. He shall realize the fallacy of his hopes, in the *union* of our citizens, and in their *eternal resistance* to his plans against constitutional liberty. We will enjoy our birth-right or perish in its defense."

XVII.

SAN JACINTO.

From the Report of Thomas J. Rusk, Secretary of War, relative to the battle of San Jacinto, April 26, 1836.

" THIS glorious achievement is attributed, not to superior force, but to the valor of our soldiers and the sanctity of our cause. Our army consisted of seven hundred and fifty effective men. This brave band achieved a victory as glorious as any on the records of history, and the happy consequences will be felt in Texas by succeeding generations. It has saved the country from a yoke of bondage, and all who participated in it are entitled to the special munificence of government and the heart-felt gratitude of every lover of liberty. The sun was sinking in the horizon as the battle commenced, but at the close of the conflict the sun of liberty and independence rose in Texas, never, never to be obscured by the clouds of despotism. We have read deeds of chivalry, and perused with ardor the annals of war. We have contemplated with the highest emotions of sublimity, the loud roaring thunder—the desolating tornado—and the withering simoom of the desert ; but neither of these, nor all of them, inspired us with emotions like those felt on this occasion. The officers and men were actuated by a like enthusiasm. A general cry pervaded the ranks, and that cry was : ' Remember the Alamo ! remember La Bahia ! ' * These words electrified all. ' Onward ' was the cry. The unerring aim and irresistible energy of the Texan army could not be withstood. It was freemen fighting against the minions of tyranny, and the result proved the inequality of the contest."

* La Bahia, the early name of Goliad.

XVIII.

A TEXAS PRAIRIE IN SPRING TIME.

(From Mrs. Holly's History of Texas.)

" IT is impossible to imagine the beauty of a Texas prairie when in the vernal season its rich luxuriant herbage, adorned with many thousand flowers of every size and hue, seems to realize the vision of a terrestrial paradise. The delicate, gay, and gaudy, are intermingled in delightful confusion ; and these fanciful bouquets of fairy nature borrow tenfold charms when associated with the verdant carpet of grass which modestly mantles around.

" One feels that Omnipotence has here consecrated in the bosom of Nature, and under Heaven's wide canopy, a glorious temple in which to receive the praise and adoration of the grateful beholder ; and cold indeed must be the soul from which no homage could here be elicited. Methinks the veriest infidel would here be constrained to bow and worship."

XIX.

A PRAIRIE SUNSET.

(From "Letters from Texas," by W. B. Dewees.)

"YOU have doubtless often read of a sunset at sea, but I presume have never read of a sunset on the prairie.

" Splendid as is the former, it does not eclipse the latter. When far away from home and kindred, upon the bosom of the mighty deep, I have sat and watched the orb of day as he slowly sank into his ocean bed, and thought the world could not afford another sight as beautiful. But when upon the wide prairie night approaches the beholder, and the dazzling, golden rays of the sun begin to redden ; and the mighty day-god lays aside his piercing appearance and permits the eye of man to gaze upon him with impunity, then, indeed, the soul is filled with wonder at the sublimity of the scene. The gorgeous clouds form a rosy pathway for him to tread, as he walks downward into his bed of flowers and verdure. Around him float airy purple clouds, while beneath are others tinged with the richest of vermilion.

" As he sinks slowly down, he resembles a huge ball of fire falling amidst the grass of the prairie. When at length the sun is hid for the night, the fleecy clouds float for a few moments beneath the azure sky, and then disappear.

"Then the bright silver stars come peeping forth, one after another, gladdening the eye with their twinkling light. Then comes up the full, round moon, attended by myriads more of bright stars, into the firmament already studded with these gems. Soon the light is sufficiently bright to enable the student to continue his labors by the moon's rays. He who is an admirer of the beauties of nature, can not look upon a scene like this unmoved. The wide prairie, which lies spread out on every side, is here and there relieved by a clump of trees, which serve to render the scene enchanting. Poets have often sung of the beauty of Italian skies, but those who have seen both, pronounce ours equally beautiful. It does not appear to me possible that there can be a land more lovely than Texas."

XX.

From President Houston's Letter to Santa Anna in March, 1842.

"You touchingly invite 'Texas to cover herself anew with the Mexican flag.' You certainly intend this as a mockery. You denied us the enjoyment of the laws under which we came to the country. Her flag was never raised in our behalf, nor has it been seen in Texas except when displayed in an attempt at our subjugation. We know your lenity—we know your mercy —we are ready again to test your powers. You have threatened to plant your banner on the banks of the Sabine. Is this done to intimidate us? Is this done to alarm us? Or do you deem it the most successful mode of conquest? If the latter, it may do to amuse the people surrounding you. If to alarm us, it will amuse those conversant with the history of your last campaign. If to intimidate us, the threat is idle. We have desired peace,— you have annoyed our frontier,—you have harassed our citizens; you have incarcerated our traders, after your commissioners had been kindly received, and your citizens allowed the privileges of commerce in Texas without molestation.

"You continue aggression—you will not accord to us peace. *We will have it?* You threaten to conquer Texas. We will war with Mexico. Your pretensions, with ours, you have referred to the world, and to the God of battles. We refer ours to the same tribunals. The issue involves the fate of nations. The event is known to the tribunal of heaven. If the experience of the past will authorize speculations of the future, the attitude of Mexico is more 'problematical' than that of Texas."

XXI.

From Governor Smith's Address to the People of Texas.

"EXECUTIVE DEPARTMENT, March, 1836.

" 'TEXAS EXPECTS EVERY MAN TO DO HIS DUTY.

"FELLOW-CITIZENS OF TEXAS : The enemy are upon us. A strong force surrounds the walls of the Alamo, and threatens that garrison with the sword. Our country imperiously demands the service of every patriotic arm, and longer to continue in a state of apathy will be criminal. Citizens of Texas ! descendants of Washington ! awake ! arouse yourselves ! ! The question is now to be decided, are we to continue freemen, or bow beneath the rod of military despotism? Shall we, without a struggle, sacrifice our fortunes, our liberties, and our lives, or shall we imitate the example of our forefathers, and hurl destruction on the heads of our oppressors? The eyes of the world are upon us ! All friends of liberty and the rights of man are anxious spectators of our conflict ; or are enlisted in our cause. Shall we disappoint their hopes and expectations? No ! Let us at once fly to arms, march to the battle-field, meet the foe, and give renewed evidence to the world that the arms of freemen uplifted in defense of their liberties and rights are irresistible. 'Now is the day and now is the hour' that Texas expects every man to do his duty. Let us show ourselves worthy to be free, and *we shall be free!* "

XXII.

President Burnet's Proclamation to the People of Texas, June 20, 1836.

"CITIZENS OF TEXAS: The enemy are again preparing to invade our soil. Intent on vengeance for their defeat, they have rallied another horde of miscreants, and hope to accomplish by their hasty levies, a conquest which the utmost exertions of their favorite chieftain has failed to effect. Urrea, the cold-blooded murderer of the gallant Fannin and his noble band, leads the returning Vandal host, and threatens to exterminate all free-born Texans. Again, fellow-citizens, you are called upon to rally to the standard of your country, to sustain the independence you have solemnly pronounced, and to preserve your homes, your domestic altars, and your sacred liberty from pollution and inthrallment. The approaching army threatens to be more formidable than that you so lately and so gloriously vanquished on the plains of San Jacinto. But Texans ! what you have once done, you can do again.

It is the peculiar property of true courage to rise in dignity, and in spirit, as the pressure of adverse circumstances increases; to brighten in cheerfulness and resolution, as the storm lowers and gathers darkness. Let us exemplfy as a people, this glorious property of the highest military attribute. Let every citizen of Texas repair with alacrity to his post. It is the sacred duty of every man who calls Texas his home, and who claims a proprietary interest in her soil, to stand forth in her defense, in this her hour of peril. Let none prove recreant. The trial of *real* patriotism is at hand. Action, prompt energetic action, is the best evidence of a patriot's zeal. Noisy and bluster-ing words may deceive for a time, but right actions carry conviction to the mind. Let us realize that the 'best security for our families is to be found in a gallant bearing before the enemy.' The army is the best buckler we can throw around our wives and children. The contest is for life, liberty, and independence. Let every man do his duty, and the glorious prize will be gloriously won."

XXIII.

Houston to Santa Anna, March, 1842.

"THEN was presented to Texas the alternative of tamely crouching to the tyrant's lash, or exalting themselves to the attributes of freemen. They chose the latter. To chastise them for their presumption you advanced upon Texas with your boasted veteran army. You besieged and took the Alamo, but under what circumstances? Not surely those which should characterize a general of the nineteenth century. You assailed one hundred and fifty men destitute of every supply requisite for defense. Its brave de-fenders, worn down by constant vigilance and unremitted duty, were at length overwhelmed by nine thousand men, and the place taken. I ask you sir, what scenes followed? Were they such as should characterize an able general, a magnanimous warrior, and the president of a great nation? No! Manliness and generosity would sicken at the recital of the scenes incident to your success, and humanity would blush to class you among the chivalric spirits of the age of Vandalism. This you are pleased to class in the 'suc-cession of your victories;' and I presume you would also include the mas-sacre at Goliad. Your triumph there, if such you are pleased to term it, was not the triumph of arms,—it was the success of perfidy! Fannin and his brave companions had beaten back and defied your veterans. Although outnumbered more than seven to one, their valiant, hearty, and indomitable courage, and holy devotion to the cause of freedom, had foiled every effort of your general to insure his success by arms. He had recourse to a flag of truce ; and when the surrender of the little patriot band was secured by the most solemn treaty stipulations, what were the tragic scenes which ensued? The conditions of the surrender were submitted to you, and, though you have denied the facts, instead of restoring them to liberty according to the conditions of the capitulation, you ordered them to be executed, contrary to every pledge given them, contrary to the rules of war, contrary to every principle of humanity. Yet at this day you have the effrontery to animadvert upon the conduct of Texans relative to your captivity after the battle of San Jacinto."

XXIV.

"'THE FLAG OF THE LONE STAR.'

(Texas Almanac, 1861.)

" It is universally believed in Georgia, that the flag of the Lone Star was the work of Miss Troutman, of Crawford county, Georgia, now Mrs. Pope, of Alabama ; and by her presented to the Georgia battalion, commanded by Lieutenant-Colonel Ward. . . .

" It was of plain white silk, bearing an azure star of five points on either side. On one side was the inscription : *'Liberty or Death,'* and on the other, the appropriate Latin motto : *'Ubi Libertas habitat, ibi nostra patria est.'*

" This flag was unfurled at Velasco on the 8th day of January, 1836, and proudly floated on the breeze from the same liberty pole with the first flag of independence, which had just been brought from Goliad by the valiant Captain William Brown, who subsequently did such daring service in the navy of Texas. . . .

" On the meeting of the first congress, the flag of the Lone Star was adopted as the national flag of the young republic.

" A correspondent of the *Central Texan* denies the claim of Georgia, and insists that the *first* Lone Star flag ever unfurled in Texas, was presented by Mrs. Sarah R. Dawson to a company of volunteers raised in Harrisburg, Texas, in 1835, and commanded by Captain Andrew Robinson. The flag was a tri-color of white, red and blue. The star was white, five-pointed, and set in a ground of red."

XXV.

From President Lamar's Message, November, 1840.[*]

" SCARCELY five years have elapsed since Texas, without money or arms, or any of the means of war, and with a population of less than forty thousand souls, first raised the standard of resistance to the despotism and misrule of a government claiming the control of boundless wealth, and of eight millions of inhabitants ; and yet, within that short period, and against such fearful odds, she has not only achieved and secured her independence beyond the reach of doubt, but has maintained a well organized government at home, established foreign relations abroad, more than quadrupled her population, and now exhibits to the world a country teeming with all that is essential to the necessities or happiness of man ; and this, too, without incurring a debt exceeding five millions of dollars including every species of liability both foreign and domestic. Can such a state of things as this produce gloom and despondency in the hearts of those whose indomitable courage and persevering resolves have achieved so much.

" Assuredly not—on the contrary we find in it abundant cause to felicitate ourselves on the almost magical change which in so short a time has already been produced, and every inducement to stimulate us in the pursuit of that policy which has thus far led to such fortunate results."

XXVI.

Speech of Hon. D. S. Kaufman welcoming M. De Saligny to the House of Representatives of Texas, November 17, 1840.

" SIR : On behalf of the House of Representatives I welcome your presence in this hall. In you we recognize an ardent and devoted friend of Texas ; and more than all, an able and faithful representative of that great and gallant nation, the very mention of whose name can not fail to excite the liveliest emotions of gratitude in the bosom of every American. Your liberal and illustrious sovereign, Louis Philippe, always jealous of his country's honor and glory, has never yet evinced an envy of another nation's success. A monarchy herself, France has always been ready to extend to republics the right hand of fellowship. We have read and heard of her magnanimity to the

---

[*] This long sentence will furnish a good exercise in reading or speaking.

United States when struggling with the gigantic power of Britain ; we have seen and felt her friendship toward us, when we were as yet unnoticed and unknown. She has taken us by the hand, and welcomed us into the family of nations. . . .

" To you, sir, as the pupil of the illustrious Lafayette, we feel much indebted for our elevated stand among the nations of the earth. You have spared no pains—you have left untried no exertions, to disabuse the European mind of unjust prejudice against our infant Republic. Go on, sir, in your friendly work. Republics are *not* ungrateful. Texas will long remember with gratitude your friendship to the cause.

" May the banners of the *tri-color* and the *Lone Star* always wave in friendship and in triumph ; and may the rude blasts of discord never disturb their peaceful folds ! In the name of the people of Texas, I greet you ! "

XXVII.

From a Speech of Honorable Forbes Britton, November 21, 1857.

" Sir : Come with me for a moment to the border dwelling. Do you see in the log cabin, that old gray-headed man, who sits over the dying embers, his head bowed in sorrow. His hearthstone is bathed in tears, his lonely cottage is draped in mourning ; his stalwart boy, the prop and staff of his declining years, rests beneath yonder oak. In a paroxysm of hope, he raises his tearful eyes to the flag of his country ; and it mocks his agony in its *violated promises of protection.* That female form crouching by his side, wringing her hands in despair, has lost her husband, her idol, her joy. Lean forward and catch the almost inaudible sounds as they escape from her quivering lips, and you will hear the meek and submissive prayer : ' Thy will be done on earth as it is in Heaven.' No marble slab tells the mournful story, but look into their hearts, and you will find inscribed there : ' My poor boy ! my husband ? ' Sir, this is the work of the scalping-knife. It is no idle picture—no *ignis fatuus* of the brain to lead off the imagination. No sir ; I speak what I *know.* It is *true.* There is not a returning season of spring that the lintels of our doors are not stained with the blood of our people. Then, sir, if it but save the life of one man, woman, or child, give us the pittance we ask ! In the name of Justice,—in the name of Mercy,—I ask the passage of the bill."

XXVIII.

From the Remarks of Chief-Justice Hemphill on the Announcement to the Supreme Court of the Death of General James Hamilton, December, 1857.

"JAMES HAMILTON can never be forgotten by Texas, the hearts of whose people can not disregard his great public services. Among all of her noble citizens, not one made greater sacrifices, or served the State with a purer or more earnest devotion. His body lies ingulfed in the ocean ; but his name, his great deeds, his illustrious example, and the memory of his virtues, remain. His fame is burnished on the proudest page of history, and will endure as long as history itself shall survive. He was endowed with the finest social qualities. His was the heart to charm, and to be loved by all with whom he had intercourse. To the beautiful proprieties of his domestic relations, the love, tenderness, and affection, which, as with a halo, encircled his family, we can only allude. In the depth and anguish of their affliction, that circle is sacred, and shall not by us be invaded."

XXIX.

From the Eulogy on the Death of Hon. James Webb, delivered by Honorable J. C. Wilson, November, 1856.

"HE is dead. A gentleman by nature, by culture, by association, but not by these alone. He would have been a gentleman anywhere and under any circumstances. His patent of nobility was stamped upon the surface ; but better far, it was stamped upon the soul. He had the heart of a true man. It was a strong, brave, and joyous heart ; cheerful, though scarred by disappointments and bereavements. Youthful and glowing, though it beat beneath the frosts of four and sixty winters. It was a feeling, generous, bold, manly heart ; and the man whose breast is warmed by such an one,—I care not where or how his lot be cast—is a nobleman of God Almighty's own making. That heart is cold and still. It will shed its genial warmth around the circle no more. No more shall we listen to his genial wit, or calm unpretending wisdom, in the social gathering ; nor hear from him the full and fluent tide of learning in the forum. He is gone—the modest, gentle, and gifted—the wise and learned, the kind and true, has passed away from earth forever."

22

XXX.

Extract from an Address Delivered by Stephen F. Austin, in Louisville, Kentucky, March, 1836.

(From Pease's History of Texas.)

"WHEN a people consider themselves compelled by circumstances or by oppression, to appeal to arms and resort to their natural rights, they necessarily submit their cause to the great tribunal of public opinion. The people of Texas, confident in the justice of their cause, fearlessly and cheerfully appeal to this tribunal. In doing this, the first step is to show, as I trust I shall be able by a succinct statements of facts, that our cause is just, and is the cause of light and liberty; the same holy cause for which our forefathers fought and bled; the same cause that has an advocate in the bosom of every freeman, no matter in what country, or by what people it may be contended for. . . . . . .

"The emancipation of Texas will extend the principles of self-government over a rich and neighboring country, and open a vast field there for enterprise, wealth, and happiness; and for those who wish to escape the frozen blasts of a northern climate, by removing to a more congenial one. It will promote and accelerate the march of the present age, for it will open a door through which a bright and constant stream of light and intelligence will flow from this great northern fountain over the benighted regions of Mexico."

XXXI.

"HYMN OF THE ALAMO.

The following poem is from the pen of Col. R. M. Potter. It has often been incorrectly published. It was furnished by the author, in his own handwriting, to the publisher from whom I obtained it.

"ARISE! man the wall—our clarion blast
Now sounds its final reveille,—
This dawning morn must be the last
Our fated band shall ever see.
To life, but not to hope, farewell.
Yon trumpet's clang and cannon's peal,

ANSON JONES.

See p. 259.

And storming shout and clash of steel,
Is *ours*,—but not our *country's* knell.
　　Welcome the Spartan's death—
　　　'Tis no despairing strife—
　　We fall—we die—but our expiring breath
　　　Is freedom's breath of life.

" Here on this new Thermopylæ,
Our monument shall tower on high,
And, ALAMO, hereafter be
On bloodier fields the battle-cry !
Thus Travis from the rampart cried ;
And when his warriors saw the foe
Like whelming billows move below,—
At once each dauntless heart replied :
　　Welcome the Spartan's death—
　　　'Tis no despairing strife—
　　We fall, but our expiring breath
　　　Is freedom's breath of life !

" They come—like autumn leaves they fall,
Yet hordes on hordes they onward rush,
With gory tramp they mount the wall,
Till numbers the defenders crush.
The last was felled the fight to gain,
Well may the ruffians quake to tell
How Travis and his hundred fell,
Amid a thousand foemen slain.
　　They died the Spartan's death,—
　　　But not in hopeless strife :
　　Like brothers died—and their expiring breath
　　　Was freedom's breath of life."

------------◆◆------------

XXXII.

From the Valedictory Address of Anson Jones, President of the Republic of Texas.
Delivered upon the Occasion of the Inauguration of the New State Government,
February 19, 1846.

" THE great measure of annexation so earnestly discussed is happily consummated.　The present occasion, so full of interest to us and to all the

peop e of this country, is an earnest of that consummation ; and I am happy to greet you, their chosen representatives, and to tender to you my cordial congratulations on an event the most extraordinary in the annals of the world —one which makes a bright triumph in the history of republican institutions. A government is changed both in its officers and in its organization—not by violence and disorder, but by the deliberate and free consent of its citizens ; and amid perfect and universal peace and tranquillity, the sovereignty of the nation is surrendered, and incorporated with that of another.

. . . .

" The Lone Star of Texas, which ten years since arose amid clouds, over fields of carnage, and obscurely seen for awhile, has culminated, and following an inscrutable destiny, has passed on and become fixed forever in that glorious constellation which all freemen and lovers of freedom in the world must reverence and adore—the *American Union.* Blending its rays with its sister States, long may it continue to shine, and may generous Heaven smile upon this consummation of the wishes of the two Republics now joined in one. May the Union be perpetual, and may it be the means of conferring benefits and blessings upon the people of all the States, is my ardent prayer.

" The first act in the great drama is now performed. The Republic of Texas is no more."

———— ▸•◂ ————

XXXIII.

From the Report of the Committee on Foreign Relations to the Senate of the Republic of Texas, January 20, 1845.

" THE annexation of Texas to the United States, already so emphatically *willed* by the people of both countries, will, when consummated, be among the most interesting events recorded in the annals of history. It will stand without a parallel in political changes. It is true that the chronicles of nations are full of the change of governments, of the extension of empire, of the partition of the weaker among the stronger powers ; but this will be the first instance where a few sovereign and independent people will have merged their government in another by their own free-will and consent.

" Other nations have lost their separate and independent existence, but they have fallen before the bloody car of conquest ; and have been appropriated as the successful spoils of ambition. They have only changed masters, and in too many instances, have had substituted a more intolerable despotism than that which preceded it. But here, how different will be the change— how incomparably different must be the results : Our weakness will become strength ; our danger, safety ; and desolation of heart will be supplanted by smiles of joy. In this change there will be no compulsion ;—no force—no rapacity—no desire for aggrandizement : nothing but the stern determination peculiar to, and characteristic of, freemen, to extend the area of rational liberty ; to render more durable republican institutions ; and to perpetuate the glory of the American name. Who would not exult in the appellation of an American citizen ?

"What country is there contiguous to the United States, that would not rejoice to share the benefits, the privileges and the protection of that government?

"Would not the incorporation of Texas into the American Union be preferable to the tardy, the uncertain, and the hazardous experiment of building up a new government, burdened with debt, and possessed of peculiar domestic institutions which invite the improper interference and misplaced philanthropy of the world?

"Ought the restoration of the mutilated province of Louisiana be longer delayed, when Providence, by a peculiar and most extraordinary series of events, seems to have pointed out the easy means of frustrating the designs of men—or at least their bad counsels? The imbecility of Spain—the anarchy of Mexico, the daring attempt of Santa Anna to destroy the constitution of the country, the resistance and bravery of the people of Texas, the carnage of San Jacinto, and the enlightened judgment of the people of the United States, have all admirably conspired to bring about that restoration. 'What God hath joined together, let not man put asunder.' Texas is a part of the great valley of the Mississippi. Her people are the people of the United States; and although separated for awhile from her natural allies, the time is at hand when the error will be remedied, and the 'lost pleiad' return again to its native sky."

XXXIV.

THE "LONE STAR" OF TEXAS.

BLACK was the night that brooded o'er the land,
  Sombre the clouds that walked athwart the sky,
Chilly the winds that whistled o'er the plain ;
  But stout the hearts that beat unitedly.
That night was Despotism's darkest hour,—
  Those clouds and winds, the foes which gathered near ;
Stout hearts might well, dismayed in terror, cower ;
  But those were *Texan* hearts that knew no fear.

See—just above th' horizon's farthest edge
　　A lone star rises in the gloomy night;
Dimly, and tremblingly, its rays are seen
　　Shining through cloud-rifts, or concealed from sight;
Faintly it glimmers o'er the *Alamo*—
　　Redly it gleams above *Jacinto's* field,—
Higher it rises—now, brave hearts, rejoice—
　　'Tis fixed in beauty on Heaven's azure shield.

Lovers of liberty,—where'er ye dwell !
　　Foes of oppression,—be ye far or near !
Hearts that with sympathy for freemen swell !
　　Ye who the name of *Washington* revere !
Behold that star !—the peer of all around,
　　Blazing from out *united stars* 'tis seen—
A " *lone star* " free,—now free amid the free,
　　Unchanged, undimmed, unclouded, and serene.

XXXV.

AD. LAWRENCE'S RIDE.

MANY a thrilling incident of border life connected with the early history of Texas will never be recorded. It has been the lot of the writer to become acquainted with some of the early settlers of that State, and to hear them tell many a tale of danger and of daring. One of them is here narrated.

Adam, or Ad, Lawrence settled near the head waters of the Trinity River, in Texas, in 1829.

No man could be by nature better adapted to the profession he had chosen. Athletic in body, and undaunted in spirit, he was especially fitted to risk the dangers of frontier life. At the time the writer of this sketch first became acquainted with him, he was upward of sixty years of age, modest in manner, simple and unaffected in language. Rough as he appeared to the casual observer, he was kind and gentle, and the following incident as it fell from his lips, bore the impress of being a simple recital of unvarnished facts. In the summer of 1832, Ad. Lawrence, with three other men, went out mustanging.

A brief account of the mode in which these hardy frontiersmen were wont to capture the wild horses of the prairie, will interest the reader.

A few expert riders, mounted upon strong and fleet horses, and each provided with a strong rope, having discovered a herd of mustangs, would gradually approach to within a short distance of them, and then making a simultaneous dash among them, would each throw a lasso over the neck of one, and after a vigorous and exciting contest of half an hour or more would generally succeed in capturing their prizes. The mustangs, after being once conquered, are easily managed, and by kind treatment soon become perfectly gentle. Some of them are beautiful animals, " pretty as a picture," and most of them being natural pacers, make excellent riding horses.

These wild horses frequented the prairies of Texas at the time of my story. Even since the writer's advent to this State, in 1850, he has seen several large herds. Of late years, they have retreated before the approach of the white man, to more distant wilds.

When about ten miles from the nearest settlement, and far out in the broad prairie, Lawrence and his companions discovered a herd of mustangs feeding, a mile or two distant. They approached them cautiously. As they came nearer, the horses, about one hundred in number, showed no signs of fear ; and when noticing this singular circumstance, the long grass of the prairie suddenly became alive with Indians. The remainder of the story will sound better in Ad's own language.

" There was one to each pony, and they all mounted at a jump, and made for us at full speed, coiling their lariats as they rode. There was no time for swapping horses, so we all turned tail and made a straight shoot for the nearest settlement on Trinity, about ten miles off. Our animals were all fine, but the nag I was on was a black mare a little ahead of any thing in that country for speed and bottom. We rather left them the first three miles, but then their ponies began to show themselves. I tell you, you've no idea how much an Indian can get out of them mustangs. Instead of being a weight to them, they seem to help them along, and they kept up such a powerful yelling, 'pears like you might have heard them to Red River. We noticed that they divided, one half striking off to the left, and we soon found out the reason, for we quickly came to the bank of a deep gully or ravine, which had to be headed, it couldn't be crossed. They knew every inch of the ground, and one party made straight for the head of it, while the balance struck in below us to cut us off in that direction. 'Twas no use talking. We had to ride about a quarter of a mile to the left, right in their very faces, and head that branch. My nag was still tolerably fresh. The others were beginning to blow right smartly. I rode just fast enough to keep in the lead. I didn't care particularly about getting off without knowing what became of my companions. Just as I came to the head of the hollow, the Indians were within about one hundred yards, and yelling awfully.

" They thought they had us sure. I gave my mare the rein, and just touched her with my spur, and turned the corner with about fifty arrows whizzing about my ears. One stuck in my buckskin jacket, and one in my mare's neck ; you may believe she didn't go any slower for that. For awhile I thought she cleared about twenty feet at a jump. Soon as I got headed right again, I looked around to see what had become of the others. One look showed me. They were all down. About half the red skins had stopped to finish them, and the balance were coming for me like red-hot lightning. I felt kind of dizzy like for a minute, and then I straightened up and determined to get away if I could. I hadn't much fears, if I didn't have to head another branch. I could see the timber of Trinity three miles away, and I gave my mare her own head. She had been powerful badly scared, and had been working too hard, and she was puffing a good deal.

"I managed to pull out the arrow which was sticking in her neck. Then I worked off my heavy buckskin coat, which was flopping about with the arrow sticking in it, catching a good deal of wind, and threw it away. I kept on about a mile further without gaining or losing much. Then I made up my mind to stop and let my nag blow a little, because I knew if I didn't she couldn't hold up much longer. So I pulled up, and alighted and looked around. Seemed as if the whole country was alive with them. About forty in a bunch a few hundred yards behind, and one not a hundred yards off. I loosened my saddle-girth so she could breathe good, took my bridle in my left hand, and pulled my butcher knife with my right. It was the only weapon I had, I had dropped my rifle when I got dizzy. The Indian was game. He never stopped until he got within ten feet of me. Then he throwed away his bow, jumped off, and came at me with a long knife like mine.

"There wasn't time for a long fight. I had made my calculations, and he was too sure he had me. He ran full against my knife, and I left him lying there. I heard an awful howl from the others, as I pulled off my heavy boots, tightened my girth, and mounted. A few minutes more and I struck the timber of the Trinity, and made the best of my way through it to the river.

"I knew that for miles up and down the banks were bluff, and fifteen or twenty feet high. Where I struck the river they were about fifteen. I knew if my mare wouldn't take the leap I had to do it without her. She stopped an instant and snorted once or twice, but hearing the savages yell close behind, she took the jump. Down—down we went, full fifteen feet, plump into the deep water. We both went under for a second, then she rose, and struck out for the opposite bank with me on her back. Poor creature, she got about two-thirds across, and then gave out under me with a groan. I tell you I fairly loved that animal that moment, and hated to leave her as bad as if she'd been human.

"I swam the rest of the way, and crawled out on the bank pretty well used up. But I was safe. I saw the howling and disappointed savages come to the bank I had left. But not one of them dared take the leap. And the distance was too great for them to shoot. So I rested awhile and then made the best of my way to the settlements."

XXXVI.

THE CURRENCY DURING THE WAR OF 1861-5

THE gigantic civil war of 1861-5 in the United States, presents in the history of our nation a momentous era. The financial condition of the South was during the time mentioned at once novel and startling. In the early part of the struggle the new government at Richmond, to meet its passing wants, provided for the issuance of an immense amount of paper money. This being put into the hands of army contractors, quartermasters, and commissaries, speedily found its way to every part of the South. Then followed a scene in commercial matters difficult to be described. Gold, ever jealous of its own value, and fearful of being depreciated by being brought into contact with this new money, immediately withdrew from the public gaze, and crept into the safe of the merchant, and the stocking and shot-bag of the countryman. In no respect behind in this money-making, the several States issued a large amount of their notes, for circulation within their borders. Following the example of the States and the general government, and big with the importance of the occasion, each county of each State, and every city in every county, poured its offering into the public lap in the shape of a large amount of county or city warrants to be used as money, in amounts varying from twenty-five cents to ten dollars.

One would suppose that money would have been plenty enough now; but no—every man in business, from the first merchant in the city down to the negro barber around the corner, boiling over with patriotism, threw out upon the public bushels of shin-plasters, which he coolly gave you in exchange for your Confederate money or State warrants, and blandly assured you that it was quite necessary for the public welfare, perfectly solvent, and an elegant circulating medium. What did it signify that his next door neighbor who sold lager beer would not receive it, but assured you that his money was current throughout the city? Or that the druggist over the way who sold you a bottle of bitters declared that they both were worthless, and that *he* had only been driven to the necessity of issuing his tickets to supply the demand for small change? This only argued envy, hatred, malice, and all uncharitableness, and detracted nothing from the intrinsic value of the circulating medium. A perfectly anomalous condition of affairs now presented itself. Scores of men who never had a hundred dollars in coin at a time in their lives, opened shops, got a box of tobacco, a barrel of whisky, and a few remnants of dry goods, and began making paper money and buying houses and lands. Every individual sovereign in the land, no matter how ragged his breeches, had his pockets full of money and could accommodate you to any thing you wanted from a confederate fifty dollar note to a twenty-five cent county warrant, or from a five hundred dollar four per cent. bond down to a ten cent "Sour Lake Volcanic Springs" shin-plaster. This was the state of things in the year 1862. During that year Confederate money fell to twenty-five cents on the dollar, and in 1864, by the first of July it had reached a point when it was worth but two cents on the dollar, or fifty for one.

The existence of the blockade, which the Federal government had strictly enforced since the beginning of the war, prevented the monetary affairs of the Southern Confederacy from affecting the rest of the world.

Thrown entirely upon their own resources, the people depended upon themselves, and the immense debt due by the Confederate government was due almost entirely to its own citizens, who regarded its settlement as doubtful, and as a matter of comparatively small consequence. During all this time the government tried to enhance the value of its money by a direct tax levied upon it. These taxes, which in amount perhaps exceeded any thing recorded in history, amounting to ten, twenty, thirty, or even fifty per cent. in some cases, were submitted to and paid by the people with a resignation which the ancient patriarch of Uz would have contemplated with profound respect.

The following scene, which the writer has located in one of the drug stores of a city in Texas, will serve to show the reader how business was transacted in those days. The reader may be assured that it is not overdrawn in any material point.

DRAMATIS PERSONÆ.

PROPRIETOR.   Exempt by being over fifty years old.
JOHN, *the clerk*.   Exempt by occupation.
CHARLIE.   Half-grown negro boy.

The scene opens in the morning. Enter PROPRIETOR *wearing a dignified face and a threadbare coat; also* CHARLIE, *wearing a dilapidated pair of breeches, one leg of which is much shorter than the other.*

Proprietor.—" Charlie, sweep out the establishment, having first sprinkled the floor with *aqua pura.*"

CHARLIE *proceeds to sweep, and in a few minutes came to his master with a handful of paper.*

Charlie.—" Here mas'r, de mice has been making a mess of de 'federate money, I 'spec."

" *Proprietor.*—" Damn those mice, here's several twenties gone ; very well, go on with your sweeping."

Enter CLERK.

Proprietor.—"John, please go out on the street and find out what **Confed**erate money is worth this morning."

JOHN *goes out, and in a few minutes returns.*

John.—"Worth forty for one, this morning."

Proprietor.—"Very well, please step around to the tax-office and **see if** any taxes are due to-day, and how much."

Exit JOHN, *and enter* CUSTOMER *clad in a squirrel-skin cap and a six-shooter.*

Customer.—"Got any quinine?"

Proprietor.—"Yes—do you want a bottle?"

Customer.—Yes—how much is it?"

Proprietor.—"Four hundred and eighty dollars an ounce."

Re-enter JOHN.

John.—"There are several taxes to pay to-day. Quarterly tax on sales —thirty per cent. on profits, five per cent. ad valorem and income tax."

Proprietor.—"How much do they amount to?"

John.—"About ten thousand dollars."

Proprietor.—"All right, please pay them."

Customer.—"How do you take new issue?"

Proprietor.—"Twenty for one."

Customer.—"How do you take one hundred dollar bills?"

Proprietor.—"Interest or non-interest?"

Customer.—"Non-interest."

Proprietor.—"Forty for one, with an additional discount of $33\frac{1}{3}$ per cent. and ten per cent. further deduction for each month since July."

Customer.—"H—ll, how much would that be?"

Proprietor.—"Don't know—take that slate and figure it up yourself."

Customer.—"How do you take fives?"

Proprietor.—"Same as new issue."

Enter another CUSTOMER.

2d Customer.—I want an ounce of laudanum."

PROPRIETOR *takes a black bottle capable of holding about a quart, and having poured an ounce of laudanum into a broken graduate, transfers it to the bottle, stops it with a corn cob, and sets it before the customer, who asks the price.*

Proprietor.—"Twenty dollars."

2d Customer. — "How do you take hundred-dollar interest-bearing notes?"

Proprietor.—" I don't know what they're worth."
2d Customer.—" What is State money going at ? "
Proprietor.—" Ten for one."

2d CUSTOMER *pays a torn twenty dollar note for his laudanum, which the* PROPRIE-
TOR *hands to* CHARLES *with an injunction to paste it and put it where the mice
can't get it.   Enter a small boy, who inquired if that establishment redeems its
own shin-plasters, and having received an.affirmative reply, produces a torn bit
of paper on which the numerals* 25 *can with some difficulty be deciphered,
and having received therefor five postage-stamps he retires.*

Proprietor.—" John, we're a great nation."
John.—" We are."

———— ▸◂ ————

XXXVII.

LAST DAYS OF THE TRANS-MISSISSIPPI DEPART-
MENT.

THE victorious march of Sherman through Georgia and the Carolinas
was followed by a few days of portentous calm.

This was followed by the crushing news of the evacuation of Richmond,
and the surrender of Lee and the army of Northern Virginia.

This stunning intelligence was received by those who expected it in silence,
by others in gloomy astonishment.   The bulwark of the Southern confederacy
was gone—the hopes of the people were dashed to earth.

The great weight of Lee's character, and the confidence which the people
of the South reposed in him, were sufficient to justify the belief that what he
had done, he had done from an honest conviction that the cause had become
hopeless ; and having reached this conclusion, he would use his influence to
put a stop to the further effusion of blood.   A few days more, and the surrender of Johnston put out the last ray of hope in the hearts of the most
sanguine.

The capitulation of Taylor was accepted as a foregone conclusion, and on
all sides it was admitted that the Cis-Mississippi department was powerless
for further resistance.

Then it was told that the Federal commissioners had reached Shreveport,
to demand of General E. Kirby Smith the surrender of the Trans-Mississippi
department.   At this juncture the mail stopped, and for two days we were
entirely in the dark as to what was transpiring.

Then half a dozen of our citizen soldiers came home and told us that the
army was disbanded.   This in a day or two. more was proved to be true, by

the arrival of hundreds of soldiers at Austin, Texas, on their way to their homes in different parts of the State.

The consequence of disbanding twenty thousand men, who had been in the service three or four years without having received any pay for their services, can be imagined only by those who have made history their study.

Discontented and disorderly, a few of them reckless and desperate, all with arms in their hands, they started home.

The writer was in Austin at the time, and some of the incidents which occurred there will furnish a theme for the remainder of this article.

Company after company of men came to the place, and the idea having occurred or been suggested to them, that there was a large amount of government stores in the quartermasters' and commissary store-houses in various parts of the city, an immediate direction was given to the uneasy spirit which prevailed. The scenes which followed beggar description. Crowds of soldiers collected in front of every government building in town, demanding the keys, and when these where not forthcoming at once, the doors were broken in, and the grab game commenced. The mania to " hold fast what you get, and catch what you can," was by no means confined to the soldiers. Numbers of men who had never taken any part in the war, together with women, children, and negroes, assembled around the places where coffee, flour, sugar, salt, bacon, cloth, rope, leather, cotton, medicines, etc., etc., were dealt out with unsparing hands. Individuals might be seen going away from these places, loaded in the most grotesque manner. Here a man with a bale of rope in his hands, and a string of tin cups around his neck ; then another with two or three saddles on his back. Here one with a can of bals. copaiba or a case of quinine ; then another staggering under the weight of a heavy side of leather.

Here a woman might be heard vociferating an order to a negro to take a sack of flour to her house ; there another who declared that her brother-in-law had been in the war all through the thing, and had never realized a cent from it yet. Here might be seen a small boy with his arms full of cotton cards, and his pocket full of epsom salts ; there another bearing off in triumph a tin bucket full of fixed ammunition.

At the cotton warehouse in another part of the town the scene was scarcely less exciting. Bales of cotton were rolled out upon the pavement, the ropes cut, and everybody invited to " pitch in." The snowy staple was borne off by the bale, sackful, armful, hatful, pocketful, by women, children, and negroes, irrespective of services rendered in the army of the Confederate States.

While affairs thus progressed in the city, a party of soldiers were busily scouring the country in search of mules, horses and wagons belonging to the government, and every quadruped having upon him C. S., or in company with those having that brand, was incontinently seized upon. Woe to the luckless wight who might chance to be riding a mule with a confederate cast of countenance. No matter if he were going for the doctor, or to preaching. No matter if a hundred miles from home, if the beast looked like a conscript, the rider was at once dismounted.

Trains of wagons were stopped and the animals taken therefrom ; and in some instances the wagons left standing in the road. These seizures were made without violence or noise. Indeed the whole performance looked more like holiday sport than reality. In most instances private property was respected. Meantime the whole country was full of direful rumors. " Houston, San Antonio, and other places, were reported sacked and burned : the country was being laid waste. Large bodies of soldiers were on their way swearing vengeance against Austin. Sixty thousand Federals had landed at Galveston and would arrive in a few days." " General Magruder was hung." Such were some of the stories which persons of weak nerves industriously circulated and believed. The State was in a fever of excitement. This condition of affairs lasted about ten days or two weeks, after which the disbanded troops quietly dispersed to their homes. Probable in no other country under the sun save in the United States could such large armies have been suddenly disbanded without spreading terror throughout the land.

Thus collapsed the Trans-Mississippi Department. Ground down with taxation, heartily tired of conscription, sick of impressment, and disgusted with the corruption of officials, and government contractors, the mass of the people accepted the result with a feeling that was almost satisfaction.

XXXVIII.

MEXICAN REVOLUTIONS.

OUR neighbors of Mexico are *au fait* at revolutionizing. The practice of centuries has made them perfect in that branch of political economy. Peopled by a class of men, who by nature and education are alike unable to appreciate the blessings of a free government, she has been the sport and fury of every political mountebank who has bayonets enough at his heels to enforce his claims. Her civil contortions have been frightful. Her revolutions are performed with as much certainty, though by no means with same regularity as those of our solar system.

For instance, each State revolves upon its own axis oftener, upon an average than the planets, but the whole claim the privilege of gyrating around the central government no oftener than it suits them. Three-quarters of a century ago the French were considered tolerably adept at overthrowing a Bourbon and establishing a Bonaparte; but then French revolutions were expensive. It was considered necessary to raise barricades, and to rake the streets of Paris with grape-shot, while the ax of the guillotine worked up and down with as much regularity as a trip-hammer. Besides this, it took at least a month in Paris to pull down a dynasty and set up a despotism. In Mexico, on the contrary, the science of revolution is so well understood that no extra time is lost, twenty-four hours being amply sufficient; no extra blood is spilt; citizens are not deprived of more than one night's rest under ordinary circumstances; a gun or two are fired, a *pronunciamento* issued, and the thing is done. True it is that fighting occasionally takes place, but I am credibly informed that after a terrific engagement of two days between the ins and the outs, at Matamoras in 1862, when the cannonading was so incessant that the innocent people on the Texas side of the Rio Grande thought that half the denizens of Mexico must be *in articulo mortis*, a careful summing up of the casualties showed a total loss of one killed and two wounded. The reason of this is obvious. Most of the fighting is done in the night, in order that individuals who might be disposed to be hostile, may not be able to see to perpetrate acts of violence upon the brave men who man the artillery. In order to give the reader some faint idea of the facility with which power is transferred in Mexico, a sketch is given below in the words of an eye-witness, a friend of the writer.

"During the summer of 1863, I was in Matamoras, the capital of the State of Tamaulipas. One morning my black servant failed to come to my room at seven o'clock, as usual. His absence remained unexplained until nine o'clock, when he came running in in a state of great excitement. 'What's the matter, Ben?' 'Don't know, massa. 'Spec dars a revolution going on— I'se been in de calaboose two hours.' Having arranged my toilet I went out for the purpose of getting my breakfast, but scarcely had I emerged from the house, when I beheld a person who I was told was Governor Ruiz, making very good time down the street, coat-tails standing out at about forty-five degrees, bare-headed, and presenting altogether a very ungubernatorial appearance. Not very far behind was a file of soldiers in hot pursuit. I at once retired to the interior, as I had been informed that the first act in the drama of a Mexican revolution was to lock up all persons who were found out, irrespective of age, sex, color, position, or occupation. Having waited about two hours, or as I supposed sufficiently long for the turbid political waters to subside, I again peered out, and discovered a person who informed me that since the previous night there had been two Chief Magistrates, and that a third, Serna, was now about being inaugurated. As I had enjoyed a slight previous acquaintance with Serna, I at once made bold to proceed to his office to obtain, if possible, a passport, to leave before the political horizon should again become darkened. I reached the office of that dignitary just as an animated discussion was taking place between two officials, each of whom claimed to be secretary of state. This having been summarily decided by one of them being marched off between two bayonets, I fortunately succeeded in obtaining my passports. Had I left at once all would have been well, but having a buggy and a pair of horses, together with my baggage at the hotel, I delayed long enough to secure them and then took my departure.

"Scarcely had I reached the suburbs of the city, my heart meanwhile growing light at the prospect of getting away safely, when—such is the uncertainty of Mexican affairs—my way was intercepted by a party of cavalry. I at once produced my passports, which the officer in command commenced diligently reading upside down.

"Finding that this operation would be likely to delay me some time, I told him that it was all right, Governor Serna had given it to me. Unfortunate blunder. His brow grew dark as he informed me that Serna was no longer governor of Tamaulipas, but that Cortina was the man. Here was a pretty affair. At this rate there would be two or three more rulers before I could get out of their jurisdiction. A bright thought struck me. I drew out five dollars. The brow of the agent relaxed, but he still held on to my passports. I drew out five dollars more. A smile broke over his face, as he handed me my papers, and with a polite '*bueno, adios senor,*' bade me farewell. Be assured I did not suffer the grass to grow under my feet until I had crossed the Rio Grande in Texas."

XXXIX.

AN AUTHENTIC ANECDOTE OF GENERAL HOUSTON HITHERTO UNPUBLISHED.

IN the year 1860, while Houston was Governor of Texas, an expedition was fitted out for frontier protection. In the purchase of medical supplies the Governor gave strict orders that no liquor should be included, under penalty of his serious displeasure. In the requisition for medical stores made by Dr. T——, surgeon of the regiment, were included, Spts. Vini Gallici, bottles 24. This was duly furnished with the other articles, and the bill was taken to General Houston for his approval. The old gentleman settled his spectacles upon his nose, and gravely putting his eagle quill behind his ear, read the bill through slowly and carefully until he came to the item in question, when he turned to the druggist and said: "Mr. B——, what is this, Spts. Vini

Gallici?" "That, General, is brandy." "Ah, yes, and do you know that I have given positive orders that no liquor should be furnished for this expedition?" "No, General, I was not aware of it?" The general rang his bell. "Call Dr. T——." The doctor was summoned. "Dr. T——, what is this Spts. Vini Gallici for?" "That, Governor, is for snake-bites." Appealing to the druggist, the Governor continued, "Mr. B——, is Spts. Vini Gallici good for snake-bites?" "Yes sir, it is so considered." "Yes," replied General Houston, in slow and measured tones, "and there is Dr. T——, who would cheerfully consent to be bitten by a rattle-snake every morning before breakfast, in order to obtain a drink of this Spts. Vini Gallici." Having thus delivered himself he approved the account.

————◦◦————

XL.

Copy of a letter, never before published, written by J. W. Fannin, a few days before his capture. The letter was found among the private papers of Colonel T. F. McKinney.

GOLIAD, 28th February, 1836.

MR. JOS. MIMS:

The advice I gave you a few days back is too true. The enemy have the town of Bexar, with a large force, and I fear will soon have our brave countrymen in the Alamo. Another force is near me, and crossed the Nueces yesterday morning, and attacked a party by surprise under Colonel Johnson, and routed them, killing Captain Pearson and several others after they had surrendered. I have about four hundred and twenty men here, and if I can get provisions in to-morrow or next day, can maintain myself against any force. I will never give up the ship while there is a pea in the ditch. If I am whipped it will be well done, and you may never expect to see me. I hope to see all Texans in arms soon. If not, we shall lose our homes, and must go east of the Trinity for awhile. Look to our property; save it for my family, whatever may be my fate. I expect some in about this time by Coagly, and wish you would receive and take care of it, I now tell you, Be always ready. . . . . . If my family arrive, send my wife this letter. Inquire of McKinney. Hoping for the best, and prepared for the worst, in a devil of a bad humor.

Farewell.

J. W. FANNIN, JR.

2\%

XLI.

DAWSON AND SIMS.

EVERY old citizen of Austin remembers Frederick Dawson, of Baltimore, Maryland, who furnished money to help Texas in her early struggles. Dawson was a jovial gentleman of huge proportions, and used to come to Austin during the sessions of the Legislature after annexation, to press his claims for settlement with the State of Texas. He was a jolly companion, a good liver, very fond of brown stout, and had a laugh which waked the echoes around Austin in a marvellous manner.

In the amplitude of his proportions and the magnitude of his laugh, Dawson was rivaled by Bart Sims, a denizen of the Colorado valley. They had never met before the occasion under consideration, consequently their points of resemblance were unknown to each other. Upon this day, the gentlemen above-named being both in town, the street boys conceived the remarkably brilliant notion to have Sims and Dawson laugh for a wager. No sooner said than done. The duello was agreed upon by the principals, drinks for the whole population were staked upon the result, judges were duly chosen, and the cachinnation commenced.

Never before or since has the sun of Texas shone upon a more peculiar spectacle. For half an hour, the log-houses within, and the hills around the seat of government of the Lone Star State, echoed and reëchoed to laughter of the most thundering description.

Dogs, pigs, chickens, and little children ran away terrified; and men, women, and larger boys and girls, who didn't know what was the matter, poked their heads out of the doors and windows adjacent, in wonderment. Gradually, the bystanders becoming infected with the fun of the thing, joined in the loud smile, and from the head of Congress Avenue to its foot, the street was one astounding roar. At one moment the star of Sims would appear to be in the ascendant in this equally matched contest, but the next instant Dawson would gather himself for a mighty effort, and roll out a peal that would put the neigh of a horse or the bray of an ass to shame unutterable. At length the match was over, and the crowd awaited the decision of the umpires, who, after due deliberation, gave the award in favor of Dawson.

"Well, boys," said Sims, after the result was announced, "he," pointing to Dawson, "laughs to the tune of half a million, while I haven't got a d—d cent to laugh on." This was a good hit for Sims, who was not rich in this world's goods, and the laugh now turned in his favor, while his antagonist stood the treat with his usual good-nature.

XLII.

TEXAS INDEPENDENCE.

THE following eloquent extract is taken from one of Thomas H. Benton's speeches :

" Goliad has torn Texas from Mexico ; Goliad has decreed independence ; San Jacinto has sealed it ! What the massacre decreed, the victory sealed ; and the day of the martyrdom of prisoners must forever be regarded as the day of disunion between Texas and Mexico. I speak of it politically, not morally ; that massacre was a great political blunder, a miscalculation, an error, a mistake. It was expected to put an end to resistance, to subdue the rebellion, to drown revolt in blood, and to extinguish aid in terror. On the contrary, it has given life and invincibility to the cause of Texas. It has fired the souls of her own citizens, and imparted to their courage the energies of revenge and despair. It has given to her the sympathies and commiseration of the civilized world. It has given her men and money, and claims upon the aid and a hold upon the sensibilities of the human race. If the struggle goes on, not only our own America, but Europe, will send its chivalry to join in the contest. I repeat it ; that cruel morning of the Alamo, and that black day of Goliad were great political faults. The blood of the martyr is the seed of the church. So the blood of slaughtered patriots is the dragons' teeth sown upon earth, from which heroes full grown and armed, leap into life and rush into battle. Often will the Mexicans guiltless of that blood, feel the Anglo-American steel for the deed of that day, if this war continues. Many were the innocent at San Jacinto, whose cries in broken Spanish, abjuring Goliad and the Alamo, could not save their devoted lives from the avenging remembrance of the slaughtered garrison and the massacred prisoners. Unhappy day, forever to be deplored, that Sunday morning, March 6, 1836, when the undaunted garrison of the Alamo, victorious in so many assaults, against twenty times their number, perished to the last man by the hands of those, part of whom they had released on parole two months before, leaving no one to tell how they first dealt out to multitudes that death which they themselves finally received.

  .   .   .   .

" Accursed be the ground on which the dreadful deed was done ! Sterile and set apart let it forever be ! No fruitful cultivation should enrich it ; no joyful edifice should adorn it ; but shut up and closed by gloomy walls, the mourning cypress and the weeping willow, and the inscriptive monument, should forever attest the foul deed of which it was the scene, and invoke from every passer-by, the throb of pity for the slain and the start of horror for the slayer. And you, neglected victims of the Old Mission, and the San Patricio, shall you be forgotten because your numbers were fewer, and your hapless fate more concealed? No! but to you justice shall also be done. One common fate befell you all, one common memorial shall perpetuate your names, and embalm your memory."

XLIII.

LAFITTE.

(From Brief History of Texas.)

RUINS OF LAFITTE'S FORT.

BETWEEN the years 1817 and 1820 this celebrated freebooter of the Gulf held sway at Galveston. He built there a town which he called Campeachy. His authority over his subjects was supreme, and he lived in almost regal splendor. His establishment was finally broken up by the United States naval force in 1821, and he abandoned Texas.

Jean Lafitte was a native of Bordeaux, France. At an early age he ran away from home and enlisted in a British ship of war. Deserting soon after, he went to South America. About 1806, he fitted out a privateer, in which he coasted in the West Indian seas, and in a few years by his bold exploits he acquired great wealth, and, by the singular attractiveness he possessed gathered around him a most devoted band of followers. From 1811 to 1813 the headquarters of Lafitte were upon the island of Grand Terre, or as it was afterward called Barrataria. This island is about sixty miles from the delta of the Mississippi. In 1813, Governor Claiborne of Louisiana, in order to break up the nest of pirates, offered a reward of five hundred dollars for the head of Lafitte, to which the buccaneer responded by offering fifteen thousand for the head of the governor. A military force was now sent by the governor to enforce his authority, but Lafitte and his force captured the command, loaded them with presents, and sent them back. The aid of the United States government was next invoked, and Commodore Patterson was dispatched with a fleet to break up the settlement.

But the pirates burned their town and retreated, and the Commodore returned. Lafitte, with his characteristic effrontery, next offered his services to the United States in the war of 1812–15, against England, on condition of his pardon. This was agreed to as the easiest way of getting rid of him, and the bold rover of the seas fought gallantly behind the breastworks at New Orleans.

In 1817, Lafitte having returned to his old habits, established himself at Galveston, where his followers numbered at one time fully one thousand. He built a fort there, and a town which he called Campeachy, and lived for years in royal style.* His authority and influence were almost without limit. In 1819, he was appointed by the Mexican Republicans, governor of Galveston island. In 1820, an American schooner was taken by one of his cruisers, and having been plundered, was sunk. This was the signal for his ruin. In 1821, an expedition was sent, under Captain Kearney, to break him up. When this force arrived, Lafitte went out to meet the captain, and inviting him and his officers to his house, he entertained them in a princely manner, trying by the blandishments he knew so well how to use, to dissuade them from the object of their mission. Finding that the officer in command was inexorably resolved to do his duty, Lafitte immediately called his followers around him, and having paid them off he bade them farewell. Then, with a few chosen followers and in his favorite vessel, he abandoned Galveston forever. Lafitte continued for years after this to cruise against the Spanish commerce. He died at Yucatan in 1826.

* A friend informs me that although possessed of immense wealth, Lafitte lived in a plain and simple manner.

XLIV.

METEOROLOGY OF TEXAS.

THE following tables, kept at Austin, Texas, for between seventeen and eighteen years, will be found of interest to those who contemplate making a home in our great State, no less than to the citizens thereof. They can be relied upon as correct:

RAIN TABLE FOR SEVENTEEN YEARS, BEGINNING AUGUST, 1857.

Rain in 1857, 4 months, . .	20 inches.	Rain in 1866, ...	41.95 inches.
" " 1858, ...	36.37 "	" " 1867, ...	27.19 "
" " 1859, ...	30.24 "	" " 1868, ...	40.09 "
" " 1860, ...	29.61 "	" " 1869, ...	38.54 "
" " 1861, ...	28.69 "	" " 1870, ...	41.23 "
" " 1862, ...	23.17 "	" " 1871, ...	29.21 "
" " 1863, ...	33.85 "	" " 1872, ...	29.81 "
" " 1864, ...	25.16 "	" " 1873, ...	44.94 "
" " 1865, ...	38.40 "	" " 1874, to Aug. 1, . .	18.06 "

Total rain-fall in 17 years, ... 576.51 inches.
Average annual rain-fall, same time, ... 33.93 "
Largest rain-fall in any one year was in 1873, ... 44.94 "
Smallest rain-fall in any one year was in 1862, ... 23.17 "
There has been a steady increase in the fall of rain, as shown below:
Aggregate rain-fall for 5 years, beginning January, 1858, ... 148.08 "
Average annual for same time, ... 29.61 "
Aggregate for next 5 years, beginning January, 1863, ... 166.55 "
Average annual for same time, ... 33.31 "
Aggregate for next 5 years, beginning January, 1868, ... 178.88 "
Average annual for same time, ... 35.78 "
The wettest month in the year is September, there being an average for that month of 4.40 inches. The driest is December, average being 1.81 inches. Largest amount of rain in any one month during above time was in October, 1870, 12.63 inches. Largest amount in any one shower was in August, 1870, 7 inches in four hours.

RANGE OF THERMOMETER FOR SEVENTEEN YEARS.

	Highest.	Lowest.		Highest.	Lowest.
1858	98	22	1867	98	17
1859	101	10	1868	96	15
1860	107	18	1869	97	19
1861	100	23	1870	96	11
1862	104	23	1871	102	22
1863	99	17	1872	99	15
1864	99	6	1873	96	13
1865	106	18	1874	102	28
1866	96	21			

XLV.

TEXAN SCENERY.

THE following, from Edwards' History of Texas, published in 1836, well describes the scenery in parts of the interior of Texas.

"Now, reader, your relator is lost for words to describe the balance of this landscape triangle after crossing the river Trinidad ; and no language can convey to the mind any thing adequate to the emotion felt by the visitor in ascending this vast iregularly regular slope of immense undulated plain which expands before the eye in graceful rolls, affording from the summits of their gentle swells a boundless prospect of verdure, blending in the distance to the utmost extent of vision, with the blue of the horizon.

"Few spectacles surpass it in beauty and magnificence. The boundless expanse, and profound repose of these great plains excite emotions of sublimity akin to those which arise from the contemplation of the ocean in its display of undulatory movements. Yea—a more grand and stupendous silence even broods over these regions, where often neither sound nor sight foreign to the scene disturbs the contemplation of the passing traveler. These rolling prairies are generally divided by a broad declivitous vale, through which meander in sweeping curves one of those brooks, creeks, or branches which enter the Trinidad (now called Trinity) Brazos or Colorado ; on which, as they approach these rivers, there is more or less of timber relieving the eye in unison with these fine airy groves of every shape with which the prairie mounds are studded, with spaces in them seemingly designed for building. Nature invites the culture of art here with the most alluring smiles. In many places these eminences or inclined plains are regularly and beautifully decorated with timber, forming rows or colonnades ; then varying into serpentine avenues, arches, or verdant alcoves, charming in their appearance and soothing in their effects.

"These rows of timber and picturesques groves are called islands, from the striking resemblance they present to small tracts of land surrounded by water. Nothing can be more natural than the comparison, as the prairies often assume the appearance of a lake, both in surface and color ; and in the remoter parts the hue melts into that of distant water. And it requires no very great effort of the imagination, especially in certain conditions of the atmosphere, to fancy that such is the reality of the scene. Yes, so much has nature contributed to the illusory appearance of these groves, that they often present all the beauty of art. For the trees are of nearly uniform size, and grow near together, without undergrowth, and present outlines perfectly well defined, and often surprisingly regular: some appearing to form exact circles or ovals, while others are nearly square or oblong, with scarcely a single tree projecting beyond:—so that it is found difficult to divest one's self of the impression that much of the land has been lately cleared, and these are the remains of the forest. Taking this interesting province in all its bearings, I doubt whether another like it could be found on the continent—from its one-mile encircled prairie to those of twenty miles, without a solitary tree, shrub, or bush. And although the music of the brooks and waterfalls is not heard to enliven nature—now leaping from rock in frolic play, and then tossing in foaming cascades over mountain scenery—yet there are but few streams which do not reveal in their clear depths every little pebble and shining grain of sand ; at one time expanding their swelling bosoms to the broad eye of day, reflecting back the sparkling sunbeams as from a thousand mirrors, at another flowing smoothly over their beds of sand, and coyly retreating beneath the shade of overhanging foliage, and the more delicate network of the skirting wood. Elevations of land, from the round ·pigmy hills of a few feet high to the elongated mountain of the fourth magnitude, are to be met with in this section of country: from whose summits there is always an elivening, sometimes a magnificent prospect.

" Out of many which might be described, there is one which is well worth the fatigue of a hundred miles' journey to see ; it is immediately on the road from Bexar to San Felipe, thirteen miles east of the Guadaloupe River. On ascending from the Colorado up this inclined plain for the first time, we are suddenly stopped on the west edge of a rather abrupt declivity, with astonishment and wonder. Well does it receive the appellation of Mount Pisgah—for with Moses of old we are made to exclaim, " Behold the land of Canaan and the best of it lies before you.' For the whole undulating valley of the Guadaloupe River, with its branches, its prairies, its woods, its hills, and its vales, as far north, west, and south as vision can extend, lies under your enraptured gaze in a full panoramic view."

XLVI.

THE WILD MAN OF THE WOODS.

CONTRIBUTED BY SWANTE PALM.

MOSES EVANS spent most of his time in the woods, locating lands on the frontier amongst the wild Indians. Occasionally he would " come into the white settlements," particularly in season for mass-meetings and camp-meetings. We all knew "Mose." He was a robust, strong frontier character, with a large sunburnt face, all in flames, had fiery red hair and long beard, deep-set black eyes. He was a man of peculiar looks, and sought to be noted particularly by " Mister-Ladies," whose company he was very fond of. One of those, he said it was, who wrote the following love-letters for him. They were published in a local paper, much to Moses' notion of " good licks." He was himself an illiterate " wild man of the woods," as he called himself, but had in his young days served as a bar-keeper, had a peculiar address and assurance, winning and " illigant." Mose died a smiling old bachelor. There were no " Mister-Ladies " on those edges of civilization where he spent his life ;—and—his "dear Forestina" was at last caught, the " Wild woman of the Navidad bottom,"and turned out to be an African negro-man, one of those wild negroes whom the famous Monroe Edwards imported direct from Africa, and who had run away and lived for many years, wild and fleet as a deer, in the woods.

MOSEANIA EVERGREENS.

THE WILD MAN TO THE WILD WOMAN.

There are some things to mortals given,
Less of earth and more of heaven ;
A tear so limpid and so meek
It would not stain an angel's cheek.

A tear, such as the Wild Man would shed
On his wild beauty's sacred head.
Celestial wood-nymph ! lovely and free,
My devoted heart I offer thee.

Here's myself, my heart, all my land !
Give, oh give me thy precious hand ;
Then in wild woods blissful and blest we roam,
Earth our paradise and heaven our home.

MOSES EVANS.

WASHINGTON, July 11, 1850.

REPLY OF THE WILD WOMAN TO THE WILD MAN.

Oh ! Moses ! my dear, as I list to your lay,
My heart, like a bird on its pinions away
O'er the forests and plains that now intervene,
Would fly to your bosom so *soft* and so *green;*
So *soft* in the strain with which you would woo ;
The wild woman's heart, that beats only for you.
And *green*, in the offer of all your lands,
To gain what is yours—the Wild Woman's hand.
Not your land, but your whiskers, bushy and long,
First fastened my heart with love's magic thong.
Indeed, my dear Moses ! they scarcely would fail,
They remind me so much of the red fox's tail—
Their color so like that strange blending of hues ;
That often hath waked the song of the muse,
Which may be produced by salt water, when warm,
If the sun lends its rays to strengthen the charm.
I'm weary, my darling, of being alone ;
Come take the *Wild Woman*, and make her your own,
Like the dove from the ark, her heart longs for rest,
And would gladly repose on your *Rattlesnake Vest*.*

THE WILD WOMAN.

WILD MAN TO THE WILD WOMAN.

My Dear Forestina :

It is with emotions of no ordinary kind that I address you. I am especially encouraged to do so from the very favorable reception my first met with, and your kind reply thereto. With great candor and sincerity did I express the sentiments of my heart toward you. In my first I poured forth the ardent emotions of a devoted heart in poetic strains ; in this I will use the plain language of prose. And now be assured that my ardent wish is still that

My heart shall ever be thine—
May thine be ever—ever mine.

You can not imagine, my dear, how much pleasure I received in reading your reply to my first communication. Oh how my heart fluttered and went pit-a-pat so I thought it would burst my very sides, so hard did it bound about. When I read in the very first line these words: "Oh Moses ! my

---

* Moses Evans, *the Wild Man*, wore a vest made of the skins of rattlesnakes.

dear, you can not imagine how queer I felt—all over so." Well, thought I, "good licks these, to begin with—I reckon it will all come out right yet." And then you say "Would fly to your bosom so soft and so green." Well, I couldn't exactly understand what you meant by "soft and green" bosom. Thought I, she is mistaken there—hard as bone. As to green bosom, never saw one, should think it very pretty though.

Again you speak of "red fox's tail." In the settlements they would say, red fox's latter end or posterior extremity. But perhaps you mean mane, instead of tail. As I wear a large flowing mane under my chin, you may have reference to that.

Again you speak of "salt water," that looks so beautiful when the sunbeams fall upon it. It may be so. As I have never been on or in salt water much, can't say how it is. I have some friends, however, who have gone up Salt River, but they have not come back again, so don't know how they find it there. Some folks have tried to get my friend General Houston to go up, but he won't go. I almost wish he would go, for he would come back again and let me know how it looks up there.

But oh! my dear Forestinia, I can't tell you how happy it made me when I read the following lines.

> "I am weary, my darling, of being alone,
> Come take the Wild Woman and make her your own."

Well, thought I, "good licks" again. I reckon that's plain language enough. So the thing is fixed sure, and no mistake about it.—Well, my dear, I'll come and no mistake, so you can make ready; but you must set the day first.

> And oh! how happy I shall be,
> My charming one, when I get thee.

I, too, my darling, am weary of being alone. Long have we wandered in these wild woodland wastes, and on these prairie-plains—solitary and alone. I have been a few times into the settlements, and am pleased with what I have seen there, as the results of civilization, education, and religion. Let us then leave our wild homes, and go in and try the experiment of civilization, with the rest of mankind. But remember before you go, and weigh the matter well that you must leave this beautiful rolling prairie, over which you have so often bounded like a timid deer, and these shady groves, and thick forests of large spreading trees, under whose shades you have so often sat to rest. And those meandering brooks, whose cooling, sparkling waters have so often slaked your thirst, and on whose banks you have watched their finny inhabitants so playful while sporting on the pebbly bottoms—apparently to gratify and interest you. I say, you must leave all these, together with all those beautiful wild flowers, so gay and so sweet—as the timid deer and the gentle young fawns with which you have associated so long—and all those woodland song-sters whose sweet music has so often lulled you into quiet and repose, and whose plaintive warblings have announced to you the early dawn, while they would sing, as it were for your special benefit, their morning hymns. And that soft moss couch, suspended under that large spreading tree, with those beautiful curtains, and fancifully arranged moss drapery, upon which you have so long and often reclined and taken sweet, quiet repose, while the cool-ing, gentle breezes were wont to waft so softly over your innocent and lovely form—and the dewlike pearl drops would dangle from your long flowing locks. Can you leave all those, my charming one? If so, then come and go with me, and I will introduce you to a greater pleasure than all these can afford.

You shall have a fine comfortable dwelling-place, instead of your wild trees, to shelter you from the pelting storm and scorching sun, (if uncle Sam don't rob me of my land) and all other things necessary for your comfort. And you will have the society of the wise and the good—warm, kind friends, and all the blessings of civilization.

But it is unnecessary for me to say more now, as I hope you will be placed soon in a position to judge for yourself. Come then, my own sweet one, and go with me—and let us be happy while we may. And as two drops of water unite and blend together in one, so may we be united inseparably, while life with us shall last.

Oh! my dear, my darling charming one,
So pure, none like thee beneath the sun—
Nature's perfect model as thou art,
Unstained by vice, and so pure in heart,
May corroding cares, in after years,
Ne'er dim thy bright eyes with sorrow's tears.
When thy sun sets in the western sky
May thy spirit soar to realms on high.
Then bask in sunbeams of immortal days,
And join in songs of angelic lays.
Is the ardent aspirations of one
Whose heart dotes on thee, and on thee alone.
Your affectionate friend and lover,
MOSES EVANS.

WASHINGTON, August, 1850.

TO THE WILD MAN OF THE WOODS.

RATTAN THICKET, TEXAS, Sept. 1, 1850.

How long in the shade of this cotton-wood tree
   Shall I wait for thy coming, my dear?
How oft shall I spread up this moss-bed for thee?
   Oh! when will you be with me here?
While amid this deep forest alone I repine,
   My thoughts often wander to man's dreaded haunts,
And then I imagine that sometimes I find
   The loved one for whom my soul ever pants.
And then in delight—while the precious thoughts play
   On my brain, for a moment I seem to be there;
But alas, the bright vision soon passes away,
   And leaves me alone in despair.
Will you come to my moss-woven couch in the tree?
   The old hollow cotton-wood ages have known,
It waves its dark branches majestic and free
   In the light of the sun and the gloom of the storm.
In sweet solitude, I had been long reposed,
   Undisturb'd by man's treachery and sin;
Until the soft words of thy letter in prose,
   Awoke the wild passions that slumbered within.
Inspired by those words, new ideas of bliss,
   Incessantly haunted my startled up brain;
The sunlight looked brighter, the moonbeams did kiss
   The pendulous dewdrops, that hung on the plain;
The wide-spreading oaks, green glades and gurgling rills,
   The pebbling brooks, timid dear, and gentle fawns;
The soft wafting breezes, the grassy clad hills,
   The cool shady bower and sweet blooming lawns;
The dew-spangled valleys, the evergreen groves,
   All glowed on my sight and swelled my lone heart,
The gay warbling songsters, sang sweetly of love,
   When I yielded my heart and deem'd myself blest.
Oh! say not that I must leave the sweet flowers,
   And the songs of the birds which have cheered me so long;
The dark shady woods and the moss draped bowers,
   The wild-cats and panthers and the wolverine throng.

No, no, my dear Moses, we can't leave the woods **wild,**
   In exchange for the horrors of civilized life,
Nor quit these bright scenes for religion's false smile :
   It groans in deep sorrow, division, and strife.
And education, it may do pretty well,
   To pamper all those who know how to use it ;
But for us, dear Moses, I'm sure we can't tell
   How far we might be induced to abuse it.
We may not try it, my Wild Man, 'tis plain,
   We never could pursue their bad measures,
The crowd would surround us and give us much pain,
   While they couldn't add one straw to our pleasures.
Besides, my dear Moses, you often are talking,
   Of " good licks," and " mister ladies," so charming,
You'd soon be induced with them to go walking—
   The very thought to me now is alarming.
Then come to my camp in the Navidad swamp,
   Far away from society's turmoil and strife,
You'll be to the Wild Woman all that she wants,
   And she'll be to you the ever-loving wife.

FORESTINA.

To MOSES EVANS, WILD MAN OF THE WOODS, BRAZOS SWAMP, TEXAS.

XLVII.

THE NORTHERS OF TEXAS.

IT is understood by many persons at a distance that the Texas " northers " are dreadful winter storms, which come on so suddenly and are so severe and extremely cold, that man and beast, caught out on the open prairies a few miles from shelter, have often been known to freeze to death in a very short time. Before I came to Texas I had heard such representations made of Texas northers. In a late " Manual of Geography " the children are taught that " Texas is famous for its north winds. These come on at times so suddenly in winter, and are so cold and severe, that both man and beast have been known to perish in them."

Now it is admitted that Texas northers have not only become famous abroad, but that they deserve notoriety for the suddenness and violence of their winds, but not, generally, for the severity of the cold which attends them. The cold spells of winter of the same latitude in Georgia and Florida, from which I came, are generally as cold, if not colder, than the winter northers of Texas. It is seldom we have frost, in the vicinity of Austin, before the middle or last of November, and be it know that Austin is about in the center of the belt of Texas northers ; for the northers are confined to the prairie portion of the State, west of Trinity River.

For the last three or four winters—since I have been in the State—not more than a half-dozen of these north winds have been cold enough to form ice at all, during any one winter, and only three or four of them during the whole time have sunk the mercury to twenty-five degrees Fahrenheit.

Let it be understood that here in Texas all north winds which come up suddenly, with any degree of violence, are called northers—even a summer thunderstorm from the north is called a norther—but the term is principally applied to the sudden north winds of winter.

The people here in Texas divide these winter storms into " wet northers " and " dry northers." The wet northers are very similar to the winter storms in the States east of the Mississippi River. A north wind blows, with more or less violence, attended with rain, and sometimes, but not often, with snow and sleet, and lasts about twelve or fifteen hours, passing off with a mode- rate north or north-west wind. But the dry northers are attended with pecu- liar and singular phenomena, never witnessed, so far as I know, in any storms east of Texas. As these notorious dry north winds have given the character and the bad reputation of the northers of Texas, I shall endeavor to describe them somewhat in detail.

For several hours preceding the most violent of these dry northers there is almost a dead calm and the air is unusually warm and sultry. A few low, sluggish bodies of cloud float about in the eddy atmosphere. A dark, muddy looking cloud wave next appears low down all across the northern horizon, which is the " precautionary signal " of the near approach of this strange Texas storm. A few minutes more, and the terrible roaring of the norther is distinctly heard. All hands in the field at work are now running to the house for shelter, where all is hurry and busttle to pile on the wood and get the fires ablaze. At the same time, the stock on the prairies have turned tail to the wind, and are fleeing as for life to some timbered ravine or bluff for shelter. All this, and more too ; but be not alarmed, for there is no danger, though the Geography says " men and beasts have sometimes per- ished in them," which may possibly be so ; but still the colts on the prairie and the children in the yard are kicking up their heels, sporting amidst the pranks of the dashing wind. But the dark, cloud-wave is now over, and no rain, except it may be a very slight mist, followed by a dry, blue, misty haze, with the peculiar smell of—some say—sulphur, but others say like a burning forest. Let this be as it may, there is evidently in these dry " blue northers " (as they are called), a state of high electrical condition of the atmosphere, which produces a thrilling sense of exhilaration in man and beast.

The force of the wind in the most violent of these dry storms is about sufficient to blow down an ordinary rail fence, where most exposed to the wind. These storms continue without abatement for about twelve hours, and then gradually subside in about twelve or fifteen hours more. The cold which attends them is variable, often not freezing at all, and then again sinking the mercury in the tube of the thermometer down to twenty-five or twenty degrees, and in one instance, at Austin, as low as six degrees ; but such extreme cold only occurs, perhaps, once in a lifetime ; as was experienced in Florida in February, 1835, when the water froze on the skin of the cheek between the washpan and the towel.

These dry northers are considered, and no doubt are, very healthy winds, coming as they do over an extended dry and elevated country. The experience is that a few "blue northers" sweeping over the malarious districts of the country, in the month of October, bring health and infuse life and energy into all the subjects of chills and fevers, and morbid livers.

W. J. BLEWETT.

XLVIII.

ADVENTURES OF A YOUNG TEXAN.

WE have been permitted to copy from the journal of John C. Duval the following extracts from his journal, giving an account of some of his adventures in Texas in the spring of 1836.

MASSACRE AT GOLIAD.

"On the morning of the 27th of March we were ordered to get ready to march to Copano, where we were told there were several American schooners upon which we were to embark after giving our parole of honor not to engage again in the war. We were formed into three divisions and marched out separately. The largest division, comprising about 150 men, in which I was, was taken out along the road leading from the Mission to the upper ford. Another division was taken out into the open prairie back of the town, and the third along the road leading to the lower ford. As one division filed through the streets of the town, I heard several of the Mexican senoritas (with whom doubtless we had frequently danced at the fandango) exclaim, "*Pobrecitos*" (poor fellows) ; and if any idea of the foul play intented us had ever entered my mind, my suspicions would then have been aroused, but as it was the incident made no impression upon me. We had marched about half a mile when a halt was ordered, and the file of Mexican soldiers on our right countermarched and formed behind the file on the opposite side. No suspicion was aroused by this movement, as we supposed the soldiers were merely making a change in the order of march. The first intimation I had of what was coming was given by some one near me saying, "Boys, they are going to shoot us," and at the same instant I heard the clicking of the musket locks; and before I fairly comprehended the situation the soldiers fired and killed nearly every man in the front rank of our division. At this moment I distinctly heard the firing upon the two other divisions. The firing upon all was nearly simultaneous, and was doubtless arranged to take place at a preconcerted signal, though I saw none. About fifty men, I think, in our rear rank were untouched. These endeavored to make their escape toward the river. The man standing in front of me was killed, and in falling knocked me over, covering me with his blood. I lay for an instant stupefied and stunned by the suddenness of the whole affair, and when I rose up the Mexican soldiers had passed over me, supposing I was killed, and were in the pursuit of those flying to the river. I followed on after them unobserved, as they did not look back, until I had got within about eighty yards of the river. Just then a soldier whose gun was empty charged upon me with his bayonet, but at the instant he drew back to give me the *coup de grace*, a man from Georgia, whose name I have forgotten, ran in between us and received the thrust intended for me. It was given with so much force that the bayonet pierced him through and through. After he fell I saw the Mexican, with his foot upon him, endeavoring to withdraw the bayonet, but just then I had pressing business elsewhere and did not stop to see how he succeeded. I ran right though the Mexican lines, and although several shot at me, I escaped untouched.

"Being a good swimmer I plunged without hesitation into the river, and quickly reached the opposite bank, for the river, though deep and swift at this point, was not more than fifty yards wide. But the bank was nearly perpendicular, and eight or ten feet high, and I had to swim down the river, the enemy meanwhile popping at me, about one hundred yards, before I could effect a landing.

"Then I came to a grapevine hanging down from a tree which leaned over the water. This I caught hold of, and by its aid had nearly reached the top of the bank, when a soldier fired his *escopeta* at me, cutting the vine entirely through just above my head and backward I fell into the river again. The Mexican had made a line shot, but I was unhurt, and when I had swum down eighty or one hundred yards farther, I came to a shelving part of the bank, up which I contrived to scramble without any great difficulty."

24

After Mr. Duval's miraculous escape from death, as recounted above, he made his way as best he could through the wilderness to the encampment of the Texas army on the Brazos. During these weeks he encountered many wonderful adventures, which he narrates with a graphic pen, and which we should like to publish in full; but our limits forbidding this, we must content ourselves with giving one or two extracts from his journal.

And first we will relate

HOW HE ESCAPED FROM THE INDIANS.

" I then pursued my course, and in a few hours came to a heavily timbered bottom which must be that of the Navidad, which is the next stream of any size east of the La Vaca. After penetrating this bottom perhaps half a mile, my attention was drawn to the barking of a dog behind me.

" At first I did not notice it particularly, supposing it to be a dog belonging to some of the settlers who lived on the Navidad before the war, and which they had left behind when they fled before the approach of the Mexican army. But at length I observed that although I was traveling at a pretty rapid walk, the bark of this dog seemed to get nearer and nearer to me. I then began to have some suspicions that the dog was on my trail, and that probably there might be some one with him. Under this impression I hurried on as rapidly as possibly. Crossing the Navidad at a shoal where the water was not more than knee-deep, and after a rapid walk of an hour, I came to the open prairie on the east side of the river. All this time I could hear the yelping of the dog behind me, at apparently about the same distance as when I first heard it. I continued my course into the open prairie for three or four hundred yards, and then turned short around and retraced my steps to the edge of the timber. I then made a spring as far as I could at one jump to the right, and continuing along the edge of the timber about two hundred yards, I concealed myself in the top of a fallen tree, whence I could have a distinct view of any one coming out of the bottom. While thus concealed, the barking of the dog drew nearer and nearer rapidly, and before long I saw the dog and three or four Indians emerge from the bottom, at precisely the point where I had left it. One of the Indians held the dog by a leash, and was armed with a gun; the other two with lances and bows. They did not pause, but continued on the trail I had made through the prairie. When they came to the point where I had turned back, the dog was evidently at fault, but the Indians, taking it for granted that I had continued on my course, kept leading and urging the dog on in the same direction, until at length they were lost from sight. Had I not played their own game upon them, I should unquestionably have lost a portion of my hair upon that occasion; and I took considerable credit to myself for the way in which I had eluded them."

DUVAL DRAWING A PIG THROUGH THE FLOOR.

To face p. 371.

He next tells

HOW HE REPLENISHED HIS LARDER.

"My provisions were exhausted. I was exhausted. To say I was hungry would be a weak expression. I followed the margin of the timber for several miles, in hopes of finding a house where I might possibly be able to renew my stock of supplies. At length, in a clearing, I saw a house, toward which I cautiously advanced, until I was satisfied there was no one about it. On close examination it was evident that a marauding party of Mexicans had been there, and had appropriated whatever eatables there might have been on the premises.

"I searched everywhere thoroughly, but could find nothing in the way of provender. By this time the sun was set, and as there was a bed in the room, which looked very inviting to one who had been sleeping so long upon the ground, I determined to occupy it at least for one night. So, after devouring the few remaining crumbs in my knapsack, I turned in, and was soon fast asleep. It must have been near midnight when I was aroused by a noise of some sort. Listening attentively I soon discovered that the noise proceeded from a drove of hogs that had taken shelter under the house. The building was upon blocks, a foot or so from the ground, and the space beneath the floor was therefore sufficiently roomy for their accommodation. The floor was of thick puncheons or slabs, which were held upon the sleepers solely by their own weight. Hunger in my case stimulated necessity to be the mother of invention, and it at once occurred to me that I could bag one of those porkers, by quietly lifting one of the puncheons so as to grab one of them from above and haul him up through the opening. I at once proceeded to put my plan into operation. So I got up, and after listening a moment to discover by their grunting exactly the spot where they were, I slowly raised the puncheon. Thrusting my arm cautiously through the opening I felt around until my hand came in contact with the leg of a hog, when I suddenly seized upon it and attempted to drag him through the floor. But unfortunately for the easy accomplishment of my undertaking I had secured hold of a large hog, and it was no easy matter to induce him to come up in the way I wanted him. Such kicking and squealing I never felt or heard before, and for some time the contest hung in an even scale; but I knew that if I let go, my chances for a breakfast were gone. Hunger gave me unwonted strength, and at last, after he had cut me severely with his hind hoofs, and knocked all the skin off my knuckles against the sharp edges of the floor, I dragged my prize by main force into the room, and, replacing the slab, I had him secure. Now, how should I kill him was the question. There was nothing in the room by which to give him the *coup de grace*. The moon was shining brightly, and I went outside to hunt up something to answer the purpose. The only thing I could find was a heavy maul, and armed with this I re-entered the room, and forth-with there ensued a peculiar and animated engagement.

"The maul was very heavy and in my weakened condition I could not wield it with sufficient celerity to strike a stunning blow with any precision. Round and round the room we went for a quarter of an hour, the hog squeal-ing and dodging, his hoofs clattering and rattling on the puncheons, with a noise like the long roll of a snare drum, and now and then my maul coming down on the floor with a tremendous bang that might answer for the bass ; the whole making a concert which might have been heard a mile. Finally, I got a fair whack at the top of his head, and so brought him down, and afterward dispatched him by repeated blows. When the contest was over, I was so com-pletely exhausted that I tumbled back into bed, and did not wake up until the sun was high in the heavens."

We must content ourselves with one more extract from Mr. Duval's journal. After making his solitary way as best he could from Goliad east through a country altogether unknown to him except by means of the map which he had ; subsisting as best he could by means of what he could find by the way or at the settlers' cabins, all of which had been deserted on the approach of the Mexican army he crossed the San Bernard by swimming, and entered a deserted house to rest. At a house where he had previously stopped he had found a large dog, who had insisted upon following him wherever he went. He says, "I entered the house, and soon had a blazing fire upon the hearth. I was not as cautious as I would otherwise have been, for I felt sure that the Mexicans had somewhere met with a serious repulse. What con-firmed me in this *belief* was that for two or three days previously I had seen small portions of troops traveling hurriedly and in apparent disorder toward the *west*, whereas all troops I had seen before were going in the opposite direction. Upon rummaging my pocket, I found a handful of corn, which I proceeded to parch for breakfast. While busily occupied in this way, my dog uttered a low growl, and looking up I saw the muzzle of a gun slowly pro-truding through the window.

"In a moment it flashed through my mind that a straggling party of the enemy had been attracted by the smoke, and I saw that I was completely entrapped, for the only door of the house was on the same side as the window. But before I had time to determine what course to pursue my dog suddenly sprung through the window, and at the same time some one uttered an excla-mation of astonishment and fear, followed closely by substantial oaths in plain English. I opened the door just in time to save the intruder from being throttled by my dog, who, fortunately for him, in place of his neck had seized upon a thick woolen comforter wrapped around it. With some difficulty I got him to let go his hold. The attack had been so sudden that he had no chance to use his gun. This gentleman, Mr. Monroe Hardeman, afterward well known through Western Texas, in company with Captain Duncan, were following on the rear of the retreating Mexican forces, and seeing the smoke from my chimney, had naturally supposed that a party of the stragglers had stopped there.

"Hardeman had dismounted and gun in hand advanced stealthily toward the house. The door being closed, there was no chance to reconnoiter except through the window, and he was just in the act, as I have stated, of slipping his gun through it preparatory to looking in, when my dog sprang out and fastened upon his neck. Mr. Hardeman told me he was never so badly frightened as at that time. In a minute Captain Duncan, who had seen the row between his companion and my dog, came up, and dismounting, we all entered the house. I then told them I was one of Fannin's men, who had escaped the fate of the others, and they, on their part, informed me of the battle of San Jacinto, which had transpired four or five days before, and in which they were participants. They told me the war was virtually over, and Santa Anna's army was in full retreat toward the Rio Grande. Noticing that I had a lean and hungry look, or else observing the wistful glances I cast at Captain Duncan's wallets, the latter proceeded to empty their contents on the floor, consisting of a liberal supply of biscuits, potatoes, meat, and so forth, and hospitably invited me to "pitch in." No second invitation was requisite, and I began, without loss of time, a vigorous attack upon the provender. After half a dozen biscuits, as many potatoes, and perhaps three or four pounds of meat, had disappeared, the captain, losing all confidence in my discretion, and without as much as saying, 'By your leave,' cleared the table at one fell swoop, and crammed what was left into the saddle-bags again. I remonstrated with him upon such treatment; told him it was a breach of hospitality to invite a guest to break bread with him, and then clear the table before he had finished the first course; that I was just fairly getting under way; but all I could say had no impression, and I did not get a peep into those wallets again until we pitched camp twenty miles distant. In company with these gentlemen I returned to the army, then on the Brazos."

XLIX.

THE SOLDIER'S SWEET HOME.

BY MRS. MARY L. WILSON, SAN ANTONIO.

(From Allan's Lone Star Ballads.)

THE soldier who o'er the lone prairie doth roam
Oft sighs for the far distant pleasures of home,
For the absent and dear ones who love him so well—
Oh! the deep pain of parting, the soldier can tell.
Home, home; sweet, sweet home,
The call of our country is dearer than home.

But who would stand idly when brave deeds are done?
Or who would heed danger where glory is won?
We'll welcome the conflict for freedom's the prize—
And hallowed his grave is, for freedom who dies.
Home, home; sweet, sweet home,
Oh who would not fight for his fair Texas home?

Dear Texas—thy soil unpolluted shall be,
Or thy bosom shall give us the graves of the free;
Nor die we revengeless, for with us shall fall
A host of the foemen—their blood be our pall.
Home home; sweet, sweet home,
We'll die to defend thee, our beautiful home.

But victory shall crown us; with wisdom our guide—
With valor, and justice, and God, on our side,
And prayers of our dear ones ascending to heaven
'T were treason to doubt that success shall be given,
Home, home; sweet, sweet home,
Then dearer than ever shall be our sweet home.

L.

UP! MEN OF TEXAS.

(From the Houston Telegraph, 1842.)

Ye men of Texas, can you see
  Yon swarthy foeman coming on,
And know that God has made you free,
  By San Jacinto's battle won?
Can you look on with careless eye,
  Regardless of your sacred right;
Or strive a shameful peace to buy?
  Up! men of Texas, to the fight.

Oh, bitter shame and deep disgrace!
  Shall Texas' star e'er sink so low,
That you should fear such foes to face,
  Forgetful of the Alamo?
Or offer, coward like, to pay
  Five millions for your conquered right?
Rouse—rouse your hearts without delay—
  Up! men of Texas, to the fight.

Ye strove before, in honored time,
  And well your rifles told the tale:
Will Texans now yield up their clime,
  Or let their noble courage fail?
Remember well the Alamo,
  And let the name your souls unite,
To deal destruction on the foe—
  Up! men of Texas, to the fight.

Tell Mexico's degraded sons,
  Their bloody debt shall yet be paid,
For Fannin and his martyred ones,
  Dire vengeance stands too long delayed.
The blood-stained soil of Goliad
  Still rises darkling on your sight,
And shows the treacherous fate they had—
  Up! men of Texas, to the fight.

And think ye others will not lend,
    In such a case, a helping hand?
Will relatives forget the end
    Of those brave men—the Georgia band?
Will Shackleford forget his boy?
    Will not Duval come with delight?
Lo—thousands hail the shout with joy—
    Up! men of Texas, to the fight.

·The "dark and bloody ground" has sons
    To whom the name of Crockett 's dear.
The western hunters, with their guns,
    Will gladly seek for glory here,
The chivalry of distant lands
    Will aid the struggle for your right.
And joyful front these savage bands,
    Up! men of Texas, to the fight.

Arouse, arouse, your flag's unfurled,
    Seek victory or win your graves.
Show proudly forth to all the world
    That Texians can ne'er be slaves.
Oh let the memory of the past
    To noble deeds your souls incite;
Be firm—be valiant to the last—
    Up! men of Texas, to the fight.

———— ►•◄ ————

LI.

LEAVE IT! AH NO—THE LAND IS OUR OWN.

BY MRS. MARY G. YOUNG.

(From Allan's Lone Star Ballads.)

LEAVE it! ah no—the land is our own,
    Tho' the flag that we love is now furled,
A Texan must roam o'er his own prairie plains,
    Or find rest in the far spirit world.
        Oh! the Lone Star State our home shall be
        While its waters still roll to the Mexican Sea.

Where shall so blue a sky ever be found,
    As the heavens that bend o'er us here?
Or when do flowers bloom so fragrant and sweet,
    The wayfaring wanderer to cheer?

Others may seek South American shores
    Orizaba and fair Monterey;
But never, because she be burdened with woes,
    Shall our feet from our own loved State stray.

Then here's to our State—our own dear State,
    Right or wrong—enslaved or free;
In poverty, wealth, enthroned or disowned,
    Our mother our queen shall be.

LII.

MY CHILDHOOD'S HOME.

BY WESTON. 1845.

FAR off on the hill tops the daylight is dying,
    Deep darkness is stealing adown the lone vale,
Thro' the old poplars zephyrs softly are sighing,
    And nature's glad anthems are borne on each gale.

The night bird is singing her welcome to even,
    The locust is trilling her song on the lawn;
While the sunbeams still linger to beautify heaven,
    Sweet emblem of those who are hallowed when gone.

Within the dark thicket the partridge is calling
    Her brood from their wanderings to come to their rest,
On the meek floweret the mild dews are falling,
    And now in her night robes all nature is drest.

Loved vale of my fathers, dear home of my childhood,
    What fond recollections have hallowed thy streams,
Thy hills and thy dales and thy oft-courted wildwood,
    And made thee, in slumbers, the scene of my dreams.

No more on the hillside at eve I may wander,
　　And hear the wild notes of the whip-poor-will's strain.
But absence will still make my heart grow the fonder,
　　And long for my home in the valley again.

Here, sweet is the spring tide, and Summer is gladness,
　　Here Autumn comes teeming with plenty and glee;
Here Winter was never a season of sadness,
　　Here piety dwells and the people are free.

'Tis thus in thy quiet forever I'd leave thee—
　　'Ere dawn of to-morrow I'll be far away—
E'en now I but linger, this sad lay to weave thee
　　And for thy long welfare most fervently pray.

But 'tis a sweet hope, for it lightens the sadness
　　Which steals o'er my heart when I think of the dead,
That my soul may revisit these life scenes of gladness
　　When low in Earth's bosom my body is laid.

Oh! God of my fathers, I humbly implore thee
　　That while our proud rivers shall roll to the sea,
Within this loved vale may be found to adore thee
　　The sons of the valiant, the wise, and the free.

Still sweet be the song on the hill-tops at even,
　　And long in the vale may simplicity dwell,
And so live her sons that their home may be Heaven,
　　When to earth they have bidden a final farewell.

———◆◆———

LIII.

THE TOLLING BELL.

BY D. W. C. BAKER.

HARK—the tolling bell
　　Sounds from far away;
And its echoes come,
　　Come, but not to stay;

Rising on the hill
  Falling in the vale,
Sinking in the calm,
  Swelling on the gale,
Till th' exhausted ear, with almost pain,
Fails to catch the dying sounds again.

Tell me, tolling bell,
  Whither goes thy sound?
Does it faint and fall
  Trembling on the ground?
Is it lost in air,
  Or in ocean waves?
Does it seek a home
  In the hidden caves?
Or does it float away to other spheres,
And mingle with the sounds of former years?

Hopes are like thy sound,
  Oh, thou tolling bell,
And alternately
  Do they sink and swell—
Do they rise and fall,
  Lost upon the sea,
Wrecked upon the wave
  Of uncertainty.
Gone forever from the longing breast,
Seeking ever for a place of rest.

Go—thou restless Hopes—
  Seeking the fleeting sound
Of the tolling bell,
  Till its home be found.
Or on mountain top,
  Or in vale or cave,
Underneath the earth,
  Underneath the wave,
Or with it wing thy flight to other spheres,
And mingle with the hopes of former years.

LIV.

LAMENT FOR A STOLEN "PET."

DEDICATED TO COLONEL HOBBY, BY MOLLY E. MOORE.

HARK! I hear the swift ring of the bugle call!
But no answering neigh from thine empty stall!
Thou wert wont to fly at that shrill command,
To bend thy neck to thy master's hand!
But the joyous rush of thy light, swift feet,
With its mystic ring and its echo sweet—
Ah, those musical sounds on the blossoming shore
And the long hard beach are heard no more.

Does that proud neck arch at the stranger's tone,
As it did when MY trumpet call was blown?
And HIS hand, my beauty! oh! does it twine
In thy shining mane with a touch like MINE?
Dost thou follow HIS form with a wistful eye?
Dost thou fret at thy rein when HIS step draws nigh?
And ah! dost thou strain thy matchless speed
At the will of the stranger? my gallant steed!

Thy master is lonely beside the sea
In the noisy camp! He cherished thee
While others battled for flower or glove,
And the glittering toys in the Court of Love,
Or the guerdon from beauty's countless store—
Or which should be first on the festal floor!

And well might they shine! 'tis a high surprise,
The first love-glance from a lady's eyes,
When their dreamy power on the soul lies ever
As the lotus blue on its orient river;
But thine, oh, my beauty! sure SOMETHING keeps
A HUMAN watch in their mystic deeps!

There are fair young forms in the lighted hall,
Where flowers are festooned on the fretted wall.

There are feet that are swift as a lightning glance,
When they move, like dreams, in the mazy dance ;
But thine, my lost darling, were fleeter far
(And softer the glow of the twilight star,
Than that light that fell from the shaded lamp !)
When we moved by the edge of the broad-spread camp,
Along the beach where the ocean hymn
Grew deep and clear in the evening dim !

Thy master is lonely beside the sea,
In the desolate place where he cherished thee !
Together your breasts have been bared to brave
The burning desert, the swelling wave ;
Ye have threaded together the forest deeps,
Ye have climbed together their rocky steeps ;
And together, with wild blood throbbing high,
Ye have shot o'er the plains 'neath the western sky !

Thou hast borne this form through the gloom of the flight,
From the flush of morn to the gathering night !
Thou hast carried him proudly where turf was red
With the blood from the breasts of the gallant dead ;
Thou hast gayly swept o'er the lonely wold,
When the night was fierce with a bitter cold.
Does the stranger tax thy glorious speed
With a careless hand, oh ! matchless steed ?
But thy stall is empty, and where thou art
Beats there for thee so warm a heart
As that thou hast left ?   Does the stranger's hand
Tighten thy bridle with fierce command ?
Oh, where art thou ?   In the distant west
Art thou spurning the turf on the prairie's breast ?
Or, beyond where the Rio Grande flows,
In the land of the orange, the land of the rose,
Has he given thy rein (where the leaves unfurl
With so free a grace !) to some dark-eyed girl ?

That dark-eyed girl—does she wreath thy brow
With rich, gay blossoms of Mexico ?
And the hand that she lays on the flowing mane,
Does it shine like a snow-flake under the rein ?

Ah ! well ! but I know she loves thee not
As thy master loved !   But be fair thy lot
In that distant land !   He shall miss the high
Proud toss of thy head.   Thou wert won't to go by
Like a fairy dream, or a lady's sigh !—
Shall miss thine eyes, with their luminous depths, the curve
Of thy stately neck, with each swelling nerve !
Thy slender hoofs, with their resonant beat.
Oh ! for the rush of thy fair swift feet !
And oh ! for the touch of thy floating mane,
And the long, wild gallop across the plain,
For one more thrill of thy reckless speed !
My prairie darling, my beautiful steed !

HOUSTON. July 1, 1864.

LV.

REPLY TO THE "LAMENT FOR A STOLEN PET.

DEDICATED TO MISS MOLLIE E. MOORE, BY COLONEL HOBBY.

YES, the bugle calls loud on that surf-beaten shore,
Whose echoes my footsteps shall waken no more.
And sad to *his* ear is that shrill-ringing call—
There's no answering neigh from my desolate stall.
In the hush of the twilight, no more shall we ride,
On the beach where the billows roll on in their pride.
No more shall my flying feet scatter the spray
That the south winds had kiss'd from the breakers at play,
And embroidered the shore with a delicate fringe,
A frost-work on sea-shell of rose-colored tinge.
No more at *his* tent, ere the sentinel's eye
Hailed the dapple of morn in the orient sky,
Shall I hurriedly go, or as patiently stand
For a sound of *his* voice and a touch of his hand.
No more to his cheek shall my own ever press,
Nor bend my proud neck to his gentle caress.
I long for a touch of that kind hand again,
I fret, for a stranger now tightens my rein.

Sorrow shadows his brow, *he* is lonely, I know,
In his camp where the billows unceasingly flow.
My heart is his own, it can never be less
For him, who mourns me in silent distress.

His companion for years, through dangers together,
Through summer's fierce heat and winter's bleak weather;
Over prairies in boundless magnificence spread,
Where pleasure more often than safety hath led.
Where flowers are gaudy, and sweetest perfume
Is wafted in freshness, from blossom and bloom,
Where sounds disturb not the repose of the day,
Save the partridge that whirr'd from my footsteps away.
Then onward through solitude still would we press,
Over mountains sublime in their bleak barrenness,
Where the eagles would scream from their summits of snow
At the speck that was threading the gorges below.
Where nature appears in her fiercest of moods,
Where none save the savage's footstep intrudes;
Rock piled upon rock, unrelieved by a bloom,
Each mountain pass shrouded in silence and gloom.
Hark! the wild sound, 'tis the Comanche's dread whoop
As he bends to his prey with a vulture's fell swoop.

He tightened my rein as I snuffed the fresh breeze,
And away from pursuers with swiftness and ease!
As free as an eagle that cleaves the calm air,
With a sure-footed bound the deep gorges I'd dare,
'Till the echoing shout of pursuers, once near,
Wax'd fainter and fainter, then died on the ear;
Sound sunk into silence, pursuers had failed
And the mountain tops, blue in their misty wreaths, paled;
Then relieved, would I watch, for there danger still lowers,
O'er my master asleep, 'mid the dew-moistened flowers,
More anxious than wearied, I'd watch by his side,
Till the morning blushed in, like a blooming young bride.
This love is the *only*, that ever endures
That confidence wins, and that danger matures.

When the silence of midnight brooded over the deep,
And the winds and the waves laid together asleep,

We have wandered along 'neath those luminous skies,
That blazed with the light of a thousand bright eyes.
The sky caught a charm from the ocean's blue wave
While its radiance illumined her deep coral caves,
And the Peri below, in their palace of pearl,
Caught the diamonds that fell with a glitter and whirl
From the silver lid stars, as in splendor they'd glide
From the measureless height down the fathomless tide,
The soft heavens bent down, ocean lifted her breast,
The wind, wooed into silence, disturbed not their rest ;
In rapture each gazed on the other's bright face,
And night paused, as she witnessed the blissful embrace.

The poems then oft would my master rehearse,
And my feet would keep time to the magical verse ;
And there would he tell, as we journey'd along,
How great was thy genius, and splendid thy song ;
How morality pure in thy verse was enshrined,
And the graces of fancy around it entwined ;
How Truth, in her grandeur, pervaded the whole,
Enlarging the mind and improving the soul ;
How sublime in its uses thy mystical art,
While it wakens new life, sweetly mellows the heart !
How it lightens the weight of His chastising rod,
And points us in penitence upward to God ;
How it cheers the desponding and lonely heart up,
And sweetens the draught of life's bitterest cup ;
How it weaves a bright hope when misfortune shall crowd,
And a lining of silver to every dark cloud !
Such province is thine, with thy heaven-born art,
And well thou succeed'st in thy beautiful part.
Thy name in the camp is held almost divine,
From Mexico's border to Maryland's line.
Thy poems are prized by the brave and the true,
And blessings unnumbered are wafted on you,
Each Texian claims thee, his being of song,
But not to Texians alone does thy genius belong,
That genius so splendid shall ne'er be confined
To a worshiping few, what was meant for mankind.
More fame to the State will thy gifted pen give
Than the thousands now here, and hereafter may live :

And such were his words by that murmuring sea,
As he told of the future bright promise for thee.

" Is thy rein now given (where the leaves unfurl
With so free a grace) to some dark-eyed girl?
That dark-eyed girl—does she wreath thy brow
With rich gay blossoms of Mexico?
And the hand that she lays on thy flowing mane,
Does it shine like a snow-flake under the rein? "

No: Woman has never yet tightened my rein,
Nor twined her fair hand in my dark-flowing mane—
At the sound of her voice I would toss my head high—
Nor touched me, nor gazed in my dark-rolling eye;
I flee from her presence with quivering limb—
I can not like those who've been cruel to him.
He cares little *now* for the love-lighted eyes
Which the passions of youth madly worship and prize.
The star of his boyhood has faded and gone,
Let its gloom, or its brightness, untroubled, sleep on:
Love's slumbering fever, disturb it not now,
Its shadowy traces still darken Hope's brow.
Its power, you sing " on the soul lies ever
As the lotus blue on the orient river. '
No, Lethe's oblivious current will roll,
And curtain the past from the dream-haunted soul.
Thrice welcome from Hades its mystical waters,
A balm to the sting of earth's loveliest daughters.
'Tis true, as he rode me, when thinking of her,
His heel would unconsciously drive the keen spur:
He told me—ah! no, let the words be unspoken,
Since the seal on the fountain of love has been broken.
In the chambers of silence, there let it now rest,
With his feet to the east and his head to the west.

Farewell to my master, and farewell to thee,
And farewell to my home by the murmuring sea.

GALVESTON, July 5, 1864.
25

LVI.

LAUREL AND CYPRESS.

D. W. C. BAKER.　1850.

"We must not forget that as we gather the laurel we scatter the cypress."—STERNE.

THE warrior who, with blood-stained hands
　And garments drenched in human gore,
Carves for himself a conqueror's name,
　And cuts his way to fame's proud door,
Forgets that as he plucks and binds
　The *laurel* wreath around his brow,
He scatters *cypress* in his path,
　And causes scalding tears to flow.

See, where when battle's strife has ceased,
　The conqueror proudly passes by,
The crowd around his praises shout,
　And added thousands join the cry:
Then come and view the field of death,
　Look where the slain in heaps are thrown,
Hark! while the wounded cry for aid,
　And hear the dying gasp and moan!

These are thy fruits, oh cruel war!
　This is the path which heroes tread;
One man—but one, has gained renown,
　Thousands are numbered with the dead.
Alas, alas! how true it is
　That man—ambitious man—forgets,
E'en as he gains a *laurel* wreath
　A mourner 'neath the *cypress* sits.

LVII.

THE TEXAS SOLDIER'S ADDRESS TO HIS FLAG.

PHELIM.

Star of my country, 'tis to thee
　　The soldier turns his dying eyes,
Still his expiring prayer shall be,
　　That long thy folds may proudly rise
Waving victorious o'er the plain
Where he may never fight again.

Thou single star—no galaxy
　　Art thou; no kindred glittering band;
Yet not the less thy light we see
　　Illumining our much loved land.
Like the sun lovely—Oh how bright,
Oh, mays't thou never fade in night.

Star of the unchained and the free,
　　We stand as ever we will stand
Around thy banner—and while we
　　Are left to battle for our land,
Our life-blood shall be freely given
In strife—for victory—or heaven.

Star of the true—a single tie
　　Unites our hearts, that gaze on thee,
A single prayer to One on high
　　Is offered when we bend the knee:
We humbly ask prosperity
For this dear land o'er-shone by thee.

Star that kind heaven itself has blest
　　With victory, when our cause seemed cast
For sure destruction—o'er the west,
　　The east, the south—where'er a blast
Of free wind blows—thou yet shalt wave,
Protector of the free and brave.

Lead on in front, thou gallant star!
We'll follow thee e'en to the last,
And crush invaders who bring war
Amidst our homes ;—or fierce and fast
We'll show them that the swords we wield
Are red from San Jacinto's field.

HOUSTON, 1840.

LVIII.

I'M THINKING OF THE SOLDIER.

MISS MARY E. SMITH.

(From Allan's Lone Star Ballads).

OH, I'm thinking of the soldier as the evening shadows fall,
As the twilight fairy sketches her sad picture on the wall ;
As the trees are resting sadly on the waveless silver deep,
Like the barks upon the ocean when the winds are hushed to sleep.

All my soul is with the absent, as the evening shadows fall,
While the ghosts of night are spreading o'er the dying light a pall ;
As the robes of day are trailing in the halls of eventide,
And yon radiant star is wooing blushing eve to be his bride.

I have shunned the cozy parlor,—for a silence lingers there
Since our loved one went to battle, and we find a vacant chair ;
And a sigh is stealing upward, as the evening spirits come,
With the zephyrs, to the bowers of this sad, deserted home.

For when soft " good nights " are ended, there's a room not like the rest,
Since a soldier left that chamber, and a pillow is unprest,
Oh, my soul is in a shadow, and my heart can not be gay,
As the eve, with low refrainings, comes to shroud the dying day :

For I'm dreaming of the soldier on his pallet bed of straw,
As the leaves are growing yellow, and November winds are raw—
And a vision comes before me of an aching, fevered brow,
And a proud form blighted, blasted—strangely, strangely altered now.

And I feel that strong heart beating, fainter, fainter with each breath,
Fluttering softly in its prison, fluttering thro' the gate of death

And a voice of sad despairing stirs my heart's deep fountain now,
As my hand is slowly wandering o'er that cold and pallid brow.

And a sigh so full of longing fills the chamber of my soul,
While the quivering heart-strings whisper, "Life's a tale that soon is told."
God of love, receive the soldier on the dim mysterious shore,
Where the weary are at rest, and souls are sad—ah, nevermore.

Still the dusky sibyl Future, on her dim prophetic leaves
Writes, that death will claim the soldier when he gathers up his sheaves;
This is why I'm ever sighing, and my heart can not be gay,
As the eve with low refraining comes to drown the dying day.

This is why I still am sighing, as the deep gray shadows fall,
As the somber twilight spirit soothes her shadows in the hall;
And I'm praying for the soldier, from a soul with sorrow sore,
For our soldier boys have left us—*gone, perchance to come no more.*

LIX.

ALWAYS · NEW.

B. MILLER. 1841.

SINCE man by sin has lost his God,
   He seeks creation through,
And vainly hopes for solid bliss
   By trying something new:

The new possessed, like fading flowers,
   Soon loses its gay hue!
The bubble now no more attracts,
   The soul wants something new.

And could we call all Europe ours,
   With India and Peru,
The mind would feel an aching void
   And still want something new.

But when we feel a Saviour's love,
   All good in HIM we view:
The soul forsakes her vain delights,
   In Christ finds all things new.

The joy a dear Redeemer gives,
　　Will bear us safely through;
Nor need we ever change again,
　　For Christ is always new.

And when we come to Jordan's wave,
　　And the dread monster view,
We then shall see HIS power to save,
　　And find that Christ is new.

At length to Zion's golden gates
　　Our journey we pursue,
Behold the bright immortal train;
　　And Christ will still be new.

LX.

TO MY SLEEPING WIFE.

BY COLONEL HOBBY.

IN Dream Land now thy spirit roams,
And blessed angels leave their homes
Awhile to meet thee, loved one, there,
Pure as themselves, and not less fair.

I see them now delighted gaze,
Thy loveliness their theme of praise,
And, joyous smiling, fondly twine
Their arms around thy form divine;

And twining in the midnight hair
That waves along thy forehead fair,
Sweet flowers steeped in fragrant dew,
And colored by the rainbow's hue.

I see them now all fondly press
Their kiss on lips of loveliness,
And wandering with thee, hand in hand
Thro' pearly walks of fairy land,

Where magic palaces arise,
Like clouds along voluptuous skies,
Elysian fields—ambrosial bowers—
To win thee from this world of ours.

Of beauty's type thy form and face,
The perfect mold of human grace ;
Thy hands clasped on thy bosom fair,
As if engaged in silent prayer.

Beneath thy folding marble arms,
Thy swelling bosom hides its charms ;
Where every virtue calmly glows,
And sacred love unceasing flows.

Thy teeth, of whitest pearl, disclose
Thro' parted lips of blushing rose ;
And graceful eye-brows, arched above,
Seem pencil'd by the hand of love.

That eye of life and love is hid
Beneath its stainless waxen lid,
Dark broider'd by its silken fringe
That shades thy cheek of vermil tinge.

How calm thy sleep, how pure thy rest !
The sabbath of an angel breast ;
Awake ! dear one, I can not bear
To see thee smileless sleeping there.

The fearful thought intrudes, that death
Has robb'd thee, sleeping, of thy breath ;
Appal'd, soul shrinks with horror dread—
For what were life if thou wert dead.

From angel worlds come back awhile,
And bless me with thy living smile.
Thou art my joy, my pulse, my breath—
Thy waking's life, thy sleeping's death !

LXI.

The following poem is from the graceful pen of Mrs. C. S. West, formerly Miss Florence Duval.

THE MARBLE LILY.

SHAKING the clouds of marble dust away,
  A youthful sculptor wanders forth alone ;
While Twilight, rosy with the kiss of Day,
  Glows like a wondrous flower but newly blown.
There lives within his deep and mystic eyes
  The magic light of true and happy love—
Tranquil his bosom as the undimmed skies
  Smiling so gently from the depths above.

All Nature whispers sweet and blissful things
  To this young heart, rich with emotions warm :
Ah, rarely happy is the song it sings !
  Ah, strangely tender is its witching charm !
He wanders to the margin of a lake
  Whose placid waves lie hushed in sleeping calm—
So faint the breeze, it may not bid them wake,
  Tho' breathing thro' their dreams its odorous balm.

A regal Lily stands upon the shore,
  Dropping her dew-pearls on the mosses green :
Her stately forehead, and her bosom pure,
  Veiled in the moonlight's pale and silver sheen.
The sculptor gazes on the queenly flower
  Until his white cheek burns with crimson flame,
And his heart owns a sweet and subtle power,
  Breathing like music thro' his weary frame.

The magic influence of his mighty art—
  The magic influence of his mighty love—
Their mingled passion to his life impart,
  And his deep nature each can widely move.
These passions sway his inmost being now—
  His art—his love—are all the world to him—
Before the stately flower behold him bow ;
  Speaking the love that makes his dark eyes dim.

" Thou art the emblem of my bosom's queen,
 And she, as thou, is formed with perfect grace ,
Stately she moves, with lofty air serene
 And pure thoughts beaming from her angel face.
While yet thy bosom holds this silver dew,
 And moonbeams pale with passion for thy sake,
In fairest marble I'll thy life renew,
 Ere the young daylight bids my love awake."

A wondrous flower shone upon the dark,
 A lily—bloom of marble, pure and cold—
Perfected in its beauty as the lark
 Soared to the drifting clouds of ruddy gold.
The sculptor proudly clasped the image fair
 To his young ardent heart, then swiftly passed
To where a lovely face, 'mid floating hair,
 A splendor o'er the dewy morning cast.

She beamed upon him from the casement's height—
 The fairest thing that greeted the new day—
He held aloft the lily gleaming white,
 While tender smiles o'er her sweet features play.
Presenting his fair gift on bended knee—
 " Wilt thou, beloved, cherish this pure flower?
'Twas born of moonlight, and a thought of thee,
 And well will grace this cool and verdant bower :

" And when these blushing blossoms droop and pine,
 Chilled by the cruel North-wind's icy breath,
Unwithered still these marble leaves will shine,
 Calm and serene, untouched by awful Death."
The summer days flew by like bright-winged dreams,
 Filling those hearts with fancies fond and sweet ;
But when the first frost cooled the sun's warm beams,
 The purest, gentlest one, had ceased to beat.

How like she seemed—clad in her church-yard dress—
 To that cold flower he chiseled for her sake !
What wild despairing kisses did he press
 On those sealed eyes, that never more will wake !

His clinging arms infold her once again
  In one long, hopeless, passionate embrace—
Then that fair child, who knew no earthly guile,
  Hid 'neath the flowers her sad and wistful face.

The world that once was fairy-land to him,
  Now seemed a dreary waste of verdure bare—
He only walked abroad in moonlight dim,
  And shunned the gaudy sun's unwelcome glare.
Each night he sits beside a small green mound,
  O'er which a Marble Lily lifts its head,
With trembling dews, and pearly moon-beams crowned,
  Fit emblem of the calm and sinless dead.

He never tires of this sad trysting place,
  But waits and listens thro' the quiet night—
"Surely she comes from mystic realms of space,
  To bid my darkened spirit seek the light.
Be patient, my wild heart! yon glowing star
  Wears the fond look of her soft, pleading eyes,
Gently she draws me to that world afar,
  And bids me hush these sad and longing sighs."

Thus mused he, as the solemn nights passed by,
  Still folding that sweet hope within his soul,
And always peering in the tender sky,
  With earnest longings for that distant goal.
One radiant night, when summer ruled the land,
  He sought the darling's bed of dreamless rest—
The wooing breeze his pale cheek softly fanned
  With balmy sighs from gardens of the blest :

A witching spell o'er that fair scene was cast,
  Thrilling his sad heart with a wild delight;
And steeped in visions of the blessed past,
  He gazed upon the Lily gleaming white.
Jewels of diamond-dew glowed on its breast,
  And the rich moonlight, mellow and intense,
In golden robes the quiet church-yard dressed,
  Pouring its glory thro' the shadows dense.

A nightingale flew from a neighboring tree,
   And on the Marble Lily folds his wings—
His full heart trembles with its melody :
   Of love, and heaven, he passionately sings.
The sculptor, gazing thro' his happy tears,
   Feels his whole being thrilled with sudden bliss—
An Angel voice, in accents soft, he hears,
   And trembles on his lips a tender kiss.

His hope bloomed ! above the marble flower,
   Radiant with heavenly beauty, see her stand !
His heart makes music like a silver shower,
   As fondly beckons that soft, snowy hand.
The golden moon faints in the crimson sky,
   And morning's blushes burn o'er land and sea,
Staining a cold, cold cheek with rosy dye—
   The sculptor's weary, waiting soul is free !

As onward glide the years, thro' bloom and blight
   Unchanged, the Marble Lily lifts its head :
Thro' summer's glow, thro' winter's snow, so white,
   Unheeding sleep the calm and blessed dead.
Wherever falls the pure and pearly dew,
   Wherever blooms the fresh and fragrant rose,
In that far world, removed from mortal view,
   Two loving souls in perfect bliss repose.

———➤◆◄———

LXII.

TEXAN HYMN.

BY J. C. PARMENTER.

ARISE, arise, brave Texians, awake to liberty :
To Mexican oppressors no longer bend the knee ;
But hasten to the combat, with freedom's flag unfurled,
That the glorious deeds of Texas may echo through the world.
     For we are determined to die or to be free,
     And Texas triumphant our watchword shall be.

The bugle sounds to battle, war desolates our land,
Proud Mexico's vile minions advance upon our band ;
But though the blood of Texians should crimson every plain
The rights that God has given us, forever we'll maintain.

Tho' justice long has slumbered, refreshed, she'll soon awake,
The tyrant that invades us, at her stern voice shall quake ;
Before the dread tribunal his haughty pride shall bend,
With honor for our bulwark, in vain shall he contend.

Our foe the lonely covert seeks, unseen to strike the blow,
He loves defenseless murder, and tears of grief and woe ;
He burns our homes and temples for his infernal glee,
But o'er their smoking ruins we'll fight for liberty.

We'll never trust his honor, assassin he is bred.
Brave Fannin and his warriors thus found a gory bed.
And Travis with his heroes on San Antonio height,
Before the foeman legions fell in unequal fight.

The blessed light of freedom on Texas shall descend,
And despotism's darkness in lustrous day shall end ;
The galling chains of bondage, Her sons shall bind no more,
Or we will fall unconquered upon the Sabine's shore.

HOUSTON, 1838.

LXIII.

ODE TO SAN JACINTO.

(From the Austin City Gazette.)

BENEATH the genial blue-arched southern sky,
Where constant spring yields flowers of every dye ;
Where San Jacinto's limpid waters glide,
And mingle with the Gulf's contending tide !
Midst grove-capped hills, adorned with ceaseless green,
Where nature represents her loveliest scene,
And gives her richest beauties to the earth
A nation's independence had its birth.

GENERAL SAM HOUSTON.

See p. 255.

In such a land—in such a matchless clime—
Where bird, and bush, and blossom seem divine,
The wild horse sported, and the savage trod—
Untutored one, and one defying God ;
Regarding neither law, nor time, nor place,
The sod their bed, their home unbounded space ;
Until the sons of Anglo-Saxons came,
To find a land so fair to reason's reign.
Yet o'er this fresh and bright luxuriant land
A soulless despot claimed supreme command,
Who, by his dark and superstitious sway,
Obscured the sacred light of moral day,
And, with his cringing, cowering minions, came
To rear his standard, and his power maintain :
Onward, enraged, he marched o'er field and flood,
Marking each footstep with a patriot's blood.

But here the sons of free-born sires unfurled
Their one-starred banner, and defied the world ;
For in no bosom dwelt a selfish thought :
All struck for vengeance, and for justice fought.
They met ! the conflict blacken'd like a storm ;
Foe fell on foe, and form was piled on form,
Until Jacinto's plains were stained with gore,
And freedom's eagle, undismay'd, could soar.

What lofty form, with brave and martial air,
Rides forth beneath the patriot's lonely star—
With steady eye, and heart without dismay,
Directs the movements of that glorious day ?
It was the master spirit of the brave—
O'er Houston's plume the banners proudly wave ;
His country's pride—her hope and boasted chief,
Who won a lasting name and fadeless wreath.

What gallant form led on the foremost rank,
Unsheath'd his sword and spurred his charger's flank ;
Then with one shout—one loud, inspiring whoop—
Gave bold examples to the rushing troop ;
And like a meteor, through the cloud of strife,
Left death behind, where all before was life ?
It was the brave, invincible Lamar—
The son of genius and the soul of war !

Hockley, with eagle eye and dauntless breast,
And Burleson, the dragoon of the West,
Soon changed the gathering whirlwind of alarm
Into a fierce and loud impetuous storm ;
And Wharton was there, whose high, devoted soul
No fear could stay, no mandate could control ;
He cheered the conquering, trampled o'er the slain—
" The keenest blade on San Jacinto's plain."
And there was Horton, near his chieftain's side,
His word to hear, his rushing lines to guide ;
Sherman, the brave, and Millard, ever true,
With Rusk, and Coleman, battling close in view ;
While Karnes, and Cook, and Somerville, and Bell,
Stood arm to arm where foemen thickest fell—
Each, bent on conquest, firmly kept his post ;
For every man was " in himself a host."

In future time, then may the pilgrim's eye
See here an obelisk, pointed to the sky,
Commemorative of each patriot's name,
Who nobly battled for his country's fame ;
And on its pedestal, and tapering spire,
Read epitaphs that freemen will admire,
Inscribed in lasting characters of gold,
To celebrate the gallant and the bold.

J. B. R.

December, 1841.

LXIV.

LONE STAR OF THE SOUTH.

J. E. DOW.

FAR southward over Sabine stream
    A young republic lifts her head,
Whose single star doth proudly gleam
    O'er valor's grave and glory's bed ;
That star of empire took its flight
    From freedom's coronal of light :
Beamed on Jacinto's deathless plain,
And watched a nation's birth again.

And then, how sad, how strangely still
   The Indian city sits alone.
No herd upon the verdant hill,
   No skeleton beneath the stone,
Forsaken mart of ages, start
   Life's current from thy marble heart,
And bid the pulse of empire beat
Through ivied hall and mossy street.

Beside the green and sculptured piles,
   Whose roofs support the ancient woods,
The hunter's home in beauty smiles,
   And joy runs through the solitudes ;
And where the western Druid trod,
   And offered human blood to God,
The Gospel bell doth sweetly chime,
At Sabbath morn and even time.

The fierce Comanche seeks his home
   Beyond the Rio Brazos' wave,
No more in battle paint to roam
   Around his father's sunken grave,
While the broad stream, whose bosom ne'er
   Knew but the swan and fallen deer,
Whirls the swift steamboat's wheel along,
And echoes to the boatman's song.

Oh, 'tis a fair and goodly land,
   Where restless spirits love to roam,
Where labor spreads his rugged hand
   And decks with flowers contentment's home :
Where prairies vast the woods embrace,
   And rivers run their endless race,
And wild winds whisper to the sea
Of ages past and yet to be.

To its green breast young nations cling,
   And raise the cry of infant life ;
While commerce spreads the ocean wing,
   And war's wild bugle wakens strife.
And there the foeman from afar
Sees on its flag a pilgrim star,

And strives the glorious hour to learn
When the lost pleiad shall return.

There shall the wave of life roll on,
    As rolled the north on Europe's shore,
Till the last boundary is won,
    And ocean voices drown its roar.
O'er martyr's grave and monarch's tomb,
O'er tyrant's throne and knighthood's plume,
O'er craven hosts to slaughter led,
The northern soldier's foot shall tread.

What! let the British Lion roam
    Along the prairies of the South?
Leave life and liberty and home
    Dependent on his gory mouth?
Oh! sooner should our children fold
In deepest shame the stars of gold,
And bury freedom's burning shield
On every deathless battle-field.

Oh! for a coal of burning fire
    That from the Almighty's censer fell,
To touch the lips of son and sire,
    And break the soul-destroying spell.
Then would scorn the name
Of him who dipped his pen in shame,
And on the revolution's urn,
Forbade a sister State's return.

LXV.

TEXAS—OUR HOME.

BY MRS. WELTHEA E. GRAHAM.

BEAUTIFUL land of fragment blooms,
Emerald carpet, and rich perfumes ;
Land of the brave, the leal, the true,
Whose skies are softer and deeper blue
Than the mellowed light of a moonlight pale
'Neath the starry gleaming of midnight's veil.

Land where in gorgeous shimmering lines
On the golden beach the warm sand shines,
And the stealthy morn drags on apace
As the sea fog mantles his heavy face,
And the jeweled drops of sea-foam lie,
Like a rainbow mist, 'gainst a sunset sky.

Land of the prairies, the wide, the free,
That sleeps to the hum of the droning bee,
Where the day-god raises his jeweled crest,
Or sinks in dreams on the twilight's breast,
With a sweeter grace and a kindlier power,
And a dainty gilding of tree and flower.

Land where the live-oak rears its head
With a knightly bearing, to list the tread—
The steady tramp of the myriad feet
That seek its shade with hoofs as fleet
As the wild gazelle ;—where the lightning's play
Tremulous steals from its limbs away.

Land where the seasons gently flee
To the measured march of eternity,
Soft as a babe that sinks to rest
New-cradled and lulled on its mother's breast ;
Where ambered grain steals to the winter's kiss,
And spring-time warms it to newer bliss.

Oh ! Texas—*friend* *—aye, a friend indeed,
That bows to the poor man's every need,
With earliest harvest, eternal flowers,
With balmiest winds and glorious showers,
With gems of dew, and coils of mist,
And the sunlight's purpling amethyst !

Glorious land, where the Lone Star gleams
O'er thy prairies wide and thy sweeping streams,
As softly now as in days gone by,
When the war-god gazed, with baleful eye,
On the little band that uprose to save—
Or shield thine honor in freedom's grave.

* Texas is an Indian word signifying friend.

26

Thine is the land whose birth hour knew
But scenes of terror, where hearts, as true
As the tempered steel, ceased to glow
Behind the walls of the Alamo—
When the Aztec minions who scourged the land,
In wedding with death, had thinned *thy* band.

And down where the San Antonio glides,
Where the purpling tint of sunset hides,
And cool winds play with the waves at will,
And the lily floats on its bosom still,
The quivering lip and moistening eye,
Will tell of dreams that come thronging by.

Of Goliad's field, where the traitor foe
Struck in the dark his *deadliest* blow,
And the jaws of death were red with blood,
As the streams rolled by with widening flood,
And a cry for vengeance went up to God
From the souls of those 'neath the new-turned sod!

On San Jacinto the foe then met,
And the turf with the dastards' blood grew wet,
For the hour had come when the patriot band
Were to win or die, as, hand in hand,
With a cry to God to defend the right,
They rushed on the foe in deadliest fight.

And history tells how the red blood ran,
As man went down with his brother-man,
With glazing eye and paling face,
On the peaceful turf, in death's embrace;
And the darksome frowns of the god of war
Were hid by the beams of thy glorious star!

Texas, our home, our haven of rest,
That we love as the wild bird loves its nest!
When winds are baleful and skies are dark,
And over the heart there gleams no spark,
No ray of hope—may we turn to thee,
The *Lone Star*, to guide us o'er life's sea!

LXVI.

LOVE AND LATIN.

D. W. C. BAKER.

I WALKED with a maiden one beautiful night,
When the moon shone clear and the stars shone bright,
And I said to the maiden, " Now listen to me,
While I teach a short lesson in Latin to thee,
We'll take the verb *Amo*, 'tis so very pleasant,
Translated—Dear maiden, *I love* thee at present.
Amare, infinitive, means, do you see,
To love, then is *infinite* pleasure to me.
Amavi, indicative perfect, my dear,
I have loved thee perfectly well for a year.
Amatum, the passive participle,
Having been loved by me so long and so well,
I pray thee to passively list to my suit,
And when thou hast heard it, to grant it ; to boot.
I promise, dear maiden, if thou wilt be mine ;
To be *perfectly passive,* and calmly *supine,*
And though I'm *imperfect,* thy *future* shall be,
A long conjugation of *amo* and me."

Then the maiden looked up in my face with a smile,
And whispered, " Now listen, I'll teach *thee* awhile.
Though you seem to be in the *imperative mood,*
I hope my instruction may do you good.
If you'll promise to be a good scholar for life,
I'll teach you the meaning of *conjux*, a wife ;
But if you should ever my anger provoke
I'll teach you *Conjugum,* which meaneth a yoke."

LXVII.

THE LAST TEAR I SHED.

BY ROBERT JOSSELYN.

THE last tear I shed was the warm one that fell
As I kissed thee, dear mother, and bade thee farewell:
When I saw the deep anguish impressed on thy face,
And felt for the last time a mother's embrace,
And heard thy choked accents, most frantic and wild,
" God bless thee forever!   God bless thee! my child."

I thought of my boyhood, thy kindness to me,
When, youngest and dearest, I sat on thy knee.
Thy love to me ever so fondly expressed,
As I grew up to manhood, unconscious how blest.
Thy praises when right, and thy chidings when wrong,
While wayward with passions unheeding and strong.

I thought of thy counsels, unheeded or spurned,
As mirth had enlivened, or anger had burned,
And how, when by sickness all helpless I lay,
Thou didst nurse me and soothe me, by night and by day,
How much I had been both thy sorrow and joy,
And my feelings o'erflowed, and I wept like a boy.

Years, years of endurance have vanished, and now
There is pain in my heart, there is care on my brow,
The visions of fancy and hope are all gone,
And cheerless I travel life's pathway alone.
Alone? ay, alone: though some kind ones there be,
There are none here to love me, to love me like thee.

My mother, dear mother, cold-hearted they deem
Thy offspring, but, oh, I am not what I seem;
Though calmly and tearless all changes I bear,
Could they look in my bosom, the feeling is there,
And now, sad and lonely, as memory recalls
Thy blessing at parting, again the tear falls.

AUSTIN, TEXAS.

LXVIII.

NAVAL HEROES.,

To COMMODORE MOORE, and those who fought and died under the naval banner of our Republic, these lines are inscribed.

(Galveston News.)

HARK, hark to the thunders that boom in the deep,
   And shake the broad plains of the sea,
Lo, the war lightnings flash, and the battle-cries sweep,
   On the ocean wind wild and free.
Loud, loud is the strife, and more dreadful it grows,
   And brighter the cannon flames glare,
And nearer in conflict the proud navies close
   And blacker with smoke frowns the air.

And now on the battle's wild tumult arise
   The shrieks of the death-stricken brave,
The patriot's last prayer, as his soul mounts the skies
   And invokes God his country to save.
Down swooned to the deck all crimsoned with gore
   Brave Wilber, a lion in fight,
And horror of horrors, young Bryant is pierced—
   Heaven shrinks from the sad, sickening sight.

Poor boy ! tho' thy young days have ended on earth,
   Tho' thy grave is deep, deep in the sea,
Yet Bryant, we'll hallow thy name and thy worth,
   And thy deeds in defense of the free.
As long as the ocean wave beats on our shore,
   And freedom a home here shall find,
So long thy misfortunes we'll weep and deplore,
   So long shall thy fame be enshrined.

Then Bryant, sleep on with the heroes who fell,
   Their homes and their lives to defend,
They went forth to glory, they welcomed their knell,
   For they heard victory's tones with it blend.

Shame, shame on the coward who dastardly sneers,
   And lifts not his voice to applaud
The heroes who dared in the battle to face
   The foes of their country, unawed.

Shame, shame on the being, vile, heartless, and base,
  Who stops not, when battle is o'er,
To blacken the fame and the honor of him
  Whose name he had clung to before.

Ingratitude carries a curse on its brow :
  And the heart that can nourish its spell
Will sink in dishonor, tho' thousands may bow
  And its praises exultingly swell.
But Moore—there are hearts in our country still true,
  There are bosoms unsullied and pure,
And long will they throb still more grateful to you,
  While freedom and life shall endure.

GALVESTON, 1842.

LXIX.

TEXAN SONG OF LIBERTY.

C. D. STUART.

THE storm of the battle no longer is o'er us,
  Freedom to Texas with glory descends ;
The flag of our triumph waves brightly before us,
  And conquest her splendor to liberty lends.
Huzza ! from our limbs the last fetter has crumbled,
And Mexico's pride in the dust has been humbled.

A shout from the banks of Jacinto's bright waters
  Goes up with the roar of the storm and the blast :
The voice of her sons and the song of her daughters
  O'er tyranny's chains that are riven at last.
Huzza ! nevermore will our Lone Star surrender,
While a true Texan heart is left to defend her.

The heroes who lie on the red field of battle
  Speak loud thro' their blood, and the triumph proclaim,
And their slumber, more potent than cannons' fierce rattle,
  Bids Texas remember her dead and her fame.
Their silence is tongued with, Huzza ! for the river *
Whence backward the foeman was driven forever !

                    * San Jacinto.

And lo! from Bexar's stained turf is awaking
  A sound from the bones of the brave who were slain,
A sound like the voice of the thunder peal breaking,
  Defying the Tyrant to trample again
Where Mexico's banner, all trailing and gory,
But marks the bright pathway of Texas to glory.

Then bright be the star and undimmed be its splendor,
  That links her free name to the love of the world,
And long as our spirit is left to defend her,
  Let freedom's broad banner be nobly unfurled:
While the lips of her brave, and her beautiful, thunder,
No tyrant shall trample our liberty under.

GALVESTON, 1844.

LXX.

THE LONE STAR OF TEXAS.

G. G. SIMCOX. 1851.

WHEN the Lone Star of Texas arose in the West,
  Pale and dimly it shone from its orbit on high,
For the Mexican Eagle had flown from his nest,
  And his broad dusky wings overshadowed the sky.

As the hordes of Sant' Anna rushed on to the fight
  And up to the Heavens their battle-cry pealed,
Oh! paler that star grew, I ween, for its light
  Was eclipsed by the glitter of helmet and shield.

On the spot where still struggled a small Spartan band,
  Who had sworn for their country to conquer or die,
Where the dark frowning walls of the Alamo stand,
  The "Lone Star," still shone from its home in the sky.

How that band bravely stood through the perilous fight—
  How they gloriously died—let history tell.
But paler than ever that star shed its light
  When Travis—the Texas Leonidas—fell.

Where the tyrant dismayed, from the battle-field fled,
　　Where the blood of his minions encrimsoned the plain,
O'er the field of Jacinto, where slumber the dead,
　　More brilliant than ever that star rose again;

And now in the flag of the Union, that star
　　In a bright constellation unceasingly glows.
And long may it shine, in peace or in war,
　　A beacon to friends, or a terror to foes.

LXXI.

A GARNERED MEMORY.

BY NETTIE POWER HOUSTON.

THERE is a blessed memory,
　　Embalmed with my love and tears,
That, buried deeply, tenderly,
　　Has hallowed my heart for years.
'Tis a bright, but a sad, sad vision
　　That hovers before my gaze,
Bringing me all of the treasures
　　I lost with my childhood days.

'Twas a winter evening hazy,
　　The cares of the day were done,
And the troops of merry school-girls
　　Came home in the setting sun:
My weary feet on the threshold,
　　I stored all my books away,
Tossed off my gloves and my bonnet,
　　To rest with the dying day.

My mother sat in the twilight,
　　Musing and dreaming alone:
Her face, in the fire-light shadows,
　　With a calm, sweet glory shone,
I knew of what she was dreaming,
　　I had studied her features so,
That I told by their softened meaning
　　When she thought of the long ago.

I threw back my dark hair's tresses,
  And sitting child-like at her feet,
Asked my mother to tell me the story
  To her memory treasured and sweet.
Her blesséd blue eyes grew wistful,
  She thought of my father now,
And a look of deep loving and longing
  Crept over her lips and her brow.

The glimpses of light through the window
  Strayed lovingly over her hair,
The daylight seemed yearning to bless her,
  And lingered caressingly there :
There never was hair like my mother's,
  'Twas jet in a setting of gold,
Like midnight asleep, in rich masses
  With daylight awake on each fold.

" No wonder my father so loved you,"
  I mused, looking up in her face,
For motherhood, freighted with trial,
  Had not stolen her beauty and grace,
Her dress was the deepest of mourning,
  And her hands were so waxen and white
I thought of the pure snowy blossoms
  That open their petals at night.

Then she told me, in tones like low music,
  The story that measured her life,
Her girlhood, its beauties, its triumphs,
  E'er the love-crown had made her a wife.
And she painted a picture so vivid,
  I fancied it dawned on my view,
Of the evening my father first met her,
  When the old life was lost in the new.

She told how her dress, white and spotless,
  And the curls of her dark flowing hair,
How her blue eyes, her fresh simple beauty,
  Chained his heart in a lifetime of snare.

She told me the scene of betrothal,
    In a beauteous garden of flowers,
Of the lovely, enchanted Bay City,
    Where glided her girlhood's bright hours.

Then she pictured the eve of her bridal,
    When, leaving behind every tie,
She followed her heart's chosen ruler,
    To dwell 'neath a far-distant sky.
Then my mother's sweet face kindled proudly,
    And she said, in a low, earnest voice,
" When I married your father, my daughter,
    Of the whole world I wedded my choice."

The shadows of night were around us,
    The story had closed with the day,
But the words of my mother still lingered
    Like the echo when songs die away.
Long I dreamed o'er the words she had spoken :
    Of the love and the pride in her voice,
And I said to myself, " Earth were heaven,
    If each woman had married her choice."

AUSTIN, TEXAS.

—————————+ ◦ ◦—————————

LXXII.

AN ESCAPE FROM THE ALAMO.

THE following remarkable story is copied from the " Texas Almanac "
for 1873.

MOSES ROSE, a native of France, was an early emigrant to Texas, and
resided in Nacogdoches where my father Abraham Zuber made his acquaintance, in 1827.   In 1830, I saw him several times at my father's house ; he
was then about forty-five years old.   Rose was a warm friend of Colonel James
Bowie, and accompanied him to the Alamo in the fall of 1835.   During the
last five days of his stay at the Alamo, the enemy kept up an incessant bombardment, and several times advanced to the wall, and the men within were
so constantly engaged that they ate and slept only at short intervals.   The
following is Rose's account of his escape.   About two hours before sunset, on
the third day of March 1836, the bombardment suddenly ceased, and the

enemy withdrew an unusual distance. During this time Travis paraded his men and calmly addressed them as follows: " My brave companions—Necessity compels me to employ the few moments now afforded to make known to you a most solemn and melancholy situation. Be prepared for the worst ! Our fate is sealed—within a few days, perhaps a few hours, we must all be in eternity. It is our destiny—we can not avoid it. It is our certain doom. I have kept you in ignorance of this, in hopes of receiving re-enforcements. I ask your pardon for it. In deceiving you, I also deceived myself. I have all along received assurances of help. Every letter I have received, and every person I have seen, has represented that our people were ready, willing, and anxious to come to our relief: and that we might expect enough help to enable us to repulse our foes. The help has not come, and our hopes are dashed to earth. My calls on Colonel Fannin remain unanswered, and the messengers have not returned.' It is my belief that his whole force has been cut off, and our couriers have perished. Relying upon help, I have kept you within these walls. Relying upon help, I have scorned the enemy's demand for a surrender. The worst has now come near us. We are surrounded by an army large enough to annihilate us at a blow, from whose arms we are sheltered for the time by these walls. We must not surrender : for should we do so, that black flag waving in our sight admonishes us as to our doom. We can not cut our way through the ranks of the foe. There is no alternative but to remain here and struggle to the last. Santa Anna is, I am convinced, determined to storm and take this fort at whatever cost. Then, let us in this emergency be men and brothers. Let us withstand our adversaries to the last : and should they, as they will, scale the walls, let us meet them as they come, and never cease to oppose and combat them hand to hand while life remains. Thus, though we perish, we shall weaken our enemies and strengthen our friends : and our memory will be cherished by posterity till history shall be erased and all noble deeds forgotten. My determination is taken : but I leave every man to his choice. Mine is to stay in this fort, and to die fighting for my country. *This will I do, if left alone.*" Colonel Travis then drew his sword, and with its point traced a line upon the ground from right to left. Then, resuming his position in front, he said, " I now call upon every man who is determined to stay here and die with me, to come across this line. Who will be first ? March !" The first was Tapley Holland, who leaped across the line with a bound, exclaiming, " I am ready to die for my country." He was instantly followed by every man in the line excepting Rose. The enthusiasm was tremendous. Every sick man who could walk, arose from his bunk and tottered across the mark. Bowie, who could not leave his cot, said, " Boys, some of you lift me up and carry me over." Four men at once ran to him, and each taking a corner of his mattress, lifted him up and carried him over the line. Rose was deeply affected. He stood still till all save him had crossed to the other side. A consciousness of the situation overpowered him. He sank upon the ground and covered his face. For awhile he seemed unconscious of what was transpiring. A determination to escape, if possible, took possession of his mind. He arose from the ground: he glanced around: he felt in a dream: he cast a searching glance at the cot of Colonel Bowie. David Crockett was leaning over him, conversing in a low tone. Bowie looked up, "You do not seem inclined to die with us, Rose." "No," he returned, "I am not prepared to die, and shall avoid it if I can." Crockett then spoke. "You might as well take your chances with us, for escape is impossible."

Rose looked up at the top of the wall. His determination was taken. He seized his wallet and sprang to the summit of the wall. Standing on the parapet, he took a last look at his friends. Turning his eyes without, he was amazed at the scene which met his gaze. The ground at the base of the wall was literally covered with dead Mexicans and pools of blood. He viewed this horrid sight but an instant. Throwing his wallet, he leaped after it. He fell prostrate in a pool of blood. Recovering himself in a few seconds, he gained his feet, and throwing his bloody wallet over his shoulder, he walked rapidly away. All this was done literally in full view of the Mexican army, and yet, strange to say, without exciting attention. He took the road down the river and crossed the ford. He passed through the town. It seemed deserted. He continued his course down the river. The stillness of death prevailed. He met no one. Suddenly the thunder of the renewed bombardment saluted his ear. Its roar continued to smite upon his ears during the night, when he heard it no more. In the morning he recrossed the river three miles below the town, and directed his course eastward toward the Guadalupe River. He traveled day and night, but made little progress, on account of the large tracts of prickly pear through which he was compelled to pass. These constantly gored him with their thorns, until he was almost unable to proceed. On the sixth of March, he reached the Guadalupe River, and rolling a log into it, he paddled himself across. He continued his journey slowly and painfully for about two weeks, when he reached the residence of my father in Grimes county. My parents had before this seen in the *Telegraph* and *Register*, an account of the fall of the Alamo, and a list of those who were slain, among whom Rose's name appeared. On his arrival, my father recognized him and exclaimed, "My God, Rose, is this you, or your ghost?" "It is me, and no spirit," was the answer. Rose remained at my father's two or three weeks, after which he departed for his home in Nacogdoches, where he soon afterward died.

LXXIII.

THE WRITING ON THE WALL.

BY SAM HOUSTON.

Lo, the sounds of mirth rise loud
   From a city in the east,
And a thousand gleaming chariots
   Gather to a royal feast ;
And a mellow, mystic radiance,
   Hangs upon the perfumed air,
While the sound of soft, sweet music
   Drives away each shade of care.

E'en this city's proudest children,
   Look with rapture on the sight,
While the throng of giddy dancers
   Glide beneath the tinted light.
On his throne of dazzling splendor
   Now Chaldea's king reclines,
While the goblets, gemmed and golden,
   Glow with rich and ruddy wine.

And to still increase the luster
   Of this glorious gala night,
Glitter Judah's sacred vessels,
   Trophies of a heathen's might.
Round the walls of this grand city
   Now the Persian armies slept,
While their stern and gloomy sentries
   Long and weary vigils kept.

But what care the gay Chaldeans,
   With their walls of wondrous height ?
What to them was haughty Cyrus,
   In his silent, sullen might ?
While, perchance, some sleepless veteran
   In the darkened foeman camps,
Looked with eyes of wistful wonder
   On the many glimmering lamps ;

With their countless scintillations
  From the windows tall and wide,
And their meteor-like reflections
  On the dark Euphrates' tide :
Or, perchance, some drowsy watcher
  Paused upon his lonely beat,
And, in silence, marked the timing
  Of the dainty, tinkling fleet :

Then resumed his measured pacing,
  As a night bird rustled by,
Thinking on the mighty changes
  That must meet the morning's eye :
How the broad Euphrates River,
  Wakened from his stony bed,
Would move on in frightful grandeur
  Through a city of the dead.

But what recks the king Assyrian,
  On his gorgeous golden throne,
'Mid the sound of music swelling,
  With its rich, voluptuous tone ;
'Mid the fairest of earth's daughters,
  Decked with gems from land and sea,
With his throngs of glittering satraps,
  Ever prompt to bend the knee.

Lightly laughs Assyria's ruler,
  Little doth he dream of harm ;
Sweetly smiles yon lovely maiden,
  Leaning on her lover's arm—
Hark ! How silent are the minstrels !
  See this proud assemblage quail !
And the god-like King Belshazzar
  Turneth strangely, ghastly pale :

For, along those walls palatial,
  There a ghostly hand doth write,
In a dark and unknown language,
  Words that scorch the very sight,

Many a deeply skilled magician,
  With his weary, restless eyes,
And in turn, each weird old seer,
  Now, this spectral problem tries.

But in vain their conjurations,
  Still those flaming letters stand
On the grand old walls emblazoned,
  Written by God's own right hand:
" Bring the Hebrew captive hither,"
  Then the trembling monarch cried,
" Since the learned of all Chaldea
  By these letters are defied."

Now, Judea's prophet enters
  'Mid that pale and trembling throng:
Through those halls that late re-echoed
  With the sounds of dance and song.
" Hebrew captive," spake the monarch,
  " If this writing thou canst read,
Costly robes and kingly honors
  Will I give to thee as meed."

He replied: " I ask not honors—
  What to me this heathen land?
One of many children, chastened
  By a father's loving hand—
But Belshazzar, king Assyrian,
  With thy broad and rich domains
With thy countless heathen altars,
  And thy strange, unholy fanes,

" 'Tis to thee that this comes greeting,
  Penned by high Jehovah's hand,
At whose throne the angels worship,
  In full many a bright-winged band.
Lo! thy days of might are numbered,
  And, ere morning dawn again,
Thou, with many a loyal subject,
  Wilt be counted with the slain.

" In the balance of High Heaven
　Hath thy wanting soul been weighed.
By great Alpha and Omega,
　By the Maker of all made.
Lo, thy kingdom shall be given
　To the Persian and the Mede—
Thus, O haughty heathen monarch,
　Doth this dreadful writing read."

Dreary silence holds dominion
　Through those grandly lighted halls,
And the noise of trampling horsemen
　On the drowsy night air falls :
Loudly wake the sounds of conflict,
　As the pale stars softly wane—
Medes and Persians hold Chaldea,
　And Belshazzar's with the slain.

Canst thou tell me, smiling skeptic,
　Why no longer, as of yore,
Doth the weary Arab rest him
　On the dark Euphrates' shore?
Yes ! a pool of stagnant blackness
　Sleeps where Babylon once stood,
And the raven and foul lapwing
　Lave their pinions in its flood.

For the satyrs hold their revels
　Where once lordly feasts were held,
And the slimy adder hisses
　In the place where music swelled.
List ! and thou wilt hear the angels
　As they worship, one by one,
Say, " Oh ! God, in Earth and Heaven,
　May Thy holy will be done."

GEORGETOWN, TEXAS, 1868.

LXXIV.

THE MIER PRISONER'S LAMENT.

(From the Galveston News.)

YE warbling birds in shady bowers,
  Your thrilling melodies how gay,
They bring to mind the rapturous hours
  I've spent with one who's far away.
When wandering by some crystal rill,
  Where fragrance floats on every breeze,
I oft have heard those notes so shrill,
  'Mid sylvan groves of spreading trees.

Those very notes I oft have heard,
  In deep wildwood on summer's day,
When I was with my gentle bird,
  My Isabel, who 's far away.
Those blissful hours of peace have passed,
  Which I so happily enjoyed,
And I am now in prison cast,
  With even worse than death annoyed.

Whene'er ye waft on airy wing,
  And through the blue expansion stray,
Go to my love and say, "We bring
  A tear from him who 's far away."
Your freedom, birds, I envy not,
  But to my fate I'm reconciled.
If to be freed shall be my lot,
  I oft may hear your warblings wild.

But if this frame be doomed to death
  E'er time shall bring another day,
Go tell my wife, my latest breath
  Was spent for her so far away.
Go, tell her that her husband died
  At peace with God,—his sins forgiven,
That the last words his spirit sighed,
  Were—"May we meet again in Heaven."

27

LXXV.

THE TEXAS RANGER.

BY J. T. LYTLE.

(From the Houston Telegraph.)

Mount, mount, and away on the green prairies,
The sword is our scepter, the fleet steed our pride!
Up, up with our flag! let its bright folds gleam out.
Mount, mount, and away, on the wild border scout.

We care not for danger—we heed not the foe,
Where our gallant steeds bear us, right onward we go;
And never as cowards will we fly from the fight,
While our belts bear a blade, and our Star sheds its light.

Then mount and away—give our horses the rein,
The ranger's at home on the prairies again.
Spur, spur for the chase, dash on to the fight—
Cry, Vengeance for Texas—and God speed the right.

The clouds of the foe gather thick round our way,
Our war-cry rings out as we rush to the fray.
What to us is the fear of the death-giving plain?
We've braved it before, and we'll brave it again.

The death-giving bullets around us may fall,
May strike us full low, but they can not appal.
Through the red field of carnage right onward we'll wade,
While our guns carry ball—our arms wield a blade.

Hurrah! my brave boys, you may fare as you please
No Mexican banner now floats on our breeze.
'Tis the flag of Columbia that waves o'er each height;
While on its proud folds our *Star* sheds its light.

DAVID CROCKETT.

See p. 262.

LXXVI.

ON THE DEATH OF DAVID CROCKETT,

WHO FELL AT THE ALAMO, MARCH, 1836.

BY T. F. SMITH.

(From the Houston Telegraph.)

HEARD ye that sigh, that melancholy wail,
Borne sadly on by evening's fitful gale,
Like some lone whisper from the silent tomb,
Shrouding a nation with its saddening gloom?
It comes from Texas, like a dying knell,
Where gloriously the immortal Crockett fell.

Like some tall giant on the field of blood,
Undaunted 'midst the gallant slain he stood,
He knew no fear—in danger's darkful storm
He boldly, proudly, reared his warrior form.
His cause—the cause of freedom and the free,
His glorious watchword—Death or liberty.

Sleep, mighty warrior, in thy tombless bed,
The bravest hero of the valiant dead!
Thy name is cherished in a nation's pride,
Whose tears for thy sad fate can ne'er be dried.
Some sculptured marble yet shall rise, and tell
How Crockett with his brave companions fell.

Freedom shall light her torch above thy tomb,
And freemen write the story of thy doom.
Tyrants shall tremble at thy honored name,
And blush to read the record of thy fame:
While millions, at their annual jubilee,
Shall boast a Crockett lost—a nation free!

LXXVII.

MY EARLY DAYS.

BY MRS. LYON (DORA DE LYLE).

THEIR memory comes, like sunshine beams,
  Across my darkened path :
Or, like the vivid lightnings, gleams
  Amid the tempest's wrath.
Or like the rainbow on the cloud,
  Its darkness to illume ;
Or like the rose wreath love hath brought
  To smile upon the tomb.

It comes to cheer my lonely way
  With many a pictured dream,
To gild life's dark and shadowy day
  With joy's reflected beam :
And while the sunlight falleth dim,
  And darkness veils the night :
To the pale star of other days
  My spirit turns for light.

For I have seen the hopes of youth
  Wither in slow decay,
The sacred promises of truth
  Like frost-work melt away.
When of the sparkling cup of bliss
  My thirsting soul would sip,
I've found the draught all bitterness,
  And dashed it from my lips.

And can it be, that in life's maze
  No happiness is found ?
Say—is there no sweet resting-place
  In all earth's varied round ?
No bright oasis for the heart
  Where love's sweet fountain flows,
To cool the parching lip and brow
  Amid a thousand woes.

Not here, not here, the mournful truth
  Is borne on every breeze:
It sighs through Autumn's fading bowers,
  And murmurs o'er the seas.
The solemn moonlight silently
  Doth whisper as we stray,
Oh! seek not here for happiness,
  It dwelleth far away.

Beyond the blue and star-lit throne,
  Where sin and change are o'er,
There is the glorious spirit home,
  Where thou shalt weep no more.
Then onward in life's thorny path,
  Its flowers shall yet be thine,
If thou wilt keep the " narrow way "
  That leads to life divine.

BASTROP, TEXAS.

LXXVIII.

THE GIRL WITH THE CALICO DRESS.

BY ROBERT JOSSELYN.

A FIG for your upper-ten girls,
  With their velvets, and satins, and laces,
Their diamonds, and rubies, and pearls,
  And milliner figures and faces ;
They may shine at a party or ball,
  Emblazoned with half they possess,
But give me, instead of them all,
  My girl with the calico dress.

She's as plump as a partridge, and fair
  As the rose in its earliest bloom ;
Her teeth will with ivory compare,
  And her breath with the clover perfume ;
Her step is as free and as light
  As the fawn's, whom the hunters hard press ;
And her eye is as soft and as bright—
  My girl with the calico dress.

Your dandies and foplings may sneer
    At her modest and simple attire ;
But the charms she permits to appear
    Would set a whole iceberg on fire :
She can dance, but she never allows
    The hugging, the squeeze and caress,
She is saving all these for her spouse—
    My girl with the calico dress.

She·is cheerful, warm-hearted, and true,
    And kind to her father and mother :
She studies how much she can do
    For her sweet little sister and brother.
If you want a companion for life.
    To comfort, enliven, and bless,
She is just the right sort for a wife—
    My girl with the calico dress.

AUSTIN, TEXAS,

LXXIX.

MARY.

BY W. T. G. WEAVER.

I SING of one I love to woo,
    Her home is in the prairie :
Her hair is brown, her eyes are blue—
    Sweet is the smile of Mary.

No dazzling belle she seeks to be,
    Tho' charming as a fairy ;
A graceful cottage girl is she—
    My own kind-hearted Mary.

She dwelleth in a humble cot,
    'Mid landscapes green and airy ;
There I delight from spot to spot
    To rove and talk with Mary.

From early spring, when violets bloom
    And alders wave so lightly !
'Till opening roses shed perfume
    And sunflowers glisten brightly :

Though all the hours it is my pride,
 Among the scenes so fairy;
Where flowerets blow and waters glide,
 To ramble with my Mary.

And while life's sands glide thro' the glass,
 May my lot never vary:
But every fleeting moment pass
 In happiness with Mary.

DALLAS, TEXAS.

LXXX.

RESURGAM.

BY GISBORNE SIMCOX.

ONE summer eve I chanced to tread
 An old cathedral's echoing aisle
Where, sacred to the tranquil dead,
 Rose monuments in every style;
But 'midst them all, an ancient stone,
 Most my attention seemed to gain,
And this the epitaph thereon—
 " *Resurgam* "—I shall rise again.

Unnoticed by admiring glance
 Of casual visitor, 'twould lie
No chiseled sculpture to entrance
 The stranger's wonder-seeking eye;
No name to tell who slept beneath,
 No flattering poet's fulsome strain;
Yet spake that sleeper, e'en in death,
 " *Resurgam* "—I shall rise again.

Be mine, I mused, when fortunes lower,
 When life is cheerless, hope deferred,
To ply my task with increased power,
 Act well my part in deed and word:
The darkest hour precedes the dawn,
 Ease may succeed long years of pain,
Be from your slab my motto drawn—
 " *Resurgam* "—I shall rise again.

To noble ends, if this resolve
   Be carried out " while yet 'tis day,"
I know that as the years revolve,
   And in my turn I pass away
To purer joys, beyond the tomb,
   Than Earth's delusive hopes contain,
To realms of light—from burial gloom,
   " *Resurgam* "—I shall rise again.

AUSTIN, TEXAS, 1850.

LXXXI.

LITTLE BABIES.

BY NETTIE POWER HOUSTON.*

THERE are babies all about us—
   Babies fresh, and sweet, and fair,
Made for seeing, loving, kissing,
   Little babies everywhere.
Who on earth can fail to love them?
   God's fair sunbeams stolen in.
Bless the little sinless babies!
   Innocent, though born in sin.

We can see them all around us,
   In the house and on the street,
Watch their rosy, dimpling faces,
   Hear their busy hands and feet.
Little babies, whose rich garments
   Bear wealth's impress o'er and o'er,
Little babies—poor men's treasures—
   Rollicking upon the floor.

Little black-eyed bonny babies,
   Brimming full of fun and glee;
Little blue-eyed sunny babies,
   There's no prettier sight to see.

* This poem is from the pen of the youngest daughter of General Sam. Houston.

If my arms were only stronger,
　So the wee ones wouldn't fall,
I could kiss them by the dozen,
　Little babies, one and all.

Yes, the world is full of babies,
　Some that just can coo and smile,
Some that dance, and laugh, and chatter,
　Bright and happy all the while.
Some have learned to think and reason,
　And can speak in baby-talk;
Some, whose little limbs are stronger,
　Have essayed alone to walk.

Little babies have their trials,
　So they sometimes sob and wail;
Telling, if we could divine it,
　Many a sad, heart-rendering tale.
'Tis a part of human nature,
　To ask sympathy in woe,
And with little baby-sorrows,
　Grown folks shouldn't grumble so.

Heaven's choice blessings are the babies,
　Blessings not denied the poor;
For the little wandering angels
　Steal in at the humblest door.
Earth is never wholly fallen,
　While these rays from God's own smile,
Say, in silence, something better
　Is beyond us all the while.

There are many little babies
　Who have crossed the river o'er,
Some, whose life-barques were too fragile,
　Perished on an earthly shore.
Little snowy, waxen babies,
　With their tiny hands at rest,
Little buds, too frail to blossom,
　Save in mansions of the blest.

Ah, 'tis much we owe to babies,
  For they fill our lives with light,
Their bright faces and sweet laughter
  Scatter all of sorrow's night.
Little hearts, all unsuspecting,
  Of the paths our feet have trod,
In their simple might possessing
  Power to lead us all to God.

LXXXII.

LINES IN MEMORY OF

MIDSHIPMAN A. J. BRYANT,*

WRITTEN IN 1844, BY WILLIAM H. RHODES OF GALVESTON.

WHEN the hero of a hundred fields
  Is stricken to the plain,
And dies amid the expiring groans
  Of thousands he has slain;

If o'er his head that banner waved
  He battled to uphold,
And triumph greets the band he led
  Where war's loud thunders rolled;

A nation's requiem wail is heard
  To mourn the warrior's doom;
And every patriot's eye is wet
  To yield him to the tomb!

And, Bryant, shall no friendly tear,
  Nor heart-felt sigh be thine,
Because thy death-bed was the wave,
  Thy grave the ocean brine?

---

* Midshipman Bryant was severely wounded in the engagements of the Texas and Mexican fleets off Yucatan, while in the service of the Republic of Texas, and was subsequently lost at sea by the foundering of the schooner Galveston.

Because thy failing hand grasped not
 The banner of the free ;
Nor, dying, waved it o'er a foe—
 Shall none lament for thee ?

So soon have all forgot the day
 That thy young breast was bared
To brave the battle's awful shocks,
 And all its dangers dared ?

When loud around thee cannon pealed
 And death's dread bolt flew by !
When angry flame and black'ning smoke
 Enveloped sea and sky ?

When cries of agonizing pain
 Rose o'er the battle's roar,
And gasping friends besprinkled thee
 With life's fast ebbing gore ?

So soon have all forgot the blows
 That drained thy tender veins—
That made thy childish frame a wreck,
 Thy life a load of pains ?

Shall base ingratitude repay
 The debt we owe to thee ?
And shall forgetfulness usurp
 Thy sacred memory ?

Oh, no ! brave boy, sleep on in peace,
 We'll cherish long thy name.
And deck thy honored memory
 With ever-living fame.

LXXXIII.

SUNBEAMS.

BY MRS. T. H. BEVERIDGE.

I saw a youthful mother
  Once, on a summer day,
Set down a smiling infant
  To watch its frolic play.
It gamboled on the flowers
  That decked the carpet o'er,
And seemed with childish wonder
  Each object to explore.

A something on the instant
  Its glad career arrests;
And earnestly it gazes where
  A golden sunbeam rests.
And now its tiny fingers clasp
  The treasure rich and rare
Which, in its baby innocence,
  It really thinks is there.

But ah!—its hand uncloses—
  Its disappointed gaze
Meets with no gem of beauty,
  No bright imprisoned rays.
And is it not thus with us all,
  Who life's dark way pursue?
We seek to grasp the sunshine,
  And darkness meets the view.

LXXXIV.

THE BEST.

BY HERMAN WILKE. 1850.

WHERE is the country, East or West,
Whose men are noblest, women best:
Where Earth is not a dismal den,
Where Nature stamps her noblemen?

Is France that favored country—say?
Sound forth her praises well I may—
I love her women gay and fair,
And men are brave and noble there.

Are Germans made of purer mold?
Toward *thee* my heart can ne'er grow cold.
Home of my youth—thou'rt dear to me,
And yet the guerdon's not for thee.

Shall ancient England proudly claim
Honor and virtue's diadem?—
Russia or Poland boast of right,
Most virtuous dame, most gallant knight?

Chivalric Spain! art thou the land
Where beauty wields most magic wand?
Dark are thy maidens' glowing eyes—
Yet beaming Orient stars I prize.

And lo—beyond the Western main—
Well might I tune a nobler strain.
For that fair land, where earnest men
Maintain the rights of citizen,
And where in beauty's smiling eyes
A sweet reward for merit lies.

Yet where's the land of all—I ask,
Where truth rejects the traitor's mask?
Where the clasped hand is good as oath,
And freedom thrives through honor's growth?

That land—is it not everywhere?
Let only virtuous hearts be there,
Where love of truth and honesty
Joins hand in hand with fair and free.
This is the land of unmixed joy,
The land with least of earth's alloy.

There woman's bosom pure and chaste,
Will ne'er its charm on recreant waste;
And beauty's love and beauty's sighs
Be aye the meed of high emprise.

LXXXV.

THE NIGHT BEFORE THE WEDDING.

BY WM. M. GILLELAND.

I'M sitting all alone to night,
  And sad November round me grieves;
The sky is misty, dark, and cold,
  And sadly sound the falling leaves.
The fire is low upon the hearth,
  My midnight lamp is burning low,
While tranquil sleep, on couch and tomb,
  The travelers of the world below.
The bells their mournful chimes have hushed,
  Where late the burial rites were read,
And they who swelled the mourning train
  To music of the banquet tread.
The windows rattle to the blast,
  Which means like some deep heart in pain,
And like the strains of saddest song,
  Comes down the cold November rain.
It is a night for memories wild,
  Or golden dreams of diamond days;
A night when ghosts the churchyards walk
  And minstrels con their tragic lays.

My books around me scattered lie,
  Old tomes of ancient days and men,
Where I have followed Cæsar's hosts,
  Or marked the march of Xenophon.
But what to me is now romance,
  Or history's page, or burning song,
Since they but cloud the golden hopes
  That to an untried life belong?
It is the last of lonely nights
  That I shall know perhaps for years;
And wine, perchance, will fill the cup
  That only brimmed before with tears.

My days have been a sad romance,
　With pain and grief and sorrow ripe;
And in my years of wintry youth,
　I've seen few pleasant scenes of life.
And yet I do not hate the world,
　For many a faithful friend I've known,
And round my heart their names are set
　Like jewels in the kingly crown.

To-morrow night I leave the shore,
　My bark is waiting on the tide,
To bear me from this single state
　To scenes that I have never tried.
And will my days like music glide?
　No clouds obscure my being's sky,
And she who is to be my bride
　Still love me till the day I die?
And will she soothe me when I'm sad,
　And roam beside me hand in hand,
Till one or both have closed the gate
　That opens to a spirit land?
And will there be no sad regrets?
　For human nature's ever frail;
Have sentiment and real life
　Been weighed within a separate scale?
All pleasure must have some alloy,
　And joy and grief are kindred born,
There is no rose, however fair,
　That still does not conceal a thorn.
Comparison is beauty's test,
　And joys are measured by its scale,
For he who Alpine snows has felt
　Will best enjoy the genial vale.

But life must change from old to new
　And 'tis a tale that soon is told;
I'll link them in the name of wife
　And bind them with a ring of gold.
The morn is rising in the east,
　My taper fades in light of day,
Lo! in the beams of wedded bliss
　My autumn shall be changed to May.

If she to whom my fate has pledged,
  Ne'er murmurs at her wedded choice,
And in my harsher nature blends
  The music of a gentler voice:
Then shall we banquet all our days,
  And life will be a song of love,
Harmonious as the spheral chimes
  Within the universe above.
Man was not made to live alone,
  Then haste ye on, ye weary hours!
Ye are the steeds that bear my life
  From barren wastes to blooming bowers.

November 26, 1862.

LXXXVI.

SWEDISH POETRY.

(Translated from the Swedish by Swante Palm. Paraphrased into English verse by D. W. C. B.)

Some curiosity having been manifested to know something of the Swedish poem, the " Sea King," we give a full translation of it, made by a gentleman of our city. We are the more ready to do this, as we have never before seen a translation of it, although we have examined the works of those who have translated Scandinavian poetry into the English language.

Of the author, Geijer, Mary Howitt has said: " Sweden has many poets—she has but one Geijer."

Being assured that the translation is a faithful one, we would recommend it to the notice of the publisher of a new edition of the " Poems and Poets of Europe," by Longfellow.

THE VIKING.

(Translated from the Swedish of E. G. Geijer.)

WHEN only fifteen years of age,
  I left my mother's home—
To herd the goats was a weary task,
  And I longed in my heart to roam.
I dreamed, I thought, I knew not what,
  But life to me no pleasure brought,
          In the woods.

With swelling heart from the mountain top,
   I gazed o'er the wide, wide sea:
I felt the charm of the billow's song,
   And they seemed to sing to me:
" We come from far off, far off lands,
No shackles hold us, we feel no bands
     In the ocean.

One morn from the shore, a ship I saw;
   Like a bird in the bay she flew,
Then beat my heart, then swelled my breast,
   Then my soul's desire I knew.
I ran from the goats and my native land,
And joined the Viking's ship and band,
     On the ocean.

The friendly wind leaped in the sails,
   And we flew o'er the billow's crest,
My native hills sank in the deep,
   But peace was within my breast.
My father's sword I grasped in hand,
And vowed to conquer throne and land
     On the ocean.

The Viking fell by my wrathful steel,
   For he called me a beardless boy.
I took the ship, and o'er the sea,
   I found in strife fierce joy.
Full many a fort I overthrew,
And shared the spoils with my trusty crew
     On the ocean.

With eager lips the foaming mead
   We quaffed on the stormy tide;
We ruled o'er the waves and every coast;
   In Walland I took me a bride.
Three days she wept and only three,
And then, was a willing bride to me
     On the ocean.

28

I had a throne and a kingdom once,
    And under a smoky roof
I used to feast, and drink, and sleep,
    And lock my doors—forsooth.
'Twas but a winter, and yet to me,
The earth grew small, I longed to be
       On the ocean.

I'd nought to do, but helpless fools
    Were ever at my back ;
They'd have me to wall the farmer's barn,
    And tie up the beggar's sack.
Of crimes and laws, I heard each day
My full, and wished me far away
       On the ocean.

At length the Winter passed, and then
    Over the hills came Spring.
" To sea, to sea," the billows sang,
    As of old they used to sing ;
And the balmy winds played o'er the lea,
And the streams, unfettered, leaped with glee
       To the ocean.

Then came the old resistless love
    To live on the stormy main—
I threw my gold, to the winds, and dashed
    My crown to the earth again ;
And with but a ship and a sword as before,
A Viking again, I went from the shore
       To the ocean.

Free as the winds, we cared not where,
    We sailed over many a sea,
And visited many a land, and saw
    That as of old did we.
So bowed all men to care's stern sway ;
But she could not follow our pathless way
       On the ocean.

In the day when I stood on the tossing prow,
    The future was bright to me,
And calm as the swan 'mid the waving reeds,
    I sailed o'er the sparkling sea.
Mine was each prize in my path that came,
And free as the boundless space my aim
      On the ocean.

But at night, I stood on the plunging prow,
    When the waves were rolling high,
And heard the Nornas * knit their woof
    In the storm that went howling by.
Like the life of man is the billow's flow,
'Tis best to be ready for weal or woe
      On the ocean.

With twice ten years, misfortune comes,
    And the dark sea craves my blood.
She knows it well, she has drank it oft,
    When in thickest fight I stood.
This beating heart that so oft has thrilled,
Must soon by Death's cold hand be chilled
      In the ocean.

Yet I will not mourn that my days are short,
    Brief have they been—but sweet,
To the halls of the Gods but one way is known,
    And I seek it with youthful feet.—
The billows are singing a dirge for me,
And where I have lived my grave shall be,
      In the ocean.

————

Thus the Viking sings,
    Wrecked on the lonely shore,
And 'neath the cruel sea
    He sinks to rise no more.
The billows sing again their song,
    And the winds go playing by:
But the memory of the brave heart lost
    In the deep, shall never die.

* According to Scandinavian Mythology, the Nornas were three Goddesses, one of whom spun, the second wove, and the third cut the thread of human life.

LXXXVII.

"NOT DEAD—BUT GONE BEFORE."

BY WELTHEA E. GRAHAM.

THEY press around me in a glorious band—
    Shadowed upon the camera of thought
        They bend ;
Unseen, their embassies of heart to hand,
    And soul to soul, throng in, unsought,
        And friend
And foe meet and embrace and glide away,
Performing deeds of love, nor falter by the way.

A sweeping host—I see them hurrying by—
    No star-crowned, white-winged *idle angels* they,
        But souls—
Souls that must tireless search the earth and sky,
    Eternity and time, and dreamless day,
        And poles
Of other, brighter, holier worlds than these,
Beyond our summer skies or summer seas.

Around, above me, and the air is full
    Of guests plucked from the highways of the land,
        And they
Fresh from the glories of Bethesda's pool,
    'Mid resurrection of soul, heart, and hand,
        For aye
Feast from the table of the wondrous Lamb,
With brows serene and spirits pure and calm !

The friendless and forsaken, orphans lone,
    And frail hearts that have bent beneath their woe
        And misery,
Stray waifs in life—mother and sire and son,
    Virtue and crime and innocence—and lo !
        Eternity
Whispers around me that the solemn air
Is partly mine, for those I love are there !

Not dead—but gone before ! A little while,
    When standing on the brink of endless day
            And love,
Unfelt, their gentle touch, unseen their smile,
    Shall trace beyond the shoals of doubt, the way
            Above :
Mayhap some little babe, with guileless hand,
Will catch our wakening in the summer land !

Not dead—but gone before ! Ah ! dreamless sleep,
    Ah ! resurrection from the silent tomb
            To life eternal,
Unveil thy mystery, that those who weep
    Shall quick embrace thee, so their souls may bloom
            In bliss supernal !
Not dead—but gone before ! A peerless band—
The wisdom seekers of the better land.

Ah ! guardian one, who dwellest with the pure,
    Hymning thy glories o'er each new-born soul,
            I plead,
Teach me thy simple way, unveil the lure
    Which waves of doubt and fear around me roll—
            I need
Thy steady grasp upon the helm, thy lustrous lore,
To prove—*thou art not dead—but gone before!*

LXXXVIII.

THE TEXAN'S SONG OF LIBERTY.

BY WILLIAM BARTON.* 1836.

WHEN the locusts of tyranny darkened our land,
And our friends were reduced to a small Spartan band,
When the Alamo reeked with the blood of the brave,
And Mexican faith slept in Goliad's grave ;
When our star that had risen so beauteously bright,
Seemed destined to set in thick darkness and night ;

   * From whom Barton's Creek, near Austin, is named.

'Twas then our proud leader addressed his brave men,
And the Prairies of Texas re-echoed—Amen.
" On, on to the conflict, ye Texians brave,
March forward to victory or down to the grave !
Let your swords be unsheathed in Liberty's cause,
And your bosoms be bared in defense of your laws !
Let your watchword be Fannin, in treachery slain
And Alamo's sons, whose bones whiten the plain !

" For your friends and your homes let your rifle be aimed,
For your country that's bleeding, exhausted, and maimed :
Go, show to the world that our handful of braves
Can never be conquered by myriads of slaves ! "
'Twas said, and the single-starred banner waved high
O'er the heads of our hero, whose deep slogan cry
Made the cravens of Mexico tremble and cower,
While our bugles rang forth, " Will you come to the bower ? "

LXXXIX.

THE GOLDEN OPPORTUNITY.

BY HORACE ROWE.

SPRING is coming on in beauty,
    Hailed by all the glorious Earth :
And her voice is sweetly ringing,
    With the songs of joy and mirth.

And her path is strewn with flowers,
    Garlands wreathed about her brow,
Robed in Nature's richest costume
    She is coming gayly now.

All the world is up and doing,
    With a heart as light and free
As the little birds that carol,
    Round them in melodious glee.

And th' industrious farmers early
    Hasten onward to the field,
For this is the time to labor,
    If their " harvest much would yield."

If abundance they would gather
　Of the fruit which Autumn bears,
They must labor now or never,
　For the present only 's theirs.

Youth ! to you this time given—
　This bright spring-time of your life :
It you must improve, or falter
　In this world's unkindly strife.

Let not petty trifles turn you,
　Such as maiden's smile of art ;
But look thoughtful down the future,
　With a proud defiant heart.

What is life without distinction ?
　What a name without a name
That shall rest in blazing letters
　On the tablet wrought of Fame ?

Would you die and be forgotten
　Like the ripples of a stream ?
Or the bare and baseless fabric
　Of a sluggard's idle dream ?

Then know this—without exertion,
　You will not behold your name
Blazon'd on the banner floating
　O'er the battlements of Fame.

Ask—Where shall my name be written ?
　Then but mark the loftiest height
Aim at this—o'ercome each barrier,
　Reach the pinnacle, and write.

Write by merit—not dishonor,
　Nor by avaricious wealth ;
For the wealth of glory fadeth,
　When 'tis won by treacherous stealth.

XC.

EPITAPH OF THE TEXAS DEAD.

BY B. H. DAVIS.

No slab of pallid marble
  With white and ghostly head,
Tells the wanderers in our vale,
  The virtues of our dead.

The wild-flowers be their tombstone,
  And dewdrops pure and bright
Their epitaph, the angels wrote
  In the stillness of the night.

AUSTIN.

XCI.

The following verses were written by N. T. Byars, of Washington, Texas, in 1835, upon the occasion of the receipt of a threatening proclamation from Santa Anna, addressed to the people of Texas. The declaration of Texas independence was written and signed in the house of N. T. Byars.

Boys, rub your steels and pick your flints,
Methinks I hear some friendly hints
That we from Texas shall be driven—
Our lands to Spanish soldiers given.
    To arms—to arms—to arms!

Then Santa Anna soon shall know
Where all his martial law shall go.
It shall not in the Sabine flow,
Nor line the banks of the Colorado.
    To arms—to arms—to arms!

Instead of that he shall take his stand
Beyond the banks of the Rio Grande;
His martial law we will put down
We'll live at home and live in town.
    Huzza—huzza—huzza!

DAVID G. BURNET.

See p. 257.

XCII.

CHARACTER OF DAVID G. BURNET.

BY COLONEL A. M. HOBBY.

THIS is fully expressed by his public acts and private life. Nothing which relates to him is obscured or uncertain ; his objects were undisguised and his motives seemed equally matters of publication. He derived from nature a well-proportioned and vigorous understanding, an amiable temper, and exquisite sensibility, and had received an education which admirably fitted him for the practice of every public and private virtue. His integrity was absolute proof against all earthly temptations ; a critical review of his conduct will justify the declaration. Obloquy and persecution, or blandishments and power, were alike unable to influence a soul inspired by virtue, and which looked beyond the vicissitudes of chance for reward. It is not strange that a man endowed with these great moral attributes should have possessed the loftiest quality of courage—a courage indeed which recognized no fear, but banished even the apprehension of danger ; yet, so little aggressive in its character, that under the most trying circumstances he preserved the perfect equanimity of his temper and the serenity of his gentle disposition. His extreme sensibility enabled political antagonists too frequently to annoy him. He attached to every charge, however groundless, and to which the authors themselves gave neither credit nor consequence, an undeserved importance ; these charges, which men of hardier natures and less sensibility would have received with coolness, or treated with indifference, he always repelled with promptness and and vigor. His devotion to truth was ardent and lofty, and shone forth in his conduct and actions with uniform and splendid luster. It is related of Petrarch that upon the trial of a cause he was summoned as a witness. On offering to be sworn, the magistrates removed the book and said, " No, Petrarch, your word is sufficient." However questionable may have been the legality of the act, it conferred at least upon that distinguished man the most distinguished compliment which history records. Ages have passed, and generations have read it ; ages and future generations will come, and still the record will be read, that love of truth was the most conspicuous virtue of the illustrious scholar and poet. The influence of that single act has been boundless, since after an interval of five hundred years no eye that has ever fallen upon his fascinating pages has ever turned away without inscribing upon memory the beautiful and refreshing record, or afterward been wholly exempt from its divine influence. Love of truth was not less deeply fixed in the soul of Bur-

net, and from devotion to its precepts he was never known to depart. Posterity and contemporaries not unfrequently differ in their opinions of public
character. The zeal of partisans, and bitterness of enemies, which discover
in the same act cause for eulogy or invective, do not affect the impartial judgment of after times. The justice of history will not permit unmerited praise
or intemperate abuse, but will appoint the proper place to all who have been
charged with the responsibility of office, and will pronounce the final judgment
of benefactor or tyrant. The pure character and consistent conduct of Judge
Burnet has left no room for differences of opinion to exist between past and
future generations, and the judgment pronounced by his contemporaries has
been confirmed by posterity.

XCIII.

TEXAS MINERALS.

BY PROFESSOR A. R. ROESSLER.

(From Texas Almanac.)

In compliance with your request, I have the honor to submit the following
information on the mineral resources of the north-western portion of Texas,
which I obtained from personal observation during the last fifteen years. In
this brief article, I mention the most prolific deposits, so far as known,
arranged according to their importance.

Copper, covering as it does a large area of the country, is almost inexhaustible, and will afford a vast fund of wealth for generations to come. A
large portion of the counties of Archer, Wichita, Clay, Haskell, territory of
Bexar, counties of Pecos and Presidio, extending to the Rio Grande, is
filled with immense hills of copper ore, some of which has been thoroughly
tested and will yield on the average 55.44 per cent. of metal ; though some
particular localities have produced specimens even as rich as 68 per cent.,
containing, besides, some silver, oxide of iron, etc.

HOW TO SECURE THE LAND.

A great portion of these lands are subject to location with land certificates,
or documents which are evidences of the right of the holder to locate and
possess a certain number of acres of the public domain of Texas, not already
located and patented. Some of these lands were granted to railroads, as
constructed, and thus brought into market and their value enhanced, depend-
ing principally on the state of the market and the knowledge of parties as to
the amount, character, and location of valuable unlocated lands, that have a
prospect of being speedily developed. These lands can be bought in some

instances as low as twenty-five and fifty cents per acre, and as the new constitution of Texas prohibits further sale or donation of lands except for homestead and pre-emption, the lands can only be obtained from the State by actual settlement and improvement. About one hundred millions of acres of land are subject to location, among which I estimate at least half a million of acres to be valuable mineral lands.

UNEXAMPLED COPPER ORE DEPOSIT.

The first intelligence I received of the existence of this unexampled deposit of copper ore, was through M. D. Bullion, of Hunt county, Texas, who sent me a small piece of this ore in an envelope, for examination, with the remark, " if this stuff is of any account, I can load up five hundred wagons, without digging, from a 320 acre tract." Upon examination, I found it to be a highly interesting specimen of copper glance (nearly a pure sulphuret), containing 55.44 per cent. of metal. Its geological connections are of the highest interest and prove that this metalliferous tract is a portion of the Permian formation, which stretches from Kansas down into Texas, and is the only example of this formation in the United States.

MINING AND SMELTING ADVANTAGES.

In 1870, after traversing the cretaceous and carboniferous series northward of Weatherford, Parker county, I was very agreeably surprised by a grand panorama of outcropping of this formation. This system (Permian), is extensively developed in Russia, between the Ural mountains and the river Volga ; in the north of England ; and also in Germany, where it is mined for its treasures of copper, silver, nickel, and cobalt ores. In Texas the ore is found on the hill-sides and also on the surface, giving no trouble for mining or drainage. Four persons, in ten hours, took out six thousand pounds, averaging sixty per cent. Coal, timber, limestone, soapstone, and all the requisites for building furnaces and smelting the ores are in the vicinity, and the projected line of of the Southern Pacific railroad passes over the locality. At present, mining operations can not be safely prosecuted, owing to the proximity of bands of prowling Indians.

The hills which I have traced throughout Archer, Wichita, Haskell, and Clay counties, are nearly barren—towering above the most beautiful and fertile mesquit prairies, fringed by the finely timbered bottoms of the tributaries of Red River, and are exceedingly picturesque.

TRUE VEINS OF COPPER.

Explorations of the copper veins, over the summits and sides of the hills, justify the conclusion that within the extent of one degree of longitude along the Little Wichita River, hardly a tract of 160 acres could be found without large accumulations of ore upon the surface. The vein lodes are parallel with the strata, but there is sufficient evidence that they partake of the nature of true veins.

MANGANESE, COBALT, NICKEL, AND BISMUTH.

Leads of manganese, cobalt, nickel, and bismuth are often met with. The copper ore contains only 25 per cent. of impurities; is far superior to the ferro-sulphuret of copper, or copper pyrites, generally worked for in England, and in native copper ore as found at Lake Superior. It is easily smelted, and the strata in which it is found is more easily excavated than in any other in which copper ores occur.

LEAD AND SILVER.

These two metals are always associated together in this State. The calciferous sand-rock—which is the lead-bearing rock of Missouri—abounds in Texas, and the varieties found in it here are carbonate of lead, sulphuret of lead, and molybdate of lead. The former two always contain such large quantities of silver as to be considered silver ore. A sample from a three feet vein in Llano county, gave a yield of 286 ounces of silver and 74.45 per cent. lead. It is the carbonate of lead in combination with the sulphuret, and owing to the large percentage of the former will be very easily reduced. The indications are very favorable for a very large quantity and excellent quality of ore. At present, lands in this section of the State are of very little value notwithstanding the abundance of minerals and timber. With a well-developed mining industry established here, no other country could compete with this region, so far as regards fuel, construction timber, and materials for building and sustaining a railroad. There are about 10,000 acres of vacant land, —and the lands already located can be had for a trifle—the rocks of which are silver and gold-bearing.

REMAINS OF SPANISH FURNACES.

The examination of shafts to a depth of fifty feet, chisel and drill marks, and other unmistakable evidences, leave no doubt that the Spaniards formerly worked these mines, and remains of the ore worked, show it to have been very rich.

IRON.

The iron deposits of North-western Texas are of the most remarkable character, equaling in extent and richness those of Sweden, Missouri, New Jersey, and New York. They include almost every variety—magnetic, spathic, specular, and hematite ores. The largest deposit of magnetic iron ores is situated in Mason, Llano, and more western counties. Immense loose masses of ore lie scattered over the surface, which have been upheaved by ingenious agencies from unknown depths below. Most of these deposits are in true veins. As no true metallic vein has ever been traced downward to its termination, the supply is inexhaustible. The analysis of an average specimen gave 96.890 per cent. of per-oxide of iron, with 2.818 per cent. of insoluble silicious substances—proving it to be a magnetic oxide, which will yield 74.93 pounds of metallic iron to 100 pounds of ore.

The prevailing rocks are red feldspathic granite, gneiss, quartz, talcose and chloritic shists. Granite ridges surround the deposits, and veins of quartz traverse it in all directions. The limestone of the paleozoic and cretaceous rocks are in the immediate vicinity, from which materials for flux can be easily obtained. A most remarkable development of hematite and limonite occurs on the waters of Red River. It is found in regular layers of from fifty to sixty feet in thickness. Associated with these ores are various oxides of iron, suitable for pigments of red, yellow, and brown colors distributed, forming regular layers of several feet in thickness. The largest amount is on vacant lands—subject to location by certificates.

COAL.

The coal-bearing rocks of Texas occupy an area of not less than 6,000 square miles, embracing the counties of Young, Jack, Palo, Pinto, Eastland, Brown, Comanche, Callahan, Coleman, and extending to the territory of Bexar. The rocks contain the characteristics belonging to the coal measures of Missouri and other western States. In general appearance, this coal resembles that from Belleville, Illinois. The analysis gives fixed carbon, 52 per cent.; volatile matter, 36 per cent.; ashes, 3 per cent.

This coal cokes with a great flame, without changing its form, and the development of this valuable mineral is destined to be of the greatest importance to the State.

ANTHRACITE COAL,

lighter and more brittle than the anthracites of Pennsylvania, has been found in various parts of the State, but I had no opportunity to visit the localities.

Lignites, tertiary, and other coals of more recent origin, occupy an area of some 10,000 square miles—in connection with the true coal formation—on many points of the Rio Grande, in Webb, Atascosa, and Frio counties. They are mostly soft and ashy, but superior to German brown coals.

ASPHALTUM.

Asphaltum has been found in Hardin, Travis, Burnet, Llano, and many counties on Red River. The earth for some distance around certain acid springs is charged with it, and may be employed for the purpose of illumination. For pavements, roofing, and other uses, this material is too well known to require further mention.

GYPSUM.

In the north-western portion of the State is the largest deposit of gypsum known to exist in the world, spreading over two hundred miles on the upper Red River and its tributaries. This will be of great value as a fertilizer. Some of the specimens are as transparent as the purest glass, easily split into thin layers.

SALT.

There are many salt springs and salt lakes in this formation. Salt is manufactured in the great laboratory of nature by solar evaporation. The most important locality, producing an almost inexhaustible amount of salt, is Sal Del Rey, the greatest salt lake in Hidalgo county, and at the Horsehead Crossing on Pecos River, Pecos county. The salt here is ready formed, and need only be shoveled up and taken to market. The water is so strongly impregnated that the human body can not be made to sink in it. The salt is very pure and fit for table use, without refining.

Petroleum springs occur over a space of about fifty square yards in Hardin county, and it is highly probable that larger supplies may be obtained by boring. The surface indications are certainly as favorable as those of the now famous oil wells of Pennsylvania and northern Ohio, prior to the discovery by deep boring. Extensive quarries of marble roofing slate, grindstone, soapstone, and asbestos, with a large class of metallic substances usually present in highly metalliferous regions—such as alum, cobalt, nickel, manganese, arsenic, etc.—are abundant.

WHAT IS WANTED.

In mineral wealth and natural advantages, Texas will compare favorably with any other portion of the United States. To insure the speedy development of these resources, there must be a wider diffusion of knowledge as to the real character of the country, and I am glad to notice that the *Industrial Age* is devoting a portion to this important region, so soon to be in communication with St. Louis. Texas needs enterprising capitalists as well as men of muscle, to develop her mines, build her railroads, erect reduction works, furnaces, foundries, rolling mills, and manufactories of all kinds. With these come skilled labor, churches, schools, and general progress in all the useful arts.

XCIV.

OUTLINE OF THE LEADING CHARACTERISTICS OF TEXAS.

MEN and women in all parts of the world are asking themselves, how shall we better our fortunes? Where shall we go to procure the necessaries and luxuries of life with greater ease? to lay by a competency for old age, and an inheritance for our children?

Such is the universal inquiry all over the old world. On the contrary, in a new and sparsely settled country like Texas the inquiry is precisely the reverse. Here it is : Where shall we get men and women to settle upon our rich lands? Where shall we get laborers to cultivate our soil? Here we suffer because our rich lands lay waste, because they are dead capital on which we have to pay taxes, while they bring no income to the State or to ourselves. The necessity for a change of population from countries where it is in excess to countries sparsely inhabited, is the same as that for the transfer of products or commodities from countries where they are not wanted to countries where they are wanted. They are without value until they are transferred, but become of great value when removed to where they are wanted. The excess of population in most parts of Europe not only causes great suffering from want and destitution, but is often a heavy burthen on the governments, requiring the expenditure of millions annually for the relief of indigence and distress. And yet these hundreds of thousands of suffering men, women, and children, when transferred to a country like this, are at once made happy, contented, and prosperous, and instead of being a burden to the country where they are now, they become a source of great national wealth and prosperity. These considerations prove beyond all doubt that this transfer of population from countries which are suffering from its great excess, to countries which are suffering for the want of it, is an object of great national concern, and there is not, perhaps, a single question more imperatively demanding the attention of the governments of Europe and America than that of immigration, for this very means for relieving the necessities of the former will supply the wants and necessities of the latter. But in the absence of proper treaty regulations by governments for thus relieving their mutual necessities, there is greater demand for individual enterprise and associated capital to accomplish the same end ; and hence the organization of immigrant associations more or less comprehensive in their scope, embracing neighborhoods and counties, and even States, is now admitted to be one of the great instrumentalities for promoting the prosperity and increasing the wealth and population of our country.

It may be set down as an established rule that a poor man has more advantages in a new country than in one which is old, for the reason that labor is more valuable in the one than in the other. Texas is a new country ; large areas of her domain have never seen the plow or been tickled with the hoe. She desires to receive a large amount of immigration ; it is to the advantage of her citizens to get this immigration ; she asks for it. She asks men and women in all parts of the world who are seeking to better their fortunes, to acquire an estate, to provide for a rainy day, to come to her territory. She offers to all such great inducements to come. To set forth these inducements, and to give the immigrant who proposes to come to Texas such directions as will make his way pleasant and profitable, is our present object. We shall set forth in such clear and concise language as we can command, the advantages of Texas, and the means by which the immigrant may avail himself of them.

EXTENT OF TEXAS.

As shown elsewhere, Texas has an empire of territory exceeding in extent most of the governments of the world. Its area in square miles is 274,365, or 175,594,560 acres. It extends from about twenty-five and one-half degrees to thirty-six and one-half degrees north, or through eleven degrees of latitude ; and from about ninety-three and one-half to one hundred and seven degrees of longitude west from Greenwich, or through thirteen and one-half degrees of longitude. Its greatest extent from north to south is therefore near one thousand miles, and nearly as much from east to west, being considerably larger than France. It of course comprises a variety of soil and climate, while the productions are equally varied. It embraces the southern portion of the temperate zone, within which belt of the earth's surface is found the mildest and most uniform temperature and most salubrious climates of the world, both in the eastern as well as western hemisphere. It will also be seen that Texas extends from the Gulf of Mexico near half across the continent to the Pacific, and the shortest line from ocean navigation on one side to the seaports on the other side must pass through this State, the saving in land transportation being near one thousand miles, as compared with the present overland route.

STOCK REGION OF TEXAS.

Nearly all that portion of Texas west of the Nueces River, and including the large counties of Presidio, Pecos, and El Paso, and also the territory of Bexar, of Young, and the Pan-handle, constitutes what is usually called the great stock region of the State, and covers about one-third of its area. It is true that there are several of the counties on the Neuces, within this region, where farming is successfully carried on, while there are large bodies of as rich land as there is in the world on the Rio Grande, and some other river valleys, but as a general rule stock raising constitutes the great paramount pursuit in all this vast region, and but a comparatively small portion of it is adapted to agricultural pursuits.

AGRICULTURAL COUNTIES OF TEXAS.

Stock raising is likewise the chief pursuit in all the counties between the Nueces and the San Antonio Rivers, extending up to the head-waters of the Colorado and Brazos Rivers, but most of this is also a good farming country, though crops are rendered rather uncertain on account of the frequent droughts. East of the San Antonio River, to the Sabine on the east and Red River on the north, the whole country is adapted to farming purposes, with a much smaller proportion of waste land unsuited to cultivation than any other State in the Union. While many of the counties have large bodies of prairie land with a light sandy soil, which will not be cultivated until the country is much more densely populated and the better lands taken up, yet there is really very little, even of the poorer lands, that could not be much more profitably cultivated, and will not yield better crops, than most of the uplands in the older Southern States. But while there is not probably one acre in ten of all this vast extent of country that will not yield handsome profits to the cultivator, yet the whole amount of lands now under cultivation is scarcely more than a twentieth part of the good farming lands of the State, and our population will probably have to increase twenty-fold what it now is before all our productive lands are brought under cultivation. We think it is not an extravagant estimate to say that Texas has a larger body of virgin soil never yet touched by the plow than all the other Southern States put together, and there is certainly no other State in the Union whose soil and climate are adapted to so large a number of the great agricultural staples, or to so large a variety of products of every kind, embracing those suited to high northern latitudes and to semi-tropical climes. Here cotton and wheat grow in the greatest perfection side by side in the same field, which can be said of no other country, and here sugar-cane, rice, tobacco, and every cereal and vegetable known, are profitably grown in nearly all our counties within the limits above named, though some of them are better adapted to certain counties than to others, some requiring one quality of soil and some another. The difference of climate between the southern or coast counties and those in the north also has its effect upon the products, causing wheat and other cereals to be more successful in the northern counties,

29

while sugar-cane and some other products succeed better in the southern counties. But we may here remark that the products most universally required for the support of every family are most universally adapted to all parts of the State, such as corn, Irish and sweet potatoes, and nearly all vegetables. And nearly the same may be said of stock ; for though, as we have said, the western portion of the State is the great stock region of Texas, yet there is no farmer in any part of the State who can not have, with the most trifling expense, as many cows, oxen, horses, sheep, goats, hogs, and poultry, as he has any use for, for the support of his family and for all farming purposes.

RAINS.

As a general rule the more western counties of the State are most liable to suffer from drought. But experience has shown that this objection is becoming less from year to year, as the country becomes more settled and more under cultivation. The prairie fires that formerly so often swept over the western plains, destroying every shrub and preventing the growth of timber, have become far less frequent, and confined to comparatively narrow limits. Hence there are now thousands of acres in nearly all the western counties growing up in mesquit and various kinds of timber, where a few years ago there was not a shrub to be seen. This growth of timber is believed to be one principal cause for the more regular fall of rain, for in all parts of the world the growth of timber has long been recognized to have this effect, and in many countries the growth of forest trees has been encouraged by government as a means to secure the more regular fall of rain. To this cause is generally attributed the fact that the counties on the San Antonio River, and others in the west, are now far more exempt from droughts than formerly, and it is now believed by many that the crops there are no more liable to suffer from too little rain than they are from too much in most of the States. In all other parts of Texas the seasons of rain are much the same as in other States, and crops are liable to as few casualties as in any part of the world. In one respect Texas has an advantage over any country we have seen, for as a general rule deep plowing and early planting will secure fair crops in nearly all parts of the State with very little rain, and sometimes with none at all. This advantage is owing to the fact that our planting season commences a month or two earlier than in other States, on account of our mild winter, and also to the fact that our soil has nearly everywhere a substratum of clay and is very retentive of moisture, with deep plowing.

CLIMATE.

It seems to be a general impression with people abroad that Texas is unhealthy ; that the climate is excessively hot ; and that foreigners especially run a great risk in coming to a State so far south. Nothing can be more remote from the truth, as thousands of foreigners from all parts of Europe can testify. The temperature in Texas in the hottest days of summer is nearly always several degrees below the greatest heat at the north, and while many deaths in most of the northern cities occur every year from sun-stroke, there is not, perhaps, a well-authenticated instance in Texas of a single death from this cause. But a comparison of the range of the thermometer there and here removes all doubt on that subject. In winter the difference in temperature between Texas and the northern States is still more manifest, the severity of the cold being many degrees greater there than here. The fact is established beyond doubt, that Texas has the most uniform, equable, and mild temperature of any State in the Union, neither the heat nor the cold being so excessive, and, other things being equal, this exemption from the extremes of heat and cold is *prima facie* evidence of a more healthful climate. But this evidence is corroborated by experience, for although certain diseases are prevalent in many parts of Texas, yet the general health of the country is not surpassed, if equaled, by any other State, while for salubrity, all western Texas is proverbial. The whole sea-coast for more than a hundred miles interior is fanned by a most delightful and health-giving breeze from the Gulf during all the summer months. This breeze partakes of the regularity of the trade winds, and prevents any feeling of oppressiveness from the heat during the highest range of the thermometer. It must also be observed that there is far less low and marshy land than in any other southern State. Indeed, there is no State of greater healthfulness than Texas, while many portions of the State, as Austin and San Antonio, and the hilly regions further north and west, are the resort of consumptives, who almost invariably recover and live many years. It is a fact not to be gainsaid or denied, that for pulmonary complaints there is no climate in the world more favorable than that of the section we have indicated.

HOW TO COME TO TEXAS.

A good deal will depend on the place you start from. Hundreds and thousands are pouring into Texas from other States. Georgia, Mississippi, and the Carolinas have sent troops of immigrants to Texas, who cross the Mississippi River in their own wagons, and make the journey in their own time and without much expense. This was the plan followed by thousands of families last year. The people are hospitable, and disposed to do all that they can to assist an immigrant. They will furnish him provisions at the lowest rate, and render him such kindly offices as will mitigate the hardships of his journey,

We are assured that many families from Kansas and Arkansas will enter

Texas this year by the Missouri, Kansas and Texas railroad (for information concerning which see article under that head). The cold climate and the high priced lands of Kansas are driving a multitude to Texas. They come where the winters are not so rigorous, and where lands can be bought for a mere fraction of that which they cost in other States. These sturdy farmers are so well acquainted with the culture necessary for Texas crops that they require no instruction, but are at once ready to begin work in an intelligent manner.

THE EUROPEAN IMMIGRANT.

To advise the European immigrant and furnish him with information suited to his necessities, requires conscientious care. We are to tell him how to get here, what to bring, what to expect and what to do ; we are to tell him what to avoid and who to avoid, how to make his little go the furthest, and how to get the most comfort from it ; we are also to warn him of the changes in the climate, and what he must do to preserve his health.

ACCLIMATION.

And here we must say that while no State surpasses and few equal Texas in healthfulness, yet the immigrant from high northern latitudes generally has to undergo an acclimation, by which we mean that during the first year of his arrival he experiences some debility or sickness from the change of climate. And during his first year it is therefore necessary for him to be more on his guard against unnecessary exposure. But after the first year no such caution is necessary, and the immigrant often enjoys better health than in his native country.

TO THE IMMIGRANT FROM OTHER STATES.

The most natural method of coming to Texas is in one's own train or conveyance. Those who come in this manner will need no direction from us, for they will choose such articles of necessity and convenience as they may possess, and make the passage with greater or less comfort, according to their means.

They will find in our pages,* under the appropriate headings, such information with regard to time and location as will aid them in getting established in season to make a crop the first year.

Our advice to the native-born immigrant is different from that which we should give a foreigner. We advise the native-born to select a location at once, and proceed to erect shelter for himself and animals, and after that to plant corn and vegetables enough for at least one year's subsistence ; while we shall advise the foreigner to hire out on some one else's farm for the first

* This article is taken from Texas Almanac.

year. The native-born immigrant is familiar with our language and habits. He is accustomed to our modes of culture. He knows the times and seasons for putting in crops. He knows almost as much as the old Texan, and is of course prepared to take hold on his own account at once—which the foreigner can not so advantageously do. But the foreigner should settle in the neighborhood of his own countrymen, who have become familiar with the proper mode of cultivation. He may then safely go to work at once on a farm of his own, under the advice and assistance of his neighbors.

SURFACE OF THE COUNTRY.

The coast counties, for a distance of fifty to one hundred miles interior, are quite level, but beyond, the country becomes rolling, with alternate gradual elevations and depressions, and this inequality of surface increases as we proceed toward the north-west, until it finally becomes hilly and then mountainous in some of the north-western counties. In fact the whole of Texas is an inclined plane, with a gradual descent from the northern or western boundary to the Gulf, Austin and San Antonio being six or eight hundred feet above the Gulf surface, and the country farther north being still more elevated. The highest of the mountains do not, however, exceed two thousand feet above their base.

STREAMS.

Nearly all the streams run in a south-east course, emptying into the Gulf of Mexico, or rather into the bays that separate the Gulf from the mainland nearly the whole extent of the coast, with narrow islands and peninsulas intervening between the Gulf and the bays. These streams have nearly all deep channels, and are subject to overflow in comparatively few places and at distant intervals. The banks of the rivers being generally high, usually afford good drainage for the bottom lands, and make them comparatively healthy, and free from malarious diseases, as well as valuable for farms. They are the richest lands in the world, being nearly all alluvial to the depth of fifteen or twenty feet.

Very few of the rivers of Texas afford reliable navigation ; and though several have been usually navigated by steamers several hundred miles in the winter months, yet most of this navigation will probably be abandoned as our railroads are extended.

TIMBER.

There is scarcely a stream in Texas that is not bordered on both sides with a growth of timber extending from a few hundred yards to six or eight miles in width on both sides. There are generally, also, groves of post-oak and other timber in the interior prairies between the rivers, of greater or less extent, even in the poorest timbered portions of the State, which embraces the western counties, but this timber is not generally suitable for building purposes. The eastern counties are, however, unsurpassed by any portion of the old States for the abundance and excellent quality of their timber, consisting chiefly of pine and cypress, and many other varieties, black walnut, ash, white-oak, with nearly a dozen varieties of oak, mesquit, bois d'arc, etc. Some of these are the finest grained and most durable timber known, and afford the best material for agricultural implements, wagons, and furniture. Though the timber in most of the western counties is unsuitable for building, yet it is used for that purpose by immigrants on their first arrival, and until they are able to procure a better quality from abroad. It is also generally used for fences, though live hedges are no doubt better and cheaper in the end.

MECHANICAL PURSUITS.

In nearly all the counties, all the mechanical pursuits and trades most required in an agricultural country are carried on. Blacksmiths and wagon-makers find encouragement everywhere, and are well remunerated. And, though most of our agricultural implements and furniture are imported, yet workshops for repairs are found in nearly all our small towns, and in many instances they manufacture far better and more durable articles than are usually imported. There is nearly everywhere an increasing demand for tradesmen, who realize better wages than in most other places,· say four to five dollars per day.

MILLS, MACHINERY, ETC.

Saw-mills by water, steam, and horse power, are in operation in most parts of the State, for though in many counties there is a scarcity of timber, yet in nearly all of them there is some timber, and as it is most valuable where the scarcity is greatest, therefore mills are established to utilize it wherever it is found. In all the heavy timbered counties of the east, and in many of the well timbered counties of Middle Texas and on the Colorado, saw-mills abound. Corn-mills are also found in connection with cotton, gins, sugar mills, and flouring mills, in all parts of the State, so that there are very few farmers who have not a corn-mill in their immediate neighborhood. Blacksmith shops, and wagon and plow manufactories, with all the latest improved machinery, are equally abundant ; so that every farmer can readily have his farming implements repaired with but little delay. In all our wheat and small grain counties there are flouring mills, and also all the most approved labor-saving implements of husbandry, such as gang-plows and cultivators, reaping and mowing and threshing machines, etc.

FARMING SEASON IN TEXAS.

While in most other countries, and most of the other States of this Union, the cultivation of the land and harvesting are confined to about one-half the year, these labors in Texas may be performed nearly every month in the whole year. There is rarely a single month in the winter when the farmers of Texas may not be seen plowing, sowing, or planting. They hardly more than get through picking cotton and gathering their corn and other crops, before it is time to commence plowing their fields for a new crop. Our best farmers usually commence plowing in December or January, and corn planted in February is generally more certain to produce a good crop than when planted later, because it is less likely to suffer from drought.

During all the cold, bleak winter months, from Nebraska and Iowa to the New England States, when nearly all that the farmers there can do is to keep themselves from freezing, and to keep their stock alive by feeding out the hay and fodder gathered during the summer—during all these dreary winter days, the Texas farmer enjoys the pleasant, balmy weather of spring, while his flocks and herds are feeding on the prairies, or in the timbered bottoms. The only interruption to the usual farming labors in the winter is the occasional Texas norther, sometimes accompanied with rain, and very rarely with sleet, which, however, never lasts more than a day or two, and is at once succeeded by the usual mild weather.

It may be safely estimated that the farm laborer in Texas is worth fully twenty-five per cent. more than in the Northern States, simply on account of the greater length of the season when he can be profitably employed. And if to this is added twenty-five per cent. more from the labor saved in gathering hay and fodder at the North during summer, and having to feed it out again in winter, scarcely any of which labor has to be performed here, as all our stock—cattle, horses, mules, sheep, and hogs, support themselves the year round, and feeding is only required for our milch cows and working animals, and perhaps for fattening hogs a month or two before killing them, and also for sheep during the few days of our winter northers. But even the working horses and oxen and milch cows do not require one-half as much feed as in northern latitudes, because nearly every farmer has a good range or pasture for them, into which they are turned when not in actual use.

FERTILITY AND CAPACITY OF THE SOIL OF TEXAS.

As we have said before, though we have large bodies of unproductive land in Texas, yet it is certainly true that fully nineteen-twentieths of all land unsuited to cultivation in this State lies in what is called the stock raising region of the extreme west. In what we have designated as the agricultural portion of the State, embracing about two-thirds of it, we venture to say that there is a smaller proportion of land unfit for cultivation than can be found in any other State, while there is certainly no State in the Union possessing such immense bodies of land of almost inexhaustible fertility. We do not think it any exaggeration to say that if all the rich alluvial or bottom lands on the Trinity, Brazos, Oyster Creek, Colorado, Guadaloupe, and other streams of Texas, and all the rich uplands capable of producing from one-half bale to a bale to the acre, were in cultivation, the whole product of the State would equal, if not exceed, the present product of the whole United States. We merely ask those who question the correctness of this statement to make an estimate of the whole number of acres of such land in the State, and they will then see that the statement is within the limits of truth. Even at this time Texas is producing probably over one-tenth of the whole cotton crop of the South, and yet there is certainly not one acre in ten of such lands now under cultivation.

FACILITY OF TILLAGE.

There is probably no country where the rich and productive lands can be cultivated with so little labor. We admit, however, that the heavily timbered lands of our river bottoms, and in all the eastern counties, require about the same amount of labor to clear and fence them as the timbered lands of other States. But when once thus prepared, the soil is generally loamy, like most all alluvial lands, and is easily turned by the plow. Our prairie land is, however, generally heavier and more tenacious, and requiring a strong team to break it up for the first time, but all the subsequent cultivation is much easier. Usually the best of our prairie land is that in which the clay predominates over the loam and lighter soil. As most of our prairie in the coast counties, for a distance of fifty to one hundred miles interior, is nearly a dead level, ditching is therefore necessary as a general rule, to drain off the winter rains and make it fit for early planting. The ditching also greatly increases the yield in wet seasons, but as yet comparatively few of our farms have as much ditching as they require, as our farmers have for many years past been compelled to get along with the least labor possible. In the interior counties the prairies are generally sufficiently undulating to afford good natural drainage, and our farmers have only to plow and plant in order to secure good crops. The hoe is seldom used in making our corn crops, and is generally required only once in making a cotton crop; so that one hand with suitable plows and a good team may easily cultivate from twenty-five to forty or fifty acres, with one-third or one-fourth in cotton and the rest in corn. Or if wheat or other small grain be raised, one man can cultivate and harvest a much larger number of acres, using, as is almost universally done, the labor-saving implements, such as reapers, threshers, etc. In speaking of the facility of tillage we should not omit to state that nearly all the farming land of Texas is free from any obstructions from rocks or stumps, which often give the farmers of other countries so much trouble. It is rarely that a stone is to be seen on any of our farms, except in some of the more interior counties, and even then they are not often in sufficient quantities to add much, if any, to the labor of cultivation. The principal portion of our stony land is in the more hilly section of the State, and of a poorer quality, used almost entirely for pasturage for cattle and sheep. Nevertheless, fine quarries of stone abound in some of the middle and in most of the frontier counties.

WATER.

Scarcity of water has often been made an objection to Texas, and though this may be well founded to some extent, yet there are few of the Southern States better supplied with good water, or where it can be more easily obtained. There is no State better supplied with rivers and small streams, as is shown by a glance at our map of the State, and yet it must be admitted that very many of these streams become very low in our dry seasons, and some few of the smaller ones often become dry, but this is also the case in most of the other States. The water of our rivers is always good stock water, and it is rarely that stock suffer for want of water, except in the extensive prairies of the west. In all the interior and middle portion of the State springs of good water abound. There are, however, many sulphur and chalybeate springs, or those possessing other medicinal or mineral properties, some of which have already become places of resort on account of their healing properties. Still there are many of our farmers who use wells or cisterns in order to have water of a better quality, or to have it more convenient, as is also done in other States. But water can be had almost anywhere by digging fifteen to thirty feet, at a very trifling expense ; but the well water is not unfrequently impregnated with sulphur or other mineral substances, and though not considered unhealthy, is not palatable to many persons, and, hence cisterns appear to be coming into frequent use in many parts of the State. These can, however, be had at a small expense, as almost any roof is sufficient to give an ample supply of water for family use.

VALUE OF TEXAS LANDS.

The effect of the late unfortunate war was to greatly reduce the value of many of the best lands in Texas, from one-fifth to one-tenth of their market value before the war. The reason is obvious: Probably more than one-half our agricultural labor was performed by slaves; that labor was at first almost all lost to the country by emancipation, and there was no other labor to supply its place. The consequence was that much the larger portion of all the cotton, sugar, and corn land of the State was thrown out of cultivation; the owners had no means to make them bring any income, and necessity compelled thousands to offer their best lands for almost any price they could get: frequently improved lands, that were previously worth fifty dollars an acre, were sold for five or ten dollars. But since the close of the war our lands have been gradually recovering from that heavy depreciation, as immigration has been increasing from year to year. There has also been considerable improvement in the labor of the freedmen, who, as a general rule, perform far more labor than after their first sudden emancipation. Having been disappointed in their anticipations of support by the government, they have been compelled by necessity to labor enough for their own support. The steady increase of the area of land required for cultivation from these causes is having the effect to enhance the market value from year to year : but though our choicest lands, especially when desirably situated and under improvement, may now command from five to ten dollars, or even twenty dollars per acre when in the vicinity of good markets and railroads, yet the great body of our unimproved lands, even of the best quality, can be bought for two, three, and four dollars per acre, according to the circumstances that affect the value of lands everywhere, independent of their quality. Tens of thousands of acres of unimproved uplands all over the State, that under proper cultivation may produce from twenty to thirty bushels of corn, or say half a bale of cotton to the acre, may be bought now for the lowest price above named, and often, perhaps, for a dollar per acre.

THE SEVERAL SUBDIVISIONS OF TEXAS.

The following, from a previous issue, may serve to give a general outline of a State embracing such a vast area as Texas :

"We will here give the several divisions of the State, to which we have referred above, more definitely :

" 1. Northern Texas—Embracing three tiers of counties on the south side of Red River, and extending west to the counties of Cook and Wise ; about thirty counties in all.

" 2. Eastern Texas—Lies south of Northern Texas, and between the Sabine and the Trinity, extending south to the Gulf ; about twenty counties.

" 3. Middle Texas—Between the Trinity on the east and the Colorado on the west, and extending south from Northern Texas to the coast ; making some twenty-five counties.

" 4. Western Texas—Extending from the Colorado on the east to the Nueces on the west ; in all, about twenty counties.

" 5. Extreme South-western Texas—extends west from the Nueces to the Rio Grande, and from the coast to San Antonio, and including Bexar and the adjoining counties ; making some fifteen large but mostly unsettled counties.

" 6. North-western Texas—Embraces the counties to the north and north-west of San Antonio, as far north as the counties are formed, or about forty counties.

" 7. The Mineral Region—Comprehending the counties of El Paso and Presidio, and the territory of Bexar and Young to the east of Presidio ; an area of fifty thousand square miles.

" 8. The Pan-handle—Extending north to the parallel of forty-two and one-half degrees, with the Indian Territory of the United States on the east and New Mexico on the west. This portion of Texas, embracing some twenty thousand square miles, has but very few inhabitants at present. The east side adjoining the Indian Territory, is represented as being an excellent farm-ing country, while the west, adjoining New Mexico, is believed to be barren, or only suited to grazing."

CHARACTER OF THE PEOPLE OF TEXAS.

" Notwithstanding all the abuse that has been cast upon the South, and especially upon Texas, we do not hesitate to say that when the immigrant settles in any of the above farming sections of Texas, he will find himself sur-rounded by a law-abiding, peaceable, and well-informed people, who will not only respect all his rights, but will extend to him all the kindness and atten-tion due to a stranger. He will also find the old settlers of Texas generally a moral and religious people, but perfectly free from all bigotry and intoler-ance. However much he may be opposed to them in politics, he will never hear an unkind word from them on the subject, unless he attempts to dis-turb the peace of the neighborhood by stirring up political excitement and using disrespectful language. All that has been said of the violent and dis-orderly character of Texans is totally false, and we here pledge ourselves that every immigrant will find it so. There may be and probably are some disorderly persons in the country, but they are not more numerous than in the Northern States. A man may travel a thousand miles in Texas, and if he does not insult the people he will receive a kind and hospitable reception everywhere, and nobody will inquire as to his religious or political opinions unless he proposes the subject. Common schools will be found in almost every neighborhood where the number of children is sufficient to make one. In some places the population is too sparse for that purpose, and this may be an inconvenience for a time, but only until two or three more families may arrive and make up the requisite number of children."

PRE-EMPTION LANDS IN TEXAS.

The immigrant should bear in mind that Texas is the only State in the Union that has public lands of its own, and has entire control over them. It will be seen elsewhere that notwithstanding the State has been deeding away these lands for the past forty years, under various laws, yet we still have near one hundred millions of acres of public lands to be disposed of by the State. Under our present laws every immigrant family may secure one hundred and sixty acres, by settling on it for a period of three years, and every single man may have half that amount, or eighty acres, on the same easy terms. They may have a choice of selection from that vast body of our public domain, and all they are required to do beyond settling on it is to pay for the survey and and title papers, not exceding ten or fifteen dollars currency. This, it will be seen, is a far more liberal encouragement to the immigrant than is given by the government of the United States, where the immigrant has to pay, besides the usual fees for title papers, the sum of $1.25 per acre. It is true the public lands of Texas, like those of the United States, are generally situated in the frontier counties, and are most of them exposed to Indian depredations at this time. We are, however, hoping for better protection from the government of the United States, but even though we may be disappointed in this, as we have been, yet our railroads, and especially the Texas Pacific, are now progressing so rapidly through that region that we have every reason to believe that within the next five years the Indians will no longer be an obstacle to the settlement of those lands, while the railroad will greatly enhance their value by making their products accessible to our markets.

PRICES OF PRODUCTS AND PROVISIONS.

There is a remarkable uniformity in the price of the usual products of our State and all the necessaries of life in all our counties. The immigrant can generally buy a good farm horse or mule for $75 to $100, a yoke of gentle oxen for $30, a milch cow and calf for $12 to $15. He can buy a few head of common stock cattle at about $5 or $6 per head, sheep at $1.50 to $2.00, and hogs at say $2.50 to $3 each. He can buy a good beef, weighing five hundred or six hundred pounds, at about $15. The usual price of butter is twelve to fifteen cents per pound, and lard and bacon about the same. Chickens are worth say fifteen cents each or $1.50 per dozen, and eggs 12 to 15 cents per dozen. The usual price of corn on our farms varies in different parts of the State from thirty to fifty cents per bushel, but in the spring season is usually about one dollar per bushel. Wheat in Northern Texas is about $2 per bushel, and flour of the best quality, made from our own wheat, is reported to be worth about $5 per one hundred pounds, or $10 per barrel. All other products are about in the same proportion. Sweet potatoes are now brought to this market (Galveston) and sold at one dollar per bushel, but in the country can be had for about half that price. We would state that nearly all the country products sell in our markets at about double or treble the above prices. We would also remark that sugar, coffee, flour, and nearly all imported staple articles, whether called the necessaries or the luxuries of life, are sold at as low a price in Texas as in most of the States of the Union. The active competition among our merchants has brought prices down to the lowest figures at which the articles can be afforded. Such is the case with all articles of furniture, hardware, crockery, medicines, boots and shoes, dry goods of all kinds, groceries, agricultural implements, corn and flouring mills, and all kinds of machinery.

MANUFACTURES.

We have in different parts of the States about a dozen woolen and cotton factories in operation. In Eastern Texas there are several smelting furnaces for iron ore, and two or three foundries for iron castings of various kinds. But manufacturing in this State is yet in its infancy, though we believe the day is now near at hand when this will prove the most profitable investment that can be made. But we want a large supply of capital and skilled labor. We have a great abundance of the raw material for cotton, wool, and iron factories, that can be had by the home manufacturer greatly below the cost to the manufacturer at the North or in Europe. In previous issues of the Texas Almanac it has been demonstrated that the home manufacturer can save on the cost of the raw material, and other ways, more than the entire profits of the manufacturer abroad.

XCV.

WICHITA AND WILBARGER COUNTIES.

(From the Texas Almanac.)

THESE counties are located on the south bank of Red River and Prairie-dog-town River, the former separating them from the Indian territory. The character of land, water, and timber, is the same in both counties, and they are therefore described as one body. The surface of the two counties forms a nearly uninterrupted rolling prairie, covered with a heavy growth of luxuriant and nutritious grasses. Within the limits of Wilbarger county, four miles above the north-west corner of Wichita county, is the junction of Pease and Red River, and eight miles north-west of the said corner is the confluence of the latter and the Kechee-aque-hono, or Prairie-dog-town River. The bed of Red River at this point is about 500, that of the other about 800 yards wide; but Red River furnishes the most water and is *always running,* while Prairie-dog River is frequently dry during the summer. The bed of Red River at the mouth of Pease River is a mile wide, and with the clouds of dust and quicksand, stirred up by every breeze, resembles a Sahara *en miniature.*

Wilbarger and Wichita counties are well watered by bold running streams and innumerable limpid and pure springs. Pease River enters Wilbarger county from the west, and runs in a nearly direct course to its junction with Red River. Wanderer's Creek is a tributary of Prairie-dog-town River and a very crooked stream, winding its way through a beautiful valley of rich lands. The Big Wichita River crosses the south line of Wilbarger county, and flows in a north-east course through this and the center of Wichita county; it is a bold running stream, but very crooked; the water has a yellowish color and a strong brackish taste. I have obtained tolerable good water by digging holes in the quicksand of the river bed; the Indians follow sometimes the same process. Beaver Creek is a large tributary of the Big Wichita, and a magnificent stream. From its sources in Hardeman county to its junction with that river, it waters one of the richest and most fertile valleys in the State. The main creek and its numerous branches and tributaries are skirted with a fine growth of timber; other water courses in Wilbarger county are Jenny's, Minna's, Lilly's, Burke's, McGee's, and numerous others, branches of Beaver Creek; Reed's, and other smaller creeks, tributaries of Big Wichita, and a number of creeks flowing into Red River. In Wichita county are Gilbert's Creek, a tributary of Red River, Plum, Baxter's, Buffalo or Tanahah, Holliday, and other creeks, branches of Big Wichita and Beaver Creek. The Little Wichita flows through the south-east corner of the county.

Some of the finest springs of pure water may be found along the banks of Red River, Pease, and Prairie-dog River. The St. Andrew Springs, near the mouth of the Pease River, have gained a reputation and have become a general camping place of military and surveying expeditions.

The soil of both counties is a rich red loam, in the elevated portions rocky and gravelly. The country in the forks of Pease and Red River is elevated, and hilly at the mouth of Prairie-dog-town River. In these hills are many brooks of pure water and cool and limpid springs; one of the finest is Pearl Spring. To the admirer of the sublime and beautiful, I can recommend a visit to this region of country: a most magnificent view presents itself at sunrise to a person standing on the precipitous hills west of the mouth of the Kechee-aque-hono. The Wichita Mountains rise in large dark-blue masses from the apparently unlimited carpet of bright buffalo and mesquit grasses.

By the dark foliage of the timber, you can follow the course of tortuous streams and copy a map of the country from the original plot. The mountains appear not very distant, and you propose a short ride—still, from your high stand, at the mouth of Kechee-aque-hono, you will find it fully twenty miles to the nearest mountains. But do not imagine this extensive prairie a region of dull monotony!—the picture is animated by droves of mustangs and herds of buffalo, deer, and antelopes, and occasionally chasing Indians will set the whole in motion with the sound of distant thunder.

The timber in Wichita and Wilbarger counties consists chiefly of mesquit, of which there are extensive forests—it covers half of Wichita county. Along the water courses, especially along Beaver Creek and the Little Wichita, walnut, pecan, post-oak, chittam, wild china, hackberry, cottonwood, etc., are found. There is also good building rock in different parts of the county; in Wichita county I found copper ore of a rich quality. In 1852, Dr. Shumard, one of our State geologists, found specimens of the same ore on the opposite bank of Red River. There can be no doubt but that this country will equal any portion of Texas or the United States as a grain country, and for stock-raising I think it will equal the range upon the Clear Fork of Brazos.

In conclusion I will remark, that the eastern border of the red lands of Western Texas (red loam) is on a nearly a direct line drawn from the mouth of the Little Wichita to the junction of the Concho and Colorado, and thence in the same course to the Rio Grande. The rich red land bottoms of the lower Red River were carried away in small particles from the highlands of the West.

Rain is sometimes scarce in the counties of the north-west, when the lower country has plenty of it; at other seasons, the north-western country is flooded when other portions of the State suffer from the drought. For instance, in the summer of 1857, when the whole country suffered from the extreme drought, the rains were excessive during the months of July and August in the country between the Upper Red River and the Brazos; these streams were level with the banks, and sometimes impassable. I am inclined to think that such rains are pretty regular, and account for the "June rises" in Red River and Brazos; these are certainly not caused by the "melting of snow in the mountains," as was formerly supposed.

The foregoing is a general description of the new and unsettled counties of north-western Texas. It would have carried me, perhaps, too far, to extend my remarks over many particulars and interesting peculiarities; still, in connection with a good map, it will suffice to illustrate the true character of a country that is little known, and which has been frequently misrepresented. There was a time, when the country west of the Trinity River was represented to be destitute of wood and water (see

Yoakum's History of Texas) and the north-west generally as a barren desert. Now we find the limits of the Llano Estacado defined, and the crossing of the plains has lost its horrors. Even if the country is elevated, and in places mountainous and dry, there are between the Trinity River and the borders of the Llano Estacado beautiful springs and streams; soil remarkable for fertility; broad and level bottom-lands clothed with luxuriant grasses; excellent timber, large and abundant; picturesque scenery and charming landscapes.

XCVI.

UNSETTLED REGIONS ON THE WESTERN LIMITS OF TEXAS AND TO THE PACIFIC. RAILROAD TO GUAYMAS, ETC. (From Texas Almanac.)

In the foregoing I have confined my remarks to the limits of counties created by the last legislature; in connection with this, I desire to make a few observations regarding the region of country west of the same.

The section of country west of the line of created counties and east of the Pecos River and the boundary of New Mexico, forms part of the territories of Bexar and Young. The boundary of the two districts runs from the sources of the South Prong of the Clear Fork of Brazos, due west to the line of New Mexico. This vast country includes about two-thirds of the Llano Estacado, the remainder of this plain being in New Mexico. Various descriptions have been given of this high table land by military and other expeditions, still the largest portion is yet unexplored. The Passage of the Llano was always dreaded, and parties crossing hurried over the endless waste, following a certain course or a trail, without ever looking right or left. Thus, suffering terribly, they passed sometimes within a short distance of water. It was always a favorite plan of mine to explore the unknown portion of the Staked Plain, but I have been delayed, and now I expect that the United States and Texas boundary expedition will unveil at least a portion of the mysterious land. I have various accounts from Indians and Mexicans of the unexplored portion of the Llano Estacado, which so far have turned out tolerably correct. The water-holes, for instance, in the sand-hills upon the Llano near the south-east corner of New Mexico, were described to me by Indians, and I had indicated them on maps long before they were found by Captains Pope and Hardeman. (One of these maps was taken off by Major Scurry, the boundary commissioner for Texas, but I don't suppose either he or the maps were ever seen in the surveyors' camp.) I have also

Houston Issuing Orders.

in my possession a sketch copied from a document in the clerk's office of Bexar county, and translated from the original Spanish by F. Giraud, Esq., the accomplished and able district surveyor of Bexar ; the document is a report of a Spanish serjeant, who crossed the Llano with a small guard, on his way from Presidoi de Pecos (a former station near the sources of the Pecos River, and, I presume, the present Pueblo of Pecos) to San Antonio. The route crosses the plain west of the sources of Red River, from north-west to south-east, below the thirty-fifth degree of north latitude.

Thus San Antonio and Santa Fé may be connected, without much difficulty, by a direct road, which would give to Texas the entire trade of New Mexico, and, with the recently discovered Lagunas, near the New Mexican corner, and perhaps other permanent watering places well defined, why may not, after this, the California stages run from Fort Chadburne due west, follow up Giraud's Creek, thence by way of the Mustang Ponds and water-holes in the sand-hills, to the mouth of Delevan Creek, thereby shortening the present route about seventy-five miles?

From this it will seem that the time is not very far distant when the Plains, over which the Comanche and the Apache speed their course amid the loneliness of rude nature, will resound with the strange sounds of cattle-bells, cracking whips, and the whistle of the locomotive.

The region of country situated upon the head-waters of the Colorado, the Conchos, and the Brazos rivers ,is of great importance. The valleys, especially along the Colorado and the Conchos are extensive, and capable of sustaining a dense population. The soil is of a rich red loam, and, on the waters of the Brazos, underlaid by a stratum of gypsum from one to three and four feet thick. A large portion of the valleys on the Colorado, the North and the Main Concho and their tributaries, can be irrigated, thereby making it less affected by dry seasons.

The great facilities for stock-raising, I regard, however, as one of the most important resources of this section of country. As a range for horses and sheep, the Colorado and Concho country has no superior in any part of the State—having an abundance of running streams of pure and unfailing water ; the valleys surrounded by hills and elevated plateaus, giving shelter to the herds against the icy northers in the winter seasons, and a Geo. W. Kendall could not find a more desirable country for innumerable flocks of sheep.

The Double Mountains are situated near the sources of the Brazos River, between the Main and Double Mountain Fork, and form a remarkable feature of the country. The two prongs of Brazos River are here twelve miles apart, the Main Fork runs eight miles north of the mountains, and four miles to the south of them the Double Mountain Fork washes their base.

The mountains rise about 500 feet above the general level of the Brazos

30

valley ; correctly speaking, there are three Peaks upon the same basis. At a distance the tops of the mountains appear to be pointed, still the largest (the south-eastern) one, is flat and covered with a horizontal layer of limestone rock from four to twelve and fifteen feet thick, and about 150 yards long. The slopes of the mountains are covered with shin-oak bushes. The action of the water is visible on all sides, and as the soil washes off, the rock on the top crumbles down. Whether these mountains are upheaved masses, or the remnants of former elevated plains, I leave to our accomplished State geologist to decide, but from the stratification I think the latter to be the case.

From the top of the Double Mountains an extensive view may be obtained : the country is spread out before your eyes like a map. To the west and north-west you see the unlimited plains, interrupted only by a few isolated mounds, dotted over the wide space ; and the tributaries of the Brazos terminating in gullies and ravines. To the east the surface presents a variety of rocky hills, and mesquit flats, whilst south of the Double Mountain Fork, a rolling mesquit prairie extends over to the waters of the Clear Fork. Around the base of the mountains and along the banks of the rivers, there are rich salt springs ; the river water up here is unpalatable.

There is a little timber along the upper tributaries of the Brazos, but along the Colorado, Concho, and their branches, considerable walnut, pecan, elm, oak, hackberry, sycamore, cottonwood, etc., and on the hills scrubby live-oak and cedar are to be found.

What gives this section of country a peculiar importance, is its nature and position on the edge of the Llano Estacado. The precipitous bluffs and broken character of the country, north and south, form a nearly impassable barrier even to common wagon roads, whilst on the Upper Colorado and Brazos, there is a gentle ascent to the Llano Estacado, and a practical point of crossing that plain. In consequence of these and other advantages, I have, years ago, in letters and reports to the leading men of the Southern Pacific Railroad Company, pointed out the country upon the head-waters of the Colorado *as the key of the southern route to the Pacific.*

The roads and thoroughfares, from east to west and south-west, of the States south of the Ohio and Missouri, will have to concentrate here ; and if a railroad to the Pacific, through the United States Territory—which has become a commercial and political necessity—be built at all, the Texas road will be the first, in spite of the action of Congress or northern sectionalism. For if our own people will oppose the progress of this road, we must look beyond the Rio Grande for assistance, and if we can not build an iron bridge to San Diego, across the deserts of Arizona, we may across the wealthy mineral regions of Chihuahua and Sonora, and make Guaymas the successful rival of San Francisco.

The most favorable crossing of the Llano Estacado for the South Pacific Railroad is certainly from the sources of the Main Concho River to Horsehead Crossing on the Pecos, thence via Fort Davis to the Rio Grande, and following up that stream to El Paso. A railroad to Guaymas, on the Gulf of California, would turn from the Pecos or from Fort Davis south-west ; cross the Rio Grande, near Presidio del Norte, and follow up the Rio Concho, of Mexico, on the most practical line to Chihuahua ; thence by the most favorable route—perhaps the valley of the Rio de Papigo—to La Junta, in Sonora, and thence to Guaymas.

PACIFIC RAILROAD TO GUAYMAS.

I will further remark with regard to this proposed railroad, which may soon attract the eyes of the world, that this line is about 400 miles shorter than that to San Diego. In our late treaty with Mexico, the right of way for this road was granted ; and at the auspicious beginning of the first Southern Pacific Railroad scheme, the Governor of Chihuahua offered favorable propositions to carry that road through his State. Guaymas is one of the finest harbors on the Pacific coast. It is perfectly secure against violent gales ; has a safe entrance, and, with some improvements and dredging, sufficient space and depth to admit a world's navy. The *Pennsylvania*, line-of-battle ship, was in the harbor in 1848, during the Mexican war.

The *Weekly Arizonian* gives the following account of

THE CITY OF GUAYMAS.

" The entrance to the harbor of Guaymas is about 200 yards wide, easy of access, and without hidden dangers. The bay is some four miles in length, elbow-shaped, and from a hundred yards to a mile in width, of which, however, only a narrow channel is fit for vessels. Those of twelve feet draught have to anchor about two miles from town. The harbor is small but good, and might be considerably enlarged by dredging. Its rocky edges abound in excellent oysters and its waters with a few species of fish. When rounding the elbow, near a mound called El Moro, the town and inner bay become visible. Ragged red barren hills rise from the very edge of the placid sheet of water.

" There is a slope on the head of the bay, about half a mile in width by a mile in length, connected with a level tract sloping to the south-west. On this slope stands Guaymas. Its present population is about 3,500 or 4,000, not counting Yaqui Indians, who have temporary camps in the suburbs. The streets are irregular, narrow, and crooked, with the exception of one, which is from seventy to ninety feet in width, and may be called the promenade of Guaymas.

"After five o'clock P. M., the sun having sunk behind those rugged hills, a cooling breeze comes over the blue waters of the Gulf, the sky is tinged with those brilliant variegated colors, so peculiar to a southern clime, and it is decidedly the most pleasant portion of the day. The grand street then assumes a more lively appearance; parties of ladies and gentlemen are out promenading. After ten in the evening the streets are deserted, except by the patrol or the solitary straggler.

"Guaymas, in a commercial point of view, is the most important place in Sonora, and is the only seaport open to foreign trade, which is far more extensive than is generally supposed. The whole commerce is concentrated in the hands of a few persons, and they, with a few government officers and owners of estates, compose the aristocracy of the country.

"The importing business, as it is managed at present, requires a large capital, as goods are chiefly bought in Europe, and eighteen months or two years are often lost between the shipment and sale. The chief imports are English and French dry goods and groceries; common cotton fabrics, etc., from San Francisco.

"The chief article of agriculture shipped from Guaymas is an excellent article of flour; there is no other farming produce to ship, and even much of this can not be exported, on account of the great distance from the agricultural regions to the port, and the difficulties of transportation. But the principal resources of this department are its mines and placers of gold, silver, and copper. Several millions of silver are annually shipped to Europe, and a great deal to the United States, notwithstanding the ruin and abandonment of many mines which formerly yielded six or eight millions yearly."   H. WICKELAND.

XCVII.

THE "PAN-HANDLE" OF TEXAS.

(From Texas Almanac.)

as nearly every body knows, is that portion of the State north of the Kecheeaque-hono or Prairie-dog-town River, and between Red River and the 100th meridian on the east, and the 103d meridian—the boundary of New Mexico—on the west. It comprises about 27,250 square miles of territory. The physical description of the "Pan-handle" may be divided into three parts—the south-eastern portion, including a part of the upper basin of Red River; the south-western, including a portion of the "Llano Estacado," and the northern, watered by the Canadian and its tributaries. The south-eastern section is decidedly the most fertile, being watered entirely by Red River and its branches, and forms a basin of about 6,000 square miles, from 800 to 1,000 feet lower than the plain to the west of it. Red River proper (sometimes called North Fork), the Salt Fork, Prairie-dog-town River, and their upper tributaries, have their sources in the deep ravines of the eastern border of the Llano Estacado, which are very narrow and sometimes several hundred feet deep. The sharp and ragged outlines of the edge of this plain, together with the deep ravines and broken character of the detached mountains, render the scenery of that region highly peculiar. Everywhere may be perceived the powerful action of the waters, which for centuries rushed down from the highlands of Texas, to assist the "Father of Waters" in creating Louisiana. It is apparent that the upper basin of Red River once formed the eastern slope of the high plain, but from the washing of the waters, the rich red substance—red clay with an admixture of dissolved sulphate of lime—has been carried off and settled gradually along the lower streams, and now forms the rich bottoms of Red River; whilst the sandy portion of the soil settled in the upper streams and caused the beds of quicksand.

Descending the prongs of Red River toward their junction, the country becomes less broken and more level and fertile, until it forms at the foot of Wichita Mountains an apparently boundless, slightly undulating prairie, out of which the granite peaks rise in gigantic masses, like the pyramids of Egypt.

Red River flows in an easterly course, until it encounters the Wichita Mountains, thence it turns south, and receives the Salt Fork (Red River is about eighty, Salt Fork, sixty feet wide at their junction), having wound its way around the mountains, and having its waters increased by those of the Kechee-aqua-hono and Pease Rivers, it resumes its eastern course.

The False Washita River, the most northern tributary of Red River, and which has its sources within the borders of Texas, between Red River and the Canadian, flows to the north of the Wichita Mountains. Thus the waters of Red River embrace as it were that beautiful mountain country, with its rich and truly picturesque and charming valleys, its pure icy springs and limpid streams, its droves of mustangs, and numerous herds of buffalo, elk, and deer, and other game feeding among orchard-like mesquit forests. But I regret to say, of all this, Texas owns but a small share. The Wichita Mountains are in the United States Indian territory, with the exception of five or six prominent peaks, which are west of Red River. They are nevertheless near and interesting neighbors, and I hope that our State geologists will not omit visiting them, and making a thorough examination of their character. The mountains are masses of granite and greenstone, upheaved by some action of volcanicity. The peaks are generally disconnected, the sides steep and bare, covered in some places with scrubby cedar and shin-oak. On the summit and in excavations of some of the mountains, where water had collected and the soil appeared to be moist generally, I also found black-berries and currants ; considerably tall and well-grown mountain cedar, chittam (gum-tree), and bois d'arc.

West of the basin of Red River, we encountered the rugged outlines of the Llano Estacado. The edge of this plain is not one continuous bluff, but is deeply indented, and bordered by detached hills, and remnants of the plain, from which they have been severed by the action of the water, and which are rapidly wearing away, so that the table-like summit will be reduced to a mere point and the elevation become a conical hill.

On reaching the table-land, a view presents itself, as boundless as the ocean. Not a tree or shrub relieves the dreary monotony of an apparently unlimited carpet of grass. The greatest breadth of this great plain west of the sources of Red River, is about 125 miles ; it is a more or less rolling prairie, with a general elevation of from 4,000 to 4,500 feet above the level of the ocean. It attains its highest elevation near the eastern line of New Mexico, where sand-ridges form a crest or " divide." Although, from the want of sufficient rains during some seasons, unfit for cultivation, this plateau is by no means value-less. For, with the exception of some sandy and gravelly belts, it is covered with a thick growth of gramma and other grasses, which will afford abundant pasturage during the whole year to unlimited herds of cattle. At some seasons of the year there are abundant rains—which I am induced to think are pretty regular—but the soil soon becomes dry on account of the per-colation of the moisture through the loose soil to the substratum of clay. A portion of the water collects in the depressions and forms ponds ; and with improvements, such as artesian wells and artificial tanks, after the Mexican system, a great portion of the Llano Estacado may be redeemed for cultivation.

The soil of this plain is a red loam or clay, more or less sandy, but that it is not an entire desert is evident from the fact—as stated in another place —that some of the richest lands on earth, the Red River bottoms, once formed part of the table-lands. Dr. G. G. Schumard, who accompanied Captain R. B. Marcy on his exploration of the sources of Red River, describes the bluffs of the Llano as consisting of horizontal layers of drift, sandstone, and red clay.

Whether any considerable portion of the Llano Estacado will ever be reclaimed for the use of mankind, and for what purposes—whether for the production of wheat and other small grain, or the cultivation of tea or the yam-root—remains with the future.

That region of the Pan-handle north of the South Fork of Canadian River is yet little known. In 1856, I explored the country along the boundary line between the Pan-handle and the United States Indian territory, as indicated by Captain R. B. Marcy, but I found this line to be incorrect. As near as I could ascertain with the means in my possession, the true boundary—the 100th degree of west longitude—is one degree west of where it was located by the United States engineers. Following Marcy's line, the Canadian River is 105 miles north of Red River.

The northern portion of the Pan-handle is a succcession of high rolling prairies, intersected by the narrow valleys of numerous streams. The principal watercourses are the South and North Fork of the Canadian, Dry River, Mesquit Creek, and other tributaries of the South Canadian. The North Fork has its sources in Texas, near its extreme northern boundary, and follows an easterly course; all the information, not very reliable, perhaps, which I have of this stream and the adjacent country, I obtained from the Indians.

The South Fork escapes the canyons of the Rocky Mountains in New Mexico, enters Texas from the west, and pursues a course nearly due east. Dry River is a southern tributary of the South Canadian, and has its fountain-head upon the Llano Estacado, immediately west of the sources of Red River and the False Washita; it has a gravelly bed, which is generally dry, and is 200 yards wide at its mouth.

The explored route of a Pacific Railroad along the 35th parallel follows up the valley of the Wichita and the Canadian River.

The northern, as well as other portions of the Pan-handle, is only moderately supplied with timber. Occasionally the eye is relieved by the sight of a line of timber, which usually marks the course of streams; I also found it in groves on the elevated lands, and in ravines along the banks of the Canadian. In the latter places I saw excellent cedar, post, and burr oak. On the north bank of the South Canadian, a few miles west of the intersection of "Marcy's boundary line," I saw a large forest of oak timber. Lieutenant Abert, in a report, says more particularly of this, that "On the 27th of September, in longitude 99° 11' on the north side of the Canadian, he passed through a country completely covered with a dense growth of oak, commonly called Black-jack; this forest stretched back from the river as far as the eye could reach." In some of the bottoms, where the trees were of a more luxurant growth, I found burr oak.

The Antelope Hills have obtained some reputation as a peculiarity of the country. These hills lie on the south bank of Canadian River, near the 100th meridian—the boundary between Texas and the United States Indian territory—and are sometimes called the Boundary Hills. They are from 100 to 130 feet high, with a table of sandstone about fifteen feet thick, very much like the Double Mountains near the heads of Brazos River. The Antelope Hills, and others similar in character and form, are apparently the last remnants of an elevated plain, which once covered the whole region. They are not, however, situated on the same meridian with the Wichita Mountains, as represented on all maps of that country ; and persons looking for them in that direction (due north of the mountains), have found themselves disappointed.

The 100th meridian, according to Captains Marcy and McLennan, I found to be the 99th degree of west longitude, and the Antelope Hills are therefore one degree westward ; and the 100th meridian, as determined by those gentlemen, is not the boundary of Texas.

A considerable portion of the Pan-handle is included in what is called the Gypsum Formation. This term was adopted for those portions of the strata "composed of red clay, sandstone, and marl containing gypsum more or less abundant." The eastern limits of the Gypsum Formation extend from the sources of the Colorado River, in a north-east direction over the heads of Red River, and crossing the Canadian about two hundred miles west of Fort Smith. Its northern extension is not fully determined. To the west, the formation is exposed in nearly every river-bed and canon, so far as the Colorado Chiquito, in New Mexico.

In the fanciful descriptions given by some persons of the character of the Pan-handle, they have no doubt been influenced by a desire to commend themselves to the favor of those interested in the location of lands, or else they knew little about the country they were describing. But be the motives what they may, it has caused disappointments, and sometimes been attended with disastrous consequences.

In the region of the Pan-handle country, situated upon the waters of the Red River, the Canadian, and their tributaries, wheat and other small grains may be raised successfully, especially where irrigation is practicable, and in the valleys formed by the numerous streams, which are clothed with a luxuriant growth of grass. The country may be more particularly recommended to a pastoral or wine-making and fruit-raising population. From the abundance of wild grapes, plums, currants, etc., in all parts of the Pan-handle, it may be inferred that the soil is admirably adapted to the cultivation of fruit-tree and the vine, and that may become applicable of this country which Major Emory observes of the Rio Grande valley : "In no part of the world does this luscious fruit (grape) flourish with greater luxuriance, than in the upper valley of the Rio Grande, as far down as Presidio del Norte, when properly cultivated." In the months of June and July, 1856, I visited the Canadian. That country, like the whole region west of the Mississippi, was then suffering from a severe drought. Water was scarce, and the ground parched ; and when we reached the Canadian River, near the 99° of west longitude, where the stream is usually from 400 to 600 feet wide, it was perfectly dry. The only water-hole we found that day, was in the bed of a small creek, and a troop of Comanches manifested a desire to dispossess us of that. Notwithstanding this drought, portions of the country were literally covered with plums, and grape-vines loaded with most delicious fruits. Of grapes I found two different kinds, both small, sweet, and of a dark blue color. The plums were frequently an inch in diameter, sweet, and of light yellow and red color, slightly differing from the "Chickasaw plum." In fact, I went on this tour with nine whites and six Indians, without any provisions, and short of ammunition, and we lived for four weeks entirely on buffalo meat and wild fruits.

All the territory of Texas north of Red River and a line drawn from its sources due west to the eastern boundary of New Mexico, belongs to the land district and jurisdiction of Cooke. The portion of the Pan-handle south of this is within the limits of Young district.

Persons visiting the Pan-handle country—in fact, the whole of North-western Texas—will be delighted with the balmy and salubrious atmosphere. The mean temperature in the summer, I found, according to several years' observation, from 80° to 82° ; in the warmest seasons the thermometer hardly ever rises to 95°, and even when at this height, the heat is mitigated by the refreshing southern breeze, which makes the nights particularly cool and comfortable.

The above is rather a hastily written sketch of an extensive portion of our territory. Not having my notes with me, I give this from memory ; and a more detailed account, interesting as it might be, would perhaps trespass beyond the space allotted to me. For a better illustration of the topography and general features of the country, I refer to any good "Map of the State." Our knowledge of the country along the western and northern boundaries of the Pan-handle is as yet limited ; but with the progress of the Boundary Survey we shall obtain reliable information of its nature.

H. WICKELAND.

XCVIII.

GAME IN TEXAS.

BY GEORGE J. DURHAM, OF AUSTIN.

IN the north-west and at present unsettled portions of our State are still to be found, in the fall and winter, large numbers of the grandest and stateliest of all the four-footed game of this continent—the buffalo. Last winter they were abundant a short distance west of Fort Belknap, in Young county, and a party of hunters who went out in their pursuit brought into and sold in this market large quantities of both tongues and skins. Indigenous to the same region is to be found the black-tailed deer and elk, although neither are now abundant, both of which, with the single exception of the northern moose, are the largest of the deciduous-horned ruminants of North America. The fleet-footed antelope is still abundant on our western and north-western frontiers, while the common deer is to be found throughout the State, and probably not one county within its wide limits can be found wholly destitute of this highly prized game, although a disease, familiarly known as " black tongue," has of late years much decreased their numbers. These embrace the principal ruminants of our fauna which can be strictly regarded as game. Among the less noted mammals we have the hare, rabbit, and squirrel species, spread with a lavish hand throughout the State, the first occupying the prairie plains, over whose surface he gambols with a speed superior to that of his European congener, but, in size, general appearance, habits, and edible qualities, he is very similar to that hare. And to those who are fond of the long-tails, I can say I know of no sport more exhilarating, in its proper season, which may be said to last from September to April—as I regret to say we have no game-laws here—than coursing the hare of our western prairies. Unfortunately, however, in some parts of the State it has become liable, since the introduction of the smaller cereals, to dropsy, in like manner as its European relative. This however, is confined to this member of the *Lepus* family ; for I have never known it to affect either of our two varieties of rabbits, the largest of which, familiarly known as the swamp-rabbit, inhabits the heavy timbered woodlands and bottoms, while the smaller species is to be found in the uplands and oak-openings. Both species are unlike their transatlantic kindred in not burrowing and being gregarious, although, where circumstances favor the lesser species, such as a dense growth of the cactus affords, they are as numerous as in an English warren. The squirrel, which a European sportsman would scarcely classify with game proper, holds here a deservedly high place, especially in the *cuisine*, for well does he grace both the bag and board. Of them we have several varieties, but the most common are the gray and fox squirrels, the graceful little flying species being too small for the larder. With these I conclude my remarks on the *fur* of our State ; for though both bear and peccaries, each possessing edible qualities in their proper season, might with propriety be classed under that head, I pass on to the more varied subject of the *feather*.

At the head of the list of land-birds, and of that class known to naturalists as *Rasores* or scratchers, stands the turkey, at once the largest of the granivorous birds, and the most eagerly sought for of all feathered game, twenty or even twenty-five pounds being no unusual weight in a favorable season for a male ; and, like the common deer, it is distributed in every portion of the State where trees of sufficient height are to be found to afford it secure roosting-places.

Of the grouse family we have but one species in our State—the prairie hen, or pinnated grouse—and it, like the red grouse of the British Isles, is an inhabitant of the open grounds or prairies, as we have nothing of the character of moor-land ; the prairies, however, form the predominant feature in the landscapes of the western portion of the State. But to make amends for the paucity of species in this family, our bird is, *par excellence*, the grouse of cisatlantic sportsmen, and many of those who have tasted his quality on the other side too. I do not mean gastronomically, but as a game bird, whether we consider his size—which in the adult male, on a good range, attains the weight of three pounds—or his strength of wing, which can be used with sufficient vigor to bear him safely out of danger even when pursued by the stoutest of our Peregrine falcons. Then, again, when the cover is good, he lies to Sancho as close as his Scotch brethren, and is withal as toothsome, especially when grain-fed, as any of his class, be it red or black game of across the water, or any of the numerous varieties, now known to be some twelve in number, of North America. Again in some portions of our State, as in the wheat region of the northern counties, his name is legion, and there the grouse-shooter, glutton or battue-lover though he be, can fill his wagon till his cheek should mantle with shame at the ruthless and often useless slaughter of so many innocents. In many counties east of this meridian, from the coast to Red River, possessing sufficient prairie-range, there is a plentiful sprinkling of this, *me judice*, the choicest of all game-birds, which is also the case with a large section of our State lying to the south ; but as a general rule the western line of its *habitat* will be found not far from the ninety-seventh parallel of longitude.

The next most useful and popular family is the quail, perhaps more generally known as partridges, of which our State can claim at least four varieties : two in the further west on the Rio Grande and country adjacent, and known respectively as Gambel's partridge and blue partridge, both handsome game-birds, occupying nearly the same section. The former, however, more affects the cultivated districts of the Upper Rio Grande, but has not yet been found east of the Pecos River. The *habitat* of the latter reaches down that stream as low as 25° north latitude. The eastern line of its range, like the former, is confined to the valley of that river. The third species, known as the black-bellied or Massena partridge, is found in limited numbers as far east as this river (the Colorado), and is sometimes met with in this vicinity, but, as it affects the hilly country, is not to be found east of this point. Westward it extends to the Pecos and perhaps beyond. The fourth and last species is our own "Bob White," familiarly known from the Hudson to the Rio Grande as one of the gamest little birds of the western hemisphere, and furnishing more sport in his capture than any other individual of our extensive fauna. These varieties are nearly all of a uniform size, being larger than the European quail, are prolific, monogamous, and generally partake of similar habits. The Western species, however, are more disposed, like the red-legged partridge of the Eastern continent, to trust to their legs rather than their wings in escaping danger, which proclivity may be induced from their inhabiting regions furnishing less grass cover than that occupied by their Eastern relative.

Of the *Phasianidæ*, or pheasant family, this State and continent, so far as at present known, does not furnish even a single member; but this is more than compensated for in the numerous varieties of both the grouse and quail tribes.

There is yet another family which should be included in the game-list of land birds, although classed among the waders, and this in point of size of each of its two members, the largest in this division. I allude, of course, to the *Grus*, or crane family, of which we have two species, the white or whooping-crane, and the blue or sand-hill crane, both noble and majestic birds, and superior as an article of food to many other better known and more popular families, being strictly granivorous, at least during their seven or eight months' stay with us in each year, feeding alternately upon the indigenous food of the prairies, upon which they become quite fat in the spring, and the cultivated food of the fields. The former stands five feet in height, the adult birds is of a snowy whiteness, with the tips of the wings black, and weighs between twelve and fifteen pounds. The immature birds of this species have the upper parts beautifully variegated with patches of reddish feathers. The more familiar and far more numerous "sand-hill" is also of the same habits and taste as his more stately congener, is about one foot less in height, three or four pounds lighter, and wears a more homely garb of grayish blue, which in the younger birds is often tinged with a sandy hue. This family now occupies in our fauna the place formerly held in Europe by the bustard, but which has long since ceased to be an ornament to the open grounds of the British Isles.

Among the *Natatores*, or swimmers, we have two species of swan, the American and trumpeter, both, I believe, spending the winter with us upon our bays and estuaries in immense flocks, but forsaking us early in the spring for their northern homes. They are seldom to be met with in the interior, only when exhausted by long flight in their autumnal migration, which not unfrequently takes place; and woe befall them should they be discovered while in this defenseless condition, when with stiffened and powerless wings they fell an easy prey to every spoiler.

Of the goose family we have at least four well-known and well marked species, two inhabiting the coast, which may be termed salt-water or bay geese, and two remaining in the interior, which may be termed fresh-water or inland geese, the former known as the Brandt goose and snow goose, the latter as the common or Canadian goose and the gray or white-fronted goose. All arrive early in October, the bay geese passing on to the coast without stopping, only for food and water, and the latter remaining with us until the latter end of April, affording abundant sport to the wild-fowl shooter, and, after a short sojourn with us, excellent eating. Yes, yonder they are, and within reach of the fence too, a glorious lot of them. The wagon is hitched, and we proceed to insinuate ourselves along the fence, briers and bull-nettles nothing daunting, until we reach the coveted point which may be shall enfilade their ranks. The barrels are cautiously inserted between the rails, and, as you look along them, you see their black and glossy necks now erect and motionless, for their eyes and ears have been at work. Not a moment is to be lost, the triggers are touched, and eight ounces of " T " shot from four barrels scatter wounds and death among them.

Early in September the ducks commence to arrive, and now is the time for those fond of duck-shooting, and of migratory duck-shooting in particular, tô closely watch the weather, and with the first " norther " to betake themselves and retrievers at the earliest dawn to some well-known jutting point or island in our rivers, and there levy tribute upon them in their passage down our streams to their winter home, which of some species is still further to the south. The first that make their appearance is the blue-winged teal, and a delicious fowl it is, both to shoot at and to eat; nevertheless, even they will at times be a little weedy. But here they come; they are upon us in a moment, in the twinkling of an eye, with the glistening sheen of their steel-blue wings dancing in the dim light of the early morning; and, as they make the turn, dip, or rise, as the case may be, huddling confusedly together for the moment, point the barrels into the darkest part of the flock, and if you have used effectively and simultaneously both your brain and muscle, and fired coolly and deliberately, your heart will be gladdened at the results produced by your sixes or sevens; and as your retrievers gather in the harvest, each congratulating the other on the glorious havoc, a flock passes by you " scot free," which largely discounts your success, and quickly brings you back to reason and the nether world.

The next in time and order of migration is the shoveler, the peer of the preceding species in all respects save one—that of not flying in as compact a body ; but in size and plumage superior, especially when dressed in his spring garb, when he may be regarded as a feathered beau among his tribe, provided our wood or summer duck be not present, which stands without a rival in beauty of plumage, and is moreover the only one who remains with us the year round. In the wake of the shoveler follows the widgeon, green-winged teal, and pintails, all choice and well-known fowls ; these, in like manner, are followed by the gray duck, ring-necks (the daintiest of all), and occasionally canvas-backs, the mallards bringing up the rear, as it is the middle of December before they are generally diffused throughout the State ; but when that has taken place, and the oak mast is abundant, every favorable stream will yield up its feathered treasures to the lover of wild-fowl shooting. The ducks above named are those only which usually follow the course of our streams in their autumnal migration, and may all, except the canvas-backs, be regarded as fresh-water or inland ducks, those whose habitat is the bays and lowlands of the coast, meandering the shore-line of the Atlantic and Gulf coasts in their route to the south. Of these there are about a dozen more varieties which spend the winter months with us, many of which afford ample sport to the punt-shooter, as well as furnishing a bountiful supply of palatable food to littoral residents, but usually of a quality inferior to those above mentioned.

Of the *Scolopacidæ*, or snipe family, we have in their proper seasons three species—the savory woodcock, in suitable localities in the timbered portions of the State ; the English, or Wilson's snipe, on the coast and throughout the interior wherever marshy ground is to be found, and along the muddy margins of smaller streams ; and the New York snipe, which, unlike his relatives, associates in flocks, and is found on the coast in the winter, but does not visit the interior until the spring.

When the winter shall have passed away, and first warm breaths of spring return, with swelling buds and genial showers, the more sensitive blue-wings and shovelers, which temporarily left us for a more southern home within the tropics, return, and with them come vast flocks of plover, curlew, tatler, sanderlings, and nearly all the varieties of what are usually termed shore-birds, many of which are eagerly sought for by both sportsmen and epicures, and remain with us until early in May.

Such is a brief outline of the principal game-birds and quadrupeds of our favored State ; and if perchance it should be the means of bringing permanently within our spacious limits one genuine sportsman, the writer will be amply repaid for this short sketch, in which he is so conscious of falling far short of doing justice to a subject well worthy of a more able pen.

XCIX.

GAME IN TEXAS—CONTINUED.

BY GEORGE J. DURHAM, OF AUSTIN.

As my remarks last year on the subject stated at the head of this article were necessarily condensed, owing to want of space in *The Almanac*,* I will now resume a brief description of the lesser feathered tribes which may be regarded as game, which term, I wish it understood, will embrace all the birds of our State—so far as my observation extends—which are considered as edible and worthy of the sportsman's attention.

Of the *Scolopacinæ*, or snipe family proper, we have but three species, namely, the woodcock (*Philohela minor*), the English snipe, or Wilson's snipe (*Gallinago Wilsonii*), and the New York, gray, or red-breasted snipe (*Macroramphus grisens*). The former visits us late in the autumn ; but owing to the want of suitable *habitat* in this portion of our State, is rarely to be met with. East of this meridian (97°), which, be it observed, may be regarded as that which generally divides the wood-land from the prairie portion of the State, he may often be " belted " in gratifying numbers. His congener, the English snipe, makes his first appearance here about the first of October, and continues to arrive throughout the fall months, as driven southward by the increasing cold of more northern regions, and can be found in almost every spongy springhead in the prairie drains. On and near the coast he is abundant ; there the snipe-shooter can load and fire until every loop in his belt is garnished to repletion with their graceful forms. I am not aware that the gray or redbreasted snipe—improperly so called—is to be found, in the autumn, in the interior of the State, as they probably migrate coastwise at this season, which is the route usually taken southward by many of our migratory birds ; but in the spring, with the first warm rains, he is to be found in the edges of the prairie slashes in flocks ; for this member of the family—while sojourning with

* This and the preceding article were taken from Texas Almanac.

us at least—is strictly gregarious, although the flocks are never large, say not exceeding fifty individuals. But fortunate is he who finds one of half that number of these unsuspicious birds engaged in probing the muddy margins of our prairie pools ; and if he is withal not too hasty, he can easily obtain an enfilading fire before they arise, and with the second barrel, on the wing, again materially diminish their numbers. Now, load quick, for they will surely be back again. Yes, here they come ! Squat ! And again and again they pay tribute, until, if you choose, you may " belt " nearly all of their number ; for I know of no bird which exhibits such tenacity to a favorite feeding-ground, or, maybe, such desire to rejoin its former companions, as this. At this season—the early spring—his dress is plain, nearly a unicolor above— ashy gray—and beneath, white ; and the condition of his flesh poor. Should you fortunately find him late in the spring, in his courting habiliments, congratulate yourself ; for, presto, change ! he is no longer the same emaciated, sober-colored Scolopax of six weeks before, but a fat, plump, gayly-dressed, feathered beau ; and should you not have been a close observer, it requires not much stretch of the imagination to deceive yourself into the hallucination that your belt is now laden with a new variety of woodcock, so closely do they now resemble in form and plumage that well-known bird ; but smaller in size they of course are, as " Philohela " in good plight averages eight ounces, while his cousin " Macroramphus " is but five. " Red-breasted " indeed he is ; but this prefixture to his name—like many others given to the feathered tribes—is an injudicious one, as it conveys an inaccurate idea that that part alone is of a red color, while the fact is, that it is the prevalent color of his entire body, as much so as that yellowish red is the prevailing color of the woodcock.*

Perhaps the next most interesting family to the sportsman, as well as that which is most useful in furnishing savory articles of diet, is that of the *Charadri-dæ*, or plovers, at the head of which stands the golden plover, or bull-head (*Charadrius Virginicus*). This also passes over our coast in its autumnal flight to the south, having a widely extended range, reaching from the islands in the Arctic Ocean far down the continent of South America, if not to Cape Horn itself. But whether it stops at all with us in that migration, even for food or rest, I am unable to say, as it is exclusively confined to the Gulf coast, or maybe, the Gulf itself ; for it has wonderful powers of continued flight. Here, inland, at that season, I have never observed it ; but early in the spring it spreads itself over our grassy plains in countless multitudes on its passage to the north for nidification. With us it remains to recuperate its wasted flesh, which it does in a very short time, and early in April is ready to continue its journey on that isotherm which warms into life and brings to the sur-

---

* The distinguishing mark of this group is : Bill straight, and longer than the naked portion of the leg, the end of the upper bill thickened and bent over the tip of the lower.

face the worms and insects which sustain and fatten it. Now is the time to sally forth with a gentle team for its capture; for this, like many other of its associate tribes, is best approached either in a wagon or on horseback. See what a oloud of them, as they wheel and circle over that depression in the prairie, now covered with water a few inches deep, through which the green grass is just beginning to appear, faintly tinting its surface with an emerald hue! Now they turn again, and, sure enough, they have lit on that little tongue of land which projects into the watery waste. With uplifted wings they wade into the grateful element, and with depressed head and ruffled plumage the spray is scattered in all directions, while the pearly drops glide from their golden spotted backs. So busily engaged are they with their morning ablutions they heed not our approach. The water seems to be fairly alive with them. So, Major (alas! he is no more), drive into that mott of timber quick, and hitch the horses at once ; which done, we cautiously advance in a stooping posture, for here there is no friendly bush or weeds to conceal us. But the desired course is kept, and the distance gained without creating alarm. Four barrels now discharge their contents into the busy, splashing throng, and twenty, thirty, and even forty of their number have been picked up from such a discharge. Should "Virginicus" remain with us until May, which it very rarely does, I have known it—on one occasion only—to assume its nuptial garb of jet black plumage of the under body surface.

In addition to the preceding, we have, in the interior at least, one other plover which is eagerly sought for by, and is quite a favorite with, sportsmen. It is locally known by the name of "whistling plover," from its continued piping while on the wing. Its ornithological name—if it has one—is unknown to me. It is about the size of the kildee plover, but more compact in form, and visits us before any other migratory plover, and remains until the end of April; is, while with us, of an olive color above and white (pure) beneath; bill obtuse black ; foot and legs of the same color ; is gregarious, and flies in a very compact body ; so much so, that a dozen can sometimes be obtained, when at a right angle from their line of flight, at a single discharge. In windy weather, they have the habit of squatting as soon as they alight, which renders their position difficult to detect, unless you are in close proximity at the time of their alighting, when, by a close scrutiny, their heads may be seen. Then select the proper distance which, of course, should be that which will secure the greatest spread of shot consistent with the requisite force, and if you have taken the precaution of advancing up the wind, should it be blowing what a "salt" would term "pretty stiff" you may possibly obtain two sitting shots before they fly, thereby cutting two lines through their ranks, which, if fired with one knee resting on the ground, will be materially lengthened over those fired from an erect position. Then gather your two or three dozen victims, and be thankful for nature's bounties ; for be assured there is no Chara-drius their superior for the table.

With the exception of the kildee plover (*Ægialites vociferus*), which I regard as of no use for the larder, the preceding species embrace all the Plover of note which occur in the interior. On the coast many other species are to be found, such as the black-bellied (*Squatarola Helveticus*), Wilson's plover (*Ægialites Wilsonii*), ring plover (*A. semipalmatus*), and the piping plover (*A. melodus*).*

Of the *Numeniæ*, or Curlews, we have also two species in the interior ; the the long-billed (*Numenius longirostris*), and the Esquimaux curlew (*N. Bore-alis*). The former stays with us throughout the year, and doubtless breeds on the Gulf coast. He is, however, by no means a favorite for culinary purposes ; for while sojourning in the interior he is always poor in flesh, even in the spring when food is abundant, and coarse in its texture, but neverthe-less generally well flavored ; hence, when opportunity offers, he is brought to bag, though it takes field artillery, or projectiles fired from like engines, to do it efficiently, so tenacious is he of life. However, when one is brought down from a passing flock, or knocked over while statelily perambulating the prairie, seemingly not noticing you, but with at least one eye upon you all the while, let him lie there a short time ; or if wounded, and disposed to hail his retreating companions—which he is tolerably certain to do—gratify the exercise of his vocal organs ; for in all likelihood by the time you have loaded, or before, if you are still blessed with a muzzle-loader, he will either call back that flock, or should there be another in the neighborhood, that is, within the radius of a mile or two, he will call up that, and give you an opportunity of adding another long-bill to diversify your bag, a couple of which really ought to suffice any reasonable being—not a taxidermist—that being presumed to be the main object for which they are desired.

The Esquimaux curlew, like the golden plover in its autumnal migration, gives us the go-by in its pasage to the south. If it then stops on our coast, it is unknown to me, as is also the time of its passage ; and whether it is per-formed nocturnally or diurnally I am also in ignorance of ; but certain it is, that it *does pass*, and that by quite a different route from the one taken in the spring ; for then they are as regular in their arrival from the south as any other migratory bird. It too, like " Virginicus," is said to have a wide geo-graphical range, reaching from the " Barren Grounds," on the northern con-fines of this continent, most probably down to the grassy plains of South America. Its range, however, in that direction has not yet been determined.

* The distinguishing marks of this group are : Bill rather cylindrical, as long as the head, or shorter toward the point, rather swollen ; hind toe rarely present, and then only rudimen-tary ; the outer and middle toes more or less connected by a membrane.

Coincident with the arrival of the golden plover, it makes its appearance on the prairies of the interior, and with them it also departs. Look at that dark patch in the distant prairie which is now assuming its spring livery. Can it be a flock of the little curlews? If so, it is a huge one. Yes, it surely is a mass of birds of some sort, which have lit there since we passed in the morning; for see it has already expanded, and now is less dark in color than it was when we were a few hundred yards back. Approaching nearer, we see individual birds moving, and soon identify our savory friends the little curlews. Glorious! Now for the nearest object where the wagon can be secured, and then for havoc in their rusty-colored ranks. An hour or two is spent in slaughter, generally lining two or three while on the ground, and occasionally getting in both barrels as they circle by you, when it "rains" curlew for the time being, so compact is the flock while on the wing. A few dozen, maybe, of their number are added to the day's bag, with joyful hearts— and a valuable addition it is; for so palatable and sizable a bird—it weighs half a pound—is always welcome.

The curlew known as the short-billed (*Numenius Hudsonicus*)—though this name is often applied to the preceding—I am not acquainted with. Mr. Audubon states, "It passes from Texas northward in the spring," and therefore at that season may for a short time be found upon our coast, but in the interior it is never to be found. I therefore infer it to be merely a bird of passage with us, and perhaps strictly maritime in its habits. Its weight is stated to be rather over one pound.*

Of the *Limosæ*, or godwits, I have but little to communicate. There are two species, the marbled godwit (*Limosa Fedoa*) and the Hudsonian godwit (*L. Hudsonica*). The former, being an exclusively maritime bird, I have never met with; but it is said to be found on our coast, though in what numbers I am unable to state. The latter is occasionally to be found as far in the interior as this point (Austin), and is both handsome and edible, and every way worthy of the sportsman's attention.†

The next group, or sub-family, that of *Totaninæ*, or tattlers, embraces some of the most popular birds, though, strictly speaking, both of the two last belong to this group. And first to be considered is Bartram's tattler, Bartram's sandpiper, grass or field plover, with many other names, both

---

* The distinguishing marks of this group are: Bill very variable in length, nearly straight at the base, then rapidly decurving to the tip, where the upper mandible thickens downward, and extends beyond the lower, as in Scolopacinæ. Outer toe webbed at its basal joint, inner one for half that distance.

† The distinguishing marks of this group are: Bill much longer than the head, nearly equaling the tarsus (lower joint of the leg) and toes together, curving slightly upward from the base, but depressed at the tip, where it is thickened, and projects a little beyond the lower. Feet same as preceding group.

common and scientific, for its proper placing and name have long been an object of dispute and uncertainty. Plover, however (of any kind), he certainly is not. Hereafter he is to be scientifically known as *Actiturus Bartramius*, and visits us from the northward—well, when do you think? Very early in midsummer ; for between the tenth and fifteenth of July, in a warm, clear summer night, his mellow whistle can first be heard ; and as he can occasionally be found even as late as the middle of October, when the last leave us for more southern climes, and again return by the end of March, and stay until the tenth or middle of May, he can not, after that date, go very far northward for nidification and return by the date above mentioned. In fact, they may almost be said to breed in our State, although I have never yet heard of their having done so ; but on a few occasions shelled eggs have been found within them when killed late in May. On their arrival in July, they are fat, and continue to advance in obesity during their sojourn, until one is at a loss to understand why so frail an epidermis—for you can scarcely pluck them without tearing—as that which encases them does not give way before so much internal pressure, and collapse ensue, which, to a limited extent, is the case when shot flying in the middle of a hot day in August, and the falling bird strikes the hard surface of the hot ground. This has frequently occurred during the present season, 1868. When picking them up, *the oil has dripped from their tail-feathers.* For edible purposes, *me judice*, they are then unfit ; and to those who affect *oleum locusta* in its most condensed form, I leave their discussion at this season of the year. On their return in the spring, they are usually much emaciated, but a short time suffices to put them in edible condition. They are generally shot singly from a buggy, and orthodoxically, with your wife or sweetheart for a driver, as the case may be ; but oftentimes, if the sportsman will come down to *terra firma*, he can align two ; and though they may be many yards apart, if he will get still closer to mother earth, (provided he hasn't white pants on!) by dropping on one knee, (mind you, to the birds!) he will lengthen the spread of shot and usually secure both ; and this I regard as the only skill exhibited in the capture of *Acti-turus Bartramius*, however much may be otherwise displayed in the capture of the fair Diana by your side, which, we trust, was sufficient to insure success. To the gentler sex of our State, both married and single, in suitable weather, I unhesitatingly say, try " plover-shooting." How many out-door pleasures are lost to my fair countrywomen, simply because none have drawn their attention to them. They fish in summer—no violence is done to public opinion in that—then why not drive in spring and autumn plover-shooting? I again repeat, try it ; and if this suggestion is acted on, I may, on some future occasion, be encouraged to offer another of like character. I should also add that this bird is well known throughout the Atlantic and Gulf States, and extends its migrations as far south as the Argentine Republic.

There is another near relative to the preceding to be found in the interior, but rather smaller in size, which is said to breed within the State, of similar general appearance and habits, but more gregarious, known by the name of buff-breasted sandpiper (*Tryngites rufescens*). Of the Willet, or semipalmated snipe (*Symphemia semipalmata*), I am unable to speak, as it is exclusively a shore bird, and never yet observed this far inland ; it is said to breed abundantly on our coast, and ranks among the most desirable and eagerly sought for of shore-birds. The greater and lesser yellow-legs (*Gambetta melanolenca* and *G. flavipes*) are to be found throughout the interior, both in the autumn and spring, in almost every suitable locality ; but, not flying in compact bodies, are no especial favorites with sportsmen. Several other members of the same group are also to be found, in the proper seasons, on our coast? but I am not familiar with them or their habits.*

The most numerous tribe of shore-birds, and perhaps the most interesting to sportsmen of the coast, is that of the *Tringæ*, or sandpipers, which, excepting in the spring, are nearly all exclusively littoral in their habits. Many of them are of sufficient size to engage individually the sportsman's attention, while all are gregarious, excepting, of course, during the breeding season—which is generally in the far north—and fly as well as rest in compact bodies. Consequently their pursuit and capture is one both of pleasure and profit to those who live contiguous to the shore. For obvious reasons little more than a mere enumeration of them must, for the present, suffice. The gray-back or robin snipe (*Tringa Canutus*) is quite a desirable bird, whether we regard its edible qualities (as it is a dainty) or its size, which, when in good condition, is between five and six ounces. The purple sandpiper (*T. maritima*) :—this rare species may only be a bird of passage with us, as it is stated to be a winter visitant to the tropics. The red-backed sandpiper (*T. Alpina*), an abundant species and general favorite for the table, of about three ounces weight. The jack-snipe (*T. maculata*) may, perhaps, be only a bird of passage with us, as its winter migration is thought to extend to South America. Weight, six ounces. Least sandpiper (*T. Wilsonii*), as its name indicates, is of small size, but good for the table ; and, as it flies in dense flocks, a mess can often be procured at a single discharge. The distinguishing marks of the preceding group are : bill nearly straight, not widened at the tip ; tarsus shorter than the middle toe and claw ; feathers of the tibia (thigh) reaching to the joint ; tail wedge-shaped.

* The distinguishing marks are : Bill nearly straight, about the length of tarsus, tapering, rather hard, and pointed ; gape extending nearly to a point below the eye ; outer toe usually webbed at the basal joint.

Omitting some of the less noted sandpipers, the sanderling (*Calidris arenaria*), which lacks the hind toe, in like manner as the plovers, and the stilt sandpiper (*Micropalama Himantopus*), though the latter is well worthy of the sportsman's attention, I will pass on to the *Rallidæ*, or rail family, none of which are to be found in sufficient numbers in the interior, for want of suitable feeding-ground, to demand attention, though the sora, or ortolan (*Rallus Virginianus*), and little black rail (*Porzana Jamaicensis*), are frequently met with in the interior; while the yellow rail (*P. Noveboracensis*), is doubtless to be found on the coast; all of which are of the short-billed varieties. The longed-billed species are the king rail (*Rallus elegans*), and the clapper rail (*R. crepitans*), both of which are to be found upon our coast, the latter an abundant species.

The coot (*Fulica Americana*), the Florida and purple gallinules (*Gallinula Galatea* and *Martinica*), with the heron and ibis families, I omit, as none of them can strictly be regarded as edible, which terminates the *Grallæ*, or waders.

We have, also, two members of the *Columbidæ*, or pigeon family, worthy of notice—the common wild pigeon (*Ectopistes migratoria*), which visits the wood-land portion of our State in the winter, and the Carolina dove (*Zenaidura Carolinensis*), the latter resident with us throughout the year. On the lower Rio Grande there are also two other species, the red-billed and white-winged doves (*Columba flavirostris* and *Melopelia Leucoptera*), and in the same region is to be found one member of a useful family—the *Penelopidæ*, or guans—which is peculiar to Central and South America; the cha-cha-la-ca (*Ortalida McCalli*), which is about the size of a pullet, arboreal in its habits, though it nests upon the ground, laying six or eight eggs. Length, twenty-three inches, of which the tapering tail is one half; stretch of wings, twenty-six inches; and weighs rather less than two pounds.

The preceding observations, especially those relating to our exclusively shore-birds, are based upon the Smithsonian edition of the general report of the United States Pacific Railroad Explorations and Surveys, and the octavo edition of " Birds of America," by John James Audubon.

C.

THE YELLOW FEVER IN TEXAS IN 1867.

THE year 1867 will long be remembered as the most disastrous ever known, in consequence of the yellow fever epidemic having extended to many interior towns of the State, which have hitherto been deemed entirely safe from such a visitation. About thirty interior towns and villages have suffered a most appalling mortality, such as has scarcely ever been known in cities subject to the the same visitation almost annually. The yellow fever first made its appearance in Indianola, we believe, early in July, and its next appearance was in Galveston, where it was first officially reported the latter part of the same month, and did not break out in Harrisburg and Austin until the first or second week in August, and was not admitted to exist in New Orleans till several weeks later, though respectable physicians reported cases in their practice there in July. It was from the middle to the latter part of August that it was reported successively in Lavaca, in Victoria, in Goliad, Hempstead, Cypress, Navasota, Millican, Brenham, Chappell Hill, La Grange, Bastrop, Alleyton, Long Point, Courtney, Anderson, Huntsville, Liberty, Lynchburg, and in many other neighborhoods and small villages. It is said to have been successfully excluded from Richmond and Columbus by a rigid quarantine, and also from Brownsville and Anderson till a very late period, though it finally broke out in both of the latter places. Soon after the great storm, or about that time, namely, early in October, there were but a few cases in Anderson and some fifty deaths in Brownsville. In most of the above places the mortality was very great. In Galveston, the whole number of deaths from the first to the last reported—November 11th—was 1332, of which number 1134 were from yellow fever. The population of Galveston early in July was found by the census of the assessor and collector, Captain Scudder, to be 22,500; but some 5,000 or 6,000 are supposed to have left before the end of that month, to escape the danger. The above mortality is variously estimated to have been from 15 to 30 per cent. of the yellow fever cases; but according to the best information we could get, up to the time of preparing this article, the mortality in all the interior towns, except Houston, must have been much greater. In Harrisburg, and some other towns, considerably more than half of all the cases died; in others, about half; and in others, perhaps a smaller proportion. The cause of this great mortality is obvious. In these interior towns the people were entirely unprepared for such a visitation, and universal consternation was generally the consequence of the first announcement of this fearful disease, and hence many people who were able left for places of safety, and it is reported that in some instances there were not enough left of the well to attend upon the sick and bury the dead. Some of the accounts given us are truly heart-rending. The proper medicines were very often wanting, and, still oftener, physicians who knew how to treat the disease, while nurses could with difficulty be had at all. This was particularly the case at the first, though, soon after, great relief was rendered by the Howard Association of Galveston, and a similar association in Houston, as well as by the voluntary efforts of many experienced physicians and nurses who went from Galveston and Houston.

We had hoped to be able to give full statistics in this work of this most fatal epidemic; but the returns in answer to the circulars sent for that purpose did not come in time. However, we are glad to learn that Colonel Yard, President of the Galveston Howards, is preparing a full and reliable report, not only of the deaths in all the afflicted towns, but of the various modes of treatment, and the success of each, so as to furnish valuable data for the medical profession.

CI.

GEOLOGICAL RESOURCES OF TEXAS.

BY S. B. BUCKLEY.

(From Texas Almanac.)

THE Geological Survey of the State having only been in progress during a portion of the three years immediately preceding July, 1861, little has yet been done in the discovery of valuable minerals, with the exception of iron and coal ; or toward defining the different geological series of rocks. We will only briefly allude to the actual and prospective mineral resources of Texas, and refer those who wish for further details to our preliminary report of the survey.

The azoic rocks of Llano county contain immense beds of magnetic iron ore—the magnetite of the mineralogists, which, as is well known to manufactures of iron, is the best of ores—yielding the greatest per cent. of metallic iron. This is the same ore as that of the celebrated iron mines of Norway and Sweden. It also occurs in the azoic rocks of the north-eastern part of the State of New York, where during the last few years it has been wrought extensively.

The largest deposit of iron ore known in Llano county is on Jackson's Creek, a tributary of the Llano River. It is near Mr. Epperson's, about twelve miles west of the town of Llano, and nearly eight miles east of the Smoothing

Iron Mountain. It is a massive iron hill, from 25 to 30 feet high above its visible base; about 800 feet long and 500 feet wide, with an estimated elevation of from 200 to 300 feet above the surface of the Llano River at low water mark. This ore has been tested on a large scale, and found to yield more than 70 per cent. of metallic iron ; which was pronounced by some blacksmiths to be equal to the best Swedish iron. Our route to it was by the way of the Smoothing Iron mountain, over a comparatively level, hard, sandy road ; a soil formed by the disintegration of granite. Nearly the whole distance (about eight miles), we passed through open post-oak woods, interspersed with hickory and black-jack, (*Quercus nigra*). We saw sufficient timber surrounding the iron hill, and in its immediate neighborhood, for manufacturing purposes during many years. Iron made by the use of charcoal is superior to that made by other fuel ; so says Overman, who is a good authority in metallurgy. The limestones of the paleozoic and cretaceous rocks are in the vicinity, from whence abundant minerals for a flux can easily be obtained. The steatites, or soapstones, of the county can be used in the construction of furnaces. The cost of obtaining the ore is little, for it lies already at or near the surface. Immense blocks of ore lie scattered over the iron hill, or near its base. It is in a dry, healthy climate, where there would be little or no loss to either the workman or manufacturer, from sickness or bad weather. Plenty of provisions can be had from German and other farmers in the surrounding country. It is in a comparatively level country, with a hard gravelly soil, over which there are good roads throughout the year. Most of the mountains of Llano county are isolated, and scattered, at distant intervals, over the plain. Constant flowing streams are in that vicinity. We make these statements to show the great advantages here presented for the manufacture of iron.

A large bed of magnetic iron ore, of a similar character to the preceding, occurs eight miles distant, in a north-westerly direction. It lies between two granite ridges, and is traversed by quartz in all directions. At both of these localities the ore has evidently been ejected up from below at the same period with the granite, and by the same igneous forces ; hence these ores are true metallic veins, and their supply is inexhaustible.

On Comanche Creek, near Comanche Mountain, in Llano county, are extensive dykes of hornblende rock, inclosing large masses of soapstone. One of these beds of steatite or soapstone is about three hundred feet wide, and extends in a westerly course toward the Hondo Creek, where, at the distance of eight miles, it appears again. It has a light gray color, a fine grain, and a very compact texture, yet so soft that it can easily be cut with a knife or sawed into thin boards. It is an excellent material for the construction of furnaces, fire-places, inkstands, etc. It can also be used for fence-posts, as is done in some parts of New England. Pounded fine, and mixed with a little grease or tallow, it forms a very durable article to lessen the friction in the axles of wagons and carriages, for which purpose wagoners from a distance obtain it, considering it neater, better, and more lasting for that use than any thing else.

There are some large veins of ore containing a small per cent. of copper on the Little Llano River, about eight miles above its mouth. It resembles the gray oxide of copper, and, on exposure to the air, becomes more or less coated with a blueish green color. Its composition is mostly iron, and it is very similar to surface indications at the copper mines of Ducktown in the south-eastern part of East Tennessee. It is there termed by the miners "gossan," or the "blossom" of copper. These Ducktown mines have been a source of great wealth to their owners; and it is possible this Llano mine may prove to be equally profitable. The ore is in veins of a few feet in thickness, between gneissoid metamorphic rocks, on the borders of the granite. These veins were partly covered with gravel and soil formed by the disintegration of the granite hills, near the base of which they are situated. Their geological position is such as to lead us to expect that mining will here be a lucrative business.

The metamorphic are those stratified rocks whose form and composition have been altered by heated granite or other rocks of igneous origin; hence they are rarely in horizontal strata, but more or less inclined, broken, and contorted by the immense power exerted upon them at the time of the upheaval of the granite and its associated rocks. The metamorphic rocks are here on the outskirts of the granite in highly inclined strata, having evidently been thus lifted up at the time of the upheaval of the granite from its fiery bed below. These metamorphic rocks are interesting, as commonly being the depositories of the precious metals, especially gold and silver. They occur over quite a large section of country, a few miles south and south-east from Fort Mason, in Mason county, from which they extend westward into geologically unexplored regions. They consist chiefly of micaceous shales, with quartzose veins, in appearance much resembling the gold-bearing rocks of some parts of North Carolina and California. At a place about eight miles south of Fort Mason we obtain a small quantity of gold in the *débris* of these rocks: but, as our stay there was less than an hour, those rocks need another and much more thorough examination.

Bowie, Davis, Marion, and other counties in North-eastern Texas abound in iron ores, some of which have been wrought to a considerable extent. They are said to yield about 50 per cent. of metallic iron, and are hematites, or peroxides of iron. In Bastrop and Caldwell counties the same species of iron ore is abundant in the sandstones of the tertiary period. Enough is already known to assure us that the State has sufficient iron, not only to supply its own wants, but also those of the entire South during many ages. These hematites, although they may yield only from forty to fifty per cent. of metallic iron, can, without doubt, be profitably manufactured, on account of the abundance of fuel in their neighborhood, the facility of transportation, and the little expense of obtaining the ore, which is generally in hills at the surface. Most of the mines of Pennsylvania afford only about 50 per cent. of metallic iron, and that State produces about half of the entire iron made in the United States.

Extensive lignite or brown coal beds are in a large portion of the tertiary region of the State, as far as has been yet examined, namely, in Bastrop and its adjoining counties, and many of the counties east of the Trinity River. On Cedar Creek, west of the Colorado River, near the town of Bastrop, we measured some of these beds of coal, which are five feet thick, in nearly horizontal layers. Lignites have generally about ten per cent. less carbon than bituminous coal, and have that proportionate value for fuel. The amount of carbon in all mineral coals varies greatly, and can only be determined by chemical analysis. Some of the brown coals are equal in value to inferior bituminous coal. Sulphuret of iron often occurs in both lignite and bituminous coals to such an extent as to render them unfit for smelting iron ores (on account of the strong affinity of sulphur for iron), until they have been made into coke ; hence the greater value of charcoal and anthracite in the manufacture of iron.

We made a hasty journey to the region about Fort Belknap, and saw that the coal measures, in their characteristic forms, occupy a large extent of country in Young and its adjacent counties. The rocks are sandstones, limestones, and shales with seams of bituminous coal. They have the well-known fossils peculiar to the coal measures of the Western States in the upper valley of the Mississippi. There is a bed of coal about three quarters of a mile above Fort Belknap, in a small ravine near the Colorado River. From this place coal was obtained both for fuel and for blacksmithing, when the fort was occupied by the government troops. After the removal of the soldiers, the bank above the coal fell in, so that now there is no good view of the coal-bed. We saw this bed of coal exposed higher up the ravine, with a thickness of about three feet. On Whisky Creek, about two miles north of Fort Belknap, there is a fine exposure of the coal, where there is the following section near its mouth, a few rods from the Colorado :

    1. Surface soil, sandy loam . . . . .1–2 feet.
    2. Sandstone (conglomerate) . . . . 44 "
    3. Coal . . . . 1½ "
    4. Sandstone and shale alternating . . . . 8 "

5. Coal .... $3\frac{1}{2}$ feet
6. Sandstone .... 26 "
7. Shale and limestone (fossiliferous) .... 2 "
8. Coal .... $1\frac{1}{2}$ "
9. Light gray friable shale to bed of stream .... 3 "

A few hundred yards higher up the stream, where coal has been mined to some extent, and where one man is said to have dug out seventy-five bushels in a day of a good quality of coal, there is the following section :

1. Slope covered with sandstone .... —
2. Black, yellow, and-ash colored shales .... 10 feet.
3. Fine grained sandstone .... $\frac{1}{2}$ "
4. Blue fire-clay .... $1\frac{1}{2}$ "
5. Coal 4
6. Clay containing selenite .... $\frac{1}{2}$ "
7. Slope to the creek .... —

Here the sandstone above the coal contains coal-plants, and is ripple marked. There are several other places on Whisky Creek where the coal crops out. North of Fort Belknap about six miles, near Judge Harmonson's, is a seam of coal five feet thick. This bed is exposed along the base of the hill from twenty to twenty-five rods. Coal has also been obtained here both for fuel and blacksmithing. On the Camp Colorado road, in several places in Buchanan county, we saw seams of coal exposed in the hill-sides. In Palo Pinto county, bituminous coal occurs, and is used by blacksmiths of that section. The rocks in the bituminous coal region are in nearly horizontal layers, or dip at small angles. There are salt springs in the eastern part of Llano county, and also in the western part of Lampasas county, where sufficient salt for the wants of the country is made.

In the geological rooms at Austin, previous to the late war, were specimens of gold, silver, copper, and lead, obtained by casual explorers in the western and north-western parts of the State. Those of gold and silver have been taken away, but there still remain in the cabinet rich specimens of copper and lead from those regions. Geological indications, and these specimens, lead us to confidently predict that those portions of the State have vast mineral wealth. Our extensive lignite and bituminous coal-beds and bituminous springs in various sections of the State, which our limits will not permit us to notice, also promise large yields of petroleum.

CII.

THE MINERAL RESOURCES OF TEXAS.

BY S. B. BUCKLEY, OF AUSTIN.

(From the Texas Almanac.)

IRON.

In the previous article we gave some account of the iron hill in Llano county, where there is a solid mass of magnetic oxide of iron, surrounded by azoic granite. This ore was smelted to a limited extent during the war. It yields about 75 per cent. of metallic iron, and there is enough of the ore to supply the iron wants of the entire South for ages. During the past season we have twice visited Llano county, and found that iron ores abound in other sections there, especially in the vicinity of Pack-saddle Mountain, where there are immense beds of the brown oxide of iron (limonite) in the Potsdam rocks, not far from the Llano River, in the eastern part of the county. These limonite beds extend at intervals to the town of Burnet, in Burnet county. About three miles south of this town, on Hamilton's Creek, an iron foundry for smelting and casting has been lately erected. This foundry is in the midst of a wooded region. The ores smelted afford about 70 per cent. of metallic iron. Limonite is one of the most important iron ores, and its purer varieties, when smelted with charcoal, are easily convertible into steel. At the time of our visit to this foundry (June, 1861), the works were so far completed that they expected soon to begin smelting, and to be able to sell castings, at about one-half of the usual prices in this portion of Texas, and realize a handsome profit. Burnet and Llano, being both timbered counties, will afford sufficient wood to make charcoal for the manufacture of iron during many years. These counties abound in hills, mountains, and streams, giving health and the best of water power, affording almost unequaled advantages to the manufacturer.

In Eastern Texas, iron ores are very abundant throughout a large part of the country east of the Trinity River and north of latitude 30°. These ores include two forms, hematites and limonites, which are the species from which most of the iron of commerce is made. At Nash's iron foundry, in Marion county, iron was made both before and during the war. The ore used at this foundry is said to yield 60 to 75 per cent. of metallic iron. Charcoal is used in its manufacture; wood is abundant in that section. The best iron ores of Texas yields a larger per cent. than those of most of the ores smelted in the older States. Not only are these superior iron ores common, but they are also at and near the surface, where they are waiting to be placed in furnaces and be smelted. With such ores in such quantities, and with such great facilities for their manufacture, it will be strange, and show a great want of economy in her people, if Texas does not, ere long, export instead of import iron.

Very little has yet been done toward smelting the iron ores of Texas. Nash's is, we believe, the oldest foundry for that purpose, and there the business has never been on a large scale, nor the machinery of the first-class, suitable to make bar iron or steel. At one or two foundries in Cherokee county, iron ores have smelted to a limited extent. Texas needs large iron foundries and rolling-mills for the manufacture of bar and railroad iron. A few hundred thousand dollars expended in this way will save millions to the State. The advantages here for the manufacture of iron are: a home market, plenty of fuel, both wood and coal, lime rocks, steatites or soap stones for furnaces, the best of water-power, a delightful and healthy climate, provisions cheap and abundant.

COAL.

The bituminous coal-fields in Young and its adjacent counties in Northern Texas were partly described by us in the preceding article, and also in our preliminary report, since which no further geological examinations of these coals have been made. The railroads projected and now in process of construction will soon make this coal available.

In March last, accompanied by Dr. Lincecum, of Washington county, we visited a large coal deposit which extends from Little River in Milam county to the east side of the Brazos in Robertson county, a distance of from fifteen to twenty miles. Here there are two beds of coal, the upper of which is from ten to twelve feet thick, and the lower has a thickness of from three to four feet, as reported by Mr. Caleb Pendarvis, who sank a well about ten feet below the lower coal strata. Mr. Pendarvis could not give a true section of his well, it having been dug several years previous. We heard of other persons finding similar beds of coal in digging wells throughout the country intervening between the coal on Little River and that of the Brazos, which, joined with a similarity of the strata of rocks at the coal-beds of both rivers, renders it pretty certain that the beds are continuous from river to river.

At Little River we measured the following section:

1. Surface dark loam .... 3 feet.
2. Yellowish-red clay and sand .... 4 "
3. Yellow and blue shales .... 10 "
4. Coal .... 8 to 10 "
5. Fire-clay and black shale to bed of stream .... 8 "

The bed·of coal crops out for several hundred feet along Little River, on the plantation of Mrs. Middleton, about six miles west of Port Sullivan. The bed of coal here varies in thickness from five to twelve feet. Both the Brazos and Little River were so high that we could not see the lower bed of coal at either place. On the east side of the Brazos the coal-bed extends about 700 yards along the banks of the river, on the plantation of Thomas P. Tindall, about nine miles above Port Sullivan. Here the thickness of coal is greater than on the Little River, the coal seam in some places being nearly fifteen feet thick. We tested this coal and found it to burn well. Mr. Tindall informed us that he intended to have grates to burn this coal put in the fire-place of a house he was about building. It is certainly a good fuel for all ordinary purposes; but, like most bituminous coals, it contains too much sulphur to be used in smelting iron unless it has previously been coked. The weather could have been scarcely more unfavorable than it was at the time of our visit there. A cold norther prevailed. Late rains had flooded the country. The roads were nearly impassable, and all streams uncommonly high, hence our examinations were hasty and very imperfect. We did not find any fossils in their native beds, so that we are uncertain in regard to the geological period of this coal. It is not older than the triassic, nor younger than the oldest tertiary. We saw undoubted cretaceous rocks but a few miles west of the coal, and also those of the eocene of the tertiary, near Owensville, in Robertson county, about twenty miles east of the coal-bed at Mr. Tindall's.

Throughout the older tertiary rocks of Texas extensive beds of brown coal, or lignite, are quite common, extending from Rusk county, in Eastern Texas, south-westward through Leon, Burleson, Bastrop, Caldwell, and Guadaloupe counties, as far west as the Nueces River. Some of these beds in Bastrop county are five feet thick, and of a pretty good quality of coal, so much so that they will, without doubt, in time be extensively used. Such brown coals are now used in Germany for all purposes except smelting and working iron, for which, it is said, they are unfit, because they will not make a good coke.

COPPER.

Copper occurs through several counties north of Fort Belknap, especially in Archer county, where extensive deposits and veins have been found during the present season. For working this copper there is a company with a large capital. The ore is remarkably rich, abundant, and easy to be obtained, lying scattered over the surface, or in veins in loose sand-rock, apparently of the upper carboniferous or Permian period. It yields 60 per cent. of copper, according to an analysis made of some ore which was sent to New York by

Governor Thockmorton. In the State cabinet we have rich specimens of copper ore from Presidio county and other parts of Western Texas. During the present season we have again visited the copper veins on the head-waters of the Little Llano River, in Llano county, which were noticed before. These copper lands have been bought by parties who intend to work for copper as soon as they can make the proper preparations. The copper interest of Texas promises to be next in importance to that of iron.

LEAD.

The State collection has numerous specimens of galena, or sulphuret of lead, from Western Texas, beyond the settlements. The calciferous sand rock, which is the lead-bearing rock of Missouri, abounds in Burnet, San Saba, and Llano counties, hence it is not improbable that lead will yet be found in that region. This is already reported to have been done. We have been told several times this summer, by different men, that they have seen bullets made from lead ore obtained in Llano county. The knowing parties will not tell where the ore is, because they wish to secure the land.

BISMUTH.

This rare metal has been found associated with copper in the copper region of Northern Texas during the present season. It is said to be quite abundant. It was at first supposed to be silver, to which it has striking resemblance in color and weight. It is the native bismuth, and occurs in massive layers, and if as abundant as represented in the letter accompanying some specimens of it which were sent to Governor Thockmorton, which were referred to us, it will be a valuable addition to the mineral wealth of Texas. Nearly if not all the bismuth used in the United States is obtained almost exclusively from Germany, where it is smelted from cobalt ores, at the rate of about 7 per cent. of bismuth. It is not as valuable as silver, but more valuable than lead. It forms useful alloys with other metals.

SILVER.

The State collection has some specimens of silver from some locality in Western Texas which is unknown to us. The old Mexicans are said to have worked rich silver mines near old Fort San Saba, and also in Llano county. The richness of these old mines has doubtless been much exaggerated, if even they were ever worked at any profit. The geological formations at these places are those of the older metamorphic rocks, and those of the Lower Silurian (Potsdam), in which silver may or may not be found. It is often found mixed with lead and copper ores.

GOLD.

Gold has been found in small quantities in Burnet, Llano, and Mason counties, in the sands of some few streams in the granite region. One of the most successful gold-hunters is said to have washed out from the sands of Sandy Creek, near Pack-saddle Mountain, in Llano county, about two ounces of gold dust, valued at thirty dollars, in three weeks. Others are said to have obtained gold to the value of fifty cents a day, and others none. This is surely not encouraging to the seekers after gold in those regions. We believe that gold has not yet been found in paying quantities in Texas. In the geological rooms we have heaps of rocks, containing either yellow mica or the sulphurets of iron or copper, which have been brought to us by parties supposing that they had found gold.

MARBLE.

Burnet and San Saba counties have large deposits of excellent marbles, comprising those which are white, variegated, and black. These are at and near the Marble Falls on the Colorado River, and also at the Mormon Mills in Burnet county, in San Saba, at Simpson's Spring, about three miles from the county-seat, and also at various other places in those counties. These marbles are in the Potsdam of the Lower Silurian rocks, and are in sufficient quantities to supply the entire South.

GYPSUM.

On the Upper Red River and its branches is the largest known deposit of gypsum in the world. The gypsum beds spread over a country of several hundred miles in extent. The time is not distant when this gypsum will be of very large value to the State, especially to the farmers of North-eastern and Eastern Texas, to be used as a fertilizer joined with red clover. We have not the least doubt but that this clover will do well in that section, if sprinkled with gypsum. The productiveness of the lands of other countries has often been more than doubled by the use of clover and gypsum, and the same results would follow their use on any of the sandy clay soils of Texas.

FELDSPAR, PORCELAIN, AND POTTER'S CLAYS.

In June last we found large veins forming large beds of feldspar on the tract of land about four miles north-east of the Pack-saddle Mountain. This will be valuable for the manufacture of the finer kinds of porcelains. We know of but one other deposit of feldspar as large as that of Llano county in the United States. This is near Middletown, Connecticut, where it is

32

quarried for manufacturing purposes. Kaolin is a decomposed feldspar. Porcelain clays, of a good quality, abound in Washington, Austin, and other counties. The common potter's clays are throughout a large portion of the State ; more than sufficient for the wants of the people.

SALT.

Salt is made extensively at Swenson's Saline, in the western part of Lampasas county ; also, in smaller quantities in the eastern part of Llano county. The salt of both these places is of an excellent quality. The salt water is obtained from the Lower Silurian rocks. Large deposits of salt exist near the Horse Head Crossing of the Pecos, in Western Texas, from whence it is hauled by teams to supply the frontier settlements. West of Corpus Christi the country in the vicinity of a large shallow salt lagoon is overflown during winter winds, which, being evaporated by the summer sun, leaves a deposit of clean white salt, several inches thick. We have specimens of this salt, in small lumps and crystals ; these, being ground in an ordinary flouring-mill, form a fine table salt. The annual supply made at these natural salt-works is very large.

PETROLEUM

has not yet, we believe, been obtained in paying quantities in Texas. The borings made for coal-oil near Nacogdoches and in the vicinity of Sour Lake have not, as far as we can ascertain, been yet successful. The present season we have examined " tar " springs in Bell county, and also near Burnet, in Burnet county, and at a place about nine miles north of Austin, on the Waco road. We have reported that the finding of large quantities of petroleum at these places would be very uncertain. Still it must be remembered that this uncertainty prevails in the best oil regions. From the best information we have, it is very certain that more fortunes have been lost than made, even in the best oil sections of Pennsylvania.

CIII.

THE COAL-BEDS OF TEXAS.

BY PROFESSOR S. B. BUCKLEY, OF THE GEOLOGICAL SURVEY.

This is but a continuation of former sketches of the mineral resources of Texas published in the *Texas Almanac* for 1867 and 1868. Since the publication of the *Almanac* for 1868, I have again visited the coal deposit in Milam and Robertson counties, and find the extent and thickness of the coal greater than I then reported. It has an exposed thickness in the Brazos, a short distance below the old dwelling of Mr. Herndon, of about twenty feet, at a place where its base can not be seen and where the coal-beds extend across the river. It crops out for nearly one mile on the river at the Herndon and Tindall plantations. It also has a large exposure, two or three miles above Mr. Herndon's, on both sides of the Brazos at the Ranger place, where it can only be seen at low water, and then only the upper portion of the coal-bed is visible.

It extends from Little River north-eastwardly to the Brazos, beyond which it continues in the same direction five or six miles, and perhaps further. A gentleman told me that he had seen a coal-bed about twelve miles east of the Brazos in the direction of Owensville, but whether it belongs to the Brazos River coal-bed or not, I can not tell.

At both the Herndon and Tindall plantations the coal has little or no rock roof, but instead it is covered with from four to six feet of clay and dark vegetable soil, as seen on the banks of the river. Hence to obtain the coal, it will be necessary to leave its upper portion for a roof, and perhaps also support it more or less with timbers and planks. This lessens the value of these coal lands very much, and may prevent their being worked in some places. However, the clay next the coal is generally hard, and it, with a portion of the upper part of the coal, which is also hard, will perhaps require very little if any support to form a firm roof. In some places, a stratum of sandstone about six inches thick is next the upper part of the coal-bed, immediately above which is tenacious blue clay, overlaid by a friable shale; while in others the sandstone is wanting, leaving the clay and shale at the top of the coal. The thickness of this clay and shale is from two to four feet, above which is a hard red or yellowish clay and soil from four to six feet thick. This occurs on the banks of the Brazos River, and also on those of the Little River. In the intervening hills between the two rivers, the coal is at a greater depth, and the mass above more solid, being sometimes rocky and at others blue clay and shale. Concretions of sand and limestone, many of them of large size, even from five to ten feet in diameter, abound in the strata of the hills which overlie the coal. These concretions are loose in large quantities in the bed of the Brazos, at the Herndon, Tindall, and Ranger plantations, and also at the outcrop of the coal on Little River. In some of these loose rocks at the Herndon and Ranger places, I found cretaceous fossils, but none in the banks *in situ*, or in their native beds. Also the soil above the coal on the rivers in several places has cretaceous fossils, but none *in situ*. They are but little water-worn, and evidently have had very little transportation. These are gryphæas, exogyras, and several other species.

This coal has been tested as a fuel for ordinary purposes, in the grate and furnace, where it burns well and leaves but little ashes. It can probably be coked, and if so, it will do very well for the manufacture of iron. It is strongly impregnated with bitumen, and will be valuable for the manufacture of gas. Taken as a whole, it is a good article of bituminous coal, and, if it can be quarried without too much expense, it will be a source of great wealth to the State.

I have not been able to obtain fossils *in situ,* so as to determine its age with certainty; but judging from those found in loose rocks in the bed of the Brazos, mixed with those derived from the strata belonging to the coal series, it belongs to the mesozoic age, and was probably deposited during the cretaceous period. There is no reason why coal should not be formed during that period as well as in the other groups of the mesozoic age, the triassic and Jurassic. Nor is it reasonable to suppose that during the long time required to form the cretaceous rocks, the earth in some places did not contain shallow seas, bogs, swamps, and a dense vegetation suited to the formation of coal. However, we need not expect to find coal in most of the cretaceous rocks of Texas, which were mostly deposited in deep seas extending over large areas, destitute of land vegetation. This is proven by their fossils, which belong to oceanic forms. The Milam and Robertson coal-bed lies on the borders of the cretaceous, near to the eocene, which is the oldest member of the tertiary age.

On and near the tops of the hills west of the Brazos, and opposite the Herndon plantation, are large deposits of iron ore in masses. It is a hematite. A gentleman, who had formerly been county surveyor of Milam county, informed me that he had taken some of this ore to Nashville, Tennessee, for analysis, and that it yielded sixty per cent. of metallic iron. I am indebted to Judge Terrill, of Houston for a knowledge of this ore, he having kindly guided me to the spot. Material for the manufacture of this ore is abundant in that neighborhood, which, joined to the nearness of the Central Railroad, and also to the cities of Houston and Galveston, will probably ere long, induce some company to undertake its manufacture.

The lignite beds of Texas occur in a belt of country extending from Zavala county, in the south-western part of the State, north-eastwardly to Bowie county, on the Red River. The intervening counties in which coal has been observed are Bexar, Bastrop, Burleson, Brazos, Robertson, Leon, Houston, Rusk, and Davis. In Bastrop county, some of these lignite beds are upward of five feet thick, as seen by the writer, on the banks of Cedar Creek.

Dr. Hayden, United States geologist for Nebraska, extended his explorations into Colorado and Dakota during the past season for the purpose of examining the great lignite deposits of the Laramie plains, where this coal

CATHEDRAL AT MEXICO.

occurs in beds of from five to eleven feet thick, extending over an estimated area of about five thousand miles. He reports some of these lignite beds to be of excellent quality, equaling the best bituminous coal. The Marshall mines, on South Boulder Creek, are very valuable : the coal of these mines has been used for several years, selling in Denver at from twelve to twenty-five dollars per ton.

Dr. Hayden also finds indications of an abundance of iron ore near some of the Laramie deposits of lignite, and says the Union Pacific Railroad Company intend to establish rolling-mills there at no distant day.

I allude to these western lignites, because I was the first geologist to call attention to the value of the lignite beds of Texas in my Preliminary Report of the Texas Geological Survey, published in 1866. Our former State geologists considered them of little or no value, and said so frequently, from whence many intelligent people of Texas still consider lignite as worthless.

There is no doubt but that these tertiary coals will yet be a source of much wealth to the State. They belong to the eocene, the oldest member of the tertiary group, and are certainly worthy of the careful examination of the geologist, and those who seek to develop the mineral wealth of the State.

The bituminous coal-field at Fort Belknap has a greater extent than has been heretofore described. It not only occurs in Young county, but also in Jack, Palo Pinto, Parker, Stevens, Throckmorton, and probably other adjoining counties. The recent discovery of rich copper ores in Archer and other counties north and north-west of Young county, adds much to the value of this coal. From the reports of explorers, and also from specimens in the State cabinet at Austin, it is probable that there is a large region abounding in copper and other valuable ores extending southwardly from Archer county into Presidio and El Paso counties. Hence, our legislators should not be in haste to sell or give way these latter counties, at least not until they have had a geological exploration and their true value been ascertained. If rich ores abound there, their development will soon attract a population which will do much toward protecting our frontiers from the Indians.

Enough is already known of the coal and iron deposits of Texas, to place her in the first rank as a State abounding in rich iron ores, which only need to be manufactured to enable her to supply the iron wants of the entire South. When this is done she will be the Empire State of the South in commerce, manufactures, and agriculture.

The example of the Pacific Railroad Company in the manufacture of its own cars and railroad iron is worthy of imitation by our Texas railroad companies, especially as we have the raw materials in iron, coal, and wood, suitable for manufactures, and equal in goodness to those of any country in the world.

CIV.

CLIMATOLOGY OF TEXAS.

BY PROFESSOR C. G. FORSHEY, SUPERINTENDENT TEXAS MILITARY INSTITUTE.

(From Texas Almanac.)

I. GEOGRAPHICAL POSITION.

THE State of Texas is bounded on the north by Red River, nearly on the 34th parallel, from the 94th to the 100th meridian ; on the east, by the Sabine, nearly along the 94th meridian ; on the south, by the Gulf of Mexico, whose coast has a south-western trend, from latitude 29° 45′, long. 93° 55′, to the 97th meridian, and thence it bears nearly south, from lat. 28° to 26°, where it reaches the 98th meridian. The Rio Grande is the western boundary, hence to lat 32°, at long. 106° 30.′

For the purposes of this paper, devoted to Texas climatology, all that portion of the State lying west of the 100th meridian will be excluded, except when expressly embraced. Further and more exact information is necessary before that region can be described ; and a much denser population must be carried thither, before that description will be needed.

II. CLIMATIC DIVISIONS.

The area of Texas presents two distinct climates, with an intermediate region, sharing, in a marked degree, the peculiarities of both. These are bounded by lines, or belts of longitude, rather than of latitude, and are dependent upon hygrometric rather than thermal considerations.

By pursuing and applying the principles announced in the chapter on meteorology ; and giving due force to geographic causes, we shall best describe and give bounds to the two climates adverted to, and account for the many discordant phenomena along the neutral area between them.

As shown in the principles of meteorology, if all the water the air can hold at 80°, were suddenly condensed upon the earth, its depth would not much exceed five inches ; and as the air never parts with all its vapor, not indeed much more than half of it, it becomes obvious that the moving atmosphere has to perform the offices of irrigation, by visiting the reservoirs of water, taking up their burden of vapor, and carrying and discharging it over the thirsty earth.

The southerly winds alone, in Texas, have such a direction as to bring us

* In writing upon climatology, we presume the reader to be familiar with the general laws of meteorology. A short synopsis of these doctrines is presented in another chapter in this volume, to which chapter we will ask the attention of the readers of this essay.

water. The Gulf of Mexico is our reservoir. All west winds and north winds are thirsty, and come to drink up and bear away the water our south winds have pumped up from the Gulf of Mexico and sprinkled over us.

III. THE SOUTH WINDS,

1. The winds of spring, summer, and autumn, and a due portion of the winter, blow from the south, across the area of Texas. Along the Gulf coast, from the Sabine to the Brazos, the direction of this wind is from a point east of south; from the Brazos to the Lavaca Bay it is from due south; and from all the Gulf and Mexican bounds of Texas, west of Lavaca, it is believed that the wind has a little westing. This last, however, lacks the testimony of systematic observations.

2. This south wind, starting from near the boundary of the regular trades, and running in a counter direction, has a mean velocity of some five miles per hour, at the coast, and diminishes in force as it progresses interior. On the parallel 34°, I found it scarcely perceptible, in August, 1858. The inhabitants say, it is usually more active. It may have a force of two miles per hour. It comes from the Gulf, charged with vapor, almost to saturation. At every degree interior, it has less and less of this vapor, so that the vigor it imparts to vegetation, even in the most obstinate droughts, within the first seventy miles of its travel from the coast, is greatly lessened, and at $2\frac{1}{2}°$ is nearly inappreciable.

3. These remarks, as to the humidity of the south wind, must of course be confined to that portion of Texas lying northwardly from the Gulf. Both theory and experience prove that in all those western portions of the State where the south wind comes not over the Gulf, it can have little or nothing of the humidity that marks the character of the same wind east of long. 97°, or 98° west. For in the travel of such wind as passes from south to north, along meridians west of the Gulf of Mexico, it is obvious they have no opportunity to imbibe humidity, after their passage over the Cordilleras. Those mountains have an average elevation of more than 10,000 feet, or two miles. All winds ascending then from the level of the Pacific, even if saturated in starting, must have their dew-point depressed by near 30° in ascending; and in descending to the plains on the side of the mountains, must be very dry winds. Hence the Dry Region of Western Texas.

4. The south wind is a thin stratum, often not exceeding two or three thousand feet, while the strata above, often two or more, have different directions, and a very different condition, as to the vapor they bear.

5. At times, and especially during winter, in the interval between northers, a stream of north wind blows briskly over the south wind, for some time before it can break through to the earth, and form the real norther. While this

is transpiring, rain s quite impossible, however well supplied with vapor the thin stratum of south wind may be; for, whenever it ascends, in a manner to produce rain, by reduction of temperature, it mingles with the north current, which is so very thirsty as to drink up every particle of vapor.

6. And even when the south wind accumulates considerable thickness— for it grows thicker by continuing long—and extends from the earth's surface up to the base of the cirrus region, the attempts to produce rain are often defeated by the greedy aridity of that great upper current, which has come over the Cordilleras. Still, rain is more abundant under these circumstances than when there is a north wind interposed between the regular south wind and upper south-west stratum of the air.

7. Hence, for these considerations, the fluctuating character of the seasons between the meridians 96° and 98° west.

8. The south winds are the source o fcomfort and positive luxury to the inhabitants of Texas during the hot weather of summer.

The nearer the sea-coast, the cooler and more brisk the current. But the entire area of prairie, and a large portion of the timbered country, feel it as a pleasant, healthful breeze, rendering our highest temperature tolerable.

Causes which produce and direct the South Wind.

9. The sun heats up the air, over the land more than over the sea; and lands not covered by forests radiate more heat than those that are shaded. The air over the prairie portion of Texas, then, has a tendency to rise, and the cooler air from the Gulf flows outward to replace it. This, in its turn, heats up, and rises as it travels onward, calling for still other supplies of refreshing air from the Gulf. As the prairie portion of the State lies chiefly west of Galveston Bay, or meridian 95°, the south wind comes from points east of south, up to this meridian.

10. This south wind is doubtless supplied, along the border of trades, by a *descent* of the upper stratum of *reflux* trades, which current has a motion northward before its descent, and thus adds considerably to the force with which it flows onward.

11. The retardation, mentioned above as noticeable at a distance from the Gulf, is caused by the large admixture of this south wind above with the south-west reflux trades. The latter *always* moves slowly, and gradually merges this Texan south wind, and bears it off north-eastwardly, between lat. 34° and 38°.

IV. TABLE SHOWING THE AMOUNT OF RAIN FOR THE SEVERAL LONGITUDES FROM THE MISSISSIPPI RIVER TO THE RIO GRANDE, LONG. 106.

PLACE OF OBSERVATION.	Lat.	Long.	INCHES OF RAIN BETWEEN LONG.					No. Years Mean.
			101–107	99–101	97–99	95–97	90–95	
	° ′	° ′						
Fort Galena, Minn....	46 19	94 19	....	....	....	....	29.48	4 years.
Fort Laramie, Neb....	42 12	104 47	19.98	....	....	....	....	2 "
Fort Des Moines, Io..	41 32	93 38	....	....	....	....	26.56	2 "
Fort Crawford, Wis. ...	40 05	91 00	....	....	....	....	31.40	7 "
Jefferson Barracks, Mo.	38 28	90 15	....	....	....	....	41.95	15 "
Fort Mass, N. Mex....	37 32	105 23	20.54	....	....	....	....	"
Fort Union, "	35 54	104 57	19.24	....	....	....	....	3 "
Santa Fé, "	35 41	106 02	19.83	....	....	....	32.35	2¼ "
Fort Gibson, Ark......	35 47	95 10	....	....	....	36.46	....	17 "
Fort Smith, Ark	35 23	94 29	....	....	....	42.10	....	13 "
Fort Arbuckle, I. Ter..	34 27	97 09	....	....	30.57	....	....	4 "
Fort Towson, I. Ter...	34 00	95 23	....	....	....	51.08	....	10 "
Fort Belknap, Tex....	33 08	98 48	....	....	20.00	....	....	2 "
Fort Worth, Texas....	32 40	97 25	....	....	40.86	....	....	3 ? "
Fort Phantom Hill, Tex.	32 30	99 45	....	17.22	....	....	....	1 "
Fort Graham, Tex....	31 56	97 26	....	....	40.58	....	....	2 "
Fort Chadbourne, Tex.	31 38	100 40	....	31.88	....	....	....	2 "
Fort Jessup, La.......	31 33	93 32	....	....	....	....	45.85	9 "
Fort McKavitt, Tex...	30 50	100 00	....	23.27	....	....	...	4 "
Fort Croghan, Tex....	30 40	98 31	....	....	36.56	....	....	3 "
Baton Rouge.........	30 26	91 18	....	....	....	....	62.10	6 "
Webberville, Tex.....	30 18	97 25	....	....	32.59	....	....	3 "
Rutersville, Tex......	29 58	96 46	....	....	....	33.12	....	2½ "
New Orleans.........	29 57	90 00	....	....	....	....	60.90	6 "
San Antonio, Tex.....	29 25	98 25	....	....	33.77	....	....	2 "
Fort Clark, Tex.......	29 17	100 25	....	21.80	....	....	....	2 "
Fort Inge, Tex.......	29 09	99 47	....	27.99	....	....	....	4 "
Fort Duncan, Tex.....	28 42	100 30	....	22.20	....	....	....	5 "
Fort Merill, Tex......	28 17	98 00	....	....	30.82	....	....	2 ."
Fort Ewell, Tex	28 05	98 57	....	....	30.82	....	....	2 "
Corpus Christi, Tex...	27 47	97 27	....	....	30.82	....	....	2 "
Fort McIntosh, Tex...	27 31	99 22	....	18.66	....	....	....	5 "
Ringgold Barracks, Tex.	26 23	97 02	....	....	20.95	....	....	5 "
Fort Brown, Tex......	25 54	97 26	....	....	33.65	....	....	5 "
Mean rain, in inches.........			19.90	23.29	31.25	42.11	47.32	

NOTE.—Along lat. 30° to 31°, from New Orleans at 9° W., to Fort McKavitt, in Menard county, Texas, 100° W., the amount of rain for the four years up to 1855, is reduced from 61 inches to 23¼ inches. And from 97°, which is nearly tangent to the Gulf of Mexico, to 100°, the reduction is from 33 inches to 23 inches.

An inspection of this table, collated from various authorities, chiefly from Reports to the War Department, will demonstrate all we have alleged as to the two climates, with a force from which there is no appeal.

V. TEXAS NORTHERS.

Number and Duration.

1. During seven or eight months of every year, Texas is liable to a class of storms, or winds, styled "*northers*" from the direction from which they come.

2. In the year 1857, there were twenty-six northers experienced at the Texas Military Institute, in Fayette county. Of these some two or three were gentle or baffled northers. They occupied fifty-seven days, having an average of two and one-fifth days in length. The latest in spring, was May 16, and earliest in autumn, was November 7.

3. In the year 1858 there were thirty-seven northers, about thirty-three of which might be classed as *well marked*, the others being either gentle or baffled northers. These occupied seventy-eight days. The latest in spring was May 9, and the earliest in autumn was October 7.

4. In the first half of 1859, there have been twenty-four northers, of which four may be described as gentle or baffled northers. They have occupied forty-seven days in their transit, and the latest was May 24.

5. It is proper to remark that nearly all the northers of May and October are mild, and rarely do much damage, or produce so low a temperature as to be severely felt. All the other months, November to April inclusive, are liable to northers of considerable severity.

6. It appears then, that in thirty months last past, of which eighteen months are liable to distinct northers, we have experienced eighty northers, not including the feeble ones of May and October. The same period has seventy-seven weeks, very nearly affirming the hypothesis of *weekly returns* of the norther. An inspection of the table shows a large number of punctual weekly recurrences of this meteor.

7. At this place of observation their duration varies from one to four days.

Area and Boundaries of Norther.

8. The region over which this peculiar storm has its sweep, is not very great, though its precise limits can not be defined: By diligent inquiry from persons of great experience, we submit the following limits:

9. On the north, by the valley of Red River, in the Indian Territory ;* on on the east, by the second tier of counties† from the east boundary of Texas, near meridian 95°, south to the Trinity, and thence south-east to the mouth of the Sabine. On the south they are felt across the Gulf, to the coast of South Mexico and Yucatan. On the west they are bounded by the Sierra Madre,

---

* Senator Throckmorton.　　　† Colonel M. T. Johnson.

up to the mouth of the Pecos, and thence by about the 101st meridian to the sources of Red River.

10. Within this area there are various degrees of violence, having their axis of intensity between meridians 97° and 98° *, and increasing in force and duration, the further south. At Red River, on this line, they are usually limited to a day or two; whereas at Corpus Christi † and Matamoras, one norther often continues till the next supersedes it; and at Vera Cruz, a twenty-days norther is not remarkable.

West of Fort Belknap, to the Pecos, the northers grow feebler and rarer.‡ North of Red River, on the route from Fort Washita to Fort Smith, they are rarely felt.

On the east margin they are much modified by the forests of the timbered region. At all points, an open prairie increases their vigor.

Forces and other Phenomena.

11. The norther usually commences with a violence nearly equal to its greatest force, if its initial point be near the observer. If it has traveled some distance, it will be warmed up, and moderated in its violence, at first attack. Its greatest force might be marked 5, in a scale between a gentle breeze at 1, and a hurricane at 10. The writer has measured one traveling at about thirty-two miles per hour—but many others at twelve to eighteen miles. The mean progress seems to be about fifteen miles per hour.

12. Just before a norther, two to six hours, the south wind lulls, and the still air becomes very oppressive. A low black cloud rolls up from the north, and when it comes near the zenith, the wind strikes with vigor. Sometimes we have a sudden dash of rain; but generally northers are intensely dry, and soon drink up all the moisture of the surface earth, and of the objects upon it, capable of yielding their humidity.

Great thirst of man, and all other animals, is experienced; an itching sensation over the skin; a highly electric condition of the skin of horses and cats; a wilting and withering of vegetation, even when the temperature would not account for it; a reduction of temperature, usually very sudden, sometimes, though rarely, a degree per minute, for twenty minutes; and in winter commonly a reduction from 70° or 75°, to 30° or 40°.

This fall of temperature is the more severely felt from the drying power of the north wind—evaporation from the surface of the skin increasing the severity of the temperature.

13. Nervous, rheumatic, and gouty persons suffer more severely than others. To invalids suffering from other maladies, it has not been found

---

* Senator Lott says they begin in the west of Titus county, none in Cass.
† Senator Taylor, of Fannin.   ‡ Senators Maverick and Britton.

unhealthy ; and for persons of weak lungs, if not too much exposed to its direct fury, it is found to be more salubrious than the humid south winds. Consumptions do not originate over the area of the norther. On the contrary, many persons afflicted with weak or diseased lungs resort to this region and find relief. The western and northern portions of this area are most salubrious, and best adapted to weak lungs.

Theory of Cause and Mode of Operation.

14. *Hypothesis.*—Suppose, by any means, a cataract or plunge of air from the great upper current, traveling to the north-east, were poured down upon the earth, about the central or northern portion of the "norther" area, what would be its characteristics, and whither would it tend ?

15. It would be cold and dry. One mile of descent would bring a temperature 17° lower, and two miles, a temperature of 33°, provided the air should retain the temperature of that elevation. Its dew-point would be very low, though its descent should be but one mile ; for its elevation in crossing the Cordilleras could not be less than two miles, or 10,000 feet. Whatever its temperature, in descending, it must be intensely dry.

16. The barometer must rise during the cataract, for these two reasons : that the whole column, being dry, would be heavier than if the dew-point were high, and that the downward plunge of the air must raise the barometric column.

17. The direction in which this torrent would flow at the earth's surface, is determined by the same physical law that occasions water to run down hill. It is heavier than humid air, and must flow into the trades, to supply the demand that causes them. The direction would be south, until the current should reach the trades, and be deflected with them to the west.

18. After the cataract fairly commenced, it would widen and deepen ; it would rush by gusts along the ground, until its course was fairly established ; it would lift up the humid south wind, now saturated, or nearly so, and would condense its vapor into a thick, black cloud on its margin, and give a shower at the beginning. Its thirstiness, however, would enable it to drink up nearly all the vapor its cold would condense, so as to give but little rain. It would commence later, both in front and in rear of its initial point. It would increase in violence in both directions, but vastly more so in advance, where it would widen, and continue in violence and duration to the tropics.

19. *Application.*—All these are marked phenomena of the real norther, and hence, for the present, we adopt the hypothesis of a plunge or cataract of air from the upper regions, as the theory of this peculiar storm.

20. The unskilled meteorologist will receive this solution with less reluctance, when he is assured that between latitude 23° and 28°, there is a well-

established region of high barometer, in which the reflux trades send down to the surface of the earth a vast flood of air—by gentle descent—to resupply the trades, and to flow in the opposite direction, and form the south and south-west winds which prevail over all the southern half of the temperate zone, on this continent.

Our own life-giving south wind is fed by this general descent of air along the border of the tropics.

Phenomena not readily explicable.

21. When a dry norther commences, the whole air, in an hour or two, curdles and becomes smoky, or rather whitish, and has a distinct smell. Its odor sometimes resembles that which is developed by a flash of lightning, though, at other times, it reminds one of fine straw smoke, in its odor.

It is highly probable that this turbidness and odor are due to the ozone set free, by the high electrical excitation, in a dry norther. Experiments instituted to test the matter, last April, were too late in the season.

22. *Sirocco.*—When the norther has a little westing, it is observed to be more intensely dry, and to be destructive to vegetation, even before the frost which usually follows it. Corn, beans, young foliage, and the grass and weeds of the prairie, bow and wither before it.* A few of these I have called *siroccos.* They occur as well in summer as in spring or autumn, and differ, in several respects, from the true norther.

23. It is not a little remarkable, that the central violence, as well as the middle region, or axis of the norther, lies along the boundary between the two climates.

24. By way of aiding the observer to recognize this boundary, without knowing his longitude, we would call attention to certain indices in the animal and vegetable kingdom, which are entirely reliable, and are peculiar, or belong chiefly, to a dry climate :

Animals.—Mule-eared rabbit, civet-cat, Mexican hog.

Reptiles.†—Coachwhip, joint-snake, spreading-adder, Amphis Benæ or blind-snake, scorpion, and tarantula.

Birds.—Mexican buzzards, swallow-tailed fly-catcher or scissor-tail, prairie hawk.

Insects.—The cutting-ant and the devouring grasshopper.

---

* The citizens of Galveston, and the southern portions of Texas, will remember the violent north-wester in 1856, which preceded and attended the storm which wrecked the *Nautilus.* It was, in my judgment, a true sirocco. In like manner the north-west wind that withered the corn-fields in Lamar, Fannin, and Grayson, and the counties south of these, on the 17th day of August, 1858, deserve a like name.

† Reptiles of all kinds are vastly more numerous over the dry region.

Vegetation, Trees.—All of stunted growth, except on streams. The mesquit tree, infallible ; cactus plants ; Agave Americana, or aloes.

These will not be limited along a definite line, but will not be found far from, or numerous east of, longitude 97°. The Lower Cross Timbers lie nearly along the limit of all these indices.

VI. GENERAL CONSIDERATIONS.

1. This essay will have shown that the climatic divisions of Texas, as alleged in Article II., are founded upon natural, and therefore permanent, laws. Human interest is best consulted in the tracing out and early announcement of these laws, for every district of country. Fortunately for the future wealth and independence of the vast Empire State of Texas, she boasts these phases of climate ; for they beckon to enterprise and industry of such varied and mutually dependent kinds, as to warrant a large, a prosperous, and a happy population, on each climatic area.

2. The great staples, the cereals, the flocks, and the vines, these are the departments for investment and industry, which, with a diversified and extremely exuberant soil, shall give an abundant population and unrivaled prosperity to every district of the State, east of the one hundredth meridian.

3. The development of her resources, and the intelligent appropriation of her various soils and climates, each to its fittest purposes, must, in a very few years, render her the most powerful and the most enviable of the sisterhood of States ; and must enable her, better than any other member of the Union, should separation ever be her misfortune, to sustain herself alone, and to command the respect of mankind, for her empire of fertile acres, and for the diversity of industry and production that shall give her independence.

CV.

THE MIGRATORY LOCUST IN TEXAS.

In the fall of 1848 the grasshoppers made their first appearance in Travis and other neighboring counties. They came with the early fall winds in October, in swarms from the north, lighting and depositing their eggs everywhere ; always when it was convenient selecting sandy land to make their deposits in. After remaining a short time, and eating the fall gardens, they suddenly disappeared, no one knowing where. The warm sun of the following March again brought the little hoppers out, and, after eating the crops up in May they suddenly rose and took flight toward the north. The crops were again planted, and the season being favorable, there was an abundant harvest. We saw nothing more of them until in October, 1856, when they again came in swarms with the early north winds. After eating the blades off the wheat, and depositing their eggs, they disappeared. In the spring of 1857 myriads of little grasshoppers, about the size of large fleas, hatched and crawled out of the ground. Until they were about three weeks old, they did not travel or eat much. At that time they were about half-grown, and after shedding they started on foot toward the north, preserving as much regularity and order in their march as an army of well-drilled soldiers. Exercise seemed to have a wonderful effect on their appetites, for as soon as they commenced traveling they became perfectly ravenous, devouring almost every kind of tender vegetation, being extremely fond of young corn, but prefering young cotton to any thing else. They had no respect for place or persons, marching through the houses with impunity; and, what was worse than all, they were *cannibals*, for if you would cripple one and throw him down, his companions would eat him up instantly. When about six weeks old they again shed their outer garments, and came forth full-grown grasshoppers, with wings well developed, but nicely folded up, only wanting a few days' sunshine to dry and unfold and fit them for use. A few days afterward they all rose at once, as if by common consent, and took their flight toward the north. In the fall of 1857 they paid us a third visit, acting precisely as they had formerly done, with one exception. On former visits, when they once bid us farewell and started on their flight, we saw no more of them ; but in the spring of 1858, after having our crops in a part of the county destroyed by our own native grasshoppers, raised on the soil, a swarm of foreigners, hatched and bred in the south, between the Colorado and the Gulf of Mexico, were met in their journey north by adverse winds and driven down upon us, the poor, hungry, half-starved things staying with us ten days—just long enough to eat the most of the remainder of our crops. In the fall of 1858 we saw them again, high up in the clouds, passing toward the south; none, however, stopped here, and we saw nothing of them returning in the spring. It is to be hoped that the last one of them found a grave in the Gulf of Mexico. In flying, their wings glitter in the sun, and the whole sky has the appearance of being filled with moving flakes of snow. They come with the north wind in the fall, and return with the south wind in the spring.

CVI.

THE MESQUIT TREE:

ITS LATE RAPID GROWTH IN THE WEST—PROBABLE EFFECT OF THAT GROWTH UPON THE CLIMATE, OR IN CAUSING MORE SEASONABLE RAINS—THE REMARKABLE TANNING PROPERTIES OF THE MESQUIT.

THE writer of the following article alludes to the mesquit gum being identical in its properties to the gum acacia of commerce. Several years ago the compiler of this volume gathered a quantity of this gum and took it to New York City, where he exhibited it to several wholesale druggists, who pronounced it an excellent article of gum arabic and proposed to pay the highest market price for any quantity that could be furnished.

SEGUIN, TEXAS, June 30, 1869.

MESSRS. EDITORS : Your Almanac* is an admirable expedient for collecting the desired information respecting the resources and natural advantages of the State, and making them known to the world. An article in the *News* of the 25th inst., on the subject of tanning and the materials for the manufacture of leather, etc., suggests a brief article on

THE MESQUIT AND ITS ECONOMICAL USES.

Botanically, the mesquit belongs to the genus *Acacia*. It is leguminous, has pennate leaves, and is thorny. It yields a gum identical pretty much with gum arabic. It is to some extent gathered and used for the purposes to which that gum is applied. It is a wood of great durability, and resists decay in a remarkable degree, making it very valuable for posts, pickets, rails, etc. It shrinks but little in drying, and is but little affected by being wetted and dried. This property adapts it for use in making furniture and certain parts of wagons and carriages, as hubs and felloes. The bean is rich and

* This article is taken from Texas Almanac.

nourishing; horses, cattle, and hogs are very fond of it, and are rapidly fattened upon it.

From the Colorado west, and particularly from the San Marcos, this tree is rapidly taking possession of the prairies, and changing them into timber lands. The change in this aspect in the last ten or twelve years is really remarkable. No one who has not seen the change could have believed that in so short a time, prairies, smooth and unobstructed by timber, could be occupied so densely by this growth, as a large portion of them are now seen to be. The next ten years will find this prairie land a timbered country, with trees large enough for useful purposes. During the late seasonable years its growth has been rapid. Two important results will follow this altered condition of the face of the country. First—stockmen this side of the Nueces River will be compelled, by the difficulty of controlling their herds of cattle and horses, etc., roaming at large over the prairies, to limit their number, improve their quality, and confine them in pastures. This will simplify the business, render it more pleasant and vastly more profitable. Second—this growth of timber will be attended with a marked climatic change. Western Texas will become much more seasonable than in its past history. It will never again be visited by such a series of droughts as desolated it in such a degree from 1856 to 1861. Uniform observation shows that the climate of countries, as to rain, is affected by the presence or absence of timber. As they are denuded of their forests, they become dryer and more subject to extremes as to the fall of rain. Egypt is a remarkable illustration of the effect of timber on climate. Some twenty or more millions of forest trees were planted by the order of one of the pachas many years ago. Their growth has given to the Delta of the Nile an annual fall of rain of about thirty days instead of three or four. The vast growth of timber over western Texas, we may reasonably conclude, will be attended with a marked climatic revolution.

MESQUIT A SUPERIOR TANNING MATERIAL.

Besides the value of mesquit for various purposes indicated, it is destined to be a source of vast wealth to Texas and the world, *as one of the best known materials for tanning and manufacturing leather.* During the war, when we were shut out from the world and cut off from the sources of our supply of the necessaries and comforts of life, we found ourselves under the necessity of meeting these wants from our own resources. Leather was an urgent necessity. Dr. J. Park, then of Seguin, an intelligent gentleman of a scientific turn of mind, directed his attention to the examination of the materials for tanning to be found in Western Texas. He tested the various barks usually used, and found the black-jack the richest in tannic acid, live-oak the next,

33

and post-oak to have the least of the oaks.   He then examined the mesquit, and found that the whole body of the wood was rich in tannin.   He ascertained that the wood was fully equal to the bark of the black-jack in quality and quantity—that it abounded in tannic acid.   This was an unexpected and very important discovery.   He made practical tests of it, and found it promptly acted in converting the hide into leather of a good quality.   He improvised a chopping machine, by which he reduced the wood and put it into a form to have the tannin extracted by boiling ; established a tannery, and successfully carried it on for some time after the war.   He was so fully satisfied of the value of the mesquit as a tanning material, that he took out a patent for his discovery.   The points established by the experiments made with the mesquit are the following, viz.

1. It is rich in tannin.

2. It is cheap, and of inexhaustible abundance.

3. By suitable machinery, it may be readily reduced into a form favorable for the extraction of the tannin by boiling or steaming.

4. It is prompt and effective as a tanning agent in precipitating the gelatine of the hide and converting it into leather.   It forms good leather in a shorter time than the tannin of the oak barks.

5. The quality of the leather is superior.

6. Its operation is such, from some peculiarity of the tannic acid it yields, that it prevents the decomposition of the hide, so that the tanning process may be successfully carried on during our hot season as well as during the winter.

The difficulty of tanning, successfully, in this climate during the hot months, with the ordinary tanning materials, is the liability of the hide to decompose or spoil in the center before the tannin, which is a powerful antiseptic, can reach it so as to preserve it.   With other materials the tanning process begins on the external surfaces of the hides, and gradually progresses toward the center.   Hence the liability of the hide to decompose in the middle and become spoiled before it is tanned.   The operation of the tannin from the mesquit is different.   When a hide is examined, by cutting it after it has been subjected for a sufficient time to the action of the mesquit ooze, it is found that the tannin has penetrated through and through it, and the tanning process has affected its center as well as its surface.   The whole body of the hide is thus preserved, so that there need be no loss from this cause, no matter how hot the weather is.   Western Texas has in the mesquit an agent which will exert a very important influence on her future—a source of exhaustless wealth which will enable her to manufacture all her millions of hides into the best of leather ; a material in sufficient quantity to manufacture leather for the whole country.   Let tanneries, then, spring up.   It is a business, properly conducted, highly profitable. And boot and shoe and harness man- ufacturing should follow, saving in our own country the immense sums we are now paying to enrich other sections and impoverish our own State.

J. M. WILSON.

CVII.

CONSTITUTIONAL GOVERNMENT IN TEXAS.

(From the Galveston News.)

I.

THE proposition for a convention to revise the present defective State constitution, and adopt one better suited to the wants of the people and the true spirit of free government, naturally calls for information and discussion on such reforms as may be regarded as necessary. On such occasions, a glance at the past, as well as an attempt to provide for the future, may not be without use, in the development of a harmonious system, embracing the lessons of experience as well as the theories of the most approved states- men of the day.

After the successful revolt of Mexico against the power of Spain, and prior to the year 1825 Texas and Coahuila were united to form a single State of the Mexican Republic, so called, though it can scarcely be said that there was any regular national government in Mexico. Under Spain it was the policy to keep the mass of the people of Mexico in a state of ignorance and vassalage. Almost every kind of useful learning was withheld from them. They were even prohibited from prosecuting an enlightened and general sys- tem of agriculture, and forbidden to manufacture any thing that could be pro- duced in Spain for exportation. They were subjected to arbitrary government. When, after the overthrow of the Spanish king, Ferdinand VII., by Napoleon, and the placing of Joseph Bonaparte on the throne, the Spanish viceroy in Mexico, Iturrigaray, endeavored to form a provisional government for the colony, partly composed of natives, the Spaniards in the Mexican capital refused to allow the native Mexicans any share in public affairs, armed them- selves, seized the viceroy at night, sent him a prisoner to Spain, and them- selves assumed control of affairs. This proceeding, which happened in 1808, was the beginning of conspiracies, on the part of the natives, to gain, in part at least, the control of their own affairs, and in 1810 a revolt broke out in the Province of Guanajuato, headed by the patriot priest Hidalgo, who was a man of ability and very much esteemed by the natives. The movement was directed to the expulsion of the Spaniards and the establishment of an independent government.   A hundred thousand natives soon united in the effort, but they were without arms or discipline, and scarcely a better match for the Spanish soldiers than their ancestors had been for those under Cortes some three centuries before.   On the death of Hidalgo, in 1811, the contest was continued by Morelos, also a priest, who called a congress, which met in 1813, declared Mexico independent, and promulgated a constitution in 1814.   Morelos, however, was captured and executed by the Spaniards in 1815.   Then the contest assumed the guerrilla character, under Guerrero, Bravo, Rayon, Teran, and other partisan leaders, until 1820, when the Spanish power seemed to be re-established and the rebels were hunted down like wild beasts.   The next year, however, Iturbide, who had distinguished himself as a royalist, headed the popular movement in favor of independence and a constitutional government, proposing what was known as the plan of Iguala.   The principal points in this "plan" were the recognition of the Roman Catholic religion as the faith of the nation, the abolition of all distinctions of caste or color, a constitutional monarchy, the crown to be offered to Ferdinand VII., and, if refused by him, to Don Carlos and Don Francisco de Paula.   Iturbide was highly successful for a time, and the whole country acknowledged his authority, with the exception of the capital, which finally gave in its adherence, and made him regent.   The next year, as the historians say, with the support of the army and the mob, Iturbide was proclaimed Emperor.   In less than a year, Santa Anna, who recently said to an American interviewer that he did not then have any idea what a republican government was, commenced a successful revolt at Vera Cruz ; overthrew Iturbide, and, with Generals Victoria, Bravo, and Negrette, established a provisional government and called a convention, which declared for a constitution somewhat similar to that of the United States, which was promulgated in 1824.   The country was divided into nineteen States and four Territories. Victoria was elected president, and Bravo, vice-president.

The Mexican constitution of 1824, however, varied in some important particulars from the constitution of the United States of the North.   The Mexican constitution failed to guarantee to the citizens the right of trial by jury; it prohibited any other than the Roman Catholic religion, and thus failed in the universal toleration guaranteed by the Federal constitution of the United States.   In Mexico the Congress, instead of the courts, was the final interpreter of the constitution, and the rights of the several States were not defined and guaranteed by the national constitution.   The States, instead of being organized political bodies prior to the establishment of a national constitution, were created by it, and had no rights except those delegated to them by the nation, thus being rather in the nature of our county and city governments, than sovereign States.   The rights of the citizen were determined by the construction of the rules of civil law, and not the clear declaration of the constitution, or even the force of legislative enactments.

At the election in 1828, Pedreza was chosen president by the party called *Escosses*, or Scots, over Guerrero, the candidate of the *Yorkincs*, or Yorkists, both parties having secret Masonic organizations under charters from the lodges indicated. Pedreza had but two majority in the Electoral College; the other party declared that they had been defeated by corruption and fraud, and Santa Anna again raised the standard of revolt; the remaining Spaniards in the country were plundered, and murdered or exiled. Pedreza assumed the office of president by force of arms. The nation, however, had no time to constiute a stable government. The Spaniards invaded the country, and President Guerrero was declared Dictator. Santa Anna defeated the Spaniards at Tampico, and, with Bustamente, then made war on Guerrero, compelled him to resign, and the army declared for Bustamente as president. Revolution succeeded revolution, until Santa Anna was, by a somewhat similar process, declared president, in 1833. Then the congress passed laws abrogating the authority of the Pope over the Catholic Church of Mexico, suppressing convents and abolishing the church revenues. It was also proposed to confiscate the properties of the church, but new insurrections followed, and ended, in 1845, in the abrogation of the constitution of 1824, and the conversion of the confederation of States into a consolidated government, with Santa Anna as Dictator, though he was nominally president. This measure was acquiesced in throughout the country, with the exception of some of the Northern portions, embracing Texas, where several thousand Americans had settled, under the colonization laws of Mexico and the guarantees of the Mexican constitution of 1824.

At the meeting of the congress or convention of Coahuila and Texas, in August, 1824, at Saltillo, provision was made for a temporary governor of the new State, with a council and other subordinate officers. All the authorities, civil, military, and ecclesiastic, citizens and soldiers, were required to take an oath of fidelity to the State and constituent congress. But, for the alleged reason that Texas was distant from the seat of the State government, and communication slow, difficult, and expensive, it was resolved to create an additional political department for that province, styled "the Chief of the Department of Texas," to be appointed by the Governor of the State, and responsible to him. He was to reside at San Antonio; to watch over the public tranquillity; inflict punishment; command the militia; examine passports, and issue the same; preside at public meetings and festivals; solve all questions raised by his subordinates and the government; see that the laws were administered, and report all to the Governor of the State. The first political chief appointed to the place was Salcedo, a Mexican, not very favorably disposed toward the

American colonists. The law for the colonization of Texas gave preferences to native Mexicans ; colonists were required to take an oath to obey the Federal and State constitutions, and observe the established religion. These regulations were the source of jealousy and misunderstandings between the races, particularly in Eastern Texas, where there were a good many Mexican colonists, and some Americans, who were not disposed to be very submissive to Mexicans.

Hayden Edwards, an empressario engaged in colonizing Americans in Eastern Texas, complained to the political chief at San Antonio of the conduct of some turbulent Mexicans at Nacogdoches, one of whom was exercising the functions of alcalde by proxy, an authority which Edwards denied, adding that if they had been natives of the United States he would have dealt with them summarily, as he was authorized to do as empressario. This gave offense to the political chief, and augmented the trouble. Frequent questions arose between settlers of the different races, which were always decided in favor of Mexicans —as for example, an American named Tramel had been authorized by the alcalde to establish a ferry on the Trinity, at the crossing of the San Antonio road. Sertoche, a Mexican, applied for the place, and it was taken from Tramel and given to him. The reason given by Salcedo was that the Mexican was entitled to the preference. These incidents are merely mentioned to show the imperfect character of political institutions in Texas at that time.

Thus the liberties of the Anglo-American colonists were assailed from within and without at the same time. In the summer of 1835 Santa Anna in person headed an army for the purpose of crushing out the opposition to his usurpation in the Northern Mexican States, including Texas, and put the Mexican city of Zacatecas, which had refused to submit to his usurpation, to the sword, destroying four thousand lives, and then marched on Texas, where he murdered nearly four thousand prisoners in cold blood.

Texas had first formally protested against this usurpation, and declared her unyielding adherence to the constitution of 1824, and finally, by a formal " declaration of the people of Texas, in general convention assembled," November 7, 1835, alleging that, whereas General Antonio Lopez de Santa Anna and other military chieftains had, by force of arms, overthrown the federal institutions of Mexico, and dissolved the social compact which existed, between Texas and the other members of the Mexican Confederacy, that the people of Texas had taken up arms in defense of their rights and liberties and in defense of the republican principles of the Federal Constitution of Mexico of 1824, and offered their support and assistance to such members of the Mexican Confederacy as would take up arms against military despotism. They denied the rights of the usurping government in Mexico to govern within the limits of Texas, and declared that the people of Texas, would not cease to carry on war against such authorities whilst their troops remained in Texas ; that the people of Texas held it to be their right, during the disorganization of the federal system and reign of despotism, to withdraw from the Mexican Union and establish an independent government, or to establish such measures as seemed best calculated to protect their rights and liberties ; but that they would remain faithful to the Mexican government so long as that nation was governed by the constitution and laws formed for the government of the political association.

This was followed by the promulgation of the Plan and Powers of the Provisional Government of Texas, the leading features of which are as follows :

The offices of governor and lieutenant-governor were established, with a general council to assist the governor in the discharge of his functions, but with no power to pass any laws except such as the emergencies of the country required, ever keeping in view the army in the field. and the means necessary for its comfort and support ; to prosecute the most effective measures to place the country in a state of defense and drive out the invaders. They had power to contract a loan, levy impost and tonnage duties, and treat with the Indians concerning their claims to lands in Texas, and to secure their friendship. Among other Indians in Texas at the time was a large body of Cherokees, who had received the right to settle in Texas from the government of Mexico. They were authorized to establish mails, grant pardons, remit fines, and hear and determine cases in admiralty, agreeably to the laws of nations. They were also authorized to create and fill such other offices as they deemed necessary ; appoint provisional judges, to try causes according to the common law of England ; grant writs of habeas corpus, sequestration, attachment, and arrest, according to the civil code and code of practice of the State of Louisiana, and exercise general jurisdiction. It was declared that all trials should be conducted by jury, and in criminal cases be regulated upon the principles of the common law of England. Officers were required to swear to "support the republican principles of the constitution of Mexico of 1824, and obey the declarations and ordinances above referred to. Many other provisions were enacted, and the convention adjourned to meet in Washington, on the Brazos, in March, 1835, when and where the constitution of the Republic of Texas was adopted. That work was done—how well, a succeeding article will show—within hearing of the cannon of an invading army, and amid the confusion and panic of a whole people fleeing for their lives. The massacres of the Alamo and Goliad had sent a thrill of horror throughout the civilized world, and Santa Anna was waging a war of extermination on the inhabitants of Texas, without regard to the claims of humanity or the usages of civilized war.

II.

On the 28th of April, 1832, the legislature of the then Mexican State of Coahuila and Texas, with a preponderance of Mexicans among its members, repealed the colonization law of 1825, and enacted a new one, limiting the grants to persons to introduce immigrants to Mexicans, and excluding natives of the United States, though recognizing existing contracts. As a set-off for this measure, however, the same body, at the instance of the members from Texas, introduced the practice of creating municipalities and giving the election of local officers to the people. These municipal bodies, two years later, became the *nuclei* around which the people rallied and under the sanction of which they organized for the support of their constitutional rights; and, as the historians of that day say, they became an object of fear to the supreme government of Mexico.

On the 1st of March, 1833, the people of Texas held an election for delegates to a convention to form a State constitution. The delegates assembled at San Felipe in April. Among them were some men of distinguished character, viz., Branch T. Archer, Stephen F. Austin, David G. Burnet, Sam Houston, J. B. Miller, and Wm. H. Wharton. Among the committees appointed by the convention was one on the proposed constitution, with Sam Houston as chairman, and one on a memorial to the Supreme Government of Mexico, with David G. Burnet, chairman. The constitution framed was republican in its character, with a few clauses retained in deference to Mexican opinions. The right of trial by jury, *habeas corpus*, the right of petition, freedom of the press, direct and universal suffrage, and the clauses common in our bills of rights, were inserted. Nothing was said on the subject of religion—either in reference to the existing establishment or "God in the constitution."

Stephen F. Austin was sent to the Mexican capital to submit this draft for a separate constitution for Texas to the Supreme Government, and ask the recognition of the new State. By the 1st of June, however, Santa Anna " pronounced " in favor of a new national government, supported by the church and the army, with himself as dictator. But the vice-president, Gomez Farias, an adherent to the constitution of 1824, took occasion, in the absence of Santa Anna from the capital, with the aid of Lorenzo de Zavala (previously Mexican minister to Washington and afterward a leading spirit in Texas, who settled and died on the San Jacinto, between Galveston and Houston), then governor of the State and City of Mexico, raised a force of Republicans and temporarily put down the outbreak. Santa Anna adroitly retired for the time being. But the national finances were exhausted and the government without resources, and resort was had to the confiscation of a part of the resources of the church. This aroused the power of the clergy, and Santa Anna again came to the surface as the champion of the church, and determined, with the aid of the army, to overthrow the constitution and establish an absolute government.

During all these troubles, Austin had been endeavoring to obtain some action by the supreme government on the objects of his mission. Congress paid little attention to this apparently unimportant matter, while civil war was spreading throughout Mexico and cholera was decimating the capital. Austin lingered throughout the summer, but met no encouragement, and on the 2d of October, 1833, wrote back, recommending that all the municipalities of Texas should unite and organize a State under the provisions of the *Acta Constitutiva* of May 7, 1824, and by union and harmony prepare for a refusal of their application by the supreme government, warning the people that if they did not take steps for their own defense Texas would be ruined forever. He succeeded, however, in procuring a repeal of the law of 1830, prohibiting citizens of the United States from removing to Texas, and started home in December. In the meantime his letter of October 2d was sent back from Texas to the Mexican·authorities at the capital ; he was arrested on the road, and imprisoned in a dungeon, without light, books, or writing materials, for three months.

In the meantime the State Government of Coahuila and Texas declared that it would not support any agreement tending, directly or indirectly, to attack the federal form of government or State sovereignty ; and that it recognized as the will of the nation only such measures as were approved by a majority of the State legislatures. This same body, however, shortly afterward denied the right of petition, and declared that any person or corporation who assumed the right of petition, usurped the rights of society and excited disorder. More than three persons were forbidden to sign a petition. Afterward, the legislature repealed the law of 1832, prohibiting persons not born in Mexico from retailing goods in the State, and gave to Madero, who was popular in Texas, the exclusive right to navigate Trinity River.

In his *pronunciamento* of May 25, 1834, Santa Anna declared that the laws against the church and those for the banishment of the monarchists, should be set aside ; that a new congress should be convened, with power to form a new constitution, etc.

The legislature of Coahuila and Texas reassembled on the 1st day of January, 1834. Among those who were present during the session was Thomas Jefferson Chambers, an American who had spent some fourteen years in Mexico, a lawyer by profession, and well acquainted with the language and leading men of Mexico. He had much influence with the legislature.

Among other measures adopted by it, was the creation of the municipalities of Matagorda. and San Augustine, the division of Texas into departments, a provision for the use of the English as well as the Spanish language in official proceedings, and Texas was allowed additional representation in the legislature, giving her three out of the eight members. This body, however, undertook to regulate the affairs of the church in some respects. It prohibited the founding of edifices by charitable donations, forbade any one to dispose of more than one-fifth of his estate for the benefit of his soul, and forbade the clergy from interfering in civil affairs. Texas was to have three political chiefs, to hold their offices for four years. Foreigners were to be allowed to purchase lands, and it was declared that "no person should be molested for political and religious opinions, provided the public order was not disturbed." .A decree was passed on the 24th of April, 1834, making Texas a judicial circuit, establishing trial by jury, and Thomas J. Chambers appointed judge.

Santa Anna released Austin from prison in June, 1834, and in October of the same year proceeded to consider the petition from Texas. He called together his four secretaries of state, three of his generals, and Zavala and Austin. Austin was heard, the petition for a separate State refused, but Santa Anna promised to place four thousand soldiers at San Antonio, "for the protection of the *coast* and frontier," under the command of General Mexia. A new election was to be ordered for governor, vice-governor, and members of the legislature of the State.

Austin was satisfied of the sincerity of Santa Anna, and wrote advising the people of Texas to sustain the adjustment of their difficulties by the president. He said : "All is changed since last year. Then there was no local government in Texas ; now there is; and the most of your evils have been remedied, so that it is important to promote union with all the State and keep down all kinds of excitement. All is going well. The president, General Santa Anna, has solemnly and publicly declared that he will sustain the Federal representative system as it now exists, and will be sustained by all parties." Wait and see.

III.

In the spring of 1834 Colonel Almonte was sent to Texas, by Santa Anna, to examine and report upon the condition of the country. He reported that the population was about twenty-one thousand, including eleven hundred negroes ; that the country was free from civil strife, and prosperous. On his return to Mexico it was proposed by Santa. Anna that he (Almonte) should return to Texas in the capacity of colonial director, and promote the introduction of a larger number of Mexicans into Texas ; but this measure was prevented by the events that led to the separation.

The first openly revolutionary meeting in Texas was held at San Antonio in October, 1834, on the recommendation of the superior judge of the department. Erasmo Seguin, a native Mexican, made a motion which was adopted, calling for a general convention of the whole colony at the same place in November following ; but the meeting did not take place.

The meeting at San Felipe, in October, mentioned in a previous article, had declared in favor of a perpetual separation between Coahuila and Texas.

The National Congress of Mexico met in January, 1835. The Centralists had triumphed everywhere, except in Zacatecas and Coahuila and Texas. The Republicans were proscribed and banished, and preparations increased for reducing the Republicans of these States to obedience, including, as the event showed, the extirpation of the American colonists in Texas. Coahuila and Texas, meanwhile, had held elections, and chosen Viesca to the office of governor, and Musquiz vice-governor. Both, as well as the members of the Legislature, were Republicans.

General Cos, military commander of the department, set out for the seat of the State Government to overrule the proceedings or disperse the legislature. Whereupon the legislature passed a decree authorizing the governor to raise " such force as he might deem necessary to secure the public tranquillity, and protect the civil authorities in the exercise of their functions, " and declared that no portion of the standing army should be stationed at the State capital, except by a direct order of the president of the nation. Viesca, in his inaugural as governor, said that Santa Anna wished to reduce Texas to the condition of a territory, " to separate her from Coahuila, in order that the people might be considered as foreigners." The legislature, in an address to the Federal Congress, declared that " distrust, discord, and a disposition to persecution and revenge " constituted the settled course of the Congress ; that the legislature was unalterably devoted to the principles of the constitution of 1824, and would continue to sustain it ; that the changes in the form of government would be dangerous in Coahuila and Texas, bordering on a flourishing sister republic and settled by people with whom the proposed changes would not agree ; that they could not conform to them, and that they involved not only the internal peace of the country, but the integrity of the nation. This language proved as prophetic as it was bold. It was, however, disregarded.

In the spring of 1835, Santa Anna left the Mexican capital, at the head of an army to subdue the republicans of Zacatecas, and Cos proceeded to Monclova with another, to disperse the legislature. During the confusion incident to this approach of troops to disperse it, that body proceeded to

enact laws extending titles to lands in Texas, and authorized the creation of
a bank, the charter of which was afterward confirmed by the Republic of
Texas and the bank itself established and conducted in Galveston for many
years, at the corner of Tremont and Market streets—Thompson's corner.
An act was passed authorizing the provisional location of the State government, and the convention adjourned.

Texas was virtually without a government, and must either await the
arrival of the Mexican army and submit to military government and extermination, or take steps for her own preservation.   She took the latter course.
A " Committee of Safety " was formed at Mina (now Bastrop) on the Colorado,
on the 17th of May, 1835.   General Edward Burleson, afterward famous as a
soldier and legislator of Texas, was among the members.   Other municipalities took the same course, under direction of the officers elected by the
people.   The people determined that they would have no more military governments than could be avoided, and drove the Mexican soldiers from Anahuac, at the head of Galveston Bay, then the principal town in this portion
of Texas, and containing several hundred inhabitants.

A meeting was held at San Felipe, on the Brazos, of which Hon. Charles
B. Stewart, at present a senator in the legislature of Texas, was secretary,
in order to concert measures to promote the peace and safety of the country.

Zavala, the late governor of the State of Mexico and minister to France,
had taken refuge in Texas, to avoid proscription on account of his republican
sentiments.   The Mexican authorities ordered his arrest, but the Texans protected him, while he assisted them in measures for the defense of the country.

The Mexican military commandant wrote to the political chief at San
Felipe to arrest Zavala, Frank W. Johnson (still alive, and one of the heroes
who took the city of San Antonio from a superior Mexican force in the fall
of 1835), R. M. Williamson (the famous Three-legged Willie), Travis, S. M.
Williams (one of the founders of the city of Galveston), and Mosely Baker
(another), and place them in military confinement on account of their revolutionary conduct.   The order, however could not be executed.   Santa Anna
wrote to General Cos : " I give this supreme order, requiring you to provide
and bring into action all your ingenuity and activity in arranging energetic
plans for success in the apprehension of Lorenzo Zavala, which person, in the
actual circumstances of Texas, must be very pernicious.   Spare no means
to secure his person and place it at the disposition of the supreme government."   A similar order was issued in regard to Travis, who was to be tried
by a military tribunal.

These measures warned the people of Texas of the policy they might
expect toward them from the military government of Mexico, and only served
to unite them in preparing for the work to be done.   Flight, extermination,

R. M. WILLIAMSON.

See p. 274.

or resistance were the alternatives placed before them. They prepared for the latter, but also prepared to make it under the forms of a constitutional government, and for principles and rights defined under the sanction of organic law. How well they did their work history has told; but a further recurrence to both the incidents and legislation of that crisis in the history of Texas may be found interesting to a generation that has since grow up, as well as to the few survivors of the period.

IV.

In the three preceding articles, have been briefly sketched the events and political questions which preceded the meeting of the first convention to form a constitution in Texas. Texas had been a portion of the Mexican republic under the constitution of 1824. That constitution had been overthrown; a military despotism established; troops were already in or marching on Texas from Mexico, to enforce the change, in October, 1835. As H. A. Alsbury said, in an address made in August of that year, all those who had immigrated into Texas from the United States, since April 6, 1830, were to be driven from the country or dealt with by the military. A number of proscribed, of which a long list was preserved, were to be arrested and tried by drum-head court, and future immigrants supplied from Mexico only.

The idea of a general consultation was urged in an " Address of the People of Columbia to the People of Texas," signed by John A. Wharton, W. D. C. Hall, Henry Smith, Silas Dinsmore, James F. Perry, John G. McNeel, Robert H. Williams, W. H. Jack, F. A. Bingham, John Hodge, William T. Austin, Isaac T. Tinsley, W. H. Bynum, Branch T. Archer, and John Hodge, of whom Messrs. McNeel and Williams are now the only survivors. Zavala favored this convention, though he still hoped for the re-establishment of a republic in Mexico. Candelle, the Mexican commandant of Goliad, imprisoned the alcalde and extorted five thousand dollars from the " administrator." He ordered the troops to be quartered on the citizens—five to a family—and supported by them. The Mexican war schooner *Mexicano*, commanded by an adventurer known as Mexican Thompson, was stationed in Galveston Bay, and, cruising along the coast, captured some small traders. The colonists procured and armed the schooner *San Felipe*, and by the aid of the steamer *Laura*, the property of McKinney & Williams, Thompson and his craft were captured.

Austin arrived at San Felipe on the 1st of September, and was welcomed with a public dinner, at which he expressed great concern at the unsettled condition of the country, but said that he would labor with the colonists for their "constitutional rights, and the peace and security of Texas;" and declared himself in favor of the proposed consultation of the people. Austin, however, said that Santa Anna had assured him that he would use his influence to "give the people of Texas a special organization, suited to their education, habits, and situation." These promises proved to be specious, and intended to mislead.

Shortly afterward a dispatch was received from the secretary of state of the Supreme Government of Mexico, declaring that the colonists of Texas were subject to the laws which a majority of the nation might establish. A new list of proscribed Texans was sent on, and the apprehension of F. W. Johnson, R. M. Williamson, Colonel Travis, S. M. Williams, Mosely Baker, John H. Moore, the well-known Mexican, Carvajal, and another named Zambrino, was ordered. An army from Mexico marched on San Antonio; five hundred more were landed at Matagorda Bay and marched into the interior. A Mexican force was sent from Bexar to demand a cannon that had been intrusted to the citizens for defense against the Indians. They refused to give it up; a fight ensued, and the Mexicans retreated. The commandant at Bexar wrote to Austin that unless the gun was promptly given up war would be commenced on the colonists.

This roused the people of all Texas. A meeting was held at San Angustine on the 5th of October, when Sam Houston and Thomas J. Rusk were present. They immediately afterward started for the scene of hostilities. The object was to capture the Mexican fortress at San Antonio, and drive the Mexican soldiers out of the country. There was as yet no military organization in Texas. Sam Houston was requested by the meeting at San Augustine to take command of the troops of Eastern Texas, and to raise others.

On the suggestion of Austin, a member of the committee of safety for each district was requested to proceed to San Felipe and form a council for the direction of affairs. Austin then proceeded to join the extempore army at Gonzales, and was elected to command it. Another body of volunteers proceeded to Goliad, surprised the Mexican garrison, and captured the ammunition and arms. The "consultation" which assembled at San Felipe, in November, 1835, consisted of delegates from the municipalities of Bevil, Nacogdoches, San Augustine, Mina, Washington, Gonzales, Viesca, and Tenehaw. These political divisions have long since been obliterated, and though it would now be possible to locate them pretty accurately, future geographers may find it hard to reconstruct the map of Texas as it stood in 1835. An ordinance establishing a provisional government was enacted. It created a governor, lieutenant-governor, a council (in lieu of cabinet), a judiciary, commander-in-chief, and subordinate offices, and adjourned to meet at Washington on the Brazos, March 1, 1836.

Henry Smith was chosen governor, James W. Robinson, lieutenant-governor, and Sam Houston, commander-in-chief. Edwin Waller and George M. Patrick are the only members of the consultation now alive, so far as is known to the writer.

In the meantime warlike operations were progressing in Western Texas. The colonists besieged the Mexican garrison of the Alamo at San Antonio, and finally fought their way into and captured the fort, after a week's fighting, on the 16th of December, 1835. Colonel Frank W. Johnson, still living, had command of the storming party after the fall of Colonel Milam, and raised the flag of the Lone Star on the fortress, after driving out an army of Mexicans three times as numerous as his own.

After the capture of Bexar, the volunteers became restless from inactivity and many of them left, either for their homes or to seek more active service, until, on the 9th of January, 1836, Colonel Neill, then in command of the Texans at Bexar, sent a dispatch to the governor informing him that the defense of the garrison was insufficient, while it was threatened by the approach of an overwhelming Mexican army. The commander-in-chief was ordered to proceed to Bexar, or some other point on the frontier. General Houston, previous to his departure, wrote "that there is but one course left for Texas to pursue, and that is an unequivocal declaration of independence and the formation of a constitution, to be submitted to the people for their rejection or ratification."

On the 11th of January, 1836, an expedition embracing two-thirds of the men from Bexar, set out for Matamoras, carrying most of the supplies of clothing, provisions, and ammunition. On the 16th of the same month, General Houston dispatched an order from Goliad to Colonel Neill to demolish the fortifications at Bexar and bring away the artillery, as it would be impossible to hold the town with the force then there. There were but eighty Texans left at Bexar; on the 17th Colonel Neill retired, but Travis called for re-enforcements to hold the place.

On the 4th of February Santa Anna set out from Monclova for Texas, at the head of an army of six thousand men, declaring his object to be to drive from Texas all who had taken part in the revolt of the province; to remove all persons of foreign birth into the interior from both the sea-coast and the country bordering on the United States; to remove from Texas all persons not entered as regular colonists under Mexican rules; divide the best lands among the officers and soldiers of the Mexican army; to prevent the frontier settlements of Anglo-Americans in Texas, and impose on Texas the expenses of the war. The army of Santa Anna came in sight of San Antonio on the 23d of February. On the 27th General Urrea arrived at San Patricio with another division of Mexicans. Santa Anna stormed the Alamo and put its

defenders to the sword on the 6th of March, after more than a week's cannonade, and several assaults with an overwhelming force.   The garrison consisted of one hundred and eighty-eight men, every one of whom was killed.
The Mexican force was nearly twenty times as great.   Colonel Fannin and
a force of three hundred and thirty Texans were overwhelmed, captured and
massacred in cold blood.   And everywhere Texans captured by the Mexicans were put to death without pity, and in violation of the terms of their
surrender, by which quarter was granted.   Probably a thousand men •were
thus slaughtered in all, out of the few thousands then citizens of Texas.   The
entire population of women and children fled toward the Sabine, while the
remnant of men capable of bearing arms kept between them and the invaders.

Such is an imperfect glance at the condition of Texas when the convention which framed the constitution of the republic met at Washington, on the
Brazos, and performed their task with arms in their hands, and in momentary expectation of the occasion to use them.   That instrument will be
exhibited in the next of these articles.

V.

The convention which framed the constitution of the Republic of
Texas met at Washington on the Brazos, on the 1st day of March, 1836, and
on the 2d declared that the people of Texas, through their representatives, constituted her a free, sovereign, and independent republic, with all
the rights and powers incident to an independent nation ; and set forth the
reasons for this declaration.   On the 4th of the same month the convention made Sam Houston commander-in-chief of the armies of the young
republic, and the convention proceeded actively to work to organize and provide her troops.   By the 16th the constitution was prepared and ready for
signatures.   David G. Burnet was elected president *pro tem.*, and a cabinet
organized.   General Houston was a member of the convention, but, after
receiving his commission, proceeded at once to join the army at Gonzales.

The declaration charged that the constitution of 1824 had been overthrown by Mexico, "anarchy prevails, and civil society is dissolved into its
original elements ;" that the law of self-preservation forced Texas to take
this course.   Mexico had invited the settlement of Texas, but Santa Anna
had now presented to the people the cruel alternative, either to abandon
their homes, or submit to the most intolerable tyranny ; that the right of trial
by jury was denied the colonists ; that no means of public education were
provided, "although it is an axiom in political science that unless a people
are educated and enlightened, it is idle to expect the continuance of civil
liberty, or the capacity for self-government ;" that local military commanders

had usurped all power, oppressing and imprisoning our citizens without law, and demanding the surrender of others, to be tried by military tribunals ; that vessels and merchandize belonging to citizens of Texas had been subjected to piratical seizures by Mexican cruisers ; that free religious exercises were inhibited ; the arms of the colonists essential for their defense against the savages and for procuring supplies of game for subsistence, were demanded to be surrendered ; that the country was invaded at the moment, both by sea and land, to lay waste the land and exterminate the people ; that Mexico had incited the Indians to murder the colonists, and no alternative but resistance, death, or flight was left. Resistance was the only course for freemen, but it was not made blindly and without aim. Amid the confusion and danger of the period a constitution was adopted, under which a government was founded that promptly commanded, not only the sympathy and respect of the people of the United States, but recognition and friendly offices from France, Great Britain, and the German States.

The objects of the Government, as declared in the preamble to the constitution, were the same as those for which the constitution of the United States was enacted, and the sovereign power was declared to be the same : " The people, in order to form a government, establish justice, insure domestic tranquillity, provide for the common defense and general welfare ; and, to secure the blessings of liberty to themselves and their posterity, do ordain and establish this constitution." This language was changed in the State constitution of 1845, under which Texas was annexed to the United States, which declared that the people of Texas, in accordance with the provisions of the joint resolution for annexing to the United States, " ordain and establish this constitution." These resolutions provided that Texas might be admitted into the Union as a State, with a republican form of government, leaving the question of boundaries to be settled by the United States, and Texas to cede to the United States her public edifices, forts, " ports, harbors, navy and navy, yards," and other public property ; but Texas to retain her own lands and pay her own debts.

The constitution of 1836 made the usual division of the powers of the government into legislative, executive, and judicial. The president could not serve two terms in succession. Congress could punish contempts by imprisonment during the session, but no longer ; no bill could become a law without being read three several days in each house, except in cases of emergency, on a suspension of the rules by a vote of two-thirds. After a bill had been once rejected no bill containing the same substance could be passed during the session. No person holding another office was eligible to a seat in Congress. No appropriation of money could be made for private or local purposes, except by a vote of two-thirds of each house. The usual veto power was

34

allowed the president. Judges were elected by joint ballot in Congress. The Supreme Court had appellate jurisdiction only, provided that no judge should sit in a case in the Supreme Court tried by him in the court below—which differs from the present practice in the Supreme Court of the United States, where a justice occasionally repeats, on an appeal, the same decision which he rendered in the case below. In the Republic of Texas the district judges, with the chief-justice, constituted the Supreme Court.

New counties were only allowed on the petition of one hundred free male inhabitants of the territory sought to be erected into counties—a rule which the State has not always followed, and the neglect of which has given us a long list of unorganized counties.

The constitution of 1836 declared that "ministers of the Gospel being, by their profession, dedicated to God and the care of souls, ought not to be diverted from the great duties of their functions. Therefore no minister of the Gospel, or priest of any denomination whatever, shall be eligible to the office of the executive of the republic, nor to a seat in either branch of Congress."

The president had power to grant reprieves and pardons, and remit fines and forfeitures, except in cases of impeachment.

In case the two houses of Congress should disagree as to the time of adjournment, he could adjourn them to such time as he might think proper.

"Every citizen of the republic" twenty-one years of age, was a voter, after six months, residence in the county where he offered to vote. Popular elections were by ballot; elections by Congress *viva voce*, and a majority of the votes necessary to a choice.

Persons convicted of bribery, forgery, and other crimes, were excluded from office and voting.

It was declared to be the duty of Congress to provide by law a general system of education. The immense dedication of public lands, and the large proportion of the public revenues since set apart for purposes of education, have been made in accordance with this brief, but clearly expressed, declaration. Some benefits have inured from it, but greater are in store, if the present and coming generations are faithful to the duty and trust thus imposed on them. In the general thirst for spoil the school funds and school lands have not always escaped the greedy efforts of speculators; but thus far it is hoped that the value of the inheritance has not been greatly impaired. The constitution of the republic prohibited the importation of Africans, a system which had prevailed in Mexico and Texas from the time of the Spanish conquest to the days of Lafitte. Indians and Africans, however, were declared not to be citizens of the republic.

The bill of rights declared that every right not delegated by the constitution is reserved to the people; that they all have equal rights, and no man or set of men are entitled to exclusive public privileges or emoluments from the community; all political power is inherent in the people, and they have at all times an inalienable right to alter their government in such manner as they may think proper; no preference shall be given by law to any religious denomination or mode of worship, but every person shall be permitted to worship God acording to the dictates of his own conscience; no law shall ever be enacted to curtail the liberty of speech or of the press, and in all prosecutions for libels the truth may be given in evidence, and the jury shall have the right to determine the law and the fact, under the direction of the court. Citizens were protected from all unreasonable searches and seizures, accused persons could be heard by themselves or counsel, "or both," and were guaranteed such other rights as are provided in the constitution of the United States, such as speedy and public jury trial, etc. Public officers were debarred from receiving presents. Excessive bail was prohibited, and the writ of habeas corpus guaranteed. Excessive fines and cruel punishments were prohibited. Imprisonment for debt was not allowed. The services or property of the citizens could not be required for public use without their consent and due compensation. The right to bear arms was protected, and the military declared to be subordinate to civil power. No retrospective or *ex post facto* law, or law impairing the obligation of contracts, was allowed. Perpetuities, monopolies, and laws of primogeniture and entailments were prohibited.

Such other incidental and general provisions as were necessary to complete a form of government quite as good as Texas has since had, were embodied in this constitution, adopted, as it was, in the midst of fugitive women and children and in the face of an invading army which devastated the country, burned hamlets, and massacred prisoners in cold blood in its then triumphant march over Texas. The men who signed it dropped the pen to hasten to the army, and a month later sealed the instrument in blood on the plain of San Jacinto. No one thought of amending it until annexation.

VI.

It has been the aim of these articles to reawaken in such persons as are already familiar with the topic, and to present to the young men of the present day, to a majority of whom the subject is not naturally attractive, though novel, such facts and considerations as are calculated to enkindle that spirit of patriotism and State pride, without which the mere form of government, whatever it may be, is but a mockery. Writers on political economy and national law place patriotism among the most important factors of a free and prosperous state. The pride and love of country is as natural as human affection, and exists in many who are not otherwise ranked as good citizens. Few are found to bear with patience insults on their State or nation, though they may find fault with it themselves, and many a man has died heroically and freely in defense of his country, who would have not scrupled to break all of the ten commandments. But the higher passion of patriotism is that which aims to serve one's country and fellow-citizens, by providing free institutions, wholesome laws, and promoting the general welfare. This can only be done through organized government and a willingness to be governed by, as well as a desire to subject others to, the constitution and laws established for the regulation of public affairs. Every foreigner on being naturalized, and every citizen on being installed in a public office, is sworn to support the constitutions of the State and the United States ; yet it may be safely assumed that many have taken this oath who never read either. The old constitution of the Republic of Texas, as a matter of course, required that the president should take an oath to support it on his inauguration. During the late civil war between the States, the newspapers and politicians, both at the North and the South, often told the people that constitutions were meant for times of peace ; that in war, necessity—and particularly military necessity—was the supreme law. Some unwritten code of martial law was invoked, and even sanctioned by lawyers, under which the most arbitrary, tyrannical, and cruel acts were perpetrated, of which the hanging of an innocent woman in the federal capital was not the least or the least disgraceful. It may be worth while at the present time—when people are looking backward as well as forward for beacons by which to steer the ship of state, to recur to an incident within the memory of many now living,' which serves to contrast the course of Texas, under her Republican Constitution, with that of Mexico, under the military despot who overthrew her liberties, and endeavored to crush those of the young Hercules who had his birth in Texas.

In 1841, Santa Anna usurped the supreme authority of Mexico, under what was known as the Plan of Tacubaya, or the military act proclaimed in the town of Tacubaya, three miles distant from the City of Mexico, in consequence of which the administration of President Bustamente was overthrown, and General Santa Anna proclaimed dictator. He appointed " deputies " for each department, and they appointed him dictator, with " authority for the organization of all the different branches of the public administration." He issued a proclamation, declaring that all persons who did not in three days accept amnesty at his hands for political offenses, should be " responsible in their persons," " and all the so-called authorities which, directly or indirectly, may counteract the said sovereign will, and may contribute to the unnecessary effusion of the Mexican blood, which shall lay upon their heads." The so-called authorities had been elected by the people of Mexico. He proclaimed a vigorous renewal of the war on Texas, and through his newspaper organs said :

" For the cause of Texas we ought to make all manner of sacrifice ; for it we ought to unite ourselves with the government, renouncing every political opinion, bearing every grievance with patience, and without complaint : and even we have said that for this reason we ought, if necessary, to defer the time of our convention until that portion of the national territory is recovered.

" In the capital of the Republic the general government and the commandants general of the departments should nominate a convention of individuals noted for their ability and true patriotism, consisting of one president and two associates, a secretary and treasurer, their duties to be as follows: To devise all the means possible to unite and place in motion all the aids for making and terminating the war of Texas. To this end they will induce all classes in their respective places to contribute each one according to his station in order to attain this patriotic and national object. There should be admitted among the contributors all foreigners, whether they have resided long in the republic, have Mexican children, or an identity of interest."

VII.

In July, 1842, the Congress of the Republic of Texas passed a bill authorizing the president, General Sam Houston, to sell or hypothecate, on on such terms as he might think proper, ten million acres of the public lands of Texas, to raise means to carry on an offensive war against Mexico, and authorize him to commence operations at such time and in such manner as he might deem compatible with the public interests. He was authorized to take command of the army in person ; to employ all the available resources of the Republic in the prosecution of the war. He was authorized to order out the militia, by draft, to include one-third of the whole population capable of bearing arms. This bill was vetoed by President Houston. He said, among other things, " In the prosecution of an offensive war, there should be no question as to the right of the government to command the services of its citizens. Unfortunately at the very outset the question arises, Has Congress the power, by the constitution, to order a draft of, and compel, the citizens of of the republic to march beyond our limits in a war of invasion ? If this power exists, it is not to found among the enumerated powers expressly delegated by the constitution to Congress ; and to me it is clear that no such power has been delegated, but is expressly reserved to the people. If Congress does not possess such power, then such a law would be unconstitutional. Were the executive to sanction any such law, with a belief that no

such power did exist, he would violate his duty to his country and to himself."
He said : "His opinion is that he has not the power, even with the sanction
of Congress, to compel the service of the militia of the republic" to engage
in such an undertaking. "It is a principle in all well-regulated republican
governments that no powers which can be exercised by the citizen in his
individual capacity should be delegated to his representative, but that such
powers should remain vested in him as an indefeasible right ; and that the
representative should never exercise power, the delegation of which is questionable, or attempt its exercise where it might be liable to abuse.   Agents
are responsible to the people under the great constitutional charter of their
liberty.   The delegated powers are defined and expressly granted—all others
remain with the people.   The concurrent will of the three departments of the
government united, could not render valid a principle, and make it binding
upon the people, which was not set forth by the constitution.   The approval
by the president of the principle set forth by Congress would not justify the
exercise on his part of the extraordinary powers rendered by the bill.   The
citizens of the republic regard him as the conservator of the constitution,
and as such he should ever feel it incumbent on him to resist every apparent
encroachment on their rights, but never to exercise one of questionable character.   He has been, and is, connected with the building up and existence of
the government, and no circumstances could ever induce him to raise a
parricidal arm against it."   He proceeded to argue the importance of adhering
to the organic law in the foundation of the government, and said that if the
bill was allowed to become law, "It might so happen in after times that great
excitement and difficulties might exist in the country, and that to remedy the
existing misfortunes of the times, measures might be contemplated of an
extraordinary character, and dangerous to liberty ; that the present act of
Congress would be brought up, referred to, and adopted as a precedent,
deriving authority from its antiquity and the associations with which it might
be connected, and some individual, clothed with similar power and deriving
authority from this example alone, in the prosecution of ambitious and selfish
ends, might exercise it to the destruction of the liberties of his country."

VIII.

The first constitution of the State of Texas, adopted August 27, 1845, and
under which the affairs of the government were conducted until the overthrow
of the State organization in 1865, by the Federal authority, was almost universally approved by the people who lived under it for twenty years.   The
Secession Convention in 1861 did not undertake to change the State constitution further than to adapt it to the new relations of the State with the

Southern Confederacy, instead of the old Union under the Federal Constitution. An ordinance was adopted by that convention, declaring that the Federal government had failed to accomplish the purpose of the compact of union between the States ; that the Northern States had violated the compact ; that the rights of the South had been violated and were further endangered by the Federal government, and therefore the ordinance adopted by the convention in 1845, under which Texas had been annexed to the United States, was repealed and annulled, and that all the powers which Texas had delegated to the Federal government were revoked and resumed, and the people absolved from all allegiance to the United States. An ordinance was adopted providing for the continuance of the existing State government, and that all officers of the same, on taking the oath to support the constitution of the Confederate States, should continue in office during the terms for which they had been elected or appointed. Governor Houston having refused to take the oath, his office was declared vacant, and Lieutenant-Governor Clark inaugurated as governor, and the secretary of state, E. W. Cave, having also refused to qualify anew, was also deposed.

It is the purpose of the present and some succeeding articles, to show the principal points of difference between the constitutions of 1845 and 1869.

The preamble in both is the same : "We the people of Texas, acknowledging with gratitude, the grace of God, in permitting us to make choice of our form of government, do hereby ordain and establish this constitution."

Article First, in the constitution of 1845, begins by saying : "That the general, great and essential principles of liberty and free government may be recognized and established, we declare that all political power is inherent in THE PEOPLE, and all free governments are founded on their authority, and instituted for their benefit ; and they have at all times the unalienable right to alter, reform, or abolish their form of government, in such manner as they may think expedient."

The first article in the so-called Bill of Rights of the present constitution ignores the supreme authority of the people, and declares that, in order that "the heresies of nullification and secession, which brought the country to grief, may be eliminated from future political discussion, . . we declare that the constitution of the United States, and the treaties made, and to be made, in pursuance thereof, are acknowledged to be the supreme law ; that this constitution is framed in harmony with, and in subordination thereto; and that the fundamental principles embodied herein can only be changed, subject to the national authority."

Here is a most radical change in the definition of the sovereign power. The constitution of 1845, which was accepted and ratified by the government of the United States, and which was allowed to exist for twenty years, was based purely upon the idea of popular sovereignty. The present constitution acknowledges the Federal government as the supreme law, and something distinct from and superior to the rights of the States and of the people, reserved under the old national constitution as it existed prior to the late civil war. Whether the framers of the present constitution meant to include the declarations of its predecessor as among the heresies of nullification and secession to be eliminated from future political discussion, and the discussion of them held as treasonable, is for the authors of this spread-eagle declaration to explain.

The second section of article first in both constitutions declares that "all free men, when they form a social compact, have equal rights ; and no man, or set of men, is entitled to exclusive separate public emoluments or privileges." In the constitution of 1845 the words " but in consideration for public services " occur after " privileges," but they are dropped in the present constitution. Both declare that " No religious tests shall be required as a qualification to any office of public trust in the State. All men have a natural and indefeasible right to worship God according to the dictates of their own consciences. No man shall be compelled to attend, erect, or support any place of worship, or to maintain any ministry against his consent. No human authority ought, in any case whatever, to control or interfere with the rights of conscience in matters of religion ; and no preference shall ever be given by law to any religious societies or mode of worship. But it shall be the duty of the legislature to pass such laws as may be deemed necessary to protect every religious denomination in the peaceable enjoyment of their own mode of public worship. Every citizen shall be at liberty to speak, write, or publish his opinions on any subject, being responsible for the abuse of that privilege ; and no law shall ever be passed curtailing the liberty of speech or of the press. In prosecutions for the publication of papers investigating the official conduct of officers, or of men in a public capacity, or when the matter published is proper for public information, the truth thereof may be given in evidence ; and in all prosecutions for libels, the jury shall have the right to determine the law and the facts, under the direction of the court, as in other cases."

In the above paragraph the word " prosecutions " has been substituted in the present constitution, for " indictments " in the constitution of 1845.

The following is substantially the same in both, though there is a slight difference in words.

" The people shall be secure in their persons, houses, papers, and possessions from all unreasonable seizures or searches ; and no warrant to search any place, or to seize any person or thing, shall issue, without describing such place, person, or thing, as near as may be, nor without probable cause, supported by oath or affirmation.

"In all criminal prosecutions the accused shall have a speedy public trial, by an impartial jury. He shall not be compelled to give evidence against himself. He shall have the right of being heard by himself, or by counsel, or both ; shall be confronted with the witnesses against him, and shall have compulsory process for obtaining witnesses in his favor ; and no person shall be holden to answer for any criminal charge, but on indictment or information, except in cases arising in the land or naval forces, or in offenses against the laws regulating the militia.

" All prisoners shall be bailable upon sufficient sureties, unless for capital offenses, when the proof is evident ; but this provision shall not be so construed as to prohibit bail after indictment found, upon an examination of the evidence by a judge of the supreme or district court, upon the return of the writ of habeas corpus, returnable in the county where the offense is committed."

The constitution of 1845 declares that " the privileges of the writ of *habeas corpus* shall not be suspended, except when in case of rebellion or invasion, the public safety may require it." In the present constitution the corresponding section reads : " The privileges of the writ of *habeas corpus* shall not be suspended, except *by act of the legislature*, in case of rebellion or invasion, when the public safety may require it."

Both say in the same words : " Excessive bail shall not be required, nor excessive fines imposed, nor cruel nor unusual punishment inflicted. All courts shall be open, and every person, for an injury done him in his lands, goods, person, or reputation, shall have remedy by due course of the law."

The constitution of 1845 says : No persons for the same offense shall be twice put in jeopardy of life *or limb*, nor shall a person be again put upon trial for the same offense, after a verdict of not guilty ; and the right of trial by jury shall be inviolate." In the present constitution the words " or limb " are omitted. The constitution of 1845 declares that " every person shall have the right to keep and bear arms, in the lawful defense of himself or the State." The constitution of 1869 makes the same declaration, but adds the words " under such regulations as the legislature may prescribe."

Both constitutions declare that " no bill of attainder, *ex post facto* law, retroactive law, or any law impairing the obligation of contracts, shall be made, and no person's property shall be taken, or applied to public use, without just compensation being made, unless by the consent of such person ; " but the present constitution contains the addition : " Nor shall any law be passed depriving a party of any remedy for the enforcement of a contract, which existed when the contract was made."

Both declare that :

"No person shall ever be imprisoned for debt.

"No citizen of this State shall be deprived of life, liberty, property, or privileges, outlawed, exiled, or in any manner disfranchised, except by due course of the law of the land.

"The military shall at all times be subordinate to the civil authority.

"Perpetuities and monopolies are contrary to the genius of free government, and shall never be allowed; nor shall the law of primogeniture or entailments ever be in force in this State.

"The people shall have the right, in a peaceable manner, to assemble together for their common good; and to apply to those invested with powers of government for redress of grievances, or other purposes, by petition, or remonstrances.

"No power of suspending laws in the State shall be exercised, except by the legislature or its authority."

The following provisions in the present constitution are not contained in the constitution of 1845:

"The equality of all persons before the law is herein recognized, and shall ever remain inviolate; nor shall any citizen ever be deprived of any right, privilege, or immunity, nor be exempted from any burden or duty on account of race, color, or previous condition.

"Importations of persons under the name of "coolies," or any other name or designation, or the adoption of any system of peonage, whereby the helpless and unfortunate may be reduced to practical bondage, shall never be authorized or tolerated by the laws of the State; and neither slavery nor involuntary servitude, except as a punishment for crime, whereof the party shall have been duly convicted, shall ever exist in the State."

The closing declaration in the Bill of Rights is alike in both, to wit: "To guard against transgressions of the high powers herein delegated, we declare that every thing in this Bill of Rights is excepted out of the general powers of government, and shall forever remain inviolate; and all laws contrary thereto, or to the following provisions, shall be void."

In future articles other discrepancies in the two instruments will be noted.

IX.

Article II. is identical in both the constitution of 1845 and that of 1869, viz.:

"The powers of the government of the State of Texas shall be divided into three distinct departments, and each of them be confined to a separate body of magistracy, to wit: those which are legislative to one, those which are executive to another, and those which are judicial to another; and no person, or collection of persons, being of one of these departments, shall exercise any power properly.attached to either of the others, except in the instances herein expressly permitted."

Article III. in the constitution of 1845, is as follows:

"Every free male person who shall have attained the age of twenty-one years, and who shall be a citizen of the United States, or who is at the time of the adoption of this constitution by the Congress of the United States a citizen of the Republic of Texas, and shall have resided in the State one year next preceding an election, and the last six months within the district, county, city, or town in which he offers to vote (Indians not taxed, Africans and the descendants of Africans excepted), shall be deemed a qualified elector, and should such qualified elector happen to be in any other county situated in the district in which he resides, at the time of the election, he shall be permitted to vote for any district officer, provided that the qualified electors shall be permitted to vote anywhere in the State for State officers, and provided further that no soldier, seaman, or marine in the army or navy of the United States, shall be entitled to vote at any election created by this constitution."

In nothing does the present constitution differ more widely from the old, than in this article; and, as a matter of course, that part of the old one which precludes Africans and their descendants from the ballot can not be revived under the fifteenth amendment to the Federal constitution. The article in the present State constitution reads as follows:

"Every male person who shall have attained the age of twenty-one years, and who shall be (or who shall have declared his intentions to become) a citizen of the United States, or who is, at the time of the acceptance of this constitution by the Congress of the United States, a citizen of Texas, and shall have resided in this State one year next preceding an election, and within the last six months within the district or county in which he offers to vote, and is duly registered—Indians not taxed excepted—shall be deemed a qualified elector; and should such qualified elector happen to be in any other county, situated in the district in which he resides, at the time of an election, he shall be permitted to vote for any district officer; provided, that the qualified electors shall be permitted to vote anywhere in the State for State officers, and provided, further, that no soldier, seaman, or marine, in the army or navy of the United States shall be entitled to vote at any election created by this constitution."

Another section in the present constitution requires a residence of only sixty days in a county to constitute a voter for county officers. The constitution of 1845 required only six months' residence in Texas previous to its adoption to constitute a citizen.

Both constitutions provide that electors in all cases shall be privileged from arrest during their attendance at elections, and in going to and returning from the same, except in cases of treason, felony, or breach of the peace.

Both use the same words in dividing the legislature into two branches and declaring that the style of the laws shall be, "Be it enacted by the Legislature of the State of Texas."

Both fix the terms of Representatives at two years.

The constitution of 1845 makes the sessions of the legislature biennial. That of 1869 makes them annual.

Both require that to be eligible to a seat in the House of Representatives the candidate shall be a citizen of the United States, and shall have been a citizen of this State two years next preceding his election, and the last year thereof a citizen of the county, city, or town from which he shall be chosen, and shall have attained the age of twenty-one years, at the time of his election.

The constitution of 1845 makes the longest term of senators four years, and divides them into classes, one half vacating their seats at the end of two years, unless re-elected. The present constitution fixes the longest term of senators at six years, and the shortest at two, dividing them into three classes, and declares that the Senate shall consist of thirty members. The old constitution declared that the number should not be less than nineteen nor more than thirty-three.

The present constitution provides for a new apportionment only once in ten years, under the United States census.

Both declare that when a senatorial district shall be composed of two or more counties, it shall not be separated by any county belonging to another district.

The constitution of 1845 required that senators should be thirty years of age. The present fixes the age at twenty-five. Both require a residence of three years in the State to constitute a senator. The present constitution declares that the House of Representatives shall consist of ninety members. That of 1845 requires a census of the population to be taken every eight years, and representatives apportioned accordingly, not to be less than forty-five or more than ninety in number.

The present constitution declares that "no person shall be eligible to any office, State, county, or municipal, who is not a registered voter in the State." The old constitution says nothing of registration.

The following is the language of both:

"The House of Representatives, when assembled, shall elect a speaker and its other officers ; and the Senate shall choose a president, for the time being, and its other officers. Each house shall judge of the elections and qualifications of its own members ; but contested elections shall be determined in such manner as shall be directed by law. Two-thirds of each house shall constitute a quorum to do business, but a smaller number may adjourn from day to day and compel the attendance of absent members in such manner and under such penalties as each house may provide."

Both declared that each house may determine the rules of its own proceedings. But that constitution of 1845 adds that each house may punish members for disorderly conduct, and expel a member by a vote of two-thirds, though not a second time for the same offense. This provision is omitted in the present constitution. Each, provides that members may protest against the passage of acts, and have the reasons for dissent entered on the journals.

Each makes the usual provision against the arrest of members of the legislature during the session ; and provides for the arrest and imprisonment, not exceeding forty-eight hours, of persons guilty of disrespectful or improper conduct in the presence of the legislature, or obstructing the proceedings.

The constitution of 1845 declares that the doors of each house shall be kept open. That of 1869 adds to this clause the words, " except upon a call of either house, and when there is an executive session in the Senate."

Both provide that neither house shall adjourn for more than three days, nor to any other place than that in which they may be sitting, without the consent of the other.

Both say " bills may originate in either house, and be amended, altered, or rejected by the other ; but no bill shall have the force of law until on three several days it shall be read in each house, and free discussion be allowed thereon, unless, in case of great emergency, four-fifths of the house in which the bill shall be pending, may deem it expedient to dispense with this rule, and every bill having passed both houses shall be signed by the speaker and president of their respective houses." To this the constitution of 1869 adds, " provided that the final vote on all bills or joint resolutions appropriating money or lands for any purpose shall be by yeas and nays."

The constitution of 1845 declares that all bills for raising revenue shall originate in the House of Representatives, but the Senate may amend or reject them as other bills. The present constitution says : " Bills may originate in either house, and be amended, altered, or rejected by the other," with the provisions requiring three several readings, on different days in each house, and requiring the final vote to be by yeas and nays on all bills appropriating money or lands.

The constitution of 1845 declares that after a bill or resolution has been rejected by either branch of the legislature, no bill or resolution containing the same substance shall be passed into a law during the same session. The present constitution embraces in substance the same provisions, and also declares that the legislature shall not authorize, by private or special law, the sale or conveyance of any real estate belonging to any person, or vacate or alter any road laid out by legal authority, or any street in any city or village, or any recorded town plat, but provide for the same by general laws." This last provision does not appear in the old constitution of 1845. The present constitution declares that the legislature shall not authorize any lottery, and shall prohibit the sale of lottery tickets ; and in another place, says no lottery shall be authorized by this State, and the buying and selling of lottery tickets in this State is prohibited.

Each prohibits the legislature from increasing the compensation of members during the session at which the increase shall be made, and excludes members from holding any office which may be created or the emoluments of which may have been increased during such term ; and both contain substantially the same provision against holding more than one office at the same time.

Each precludes defaulters to the State from office.

The present constitution declares that it shall be the duty of the legislature immediately to expel from the body any member who shall receive or offer a bribe, and excludes such parties from holding office thereafter.

The constitution of 1845 excludes ministers of the Gospel from the legislature. The present constitution, in lieu of this provision, declares that such parties, after having accepted a seat in the legislature, shall not be allowed to claim exemption from military service, road duty, or serving on juries by reason of their religious profession.

These are the only material points of difference in the two instruments relating to the legislative department of the government.

X.

The following are the only material points upon which the State constitutions of 1845 and 1869 differ, as regards the executive department of the State government :

The constitution of 1845 declares that the supreme executive power of this State shall be vested in the chief magistrate, who shall be styled the Governor. That of 1869 says the executive department shall consist of the governor, lieutenant-governor, secretary of state, comptroller, treasurer, commissioner of the General Land Office, attorney-general and superintendent of public instruction. Certain powers and duties of the governor are defined by both instruments, and both declared that he shall see that the laws are faithfully executed. Both declare that he may require information in writing from the officers of the executive department on any subject relating to the duties of their respective offices ; but the present constitution seems to make the other elective officers of the executive department as independent of the governor as he is of them, and to allow of such dead-locks between members of the department as were exhibited in the case of Governor Davis and Comptroller Bledsoe. The mode of electing the governor is the same in both instruments ; but the present constitution adds the words, " or any of the executive officers to be elected by the qualified voters of the State " to the provision for settling contested elections in regard to the office of governor.

Under the constitution of 1845, the term of office for the governor was two years. Under the present constitution all the executive officers are chosen for four years—a provision which was intended to prolong the tenure of the minority officers chosen by means of the disfranchisement of so many white voters at the time of the first election under the present radical constitution. Under the constitution of 1845 the same man could not serve more than two out of three successive terms in the office of governor. This provision does not appear in the present constitution. Both require substantially the same qualifications for the office of governor ; but under the fourteenth amendment to the Federal constitution, a person who had held office and taken the oath to support that instrument, and afterward engaged in the rebellion can not hold office either under the State or the United States, until Congress has removed his disabilities.

The constitution of 1845 fixed the salary of the first governor at two thousand dollars ; that of 1869 fixed the salary at five thousand dollars, exclusive of the executive mansion, fixtures, and furniture. Both allow the legislature to change the salaries of succeeding governors. The present constitution authorizes the governor to fill vacancies in other executive offices until the meeting of the legislature, and if the appointments are confirmed by the Senate, the appointees hold office until the next regular election.

To the provision authorizing the governor to grant reprieves and pardons, in both constitutions, the present adds, that " in all cases of remission of fines and forfeitures, or grants of reprieve or pardon, the governor shall file, in the office of the secretary of state, his reasons therefor."

The present constitution requires that nominations to fill vacancies occurring in the recess of the legislature shall be made by the governor during the first ten days of its session, and declares that should any nomination be rejected, the same person shall not again be nominated during the session to the same office.

By the constitution of 1845, as well as that of 1869, every bill presented to the governor one day previous to the adjournment of the legislature and not returned to the house in which it originated, before the adjournment, is declared to be a law, and to have the same force and effect as if signed by the governor. This time is too short for the proper discharge of the duty generally devolved on the governor during the last day of the session. Most of the important acts are only passed finally on the last day of the session, either in the legislature or in Congress, and it is utterly impossible for the executive in either case to give full and deliberate attention to the bills brought to him for signature. The fact is notorious that many laws have been signed without having been read by the executive.

The present constitution contains one provision (that may be considered an improvement on the old one), under which the governor may approve any appropriation, and disapprove any other appropriation in the same bill, by designating the appropriation disapproved, after which it requires to be passed over the veto like other bills, in order to become a law ; and if the legislature shall have adjourned before it has been returned, he may be suspend it until submitted to the succeeding session.

The constitution of 1845 made the offices of treasurer and comptroller, as well as the judges of the supreme court, elective by the legislature, but was amended previous to the war, so as to make them all depend on a vote of the people.

Under the constitution as it stood before the war, the attorney-general was elected by the people. He is now appointed by the governor.

These are only the material points in which the present and old constitutions differ as regards the powers, duties, and modes of selecting the executive officers of the State.

The following are the only points on which the State constitutions of 1845 and 1869 differ as regards the judicial department:

The constitution of 1845 says that the judicial power of the State shall be vested in one supreme court, in district courts, and such inferior courts as the legislature may from time to time ordain and establish, and such jurisdiction may be vested in corporation courts as may be directed by law. The corresponding section in the present constitution adds, after the words "inferior courts," the term "magistrates," and authorizes the legislature to establish criminal courts in cities, with jurisdiction over the whole county in which they may be situated.

Under the constitution of 1845, the supreme court consisted of a chief justice and two associates, to hold their offices for six years. The original constitution of 1869 made the number the same ; but it was amended in 1873–4 so as to make the court consist of a chief justice and four associates, who hold office for nine years, and hold courts at the capital and two other places in the State. Both declare that the supreme court shall have appellate jurisdiction only ; but the present constitution adds that " in criminal cases no appeal shall be allowed to the supreme court, unless some judge thereof shall, upon inspecting a transcript of the record, believe that some error of law has been committed by the judge before whom the case was tried, provided that said transcript of the record shall be presented within sixty days of the date of the trial." Both allow appeals from interlocutory judgments, with such exceptions and under such regulations as the legislature shall prescribe. Both permit the supreme court and the judges thereof to issue the writ of *habeas corpus;* the writ of *mandamus,* and such other writs as may be necessary to enforce its own jurisdiction. The constitution of 1845 says the supreme court may compel a judge of the district court to proceed to trial and judgment in a cause. This provision does not appear in the present constitution, which in lieu of the declaration, says the supreme court shall have power to ascertain such matters of fact as may be necessary to the proper exercise of its jurisdiction.

The constitution of 1845 says the supreme court shall hold its sessions once every year, between the months of October and June, and in not more than three places.

The present constitution originally said "that the supreme court should hold its sessions annually at the capital of the State; but this section has been amended, and the court now also holds sessions at Galveston.

The constitution of 1845 required semi-annual terms of the district courts in each county. The present constitution requires three terms.

District judges held office for six years under the constitution of 1845. The term is now eight years.

Judges may be removed by impeachment or address under either instrument.

The constitution of 1845, gives the district court jurisdiction in all criminal cases, suits to recover penalties, forfeitures, and escheats, and cases of divorce, but the present constitution amplifies these declarations by adding: "All suits for slander or defamation of character," suits for the trial of title to land, and enforcement of liens; both fix the lowest value of the amount in controversy to give the court original jurisdiction at one hundred dollars, exclusive of interest.

The constitution of 1845 provided for the establishment of inferior tribunals for appointing guardians, granting letters of administration and the transaction of business pertaining to estates, giving the district court also both original and appellate jurisdiction and control over such matters. The present constitution declares that the district court shall have original and exclusive jurisdiction over such matters. Both constitutions embrace substantially the same matter in declaring that judges shall not sit in the trial of causes in which they are interested, or where they may be related to the litigants, or may have been of counsel, and providing for the manner of try-

35

ing such causes by other judges ; and also authorizing judges to exchange districts in certain cases.

The constitution of 1845 gives parties the right to trial by jury in cases of equity as well as law. The present constitution adds, "except in cases where a defendant may fail to appear and answer within the time prescribed by law, and the cause of action is liquidated and proved by an instrument in writing."

The constitution of 1845 declares that in all cases where justices of the peace or other judicial officers of inferior tribunals shall have jurisdiction in the trial of causes where the penalty for the violation of the law is fine or imprisonment (except in cases of contempt), the accused shall have the right of trial by jury. In lieu of this provision, the present constitution says: " Every criminal offense that may by law be punished by death, or in the discretion of the jury by imprisonment to hard labor for life ; and every offense that by law may be punished with imprisonment in the State Penitentiary, shall be deemed a felony, and shall only be tried upon an indictment found by a grand jury ; but all offenses of a less grade than felony may be prosecuted upon complaint, under oath, by any peace officer or citizen, before any justice of the peace or other inferior tribunal that may be established by law ; and the party prosecuted shall have the right of trial by jury."

The constitution of 1845 was silent as regards the number of justices of the peace for each county. The present constitution requires five, to hold their offices for four years, and to constitute the county court, having the jurisdiction previously exercised by county commissioners and police courts. Justices of the peace are now also *ex officio* notaries public and coroners. Constables are appointed by the justices, sitting as a county court.

Under the present constitution, all county and district officers whose duties are not otherwise provided for, may be removed, on conviction by a jury, after indictment, for malfeasance, or misfeasance in office.

These are the principal, if not substantially the only, variations between the constitution of 1845 and the present constitution, under the title of Judicial Department. In former articles similar comparisons were made with reference to the legislative and executive departments. Other articles remained to be noticed.

XI.

In previous articles of this series a comparison was made between the State constitution of 1845 and that of 1869, so far as the Bill of Rights and the legislative, executive, and judicial departments of the government are concerned. Several other aspects of these instruments remain to be noted.

The constitution of 1845 requires the legislature to provide for the organization of the militia, and provides that any person who conscientiously scruples to bear arms shall not be compelled to do so, but shall pay an equivalent for personal service ; that no licensed minister of the Gospel shall be required to perform military duty, work on the roads, or serve on juries ; and declares that the governor shall have power to call forth the militia to execute the laws of the State, suppress insurrections, and repel invasions. The present constitution simply confers this power to call out the militia on the governor ; but makes no provision for its organization, or any exception exempting any one from militia duty.

The constitution of 1845 declares that the legislature shall make suitable provision for the support of public schools, establish free schools throughout the State, furnish means for their support by taxation on property, and set apart for the purpose not less than *one-tenth* of the revenues of the State derivable from taxation ; and forbids the passage of any law diverting the fund to any other use ; declares that the public lands granted to the counties for school purposes shall not be alienated in fee, or disposed of otherwise than by lease, for a term not exceeding twenty years. The present constitution amplifies on this head, and says that public schools shall be established " for the gratuitous instruction of all the inhabitants of the State between the ages of six and eighteen years " ; provides for a superintendent of public instruction, to hold office for four years, and fixes his salary at $2,500 a year ; authorizes the legislature to " give the district (school) board such legislative powers, in regard to the schools, school-houses and school fund of the district as may be deemed necessary and proper " ; declares that " the legislature shall establish a uniform system of public free schools throughout the State " ; authorizes the enactment of laws to compel attendance of children at school four months in the year ; declares that all the funds, lands, and other property heretofore, or that may be hereafter set apart for the endowment of public schools, shall constitute a school fund ; that " all sums of money that may come to this State hereafter from the sale of any portion of the public domain shall constitute a part of the school fund ; that the legislature shall set apart for the support of public schools ONE-FOURTH of the annual revenue from taxation ; collect a poll tax of one dollar on all male persons between the ages of twenty-one and sixty, for the benefit of public schools ; and that no law shall ever be passed appropriating these funds for any other use or purpose whatever. The legislature is further authorized to provide for raising such amount by taxation, in the several school districts, as will be necessary to provide school-houses in each district, and insure the education of all the scholastic inhabitants in the same. But the present constitution goes, or attempts to go, still further, and declares that " the public lands heretofore given to the counties shall be under the control of the legislature, and may be sold under such regulations

33

as the legislature may prescribe"; and the proceeds added to the school fund." It also declares that the legislature shall invest the school fund in the bonds of the United States government and in no other security.

This attempt to expropriate the lands of the several counties, located by them and held for their individual use, and to throw them into hodge-podge for the use and benefit of all the counties, thus placing improvident and new counties on the same footing with old ones that have been provident in the location and preservation of their lands, is in conflict with the whole theory of vested rights. The famous opinion of Chief-Justice Marshall in the Dartmouth College case, in which the principle of the inviolability of chartered property is fully established, would seem to apply to this case.

XII.

There are few questions of more interest for the consideration of the coming convention than the subject of Public Schools. The maintenance of a system of free schools has been a favorite theory in Texas since the foundation of the Republic in 1836. Every constitution adopted has made, or attempted to make, provision for the support of schools ; but none has gone so far as the present, which makes an absolute appropriation of one-fourth of all the revenues of the State for the support of schools, besides the use of the pre-existing fund, and also authorizes the assessment of additional local taxes for the purpose ; provides for the election of a superintendent of public Instruction, authorizes compulsory attendance at school; appropriates the proceeds of the sale of all public lands of the State to the support of schools ; levies a poll tax for the same object ; declares that no law shall ever be enacted diverting any of these funds to any other purpose ; authorizes special taxes to build school houses ; and provides that the school lands of the counties shall be under the control of the legislature, and may be sold by it, and the proceeds added to the general school fund. This last provision is an obvious usurpation of the rights and property of the old counties, in which these lands had vested, and which have been at the expense of locating and preserving them. The endowments of our public schools have been liberal, and, if preserved, will be of incalculable advantage.

On the 26th of January, 1839, the Congress of the Republic passed "An act appropriating certain lands for the establishment of a general system of education," and granted three leagues of land to each organized county of the Republic.

On the 5th of February, 1840, Congress granted an additional league, in all 17,712 acres, nearly twenty-eight square miles, to every organized county.

On the 16th day of January, 1850, the legislature granted a like amount of land, for the same purpose, " to each and every county in this State which has been established and organized since the 16th day of February, 1846, or which may hereafter be established by law."

On the 13th day of May, 1846, one-tenth of the general revenues of the State was set apart for educational purposes, and the money thus appropriated was invested in interest-paying bonds and became a part of the permanent school fund.

On the 31st of January, 1854, two million of dollars in United States bonds were set apart as an addition to the permanent school fund, which fund, at the present time, amounts to over $2,500,000. The interest arising from this fund—about $150,000 annually—is distributed among the counties for the support of public schools.

On the 24th of April, 1874, the governor approved an act to provide for the sale of the alternate sections of the land surveyed by railroad companies, and set apart for the benefit of the school fund.

No more important interest will require consideration in the coming convention than that involved in this subject.

The constitution of 1845 simply declared that the legislature should, as early as practicable, establish free schools, and furnish means for their support by taxation on property, and set apart not less than one-tenth of the annual revenues from taxation as a school fund ; declared that the school lands of the counties should not be alienated in fee or disposed of otherwise than by lease, for a term not exceeding twenty years, leaving the legislature free, within these limitations, to establish such a system of schools as it might deem best adapted to the changing wants and condition of the people.

With this article will close the series we proposed for the purpose of tracing the leading ideas of free government which have controlled the people of Texas since the inauguration of the Republic in 1835-'36. The whole history of the government has been consistent and harmonious, with the exception of the innovation forced upon the organic law through force and outside pressure by the events of the late war, leaving the State with a constitution which was not the work of her own people or in accordance with the popular sentiment in many important particulars, though the preamble is made falsely to allege that the people are permitted to make choice of their own form of government. In this case it was literally Hobson's choice.

The preceding articles have sketched the most important particulars in which the present instrument varies from its predecessors. The following are about all of any interest that remain to be noted :

XIII.

The provisions for the impeachment of public officers and the temporary appointment of persons to fill the vacancies thus created, are identical in both the constitutions of 1845 and 1869.

The article in the constitution of 1845, declaring what fraudulent land certificates are void, is omitted in the present constitution.

The constitution of 1845 has but one section in the article on the land office. The present constitution has eight additional sections, declaring that all surveys not returned to the General Land Office, in accordance with the provisions of the act of February 10, 1852, are null and void ; that all certificates located after the 1st of August, 1856, upon lands which were titled before of certificate, are null and void, with certain exceptions where surveys conflict ; requiring that all genuine certificates at the time of the adoption of the constitution should be surveyed and returned to the Land Office by January 1, 1875, or forever barred ; declaring that all lands previously reserved for the benefit of railroads shall be subject to location ; and prohibiting the legislature from granting lands to any person except actual settlers, and releasing to the owner of the land all mines discovered on it. This article has been amended so as to allow the legislature to grant not exceeding twenty sections of land to the mile to aid in the construction of railroads.

The constitution of 1869 provides for the creation of a bureau of immigration—which was not done by the constitution of 1845. This article will probably form a subject of considerable discussion in the convention.

Under the head of General Provisions, the oath of public officers is the same in both constitutions, excepting the addition in the present constitution, in which the officer is required to swear that he is not disqualified by the fourteenth amendment to the Federal constitution, and that he is a qualified voter.

The provision in the constitution of 1845, in regard to the crime of treason against the State, is omitted in the present constitution, as is also the provision that every person shall be disqualified from holding any office of trust or profit in this State, who shall have been convicted of having given or offered a bribe to purchase his election or appointment, and excluding from juries and the right of suffrage persons guilty of bribery, perjury, forgery, and other high crimes. Duelists are excluded from office under either.

Both require that all popular elections shall be by ballot ; elections by the legislature *viva voce*.

Both prohibit extra compensation to officers and contractors under the State, or the payment of claims not founded on pre-existing laws.

Both prohibit the payment of public money before it has been appropriated by law. Both require a vote of two-thirds of each house of the legislature to make appropriations for private purposes, or internal improvements, and prohibit the legislature from issuing paper of any description to circulate as money.

Holding office under the United States or foreign powers excludes the incumbent from a seat in the legislature, under both constitutions.

The constitution of 1845 required the legislature to pass laws to provide for the settlement of differences between citizens by arbitration. This provision appears in the present constitution also, but has never been of much use.

The constitution of 1845 provides for the exemption from forced sale of the homestead of a family to the value of $2,000. The present constitution increases the amount to $5,000, besides the improvements. Each exempts 200 acres of land.

Each declares that taxation shall be uniform throughout the State, and all property, except such as two-thirds of the legislature may exempt, be taxed in proportion to its value. The present constitution declares that the assessments for taxes on lands shall be a lien upon them, but prohibits the sale of lands for taxes except under a decree of court, and provides for such sales once in every five years.

The present constitution contains a provision, not in the old one, making it the duty of the legislature, in all cases where a State or county debt is created, to provide by law means for the payment of the interest and a two per cent. sinking fund to pay the principal, and makes all such laws irrepealable until the debt is paid.

The present constitution permits pensions to be granted to Texas veterans and Union soldiers, but not to Confederate soldiers.

It requires counties to establish poor-houses for the employment and care of indigent persons.

It legalizes all marriages made prior to or during the war by slaves. If the laws against bigamy were enforced under this provision, fifty penitentiaries would not hold the convicts.

Both instruments required the laws to be digested once in every ten years.

Lotteries and dealing in lottery tickets are prohibited by both.

No divorce is allowed to be granted by the legislature under either.

The constitution of 1845 secures to the wife all property owned by her before marriage. This provision reads as follows : " All property, both real and personal, of the wife, owned or claimed by her before marriage, and that acquired afterward by gift, devise, or descent, shall be her separate property ; and laws shall be passed clearly defining the rights of the wife in relation, as

well to her separate property as that held in common with her husband.
Laws shall also be passed providing for the registration of the wife's separate
property." In the present constitution the corresponding provision reads :
" The rights of married women to their separate property, real and personal,
and the increase of the same, shall be protected by law, and married women,
infants, and insane persons, shall not be barred of their rights of property by
adverse possession or law of limitation of less than seven years, from and
after the removal of each and all of their respective legal disabilities."

Both constitutions contain a clause declaring that every law shall embrace
but one object, to be expressed in the title, and prohibiting the amendment
of laws by a simple reference to the title.

The constitution of 1845 declares that no private corporation shall be
created, except by a vote of two-thirds of each house of the legislature,
authorizes charters to be revoked by a similar vote, and prohibits the State
from being part owner in the stock or property of any corporation. This
provision does not appear in the present constitution, which, however, declares
that corporations shall be responsible in exemplary damages for the loss of
life through willful acts or neglect on the part of their employés, a provision
not in the constitution of 1845.

The present constitution authorizes " the inferior courts " of counties, on
a vote of " two-thirds of the qualified voters," to assess taxes in aid of internal improvements—not to exceed two per cent. of the value of the property
taxed. This provision was not in the old constitution, and will form another
subject of debate in the approaching convention.

The present constitution declares that all civil officers of this State shall
be removable by an address of two-thirds of the members of each house of the
legislature, where the constitution does not otherwise provide for removals
from office. This provision did not appear in the old constitution. Neither
did that declaring that " all usury laws are abolished in this State " ; that giving mechanics a lien on articles manufactured or repaired by them ; or that
authorizing the prohibition of the sale of spirituous liquors in the vicinity of
colleges and seminaries not located at county seats.

This ends the statement of the principal points of difference between the
old and present State constitutions, leaving the discussion of their compara-
:ive merits for further debate.

CVIII.

EXTRACT FROM THE ADDRESS OF HON. ASHBEL SMITH TO THE VETERAN ASSOCIATION.

HOUSTON, May, 1875.

"I COME back from this seeming digression to our historical thread. The battle of San Jacinto was fought. It was one of the decisive battles of the world. Battles are not important from the numbers engaged in the shock, or the dead that strew the field. The victory of San Jacinto redeemed a territory of imperial extent, and consecrated it to liberty. And then look at the vast regions, California and other new States, whose acquisition and incorporation into the American Union grew out of the Independence of Texas achieved at San Jacinto. Had the campaign which was crowned so gloriously on the battle-field of San Jacinto closed with victory to the Mexicans, and in their ultimate success, the vast territories of more than a million of square miles in extent now constituting the great States of California and Texas, and the great States intervening, forming the south-western border of the American Union, these vast territories, I say, would have still remained a useless wilderness, under Mexico, cursed with the same dead palsy in which they had lain for more than two centuries. Veterans, the victory of you and yours at San Jacinto was of vast and inappreciable consequences— it was no slender, no stinted dower which Texas brought into the Union. But it is not my purpose to dwell on this topic; but to view the great closing campaign of the Texas revolution in a different point of view. It is to vindicate the truth of history from flings not unfrequently made, and often believed, in the long and sharp political contests waged between parties in the United States, that the old Texas army was a sort of insurrectionary mob, and that San Jacinto was a sort of helter-skelter massacre. You, veterans, know that it was war; not wild, unorganized disconnected skirmishes and raids, but war in its sternest form waged by the Mexican Government, under Santa Anna who was that government, a general and chieftain of great ability, commanding an army of well-organized, well-disciplined, well-appointed soldiers, themselves veterans with unbounded confidence in themselves and in their commander, waging a war of extermination, giving no quarter.

"But it is the campaign as conducted by General Houston, commanding the Texan army, which I shall briefly consider, in its conception and in its general strategic execution. With the distinguished soldier on my right—Mr. Davis—I may well fear the sarcasm on the old philosopher who discoursed on war before Hannibal. But having myself gone through several good campaigns, I may feel a just confidence in my criticism, as I am laying no claim to power of execution. And after careful study, I assert that the campaign of 1836, from the Colorado to the San Jacinto, may safely challenge the most searching analysis by the most competent masters of the art of war, Gustavus Adolphus, Turenne, Frederick, by Napoleon or Napier if they were living. When on the Colorado, some 1300 or 1400 men were present, under arms, of the Texas army. At San Jacinto there were only some 700. Many of our own people thought we ought to have made a stand on the Colorado and given the enemy battle there. Menacing us, in pursuit of us, there was approaching the Mexican army—ten thousand veterans, compact, wary, watchful. With us battle must needs have been defeat : for there is a dis- parity of numbers which no valor can over balance ; and what would our defeat have meant?—not merely the utter waste of the country but the brutal mas- sacre and worse than murder of the thousands of women and children flying eastward. But wiser counsels prevailed. Under Houston our army slowly retreated ; our retreat covered that of the women and children. As Houston continued the retreat, Santa Anna pursuing, extended his line of operations to the right and to the left so widely that every portion of his line became weak. Santa Anna and his officers, advancing without serious opposition became confident and careless. In the eagerness of pursuit and fear lest the Texan army should escape him, Santa Anna forgot the wariness of a general. Houston proceeding down Buffalo Bayou to the nook made by it and the San Jacinto River, seemed to have gone heedlessly into a trap, Santa Anna followed him, thinking he had now an easy and certain prey.

"Houston indeed made it a trap, but a trap for Santa Anna, by destroying the bridge across Vince's Bayou. And now for the wisdom of the conception of the campaign. The Texas commander suddenly turned upon the Mexican army, hurled the Texans on the vital part of it that portion commanded by Santa Anna, now advanced beyond its supports ; and by the destruction of this corps and the capture of the commander-in-chief, by a single, decisive, wisely timed blow, ended the campaign, terminated the war, and secured your independence. It would be unjust to the Texas soldiers, that is, to the Texas men of that day—for the army was the people ; it would be unjust not to recall a fact known to every one of you veterans : it is, that amid the dis- couragements, the privations incident to the long retreat, instead of the demoralization so often caused by a long and painful retreat, the spirit of the men was maintained to the very highest fighting pitch of valor. Nay, so rampant was it, that subordinate officers and men complained, nay, begged to be marshaled for fight. But the consummate wisdom of the campaign and de- termined valor of the men are equally fearless of criticism and worthy of praise.

"Veterans of Texas, citizens of Texas all, we do not beg forbearance, we do not plead human infirmity nor new and straitened circumstances. We simply and resolutely demand only truth."

PART IV.

STATISTICAL.

STATISTICAL.

I.

AUSTIN'S "ORIGINAL THREE HUNDRED."

A list of the names of the original "Three Hundred" Colonists introduced by Stephen F. Austin, under his first contract, as shown by the original records in the General Land Office at Austin, Texas.

Andrews, John.
Alsbery, Thomas.
Allcorn, Elijah.
Andrews, William.
Allen, Martin.
Austin, John.
Alley, Thomas and William.
Alley, Rawson.
Alsbery, Charles G., Harvey, and Horace A.
Anderson, Simon Asa.
Angier, Samuel T.
Austin, Santiago E. B.
Angier, S. T.
Alley, John.
Alley, William.
Austin, Stephen F.
Baily, James B.
Bradley, John.
Bigham, Francis.
Burnet, Thomas.
Bright, David.
Byrd, Micajah.

Bridges, William B.
Bucknor, Aylett C.
Bostick, Caleb R.
Brotherton, Robert.
Burnet, Pumphrey.
Boatwright, Thomas.
Brown, William S.
Beason, Benjamin.
Bunson, Enoch.
Bell, Josiah H.
Bloodgood, William.
Berry, Manders.
Bradley, Edward R.
Beard, James.
Brooks, Bluford.
Bell, Thomas B.
Burnham, Jesse.
Best, Isaac.
Betts, Jacob.
Brown, John.
Bowman, John.
Belknap, Charles.
Brown, George.

Breen, Charles.
Buttle, Mills M.
Barrett, William.
Bradley, Thomas.
Cummins, James.
Castleman, Sylvanus.
Carter, Samuel.
Chrisman, Horatio.
Clarke, John C.
Coats, Merit M.
Cummins, William.
Cummins, John.
Cummins, Rebecca.
Callahan, Morris.
Curtis, James, Sr.
Crownover, John.
Calvit, Alexander.
Curtis, Hinton.
Cooke, John.
Cartwright, Thomas.
Cooper, William.
Cummins, James.
Curtis, James.
Coles, John P.
Clarke, Anthony R.
Carson, William C.
Crier, John.
Cartwright, Jesse.
Cooke, James.
Carpenter, David.
Duty, Joseph.
Duty, George.
Davidson, Samuel.
Duke, Thomas.
Demos, Peter.
Demos, Charles.
Dewees, Bluford.
Dyer, Clement C.
Dillard, Nicholas.
Dickenson, John.
Earle, Thomas.
Elam, John.

Edwards, Pastorus E.
Elder, Robert.
Fitzgeral, David.
Foster, John.
Fulchear, Churchill.
Foster, Randolph.
Flannakin, Isaiah.
Flowers, Elisha.
Fisher, James.
Fenton, David.
Foster, Isaac.
Falmash, Charles.
Fields, John T.
George, Freeman.
Gates, Samuel.
Garrett, Charles.
Gates, William.
Guthrie, Robert.
Gorbet, Chester S.
Groce, Jared E.
Gilliland, Daniel.
Grey, Thomas and
Moore, Jno. W.
Gouldrich, Michael.
Gilbert, Sarah.
Gilbert, Preston.
Hall, John.
Harris, William.
Hall, William.
Huff, John.
Hope, James.
Harvey, William.
Harris, William J.
Hunter, Eli.
Hudson, Charles S.
Hadden, John.
Hensley, James.
Holland, William.
Holland, Francis.
Holliman, Kurchen.
Hunter, Johnson.
Harris, William and P.

Harrison, George.
Harris, John R.
Haynes, Thomas S.
Hady, Samuel C.
Harris, David.
Huff, George.
Hamilton, David.
Hodge, Alexander.
Hill, Geo. B.
Harris, Abner.
Hughes, Isaac.
Jones, Henry.
Isaacs, Samuel.
Jones, Randall.
Irons, John.
Jackson, Alexander.
Johnson, H. W. Walker, and Thos. H. Borden.
Ingram, Seth.
Irams, John.
Isaac, Jackson.
Jones, Oliver.
Jones, James.
Jackson, Humphrey.
Ingram, Ira.
Kennedy, Samuel.
Kuykendall, Abner.
Kuykendall, Joseph.
Kinchelve, William.
Kuykendall, Robert.
Kelley, John.
Kennon, Alfred.
Keep, Imla.
Kuykendall, Brazilla.
Kew, Peter and William.
Kerr, James.
Kingston, William and Powell, Peter.
Keller, John.
Little, William.
Lynch, James.
Lynch, Nathaniel.

Linsey, Benjamin.
Long, Jane H.
Leayne, Hosea H.
Lakey, Joel.
Little, John.
Mitchell, Asa.
Marsh, Shubart,
McFarlan, Achilles.
Morton, William.
Millican, Robert.
Millican, James D.
Millican, William.
McWilliams, William.
Mathis, William.
McNutt, Elizabeth.
McCormick, David.
McCoy, Thomas and Deckro, Daniel.
Morrison, Moses and Cooper, William.
McLain, A. W.,
McNair, James.
Milburn, David H.
Davis, Thomas.
Martin, Wyly.
McNeil, John.
Moore, Luke.
McNeil, Daniel. •
McNeil, Pleasant D.
Miller, Simon.
McCormick, Arthur.
McNeil, John G.
McNeil, George W.
McFarlan, John.
Monks, John.
McCloskey, John.
McKenny, Thomas F.
McNeil, Sterling.
Morser, David.
Miller, Samuel R.
Miller, Samuel.
Mims, Joseph.

Nuckels, M. B.
Nelson, James.
Newman, Joseph.
Orrick, James.
Parker, William.
Pettus, William.
Prator, William.
Phillips, Zeno.
Picket, Pamelia.
Parker, Joshua.
Park, William.
Print, Pleasant.
Chance, Samuel.
Pettus, Freeman.
Petty, John.
Phelps, James A. E.
Polley, Joseph H.
Penticost, George S.
Pryor, William.
Phillips, Isham B.
Peyton, Jonathan C.
Rankin, Frederick.
Rubb, John.
Robinson, George.
Roberts, William.
Robinson, Andrew.
Richardson, Stephen.
Rourk, Elijah.
Roberts, Noel F.
Ross, James.
Robbins, Early.
Robbins, William.
Rabb, William.
Rawls, Amos.
Rawls, Daniel.
Rabb, Thomas.
Rawls Benjamin.
Stout, Owen H.
Randon, David.
Perrington, Jsaac.
Rabb, Andrew.
Raleigh, William.

Randon, John.
Reels, Patrick and
Trobough, John.
Roberts, Andrew.
Ramey, Lawrence.
Robertson, Edward.
Smithers, William.
Smith, Christian.
Shipman, Moses.
Shelly, David.
Frazier, James,
McCormick, John.
Smith, John.
McKensie, Hugh.
Scobey, Robert.
Strawsnider, Gabriel.
Scott, James.
Stevens, Thomas.
Sims, Bartlett.
Smith, Cornelius.
Selkirk, William.
Sutherland, Walter.
Stafford, William.
Singleton, Philip.
Spencer, Nancy.
Scott, William.
Stafford, Adam.
San Pierre, Joseph.
Strange, James.
Singleton, George W.
Shipman, Daniel and Charles Isaac N.
Sojourner, A. L.
Tone, Thomas J., and Jameson Thomas.
Teel, George.
Thompson, Jesse.
Taylor, John D.
Talley, David.
Tumlinson, Elizabeth.
Tong, James F.
Thomas, Ezekiel.
Tumlinson, James.

Thomas, Jacob.
Toy, Samuel.
Varner, Martin.
Vince, William.
Vince, Richard.
Vince, Robert.
Van Dorn, Isaac.
Bayless, Daniel E.
Vince, Allen.
White, Walter C.
Knight, James.
Whitesides, James.
Whitesides, William.
Westall, Thomas.
Wells, Francis F.
Walker, James.
Whiting, Nathaniel.
Osborn, Nathan.
Williams, John R.

Williams, Solomon.
Williams, Samuel M.
Whitesides, Henry and Boulin.
White, Joseph.
Williams, Thomas.
Whitlock, William.
White, Any, (widow).
White, Reuben.
Williams, George T.
Williams, Robert H.
White, William C.
Williams, John, Jr.
Woods, Zeddock.
Wightman, Elias R.
Wilkins, Jane.
Wallace, Caleb.
Williams, John.
Williams, Henry.

The grants of land to the above persons are all signed by

STEPHEN F. AUSTIN, *Empressario.*

SAMUEL M. WILLIAMS, *Secretary.*

GASPAR FLORES, *Commissioner on the part of the Imperial Government.*

TOMAS M. DUKE, *Alcalde.*

IRA INGRAM, *Witness.*

The original contract was made between Stephen F. Austin and the Spanish government, on the 4th of January, 1823, and was ratified by the Mexican Empire, on the 18th of February, and the 11th of April, following. The records are in the hands of Samuel M. Williams, and the writer has never seen a more beautiful specimen of correct chirography than is exhibited in these old books. Thanks are hereby tendered to Messrs. W. M. Gilleland and Whiting for their kind aid in making out the above list.*

* It will be observed that there are more than three hundred names in the above list. This is accounted for by the fact that the contract specifies the introduction of *three hundred families,* and in several instances two or three young men were together considered a family, and the patent was issued to each of them severally.

36

II.

LIST OF ALL THE MEN IN THE TEXAS ARMY AT THE BATTLE OF SAN JACINTO.*

RETURN OF KILLED AND WOUNDED, IN THE ACTIONS OF THE 20TH AND 21ST APRIL, 1836.

MAJOR-GENERAL SAM HOUSTON, wounded severely.

First Regiment Texan Volunteers.

Company A.—George Waters, private, slightly wounded on the 21st.

Company B.—James Ownby, private, badly wounded on the 21st; William G. Walker, private, badly wounded on the 21st.

Company C.—Captain Jesse Billingsly, slightly wounded on the 21st; Lemuel Blakely, private, killed on the 21st; Logan Vandeveer, private, badly wounded on the 21st; Washington Anderson, private, slightly wounded on the 21st; Calvin Page, private, slightly wounded on the 21st; Martin Walker, private, badly wounded on the 21st.

Company D.—Captain Mosely Baker, slightly wounded on the 21st; C. D. Anderson, private, slightly wounded on the 21st; Allen Ingram, private, slightly wounded on the 21st.

Company F.—Leroy Wilkinson, private, slightly wounded on the 21st; James Nelson, private, wounded on the 21st; Mitchel Putnam, private, wounded on the 21st.

Company H.—A. R. Stephens, private, wounded on the 21st; J. Tom, private, killed on the 21st; J. — Cooper, private, badly wounded on the 21st; B. R. Brigham, private, killed on the 21st. Total—killed, 3; wounded, 15.

Second Regiment Texan Volunteers.

Company D.—Second Lieutenant, Lamb, killed on the 21st; G. W. Robinson, private, several wounded on the 21st; William Winters, private, severely wounded on the 21st; First Sergeant, Albert Gallatin, slightly wounded on the 21st; E. G. Rector, private, slightly wounded on the 21st.

---

* This list of the officers and men composing the Texas army at San Jacinto, was published originally in New Orleans, shortly after the battle, and copied into the Texas Almanac of 1859. We have had it examined and corrected as far as possible, but there are doubtless some omissions and inaccuracies in it still.—COMPILER.

Company E.—Washington Lewis, private, severely wounded on the 21st.

Company F.—Alphonso Steel, wounded on the 21st.

Company K.—First Lieutenant, J. C. Hale, killed on the 21st.

Company J.—Captain Smith, slightly wounded on the 21st; First Sergeant Thomas P. Fowl, killed on the 21st; W. F. James, private, severely wounded on the 21st. Killed, 3; severely wounded, 5; slightly, 3—total, 11.

Dr. William Motley, wounded severely on the 21st—died since; A. R. Stevens, wounded severely on the 21st—died since; Lieutenant-Colonel J. C. Neil, of the artillery, wounded on the 20th; William A. Park, of the artillery, wounded slightly on the 21st; Devereau J. Woodlief, of the cavalry, wounded severely on the 20th; Olwyn J. Trask, private, cavalry, wounded severely on the 20th.

A List of Officers, Non-Commissioned Officers, and Privates, engaged in the Battle of San Jacinto, on the 21st of April, 1836:

Major-General SAM HOUSTON, Commander-in-Chief of the Texan forces.

Staff.—Adjutant-General, John A. Wharton; Inspector-General, George W. Hockley; Commissary-General, John Forbes; Assistant Inspector-General, William G. Cooke; Aids-de-Camp, A. Horton, William H. Patton, James Collinsworth; Volunteer Aids, James H. Perry, R. Eden Handy, R. M. Coleman; Secretary of War, Hon. Thomas J. Rusk; William Motley, M. D.

Medical Staff.—Alexander Ewing, surgeon First Regiment Artillery, acting surgeon-general; Davidson, surgeon First Regiment Volunteers; Fitzhuch, assistant surgeon First Regiment Volunteers; A. Jones, surgeon Second Regiment Volunteers; Booker, surgeon Second Regiment Volunteers; Labadie, surgeon.

Artillery Corps.—Lieutenant-Colonel J. C. Neil, wounded the 20th; Captain J. N. Moreland; First Lieutenant, W. Stillwell.

Privates.—T. O. Harris, John M. Wade, Hugh M. Swift, William A. Park, wounded on the 21st; Thomas Green, Clark M. Harmon, T. J. Robinson, M. Baxter, Thomas Plaster, second sergeant, Willis Collins, Benjamin M'Culloch, Richardson Scurry, first sergeant; Joseph White, Thomas N. B. Green, John Ferrill, Joseph Floyd, Alfred Benton, D. T. Dunham, T. C. Edwards, S. B. Bardwell, assisted by the following regulars from the companies of Captains Teal and Turner: Campbell, Millerman, Gainer, Cumberland, of Teal's company; Benson, Clayton, Merwin, Legg, of Turner's company.

Cavalry Corps.—Mirabeau B. Lamar, commander; Henry Carnes, captain; J. R. Cook, first lieutenant; William Harness, second lieutenant; W. H. Smith, captain; Lem Gustine, M. D.; W. Secretts, F. Secretts, A.

Allsbury, W. B. Sweeney, Benjamin F. Smith, Thomas Robbins, S. C. Tunnage, D. W. Reaves, E. R. Rainwater, J. D. Elliott, J. P. Davis, J. Neil, N. Nixon, G. Deaderick, J. Nash, Isaac W. Benton, Jacob Duncan, J. W. Hill, P. Allsbury, D. McKay, W. J. C. Pierce, W. King, Thomas Blackwell, Goodwin, J. Coker, Elisha Clapp, H. Henderson, George Johnson, J. W. Williamson, Wilson C. Brown, J. Thompson, John Robbins, William F. Young, James Douthatt, John Carpenter, William Taylor, Anthony Foster, Z. Y. Beauford, Spenser Townsend, James Shaw, William D. Redd, Clopper, P. H. Bell, J. W. Robinson.

Regulars.

Lieutenant-Colonel Henry Millard, commanding; Captain John M. Allen, acting major.

Company A.—Andrew Briscoe, captain; Martin K. Snell, first lieutenant; Robert McCloskey, second lieutenant; Lyman F. Rounds, first sergeant; David S. Nelson, second sergeant; Daniel O. Driscoll, third sergeant; Charles A. Ford, fourth sergeant; Richardson, first corporal; Harry C. Craig, second corporal; Bear, third corporal; Flores, musician.

Privates.—Bruff, Bebee, Benton, H. P. Brewster, Cassady, Dutcher, Darrl, Elliott, Flyn, Farley, Grieves, Warner, Henderson, Lang, Larbartare, Limski, Mason, Montgomery, Marsh, Morton, O'Neil, Pierce, Patton, Rheinhart, Kainer, Richardson, Smith 1st, Smith 2d, Sullivan, Saunders, Swain, Tindall 1st, Taylor, Van Winkle, Wilkinson, Webb.

Volunteers.

Company B.—A. Turner, captain; W. Millen, first lieutenant; W. W. Summers, second lieutenant; Charles Stewart, first sergeant; Swearinger, second sergeant; Robert Moore, Thomas Wilson, and M. Snyder, corporals.

Privates.—Bernard, Browning, Bissett, Belden, Colton, Harper, Hogan, Harvey, Johnson, Keeland, Nirlas, Paschal, Phillips, Smith 1st, Smith 2d, Callahan, Christie, Clarkson, Dalrymple, Eldridge, Edson, Ludus, Lind, Minuett, Mordorff, Massie, Moore 2d, Scheston, Sigman, Tyler, Woods, Wardryski.

Company B.—A. R. Romans, captain; Nicholas Dawson, second lieutenant; James Wharton, A. Mitchell, S. L. Wheeler, sergeants; A. Taylor, J. D. Egbert, Charles A. Clarke, W. P. Moore, corporals.

Privates.—Angell, G. Brown, Joseph Barstow, J. B. Bradley, B. Coles, J. S. Conn, J. W. T. Dixon, William Dunbar, H. Homan, J. M. Jett, Stev Jett, A. S. Jordan, S. W. Lamar, Edward Lewis, J. B. W. M'Farlane, A. M'Stea,

EDWARD BURLESON.

See p. 268.

H. Miller, W. G. Newman, W. Richardson, D. Tindale, J. Vinater, C. W. Waldron, F. F. Williams, James Wilder, W. S. Walker, James Ownby.

Company I.—W. S. Fisher, captain ; R. W. Carter, second lieutenant ; Jones, sergeant.

Privates.—George W. Leek, N. Rudders, J. W. Strode, Jos. Sovereign, W. Sargeant, R. J. L. Reel, Rufus Wright, Jos. McAlister, B. F. Starkley, Day, John Morgan, W. S. Arnot, M. W. Brigham, P. Burt, Tewister, Slack, R. Banks, Jac. Maybee Graves, B. F. Fry, E. G. Mayrie, M'Neil, J. M. Shreve, W. Pace, Ch. Stibbins, H. Bond, Geo. Fennell, W. Gill, R. Critten-den, Adam Mosier, J. S. Patterson, Jos. Douane, G. W. Mason, Thomas Pratt, E. Knoland, A. H. Miles, Jno. Llewelyn, James Joslyn, Jo Gillespie, A. J. Harris, D. James.

Staff of the Command.

Nicholas Lynch, adjutant ; W. M. Carper, surgeon ; John Smith, ser-geant-major ; Pinkey Caldwell, quartermaster.

First Regiment Texan Volunteers.

Edward Burleson, colonel ; Alex. Sommerville, lieutenant-colonel ; Jas. W. Tinsley, adjutant ; Cleveland, sergeant-major.

Company A.—William Wood, captain ; S. B. Raymond, second lieu-tenant ; J. C. Allison, first sergeant ; James A. Sylvester, second sergeant ; O. T. Brown, third sergeant ; Nathaniel Peck, fourth sergeant.

Privates.—Irwin Armstrong, W. H. Berryhill, Uriah Blue, Seym Bottsford, Luke W. Bust, James Cumbo, Elijah V. Dale, Abner C. Davis, Jacob Eiler, Simon P. Ford, Garner, G. A. Giddings, James Greenwood, William Griffin, W. C. Hays, T. A. Haskin, Robert Howell, William Lockridge, J. D. Loder-back, Edward Miles, Benjamin Osborne, J. R. Pinchback, Joseph Rhodes, John W. Rial, Ralph E. Sevey, Manasseh Sevey, Edward W. Taylor, John Viven, George Waters, James Welsh, Ezra Westgate, Walker Winn.

Company C.—Jesse Billingsly, captain ; Micah Andrews, first lieuten-ant ; James A. Craft, second lieutenant ; Russel B. Craft, first sergeant ; William H. Magill, second sergeant ; Campbell Taylor, third sergeant.

Privates.—L. S. Cunningham, John Herron, Preston Conly, Jackson Berry, Jefferson Barton, Demry Pace, John W. Bunton, William Crisswell, Sam M'Clelland, Lemuel Blakely, George Self, Thomas Davy, Jacob Standerford, Wayne Barton, Sampson Connell, Calvin Gage, Martin Walker, Gern E. Brown, Log Vanderveer, Wash Anderson, William Standerford, William Simmons, George Green, George P. Erath, T. M. Dennis, James R. Pace,

John Hobson, Lewis Goodwin, Jos. Garwood, Willis Avery, Jesse Walderman, Charles Williams, Aaron Burleson, R. M. Cravens, Walker Wilson, Prior Holden, Thomas A. Mays, A. M. H. Smith, James Curtis, V. N. Rain, Robert Wood, Dugald M'Lean, Thomas A. Graves.

Company D.—Mosely' Baker, captain; J. P. Borden, first lieutenant; John Pettus, second lieutenant; Joseph Baker, first sergeant; E. C. Pettus, second sergeant; M. A. Bryan, third sergeant; James Bell, first corporal; James Friel, second corporal; J. L. Hill, third corporal.

Privates.—O. D. Anderson, J. B. Alexander, John Beachom, T. H. Bell, S. R. Bostick, P. P. Borden, J. Carter, Samuel Davis, G. W. Davis, J. R. Foster, A. Greenlaw, Fowler, Hugh Frazier, William Isbell, R. Kleburg, Mat Kuykendall, Robert Moore, Jos. McCrabb, Louis Rorder, V. W. Swearengen, Jos. Vermilion, I. E. Watkins, A. W. Wolsey, W. R. Williams, Ellison York, Patrick Usher, J. S. Menifee, Paul Scarborough, John Flick, J. H. Money, Weppler, John Marshall, William Bernbeck, Millett, Philip Stroth, Andreas Voyel, Nicholas Peck, William Hawkins, John Duncan, George Sutherland, Thomas Gay, Joseph Miller, G. W. Gardner, William Mock, S. H. Isbel, James Tarlton, Allen Ingraham; McHenry Winburn, W. R. Jackson, D. D. D. Baker, officers belonging to the regular service.

Company K.—R. J. Calder, captain; J. Sharper, first lieutenant, M. A. Bingham, first sergeant.

Privates.—B. Brigham, J. Conner, F. S. Cooke, T. Cooke, S. Conner, G. J. Johnstone, Granville Mills, Elias Baker, H. Dibble, T. M. Fowler, H. Fields, B. C. Franklin, J. Green, W. C. Hogg, J. Hall, E. B. Halstead, J. W. Hassel, W. Lambert, B. Mims, W. Muir, P. D. M'Neil, C. Malone, J. Plunkett, W. P. Recse, C. K. Reese, J. A. Spicer, H. Stonfer, J. Threndgil, W. P. Scott, R. Crawford, S. B. Mitchell, B. F. Fitch, W. W. Grant, J. S. Edgar, J. Smith, T. D. Owen, W. Hale, A. G. Butts, D. Dedrick, C. Forrister, W. K. Denham.

Company F.—William J. E. Heard, captain; William Eastland, first lieutenant; Eli Mercer, first sergeant; Wilson Lightfoot, second sergeant; Alfred Kelso, first corporal; Elijah Mercer, second corporal.

Privates.—Robert M'Laughlin, Leroy Wilkinson, William Lightfoot, Daniel Miller, Jesse Robinson, Josiah Hagans, John M'Crab, Maxwell Steel, John Bigley, Hugh M'Kenzie, Jos. Elinger, John Halliet, J. Robinson, D. Dunham, William Passe, James S. Lester, Phillilla Brading, Christian Winner, James Nelson, John Tumlinson, F. Brockfield, Charles M. Henry, James Byrd, Nathaniel Reid, Andrew Sennatt, P. B. O'Conner, Thomas Ryons, John Lewis, Jos. Highland, Leander Beason, S. T. Foley, Allen Jones, Thomas Adams, Mitchell Putnam, T. M. Hardiman, Charles Thompson, William Waters.

Company H.—William W. Hill, captain (sick), commanded by R.

Stephenson; H. H. Swisher, first lieutenant; C. Raney, first sergeant; A. R. Stevens, second sergeant; William H. Miller, fourth sergeant.

Privates.—E. Whitesides, J. S. Stump, J. M. Swisher, Moses Davis, John Lyford, John Tom, Nicholas Crunk, Lewis Clemins, William Hawkins, J. W. Cannon, James Farmer, R. Bowen, A Lesassiem, W. K. Dallas, M. B. Gray, James Gray, B. Doolittle, John Graham, James M. Hill, J. Ingraham, John Gafford, N. Mitchell, David Korneky, George Petty, James Everett, Prosper Hope, J. Powell, Matthew Dunn, J. D. Jennings, John C. Hunt, Jacob Groce, F. B. Gentry, J. G. Wilkinson, A. Dillard, F. K. Henderson, Uriah Saunders, John Craddick, J. Lawrence, A. Caruthers, Daniel McKay.

Second Regiment Texas Volunteers.

Sidney Sherman, colonel; Joseph L. Bennett, lieutenant-colonel; Lysender Wells, major; Edward B. Wood, adjutant; Bennett McNelly, sergeant-major.

First Company.—Hayden Arnold, captain; R. W. Smith, first lieutenant; Isaac Edwards, second lieutenant.

Privates.—Sam Leiper, Peter W. Holmes, W. P. Kincannon, Daniel Doubt, John Moss, E. E. Hamilton, David Rusk, W. F. Williams, J. W. McHorse, H. Malena Alexin, John Harvey, M. G. Whitaker, John Yancy, S. Yarbrough, Thomas G. Box, Nelson Box, G. R. Mercer, William Nabors, William T. Saddler, James Mitchell, James E. Box, Sam Phillips, John B. Trenay, Levy Perch, Crawf Grigsby, John McCoy, Dickins Parker, Jesse Walling, J. W. Carpenter, John Box, W. E. Hallmask, Thomas D. Brooks, S. F. Spanks, Howard Bailey, H. M. Brewer, Stephen McLin.

Second Company.—William Ware, captain; Job S. Collard, first lieutenant; George A. Lamb, second lieutenant; Albert Gallitin, first sergeant; William C. Winters, Second sergeant.

Privates.—J. — Winters, J. W. Winters, C. Edenburg, Lewis Cox, G. W. Robinson, G. W. Lawrence, W. Cartwright, John Sadler, James Wilson, James Deritt, Matthew Moss, Jesse Thomson.

Third Company.—William M. Logan, captain; Franklin Harden, first lieutenant; B. J. Harper, second lieutenant; E. F. Branch, first sergeant.

Privates.—John Biddle, J. M. Maxwell, M. Charencan, E. Bulliner, P. Bulliner, J. Sleighston, Patrick Carnel, William M. Smith, David Choat, David Cole, Q. Dykes, David M'Fadden, Thomas Orr, Luke Bryant, W. Kibbe, E. M. Tanner, H. R. Williams, Michael Poveto, Lefray Gedrie, Joseph Farewell, C. W. Thompson, Cornelius Devois, M. J. Brakey, Thomas Belnop, William Duffee, Joseph Ellender, William Smith, William Robertson, W. A. Symth, James Call.

Fourth Company.—William H. Patton, captain (before entered as aid to General H.) ; David Murphy, first lieutenant ; Peter Harper, second lieutenant ; John Smith, first sergeant ; Pendleton Rector, second sergeant ; A. W. Breedlove, third sergeant ; G. L. Bledsoe, first corporal.

Privates.—James Bradley, J. C. Boyd, Robert Carr, A. J. Beard, Alexander Bailey, J. J. Childs, St. Clair Patton, Claiborn Rector, Phineas Ripley, Thomas Leveney, J. B. Taylor, L. Willoughby, G. Wright, M. B. Atkison, Holden Denmon, Edward Daist, R. B. Daist, J. K. Davis, E. Gallaher, James Hall, S. Phillips, Thomas M'Gay, J. A. Barkley, Francis Walneet, Hinson Curtis, J.B. Grice, Nat Hager, B. F. Cage, J. M. McCormack, James Haye, Charles Hick, A. D. Kenyon, G. W. Lewis, J. Pickering, James Harris, William Brennan, William H. Jack, Dr. Baylor, Thomas F. Coney, A. Lewis, W. P. Lane, E. G. Rector.

Thomas H. M'Intire, captain ; John P. Gill, first lieutenant ; Bazil G. Gians, second lieutenant ; Robert D. Tyler, first sergeant ; John Wilkinson, second sergeant ; E. G. Coffman, first corporal.

Privates.—William Boyle, Benjamin Bencroft, George Barker, William Bennett, John Clarke, J. B. Coliant, J. Campbell, Cooper, T. Davis, Oscar Farish, Thomas Hopkins, Jack Lowrie, Placido M'Curdy, David Oden, G. W. Penticost, S. W. Pebbles, Samuel Sharpe, Isaac Jacques, John Chevis 1st, John Chevis 2d, Thomas Cox, Cyrus Cepton, Ambrose Mayor, Moses Allison, Isaac Maiden, F. Wilkinson.

James Galsaspy, captain ; William Finch, first lieutenant ; A. L. Harrison, second lieutenant ; R. T. Choderick, first sergeant.

Privates.—John Sayers, F. B. Lasiter, M. K. Gohoen, T. H. Webb, John Peterson, J. Montgomery, T. F. Johnson, Hez Harris, W. F. Ferrill, Samuel Wyley, William Fertilan, A. Montgomery, A. Lolison, E. M'Millan, S. Daling, J. W. Scolling, J. Richardson, Obanion, Willis L. Ellis, James Walker, Alphonzo Steel, Benjamin Johnson, F. M. Woodward, William Peterson, J. C. White, Robert Henry, Elijah Votan, G. Crosby, Joel Dederick, L. Raney.

B. Byrant, captain ; John C. Hale, first lieutenant ; A. S. Lewis second lieutenant

Privates.—William Earle, J. S. P. Irven, Sim Roberts, Joseph P. Parks, C. Rockwell, R. B. Russel, L. H. White, A. M'Kenzie, A. Cobble, John F. Gilbert, D. Roberts, William B. Scates, J. R. Johnson, William Pate, B. Lindsay, James Clarke, Robert Love.

William Kimbo, captain; James Rowe, first lieutenant; John Harman, first sergeant; William Fisher, second sergeant; Henry Reed, third sergeant.

Privates.—D. Brown, William Bateman, J. A. Chaffin, H. Corsine, Joel Crane, R. T. Crane, Joshua Clelens, W. H. Davis, S. Holeman, H. Hill, G. D. Hancock, E. C. Legrand, D. Love, D. H. M'Gary, Thomas Maxwell, A. G. M'Gowan, J. W. Proctor, Benjamin Thomas, D. Watson, Lewis Wilworth, R. Stevenson, G. W. Jones, W. B. Brown, B. Green, J. Kent, Caddell, R. Hotchkiss, Thomas M. Hughes, A. Buffington, James Burch, R. Burch, A. E. Manuel.

Juan N. Seguin, captain; Manuel Flores, first sergeant; Antonio Menchasen, second sergeant; Nep Flores, first corporal; Ambro Rodridge, second corporal.

Privates.—Antonio Cruz, Jose Maria Mocha, Eudnado Samirer, Lucin Ennques, Maticio Curvis, Antonio Cueves, Simon Ancola, Manuel Tarin, Pedro Henern, Thomas Maldonart, Cecario Cormana, Jacinto Pena, N. Navarro, A. Varcinas, Manuel Avoca.

Texas Spy Company.

Erastus (Deaf) Smith, Captain Karnes, Wash Secrets, Fieldings Secrets, R. O. W. M'Manus, — Pierce, — Kohn.

III.

(From the " Telegraph and Texas Register.")

A LIST OF THE OFFICERS AND MEN UNDER COMMAND OF COLONEL J. W. FANNIN,

WHO SURRENDERED TO THE MEXICAN FORCES UNDER GENERAL URREA, IN MARCH, 1836, AND WERE AFTERWARD SHOT IN VIOLATION OF THE TERMS OF SURRENDER, MARCH 27, 1836.*

J. W. Fannin, colonel commandant; William Ward, lieutenant-colonel; Benjamin C. Wallace, major Lafayette Battalion; Warren Mitchell, major Georgia Battalion.

* The * indicates those who were marched out to be shot with the others, but made their escape. The † those who were spared for laborers and surgeons, and the ‡ those who escaped from Colonel Ward's division on his retreat, and did not fall into the hands of the enemy.

STAFF.

— Shadwick, adjutant ; J. S. Brooks, adjutant ; Gideon Rose, sergeant ; major ; David I. Holt,‡ quartermaster ; James Field,† James H. Barnard,† surgeons.

CAPTAIN DUVAL'S COMPANY.

First Regiment Volunteers.

Captain, B. H. Duval ; Lieutenants, Samuel Wilson, J. Q. Merifield ; Sergeants, G. W. Daniel, J. S. Bagly, E. P. G. Chisem, W. Dickerson ; Corporals, N. B. Hawkins, A. B. Williams, A. H. Lynd, R. C. Breshear ; Privates, T. G. Allen, J. M. Adams, J. F. Bellows, William S. Carlson, Thomas S. Churchill, William H. Cole, John C. Duval,* H. M. Dawnman, John Donohoo, George Dyer, John Holiday,* C. R. Heaskill, — Johnson, Q. P. Kimps, A. G. Sermond, William Mayer, J. McDonald, William Mason, Harvey Martin, Robert Owens, R. R. Rainey, — Sharpe,* L. S. Simpson, — Sanders, C. B. Shaine,* L. Tilson, B. W. Tolover, J. Q. Volckner, John Van Bibber,† — Batts, Woolrich, William Waggoner.

CAPTAIN KING'S COMPANY.

Auxiliary Volunteers.

Captain, Aaron B. King ; Sergeants, Samuel Anderson, George W. Penny, J. H. Callison, William R. Johnson ; Privates, J. P. Humphries, H. H. Kirk, L. C. Gibbs, L. G. H. Bracy, J. C. Stewart, T. Cooke, James Henley, F. Davis,‡ Jackson Davis, J. Coleman, Gavin H. Smith, Snead Leadbeater, R. A. Toler, William S. Armstrong, Benjamin Oldum,† Joel Heth, — Dedrick,† — Johnson.

CAPTAIN PETTUS' COMPANY.

San Antonio Grays.

Lieutenant, John Grace ; Sergeants, E. S. Heath, William L. Hunter,* — James, Samuel Riddell ; Privates, C. J. Carriere, Allen O. Kenney, Jos. P. Riddle, F. H. Gray, George Green, Charles Seargent, Holland,* Cozart, William G. Preusch, John Wood, Dennis Mahoney, Noah Dickinson, George M. Gilland, George Voss,† David J. Jones,* Wallace, William Harper, William Brennan,* Edw. Moody, Escott, John Reese,* Manuel Carbajal, R. J. Scott, Gould, W. P. Johnson, A. Bynum, Hodge, Charles Philips, West, J. M. Cass, Perkins, Peter Griffin,† — Logan, Milton Irish.*

CAPTAIN BULLOCK'S COMPANY.

First Regiment Texas Volunteers.

Captain, U. J. Bullock, left sick at Velasco; F. M. Hunt,* first sergeant; Bradford Fowler, second sergeant; Allison Arms, third sergeant; J. R. Munson, first corporal; T. S. Freeman, second corporal; S. T. Brown, third corporal;* G. M. Vigal, fourth corporal; Privates, Joseph Andrews,‡ Isaac Aldridge, William S. Butler,‡ J. H. Barnwell,† George Washington Cumming, William A. J. Brown, Joseph Dennis, Michael, Devraux Ellis, Charles Fine, Gibbs, Pearce Hammock,† Samuel G. Hardaway,‡ Perry H. Minor, John O. Moore, Benjamin H. Mordecat,† John Moat, Mckenie, L. T. Pease,‡ Robert A. Pace, Austin Perkins, Samuel Rowe, John T. Spillers,† John S. Scully, Thomas Smith,† Thomas Stewart,† Joseph A. Stovall, Trevesant,‡ William L. Wilkerson,† Weeks, Wood, James McCoy, Moses Butler, A. H. Osborne (left wounded in the church at the Mission, afterward escaped), J. Bridgman.†

CAPTAIN JAMES C. WINN'S COMPANY.

First Regiment Texas Volunteers.

Wiley Hughs, first lieutenant; Daniel B. Brooks, second lieutenant; Anthony Bates, first sergeant; John S. Thorn, second sergeant; J. H. Callagham,† third sergeant; Wesley Hughs, fourth sergeant; John M. Kimble, first corporal; Walter W. Davis, second corporal; Abraham Stevens, third corporal; J. M. Powers, fourth corporal; Ray, corporal; Privates, John Aldridge, John M. Bryson, Michael Carrol, Thomas H. Corbys, John Ely, George Eubanks, Dominic Gallaghe, Wilson Helms, Grier Lee, Joseph Loving, Alexander J. Loverly, Martin Moran,‡ Aaron S. Mangum, Watkins Nobles, John M. Oliver, Patrick Osburn, William Parvin, Gideon S. Ross, Anderson Ray, Thomas Rumley, William Shelton, James Smith, Christopher Winters, Harrison Young, Josias B. Beall, John Bright,‡ Reason Banks, H. Shults.

CAPTAIN WADSWORTH'S COMPANY.

First Regiment Texas Volunteers.

Thomas B. Ross, first lieutenant; J. L. Wilson, second lieutenant; S. A. J. Mays, second sergeant; Samuel Wallace, third sergeant;* J. H. Neely, fourth sergeant;† Josiah McSherry, first corporal; J. S. Brown, second corporal; J. B. Murphy, third corporal; Privates, George Rounds,‡ William Abercrombie, T. B. Barton, J. H. Clark, W. J. Cowan, E. Durrain,† J. A. Foster, Joseph Gramble,† F. Gilkerson, William Gilbert, Thomas Horry,† A. J. Hitchcock,† Allen Ingram,‡ John C. P. Kennymore,† J. H. Moore, C. C. Milne, M. K. Moses,‡ J. B. Rodgers, R. Slatter, J. H. Sanders, W. S. Turberville, E. Wingate, H. Rogers.‡

CAPTAIN TICKNOR'S COMPANY.

First Regiment Texas Volunteers.

Memory B. Tatom, first lieutenant; William A. Smith, second lieutenant; Edmund Patterson, first sergeant;† Nicholas B. Waters, second sergeant; Richard Rutledge, third sergeant;‡ Samuel C. Pitman, fourth sergeant; Joseph B. Tatom, first corporal;‡ James C. Jack, second corporal; Perry Reese, third corporal; Thomas Rieves, fourth corporal; Thomas Weston, musician; Privates, D. Greene,‡ John McGowen, David Johnson, Samuel Wood, W. Welsh,† Isaac N. Wright, William L. Alison, Washington Mitchell, Stephen Baker, Henry Hasty, James A. Bradford, Cornelius Rooney, Seaborne A. Mills, Cullen Conard, James O. Young, Edward Fitsimmons, Hezekiah Fist, C. F. Hick,‡ O. F. Leverette, William Comstock, John O'Daniel, Charles Lantz, Evans M. Thomas, A. M. Lynch, G. W. Carlisle, Leven Allen, Jesse Harris, Swords, Williams, William P. B. Dubose.

CAPTAIN P. S. WYANT'S COMPANY.

Louisville Volunteers.

Captain, P. S. Wyatt, on furlough; B. T. Bradford,‡ first lieutenant; Oliver Smith, second lieutenant; William Wallace, first sergeant; George Thayer, second sergeant; Henry Wilkins, third sergeant; J. D. Rains,‡ fourth sergeant; Oliver Brown, quarter-master; Peter Allen, musician; Privates, Bennett Butler,* Gabriel Bush, Ewing Caruthers, N. Dembrinske, Perry Davis,‡ Henry Dixon, T. B. Frizel, I. H. Fisher, Edward Fuller, Frederick Gebinrath, James Hamilton, E. D. Harrison, H. G. Hudson,‡ J. Kortickey, John Lumkin,† C. Nixon, — Clennon, J. F. Morgan, F. Petreswich, William S. Parker, Charles Patton, John R. Parker, William R. Simpson, Frederick Sweman, Allen Wren.

CAPTAIN WESTOVER'S COMPANY.

Regular Army.

Ira Westover, captain; Lewis W. Gates, second lieutenant; William S. Brown, first sergeant; George McNight, second sergeant; John McGloin, third sergeant; Privates, Augustus Baker, Matthew Byrne, John Cross, John Fagan, William Harris, John Kelly, Dennis McGowan, Patrick Nevin, A. M. Boyle,† George Pettick,† Thomas Quirk, Edward Ryan, Thomas Smith, E. J. A. Greynolds, Daniel Buckley, Marion Betts, C. W. Goglan, Matthew Eddy, Robert English, John Gleeson, William Hatfield, John Hilchard, Charles Jenson, William Mann, John Numlin, Stephen Pierce, Siddey Smith, Daniel Syers, Lewis Shotts, Charles Stewart, Joseph W. Watson, James Webb, William Winningham, Ant. Siley, John James.

CAPTAIN BURKE'S COMPANY.

Mobile Grays.

David N. Burke, captain, on furlough; J. B. Manomy second lieutenant : James Kelly, orderly sergeant; H. D. Ripley, sergeant; Privates Kneeland Taylor, Charles B. Jennings, P. T. Kissam, John Richards, Orlando Wheeler, John D. Cunningham, William Rosenbury,† William McMurray, Alvin E. White,† John Chew, M. P. King, Jacob Coleman, W. P. Wood, William Stephens, Peter Mattern, Herman Ehrenberg,* Conrad Egenour, G. F. Courtman, Joseph H. Sphon,† Thomas Kemp,* N. J. Dwenny,* James Reid, William Hunter, M. G. Frazier, S. M. Edwards, William J. Green, A. Swords, Z. O'Neil, Charles Linley, William Gatlin, Randolph T. Spain.

CAPTAIN JACK SHACKLEFORD'S † COMPANY.

Red Rovers.

F. S. Shackelford, orderly sergeant; J. D. Hamilton,* second sergeant, A. G. Foley, third sergeant; Z. H. Short, fourth sergeant; H. H. Hentley, first corporal; D. Moore, second corporal; J. H. Barkley, third corporal; A. Winter, fourth corporal; Privates, P. H. Anderson, Joseph Blackwell, Z. S. Brooks,* B. F. Burts, Thomas Burbridge, J. N. Barnhill, W. C. Douglas, J. W. Cain, D. Cooper,* Harvey Cox, Seth Clark, J, G. Coe, Alfred Dorsey, G. L. Davis, H. B. Day, A. Dickson, J. W. Duncan, R. T. Davidson, J. E. Ellis, Samuel Farney, Robert Finner, E. B. Franklin, Jos. Ferguson, M.

C. Garner, D. Gamble, William Gunter, J. E. Grimes, William Hemphill, John Eiser, John Jackson, H. W. Jones, John N. Jackson, John Kelly, Dan. A. Murdock, Charles W. Kinley, J. H. Miller, W. Simpson,‡ J. N. Seaton, W. J. Shackelford, B. Strunk, W. F. Savage, W. E. Vaughn, James Vaughn, Robert Wilson, James Wilder, William Quinn, Henry L. Douglas.

PART OF CAPTAIN HORTON'S COMPANY.

Privates, Elias Yeamans, Erastus Yeamans, Daniel Martindale,* William Haddon,* Charles Smith,* Francisco Garsear,† Ransom O. Graves, Napoleon B. Williams, Lewis Powell, Hughs Witt, George Pain, Thomas Dasher, John J. Hand, Duffield, Spencer, — Cash.

The following persons, who had not attached themselves to any company, were with Fannin:

Captain William Shurlock, Lieutenant — Hurst, — Bills, Nat. Hazen,* William Murphy,* Captain Dusanque, John Williams,* Sam. Sprague, Hughes,† James Pitman, C. Hardwick, R. E. Petty, Charles Hec,‡ Nathaniel R. Brister.

IV.

CONSTITUTION OF THE TEXAS VETERAN ASSOCIATION.

PREAMBLE.

WE, the undersigned, soldiers and seamen of the Republic of Texas, having met at the city of Houston, on this the fourteenth day of May, A. D. 1873, to interchange greetings and fellowships in commemoration of the memorable days of the Republic of Texas, do hereby adopt the following Constitution and By-Laws as declaratory of the objects of our Association, and for the government of the same.

One of the objects contemplated by the Association is to have enrolled in a bound book, for better preservation and future reference, the full name, age, nativity, date of immigration, and present residence of every surviving soldier and seaman of the Republic of Texas. Another object is to bring about a more intimate acquaintance and intercourse for mutual assistance and pleasure, to assist such of the veteran soldiers and seamen as misfortune or poverty may have overtaken in their declining years, and assist such in bringing their claims before the country; and also to assist the State of Texas in deciding who are justly entitled to pensions; also to bring about general and partial meetings, from time to time, for mutual greeting and pleasure.

CONSTITUTION.

ARTICLE I.

SECTION 1. All the survivors of "The Old Three Hundred," the soldiers and seamen of the Republic of Texas, who were enrolled into proper and legally authorized companies or detachments, or served a tour of duty against Mexicans or hostile Indians, from the year 1820 up to the period of annexation of Texas with the United States of America, in the year 1845, and were honorably discharged, and produce the proof required by this Constitution, that they served in good faith the object for which they were enrolled, shall be entitled to membership in this Association.

SECTION 2. All citizens who were appointed by the Government, or elected by the people, to positions of trust from the year 1820 up to the 15th day of October, 1836, shall also be entitled to membership in this Association.

SECTION 3. The members of this Association shall be divided into three classes. The first class shall include the survivors of the "Old Three Hundred," all soldiers, seamen, and citizens who produce the proof required of service from the year 1820 till the 15th day of October, 1836.

SECTION 4. The second class shall include all those soldiers and seamen who produce the proof required of service at any time between the 15th of October, 1836, and the 1st day of November, 1837.

SECTION 5. The third class shall embrace all soldiers and seamen who produce the required proof of service between the first day of November, 1837, and the period of annexation of Texas to the United States of America, in the year 1845.

SECTION 6. To acquire full membership in either of the *three classes* of this Association, the person must be a resident citizen of the State of Texas, but all persons now non-residents of the State, who rendered service to Texas, may become honorary members of the Association.

SECTION 7. "The Old Three Hundred," and all who participated in the service during the first period named, and were entitled to bounty land warrants and donation land from the Government, for services in any of the battles of the Revolution, or in the campaigns of 1832, 1835, and 1836, shall be styled "*The Veteran Guard of Texas*," and shall take rank according to their merits.

SECTION 8. The character of proof required for the classes other than the *Veteran Guard* shall be the written statement of the interested person, sustained by two reputable persons, on their word of honor, that the facts set forth are true.

SECTION 9. The power to accept or reject applicants for membership shall be exercised by the Association, under such rules and by-laws as they may adopt from time to time.

ARTICLE II.

SECTION 1. The officers of this Association shall be a president, two vice-presidents, a treasurer, a recording and corresponding secretary, and such number of district committeemen as may be found necessary to carry out the objects contemplated by the Association. The treasurer and recording secretary may be filled by the same person, if deemed advisable.

SECTION 2. The officers shall hold their offices for one year, unless otherwise determined by the Association, and may be elected by ballot, or *viva voce*, as the members present may determine, and all members who may be prevented or are unable to attend the annual or called meetings, shall be entitled to vote by proxy; and all officers shall hold their offices until their successors are elected and qualified.

SECTION 3. The president shall have power to call meetings on any occasion that he may think proper, and in case of vacancies in any of the offices, from any cause, the president shall have power to fill the same for the time being.

SECTION 4. The president shall preside at all meetings, and see that proper order and decorum be maintained; shall give timely notice of all meetings, through the press; and in his absence, the first vice-president shall preside and discharge all the duties of the president. In the absence of the president and the first vice-president, the second vice-president shall discharge all the duties of President; and in the absence of all three of these officers, the veterans at any meeting can call any member present to the chair, who shall have the authority to discharge the duties of president.

SECTION 5. The recording secretary shall have well-bound books, in which he shall keep a full and true record of all the proceedings of the Association, and such other documents as he may be ordered to record by a vote of the Association; also to file and preserve all papers and documents that are received by him, touching the interest of the Association; shall issue all notices required by the president of meetings, or other matter, relating to the Association; shall turn over to his successor in office all books, papers, and documents in his possession, taking his receipt for the same.

SECTION 6. The treasurer shall receive all moneys due or donated to the Association, receipting for the same if required; keep a true record of all money received and paid out, and make quarterly reports to the president on the 1st of April, 1st of July, 1st of October, and 1st of January. The treasurer shall pay out such moneys as may be in his hands, on the orders of the president, or on the order of the financial committee, that the president may appoint.

Section 7. The corresponding secretary shall perform such duties as may be directed by the president and Association.

Article III.

Section 1. The members present at any regular or called meeting shall have power to adopt any and all by-laws, rules, and regulations for their government that may to them seem necessary ; to divide the State into districts, and to appoint one or more of the veterans in each district to discharge the duties required of him or them of such district.

Section 2. It shall be the duty of each district committee to ascertain the name, nativity, age, date of immigration to Texas, post-office of every veteran coming within either of the classes named, with such proof as the party applying for such membership may furnish such committee.

Section 3. The district committees shall have authority to call the veterans of their district together, if it should be desired by them, at any time and place that may be selected, for the transaction of business, or for mutual greetings and pleasure ; and it shall be the duty of the district committee to record the place and date of demise of any veteran, and the class to which he belongs, and promptly forward the same to the recording secretary. And they shall also report to the same officer the name and post-office of any veteran in their district, who may be, from any cause, suffering for the necessaries of life, or other necessary attention ; and it shall be the duty of said committee to place before the veterans of their district, without delay, the suffering condition of such veteran, and ask from them such assistance as humanity and the objects of the Association require, reporting the same, with the amount of assistance rendered, to the recording secretary, to be by him reported to the next general meeting of the Association for its action.

Section 4. The districts may be represented at the annual or general call meetings of the Association by delegates, where all can not attend in person.

Section 5. The president, or presiding officer, shall appoint all committees, unless otherwise ordered by the members present, at any meeting, and shall have authority to do any and all things necessary to carry out the objects of the Association that may not have been specified in the Constitution and By-Laws.

BY-LAWS.

Section 1. The rules governing the business of the Association shall be those governing ordinary parliamentary bodies.

Section 2. The president, or member elected for the time being, shall

37

preside at all meetings, and shall see that the proper order and decorum are maintained, and that the rules governing the Association are observed.

SECTION 3. Every member, in addressing the president, shall rise to his feet; and in case two or more shall rise at the same time, the president shall decide who is entitled to the floor, and the others shall be seated. And no member shall be allowed to speak more than once on the same subject, until all who desire to do so shall be heard, and the president shall see that the speaker is strictly confined to the subject before the meeting.

SECTION 4. The president shall appoint a committee of finance—to consist of three or five persons, as he may deem best—whose duty it shall be to ascertain the best plan of raising the funds necessary to carry out the objects of the Association ; which committee shall be authorized to receive any contributions in money or other articles, and they shall also make an estimate of what amount of funds may be necessary to annually carry out the objects of the Association ; which committee shall be authorized to receive any contributions in money or other article ; to make an estimate of the amount each member shall be asked to contribute annually, voluntarily, for the same purpose.

SECTION 5. It shall be the duty of the finance committee, and every member of the Association, to send to the recording secretary the amount donated as given to any needy veteran of either class, with the full name of the donor, for record in a bound book, to be kept for that purpose, and the names of such donors shall be read out at the annual meetings.

SECTION 6. The order of business shall be :

1. Reading and adopting minutes of preceding meeting.
2. Reports of standing committees.
3. Reports of special committees.
4. General business.
5. Election and installation of officers.
6. Annual oration.
7. Motions and resolutions.

V.

TEXAS NECROLOGY.

DEATHS REPORTED AT THE ANNUAL MEETING, MAY, 1874.

Austin, Wm. T., aged 70 ; nativity Connecticut ; emigrated in 1830 : served at the storming of San Antonio and as aid to General S. F. Austin, General Edward Burleson, and aid to Colonel Johnson in taking San Antonio ; died at Galveston, February, 1874.

Allen, Clement; died 1873.

Amsler, Charles C., aged 66 ; died May, 1874.

Augustin, Major; died August, 1874, in Polk county, Texas.

Burnet, David G. ; died January, 1872, age 82 years, Galveston.

Burleson, John; died 1874, age 66 years, Austin.

Borden, Gail ; died January, 1874, age 73, Colorado county.

Bostick, Sam R ; died ——, age ——, Fayette county.

Brooks, Thomas D. ; died 13th May, 1874, age 70, Hopkins county.

Box, John ; died at Crockett, Houston county, August 2, 1874, in his 72d year.

Conley, Preston ; died 1874, age 72, Cooke county.

Cole, James; died ——, age 78, Austin, Travis county.

Clayton, Joseph A. ; died July, 1873, Rice, Navarro county.

Calvit, Joseph F. ; died May, 1874, age 84, Velasco, Brazoria county.

Chesher, James ; died 1874.

Cherry, Wilbur ; died 1873, city of Galveston.

Duffau, F. T. ; died at city of Austin.

Dunlavy, W. T. ; died August 1873, age ——, Colorado county.

Foster, Anthony; died February 8, 1874, Panola county, Mississippi.

Falvel, Luke A. ; died in the city of Galveston, age 67, native of Ireland.

Franklin, B. C. ; died December 25, 1873, age 66, city of Galveston.

Fowler, J. H. ; died December, 1873.

Fentress, James ; died July, 1872, age 70, Prairie Lea, Caldwell county.

Hodges, Robert ; died 1872, age 67, Fort Bend county.

Hays, James ; died 1873, age 70, Columbia, Brazoria county.

Hardeway, S. G.

Holman, W. W. ; died October 1873.

Heck, Randle B. ; died 1874, Evergreen, Lee county.

Jones, Randle ; died June, 1873, age 87, city of Houston.

Love, Wm. M. ; died May, 1873.

McNeel, Pleasant; died December, 1871, age 74, Gulf Prairie, Brazoria county, Texas.

McNeel, Pinckney S; died November, 1871 ; age 58, Cedar Lake, Matagorda county.

McKinney, Thomas F. ; October, 1873, age 72 ; Onion Creek, Travis county.

Paschal, Samuel ; died June 6, 1874, age 58, city of Houston.

Palmer, Isham, age 61 ; died February, 1874, Bryan, Brazos county.

Perry, Albert G. ; died May, 1874, Falls county, Texas.

Rector, Claiborne.

Roberts, George H. ; died 1874.

Robbins, John ; died June, 1872.

Sellers, Wm. H. ; died April, 1874, city of Galveston.

Sherman, Sidney ; died in June, 1873, age 65, city of Galveston, colonel of a regiment at San Jacinto.

Thompson, A. P. ; died at the city of Houston.

Townsend, William ; died August, 1873.

Tinsley, Isaac T. ; died March, 1874, age 73 years, Columbia, Brazoria county.

Ward, Thomas William ; died in 1872, city of Austin (lost a leg at the storming of San Antonio).

Heard, W. J. E; died the 8th August, 1874, at Chappell Hill, Washington county, 73 years old (captain of a company at the battle of San Jacinto).

———•◆•———

VI.

A LIST OF OLD TEXANS WHO HAVE DIED AND BEEN KILLED BY MEXICANS AND INDIANS FROM 1828 TO 1874.

COMPILED BY REV. H. S. THRALL.

1828—Baron de Bastrop, first commissioner appointed to issue titles to S. F. Austin, first settler, in his first colony, the Old Three Hundred.

1829—James Brown Austin, died in New Orleans of yellow fever in August.

1833—Captain John Austin, D. W. Anthony, Thomas Westall, of cholera in Brazoria county.

1834—Martin De Leon, at Victoria, of cholera. Captain Henry S. Brown.

1835—Colonel Benjamin R. Milam, killed at the storming of San Antonio.

1836—March 6—William Barrett Travis, James Bowie, David Crockett, J. B. Bonham, and twenty-six officers and eighty-six men, privates, fell in the Alamo ; Colonels James Grant and Morris, on the Agua Dulce ; March 27th, James W. Fannin and three hundred and twenty others massacred at Goliad ; April 21st, Dr. M. Motley and seven others killed at San Jacinto ; Davis Thomas, killed accidentally at San Jacinto. Died—Stephen Fuller Austin, at Columbia ; Lorenzo de Zavala, first vice-president of the Republic of Texas ; Colonel Jared E. Groce : Bailey Hardeman, first secretary of treasury of the Republic of Texas ; John G. Robinson, killed on Cummings' Creek by Indians. One hundred and fifty-two men perished with Travis. Placido Benevides.

1837—George B. McKinstry, Erastus (Deaf) Smith, Colonel Henry Teal (assassinated in camp), Walter C. White, one of the first merchants in

Austin's colony; J. S. D. Bynum, A. H. Mills, killed by Indians; Colonel Robert H. Coleman, drowned at the mouth of Brazos River, James Coryell, killed by Indians.

1838—Judge James Collinsworth, aid to General Houston and first chief-justice Republic of Texas; Samuel P. Carson, Robert Eden Handy, aid to General Houston at San Jacinto; Peter W. Grayson, first aid to General S. F. Austin in the fall of 1835, at the beginning of the war with Mexico; John A. Wharton, adjutant-general at the battle of San Jacinto; John K. Allen, the father and founder of the city of Houston; Captain Andrew Brisco, commanded company at battle of Concepcion, October, 1835; Josiah H. Bell, one of the "Old Three Hundred," first settlers on the Brazos; James Gilliland, killed by Indians; Robert Potter, killed on Caddo lake, Mons. Lapham and ninety others killed by Indians near San Antonio.

1839—Shelby Corzine, William H. Wharton, minister of the United States of America, 1836; Robert Barr, postmaster-general; John Birdsall, S. Rhodes Fisher, secretary of navy; John W. Moody; Juan Antonio Patilla, land commissioner; John B. Denton; Byrd Lockhart, Colonel Reuben Ross; Robert Potter, killed; James Barbour, killed; W. Pettus, Thomas Gay, John W. Hall.

1840—Colonel Henry Karnes, Captain John M. Allen, a captain at San Jacinto; Captain A. B. Switzer, William Burton, Richard Ellis, president of the Convention, 1836; George W. Poe, in battle of San Jacinto; R. R. Royall, member first Provisional Government of Texas; Switzer was killed, 1841; H. C. Watts, killed by Indians.

1841—Captain Philip Dimitt, Richard G. Dunlop, William Fairfax Gray, S. W. Jordan, Major Ben Fort Smith, in battle of San Jacinto; Thomas Rabb, one of the "Old Three Hundred;" George C. Childress, author of the Declaration of Independence.

1842—Captain Wiley Martin, Cornelius Van Ness, Matthew Caldwell, Old Paint; Elijah Stapp, Colonel Henry Millard, commanded a battalion at San Jacinto; Nicholas Dawson and his company from Fayette county, killed on the Salado, in 1842.

1843—Thomas S. Torrey, John M. Handsford, Thomas Barnet, Dr. R. F. Brenham, killed at Salado, at the time of the rise of the Mier prisoners on the guard; William M. Eastland and sixteen others, decimated and shot; Ewin Cameron, shot by order of Santa Anna; Hugh P. Kerr.

1844—Judge Patrick C. Jack, Colonel William H. Jack, Judge Richard Morris, Commander J. K. T. Lathrop, Asa Brigham, treasurer of the Republic; G. W. Barnett, killed by Indians on the Guadaloupe; John W. Potter. Elijah Stapp.

1845—John Rice Jones, postmaster-general of the Republic; Kenneth L. Anderson, Josiah Wilbarger, from the effects of Indian wounds inflicted when he was scalped; G. A. Parker, Dr. J. A. E. Phelps, Colonel.William S. Fisher.

1846—Captain R. A. Gillespie, James Gillespie, Judge John P. Coles, one of the "Old Three Hundred;" his wife, Mrs. Elleanor Coles, died in 1874. Joseph Baker.

1847—John M. Allen, mayor of Galveston; Colonel William G. Cook, Dr. John G. Chalmers, Munroe Edwards, at Sing Sing, N. Y.; Thomas I. Smith, Isaac Van Zandt, Captain Samuel H. Walker, John H. Walton, E. L. R. Wheelock, Van R. Irion.

1848—Captain Mosely Baker, commanded the largest company at the battle of San Jacinto; Captain M. B. (Mustang) Gray, Thomas (Ramrod) Johnson, Richard Bache. Ferdinand De Leon, Fr. Bonnett.

1849—Nicholas Boyce, Dr. C. A. Perry, General Ed. Moorehouse, General Worth, S. H. Everett, Joseph L. Bennett, Colonel Lewis P. Cook, John W. Brown, Captain Samuel Highsmith, Oliver Buckner.

1850—James Kerr, David S. Torrey, killed by Indians; Middleton M. Hill, John Keenan, James Gilbert White, Josiah J. Crosby, William H. Ewing, W. D. Hargrove, Edward Eitzgerald, Hiram Baldwin, Charles A. Bullard.

1851—General Edward Burleson, David S. Kaufman, Mrs. Emily M. Perry, sister of Stephen F. Austin; Thomas M. Wooldridge, George W. Hockley, inspector-general and commanded the artillery at San Jacinto; Albert G. Vail, John Durst, of Leon county; Don Jose Antonio de la Garza, at San Antonio, aged 62 years; Francis Bingham, one of the "Old Three Hundred;" Thomas M. R. Bankhead, Asbury James, Lamar Moore.

1852—James Franklin Perry, brother-in-law of Stephen F. Austin; Wm. M. Cushney, Taylor White, Adolphus Sterne, Francis Berry, M. M. Chevalie, Charles L. McGehee, Glover W. Blanton, B. H. Martin, Wm. McDonald, Ignacio Perez, Sam'l H. Lackie.

1853—Ex-Governor Henry Smith and ex-Lieutenant-Governor Jas. W. Robinson, both in California; Colonel Barnard E. Bee, secretary of war of Republic of Texas; A. S. Cunningham, James Powers, Dr. Moses Johnson, Matthias Wilbarger, James Hodges, Robert Smithers, Dr. Enos Mabry, James H. Cocke, L. R. B. Jasper. Thomas Simons and Isaac Mitchell.

1854—Dr. James B. Miller, David Gage, General Memucan Hunt, Major McNutt, in command of camp guard at the time of the battle of San Tacinto; General Alexander Somerville, lieutenant-colonel in battle of San Jacinto, a good and brave man; Thomas J. Hardeman, the one who proposed the name for the capital of Texas in 1839, James F. Leyttle, Wash Secrets, one of Deaf Smith's spies; Virgil A. Stewart, William C. Henry.

1855—Thomas P. Cartmel, George Sutherland, had his horse shot on the 20th, at San Jacinto, from under him when Sherman attacked the Mexicans; John Duty, of Webberville; L. D. Barry, Captain G. K. (Legs) Lewis, Daniel Mosely.

1856—Dr. Branch T. Archer, secretary of war under the republic; James H. Callahan, Judge A. S. Lipscomb, Robert Wilson (Honest Bob), Judge James Webb, secretary of state under the republic; Henderson Yoakum, Richard Bache, James P. Caldwell, Judge Nelson H. Munger, ex-Governor George T. Wood, Jim Campbell, one of Lafitte's men.

1857—Seth Ingram, one of S. F. Austin's first surveyors; General Felix Huston, ex-Governor J. Pinckney Henderson, General Thomas J. Rusk, first secretary of war under the Republic of Texas, and in battle of San Jacinto; Dr. John Shackelford, captain of company under Colonel J. W. Fannin, and was saved to doctor wounded Mexicans at the Alamo in 1836: Hiram G. Runnels, ex-governor of Mississippi; General James Hamilton, of South Carolina, went down in the steamer Nautilus; J. A. Greer, Leonidas B. Aldridge; Erasmo. Seguin, Spanish commissioner to show Stephen F. Austin the territory he was to colonize.

1858.—James H. Durst, Judge Robert M. (Three-legged Willie) Williamson, (the great orator of Texas); Michel B. Menard, the founder of the city of Galveston; William Fields, ex-President Anson Jones, the last president of the Republic of Texas; Captain Timothy Pillsbury, General E. H. Tarrant, Colonel Samuel M. Williams, secretary of Stephen F. Austin's several colonies, and navy agent of the Republic of Texas.

1859—Major Robert S. Neighbors, ex-President Mirabeau B. Lamar, Judge Isaac W. Breashear, J. W. Latimer.

1860—Judge M. P. Norton, B. B. Goodrich, Collin McKinney; Commodore E. W. Moore, Colonel Matt Ward, James C. Wilson, John Rabb, Samuel A. Bogart, Henry L. Kinney, John D. Pitts of Hays county, Eliot M. Millican.

1861—Forbes Brittan, John Cameron, an empresario; Colonel Benjamin Frank Terry, killed in Kentucky; General Hugh McLeod.

1862—Colonel Clark L. Owen, Henry L. Allen, Captain James G. Swisher at the storming of San Antonio in December, 1835; Judge John Hemphill, General A. Sidney Johnston, Colonel Thomas S. Lubbock, General Benjamin McCulloch, Judge Richardson Scurry, General Allison Nelson, William C. Young, Judge Samuel Lusk, General James L. Hogg.

1863—Ebenezer Allen, A. C. Allen, General Sam Houston, " the Hero of San Jacinto ;" Colonel James Riley, ex-attorney-general ; James Willie, Alexander Thompson, a member of the first Provisional Government of Texas ; Dr. Asa Hoxie.

1864—General Tom Green, General John Gregg, General Thomas Jefferson Green, in North Carolina ; Dr. Francis Moore, former editor of the *Telegraph ;* J. W. Cruger, General William R. Scurry, John A. Wilcox, Henry J. Jewett, S. H. Morgan, A. P. Wiley, Judge C. W. Buckley, Judge Royal T. Wheeler, B. M. Hatfield, August Buchel.

1865—General John A. Wharton, Thomas J. Chambers, George T. Howard, ex-Governor Pendleton Murrah, Dr. Joseph Rowe, General Philip M. Guney, ex-Governor A. C. Horton, Shirbal Marsh, M. K. Snell.

1866—Ben. F. Hill, George W. Smythe, Jesse Grimes, Lorenzo Sherwood.

1867—Major Ben. White, Colonel Ira. R. Lewis, Judge W. B. Ochiltree, James Scott, C. C. Herbert, Dr. W. P. Kitrell, George Wilkins Kendall, Colonel Warren D. C. Hall, adjutant-general in 1835.

1868—Colonel Oliver Jones, one of the " Old Three Hundred ;" Judge W. S. Oldham, Ira A. Paschal, Judge James J. Holt, Colonel John M. Dancy, George W. Glasscock, Rev. Hugh Wilson, H. R. Cartmell, Abram Clare.

1869—Dr. N. D. Labadie, Andrew Rabb, one of the " Old Three Hundred ; John S. Sydnor, S. Addison White, George W. Crawford, Joseph Polly, one of the " Old Three Hundred ;" T. Scott Anderson, Matthias Feelcood.

1870—Jose Antonio Navarro, ex-President David G. Burnet, John Caldwell, Samuel A. Maverick, Captain John Dix, Doctor James Hewitson, an empresario, died at Saltillo ; Judge William E. Jones, Dr. C. G. Keenan, Samuel A. Roberts, David Cole, Judge William Pinckney Hill, Milton Irish (in California) ; Samuel K. McClelland, Jesse Amason, Matthew Cartwright, Eli Mitchell, N. W. Tiveson, Dr. William P. Smith, Darius Gregg, Rev. A. J. McGown, W. B. Jaques, George Noessel, Alfred Allec, Tipton Walker, H. January, Captain W. Hurd, Albert G. Haines.

1871—William M. Varnell, Thomas H. McMahan, William Dever, one of the " Old Three Hundred ; " Charles Shearn, F. H. Merriman, Milton Stapp, Stephen Southwick, Don Campbell, W. W. Browning, C. G. Young.

1872—Thomas William Ward, one of those who stormed San Antonio, December 1835 ; S. Holland, Nat. Benton, David Snively, Willis L. Robards, Captain N. Hand, of the navy ; B. Ed. Tarver, General A. B. Nichols, E. P. Hunt, Dr. William McCraven, Algernon Thompson, John K. Fowler.

TOM GREEN.

See p. 270.

1873—William Holman, Captain Randall Jones, one of the " Old Three Hundred "; ex-Governor Hardin R. Runnels, C. K. Hall, Alexander Sessums, Rev. W. C. Blair, Henry Runge, Colonel John Goodwin, Pleas-ant Childress, T. B. J. Hill, Thomas H. Stribbling, Doctor William R. Smith, George Fisher, Judge B. F. Neal, Henry E. Perkins, General Sidney Sherman, Colonel Leonard W. Groce, one of the " Old Three Hundred "; Captain William Hendley, Thomas F. McKinney, Judge G. W. Smith, P. J. Willis, Judge B. C. Franklin, Judge Robert E. B. Baylor.

1874—Gail Borden, Charles Railey, J. Lancaster, Leslie A. Thompson, J. A. Sauters, John B. Banks, James Little, John Cronican Washington, G. L. Foley, General Lewis T. Wigfall, Colonel William T. Austin, E. W. Rogers, Aaron Burns, Texas Navy; Isaac T. Tinsley, James A. Moody, William Harvey Sellers, Charles C. Amsler, G. H. Roberts, a soldier of San Jacinto; Joseph F. Calvert, one of the " Old Three Hundred;" Captain W. J. E. Heard, Colonel James Gilliam, S. B. Brush, Henry W. Augustin, Jacob Schmitz, Jose Maria Carravahal, in Mexico (Colonel Carravahal married a daughter of Martin de Leon, empresario; he procured and published the Decrees of Coahuila; in 1835 he was arrested by Cos, and sent prisoner to Mexico) ; Judge Peter W. Gray.

VII.

NAMES OF VETERANS.

FIRST CLASS.

Askins, Wesley, age 75 years ; born in Kentucky ; emigrated in 1835 ; in service in 1836. Paris, Lamar county, Texas.

Anderson, Holland L., age 65 ; native of Kentucky ; emigrated in 1830 ; San Antonio, Bexar county, 1835. Post-office, Elysian Fields, Harrison county, Texas.

Allcorn, T. J., age 65 years ; born in Georgia; emigrated in 1821; siege of Bexar, 1853. Post-office, Brenham, Washington county.

Alexander, Lyman W., age 58 ; native of Pennsylvania; emigrated in 1832 ; San Antonio, 1835. Post-office, Columbus, Colorado county.

Anderson, Washington, age 57 ; Virginia; emigrated in 1835 ; in battle of San Jacinto. Residence, Austin, Travis county.

Allbury, Y. P., age 56 ; native of Kentucky ; emigrated in 1823 ; in battle of San Jacinto. Residence, San Antonio, Bexar county, Texas.

Avery, Willis, age 61 ; spring campaign in 1836 ; in battle ot San Jacinto. Williamson county, Texas.

Alley, William, age 67; native of Missouri ; emigrated in 1822 ; San Antonio campaign in 1835. Post-office, Colorado county.

Atkinson, John, age 80; in campaign of 1836. Bellville, Austin county.

Abbotts, Lancelott; England ; in battle of San Jacinto. Residence, Warwick, England.

Addison, Nathaniel, age 59 ; nativity, Louisiana ; emigrated in 1836 ; served in Captain Cheshier's company in 1836. Residence, Hill county, Texas.

Armstrong, James, age 61 ; served in 1836. Post-office, Beaumont, Jefferson county.

Able, Joseph S., age 66 ; entered service the summer of 1836. Residence, Robertson county.

Allen, Lodger, age 57 ; native of Louisiana ; emigrated in 1827 ; served in 1836. Post-office, Chappell Hill, Washington county.

Anglin, A., age 56; native of Kentucky; emigrated in 1833 ; served in 1835. Post-office, Groesbeeck, Limestone county.

Anderson, Elijah, age 72 ; native of South Carolina ; emigrated in 1832 ; served in army in 1836. Residence, Uneca, Navarro county.

Anderson, John W., served in army in 1836. Residence, Nacogdoches county.

Adriance, John, age 55 ; nativity, New York ; emigrated in 1835 ; served in Captain Eberly's company in 1836. Residence, Columbia, Brazoria county.

Ayres, David, age 81 ; nativity, New Jersey ; emigrated in 1832 ; rendered important aid in War of Independence. Residence, Galveston city, Texas.

Austin, Norman, age 63 ; served in Colonel Albert C. Horton's company, Colonel Fannin's command, in 1836. Residence, Belton, Bell county.

Allen, Elisha, served in Captain Cheshier's company in 1835.

Alford, Winfield, age 71 ; entered army 1835. Residence, Gonzales county.

Adair, A. M., Hickman county, Tennessee ; served in army in 1836.

Area, Alexander, age 60, served in army in 1836.

Atkins, Joseph, age 74 ; emigrated in 1834 ; in the expedition that disarmed the garrison at Anahuac in June, 1835. Residence, Galveston, Galveston county, Texas.

Atkinson, Jno, age 76 ; in battle of San Jacinto. Residence, Los Angelos, Coahuila.

Anglin, Henry, age 101, nativity, North Carolina, emigrated in 1834; in service in 1836.

Benson, Ellis, age 66 ; native of Vermont; emigrated January, 1836; in battle of San Jacinto. Residence, Houston, Harris county.

Blount, Stephen W., age 66 ; native of Georgia; emigrated July, 1835 ; three months' service. Post-office, San Augustine, San Augustine county, Texas.

Burleson, Jonathan, age 66 ; native of Tennessee ; emigrated April, 1829; at the battle of Velasco and the storming of San Antonio.

Boyce, Robert P., aged 56; native of Ohio; emigrated April, 1836; T. J. Green's brigade in 1836. Houston, Harris county, Texas.

Bledsoe, George L., age 69 ; native of Georgia; emigrated in 1834; in battle San Jacinto. Residence, Honey Grove, Fannin county.

Browning, George W., age 69 ; native of Scotland ; emigrated in 1834 ; in battle of San Jacinto. Austin, Travis county, Texas.

Bruce, Willis, age 62 ; native of Tennessee ; emigrated in 1835 ; in battle of San Jacinto. Bell county.

Bates, Silas H., age 60 ; nativity, Ohio; emigrated in 1834 ; in service in 1835. Residence, Groesbeeck.

Bryan, Moses Austin, age 56 ; native of Missouri ; emigrated January, 1831 ; in service in 1835, in battle of San Jacinto, 1836, and the campaign under A. Somerville, 1842. Residence, Independence, Washington county.

Box, John, age 71; nativity, Tennessee ; emigrated in 1834 ; in battle of San Jacinto. Residence, Crockett, Houston county.

Blair, John, age 68 ; Tennessee ; emigrated in 1836 ; in Captain Switzer's company in 1836. Crockett, Houston county.

Bringhurst, George H., age 64; native of Pennsylvania ; emigrated January, 1835; taken prisoner at Copano. Houston, Harris county.

Bennett, Jake, age 60 ; nativity, Mississippi ; emigrated in 1836 ; in Felix Huston's command in 1836.

Bartlett, J. C., age 60 ; Tennessee ; emigrated in 1831 ; in army of 1836. Rice, Navarro county.

Buffington, A., age 68 ; native of South Carolina ; emigrated in 1835 ; in Cherokee campaign in 1839, and Santa Fé prisoner ; in battle of San Jacinto. Anderson, Grimes county.

Bryan, John, age 68 ; nativity, New York ; emigrated in 1836 ; in army of 1836. Burton, Washington county.

Brooks, Gilbert, age 67 ; nativity, Connecticut; emigrated in 1831 ; Colonel Morgan's command in 1836. Cedar Bayou, Harris county.

Borden, John P., age 61 ; New York ; emigrated in 1829 ; in battle of San Jacinto. Borden, Colorado county, Texas.

Barnhart, J., age 56 ; nativity, Pennsylvania ; emigrated in 1836; served in Captain Burrows' company in 1836. Manor, Travis county.

Berry, A. J., age 54; Indiana ; emigrated in 1827 ; in battle of San Jacinto. Georgetown, Williamson county.

Brown, Reuben R., age 66 ; nativity, Georgia ; emigrated in ˙ 1835 ; Johnson and Grant's command. Velasco, Brazoria county.

Bryan, William J., age 58; Missouri ; emigrated in 1831 ; in army in 1835 and 1836. Perry's Landing, Brazoria county, Texas.

Bryan, Guy M., age 53; Missouri ; emigrated 1831 ; in service in 1836. Galveston, Galveston county, Texas.

Berry, J. B., age 62 ; Indiana ; emigrated in 1827 ; in campaign of 1836. Residence, Fort Mason, Mason county.

Burleson, A., age 63 ; nativity, Tennessee ; emigrated in 1830 ; in battle of San Jacinto. Residence, Webberville, Travis county.

Brooks, George W., age 65 ; native of Virginia ; battle of Velasco ; emigrated in 1831, and in army of 1836. Clinton, De Witt county.

Byerly, William ; siege of San Antonio. Jasper, Texas.

Bradberry, James, age 69 ; in campaign of 1835. Residence, Fredericksburg, Gillespie county.

Bowman, James H., age 54 ; in the campaign of 1835. Alto, Cherokee county.

Bowman, John J., age 66 ; in campaign of 1835. Alto, Cherokee county.

Burton, Stephen H. ; in Colonel Miller's command at Copano, 1836. Hamilton county, Ohio.

Begly, John, age 63 ; nativity ——; emigrated in 1832 ; in battle of San Jacinto, 1836. Residence, Hawkins county, Tennessee.

Brewster, H. P., age 58 ; native of South Carolina ; emigrated in ˙1836 ; in battle of San Jacinto. San Antonio, Bexar county.

Billingsly, Jesse, age 60 ; Captain of company in battle of San Jacinto. McDade, Bastrop county.

Bunton, John W., age 63 ; nativity, Tennessee ; served in siege of San Antonio and in battle of San Jacinto. Mountain City, Hays county.

Balch, John, age 62 ; emigrated in 1835 ; in campaign of 1835 and in battle of San Jacinto. Residence, Chireno, Nacogdoches county.

Buckley, Lyre ; served in campaign of 1835. Shelby county, Texas.

Bennett, Miles, aged 57 ; served in summer of 1836. Residence, Anderson county, Texas.

Burleson Joseph, aged 67; served in campaign of 1835 and in summer of 1836. Residence, Lee county, Texas ; emigrated in 1833.

Bisbee, Ira, aged 64 ; served in summer of 1836. Residence, Lockhart, Texas.

Bennett, Joseph, aged 58 ; served in summer of 1836. Residence, Rankin county, Mississippi.

Bissell, Theodore, aged 70 ; summer of 1836. Residence, Bastrop, Texas,

Blanton, Jacob ; in service in Captain Becknell's company, in 1836.

Brayles, Joseph, aged 60 ; nativity, Tennessee ; emigrated in 1836 ; served in Captain J. Smith's company in 1836. Residence, Honey Grove, Fannin county, Texas.

Brooks, George W., age 50; emigrated in 1835 ; in Colonel Fannin's command. Residence, Washington county.

Burnham, Jesse ; emigrated in 1821 ; member of Consultation, November, 1835.

Brattan, William ; served in Captain Price's company, June, 1836. Residence, Mifflin county, Pennsylvania.

Browning George W. ; served in Captain Turner's company ; in battle San Jacinto, 1836.

Bailey, Eli, age— ; in service in 1836. Residence, Palestine, Anderson county, Texas.

Bell, P. Hansborough, age — ; native of Virginia; emigrated in 1834 ; served in 1835 and 1836 ; in battle Jacinto. Residence, North Carolina.

Byrne, James ; served in Colonel J. W. Fannin's command in 1836. Residence, Victoria county, Texas.

Barclay, Anderson, age 63 ; siege of San Antonio. Residence, Tyler county, Texas.

Bertrand, Thomas ; served in campaign of 1835 and 1836. Residence, Coryell county, Texas.

Burk, David N., age 64 ; in army of 1835 and 1836. Galveston, Galveston county.

Burdett, William B., age — ; in battle of San Jacinto in 1836. Residence, Bee county, Texas.

Byerly, Adam, age 73 ; storming of San Antonio.

Borden, Thomas H., age 69 ; campaign of 1835. Residence, Galveston, Galveston county.

Bradley, Daniel, age 57 ; in army of 1836. Robertson county.

Brill, Solomon W., age 68; served in summer of 1836. Residence, Seguin, Guadaloupe county.

Brenan, Thomas H., age 63 ; emigrated in 1832 ; siege of Anahuac in 1832. Rockdale, Milam county.

Blair, Payton, age 55 ; service in 1835 and 1836, in Grass Fight. Residence, Orange county, Texas.

Burkham, James ; in Wm. Becknell's company 1826. Residence, Sulphur Springs, Hopkins county, Texas.

Byrn, Rezin, age 65 ; served in J. W. E. Wallace's company in 1836. Residence, Calhoun county.

Barclay, James, died in Tyler county, December 14, 1873.

Burroughs, G. H., age 67 ; came to Texas, September, 1836 ; brought a company from Zanesville, Ohio. Residence, Bellville, Wayne county, Michigan.

Bustilla, Clement, age 60; native of San Antonio, Texas; in siege of Bexar.

Cochran, Thomas, age 62; nativity, New Hampshire; emigrated in 1834; under Baker's command in 1836. Residence, Buckhorn, Austin county, Texas.

Collard, J. H., age 58; Missouri; emigrated in 1832; in campaign in 1836. Bremond, Robertson county.

Childress, B. F., age 68; nativity, Tennessee; emigrated in 1836; Teel's command in 1836. Cleburne, Johnson county, Texas.

Collins, Bela, age 73; nativity, Massachusetts; emigrated in 1836; Captain Burrough's company, 1836. Residence, Bastrop county, Texas.

Craddock, John R., age 61; nativity, Virginia; emigrated in 1833; in battle of San Jacinto. Residence, Davilla, Milam county.

Chriesman, Horatio, age 77; native of Virginia; emigrated in 1822; in the army in 1835 and 1836.

Chattam, Tom, age 72; nativity, South Carolina; emigrated in 1834; under Captain Wade in 1836. Residence, Montgomery, Texas.

Calder, Robert J., age 64; nativity, Maryland; emigrated in 1832; commanded a company in the battle of San Jacinto, battle of Velasco, and served in 1835. Richmond, Texas.

Clemons, Lewis C., age 58; native of Kentucky; emigrated in 1833; in battle San Jacinto. Brenham, Washington county, Texas.

Crittenden, William, age 61; native of Virginia; emigrated in 1835; in battle of San Jacinto. Gatesville, Coryell county.

Chissum, J., age 65; nativity, Tennessee; emigrated in 1833; served in Captain Blount's company, 1836. Residence, Whitesborough, Grayson county.

Campbell, D. W., age 62; Kentucky; emigrated 1833; Captain Chance's company in 1836. Residence, Dresden, Navarro county.

Clary, Jesse, age 58; nativity, North Carolina; emigrated in 1834; in Captain Bird's company in 1835. Corsicana, Navarro county.

Collard, J. S., age 67; nativity, Kentucky; emigrated in 1835; served in army in 1835-'36. Residence, Willis, Montgomery county.

Cunningham, L. C., age 60; in battle San Jacinto. Residence, Schulenburg, Fayette county.

Callahan, Thomas J., age 52; in battle San Jacinto. Liverpool, Brazoria county.

Crier, Andrew, age 54; in battle San Jacinto. Fayette county.

Coy, Alexander, age 63; native of Maine; emigrated in 1835; Major Miller's command. Clear Creek, Harris county.

Cooper, Dillard, age 59; nativity, South Carolina; emigrated 1835; Fannin's command 1836. Residence, Columbus, Colorado county.

Chambliss, S. L., age 60; nativity, Mississippi; emigrated in 1835; in army in 1835 and 1836. Residence, Corsicana, Navarro county.

Caruthers, William, age 65; nativity, Illinois; emigrated in 1833; in campaign 1836. Residence, Somerset, Atascosa county.

Crist, Daniel, age 59; nativity, Indiana; emigrated in 1833; in M. Castley's company in 1836. Barton post-office, Anderson county.

Crain, J. B., age 61; nativity, Tennessee; emigrated in 1834; in battle of San Jacinto. Residence, Waco.

Cartwright, M., age 60; nativity, Alabama; emigrated in 1832; in battle of San Jacinto. Montgomery, Montgomery county.

Carey, Seth, age 68; Vermont; emigrated in 1835; campaign of 1835. Cedar Bayou, Harris county.

Covington, Charles, 64; nativity, Tennessee; emigrated in 1832; in battle of Velasco and army of 1836. Caldwell, Burleson county.

Clark, Henry, age 56; in campaign of 1836. Cherokee county.

Cannon, William J., age 65; nativity, South Carolina; emigrated in 1835; in battle of San Jacinto. Residence, Velasco, Brazoria county.

Cayce, Henry P.; native of Tennessee; emigrated in 1829; in campaign of 1835. Residence, Wharton, Wharton county, Texas.

Campbell, Rufus E., age 62; in the campaign of 1836. Residence, Travis, Austin county, Texas.

Campbell, John, age 56; in campaign of 1836. Travis, Austin county.

Chaffin, James A., age 67; in battle of San Jacinto. Residence, San Augustine. .

Cleveland, J. A. H., age 67; in campaign of 1836. Residence, Galveston, Galveston county.

Cooke, Frank J., age 57; nativity, North Carolina; emigrated in 1835; in battle San Jacinto. Residence, Hempstead, Waller county, Texas.

Crain, R. T.; served in 1836; in battle of San Jacinto. Residence, Waco, McLennan county, Texas.

Cruse, Squire; served in campaign of 1835. Residence, Woodville, Tyler county.

Copeland, George, age 58; nativity, Philadelphia, Pennsylvania; emigrated 1835; served with Colonels Grant and Johnson, 1836. Residence, Contra Costa county, California.

Crawford, Robert; in battle of San Jacinto. Residence, City of Bryan, Brazos county, Texas.

Crawaner, A., age 60; emigrated in 1830; served in army of 1836. Residence, Burnet county.

Choate, David, age 63; in battle of San Jacinto.

Chapman, George W., age 58; served in the army of 1836. Residence, Atascosa county.

Coffin, A. G., emigrated in 1836 ; served in General Quitman's command, in 1836.   Residence, San Francisco, California.

Carlisle, Robert, age 72 ; native of Kentucky ; served in Captain Dimmitt's command in 1835–'36.   Residence, Nueces county, Texas.

Capell, J. B., age 56 ; in the army of 1836.   Residence, Fort Bend county.

Carvier, Matrias, age 59 ; nativity, Texas ; San Jacinto battle.   Residence, Bexar county.

Childress, Robert, in the army of 1836.   Residence, Bell county.

Campbell, Michael, age 61 ; Sante Fé prisoner.   Residence, Bastrop county.

Callicoatte, John B., age 59 ; nativity, North Carolina ; siege of San Antonio and in the battle of San Jacinto.   Residence, Hopkins county, Texas.

Chisholm, Enoch P., age 61 ; nativity, Tennessee ; emigrated in 1835 ; served in Captain Collins' company in 1836.   Residence, Kaufman county.

Cullen, E. W.; nativity, Georgia ; emigrated in 1835 ; served at the siege of San Antonio in 1835.   Residence, Dallas county, Texas.

Cayce, Shadrack, age 67 ; served in army in 1835–36.   Residence, Gonzales county, Texas.

Coleman, Young, age 72 ; served in army in 1836.   Residence, Gonzales county.

Cockrill, Simon, age 62 ; in service from 3d October, 1836.   Residence, Tarrant county.

Callender, Sidney S., age 67 ; served in 1835.   Residence, New Orleans, Louisiana.

Chamberlain, Willard, age 60 ; in Hill's company in 1836.   Residence, Warren county, Mississippi.

Collard, L. M. ; in Jno. M. Wade's company in 1836.   Residence, Walker county.

Cassillas, Pablo, age 62 ; native of Texas ; in storming of Bexar.   Residence, San Antonio.

Cassillas, Matea, age 71 ; native Texan ; in storming of Bexar.   Residence, San Antonio.

Chacon, Carlos, age 60 ; native Texan ; in service in 1835.   Residence, San Antonio.

Contis, Julian, age 68 ; native of Texas ; in service in 1835 ; in siege of Bexar.   Residence, San Antonio.

Davis, John, age 61 ; nativity, Illinois ; emigrated in 1833 ; in service in 1836 with Major McNutt.   Residence, Burnet county, Texas.

Dawess, Isaac, age 58 ; in service in 1836.   Residence, Indianola, Calhoun county.

De Bard, E. J., age 63 ; served in army of 1836. Residence, Anderson county, Texas.

DeMorse, Charles, age 59 ; nativity, Massachusetts ; emigrated March, 1836 ; in the campaign in 1836. Clarksville, Red River county.

Duval, John, C., age 58 ; native of Kentucky ; emigrated in 1835 ; one of the survivors of Fannin's massacre. Waco, McLennan county.

Dewees, William B., age 75 ; native of Virginia ; emigrated in .1822 ; in campaign 1836. Residence, Columbus, Colorado county, Texas.

Davis, George W., age 64 ; Tennessee ; emigrated in 1835 ; Scurlock's company in 1836. Residence, Austin, Travis county.

Davie, Tom P., age 65 ; nativity, England ; emigrated in 1833 ; in battle of San Jacinto. Residence, Tyler, Smith county, Texas.

Dean, Calloway, age 63 ; nativity, Tennessee ; emigrated in 1835 ; in Grass Fight in 1835. Residence, Starrville, Smith county, Texas.

Doom, R. C., age 63 ; nativity, Kentucky ; emigrated in 1836 ; in the army of 1836. Residence, Jasper, Jasper county, Texas.

Dunlavy, Alexander, age 55 ; native of Virginia ; emigrated in 1833 ; at the siege of San Antonio in 1835. Residence, Columbus, Colorado county, Texas.

Deffenbaugh, A., age 57 ; nativity, Ohio ; emigrated in 1836 ; in Captain Burroughs' company in 1836. Residence, Austin City, Travis county, Texas.

Duty, William, age 65 ; in service in 1835. Residence, San Bernardino, California.

Duncan, John, age 86 ; native of Pennsylvania ; emigrated in 1835 ; in battle of San Jacinto. Residence, Caney, Matagorda county.

Dykes, L. P., age 63 ; nativity, Louisiana ; emigrated in 1833 ; served in San Antonio campaign in 1835. Residence, Circleville, Williamson county.

Dyches, Josiah, age 74 ; nativity, South Carolina ; emigrated in 1832 ; served in Captain Logan's company in 1836. Residence, Circleville, Williamson county.

Dunman, James T., age 64 ; nativity, Louisiana ; emigrated in 1824 ; served in San Antonio campaign in 1835. Residence, Lynchburg, Harris county.

Dunbar, William, age 56 ; served in San Antonio campaign in 1835. Residence, Galveston.

De Vare, Cornelius ; in battle of San Jacinto. Residence, Liberty, Liberty county, Texas.

Davis, George W. A., age 55 ; served in campaign of 1835. Residence, Clinton, De Witt county.

Douglass, Freeman W., age 51 ; a native of Georgia ; in the army of

38

1835 and 1836, and also a Mier prisoner. Residence, Columbia, Brazoria county.

Durst, E. H., age 60; nativity, Missouri; in battle of San Jacinto; emigrated in 1829; in the battle of Velasco in 1832 and service in 1835. Post-office, Richmond, Fort Bend county.

Dennis, Thomas M., age 66; emigrated in 1835; in battle of San Jacinto. Residence, Rockport, Aransas county, Texas.

Dyer, Leon (honorary member); emigrated in 1836: served in General T. J. Green's command. Residence, St. Louis, Missouri.

Dexter, Peter B.; in battle of San Jacinto. Residence, California.

Deadrick, Fielding; in battle of San Jacinto. Residence, Nashville, Tennessee.

Dale, Elijah V., age 63; in battle of San Jacinto. Residence, Seguin, Guadaloupe county.

Daman, Samuel, age 65; nativity, Maine; emigrated in 1832; at the siege of San Antonio in 1835 and in campaign of 1836. Residence, Columbia, Brazoria county, Texas.

De Witt, C. C., age 53; native Missouri; emigrated in 1826; in campaign of 1835. Residence, Gonzales, Gonzales county.

Dikes, M. W., age 63; in army of 1836. Residence, Bell county, Texas.

Duplex, J. B., age 73; in army of 1835 and 1836. Residence, Kinney county, Texas.

Dickson, David H., age 59; in the army of 1836. Residence, Hinds county, Mississippi.

DeBard, E. J., age 63; in the army of 1836. Residence, Anderson county, Texas.

Darden, Stephen H., age 57; native of Mississippi; emigrated in 1836; served in army of 1836.

Dever, Thomas: emigrated in 1824; in service in 1866. Residence, Liberty county, Texas.

Deleplain, A. C., age 66; served in army in 1835 and 1840. Residence, Benton, Washington county.

Doren, Jno., Santa Fé prisoner. Residence, Washington county, Texas.

Dunnettell, Henry, age 59; entered service February 22, 1836. Residence, Seymour, Jackson county, Indiana.

Doyal, M. A., age 72; served in army in 1835. Residence. Mason county, Texas.

Dugah, J. L., age 62; entered service in July, 1836. Residence, Refugio county.

Duncan, Charles R., age 57; emigrated in 1836; in Price's company in 1836. Residence, Milam county, Texas.

Dallas, James L., age 56; emigrated in 1833; entered army July, 1836. Residence, Washington county, Texas.

Diaz, Francisco, age 73; native; served in army in 1835. Residence, San Antonio, Texas.

Dodson, A. B., age 64; served in army in 1835. Residence, Live-oak county.

Etheridge, Howard, age 65; nativity, Adams county, Mississippi; emigrated in 1836; in battle of San Jacinto. Residence, Fannin county, Texas.

Eastland, N. W., age 71; native of Kentucky; emigrated in 1835; army of 1836. Residence, Snake Prairie, Bastrop county, Texas.

Erath, George B., age 61; native of city of Vienna, Austria; emigrated in 1833; in battle of San Jacinto. Residence, Waco, Texas.

Ewing, George, age 82; nativity, Pennsylvania; emigrated 1829; in Grass Fight in 1835.

Eubank, E. N., age 56; native of Virginia; emigrated in 1834; campaign of 1835. Residence, Kosse, Limestone county, Texas.

Evetts, S. G., age 63; at the siege of San Antonio in 1835. Residence, Coryell county.

Edgar, Alexander, age 76; at the siege of San Antonio in 1835. Residence, Galveston.

Elley, Gustavus, age 58; in army of 1836, and San Antonio prisoner. Residence, Guadaloupe county.

English, George, age 66; nativity, Tennessee; emigrated in 1830; served in campaign of 1835. Residence, Houston county.

Edwards, Charles 'O.; emigrated in 1832; served in Captain Wiley Martin's company in 1836. Residence, Rockport, Aransas county, Texas.

Egry, C. W., age 68; emigrated in 1836; served in General T. J. Green's command in 1836. Residence, St. Mary's, Refugio county, Texas.

Edmonson, James, age 50; served in 1836. Residence, Tulare county, California.

Earl, William, age 57; in battle of San Jacinto. Residence, Houston county, Texas.

English, Joshua, age 64; in campaign of 1835. Residence, Houston county, Texas.

Edens, D. H., age 60; served in army from July 1836. Residence, Houston county, Texas.

Eaton, Thomas H., in service in 1836 and 1837. Residence, Brazos county, Texas.

Erhard, Antonio M., age 50; served in and made prisoner on Santa Fé, expedition. Residence, Matamoras, Mexico.

Espinosa, Ygnacio, age 62; native; served in army in 1835. Residence, Bexar county, Texas.

Francis, Miller, age 64 ; native of Tennessee ; emigrated in 1833 ; at battle of San Jacinto. Residence, Buckhorn, Austin county.

Ford, John S., age 59 ; native South Carolina ; emigrated in 1836 ; Kimbro's company, August, 1836. Residence, Brownsville, Cameron county, Texas.

Fitzhugh, J. P. T., age 68 ; native of Virginia ; emigrated in 1835 ; in battle of San Jacinto. Residence, Canton, Van Zandt county, Texas.

Forbes, John, age 78 ; native Ohio ; emigrated in 1834 ; in battle of San Jacinto. Residence, Nacogdoches, Texas.

Foster, Randal, age 84 ; native of Mississippi ; emigrated in 1821 ; in Captain Wiley Martin's company, 1836.

Farish, Oscar, age 58 ; in battle San Jacinto. Residence, Galveston city, Galveston county, Texas.

Fulshear, Churchill, age 72 ; nativity, Tennessee ; emigrated in 1824 ; in battle of San Jacinto. Residence, Richmond, Fort Bend county.

Flores, Nepomuceno, age 63 ; native of San Antonio ; in battle San Jacinto. Residence, San Antonio, Bexar county, Texas.

Ferrill, John P., age 54 ; emigrated in 1836 ; in battle San Jacinto. Residence, McDade, Bastrop county, Texas.

Farmer, James, age 73 ; nativity, North Carolina ; emigrated in 1830; in battle San Jacinto. Residence, Comanche county.

Fisk, Greenlief, age 63 ; in the campaign of 1836. Residence, Brown county, Texas.

Faires, William A., age 68 ; in the army of 1835 and 1836. Residence, Fayette county, Texas.

Foster, B. F., age 57 ; in the army of 1835 and 1836. Residence, Bellville, Austin county.

Fowler, J. H., age 76 ; nativity, Tennessee ; emigrated in 1818. Residence, Paris, Lamar county, Texas.

Field, Joseph E. ; emigrated in 1833 ; at the storming of San Antonio in 1835, and in Fannin's command in 1836. Residence, Corpus Christi, Nueces county, Texas.

Faris, Isham ; served in Captain Becknell's company in 1836. Residence, Lamar county, Texas.

Fisk, James N., age 55 ; in service in 1836. Residence, San Antonio, Texas.

Ford, Simon P., age 58 ; in battle of San Jacinto in 1836. Residence, Jefferson county, Texas.

Farmer, Alexander, Sr., age 76 ; in campaign of 1835. Residence, Sunrise, Bastrop county.

Fields, Henry, served in army in 1836 and 1857. Residence, Anderson county, Texas.

Foygnet, Francis A., age 61; emigrated in 1836; served in army from May 18, 1836. Residence, New Orleans, Louisiana.

Ferguson, James, age 60; Santa Fé prisoner. Residence, Galveston, Texas.

Gailan, Victor E., age 69; nativity, Normandy; emigrated May, 1836. Residence, Beeville, Bee county, Texas.

Grayham, James, age 63; native of Tennessee; emigrated in 1836; army of 1836. Pattenville, Lamar county, Texas.

Gassett, A. E., age 62; nativity, Tennessee; emigrated in 1833, army of 1836. Residence, Crockett, Houston county, Texas.

Goodloe, R. R., age 61; nativity, Virginia; emigrated in 1836; in battle of San Jacinto. Residence, Sabinetown, Sabine county, Texas.

Gaines, W. B. P., age 65; nativity, South Carolina; emigrated in 1835; in the army of 1835 and 1836; Paymaster-General under General T. J. Rusk. Residence, city of Austin, Travis county.

Gallatin, Ed., age 64; nativity, Kentucky; emigrated in 1832; storming of San Antonio and in battle of San Jacinto. Residence, Bryan, Brazos county.

Gates, Amos, age 75; nativity, Kentucky; emigrated in 1821; in army of 1836. Residence, town of Washington, Washington county.

Green, George, age 60; native of Maryland; emigrated in 1835; in army and battle of San Jacinto in 1836. Residence, Cameron, Milam county, Texas.

Grimes, Rufus, age 55; nativity, Alabama; emigrated in 1826, in army of 1836. Residence, Navasota, Grimes county, Texas.

Gorman, J. P., age 61; nativity, Tennessee; emigrated in 1835; at the storming of San Antonio. Residence, Giddings, Lee county.

Gentry, F. B., age 63; nativity, Tennessee; emigrated in 1835; in battle of San Jacinto. Residence, Hamilton county.

Green, James, age 68; in battle of San Jacinto. Residence, Burnet county.

Good, Hannibal, at the siege of San Antonio. Jasper county, Texas.

Gallatin, Albert, age 64; in battle of San Jacinto. Residence, Bryan, Brazos county, Texas.

Goodman, J. B., age 59; in army of 1836. Residence, Fayette county, Texas.

George, David, age 58; Captain Dimmitt's company in 1835. Residence, Hays county, Texas.

Grimes, George W., age 56; army of 1836. Austin county, Texas.

Grimes, Frederick, age 70; in army in 1835 and 1836. Residence, Coryell county.

Gibson, Archibald, age 75 ; nativity, Kentucky ; army of 1836 ; emigrated April, 1836. De Witt county, Texas.

Gates, Wm. N., age 56; nativity, Tennessee; at the storming of San Antonio in 1835. Residence, San Antonio.

Gossett, A. E. ; served in Clapp's company in 1836.

Golden, Philip ; entered the army June 1, 1836.

Goff, Felix W., age 62 ; in service in 1836. Residence, Bastrop county.

Gorham, William, age 73 ; in campaign of 1835. Residence, Black Jack Springs, Fayette county, Texas.

Greenwood, James, age 69 ; in battle of San Jacinto in 1836. Residence, Montgomery county, Ohio.

Goodwin, William, age 60 ; served in the army in 1835 and 1836. Residence, Oakville, Live-oak county, Texas.

Gilliam, L. W., age 62 ; served in 1836. Residence, San Augustine county, Texas.

Garner, Isaac, age 64 ; served in army from May 8, 1836. Residence, Milam county, Texas.

Gray, James, age 59 ; served in army in 1836 and 1837. Residence, Wilson county, Texas.

Gellatley, Robert, served in E. M. Callin's company from July 8, 1836. Residence, Sabine county, Texas.

Grover, George W., age 53 ; native of New York ; emigrated in 1840, Santa Fé prisoner. Residence, Galveston, Texas.

Hawford, Henry, age 63 ; nativity, Bedford, England ; emigrated in 1836 in army of 1836. Residence, East Feliciana, Louisiana.

Horton, Alexander, age 65 ; nativity, North Carolina ; emigrated in 1824 ; in battles of Nacogdoches and San Jacinto. Residence, San Augustine, Texas.

Hopkins, J. E., age 69 ; nativity, Kentucky ; emigrated in 1822 ; served in Captain Smith's company in 1836. Clarksville, Red River county, Texas.

Hearn, Thomas B., age 55 ; nativity, Tennessee ; emigrated in 1836 ; in Captain Allen's company in 1836.

Hill, G. B., age 60 ; native, Georgia ; emigrated in 1835 ; in army of 1835. Residence, Gonzales county.

Hopson, Lucien, age 63 ; nativity, Ohio ; emigrated in 1836 ; in battle of San Jacinto and army of 1836. Lampasas county, Texas.

Harvey, John, age 64 ; native Tennessee ; emigrated in 1834 ; in battle of San Jacinto. Residence, Salado, Bell county.

Hill, James M., age 56 ; nativity, Georgia ; emigrated in 1835 ; in battle of San Jacinto. Residence, Fayetteville, Fayette county, Texas.

Hill, Isaac L., age 59 ; nativity, Georgia ; emigrated in 1835 ; in battle of San Jacinto. Post-office, Round Top, Fayette county, Texas.

Hallmark, W. O., age 70; nativity, Tennessee; emigrated 1834; in battle San Jacinto. Residence, Crockett, Houston county, Texas.

Hallmark, A. M., age 57; nativity, Alabama; emigrated 1834; in battle San Jacinto. Residence, Crockett, Houston county, Texas.

Henderson, J. W., age 59; nativity, Tennessee; emigrated 1836; served in army of 1836. Residence, city of Houston, Harris county, Texas.

Hardeman, W. P., age 57; nativity, Tennessee; emigrated 1835; in the army of 1835 and 1836. Residence, Galveston city, Texas.

Haggard, Squire, age 63; nativity, Georgia; emigrated 1836; served under George W. Jewell. Residence, Johnson county, Texas.

Ham, E. L., age 61; nativity, Tennessee; emigrated, 1836; Tinsley's company, in 1836. Residence, Ennis, Ellis county, Texas.

Hubble, John, age 72; nativity, Louisiana; in army of 1836. Residence, Cleburne, Johnson county, Texas.

Hunter, William L., age 65; nativity, Virginia; emigrated, 1835; in siege of San Antonio, and survivor of Fannin's massacre. Residence, Goliad, Goliad county, Texas.

Hunt, William G., age 60; nativity, Virginia; emigrated, 1831; in siege of San Antonio. Residence, Columbus, Colorado county, Texas.

Herder, George, age 56; Germany; emigrated in 1834; in army of 1836. Residence, High Hill, Fayette county.

Haley, Richard, age 65; Tennessee; emigrated in 1824; in San Antonio campaign, 1835. Residence, Cotton Gin, Freestone county, Texas.

Hensley, Johnson, age 67; nativity, Tennessee; emigrated in 1818; in army of 1836. Residence, Hempstead, Waller county, Texas.

Haley, Charles Q., age 55; native Mississippi; emigrated in 1824; in San Antonio campaign, 1835. Residence, Kosse, Limestone county, Texas.

Hancock, George, age 65; nativity, Tennessee; emigrated in 1835; in battle San Jacinto. Residence, City of Austin, Travis county.

Hill, A. W., age 59; nativity, Georgia; emigrated in 1835; in battle of San Jacinto. Residence, Bastrop county, Texas.

Hardeman, John, age 70; nativity, Tennessee; emigrated in 1836; served in Scurlock's company in 1836. Residence, Chambers Creek, Ellis county, Texas.

Harris, S. M., age 63; native of New York; emigrated in 1831; naval service in 1835 and 1836. Residence, city of Houston.

Highland, Joseph, age 65, in battle San Jacinto.

Hill, David, age —; served in 1836. Residence, Burnet county, Texas.

Hardin, Franklin, age 67; in army of 1835 and 1836, and battle of San Jacinto. Residence, Liberty county, Texas.

Haley, Michael, age 63 ; in Colonel Fannin's command in 1836. Residence, Oakville, Live-oak county, Texas.

Harbour, James M., age 53 ; in battle of San Jacinto. Residence, Brenham, Washington county.

Harris, Temple O., age 63 ; in battle of San Jacinto. Residence, Sumner county, Tennessee.

Heard, W. J. E., age 72 ; captain of a company in battle of San Jacinto. Residence, Chappell Hill, Washington county, Texas.

Hawkins, W. W., age 61 ; nativity, Missouri ; emigrated in 1832 ; served in army of 1836 and in battle of San Jacinto. Residence, Lexington, Lee county.

Hensley, John M., age 67 ; in battle of San Jacinto. Residence, Hempstead, Waller county.

Harris, Isaac, age 68 ; emigrated in 1824 ; campaign of 1836. Residence, Merced county, California.

Hotchkiss, R., age 56 ; in battle of San Jacinto. Residence, city of Galveston, Galveston county.

Hall, George H., age 60 ; served in 1836. Residence, Navidad, Jackson county, Texas.

Hardin, W. B., age 64 ; in campaign of 1835. Residence, Polk county, Texas.

Hallien, John F., age 63 ; in service in 1836. Residence, Bellville, Austin county.

Hoffman, Michael T., age 65 ; in service in 1836. Residence, Crosstimbers Post-office, Johnson county.

Hayden, Nathaniel, age 53 ; served in 1835. Residence, Hemphill, Sabine county, Texas.

Harwood, B. F., age 67 ; in service in 1836. Residence, Concrete, De Witt county.

Hall, Hudson H., age 68 ; served in 1836. Residence, San Augustine county, Texas.

Hillyer, W. D., age 66 ; in service in 1836. Residence, Monroe county, Wisconsin.

Hape, Richard, age 59 ; in service in 1835 and 1836. Residence, Washington, Washington county, Texas.

Henderson, John, age 62 ; in spring campaign of 1836.

Harbour, George W., age 52 ; served in siege of San Antonio. Brenham, Washington county.

Hawley, William, age 60 ; in service 1836. Residence, city of Galveston.

Herron, John H., age 59 ; in battle San Jacinto. Residence, Ledbetter, Bastrop county.

SIDNEY SHERMAN.

See p. 268.

Hensley, A. J., age 53 ; emigrated in 1829 ; in service 1836. Residence, Ledbetter, Lee county, Texas.

Hynes, John, age 50 ; in service 1835 and 1836. Rockport, Aransas county, Texas.

Hanks, Wesley W.; served from June to September, 1836. Residence, Bosque county.

Howard, Philip, age 60 ; in service August, 1836. Residence, Bosque county, Texas.

Harward, John ; in service July, 1836. Residence, Gonzales, Texas.

Houston, Andrew D., age 60 ; in service July, 1836. Residence, Williamson county, Texas.

Hamilton, Nathan, age 57 ; in service July, 1836. Residence, Navarro county, Texas.

Harding, T. B., age 60 ; nativity, Maryland ; emigrated in 1836 ; entered service 3d June, 1836, in Captain Faley's company ; served in Captain J. B. Robertson's company in 1836 and 1837. Residence, Huntsville, Walker county.

Higgins, James ; emigrated in 1836 ; served in army from September, 1836. Residence, Ashland City, Cheatham county, Tennessee.

Hitchcock, A. J., age 54 ; served in army from 1835. Residence, Shreveport, Louisiana.

Harmon, Clark M.; emigrated in 1836 ; served in army from January, 1836. Residence, Decatur county, Tennessee.

Hurd, Norman, age 85 ; served in navy, from December, 1835, as purser of *Brutus*.

Hurd, James C., age 60 ; served in navy in 1836. Residence, Galveston, Texas.

Ijams, Bazel G., age 70 ; nativity, North Carolina ; emigrated in 1835 ; in San Antonio campaign in 1835 and at San Jacinto.

Ijams, John H., age 65 ; nativity, Ohio ; emigrated in 1822 ; in battles of Concepcion and San Jacinto. Residence, City of Houston, Harris county, Texas.

Isbell, William, age 58 ; nativity, Tennessee ; emigrated in 1834; in battle of San Jacinto. Residence, Caldwell, Burleson county.

Isaacks, Sam, age 65 ; emigrated in 1823 ; in service in 1835 and 1836. Residence, Lynchburg, Harris county.

Ingram, John, age 62 ; emigrated in 1821 ; siege of San Antonio and in battle San Jacinto.

Irvine, W. D., age 53 ; nativity, Tennessee ; emigrated in 1830 ; served in Captain Scurlock's company, 1836. Kaufman county.

Isaacks, William, age 70; served in 1835 and in 1836. Residence, Cherokee county, Texas.

Irvine, Josephus S., age 51; served in 1835 and 1836. Residence, Newton county, Texas.

Jarman, Asa, age 69; nativity, Nashville, Tennessee; emigrated in 1831; in battle of Nacogdoches. Residence, Houston, Harris county.

Johnson, Samuel, age 64; nativity, Georgia.; emigrated March, 1836; in army of 1836. Residence, Fannin county, Texas.

Jenkins, John H., age 51; nativity, Alabama; emigrated in 1828; in Captain Billingsby's company, 1836. Residence, Bastrop county.

Jones, George W., age 65; nativity, Tennessee; emigrated in 1827; in battle of San Jacinto. Residence, Waco, McLennan county.

Jackson, Joseph, age 57; nativity, Georgia; emigrated in 1822; in battle San Jacinto. Residence, Caldwell, Burleson county.

Jones, A. H., age 61; nativity, Georgia; emigrated in 1835; in battle of San Antonio in 1835. Residence, Gonzales, Gonzales county, Texas.

Johnson, William, age 60; served in 1836. Residence, Williamson county.

January, J. P. B., age 59; emigrated in 1835; served spring campaign, 1836. Residence, Victoria, Texas.

Johnson, Frank W.; commander at the surrender of General Cos at San Antonio, and in service in 1836. Residence, Round Rock, Williamson county.

Jones, Kelton M., age 51; in service in 1836. Residence, Belton, Bell county.

Jean, James M., age 61; in service 1835. Residence, Calcasieu parish, Louisiana.

Jones, Lorenzo, age 69; emigrated in 1836; in service in September, 1836. Residence, Knox county, Ohio.

Jackson, E. D.; in Grass Fight; in 1835. Residence, Washington county, Texas.

Jacobs, Madison G., age 61; native of Virginia. Residence, De Witt county, Texas.

Kennard, William E., age 54; in service in 1835. Residence, Cleburne, Johnson county, Texas.

Keller, Francis G., age 70; served in Captain Dimmitt's company, 1835. Morales, Jackson county.

Kerr, George A., age 64; nativity, Georgia; emigrated in 1830; served in campaign of 1835. Residence, Thompsonville, Gonzales county.

Kennard, Michael, age 65; nativity, Tennessee; emigrated in 1830; campaign of 1836. Anderson, Grimes county, Texas.

Kerr, William P., age 59 ; nativity, Pennsylvania ; emigrated in 1831 ; campaign of 1836.

Keaghsy, William S., age 63 ; nativity, Ireland ; emigrated in 1836 ; in Captain Chesshier's company, 1836. Residence, Burksville, Newton county.

Karner, John, age 56 ; nativity, Bavaria ; emigrated in 1835 ; in battle San Jacinto. Residence, Fairfield, Freestone county, Texas.

Kokernot, D. L., age 69 ; nativity, Holland ; emigrated in 1830 ; in Grass Fight, 1835, and in service in 1836. Gonzales, Gonzales county, Texas.

Kendricks, B. H., age 54 ; nativity, Georgia ; emigrated in 1835 ; in Captain Jones' company in 1835. Caney, Matagorda county.

Kleburgh, Robert, age 70 ; nativity, Germany ; emigrated in 1834 ; in battle of San Jacinto. Residence, Clinton, De Witt county.

Kelley, Connell O. D. ; in battle of San Jacinto. Residence, California.

Kent, David B. , age 56 ; in campaign 1835. Residence, Blanco county.

Kelso, Alfred, age 65 ; in battle of San Jacinto. Residence, City of Austin, Travis county, Texas.

Kibby, William, age 69 ; in battle of San Jacinto. Residence, Iberville parish, Louisiana.

Kinchloe, Daniel, age 55 ; served in the army, 1836. Residence, Wharton county, Texas.

Kuykendall, J. H. , age 54 ; served in the army in 1836. Residence, Rockport, Refugio county.

Kirby, George, age 57 ; in service in 1836. Residence, McLennan county.

Kennedy, A. S. , age 56 ; native of Tennessee ; one of the survivors of Dawson's company. Residence, Fayette county, Texas.

Keizer, B. P. , served in army in 1836. Residence, Bryan, Texas.

Lawson, J. D., age 69 ; nativity, Kentucky ; emigrated in 1824 ; in the army of 1836. Clarksville, Red River county.

Leman, John, 65 years ; nativity, Pennsylvania ; emigrated in 1836 ; in the army of 1836 and Santa Fé prisoner. Residence, Burns Station, De Witt county.

Lyon, H. C., age 59 ; nativity, Tennessee ; emigrated in 1836 ; served in Parker's infantry in 1836. City of Bryan, Brazos county.

Lester, James S., age 76 ; nativity, Virginia ; emigrated in 1834 ; campaign of 1835 and in the battle of San Jacinto in 1836. Residence, Winchester, Fayette county.

Little, Hiram, age 65 ; nativity, Illinois ; emigrated in 1835 ; in service in 1835 and 1836. Residence, Willis, Montgomery county.

Lusk, R. O., age 62 ; nativity, Kentucky ; emigrated in 1834 ; in Grass Fight of 1835. Residence, Jewett, Leon county.

Lewis, Jacob, age 61; nativity, Georgia; emigrated in 1834; campaign of 1835. Residence, Nacogdoches county, Texas.

Langley, Campbell, age 57; nativity, Tennessee; emigrated in 1836; in Parker's company in 1836. Residence, Salado, Bell county.

Lawrence, Joe, age 74; nativity, North Carolina; emigrated in 1833; in battle of San Jacinto. Residence, Hackberry, Navarro county.

Lewis, John E., age 66; nativity, New York; emigrated in 1834; in battle San Jacinto. Residence, La Grange, Fayette county.

Love, G. H., age 54; nativity, Tennessee; emigrated in 1836; in service summer of 1836. Residence, Wheelock, Robertson county.

Linn, John J., age 74; nativity, Ireland; emigrated in 1829; campaign of 1835. Residence, Victoria, Victoria county.

Lee, Theodore S., age 75; nativity, New York; emigrated in 1835; in campaign of 1835 and battle San Jacinto. Residence, Gonzales county.

Langerheirmer, William, age 66; storming of San Antonio in 1835. Residence, Philadelphia, Pennsylvania.

Lowe, Barney C., age 57; nativity, Kentucky; emigrated 1832; served in San Antonio 1835 and in 1836.

Linsey, Joseph, age —; nativity, Tennessee; emigrated 1827; in San Antonio campaign in 1835. Residence, Mexia, Limestone county.

Lee, Isaac, age 74; nativity, ——; emigrated in 1828; served in Nacogdoches campaign in 1832. Residence, Alto, Cherokee county, Texas.

Labinski, Victor: belonged to Colonel Morehouse's New York battalion in 1835.

Latimer, H. R.; served in Captain Becknell's company, 1836. Residence, Red River county.

Latimer, A. H.; member of Convention of 1836; served in Captain Becknell's company. Residence, Clarksville, Red River county.

Lang, John J., age 64; nativity, Tennessee; emigrated in December, 1835; served in the army of 1836. Residence, San Saba county.

Lewis, M. B., age 68; nativity, Indiana; emigrated in 1830; served at Nacogdoches in 1832 and in 1835–'36. Residence, Fresno county, California.

Lindheimer, Ferdinand, age 68; served in the army in 1836. Residence, New Braunfels, Comal county, Texas.

Lewis, John S., age 61; served in 1835. Residence, Newton county, Texas.

Littlefield, H. B., age 60; served in the siege of San Antonio in 1835. Residence, Gonzales county.

Lewis, George W., age—; served in campaign of 1835. Residence, San Augustine county, Texas.

Lane, Walter P.; served in 1826, and in battle of San Jacinto. Residence, Marshall, Harrison county, Texas.

Lewis John T., age 62 ; in siege of Bexar. Residence, Newton county, Texas.

Lindsay, James, age 60; served in army from June 4, 1836. Residence, Kerr county, Texas.

Lacy, W. Y., age 60; served from May 1836. Residence, Anderson county, Texas.

Low, B. C., age 63 ; served in Cheshier's company in 1835, in siege of Bexar. Residence, Sabine county, Texas.

McDonald, Donald, age 80; in service in 1836. Residence, San Augustine, Texas.

Miller, Leroy, age 65 ; in service in 1836. Residence, San Augustine county.

Martin, Thomas, age 54; nativity, Pennsylvania; emigrated in 1836 ; in service in 1836. Residence, Houston, Harris county, Texas.

McKneely, Samuel W., age 56 ; nativity, Louisiana ; emigrated in 1835 ; in campaign with Colonels Johnson and Grant in 1836. Residence, Point Coupee parish, Louisiana.

Matthews, William H., age 78 ; nativity, Georgia; emigrated in 1823 ; in the army of 1835. Residence, Lagrange, Fayette county, Texas.

Merchant, J. D., sen., age 74 ; nativity, Tennessee; emigrated in 1831 ; in Grass Fight in 1835. Residence, Pilot Point, Denton county.

Montgomery, James, age 62; nativity, Virginia; emigrated in 1836 ; in service summer of 1836. Residence, City of Houston, Harris county.

Madden, R. W., age 58 ; nativity, Tennessee ; emigrated in 1836 ; Captain Becknell's company in 1836. Residence, Ashland, Hunt county.

Mahan, P. Jenks, age 60 ; nativity, Pennsylvania; emigrated in 1832 ; with Grant and Johnson in 1835. Residence, Houston, Harris county.

McGehee, Thomas G., age 64 ; nativity, Georgia ; emigrated in 1834 ; campaign of 1836. Residence, San Marcos, Hays county, Texas.

Moore, John H., campaign of 1835. Residence, La Grange, Fayette county, Texas.

Marton, J. P., age 63 ; emigrated July, 1836 ; served in General Green's brigade. Residence, Colorado county.

Menifee, William, age 78 ; nativity, Tennessee; emigrated in 1830 ; member of Convention in 1836. Residence, Oso, Fayette county, Texas.

Massey, J. W., age 67 ; nativity, Virginia ; emigrated in 1836 ; in campaign 1836. Residence, Longview, Usphur county.

McMaster, William, age 55 ; nativity, Louisiana; emigrated in 1835 ; in campaign of 1836.

Masters, Jacob, age 66 ; nativity, North Carolina ; emigrated in 1829 ;

Captain Scurlock's company in 1836.   Residence, Waco, McLennan county, Texas.

McGriffin, J. T., age 60 ; nativity, South Carolina ; emigrated in 1827 ; in Grass Fight in 1835.   Residence, Montgomery, Texas.

Moore, T. W., age 70 ; nativity, Georgia ; emigrated in 1827 ; in battle of Velasco in 1832, and in service in 1836.   Residence, City of Austin, Travis county.

Marshall, Joseph T., age 58 ; nativity, Illinois ; emigrated in 1829 ; in battle of San Jacinto.   Residence, Corsicana, Navarro county.

Mangum, Aaron S., age 61 ; nativity, South Carolina ; emigrated in 1835 ; in Fannin and Ward's command in 1835 and 1836.   Residence, Sherman, Grayson county.

Morgan, John D., age 55 ; nativity, Kentucky ; emigrated in 1836 ; served in army of 1836, and Mier prisoner.   Residence, Bastrop, Texas.

Morrison, Gwyn, age 66 ; nativity, New York ; emigrated in 1836 ; in service in 1836.   Residence, Navasota, Grimes county.

Mackey, John, age 53 ; nativity, Tennessee ; emigrated in 1831 ; in service in 1836.   Residence, Colorado county.

McFaddin, D. H., age 58 ; nativity, Tennessee ; emigrated in 1828 ; in battle San Jacinto.   Residence, Circleville, Williamson county, Texas.

McGill, W. H., age 61 ; nativity, Kentucky ; emigrated in 1835 ; in campaign of 1835, and in battle San Jacinto.   Burnet county.   •

McAnnelly, R. D., age 68 ; nativity, Kentucky ; emigrated in 1835 ; siege of San Antonio.   Lampasas county, Texas.

McMillan, Andrew, age 60 ; nativity, Ireland ; emigrated in 1834 ; in the army of 1835.   Residence, Owensville, Robertson county.

Martin, Philip, age 70 ; nativity, North Carolina ; emigrated in 1824 ; in battle of San Jacinto.   Residence, Willis, Montgomery county.

McBride, P. H., age 64 ; nativity, Pennsylvania ; emigrated in 1836 ; Captain Stephenson's company, 1836.   Residence, Galveston city.

McCormic, Michael, age 55 ; nativity, Ireland ; emigrated in 1824 ; campaign of 1836.   Residence, City of Galveston.

McAnnelly, Pleasant ; at the storming of San Antonio in 1835.   Residence, Guadaloupe county, Texas.

McHorse, J. W., age 51 ; in the army in 1836, and in battle of San Antonio.   Residence, Milam county, Texas.

Menifee, John S., age 59 ; in battle of San Jacinto.   Residence, Texana, Jackson county.

Manchaca, Antonio, age 74 ; nativity, Texas ; in the battle of San Jacinto. Residence, San Antonio, Bexar county.

Marshall, Lewis, age 60 ; in service in 1836.   Residence, Bell county.

Marshall, Samuel, age 65 ; in service in 1836. Residence, Bell county.

Marshall, John, age 62 ; in battle of San Jacinto. Residence, Bell county.

McCracklin, Jesse L.; native of Kentucky ; in service in 1835 and 1836. Residence, Blanco, Texas.

Miles, Edward, age 56 ; nativity, Mississippi ; in spring campaign and in battle of San Jacinto in 1836. Residence, San Antonio, Bexar county.

Moore, A. G., age 63 ; in service in 1836. Residence, Limestone county, Texas.

Millerman, Ira, age 58 ; in battle of San Jacinto. Residence, Caldwell, Burleson county.

Marshall, T. W., age 66 ; nativity, New York ; emigrated in 1836 ; pilot on steamer *Laura*, Captain Thomas W. Greyson. Residence, Houston.

McKay, Daniel, age 57 ; in battle of San Jacinto. Residence, Bell country, Texas.

Menifee, George, age 58 ; in service 1835. Residence, Jackson county, Texas.

McHenry, John, age 73 ; in service 1835. Residence, Jackson county, Texas.

McCay, John, age 80 ; in service 1835. Residence, Blanco county.

McNeil, John G. ; nativity, Kentucky ; emigrated in 1822 ; in battle of Velasco, in 1832. Residence, Brazoria, Brazoria county.

Mason, Charles, age 62 ; nativity, Georgia ; emigrated 1834 ; in service in 1835 and 1836. Residence, Gonzales, Gonzales county, Texas.

McCay, Prosper C., age 56 ; in service in 1835 and 1836. Residence, Gonzales, Texas.

Mitchell, Nat ; in battle of San Jacinto. Residence, Cameron county.

McCullock, Samuel, age 58 ; nativity, South Carolina ; at the capture of Goliad, 1835. Residence, San Antonio, Bexar county.

. McGahey, James S., age 65 ; emigrated in 1829 ; served against Anahuac and campaign of 1835. Residence, Grimes county.

Moss, Matthew, age 68 ; in service in 1836 and in battle of San Jacinto. Residence, Llano county, Texas.

Montgomery, McGrealy, aged 62 ; in service in 1836. Residence, Austin county.

McCutcheon, William, age 61 ; in service in 1836. Residence, Williamson county.

Mizell, Augustine, age 57 ; in service in 1836. Residence, Hinds county, Mississippi.

Meisenhetter, Emanuel ; served in Colonel Rogers' regiment in 1836.

McManus, R. W. O., age 62 ; nativity, New York ; emigrated in 1832 ; served in 1836 with Deaf Smith. Residence, Moss Bluff, Liberty county.

McCallister, Joseph ; in battle of San Jacinto. Sonora county, California.

Moffitt, William ; in service in 1836. Walker county, Texas.

Morris, George W ; Santa Fé prisoner, Galveston, Texas.

Mott, Samuel ; in service in 1836. Residence, St. Mary's, Ohio.

Morgan, George W ; emigrated in 1836, in service from September, 1836. Residence, Mount Vernon, Ohio.

McCormack, M. age 55 ; in service in 1836. Residence, Galveston, Texas.

Newell, John D., age 63 ; nativity, North Carolina ; emigrated in 1831 ; in battle of Velasco in 1832. Residence, Richmond, Fort Bend county.

Navarro, Nepomuceno, age 63 ; nativity, Texas ; in battle of San Jacinto. Residence, San Antonio, Bexar county, Texas.

Neill, Andrew, age 61 ; in service in 1836 and a San Antonio prisoner. Residence, City of Galveston.

Norris, Thomas, age 59 ; in service in 1836. Residence, Travis county.

Nettles, William, age 68 ; nativity, South Carolina ; emigrated in 1833 ; served in Captain James Smith's company. Residence, Houston, Harris county, Texas.

Northington, M., age 54 ; emigrated in 1833 ; served under General Green in 1836, and the campaigns of 1842. Residence, Chappel Hill, Washington county.

Norvell, Lipscomb, age 78 ; nativity, Kentucky ; emigrated in April, 1835 ; service in Captain Scurlock's company in 1836. Residence, Sabine county.

Neal, Lewis, age 74 ; nativity, Virginia ; emigrated in 1832 ; served in 1836. Residence, Montgomery county, Texas.

Norvell, William L., in service in 1835 and 1836. Residence, Brooklyn, New York.

Neel, Felding ; in service in 1836. Residence, Shelby county, Kentucky.

O'Bannion, Jennings, age 59 ; nativity, South Carolina ; emigrated 1836 ; in battle San Jacinto. Residence, San Marcos, Hays county, Texas.

O'Connor, Thomas, age 54 ; in service 1835. Residence, Refugio, Refugio county, Texas.

Osborn, John L., age 64 ; emigrated 1826 ; in service 1835 and 1836. Residence, Bastrop county, Texas.

Osborn, Thomas, age 58 ; in service 1835 and 1836. Residence, Bastrop county, Texas.

Ogsbury, C. A., age 57 ; in service 1836. Residence, Indianola, Calhoun county, Texas.

Pevehouse, Preston, age 59 ; served in siege of San Antonio and 1836. Residence, Milam county, Texas.

Phillips, William, age 57 ; served in 1836. Residence, San Augustine, Texas.

Payne, Thomas P., age 60 ; nativity, Tennessee ; emigrated 1835 ; served in Captain Bradley's company, 1836. Residence, Shelby county, Texas.

Pannell, Hugh G., age 60 ; nativity, Virginia ; emigrated 1836 ; in service 1836. Residence, Houston, Harris county, Texas.

Parker, Isaac, age 81 ; nativity, Georgia ; emigrated in 1833 ; Captain Clapp's company. Residence, Weatherford, Parker county.

Pitts, John G., age 57 ; nativity, Georgia ; emigrated in 1831 ; in service 1836. Residence, Courtney, Grimes county.

Price, William B., age 56 ; nativity, Kentucky ; emigrated in 1836 ; Captain Holliday's company in 1836. Residence, Austin county, Texas.

Patrick, George M., age 73 ; nativity, Virginia ; emigrated in 1828 ; in service 1836. Residence, Anderson, Grimes county, Texas.

Plunkett, John, age 61 ; nativity, Ireland ; emigrated in 1834 ; in battle of San Jacinto. Residence, Matagorda county, Texas.

Patten, A. B., age 59 ; nativity, Tennessee ; emigrated in 1835 ; in service 1836. Residence, Cherino, Nacogdoches county.

Patten, Moses L., age 68; nativity, Georgia ; emigrated in 1833 ; in service 1835 and 1836. Residence, Nacogdoches county.

Pilgrim, Thomas J., age 68 ; nativity, New York ; emigrated in 1828 ; in service 1835, and in the Plum Creek fight, 1840. Residence, City of Austin, Texas.

Petty, George W., age 63 ; native of Tennessee ; emigrated in 1835 ; in battle of San Jacinto. Residence, Brenham, Washington county.

Pierce, P. R., age 61 ; nativity, North Carolina ; emigrated in 1836 ; in service in 1836. Residence, City of Bryan, Brazos county, Texas.

Pier, J. B., age 61 ; nativity, Ohio ; emigrated in 1835 ; in service in 1836. Residence, Austin, Travis county, Texas.

Post, J. C., emigrated in 1836 ; in service in 1836. Residence, Wichita, Kansas.

Pace, James R., age 62 ; emigrated in 1828; in battle of San Jacinto. Residence, Austin, Travis county.

Pleasants, George W., age 65 ; nativity, North Carolina ; emigrated in 1830 ; in battle of San Jacinto. Residence, Richmond, Fort Bend county.

Price, Robert, age 63 ; nativity, South Carolina ; emigrated in 1828 ; in service in 1836. Residence, Round Mountain, Blanco county.

Pettus, John F., age 65 ; nativity, Alabama ; emigrated in 1824 ; in battle of San Jacinto. Residence, Bee county.

Perry, M., age 73 ; in service in 1836. Residence, San Marcos, Hays county, Texas.

Perry, C. R., age 52 ; emigrated in 1822 ; in Captain Hill's company in 1836. Residence, Blanco county.

39

Putman, Michael, age 80 ; nativity, Alabama ; emigrated 1835 ; in battle San Jacinto. Residence, Kendall county, Texas.

Prewett, Elisha, age, 56 ; nativity, Louisiana ; emigrated in 1820 ; in service 1836. Residence, Merced county, California.

Prissick, William, age 68 ; in service 1836. Residence, Matagorda county.

Paine, John, age 72 ; nativity, North Carolina ; emigrated in 1835 ; in campaign 1835. Residence, Fayette county, Texas.

Polk, Thomas, age 80 ; in the siege of San Antonio, and in campaign of 1836. Residence, Gonzales, Gonzales county.

Patterson, J. S., age 75 ; in battle San Jacinto. Residence, Austin, Travis county, Texas.

Pease, E. M., age 62 ; nativity, Connecticut ; emigrated in 1835 ; in campaign 1835. Residence, City of Austin, Travis county, Texas.

Peebles, R. R., age 67 ; in campaign of 1836. Residence, Hempstead, Waller county, Texas.

Paschal, Frank L., age 64 ; nativity, Georgia ; emigrated in 1836 ; in service 1836. Residence, San Antonio, Bexar county, Texas.

Parker, Daniel, age 60 ; nativity, Illinois ; emigrated 1833 ; in service 1836. Residence, Anderson county, Texas.

Pratt, Thomas, age 65 ; nativity, Georgia ; emigrated in 1836 ; in battle of San Jacinto. Residence, Lampasas county.

Parr, Samuel, age 70 ; nativity, England ; in service, 1836. Residence, Galveston county, Texas.

Pittman, Edward W., age 72 ; emigrated in 1836 ; in service, 1836. Residence, Shelbyville, Shelby county, Texas.

Pallan, John, age 64 ; served in Captain Dimmit's company in 1835–'36. Residence, Corpus Christi, Nueces county, Texas.

Payne, John C., age 53 ; served in the fall of 1835. Residence, Centre, Shelby county.

Prewett, John M., age — ; served on the steamer *Cayuga* in 1835–'36. Residence, Brazoria, Brazoria county, Texas.

Placias, Juan J., native in siege of Bexar. Residence, Bexar county Texas.

Pate, Wm. H., in service in 1836. Residence, Grath county, Texas.

Price, H. W. B., in service in 1836. Residence, Barbour county, Alabama,

Philips, Bennet, in service in 1836. Residence, Llano county.

Robinson, Zoroaster, age 66 ; emigrated 1835 ; served in 1835 and 1836. Residence, Leon county, Texas.

Roberts, Moses F., age 71 ; nativity, Tennessee ; emigrated 1836 ; served in Captain Cheshier's company 1836. Residence, Shelbyville, Shelby county, Texas.

Ramsdel, G. L., age 54; nativity, England: emigrated 1834; in service 1836. Residence, Wise county, Texas.

Roberts, Charles, age 59; nativity, Georgia; emigrated 1833; in service 1836. Residence, Kosse, Limestone county, Texas.

Ragsdale, Peter C., age 64; nativity, Virginia; emigrated 1835; in service 1836. Residence, San Marcos, Hays county, Texas.

Robinson, Joel W., age 59; nativity, Georgia; emigrated 1832; in battle of Velasco, and served in 1835, and in battle of San Jacinto, 1836. Residence, Warrenton, Fayette county, Texas.

Robertson, E. S. C., age 54; nativity, Tennessee; emigrated 1832; served in Captain S. C. Robertson's company 1836. Residence, Salado, Bell county, Texas.

Ragsdale, William J., age 63; nativity, Virginia; emigrated 1835; in service 1836. Residence, Jacksonville, Cherokee county, Texas.

Russell, William J., age 72; nativity, North Carolina; emigrated 1826; in battles of Anahuac and Velasco, 1833. Residence, City of Austin, Travis county, Texas.

Roddy, Anthony, age 69; in service 1836. Residence, San Augustine county, Texas.

Ragsdale, E. B., age, 57; nativity, North Carolina; emigrated in 1835; in service 1836. Residence, Jacksonville, Cherokee county, Texas.

Rusk, David, age 60; nativity, South Carolina; emigrated in 1835; in battle San Jacinto. Residence, Nacogdoches.

Russell, R. B., age 57; nativity, Connecticut; emigrated in 1835; in battle San Jacinto. Residence, Orange county, Texas.

Rolls, R., age 62; nativity, Washington City; emigrated in 1836; in Colonel Teal's command in 1836. Residence, Galveston, Texas.

Reamos, S. Y., age 62; South Carolina; emigrated in 1834; in battle San Jacinto. Residence, Austin county.

Reed, Nathaniel, age 69; nativity, Tennessee; emigrated in 1835; in battle San Jacinto. Residence, Bellvilre, Austin county.

Reed, T. J., age 66; nativity, Tennessee; emigrated in 1830; in Captain Collingsworth's company in 1835 and service 1836. Residence, Marlin, Falls county.

Roberson, Jerome B., age 58; nativity, Kentucky; emigrated in 1836; first regiment permanent volunteers 1836. Residence, City of Houston, Harris county.

Redfield, H. P., age 53; nativity, New Hampshire; emigrated in 1831; in campaign 1835. Residence, Giddings, Lee county, Texas.

Rogers, Lieuen M., age 45; nativity, Alabama; emigrated in 1836; served under Colonel Clark L. Owen in 1836. Refugio, Refugio county.

Robinson, George W., age 59; in battle of San Jacinto. Residence, Madison county, Texas.

Ryan, James, age 69; in campaign of 1835; Residence, Beeville, Bee county, Texas.

Robinson, Ben W., age 61; in service in 1836. Residence, Huntsville, Walker county, Texas.

Robinson, Jesse, age 73; in battle of San Jacinto. Residence, Live-oak county, Texas.

Rector, E. G., age 57; in battle of San Jacinto. Residence, Merced county, California.

Rector, Pendleton, age 66; nativity, Tennessee; in battle of Velasco in 1832, and campaign of 1835, and in battle of San Jacinto. Residence, Prairie Lee, Caldwell county, Texas.

Rogers, S. C. A., age 63; in campaign of 1835.

Raman, Richard; emigrated in 1836; captain of a company in battle of San Jacinto. Residence, California.

Ricks, G. W., age 60; emigrated in 1835; in service in 1836. Residence, Bastrop, Texas.

Read, Ezra, age 62; in service in 1836. Residence, Terre Haute, Indiana.

Reed, Jefferson, age 56; in service in 1836. Residence, Bell county, Texas.

Reed, William, age 58; in service in 1836. Residence, Bell county, Texas.

Reed, Elijah B., age 68; in service in 1836. Residence, McLennan county, Texas.

Raglin, H. W., age 57, nativity, Mississippi; emigrated in 1836; in service 1836. Residence, Austin, Travis county, Texas.

Ramsdale, M. F., age 62; nativity, England; served in Captain Ingram's company in 1835, and under Colonel Nail, 1839.

Ragsdale, M. H., age 60; nativity, Tennessee; emigrated in 1820; served in 1836. Paris, Lamar county.

Rankin, Frederick H., age 79; nativity, Kentucky; emigrated in 1822; in service in 1835 and 1836. Residence, Chambers Creek, Ellis county, Texas.

Ruble, Fielden; emigrated in 1828; served under Colonel Johnson at Anahuac.

Randall, O. M., age 54; served in 1836. Residence, Nacogdoches county, Texas.

Roberts, David, age 67; served in 1836 and in battle San Jacinto. Residence, Cleburne, Johnson county, Texas.

Roberts, John S., age 74; served in campaign in 1835. Residence, Nacogdoches, Nacogdoches county, Texas.

Richards, William B; emigrated in 1834; served in 1836. Residence, Clinton, Bosque county, Texas.

Ross, Richard; in campaign of 1835. Residence, Story county, Nevada.

Rogers, James; in Hardin's company in 1836. Residence, Liberty county, Texas.

Redfield, Jno. A., age 53; one of the survivors of Dawson's company. Residence, Lee county, Texas.

Routt, Henry T.; served in 1836. Residence, Clark county, Illinois.

Stout, Henry, age 75; nativity, Logan county, Virginia; emigrated in 1818; in service in 1836. Residence, Quitman, Wood county, Texas.

Scurlock, William, age 66; nativity, North Carolina; emigrated in 1834; in Grass Fight in 1835, and Fannin's command in 1836. Residence, Milam, Sabine county, Texas.

Savneign, Jo., age 64; nativity, Portugal; emigrated in 1835; in battle of San Jacinto. Residence, City of Houston.

Steele, John, age 60; nativity, Kentucky; emigrated in 1836; in service in 1836. Residence, city of Houston, Harris county.

Singleton, J. H., age 56; nativity, Kentucky; emigrated in 1836; in service in Captain Love's company in 1836. Residence. Waxahachie, Ellis county.

Stout, B. O., age 57; nativity, Kentucky; emigrated in 1836; in service in 1836. Residence, Goliad, Goliad county, Texas.

Stem, Isaac P., age 55; nativity, Tennessee; emigrated in 1836; in service in 1836. Residence, Kosse, Limestone county, Texas.

Simpson, William, age 72; nativity, Missouri; emigrated in 1833; in service in 1836. Residence, City of Austin, Travis county.

Steele, Alfonso, age 57; nativity, Kentucky; emigrated in 1835; in battle of San Jacinto. Residence, Mexia, Freestone county, Texas.

Sadler, John, age 66; nativity, Tennessee; emigrated in 1833; in battle of San Jacinto. Residence, Kosse, Limestone county, Texas.

Sharp, John, age 61; nativity, North Carolina; emigrated in 1830; in siege of San Antonio and at the battle of San Jacinto. Residence, Caldwell, Burleson county, Texas.

Stout, J. S., age 56; nativity, Arkansas; emigrated in 1820; in Captain Becknell's company in 1836. Residence, White-oak, Hopkins county, Texas.

Shaw, James, age 65; nativity, Ohio; emigrated in 1835; in battle of San Jacinto. Residence, Lexington, Lee county, Texas.

Smith, Lemuel, age 63; nativity, Virginia; emigrated in 1836; in Sweitzer's company in 1836. Residence, Longstreet, Montgomery county.

Stewart, C. B. age 68 ; nativity, South Carolina ; emigrated in 1830 ; in Frank W. Johnson's command in 1832, and member of convention in March, 1836. Residence, Montgomery, Montgomery county, Texas.

Smith, Manaan, age 70 ; nativity, Georgia ; emigrated in 1821 ; in Grass Fight in 1835. Keachie, Leon county, Texas.

Sarby, William A., age 57 ; nativity, North Carolina ; emigrated in 1836 ; in Felix Houston's command in 1836. Washington county, Texas.

Scates, W. B., age 72 ; nativity, Virginia ; emigrated in 1831 ; in San Antonio campaign and in battle of San Jacinto. Residence, Weimar, Colorado county.

Scott, Levy P., age 57 ; nativity, Alabama ; emigrated in 1829 ; in Fannin's command in 1836. Richmond, Fort Bend county.

Smith, Thomas J., age 65 ; nativity, Georgia ; emigrated in 1835 ; in Colonel Fannin's command in 1835 and 1836. Residence, Richmond, Fort Bend county, Texas.

Sparks, W. F., age 60 ; nativity, Mississippi ; emigrated in 1834 ; in army of 1836. Cleburne, Johnson county.

Sparks, S. F., age 55 ; nativity, Mississippi ; emigrated in 1834 ; San Antonio campaign in 1835, and in battle San Jacinto, 1836. Residence, Waco, McLennan county, Texas.

Smith, M. C., age 56 ; nativity, North Carolina ; emigrated in 1836 ; in army 1836 ; and in Woll campaign in 1842. Residence, Round Rock, Williamson county.

Swisher, John M., age 55 ; nativity, Tennessee ; emigrated in 1833 ; in battle San Jacinto. Residence, City of Austin, Travis county, Texas.

Sanders, John, age 57 ; in battle San Jacinto. Residence, Shelby county, Texas.

Shipman, Daniel, age 72 ; nativity, Kentucky ; emigrated in 1822 ; in army in 1835 and 1836. Residence, Brenham, Washington county.

Stapp, D. M., age 58 ; in campaign of 1835. Residence, Victoria county, Texas.

Stebbins, Charles C., age 63 ; in battle San Jacinto. Residence, McKinney, Collin county, Texas.

Simmonds, William, age 73 ; in battle San Jacinto. Residence, Bastrop county, Texas.

Sheppard, J. H., in the army in 1835 and 1836. Residence, Huntsville, Walker county, Texas.

Smith, Henry M., age 52 ; in the army of 1836.

Slaben, John, age 62 ; in the army of 1836.

Standefer, Jacob L., age 55 ; emigrated in 1829 ; in battle of San Jacinto. Residence, Perryville, Bastrop county, Texas.

Standefer, Wm. B. age 62 ; emigrated in 1829 ; in battle of San Jacinto Residence, Perryville, Bastrop county, Texas.

Swearengen, E., age 68 ; in army in 1836 and a Mier prisoner. Residence, Bellville, Austin county, Texas.

Sadler, W, T., age 73 ; in battle of San Jacinto. Residence, Anderson county, Texas.

Smith, Edward, age 70 ; in army of 1836. Residence, McLennan county, Texas.

Shipman, James R., age 61 ; nativity, South Carolina ; served in the fall of 1835. Residence, Fort Bend county, Texas.

Smithwick, Noah, age 66 ; in service in 1836. Kern county, California.

Scott, Philip B., age 60 ; in service in 1835 and 1836.

Sevey, Joseph S., age 66 ; nativity, Maine ; emigrated in 1834 ; lieutenant in navy in 1836. Residence, Wiscassett, Maine.

Sevey, Ralph E., nativity, Maine ; emigrated in 1835 ; in battle of San Jacinto. Residence, Michigan.

Sewell, Andrew J., age 59 ; in the army of 1835 and 1836. Residence, Seguin, Texas.

Sellers, Robert, emigrated in 1836 ; served in the army in 1836. Residence, La Grange, Fayette county, Texas.

Spear, John, age 60 ; served in 1836. Residence, Melrose, Nacogdoches county.

Sweeny, John, age 58 ; served in Captain Bird Lockart's company in 1836 and in Somerville campaign in 1842. Residence, Columbia, Brazoria county, Texas.

Sewell, Ransom, age 65 ; in service in 1836. Residence, San Augustine county, Texas.

Stringer, E. N., in service in 1836. Residence, New Orleans, Louisiana.

Salinas, Pablo ; in service in 1835 ; in siege of Bexar. Residence, Bexar county, Texas.

Spillers, John T., in service in 1836. Residence, Crawford county, Georgia.

Taylor, Campbell, age 62 ; nativity, North Carolina ; emigrated in 1835 ; in battle of San Jacinto. Residence, Bastrop county, Texas.

Thomason, W. D., age 60 ; nativity, Alabama ; emigrated in 1835 ; in Grass Fight in 1835. Cleburne, Johnson county, Texas.

Turner, Amasa, age 74 ; nativity, Massachusetts ; emigrated in 1835 ; captain of a company in the battle of San Jacinto. Residence, Gonzales, Gonzales county, Texas.

Thompson, Jesse, age 56 ; nativity, Alabama ; emigrated in 1322 ; in service in 1836. Residence, Richmond, Fort Bend county, Texas.

Tandey, A. M., age 60 ; nativity, Virginia ; emigrated in 1835 ; in the army of 1836. Residence, Hallettsville, Lavaca county.

Thomas, Benjamin, age 68 ; nativity North Carolina ; emigrated in 1823, in service in 1836 ; at the battle of San Jacinto. Residence, Bexar county.

Thompson, Cyrus W., age 63 ; in battle of San Jacinto. Residence, Liberty county.

Tom, John F., age 56; nativity, North Carolina; emigrated in 1834 ; in battle of San Jacinto. Residence, Atascosa county, Texas.

Thornton, William, age 61 ; in the siege of San Antonio, 1835. Residence, Atascosa county, Texas.

Thompson, Hiram M., age 62 ; nativity, Alabama; emigrated in 1822; in the battle of Velasco in 1832 ; storming San Antonio, 1835, and in army of 1836. Residence, Richmond, Fort Bend county, Texas.

Tumlinson, Peter, age 72 ; nativity, North Carolina; in army of 1836. Residence, Pleasanton, Atascosa county, Texas.

Taylor, Creed, age 56 ; in army 1835 and 1836. Residence, Wilson county, Texas.

Tomlinson, Joseph, age 63 ; served in army 1835. Residence, Clinton, De Witt county.

Tom, William, age 80; served in fall 1835. Residence, Guadaloupe county.

Thorn, John S., age 59 ; served in 1836. Residence, Nacogdoches county, Texas.

Thomas, Theophilus, age 65 ; in battle Nacogdoches in 1832. San Augustine county.

Thomas, J. D., age 75 ; in battle Nacogdoches in 1832. San Augustine county, Texas.

Thomas, Benjamin R., age 67 ; in service in 1836. Chappell Hill, Washington county, Texas.

Thomas, Wiley, age 73 ; served in army in 1835 and 1836. Residence, Atascosa county, Texas.

Travieso, Justo, age 66; served in 1835, in siege of Bexar. Residence, San Antonio, Texas.

Thompson S. J., age 59 ; served in army in 1835 and 1836. Residence, Cherokee county, Texas.

Troutz, C., age 65 ; made prisoner on Santa Fé expedition. Residence, Sommerset, Atascosa county, Texas.

Underwood, Ammon, age 64 ; nativity, Massachusetts ; emigrated in 1834 ; in service in 1835 and 1836. Residence, Columbia, Brazoria county, Texas.

Vanvechten, D. H., age 55 ; nativity, Pennsylvania ; emigrated in 1836 ; in Colonel Robertson's command in 1836 and a Mier prisoner. Residence, Hempstead, Waller county, Texas.

Votaw, Elijah, age 53 ; in battle of San Jacinto. Residence, Oakville, Live-oak county, Texas.

Vallentine, Henry, age 67 ; in campaign of 1835. Residence, Lavaca county, Texas.

Vanbibber, John, age 77 ; served in the army in 1836. Residence, Victoria, Victoria county, Texas.

Valentine, Charles F., age 59 ; served in army in 1835. Residence, Mariposa, California.

Vinator, James, age 78 ; served in 1836 ; in battle of San Jacinto. Residence, Nacogdoches county, Texas.

Waller, Edwin, age 74 ; nativity, Virginia ; emigrated in 1831 ; in battle of Velasco in 1832 and in campaign of 1835, and member of convention in March, 1836. Residence, Hempstead, Waller county, Texas.

Watson, John, age 60 ; nativity, Tennessee ; emigrated in 1836 ; in Captain Becknell's company in 1836. Residence, Ladonia, Fannin county, Texas.

Wilson, J. T. D., age 53 ; nativity, St. Louis, Missouri ; emigrated in 1835 ; in service in 1835 and 1836. Residence, City of Houston, Harris county, Texas.

Wallace, J. W. E., age 77 ; nativity, Pennsylvania ; emigrated in 1830 ; in campaign of 1835 and 1836. Residence, Columbus, Colorado county, Texas.

Walker, R. H., age 68 , nativity, Virginia ; emigrated in 1835 ; in campaign of 1835 and in battle of San Jacinto. Residence, Alum Creek, Bastrop county.

Wilcox, Oswin, age 63 ; nativity, Connecticut ; emigrated in 1836 ; in battle of San Jacinto. City of Austin, Travis county, Texas.

Walker, Sanders, age 56 ; nativity, Kentucky ; emigrated in 1835 ; in San Antonio campaign in 1835. Residence, Mexia, Freestone county.

Williams, James, age 56 ; nativity, Missouri ; emigrated in 1833 ; in San Antonio campaign in 1835. Waco, McLennan county.

Wilson, Walker, age 73 ; nativity, Virginia ; emigrated in 1833 ; in San Antonio campaign in 1835 and in battle of San Jacinto in 1836. Residence, San Marcos, Hays county, Texas.

Wade, John M., age 59 ; nativity, New York ; emigrated in 1835 ; in battle of San Jacinto. Residence, Montgomery, Montgomery county, Texas.

Wells, Louis, age 60 ; nativity, Tennessee ; emigrated in 1835 ; in Grass Fight in 1835. Residence, Llano county, Texas.

Whittaker, M. G., age 63 ; nativity, Tennessee ; emigrated in 1835 ; in battle of San Jacinto. Residence, Nacogdoches, Texas.

White, J. C., age 59 ; nativity, Georgia ; emigrated in 1835 ; in battle of San Jacinto.   Residence, Navasota, Grimes county, Texas.

Walker, John, age 54 ; nativity, South Carolina ; emigrated in 1836 ; in battle of San Jacinto.   City of Bryan, Brazos county, Texas.

Wheeler, S. L., age 74 ; nativity, New York ; emigrated in 1831 ; in battle of San Jacinto.   Residence, Richmond, Fort Bend county, Texas.

Williams, W. T., age 60 ; nativity, Tennessee ; emigrated in 1836 ; in battle of San Jacinto.   Residence, Kosse, Limestone county, Texas.

Whitesides, E. T., age 61 ; nativity, Tennessee ; emigrated in 1822 ; served in General Felix Huston's command in 1836.   Residence, Courtney, Grimes county.

Weaver, L. G., age 58 ; nativity, Maryland ; emigrated in 1836 ; served in Captain Allen's company in 1836.   Residence, Hockley, Harris county, Texas.

Weathered, F. M., age 55 ; nativity, Tennessee ; emigrated in 1835 ; in the army of 1836.   Residence, Hillsboro, Hill county, Texas.

Williams, Thomas J., in campaign of 1835.   Residence, Columbus, Colorado county, Texas.

Walker, Martin, age 57 ; in battle of San Jacinto, 1836.   Residence, Bastrop, Texas.

Wells, Wayman F., in campaign of 1835.   Residence, City of Austin, Travis county, Texas.

Whitlock, Robert, age 55 ; in the army in 1836.   Residence, Liberty county, Texas.

Wade, John R., age 54 ; in the army in 1836.   Residence, La Grange, Fayette county, Texas.

White, John, age 51 ; in service 1836.   Residence, Texana, Jackson county, Texas.

White, Francis M,. age 32 ; at the storming of San Antonio in 1835. Residence, Texana, Jackson county, Texas.

Winn, Walter, emigrated in 1835 ; in battle San Antonio.   Residence, Virginia City, Nevada.

Williams, Robert H., age 77 ; nativity, Tennessee ; emigrated in 1822 ; in battle of Velasco in 1832.   Residence, Matagorda county, Texas.

Williams, Stephen, age 62 ; in the siege of San Antonio in 1835.   Residence, Jasper county, Texas.

Wright, Ralph, age 68 ; in Colonel J. W. Fannin's command, 1835. Residence, Colorado county.

Winters, James W., age 56 ; emigrated in 1834 ; in battle of San Jacinto. Residence, Rockport, Aransas county, Texas.

Ware, Joseph, age 66 ; in the siege of San Antonio.   Residence, Jackson county, Texas.

Wicksan, Cyrus·; in service in 1836. Residence, Richmond, Fort Bend county, Texas.

White, John M., *first*, age 66 ; at the storming of San Antonio in 1835. Residence, Pulaski, Tennessee.

Willoughby, Leiper, age 63 ; in battle San Jacinto. Residence, Lavaca county, Texas.

Wells, Samuel G., age —; in service in 1836.

Walters, George T., age 80 ; in service in 1836. Residence, Hood county, Texas.

Williams, Richard, age 65 ; nativity, Georgia ; emigrated in 1833 ; served in army of 1835, and in the Grass Fight. Residence, Montgomery county, Texas.

Wright, Travis G.; nativity, Tennessee ; emigrated in 1816 ; served in various Indian campaigns previous to 1836. Residence, Paris, Lamar county.

Wood, William Riley, age 54 ; nativity, Tennessee ; emigrated in 1831 ; served in army in 1836. Residence, San Saba county.

Walker, Philip, age 59 ; served in 1836. Residence, Johnson county, Texas.

White, John M., age 65 ; served in campaign of 1835. Residence, Navidad, Jackson county, Texas.

Wright, George W., age 72 ; served in campaign of 1835, and in battle of San Jacinto. Residence, Live-oak county, Texas. ·

Wood, John H., age 58 ; served in 1836. Residence, Refugio county Texas.

Wells, Martin J., age 53 ; served in Captain Billingsley's company in 1836. Residence, Georgetown, Williamson county, Texas.

Withered, W. C., age 60 ; in service in 1836. Residence, Hill county, Texas.

Walters, Alexander, age 54 ; in service in 1836. Residence, Bell county, Texas.

Wood, James, age 59 ; served in 1836. Residence, Nelson county, Kentucky.

Watson, H. E., age 65 ; first lieutenant in Anderson's company, in 1835. Residence, Calaveras county, California.

Wheelock, G. R.; served in army, 1835. Residence, Brazos county, Texas.

Wade, Nathan, age 64 ; served in army in 1835. Residence, Nacog-doches county, Texas.

Williams, W., age 71 ; served in army in 1836. Residence, Limestone county, Texas.

Ward, Paul S., age 65 ; served in army in 1836. Residence, Calcasieu parish, Louisiana.

White, K. B.; in service in 1836.   Residence, De Witt county, Texas.

Young, W. F., age 74 ; nativity, South Carolina ; emigrated in 1836 ; in battle of San Jacinto.   Residence, Midway, Madison county, Texas.

Young, Michael, nativity, Georgia ; emigrated in 1829 ; in service in 1836. Residence, Bell county, Texas.

Young, James, age 60 ; in service in 1836.   Residence, City of Austin, Travis county, Texas.

Yeomans, Horace, age 63 ; served in siege of San Antonio in 1835, and in service in 1836.   Residence, Cash Creek, Matagorda county, Texas.

Young, William ; in service in 1836.   Residence, Milam county.

Zuber, William P., age 54 ; nativity, Georgia ; emigrated in 1830 ; in service in 1836.   Residence, Hearne, Robertson county, Texas.

Zumwalt, Andrew, age 55 ; in battle of San Jacinto.   Residence, Gonzales county, Texas.

Zumwalt, F. B., in service in 1835.   Residence, Gonzales county, Texas.

Zumwalt, Adam ; in service in 1835 and 1836.   Residence, Gonzales county, Texas.

SECOND CLASS.

Anderson, Joseph S., age 55 ; nativity, Virginia ; emigrated in 1839 ; served under Colonel Edward Burleson in Cherokee campaign, 1839, and under General Alex. Somerville, in 1842.   Residence, Fort Bend county, Texas.

Askins, Charles S., age 52 ; nativity, Illinois ; emigrated in 1837 ; served in Captain Edmonson's company, 1838.   Residence, Paris, Lamar county, Texas.

Addison, Oscar M., age 53 ; nativity, Maryland ; emigrated in 1835 ; under Burleson and Erath in 1842.   Residence, Salado, Bell county.

Anglin, J., age 50 ; nativity, Illinois ; emigrated in 1833 ; in Somerville campaign, 1842.   Residence, Groesbeeck, Limestone county.

Alexander, J. R., age 56 ; nativity, Missouri ; emigrated in 1838 ; Mier prisoner.   Residence, La Grange, Fayette county, Texas.

Armstrong, James C., age 57 ; Mier prisoner.   Bell county, Texas.

Alexander, M. W., age 52 ; Mier prisoner.   Residence, Jackson county, Texas.

Bowers, John H., served in 1837.

Berry, James, age 65 ; nativity, Kentucky ; emigrated in December, 1836 ; served under Colonel Teal in 1837.   Residence, Houston city, Texas.

Buchman, J. Sr., age 58 ; nativity, Germany ; emigrated 1837 ; in Captain Morgan's company, 1837.   Residence, Hempstead, Walker county, Texas.

Baker, William, age 51 ; nativity, Tennessee ; emigrated in 1837 ; served under General Tarrant in 1841. Residence, Ellwood, Fannin county, Texas.

Bloodworth, John D., age 64; nativity, Tennessee; emigrated in 1837; in Captain Becknell's company in 1837. Residence, Hailsborough, Red River county, Texas.

Buroughs, W. M., age 74; nativity, Kentucky; emigrated in 1837; in Captain B. Stout's company in 1838. Residence, Pattenville, Lamar county, Texas.

Bell, A. J., served in 1842. Residence, Nelsonville, Austin county.

Brown, John H., age 54; nativity, New York; emigrated in 1836; Santa Fé prisoner. Residence, City of Austin, Texas.

Darnard, George, age 55; nativity, Connecticut; emigrated in 1838; in Santa Fé expedition. Residence, Waco, McLennan county, Texas.

Bozman, T. B., age 53; nativity, Alabama; emigrated in 1837; Santa Fé prisoner. Residence, Midway, Madison county, Texas.

Billingsley, W. B., age 61; nativity, Tennessee; emigrated in 1837; served in the Woll compaign in 1842. Residence, Mc Dade, Bastrop county, Texas.

Boles, H., age 62; nativity, Missouri; emigrated in 1837; served in Cherokee campaign in 1839. Residence, Rockdale, Milam county.

Blackbourn, A. J., age 61; nativity, South Carolina; emigrated in 1836; in the Woll campaign in 1842, and under J. H. Moore in 1839. Residence, town of Burton, Washington county, Texas.

Bridger, Henry, age 63; nativity, Pennsylvania; emigrated in 1826; Mier prisoner in 1842. Residence, Lavaca county, Texas.

Boone, Benj. Z., age 57; nativity, Missouri; emigrated in 1837; Mier prisoner. Residence, Wharton county.

Buster, Claudius, age 58; nativity, Kentucky; emigrated in 1836; Mier prisoner. Residence, Brenham, Washington county.

Barclay, David, age 80; nativity, North Carolina; emigrated in 1837; served in Indian campaign under Captain Matthews in 1839. Residence, Bremond, Robertson county.

Barclay, C. T., age 60; nativity, Tennessee; emigrated in 1837; served against Indians under Captain Thomas J. Smith in 1843 and 1844. Residence, Bremond, Robertson county.

Bruce, William M.; emigrated in 1836; served in Cherokee campaign in 1839. Residence, Harrison county.

Baylor, John R., age 52; nativity, Kentucky; emigrated in 1840; in battle of Salado in 1842. Residence, San Antonio, Bexar county, Texas.

Brown, John B., age 59; nativity, Scotland; in Vasquez campaign in 1842.

Brown, Edward; San Antonio prisoner.

Beeman, John S., age 57 ; nativity, Illinois ; emigrated in 1840 ; served under General Tarrant against Indians in 1841.   Residence, Dallas county.

Brooks, A. M., age 66; nativity, Kentucky ; emigrated in 1838 ; served three months in the Indian campaign.   Residence, City of Houston.

Brigance, Alfred F.; served under General Somerville in 1842.   Residence, Brazos county, Texas.

Blair, W., age 53 ; native of Tennessee ; emigrated in February, 1838 ; served in Captain John Bird's company, Frontier Regiment, 1839 ; also in Vasquez and Woll campaigns, in spring and fall of 1842.   Residence, Clinton, De Witt county.

Beitel, Joseph, age 68 ; nativity, Wirtemberg, Germany ; in battle Plum Creek, 1841 ; in battle Salado in 1842.   Residence, Bexar county, Texas.

Brown, John Henry, age 54 ; native of Missouri ; emigrated in 1824 ; in battle Plum Creek, August 1840 ; in spring campaign, 1842 ; in battle Salado, fall of 1842.   Residence, Dallas, Dallas county, Texas.

Bunton, DeSha ; nativity, Tennessee ; emigrated in 1837 ; served in Woll campaign.   Residence, Travis county.

Brown, W. A. ; age 60 ; nativity, Mississippi ; emigrated in 1838 ; served under Hayes and Karnes, and at the battle of Salado in fall of 1842.   Residence, Uvalde county, Texas.

Buquar, P. L., age 56 ; nativity, Louisiana ; emigrated in 1838 ; served in the Cherokee campaign under General T. J. Rusk and under Captain Hayes.

Burt, James Ross ; native of Missouri ; emigrated in 1840 ; served under Colonel William G. Cook in 1840 and 1841.   Residence, Red Rock, Bastrop county, Texas.

Baker, John R., age 62 ; Mier prisoner.   Residence, Refugio county, Texas.

Bell, Thomas W., age 76 ; Mier prisoner.   Residence, Gonzales, Texas.

Brown, Richard ; Mier prisoner.

Boswell, Rawson P. ; Mier prisoner.   Residence, Los Angeles county, California.

Colquhoun, Ludovic, age 71 ; nativity, Virginia ; San Antonio prisoner in 1842.

Cox, John H. ; nativity, Illinois ; emigrated in 1840 ; served under General Tarrant against Indians in 1841.   Residence, Dallas county, Texas.

Cox, George W. ; nativity, Illinois ; emigrated in 1840 ; served under General Tarrant against Indians in 1841.   Residence, Dallas county, Texas.

Chatham, Thomas, age 73 ; nativity, South Carolina ; emigrated in 1832 ; served under Captain J. M. Wade.

Criswell, John Y. ; emigrated in 1830 ; in Indian campaigns from 1838 to 1842, and in P. H. Bell's Rangers in 1845. Residence, Oso, Fayette county, Texas.

Calvert, James H. ; Mier prisoner. Residence, Falls county, Texas.

Crawford, Jacob, age 56 ; nativity, North Carolina ; emigrated in 1837 ; served in 1838. Residence, Anderson county, Texas.

Chalk, Whitfield, age 63 ; nativity, North Carolina ; emigrated in 1839 ; served in campaign of 1842 ; Mier prisoner. Residence, Lampasas county, Texas.

Chambers, George W. ; emigrated in 1838 ; served in 1840. Residence, New York city.

Cabler, E. S., age 64 ; nativity, Tennessee ; emigrated in 1835 ; served in 1842. Residence, Navasota, Grimes county, Texas.

Chism, J. E. ; served under Captain W. Stout in 1840. Residence, Kosse.

Clary, Francis M., age 53 ; nativity, Alabama ; emigrated in 1834 ; in Somerville campaign in 1842. Residence, Corsicana, Navarro county, Texas.

Carrington, D. C., age 53 ; nativity, North Carolina ; emigrated in 1838 ; in service in 1839. Residence, Leon county, Texas.

Clopton, William A., age 61 ; nativity, Tennessee ; emigrated in 1837 ; in Mier expedition. Residence, McDade, Bastrop county, Texas.

Crittenden, George B., age 61 ; nativity, Kentucky ; emigrated in 1836 ; Mier prisoner. Residence, Franklin county, Kentucky.

Clark, George Wilson ; Mier prisoner.

Crawford, A. C. ; served in Galveston artillery company for coast defense in 1842. Residence, Galveston city.

Davis, Daniel, age 58 ; nativity, Kentucky ; emigrated in 1836 ; Mier prisoner.

Davis, William K., age 52 ; nativity, Alabama ; emigrated in 1830 ; served in Indian campaign under Colonel Neil in 1839, and Mier prisoner. Residence, Richmond, Fort Bend county.

Dunham, James H., age 55 ; nativity, Tennessee ; emigrated in 1837 ; served in Colonel Neil's campaign against Indians in 1839. Residence, Courtney, Grimes county, Texas.

Darnell, N. H., age 68 ; nativity, Tennessee ; emigrated in 1838 ; in Cherokee campaign in 1839. Residence, Fort Worth, Tarrant county, Texas.

Dusenbury, John E., age 55 ; nativity, New York ; emigrated in 1838 ; Mier prisoner. Residence, Harris county, Texas.

Dorsett, Theodore J., age 52 ; nativity, —— ; emigrated in 1827 ; in Cherokee campaign, and with Colonel T. J. Rusk and General Douglass. Residence, Georgetown, Williamson county.

Dean, Alexander; served in company of Galveston artillery for coast defense in 1842. Residence, City of Galveston.

Edwards, W. C., age —; emigrated in October, 1836; served twelve months. Residence, Indianola, Calhoun county, Texas.

Erhard, C., age 52; nativity, Germany; emigrated in 1839; Sante Fé prisoner. Residence, Bastrop, Bastrop county, Texas.

Edrington, James F., age 58; emigrated in 1839; served in Cherokee campaign in 1839. Residence, City of Bryan, Brazos county, Texas.

Forbes, R. M., age 64; nativity, Virginia; emigrated in 1836; served in campaign 1842.

Forrester, John, age 55; emigrated in 1837; in service 1837. Residence, City of Houston.

Fowler, A. J., age 58; nativity, Kentucky; emigrated in 1837; under General Tarrant 1841. Residence, Palestine, Anderson county, Texas.

Faulkenburg, E. W.; served in Captain Box's company, 1839. Residence, Johnson county, Texas.

Foster, Robert, age 54; nativity, England; emigrated in 1839; served under Colonel Fisher 1839 and 1840. Residence, Burnet, Burnet county, Texas.

Follet, Alonzo B.; emigrated in 1839; served in army in 1842. Residence, San Luis, Brazoria county.

Follett, Alexander; served in army in 1842. Residence, Velasco, Brazoria county, Texas.

Frederich, John, age 64; emigrated January, 1837; served under Captain Leftwich. Post-office, Houston, Harris county.

Gallagher, Peter, age 62; nativity, Ireland; Sante Fé prisoner, 1841. Bexar county.

Gray, E. Fairfax, age 46; nativity, Virginia; emigrated in 1838; served with Commodore Moore in the navy. Residence, Galveston.

Griffith, L. A., age 52; nativity, New York; emigrated, 1838; Somerville's command in 1842. Residence, Salado, Bell county.

Gillmore, Charles, age 78; nativity, Georgia; emigrated in 1838; served Cherokee campaign, 1839. Residence, Wheelock, Robertson county.

Gentry, George W., age 65; nativity, Tennessee; emigrated in 1837; served in Vasquez and Woll campaigns, 1842. Residence, Long Point, Washington county, Texas.

Gentry, W. N., age 51; nativity, Tennessee; emigrated in 1841; served in Somerville campaign in 1842. Residence, McDade, Bastrop.

Gentry, Thomas N., age 53; nativity, Tennessee; emigrated in 1841; served in Somerville campaign, 1842. Residence, Brenham, Washington county.

Goodman, Stephen, age 55 ; Mier prisoner. Residence, Washington county.

Grush, H. L.; Sante Fé prisoner. Residence, New Orleans, Louisiana.

Griffith, Leroy ; served in Somerville campaign in 1842.

Guest, Martin ; served in army in 1842.

Garner, John ; nativity, Tennessee ; in Cherokee war in 1839. Residence, Corpus Christi, Nueces county.

Gilmore, Charles ; emigrated in 1838 ; served under General T. J. Rusk. Residence, Wheelock, Robertson county.

Grady, Dan ; emigrated in 1838 ; served in Vasquez and Woll campaigns in 1842. Residence, Bastrop county, Texas.

Harnes, Abel, age 62 ; nativity, Virginia ; emigrated in October, 1836 ; served in Captain Eastland's company in 1837. Residence, Burnet county, Texas.

Hyde, A. C., age 60 ; nativity, Connecticut ; emigrated in the fall of 1836 ; served under Burleson in Indian campaign from 1839 to 1842 ; in the Somerville campaign in 1842, and in the Mier expedition and escaped. Residence, Fort Quitman, El Paso county, Texas.

Humphreys, P. W., age — ; nativity, Kentucky ; emigrated June 1, 1836 ; lieutenant and commander in the navy in 1836, and in Somerville campaign in 1842.

Hendricks, S. B., age 53 ; nativity, Alabama ; emigrated in 1841 ; served in Somerville campaign in 1842.

Highsmith, B. F. ; served in Somerville campaign in 1842.

Hefflefinger, James ; served in Captain Becknell's company in 1838. Residence, Lamar county, Texas.

Herndon, John H. ; nativity, Kentucky ; emigrated in 1838. Residence, Velasco, Brazoria county.

Heard, S. R., emigrated in 1820 ; served in General Somerville's campaign. Residence, Fayette county.

Hamilton, John E., emigrated in December, 1836 ; served against Indians. Residence, Pilot Point, Denton county.

Howard, John C., age 43 ; nativity, District of Columbia ; Santa Fé prisoner. Residence, San Antonio, Bexar county.

Hemsworth, Thomas ; nativity, England ; served under Captain Andrew Neill in 1837. Residence, Velasco, Brazoria county, Texas.

Humphrey, William, age 69 ; nativity, Tennessee ; emigrated in 1818 ; served in Hopkins county in 1838. Residence, Maple Springs, Red River county, Texas.

Hanover, Hiram, age 64 ; nativity, Maine ; emigrated in 1838 ; in Colonel Snively's campaign in 1843.

40

Howard, T. B., age 53; nativity, North Carolina; emigrated in 1838; served in 1842. Residence, City of Houston, Texas.

Hackworth, W. W., age 60; nativity, Tennessee; emigrated in 1837; Somerville campaign in 1842. Residence, Brenham, Washington county, Texas.

Hurd, S. R., age 52; nativity, Alabama; emigrated in 1830; in Somerville campaign in 1842. Residence, Flatonia.

Hill, Jeffrey B., age 59; nativity, Georgia; emigrated in 1835; Mier prisoner. Residence, Gonzales county, Texas.

· Harrill, Milvern, age 50; Captain Dawson's company. Residence, Gonzales county, Texas.

Isam, James, age 58; nativity, Tennessee; emigrated in 1840; served under General Tarrant in 1841. Residence, Fannin county, Texas.

Jeffries, A. M., age 54; nativity, Tennessee; emigrated in 1836; served under General Tarrant in 1841. Residence, Lamar county, Texas.

Johnson, T. A., age 52; nativity, Alabama; emigrated in 1837; served in 1842. Residence, Waco.

Jordan, John, age 58; emigrated in 1830; served in Somerville campaign in 1842. Residence, Robertson county, Texas.

Joeb, Peter W., age 42; native of Indiana; emigrated in 1839; in Vasquez campaign of 1842. Residence, City of Austin, Travis county, Texas.

Johnson, J. R., Mier prisoner.

Justice, Milton M., age 54; Santa Fé prisoner.

James, T. B., age 59; native of Pennsylvania; emigrated in 1837 in Woll campaign of 1842. Residence, Prairie Lea, Caldwell county.

Johns, C. R.; nativity, Tennessee; served under General E. H. Tarrant in 1841. Residence, City of Austin, Travis county.

Jones, Wm. J., age 64; nativity, Virginia; emigrated in 1837; served in 1838 in the Bonnell expedition, and in 1839, in the Cherokee campaign. Residence, Virginia Point, Galveston county.

King, John E., age 59; nativity, North Carolina; emigrated in 1838; served in Captain Sam. J. Smith's company in 1842. Residence, Salado, Bell county, Texas.

Kennard, Wm. E.

Kennard, A. D.; served in 1836. Residence, Cleburne, Johnson county, Texas.

King, R. B.; Mier prisoner.

Lemmans, John, age 65; nativity, Pennsylvania; emigrated in 1835; Santa Fé prisoner. Residence, DeWitt county.

Lord, George, age 50; nativity, England; emigrated in 1837; served in army of 1837, 1838, and 1839, and Mier prisoner.

Lamon, John, age 58 ; nativity, Germany ; San Antonio prisoner in 1842. Residence, San Antonio.

Ladner, Nicolas, age — ; nativity, Germany ; Santa Fé prisoner. Residence, San Antonio.

Leslie, A. J., age 62 ; nativity, Tennessee ; San Antonio prisoner in 1842.

Longcope, C. S., age 68 ; nativity, Pennsylvania ; emigrated in 1838 ; Santa Fé prisoner. Residence, City of Houston, Texas.

Lockhart, J. W., age 49 ; nativity, Alabama ; emigrated in 1824 ; Woll campaign in 1842. Residence, Chappell Hill, Washington county, Texas.

Livergood, J. H., age 59 ; nativity, Pennsylvania ; emigrated in 1837 ; Mier prisoner. Residence, Halletsville, Lavaca county, Texas.

Leonard, William R., age 52 ; nativity, Alabama ; emigrated in 1842 ; Captain Hood's company in 1842. Residence, Waco, McLennan county, Texas.

Love, Y. E., age 54 ; nativity, Georgia ; emigrated in 1838 ; in the Somerville campaign in 1842.

Lyon, Samuel C., age 60 ; nativity, England, Mier prisoner. Residence, Velasco, Brazoria county, Texas.

Lawrence, J. W., age 59 ; nativity, North Carolina ; emigrated in 1841 ; served in Vasquez campaign in 1842. Residence, City of Austin, Travis county, Texas.

Lynch, E. O. ; served in Galveston artillery for coast defense in 1842. Residence, City of Galveston.

Laforge, A. B ; Mier prisoner. Residence, San Francisco, California.

Lee, Pleasant M., age 54 ; nativity, North Carolina ; emigrated in the fall of 1838 ; served in the navy in 1842, in the schooner *San Bernard.* Post-office, Houston, Harris county.

Miller, S. A., age 68 ; nativity, Virginia ; emigrated in 1839 ; served under General James Smith against the Indians in 1840 and in Colonel Snively's expedition in 1843.

Moody, Miles W., age 64 ; nativity, Tennessee ; emigrated in 1835 ; served under Captain Haley, 1839.

Minton, S. F. age 52 ; nativity, Georgia ; emigrated in 1837 ; served in Captain J. Everett's company, 1842. Residence, Prairie Plains, Grimes county.

Moore, L. V. age 65 ; nativity, Georgia ; emigrated in November, 1836 ; served in Captain Edmonson's company, 1838. Residence, Paris, Lamar county.

McCawn, J. W., Sr., age 71 ; nativity, Kentucky ; emigrated in 1837 ; served under Colonel Morehouse, 1841. Residence, Washington, Washington county, Texas.

Morrel, Z. N., age 72; nativity, South Carolina; emigrated in 1835; served in Plum Creek campaign, 1840, and in Woll campaign, 1842. Residence, Bremond, Robertson county.

Martin, M. W., age 49; nativity, Texas; served in Captain Broughton's company, 1841. Residence, Red River county.

McCay, A. L., age 59; nativity, Georgia; emigrated in 1837; served in W. J. Jones' battalion in 1839. Residence, Millican, Brazos county, Texas.

Merrell, Nelson. Residence, Round Rock, Williamson county.

Marrow, Jacob, age 61; nativity, Tennessee; emigrated in 1837; served in Captain Brown's company of rangers, 1839. Residence, Cleburne, Johnson county.

Moore, Z. W., age 50; nativity, Tennessee; emigrated in 1835; served in 1840. Residence, Kaufman county, Texas.

McNabb, John, age 55; nativity, Scotland; emigrated in 1837; Santa Fé prisoner. Richmond, Fort Bend county.

Moore, W. J., age 55; nativity, Virginia; emigrated in 1839; under Colonel Tarrant in 1841. Residence, Burnet county.

Matson, James V., age 50; nativity, Missouri; emigrated in 1836; Somerville campaign in 1842. Residence, Burton, Washington county.

Manton, Edward, age 53; member Captain Dawson's company, 1842. Fayette county, Texas.

Mayes, J. W., age 56; in service 1836; Mier prisoner, 1842. Residence, Bastrop county.

Miller, Alsey S., age 54; Captain Dawson's company, 1842. Residence, Gonzales county, Texas.

McDonald, John; emigrated in 1839; served in campaign of 1842. Residence, Matagorda county.

Mims, W. D.; emigrated in the fall of 1838; Santa Fé prisoner. Residence, Nacogdoches.

Monroe, A. T., age — ; nativity, New York; served, 1841. Residence, Crockett, Houston county.

Munson, Mordello S., age 49; nativity, Texas; served under Captain Dawson and Colonel J. H. Moore in 1840–'41, and in Somerville campaign, 1842. Residence, Brazoria, Brazoria county, Texas.

Matthews, Z. W.; emigrated in 1837; served in fall of 1842. Bellville, Austin county.

Middleton, W. B.; Mier prisoner. Residence, Leon county, Texas.

Mitchell, J. W.; in service, 1842.

Menifee, Thomas; emigrated in 1830; served in Somerville campaign, 1842. Residence, Fayette county, Texas.

Nicholson, James, age 59 ; nativity, England ; emigrated in 1838 ; in Woll campaign, 1842. Bastrop county.

Nelson, A. A., age 60 ; emigrated in 1838 ; served in Cherokee campaign, 1839. Residence, Nacogdoches.

Owen, Harrison, served in 1838. Residence, Brazos county.

Peacock, James T., 57 ; nativity, Tennessee ; Mier prisoner. Residence, San Antonio.

Patten, Wm. G., age 68 ; nativity, Tennessee ; emigrated in 1837 ; served in Captain Askew's company, 1838. Lamar county.

Parker, Isaac, D., age 52 ; nativity, Illinois ; emigrated in 1833 ; served in Captain Harrison's company, Cherokee campaign, 1839. Residence, Tarrant county, Texas.

Pilant, G. B., age 62 ; nativity, Alabama ; emigrated 1836 ; Mier prisoner, 1842. Residence, City of Houston.

Phelps, Orlando C., age 52 ; nativity, Mississippi ; emigrated in 1831 ; Mier prisoner. Residence, Columbia, Brazoria.

Phelps, Virgil H., age —; nativity, Mississippi ; emigrated in 1831 ; Mier expedition in 1842. Residence, Columbia, Brazoria county.

Pennington, Elijah, age 54 ; native of Illinois; emigrated in 1837 ; in Somerville campaign in 1842. Residence, Brenham, Washington county.

Patrick, C. H., age 51 ; nativity, Kentucky; emigrated in 1841 , in ranging service in 1841 ; in ranging service in 1842. Residence, Dallas county, Texas.

Pipkin, W. R., age 54 ; nativity, Tennessee ; emigrated in 1838; served under General Alexander Somerville in 1842. Residence, Fayette county, Texas.

Patton, J. M. ; served in Captain Hopkins' company in 1838. Residence, Lamar county, Texas.

Pearson, William H. ; emigrated in 1839 ; served in the spring and fall of 1842. Residence, Williamson county, Texas.

Ryan, William, age 66 ; nativity, Kentucky ; emigrated in 1837 ; served in Colonel Neil's expedition against the Indians in 1839, and Mier prisoner in 1842. Residence, Richmond, Fort Bend county.

Rice, Z. B., age 65 ; nativity, Alabama ; emigrated in 1838 ; served under General Tarrant in 1841.

Rodgers, A. G., age 54 ; nativity, Alabama ; emigrated in 1831 ; served in 1841. Residence, Leona, Leon county, Texas.

Rucker, B. F., age 59 ; nativity, Tennessee ; emigrated in 1838 ; in service in 1842. Residence, Navasota, Grimes county, Texas.

Rice, James O., age 57 ; Mier prisoner. Residence, Travis county, Texas.

Rupley, William, age 61 ; Mier prisoner.   Residence, Victoria, Texas.
Runyan, W. J. ; Mier prisoner.

Robertson, H. A. ; nativity, North Carolina ; emigrated in December, 1836 ; served in the army of 1837.   Residence, Rockport, Aransas county.

Rucker, Lindsey P., age 60 ; nativity, Tennessee ; emigrated in September, 1837 ; served in the Vasquez campaign in 1842.   Residence, Brenham, Washington county, Texas.

Stockbridge, Elam, age 61 ; nativity, New York ; emigrated in 1837 ; served in Indian campaigns.   Residence, Houston, Harris county, Texas.

Simmons, J. B., age 65 ; nativity, Tennessee ; emigrated in 1835 ; served in 1838.

Shaw, P. V., age 55 ; nativity, Kentucky ; emigrated in 1840 ; served in army in 1840 and 1842.   Residence, City of Austin.

Smith, Jackson, age 60 ; nativity, Kentucky ; emigrated in 1836 ; served under Captain Renfro in 1838.   Residence, Jacksonville, Cherokee county, Texas.

Shearn, John, age 49 ; nativity, England ; emigrated in 1834 ; in Woll campaign in 1842.   Residence, City of Houston, Texas.

Smelser, John, age 52 ; nativity, Tennessee ; emigrated in 1826 ; served under Captain Gill against Indians in 1839.   Residence, Brazoria county.

Smith, Ashbel, age 67 ; nativity, Connecticut ; emigrated in 1837 ; served on General's staff as surgeon in 1837.   Residence, City of Houston, Texas.

Stevenson, J. B., age 53 ; nativity, Florida ; emigrated in 1822 ; served under Captain Bird in 1839.   Residence, Courtney, Grimes county, Texas.

Shaw, Josiah ; nativity, Kentucky ; emigrated in 1837 ; served under Colonel John H. Moore in 1839 ; in Plum Creek fight with Indians and in battle of Salado in 1842.   Colorado county.

Scarborough, D. B., age 69 ; nativity, Georgia ; emigrated in 1837 ; served under General Edward Burleson in 1838 and 1839.   Residence, Hearne, Robertson county.

Scarborough, L., age —, nativity, Mississippi ; emigrated in 1837 ; with General Felix Huston, and served in the army.   Residence, McDade, Bastrop county, Texas.

Sinickson, John J., age 65 ; nativity, New Jersey ; emigrated in 1836 ; served in army in 1837, and Mier prisoner.   Residence, Philadelphia, Pennsylvania.

Smith, Joseph F., age 63 ; Mier prisoner.   Residence, Refugio, Refugio county, Texas.

Sinks, George W. ; emigrated in the fall of 1836 ; acting postmaster-general under General Houston.   Residence, La Grange, Fayette county.

COLONEL JOHN CALDWELL.

See p 292.

Stephens, A. J.; emigrated in 1836; served in Somerville campaign in 1842. Residence, Navasota, Grimes county, Texas.

Smothers, Isaac; served under General Dyer in 1838. Residence, Red River county.

Shannon, J. T.; emigrated in 1840; served in the army in 1841. Residence, Velasco, Brazoria county, Texas.

Settle, J. A.; nativity, Virginia; served in Galveston artillery for coast defense in 1841–'42. Residence, City of Galveston.

Smith, S. R.; emigrated in 1838; served in Somerville campaign in 1842. Residence, Huntsville, Walker county.

Shivers, Dr. O. L.; honorary member. Residence, Marion, Perry county, Alabama.

Truehart, James L., age 58; nativity, Virginia; emigrated in 1838; San Antonio prisoner.

Twohig, John, age — ; nativity, Ireland; San Antonio prisoner.

Taylor, E. W., nativity, Massachusetts; emigrated in 1837; served in the Somerville campaign in 1842. Residence, City of Houston, Texas.

Todd, John G., age 64; nativity, Kentucky; emigrated in 1837; served in the navy in 1837 and until annexation. Residence, Harrisburg, Harris county, Texas.

Thompson, Thomas C., age 52; nativity, Tennessee; emigrated in 1831; served in Captain G. B. Erath's company in 1841. Residence, Caldwell, Burleson county, Texas.

Terrell, E. R., emigrated in 1839; served in Captain Snively's expedition. Terrell, Kaufman county, Texas.

Thurman, Alfred S., age 58; Mier prisoner. Residence, Rockport, Aransas county, Texas.

Trahurn, G. W., age 50; Mier prisoner. Residence, Stockton, California.

Vandyke, Wilson, age 57; Mier prisoner.

Ward, John, age 56; nativity, Missouri; emigrated in 1827; served in army in 1838. Residence, Paris, Lamar county.

Wynne, W. H., age 68; nativity, North Carolina; emigrated in 1839; served under General Tarrant in 1839. Residence, Paris, Lamar county.

Westcott, R. D., age 65; nativity, New Jersey; emigrated in 1837; served in Somerville campaign, 1842. Residence, City of Houston, Texas.

Wood, Isaac, age 54; nativity, Arkansas; emigrated in 1837; served under Captain Stout, 1838. Residence, Hortonville, Red River county.

Woollam, J. C. Rev., age 61; nativity, South Carolina; emigrated in 1838; served in Captain Bennett's company, Burleson's brigade, in 1839. Residence, Houston county, Texas.

Walling, Elisha, age 52 ; nativity, Tennessee ; emigrated in 1837 ; Santa Fé prisoner. Residence, Houston county.

Webb, David F., age 64 ; nativity, Kentucky; emigrated in 1837 ; and in Cherokee campaign in 1839.

Wallace, William A. A., age 69 ; nativity, Virginia ; Mier prisoner. Residence, San Antonio.

Webb, Alexander W., age 63 ; nativity, Ohio ; emigrated in 1840 ; served under General Tarrant in 1841. Residence, Dallas county, Texas.

Walling, Vance, age 52 ; emigrated in 1835 ; served against the Indians at different times. Residence, Burnet county.

Wolf, Thomas H., age 55 ; nativity, Tennessee ; emigrated in 1837 ; served under General Rusk against the Indians. Residence, Burnet county, Texas.

Wood, W. H., age 60 ; nativity, Kentucky.; emigrated in 1837 ; served under Colonel Neill in 1839. Residence, Willis, Montgomery county, Texas.

Whitehead, H. S.; emigrated in January, 1841 : served in Woll campaign in 1842. Residence, Halletsville, Lavaca county, Texas.

Wells, J. A.; served in Jordan's company in 1837. Residence, Lavernia, Wilson county, Texas.

Young, Hugh F., age 66 ; nativity, Virginia ; in Colonel Snively's expedition. Residence, San Antonio.

West, Gilford, age 58 ; nativity, North Carolina; emigrated in 1841 ; Somerville campaign, 1842. Residence, Kosse, Limestone county.

Watkins, H. M., age 63 ; nativity, South Carolina; emigrated in 1840; in Vasquez campaign, 1842. Residence, Huntsville, Walker county, Texas.

Wood, A. H., age 50 ; nativity, Tennessee ; emigrated in 1829 ; in Woll campaign, 1842. Residence, Brenham, Washington county.

Woodland, Henry, age 52 ; nativity, Indiana ; emigrated in 1837 ; Mier prisoner. Residence, Bremond, Robertson county.

Woodard, W. H., age 54 ; nativity, North Carolina; emigrated in 1838 ; in Somerville compaign, 1842. Residence, Dresden, Navarro county, Texas.

Willis, R. S., age 53 ; nativity, Maryland ; emigrated in 1837 ; in Somerville campaign, 1842. Residence, Galveston.

Wesson, J. M., age 54 ; nativity, England ; emigrated 1840 ; served under Captain Goodall in 1841. Residence, Navasota, Grimes county, Texas.

Williams, Sol. M., age 49 ; nativity, Missouri ; emigrated in 1831 ; served in Somerville campaign, 1842. Residence, Brenham, Washington county, Texas.

VIII.

THE GENERAL CONSULTATION.

(Texas Almanac.)

THE first organized movement in Texas, in opposition to the despotic measures pursued by Santa Anna, was the assembling of the General Consultation, which was composed of the following-named persons elected by the several municipalities, viz.:

Municipality of Austin—William Menifee, Wily Martin, Thomas Barnett, Randall Jones, and Jesse Burnham; of Bevil (afterward Jasper)—John Bevil, Wyatt Hanks, Thomas Holmes, S. H. Everett, and John H. Blount; of San Augustine—A. Huston, Jacob Garrett, William N. Sigler, A. E. C. Johnson, Henry Augustine, Alexander Horton, and A. G. Kellogg; of Harrisburg— Lorenzo de Zavala, Clement C. Dyer, William P. Harris, M. W. Smith, John W. Moore, and David B. Macomb; of Matagorda—Ira R. Lewis, R. R. Royall, Charles Wilson, and John D. Newell; of Viesca (afterward Milam)—J. G. W. Pierson, J. L. Hood, Samuel T. Allen, A. G. Perry, J. W. Parker, and Alexander Thompson; of Nacogdoches—William Whitaker, Sam Houston, Daniel Parker, James W. Robinson, and N. Robins; of Columbia (afterward Brazoria)—John A. Wharton, Henry Smith, Edwin Waller, and J. S. D. Byrom; of Liberty—Henry Millard, J. B. Wood, A. B. Harden, and George M. Patrick; of Mina (afterward Bastrop)—D. C. Barrett, Robert M. Williamson, and James S. Lester; of Washington—Asa Mitchell, Elijah Collard, Jesse Grimes, Philip Coe, and Asa Hoxie; of Gonzales—William S. Fisher, J. D. Clements, George W. Davis, Benjamen Fuqua, James Hodges, and William W. Arrington; of Tenehaw (afterward Shelby)—Martin Parmer; of Jefferson —Claiborne West.

This body assembled at San Felipe, and was organized on the 3d of November, 1835; Branch T. Archer was elected president, and P. B. Dexter, secretary. It adopted a declaration against the Central Government of Santa Anna, and in favor of the Republican principles of the Federal Constitution of Mexico of eighteen hundred and twenty-four. It established a Provisional Government, composed of a governor, a lieutenant-governor who was *ex officio* president of the council, and a general council of one member from each municipality, selected by the delegation therefrom, in the consultation. An ordinance was adopted, defining the powers of the Provisional government, and directing an army to be raised and organized for the defense of the country.

OFFICERS OF THE PROVISIONAL GOVERNMENT.—The consultation elected as governor, Henry Smith ; lieutenant-governor, James W. Robinson ; commander-in-chief of the army to be raised, Sam Houston ; commissioners to the United States, Branch T. Archer, Stephen F. Austin, and William H. Wharton. The consultation adjourned on the 14th of November, 1835, and the Provisional Government commenced its duties on the 14th of November, 1835.

The following-named persons were at different times members of the General Council from their several municipalities :

Austin—Wily Martin, Thomas Barnett, and Randall Jones ; Colorado—William Menifee and Jesse Burnham ; San Augustine—A. Huston and A. E. C. Johnson ; Nacogdoches—Daniel Parker ; Washington—Jesse Grimes, Asa Mitchell, Asa Hoxie, Philip Coe, and Elijah Collard; Milam—A. G. Perry and Alexander Thompson ; Liberty—Henry Millard ; Shelby—Martin Parmer and James B. Tucker ; Gonzales—J. D. Clements ; Bastrop—D. C. Barrett and Bartlett Sims ; Matagorda—R. R. Royall, Charles Wilson and I. R. Lewis ; Harrisburg—William P. Harris ; Brazoria—John A. Wharton and Edwin Waller ; Jasper—Wyatt Hanks ; Jefferson—Claiborne West and G. A. Patillo; Victoria—J. A. Padilla and John J. Linn ; Refugio—James Power and John Malone ; Goliad—Ira Westover ; San Patricio—Lewis Ayres and John McMullen; Jackson—James Kerr ; Sabine—J. S. Lane.

The following were also officers of the Provisional Government :

Secretaries of the Council—P. B. Dexter and E. M. Pease ; secretaries of the governor—Charles B. Stewart and Edward B. Wood ; treasurer—Joshua Fletcher ; auditor—J. W. Moody ; comptroller, H. C. Hudson ; postmaster-general—John R. Jones.

THE CONVENTION OF TEXAS—The Provisional Government was superseded by the convention that met at Washington, on the 1st day of March, 1836. This convention was composed of the following members, viz.:

Muncipality of Austin.—Charles B. Stewart and Thomas Barnett ; of Brazoria—James Collingsworth, Edwin Waller, Asa Brigham, and J. S. D. Byrom ; of Bexar—Francis Ruis, J. Antonio Navarro, Jesse B. Badgett, and William Motley ; of Colorado—William Menifee and William D. Lacey ; of Gonzales—John Fisher and Matthew Caldwell ; of Nacogdoches—John S. Roberts, Robert Potter, Charles S. Taylor, and Thomas J. Rusk ; of Refugio—James Power and Sam Houston ; of Shelby—Martin Parmer and Sidney O. Pennington ; of Sabine—James Gaines and William Clark, Jr. ; of Harrisburg—Lorenzo de Zavala and Andrew Briscoe ; of Jasper—George W. Smyth and S. H. Everett ; of Jackson—Elijah Stepp ; of Jefferson—Claiborne West and William B. Scates ; of Liberty—M. B. Menard, A. B. Harden, and J. B. Wood ; of Bastrop—John W. Bunton, Thomas J. Gazley and Robert M.

Coleman ; of Milam—Sterling C. Robertson and George C. Childress ;.of Matagorda—Bailey Hardeman and S. Rhodes Fisher ; of San Patricio—John Turner and John W. Bower ; of Washington—Benjamin B. Goodrich, James G. Swisher, George W. Barnett and Jesse Grimes ; of San Augustine—E. O. •Legrand and Stephen W. Blount ; of Red River —Robert Hamilton, Collin McKinney, A. H. Latimer, Samuel P. Carson, Richard Ellis, and William C. Crawford ; of Goliad—David Thomas and Edward Conrad. Richard Ellis was elected president, and H. S. Kimble, secretary. This convention adopted a Declaration of Independence, and the Government of the REPUBLIC OF TEXAS was thus inaugurated. They elected Sam Houston as commander-in-chief of the army ; framed a constitution, and adopted an ordinance organizing and defining the powers of a government to continue until an organization could take place under the constitution. This was called the government *ad interim.* The principal officers of the government *ad interim,* elected by the convention, were as follows, viz :—David G. Burnet, president ; Lorenzo de Zavala, vice-president ; Samuel P. Carson, secretary of state ; Thomas J. Rusk, secretary of war ; Bailey Hardeman, secretary of the treasury ; Robert Potter, secretary of the navy ; David Thomas, attorney-general. During this government, which continued until the 22d of October, 1836, there were many changes, and the following-named persons were, for a time, members of the cabinet, viz. : James Collingsworth and William H. Jack, secretaries of state ; M. B. Lamar, F. A. Sawyer, A. Somerville, and John A. Wharton, secretaries of war ; Peter W. Grayson, attorney-general ; Barnard E. Bee, secretary of the treasury ; John R. Jones, postmaster-general. The following persons were also in office under the government *ad interim:* Asa Brigham, auditor ; H. C. Hudson, comptroller ; Benjamin C. Franklin, judge for the district of Brazos.

When hostilities commenced in September, 1835, and the volunteers assembled at Gonzales, John H. Moore was elected to command them ; subsequently, when their numbers had increased, and General Austin arrived in camp, he was elected to command them, and continued in command until toward the 1st of December, when he resigned, and went to the United States as a commissioner, with Archer and Wharton. Edward Burleson was then elected commander, and continued in command until a few days after the surrender of Bexar by General Cos, on the 10th of December, 1835. After this time the whole military force was placed under the orders of General Houston, as commander-in-chief, until General Rusk took the command a few days after the battle of San Jacinto.

The first Congress assembled on the 3d of October, and on the 22d of the same month, a Constitutional Government of the REPUBLIC was organized under Houston's first administration.

IX.

HOUSTON'S FIRST ADMINISTRATION.

OCTOBER 22, 1836.

SAM HOUSTON, president ; Mirabeau B. Lamar, vice-president ; Stephen Fuller Austin, R. A. Irwin, J. Pinckney Henderson, secretaries of state; Thomas J. Rusk, William S. Fisher, Barnard E. Bee, George W. Hockley, secretaries of war; Henry Smith, secretary of the treasury ; S. Rhodes Fisher, William M. Shepperd, secretaries of the navy ; J. Pinckney Henderson, Peter W. Grayson, John Birdsall, A. S. Thurston, attorney-generals ; Robert Burr, postmaster-general ; E. M. Pease, Francis R. Lubbock, comptrollers ; John W. Moody, first auditor; J. G. Welshinger, second auditor ; William G. Cooke, stock commissioner; William H. Wharton, Memucan Hunt, Anson Jones, ministers to the United States ; J. Pinckney Henderson, minister to Great Britain and France; W. F. Catlett, secretary of legation to the United States; George S. McIntosh, secretary of legation to Great Britain and France.

------◆◆------

X.

LAMAR'S ADMINISTRATION.

COMMENCED DECEMBER 10, 1838.

MIRABEAU B. LAMAR, president ; David G. Burnet, vice-president. Lamar's cabinet was composed as follows, at different times : Barnard E. Bee, James Webb, Abner S. Lipscomb, James S. Mayfield, Samuel A. Roberts, secretaries of state ; A. Sidney Johnson, Branch T. Archer, secretaries of war ; Richard G. Dunlap, James H. Starr, J. G. Chalmers, secretaries of treasury ; Memucan Hunt, and Louis P. Cooke, secretaries of navy ; J. C. Watrous, James Webb, and F. A. Morris, attorney generals; Robert Burr, Edwin Waller, and John R. Jones, postmasters-general ; Asa Brigham and James W. Simmons, treasurers ; James W. Simmons and James B. Shaw, comptrollers ; John W. Moody and Charles Mason, first auditors ; Musgrove Evens, second auditor ; John P. Borden and Thomas William Ward, commissioners of General Land Office ; Thomas R. Stiff, Jackson Smith, Joseph Moreland, and Charles de Morse, stock commissioners ; Richard G. Dunlap and Barnard E. Bee, ministers to the United States ; James Hamilton, minister to Great Britain ; William Henry Dangerfield and George S. McIntosh, ministers to France ; Barnard E. Bee, and James Webb, ministers and agents to Mexico ; M. Austin Bryan, Samuel A. Roberts and Nathaniel Amory, secretaries of legation to the United States ; George L. Hammeken, secretary of legation to Mexico ; James Hamilton, commissioner to treat with Holland, Belgium, Great Britain, and France; Samuel M. Williams, A. T. Burnley, James Hamilton, and James Reiley, loan commissioners.

XI.

HOUSTON'S SECOND ADMINISTRATION.

COMMENCED DECEMBER 13, 1841.

SAM HOUSTON, president ; Edward Burleson, vice-president; Anson Jones secretary of state ; George W. Hockley and George W. Hill, secretaries of war and navy, (consolidated into one office) ; William Henry Dangerfield and James B. Miller, secretaries of the treasury; George W. Terrill and Ebenezer Allen, attorney-generals ; Asa Brigham, treasurer; Francis R Lublock and James B. Shaw, comptrollers ; Charles Mason, auditor ; John P. Borden and Thomas William Ward, commissioners of the General Land Office; James Reiley, Isaac Van Zandt, and J. Pickney Henderson, ministers to the United States ; Ashbel Smith, minister to France; William Henry Dangerfield, minister to the Netherlands, Belgium, and the Hanse Towns ; Charles H. Raymond, secretary of legation to the United States ; Samuel M. Williams and George W. Hockley, commissioners to Mexico.

XII.

ANSON JONES' ADMINISTRATION.

COMMENCED DECEMBER 9, 1844.

ANSON JONES, president ; K. L. Anderson, vice-president ; Ashbel Smith and Ebenezer Allen, secretaries of state ; George W. Hill and William G. Cooke, secretaries of war and navy, (one office); William B. Ochiltree and John A. Greer, secretaries of the treasury ; Ebenezer Allen, attorney-general ; Moses Johnson, treasurer; James B. Shaw, comptroller ; Thomas William Ward, commissioner of the General Land Office; Charles Mason, auditor; George W. Terrill and Ashbel Smith, ministers to Great Britain, France, and Spain ; James Reiley and David S. Kauffman, ministers to the United States; William D. Lee, secretary of legation to the United States ; James Collingsworth, John Birdsall, (by appointment of the president), Thomas J. Rusk, and John Hemphill, chief-justices of the Supreme Court during the Republic ; William Fairfax Gray and Thomas Green, clerks of the Supreme Court during the Republic.

XIII.

PROMINENT OFFICIALS OF THE REPUBLIC.

JUDGES OF THE DISTRICT COURTS DURING THE REPUBLIC.

Shelby Corzine	1st District.	John M. Hansford....	7th District.
Benjamin C. Franklin..	2d do	R. E. B. Baylor	3d do
R. M. Williamson.....	3d do	Anderson Hutchinson.	4th do
James W. Robinson ...	4th do	George W. Terrill	5th do
Edward T. Branch	5th do	Thomas Johnson	1st do
John T. Mills	3d do	Patrick C. Jack	6th do
Ezekiel W. Cullen	1st do	Richard Morris	1st do
Henry W. Fontaine ...	2d do	William B. Ochiltree...	5th do
John Scott...........	2d do	John T. Mills........,.	7th do
Anthony B. Shelby	1st do	William E. Jones	4th do
William J. Jones	2d do	M. P. Norton	6th do
John Hemphill	4th do	John B. Jones........	1st do
Richardson Scurry	6th do	R. T. Wheeler	5th do

DISTRICT-ATTORNEYS DURING THE REPUBLIC.

Richardson Scurry....	1st District.	W. R. Scurry.........	5th District.
A. M. Tompkins......	2d do	Peter W. Gray........	1st do
H. C. Hudson........	3d do	Peter Mac Grea.......	2d do
John Record	4th do	J. M. Ogden.........	3d do
Napoleon Thompson...	1st do	C. W. Peterson.......	4th do
John D. Morris.......	4th do	R. T. Wheeler	5th do
John R. Hubert	5th do	Henry W. Sublett	6th do
Frederic W. Ogden....	1st do	Jesse Benton, Jr......	7th do
John R. Reid	2d do	Henry W. Sublett	6th do
Charles S. Taylor.....	5th do	James Tabor	5th do
Charles M. Gould.....	5th do	K. L. Anderson	5th do
Patrick C. Jack.......	6th do	John D. Anderson....	3d do
Wm. M. Williams.....	7th do	Peter Mac Greal......	1st do
James Armstrong	6th do	Andrew Neill.........	2d do
E. M. Pease	2d do	Peter W. Gray	6th do
William T. Henderson.	5th do	F. H. Merriman......	1st do
H. P. Brewster	2d do	George W. Brown	2d do
George W. Terrill.....	5th do	Thomas Johnson	3d do
Henry J. Jewett	3d do	John D. Anderson....	4th do
William Fairfax Gray..	1st do	O. M. Roberts	5th do

William C. Young..... 7th District. | William Byrne .... 2d District.
Abner S. Lipscomb ... 1st do | Thomas Newcomb.... 4th do
James W. Henderson.. 6th do | George Quinan....... 1st do
William H. Palmer.... 6th do

SPEAKERS OF THE HOUSE OF REPRESENTATIVES DURING THE REPUBLIC.

1st Congress—Ira Ingram, 1st session ;
    Branch T. Archer, 2d session.
2d Congress—Joseph Rowe,
3d   "   —John M. Hansford,
4th   "   —David S. Kaufman,

5th Congress—David S. Kaufman,
6th   "   —K. L. Anderson,
7th   "   —N. H. Darnell,
8th   "   Richardson Scurry,
9th   "   —John M. Lewis.

CHIEF CLERKS OF THE HOUSE.

1st Congress—Willis A. Faris, 1st ses.;
    Wm. Fairfax Gray, 2d session.
2d Congress—John M. Shreeve,
3d   "   —John W. Eldridge,
4th   "   —Thos. W. Ward,

5th Congress—P. W. Humphreys,
6th   "   —James H. Raymond,
7th   "   —James H. Raymond,
8th   "   —James H. Raymond,
9th   "   —James H. Raymond.

PRESIDENTS PRO TEM. OF THE SENATE DURING THE REPUBLIC.

1st Congress—Richard Ellis, 1st ses'n;
    Jesse Grimes, 2d session.
2d Congress—S. H. Everett,
3d   "   —S. H. Everett,
4th   "   —None appear elected,

5th Congress—Anson Jones,
6th   "   —John A. Greer,
7th   "   —John A. Greer,
8th   "   —John A. Greer,
9th   "   —John A. Greer.

SECRETARIES OF THE SENATE.

1st Congress—Richardson Scurry, 1st
    session ; Arthur Robertson, 2d
    session.
2d Congress—Arthur Robertson, 1st
    session ; Wm. Fairfax Gray, 2d
    session.
3d Congress—John D. McLeod,

4th Congress—John D. McLeod,
5th   "   —John D. McLeod,
6th   "   —A. C. McFarlan,
7th   "   —Stephen Z. Hoyle,
8th   "   —Thomas Green,
9th   "   —Henry J. Jewett.

APPENDIX.

JAMES W. FANNIN—COMMISSION, ORDERS, AND CORRESPONDENCE.

COPY OF FANNIN'S COMMISSION.

To JAMES W. FANNIN, JR. ESQ:

In the name of the people of Texas free and sovereign. We, reposing especial trust and confidence. in your patriotism, valor, conduct, and fidelity, do by these presents constitute and appoint you a colonel of artillery in the regular army of Texas, for the defense of the republican principles of the constitution of 1824, and for expelling every hostile invasion thereof.

And we do also enjoin and require you to regulate your conduct in every respect by the rules and discipline adopted by the United States of North America in time of war, or such laws and regulations as may be adopted by this government; and punctually to observe and follow such orders and directions from time to time as you shall receive from your superior officers. And we do hereby strictly charge and require all officers and soldiers under your command to be obedient to your orders, and diligent in the exercise of their several duties. This commission to continue in force until revoked by this or a future government.

Done at San Filipe de Austin on the eighth day of January eighteen hundred and thirty-six.   HENRY SMITH, *Governor.*

CHARLES B. STEWART, *Secretary of Executive.*

Printed by Baker and Bordens, San Filipe de Austin.

VELASCO, August 20, 1835.

To COLONEL J. W. FANNIN, JR.

SIR: You are appointed as a confidential agent, by the Committee of Safety and Correspondence of the Jurisdiction of Columbia, to proceed to San Filipe and use your utmost exertions to persuade Wyly Martin and all other persons with whom you may have influence to co-operate with us in the call of a consultation of all Texas, through her representatives.

B. T. ARCHER, *Chairman.*

WM. T. AUSTIN, *Secretary Committee of Safety and Correspondence.*

BRAZORIA, September 18, 1835.

MAJOR J. W. FANNIN, JR.

DEAR SIR: Yours under date of this day giving us information of the landing of arms and ammunition from Vera Cruz, has been received. This information has been forwarded to the Committee of Vigilance, and I have no doubt they will correspond with the political chief, at least I think it should be made known to the people of San Filipe as early as possible. A copy of your letter has been sent to Colonel Hall, and Velasco, where Archer is all this time.

I am, your obedient servant,

EDMUND ANDREWS.

AT CAMP ABOVE SAN ANTONIO, October 9, 1835.

TO GENERAL STEPHEN F. AUSTIN:

I have declined further action under the appointment given to me by yourself. This you will therefore look upon as my resignation.

I will be found in Captain Fannin's company, where my duty to my country and the principles of human rights shall be discharged on my part to the extent of my abilities as private.

Respectfully,

JAMES BOWIE.

GENERAL ORDERS.

HEAD-QUARTERS, October 27, 1835.

The guard will be detailed and ordered to parade every morning at nine o'clock.

The commandant of each company is positively ordered to turn out the officers and men from their respective companies, and have them marched to the place where the guard parades, precisely at nine o'clock in the morning and report them to the adjutant.

The adjutant of the regiment is positively ordered to parade the guard, call the roll, and deliver them to the officer of the day precisely at nine o'clock in the morning.

He and the officer of the day will then report to the adjutant-general, receive the countersign and instructions.

He will then post the guard, accompanied by the officer of the day.

He will then dismiss the guard.

(Signed)   S. F. AUSTIN.

By order, WARREN D. C. HALL, *Adjutant and Inspector-General.*

HEAD-QUARTERS, MISSION ESPADA, October 27, 1835.

To COLONEL JAMES BOWIE, *Volunteer Aid:*

You will proceed with the first division of Captain Fannin's company and others attached to that division, and select the best and most secure position that can be had on the river, as near Bejar as practicable, to encamp the army to-night—keeping in view in the selection of this position, pasturage, and the security of the horses, and the army, from night attacks of the enemy.

You will also reconnoiter, so far as time and circumstances will permit, the situation of the outskirts of the town, and the approaches to it; whether the houses have been destroyed on the outside, so as to leave every approach exposed to the raking of cannon.

You will make your report with as little delay as possible, so as to give time to the army to march and take up its position before night. Should you be attacked by a large force, send an express *immediately* with the particulars.

S. F. AUSTIN.

By order, P. W. GRAYSON, *Aid-de-camp.*

GOLIAD, October 27, 1835.

DEAR MAJOR: Yours of the 21st came to hand a short time since, and has been partly attended to by the wagons. You will receive one wine box of liquors, etc., also two small bags sugar and coffee. The people here are opposed to sending anything like provisions privately. I have therefore had to send you as little as possible. The articles sent are put up in good order and directed to J. W. Fannin.

As regards Southerland, I have attended to him some time since, and I believe satisfied nearly all—these things are sent under his charge—no other chance. I am not permitted to leave here—I should be glad to be with you if there is a probability of your remaining before Bejar any length of time. I would be glad if you would get a permit for me to go to your camps (from General Austin), this you can do as we have business together.

General Austin ought to be made acquainted with the situation of affairs here: if some persons are not sent here who can have no possible interest in this section of country every particle of provisions taken at this place will be proven to be private property. Some person ought, I think, to be sent to investigate this matter so soon as Bejar falls. It might be a very great saving to Texas. We do not want to set up for ourselves with a heavy public debt.

I have been on my horse for the last twenty hours, night and day, procuring wagons and teams to send to you, and am now very unwell, not able to write as I would wish. Your friend, truly, etc.

A. H. JONES.

MAJOR J. W. FANNIN, JR., *Camp near Bejar.*

HEAD-QUARTERS ON THE CANAL ABOVE BEXAR, October 31, 1835.

To COLONEL JAMES BOWIE AND CAPTAIN FANNIN:

I have taken a position on the Alamo Canal, at the mouth of a dry gully about one mile from town. There is one, a little nearer, but it can not be occupied to day. I have certain information that all the surplus horses, except about 150 or 200, were started to Laredo last night. . The number that left is reported 900 head. The escort does not exceed twenty or thirty men.

I have dispatched Captain Travis, with 50 men, to overtake and capture them. He has guides, and I have no doubt will succeed.

I have to inform you that a servant of Antonio de la Garza came into camp to-day, bringing a proposition from the greater part of the S. Fernando company of cavalry, and the one of Rio-Grande—to desert. This man was sent to procure a guarantee for them, when they came out. I have given the guarantee and have now to communicate to you the mode in which they will come out to us—when, etc. He says they will be obliged to come in the day-time, upon some occasion of alarm, when they are ordered out. These troops are stationed in the house of Padilla, in one of the lower labors which Colonel Bowie understands the situation of. It would be well,.then, for you to-morrow to make a diversion on that side, so as to produce the necessary stir ; so that they may be ordered out, and thus give these men the chance to come out as it were on duty, and then escape. They will present themselves with the billet of their guns advanced, or a white flag. Padilla has many acquaintances in those companies, who sent in Garza's servant (José Ortiz) to have an understanding with him as to the guarantees and the mode of joining us.

In regard to the measure of harassing the enemy to-night, as was spoken of before we parted, by simultaneous firing on the town, I have to say that I am obliged to decline it, owing partly to the condition of the men here at present, having lost so much sleep last night ; and partly to the difficulty of crossing the river, from here, so as to co-operate in time with the men on foot. As you will make a diversion to-morrow for the purpose of bringing out the deserters, you will therefore decline any thing of the kind to-night, unless you think it better to proceed on your part. If you think so, you can act as you think best, in that respect, but without expecting any co-operation from this quarter, for the reason I have mentioned. I will, however, mention that a few men from here may probably fire on the Alamo, which is, you know, on this side of the river—about moon down.

As there is abundance of corn here, you can use that brought by Seguin for your detachment.

I wish you to send to Seguin's ranch for some rockets that are there—two or three dozen. In Spanish they are called *guites*, pronounced quates—we may want them.

Please to give me your opinions, and those of your officers, as to the mode of further operations on the enemy. S. F. AUSTIN.

By order W. D. C. HALL.

Dispatch the bearer with your answer to-night, as soon as possible.

S. F. A.

I wish your opinions as to storming or besieging.

S. F. AUSTIN.

CAMP CONCEPCION, 9 o'clock P. M., October 31, 1835.

GENERAL S. F. AUSTIN.

DEAR SIR: Yours of this date has this moment been received, and contents duly considered.

We will make the desired diversion on to-morrow, in order to afford those companies protection should they determine to join us, as early as circumstances and the weather will admit, say nine o'clock.

We have received many reports with regard to the disposition of the troops, and some of the officers, but so various as to make it doubtful what degree of credit should be attached to them. No doubt, however, exists but provisions are short, and we can compel them by close *siege* to fight us outside, starve, or run away. If these troops join us on to-morrow or any other time, we propose to you to be in readiness to enter the town forthwith.

In order to effect this object, let us agree to send our respective parties at the *same hour* in the *morning* and *evening*, so as to be *always* ready to act in concert, and thereby effect our object with as little loss and as much certainty as practicable.

If this is done, and all communication of every sort, with the city, *stopped at once*, and these two companies do not join us in a given time (say five days or some certain day), let us storm the town simultaneously. We can not doubt for a moment the result.

The corn from Seguin's ranch was received this evening, and quite acceptable.

In conclusion, we will endeavor to perform our duty below town, and do most earnestly request, nay urge, that a more regular communication with each other, twice a day if possible, be kept up.

JAMES BOWIE.
J. W. FANNIN, JR.

HEAD-QUARTERS, November 1, 1835.

To COLONEL JAMES BOWIE AND CAPTAIN FANNIN.

Your communication of this morning was received, and is satisfactory in every respects to myself and all others.

I sent in a demand to-day for a surrender. General Cos stated that his duty would not permit him to receive any official communication, and of course it was returned unopened. He in a short time after sent out Padre Garza with a flag, to say to me verbally, that he had absolute orders from his Government to fortify Bexar and hold it at all hazards, and that as a military man his honor and duty *required* obedience to these orders, and that he would defend the place until he died, if he had only ten men left with him.

This is all that has passed between us. I approached on this side to-day within cannon-shot—they fired four at us. One shot (ball) passed over our heads, and one of grape fell in the lines, but fortunately injured no one.

From every information the fortifications are much stronger than has been supposed, and the difficulty of storming of course much greater. The system of alarms will be kept up as much as possible, night and day, and the place invested as closely as practicable. For this purpose I expect to station the adjutant-general, with a competent force, at the old mill, a short distance from town.

I have no information yet of Travis. A report reached camp this afternoon through a person from Bexar, that an express had just been received there, stating that Savariego had escaped from S. Filipe and had reached the Irish on the Nueces, and in union with the troops at that place had attacked Goliad. It is, however, only a report.

The inclosed paper is from a confidential source. I had forgotten to mention that the adjutant-general made a demonstration on the other side, with a detachment.

S. F. AUSTIN.

Since the within was written I have received yours of this afternoon.

The forces are not so *unequally* divided as appears at first view. Travis is constantly out on some extra duty. He is now out. I expect him to-night, and must then send him to escort the cannon. I wish to occupy the mill and another position. Our provisions are daily increasing and *require* a strong guard. However, as equal a division will be made as is compatible with the service. We have many sick. Every thing shall be done on my part possible for the service and to keep up harmony. Our position here is far from being a strong one. We have no bank for defense. A good position can not be found without going too far off. I submit these matters to your calm judgment. It is known that head-quarters are here, and the main attack will be here if any is made. I have just heard from Travis; he will not be back until late to-morrow.

S. F. AUSTIN.

TRANSLATION.

All are busy in preparing to do their duty, they are clearing away fences, cutting down fruit-trees, etc. Three more cannons are to be mounted *to-day*. This side of the town is more accessible from behind the custom-house buildings and the priests' houses, and a tolerable strong force down along the edge of the river : to keep off any aid from the Alamo and prevent a retreat to that place, a few are placed on the roofs of the houses which are accessible from the back side.

Or, a tolerably strong party to come down the river and cut off the communication from here to the Alamo, through the ditch into the creek, and then guard the creek and two points on the river, which is come-at-able from the creek without difficulty ; a few days would compel them to surrender, for without water none can stand, and their cannon would fail.

The Alamo is very strongly arranged, but throwing the main ditch into the river, and guard the river, which has a good bluff bank, a few days would adjust matters and compel them to come out.

Keep clear of the streets, for these are prepared with their cannon. You know that this is a business that I am not much acquainted with, but think that 51,00 men would not take the place with the same ease that 200 would a month ago. We are closely watched, and if it was found out that we corresponded with you, *death* without doubt would be our portion instantly. Every day they are adding to the fortifications, as well as arming guns. Cos reports that Santa Anna has left Vera Cruz with five or six thousand men for the campaign. This is done to encourage his men. The bearer will not return here.

HEAD-QUARTERS ABOVE BEXAR, November 2, 1835.

TO COLONEL BOWIE AND CAPTAIN FANNIN :

I inclose you the result of the council of war held this morning by the officers of this division. You will see that the council has decided it is inexpedient to attempt to take Bexar by storm at present ; that the army should take such position as will enable it to harass the enemy as much as possible, out of reach of cannon ; that until the eighteen-pound battering pieces and additional re-enforcements arrive. This decision is submitted to the consideration of the officers of your division.

In addition I will add several suggestions that were made. One of them is to occupy the mill with two hundred men, and post the balance on the river under cover of a bank above, and continue the battalion below in the position it now occupies. To this it is objected, that our force is not sufficient to invest the town, so as to prevent supplies from entering, and that no important object can be effected in that way ; that more can be done by uniting the whole force above town and sending out parties of fifty men, every day and night, to range round, drive off cattle, etc. As to corn, it is certain they have a large supply inside. This point is therefore also submitted to your consideration; whether or not the whole force ought to be united above town, where corn is plenty, and harass the enemy by keeping out beeves by means of detachments, and wait until the battering cannon and re-enforcements arrive, or whether the army should remain divided as it now is.

To decide this point, the only question is this, Can the present force invest Bexar all round? If it can not, how can beeves be prevented from going in, except by keeping detachments constantly out? Can these detachments be sent and kept out, while the army is divided?

I will now make a suggestion of my own for your consideration. It is this : You will take a *safe* position below. I will do the same above. Each division will be subdivided into parties of twenty or twenty-five men. One of these parties will leave the upper division at daylight and range round on the west and sleep with you at night. A similar party will start from your division at the same time and range from the mouth of Salado and the Missions, up the Salado, and sleep there at night. A similar detachment will start at night from each camp and range round in the same way until they make the circle and get back to their respective divisions. I prefer this arrangement to the other.

I shall await your answer before I come to a final conclusion.

I shall dispatch a confidential man back to bring out the eighteen-pound cannon and shot, and also send Farmer to Gonzales to make round ball; but shall not do it until I receive an answer from you to this communication. I therefore wish you to give an answer as soon as possible.

Should you be decidedly of opinion that the whole force should be united, you can act on that decision at once, without any farther order from me. Should you prefer remaining, do so, and give your opinions as to the best mode of keeping out beeves. Yours respectfully.

S. F. AUSTIN.

Three hundred blankets, three hundred pairs shoes, cloths for tents, are are on the way out. This information was received last night. The three cannon—one six-pounder, two four-pounders—will be at the Cibola to-morrow night.

The mill will be occupied to day.

S. F. AUSTIN.

HEAD-QUARTERS, November 2, 1835.

At a council of war called this morning, consisting of General S. F. Austin, commander-in-chief, Colonel Warren, D. C. Hall, adjutant-general, Colonel

John H. Moore, Lieutenant-Colonel Burleson, Major William H. Jack, Colonel Patrick Jack, Quartermaster-General Major Sommerville, Major Benjamin W. Smith, Captain Caldwell, Captain Ebberly, Captain Bennett, Captain Switcher, Captain Bird, Captain Gonsen, Captain John Alley, Captain Nail, Lieutenant Aldridge, Lieutenant Splan, Lieutenant Hassell, Lieutenant Barnett, Lieutenant Money, Lieutenant Hunt, Lieutenant Pivey, Lieutenant Stapp, Leiutenant Hensley, and Lieutenant Dickenson.

The object of the call of the council being explained by the commander-in-chief to be, to have the opinion and determination of the officers in regard to the best measures of immediate operation, on the enemy, whether by closer investment simply, or *by storm*, after much conversation and discussion, it was proposed by Major William H. Jack that the question be directly put to the council whether *a storm* would or would not be expedient at the present moment; all the information in possession of the commander-in-chief in regard to the state of fortifications in Bexar being submitted. The question was accordingly put by the commander-in-chief, and the same was decided in the negative by all officers present, with the exception of Major Benjamin W. Smith, who voted substantially in the affirmative, saying that in his opinion the town ought to be taken *immediately*.

It was then decided unanimously by the council that such positions should be taken for the army at present, as would best secure it from the cannon-shot of the enemy and enable it at the same time to carry on offensive operations while we are waiting for the large cannon (eighteen-pounder) and additional re-enforcements.

S. F. AUSTIN.

CAMP BELOW BEXAR, November 2, 1835.

To GENERAL S. F. AUSTIN:

SIR: I take the liberty to tender you my resignation of the nominal command I hold in the army. I hope you will appoint some other person to occupy the post, more capable than myself.

Very respectfully,

JAMES BOWIE.

N.B.—I deem it of the utmost importance for you to effect a union of the two divisions of the army, as soon as practicable. Great dissatisfaction now exists in this division, and unless counteracted by the measure suggested I seriously apprehend a dissolution of it. The causes which have produced this state of things will be explained when I see you; when I will also explain my motives for taking the step I have taken in reference to myself.

Very respectfully,

JAMES BOWIE.

A true copy, W. RICHARDSON.

HEAD-QUARTERS, November 2, 1835.

To COLONEL BOWIE AND CAPTAIN FANNIN:

In accordance with the decision of a majority of your officers, and my own views, you will march the detachment under your command to this encampment either to-night or in the morning, as you may choose. It may be inconvenient to march to-night after receiving this dispatch, of this you will, however, be able to judge, and can use your discretion.

I send you a good guide.

The mill is at present occupied by a detachment under Colonel Burleson.

S. F. AUSTIN.

W. D. C. Hall, *Adjutant-General.*

HEAD-QUARTERS, CONCEPCION, November 9, 1835.

Information has been received from various channels that a large number of packs, with supplies of flour and other articles for the enemy in Bexar, escorted by fifty or sixty men, who are also bringing on seventy or eighty convicts as recruits for the besieged, are on the way from Laredo.

It is of the greatest importance to the service that these supplies should be taken, and the party destroyed or dispersed who are bringing them on, so as to prevent their reaching the enemy.

You will therefore proceed as speedily as possible, with not less than one hundred men nor more than one hundred and fifty, with the best guides you can procure in the two encampments, in the direction of the Laredo road, to intercept the said convoy.

Your detachment will be composed of as many men of your own company as have horses able to perform the trip; of volunteers from the Nacogdoches battalion, and by a detail from Colonel Burleson's command above town.

In the discharge of this duty much must be left to your own discretion. According to the information, the convoy ought to reach the Atascosa, distant about thirty miles from here, to-night; at or before reaching said creek it will leave the road, probably on the north side, and travel principally in the night through the woods and by-paths.

This will render it indispensably necessary for you to keep out spies in every direction, so as to find the trail and examine every road and by-way, for which purpose it will be important to establish a stationed camp at some concealed place on the Atascosa, so that your spies may know where to find you; this, however, you will regulate according to your judgment and circumstances.

The greatest dispatch and rapidity of movement are necessary to succeed in this matter; you will therefore lose no time.

You will have the inclosed directions delivered to the inhabitants on the Medina and Atascosa, prohibiting them from taking any beeves, or any other supplies, to Bexar, or having any communication with that place.

Travis was to have stayed at Salina's rancho on Atascosa, last night. You will inquire for him and incorporate his party with yours.

I need not urge upon you the importance of this expedition. You are fully aware of it.

Yours respectfully,

S. F. AUSTIN.

To Captain J. W. Fannin.

HEAD-QUARTERS, CONCEPCION, November 14, 1835.

CAPTAIN J. W. FANNIN:

This will be delivered to you by D. Salvador Floris, the brother-in-law of Captain Juan Seguin. Floris and his company have engaged to go on as far as beyond the Nueces, to examine whether any troops are on the road; they will also burn the whole country as far as they go. I wish you to get eight or ten volunteers to go with them. This service is important, and I have told the men of this party, that should they take public horses, they can appropriate two horses or mules apiece to their own use and property.

If you have heard nothing of the re-enforcement, I wish you to return to camp.

Burleson's division sent him and Wharton down yesterday with an unanimous request that the two divisions should be united at that place. The nature of this request, and many circumstances, render it necessary to comply with it. This division will therefore march to the mill above town to-morrow, and you will return to that camp.

Some re-enforcements have arrived, and they will now come on in great numbers. The sooner you can return the better, provided you find that nothing can be done there. Yours respectfully,

S. F. AUSTIN.

The foraging party is out from Bexar or Leon every day—about one hundred men. A strange misunderstanding prevented Ebberly's company from joining you.

GOLIAD, November 12, 1835.

MAJOR J. W. FANNIN, *Head-quarters near Bexar.*

DEAR MAJOR: Yours of the 3d instant was handed me on my arrival at this place yesterday. It was truly satisfactory to learn that my last to you had received your attention and had the desired effect the contents of which you vouched for are strictly true, not one syllable but of that character. I also have the pleasure of informing you that the whole matter has been adjusted between Captain Dimitt and myself ; he has pledged me his honor in every manner, that he never has intended anything to injure me in any way, and I have been assured by my friends here, that he, Capt. D., has spoken of the matter often, and with *tears* declared his innocence of an attempt to injure Lieutenant C. or myself, and regretted the perverse course which he had pursued. I have always been of opinion that the aim would be at Dr. Erwin ; he has, I have no doubt, acted incorrectly, in fact I am sure of it ; but let me add, he may have cause, and Dear F., I am not the man to desert a friend because the world does. Captain Dimitt refuses to speak to him, others follow the example. Doctor Erwin has joined the Volunteer Grays.

On the 5th instant we, forty in number, had a battle with seventy odd of the enemy, on the bank of Nueces River, and " flogged them like hell." From our situation not more than fifteen of our men were brought into action. The enemy commenced the attack while we were crossing the river ; they admitted three killed and about fourteen wounded, several mortally ; information since says five killed, seventeen wounded, and twenty missing. The best of the story is yet to come. By some means about twenty of the Irish in that quarter had been induced to join the enemy ; among these the alcalde, judge, and sheriff, all three were badly wounded. We have the pleasure of saying that we shot the (" twelve pokers "). You can hear the particulars of Erwin. I had intended going with the Grays, but Captain D. has promised his men to leave here in a few days—two or three—for Bexar.

Captain Dimitt says that he numbers ninety men, and can leave this place with sixty. His enemies here say that he will not leave here at all, but will hold this place to protect his own property in this section of country. The captain of the Grays can give you any information that you may desire from here, etc.

A. H. JONES.

Captain Dimitt has refused to receive Viesca as governor ; it has caused some dissatisfaction among the men. Colonel Gonzales, with thirty troops from the interior, is here, and from the manner in which he was received does not know what course to pursue. He, it is said, is very much mortified.

I understand that he says, if he was at Bejar, two hundred and fifty of Cos' cavalry, which he has once commanded, would force their way out and join him.

Martial law has been proclaimed in this place—that has also caused deserters—nobody will come to town. The citizens, or many of them, have left this section altogether. To keep peace in camp I hope we will be able to move shortly.

A good deal of sickness in camp; fifteen reported this morning, quite unwell. As the men are not permited to go to Bejar may make excuse to go home, and such as can not be denied—or will not be.

N. B.—I write you thus for your own information, knowing that you get nothing of this kind correctly.

With the hope of seeing you soon, I am your friend, etc.

A. H. JONES.

Confidential.

SAN FILIPE, November 13, 1835.

DEAR SIR : On yesterday the convention, without the expression of any wish on my part, elected me general-in-chief of the forces to be raised in Texas, and commander of all those who may hereafter be called into service.

Thus situated, I take leave to offer you the appointment of inspector-general of the army, it being within my gift. You will please intimate your acceptance, if the same should be agreeable to you. Your rank, of course, will be that of a colonel in the line.

So soon as convenient (should you accept the appointment) I will require you to join me, at this place, or wherever the head-quarters of the army may be established. But, my dear sir, if your presence is necessary for the safety of the army in camp, or is in *any wise* necessary, *do not abandon it!* Two days since the agent started to New Orleans for artillery and means to reduce San Antonio. When can they reach camp? not before March next ! Would it not be best to raise a *nominal siege;*—fall back on La Bahia and Gonzales, having a sufficient force for the protection of the frontier (which, by the by, will not be invaded) furlough the balance of the army to comfortable homes, and when the artillery is in readiness, march to the combat with sufficient force, and at once reduce San Antonio ! The army, at present without tents and necessary comforts for the men, I fear may produce an epidemic and destroy more than would have fallen in storming the place. Recommend the safest course. All admit that nothing can be done until the cannon arrive, and so long as there is subsistence in the neighborhood, the enemy will command it as well as you ! So that by the time they are starved out you will have nothing to subsist the troops of the people.

I hear our friend Colonel Bowie is at the head of the army. Bid him God speed. I am glad of it. I congratulate him and the army. You may show him this letter. Salute Dr. Richardson, and say to him the appointment of surgeon-general of the army is for his acceptance, if it will be agreeable to him.

Remember our maxim, It is better to do well, *late than never !* The army, without means, ought never to have dassed the Gaudaloupe without the proper munitions of war to reduce San Antonio. Therefore the error can not be in falling back to an eligible position.

Your obedient servant, and friend,
SAM HOUSTON.

CAPTAIN J. W. FANNIN, JR., *Army of the People, Bexar, Texas.*
Express Mr. M. H. Hanks.

SAN FELIPE, November 15, 1835.

MAJOR FANNIN.

DEAR SIR : Your letter of the 8th instant is before me and for reply.

The government here is now organized, and will in the morning proceed to appointments and to business generally. Henry Smith is governor, and Colonel Robinson of Nacogdoches lieutenant-governor; S. F. Austin, B. F. Archer, and W. H. Wharton, agents to United States. On to-morrow the council will proceed to appoint officers, treasurer, etc. I am spoken of as treasurer, but decline, if it can be filled otherwise satisfactorily. But as it is urged, I suppose it will be tendered to me, which my interest in the country will prompt me to accept. Where the council will hold its sessions is yet undetermined. I believe it will be in Washington or Matagorda, probably in the latter. The convention, however, will meet in Washington on 1st March, if not sooner called. I shall go home on to-morrow, but will return if it is not determined on to-morrow that the council removes to Matagorda.

Your army certainly has been badly conducted. We have forwarded all times even to recruits so far as has been called for, and several wagons have been dispatched which have not been called for, and yet we are publicly complained of. If your commander, or his staff, could see two inches from their noses, and order supplies in time, the country has means, men, and all that is necessary, if system was pursued and timely application made. The time, however, of the sitting of the convention has produced some delay, but I hope the same energy now on the organization of the government will be observed, and you will have no room to complain of the attention to your calls in future. Our lieutenant-governor appears to be a man of industry and correct ideas.

I think as an individual the troops ought not to leave Bexar, if they can possibly help it, but if you cannot leave it in good order, when I go home I will cause a suitable number of tents to be made and sent immediately to Copino, or Dimitt's on Lavaca, and from that packed out to camps. If the eighteen-pound cannon is at Matagorda it shall also be sent. But you ought not to look now for a suitable quantity of battering cannon and ball sooner than eight weeks. Now the question is, Will your men stay, or will they not, or can you take the place without the large cannon ? If not, then take time by the forelock.   Retire in order to Gonzales and fortify ; or you can, if sufficient supplies in camp, remain at Bexar.

We have various accounts of much interest here, all of which being communicated to the commandant I will omit them here.

You write me and Mr. Newell relative to your negroes and the purchase of my land.   I wish you to be more definite, as if I sell I must have half the amount in March or April next, either in cash or negroes.   This will be necessary, as we don't know how long we may be detained in public service, and in the meantime I must, as well as you, keep my negroes employed to an advantage.   But any service I can render you in your absence will be done to the utmost.   If you advise me to buy a place for you, or any thing else you may request, it shall be promptly complied with.   But for the present I will have your negroes collected and as soon as you write me will do as you desire.

Your pants and coat I fear I can not find in this place, but will try this evening.   If I can not find any, I will send you a stout suit immediately from Matagorda.   Your orders will be at all times attended to with pleasure.

I remain truly your friend,

R. R.. ROYALL.

HEAD-QUARTERS BEFORE BEXAR, November 22, 1835.

Captain J. W. Fannin having represented to me the absolute necessity of returning home, I have granted to him an honorable discharge, and have to say that he has uniformly discharged his duty as a soldier and as an officer.

S. F. AUSTIN, *Commander-in-Chief.*

INDEX

There are two sections to the index: (1) a general index to *A Texas Scrap-Book* (p. 661) and (2) an index to authors of pieces in the *Scrap-Book* and to sources—books, almanacs, etc.—contained in whole or in part in the *Scrap-Book* (p. 725). References to separate articles in the *Scrap-Book* are in all capital letters. Personal names that appear in a list in the *Scrap-Book* have entries that include the name of the list. For example, the index entry "Anderson, Simon Asa, Old 300, 557" indicates that Simon Anderson is in the list of Austin's Original Three Hundred on page 557 of the *Scrap-Book*.

The following is an outline of the short titles and the lists they represent:

Tx Necrology	Texas Necrology: Deaths Reported at the Annual Meeting, May, 1874 (Veterans Association), p. 578
Pioneers killed	List of Old Texans Who Have Died and Been Killed by Mexicans and Indians, 1828–1874, p. 580
S. Jacinto Army	List of All the Men in Texas Army at San Jacinto, p. 562
Veteran	Names of Veterans, p. 585
Fannin Massacre	List of Officers and Men under Col. Fannin, p. 569
Old 300	Austin's Original 300, p. 557
Gen. Consultation	Attendees of the Gen. Consultation, 1835, p. 633
Convention	Convention of March 1836, p. 634

Prov. Govt.   Provisional Government, Nov. 1835, p. 634

Houston 1st Admin   Houston's First Administration, 1836, p. 636

Lamar Admin   Lamar's Administration, 1838, p. 636

Houston 2nd Admin   Houston's Second Administration, 1841, p. 637

Jones Admin   Jones' Administration, 1844, p. 637

Judges   Judges of District Courts, Republic, p. 638

DA's   District Attorneys, Republic, p. 638

Speaker   Speakers of the House, Republic, p. 639

Clerk   Chief Clerks, Republic, p. 639

Pro Tem   Presidents Pro Tem, Senate, Republic, p. 639

Sec. Senate   Secretaries of the Senate, Republic, p. 639

In compiling the index, I have not tried to correct all the typographical errors in the *Scrap-Book*. I listed items as they appeared unless I was sure it was a mistake. I take full responsibility for all errors in the index.

I want to thank Kent Keeth at the Texas Collection, Baylor University, for loaning me a copy of *A Texas Scrap-Book* to use in compiling this index.

RICHARD MORRISON
AUSTIN, TEXAS

A

Abbots, Lancelott, Veteran, 586
Abercrombie, William, Fannin Massacre, 572
Able, Joseph S., Veteran, 586
ABORIGINAL ANTIQUITIES OF TEXAS, 238
Acclimation, 452
Adaes Mission, 17
Adair, A. M., Veteran, 586
Adams, Captain, 28
Adams, J. M., Fannin Massacre, 570
Adams, Thomas, S. Jacinto Army, 566
Addison, Nathaniel, Veteran, 586
Addison, Oscar, Veteran, 620
Address of People of Columbia, 525
Adriance, John, Veteran, 586
ADVENTURES OF A VOLUNTEER, 160
Aes Indians, 17
Alabama Indians, 132, 236
ALABAMAS, LAST OF THE, 236
Alamo, 18, 218, 583, 646, 649
Alamo Canal, 646
ALAMO, DESCRIPTION, 115
ALAMO, ESCAPE FROM, POEM, 410
ALAMO HYMN, 338
Alamo, Monument, 112, 115
Alamo, Names of Defenders, 113
ALAMO, THE FALL OF THE, 106
Alcade of Austin, 25
Aldrete, Miguel, 65
Aldridge, 651
Aldridge, Isaac, Fannin Massacre, 571
Aldridge, John, Fannin Massacre, 571
Aldridge, Leonidas B., Pioneers killed, 583
Alexander, J. B., S. Jacinto Army, 566
Alexander, J. R., 620
Alexander, Lyman, Veteran, 585
Alexander, M. W., Veteran, 620
Alexin, H. Malena, S. Jacinto Army, 567
Alford, Winfield, 586
Alison, William L., Fannin Massacre, 572
Alispa, schooner, 78
Allbury, Y. P., Veteran, 585
Allcorn, Elijah, Old 300, 557

Allcorn, T. J., Veteran, 585
Allec, Alfred, Pioneers killed, 584
Allen, A. C., Pioneers killed, 584
Allen, Clement, Tx Necrology, 579
Allen, Ebenezer, Pioneers killed, 584
Allen, Ebenezer, Houston 2nd Admin, 637
Allen, Elisha, Veteran, 586
Allen, Henry L., Pioneers killed, 583
Allen, John K., Pioneers killed, 581
Allen, John M., S. Jacinto Army, 564
Allen, John M., Pioneers killed, 581, 582
Allen, Leven, Fannin Massacre, 572
Allen, Lodger, Veteran, 586
Allen, Martin, Old 300, 557
Allen, Peter, Fannin Massacre, 572
Allen, R., 113
Allen, Samuel T., Gen. Consultation, 633
Allen, T. G., Fannin Massacre, 570
Alley, John, 220, 651
Alley, John, Old 300, 557
Alley, Rawson, Old 300, 557
Alley, Thomas, Old 300, 557
Alley, William, Old 300, 557
Alley, William, Veteran, 586
Alleyton, 487
Allison, J. C., S. Jacinto Army, 565
Allison, Moses, S. Jacinto Army, 568
Allsbury, A., S. Jacinto Army, 564
Allsbury, P., S. Jacinto Army, 564
Almonte, Col., 193
Almonte, Gen., 171
Alsbery, Charles G., Old 300, 557
Alsbery, Harvey, Old 300, 557
Alsbery, Horace A., Old 300, 557, 525
Alsbery, Thomas, Old 300, 557
Alsbury, Y. P., 99
Alto, 588, 604
Alum Creek, 617
ALWAYS NEW, POEM, 389
Amason, Jesse, Pioneers killed, 584
Amory, Nathaniel, Lamar Admin, 636
Ampudia, Gen., 127, 174
Amsler, Charles C., Tx Necrology, 579
Amsler, Charles C., Pioneers killed, 585
Anadarkos, 133
Anahuac, 586, 598, 607, 612

Anahuac Affairs, 187
Anahuac Battle, 1835, 93, 611
ANAHUAC OR OPENING CAMPAIGN
   OF THE TEX. REV., 24
Anastase, Father, 180
Ancola, Simon, S. Jacinto Army, 569
Anderson, 113, 487, 587, 602, 609
Anderson County, 198, 588, 589, 591,
   593, 594, 596, 605, 610, 615, 623,
   624
Anderson, C. D., S. Jacinto Army, 562
Anderson, Holland L., Veteran, 585
Anderson, John D., DA's, 638
Anderson, Joseph S., Veteran, 620
Anderson, John W., Veteran, 586
Anderson, K. L., 23, 216, 638, 639
Anderson, K. L., Jones Admin, 637
Anderson, K. L., DA's, 638
Anderson, K. L., Speakers, 639
ANDERSON, KENNETH LEWIS, 280
Anderson, Kenneth L., Pioneers killed,
   582
Anderson, O. D., S. Jacinto Army, 566
Anderson, P. H., Fannin Massacre, 573
Anderson, Samuel, Fannin Massacre, 570
Anderson, Simon Asa, Old 300, 557
Anderson, T. Scott, Pioneers killed, 584
Anderson, Wash, S. Jacinto Army, 565
Anderson, Washington, S. Jacinto Army,
   562
Anderson, Washington, Veteran, 585
Andrade, General, 170
Andress, M., 113
Andrews, John, Old 300, 557
Andrews, Joseph, Fannin Massacre, 571
Andrews, Micah, S. Jacinto Army, 565
Andrews, Robert, 67
Andrews, William, Old 300, 557
Angelina River, 231
Angell, —, S. Jacinto Army, 564
Angier, Samuel T., Old 300, 557
Anglin, A., Veteran, 586
Anglin, Abram, 198
Anglin, H., Veteran, 586
Anglin, J., Veteran, 620
Antelope Hills, 471
Anthony, D. W., 52

Anthony, D. W., Pioneers killed, 580
Antone, Sayle, 65
Aransas Bay, 70, 244
Aransas County, 594, 595, 601, 618, 630,
   631
Archer County, minerals, 442
Archer, Branch T., 23, 192, 216, 633,
   634, 656
ARCHER, BRANCH T., 265
Archer, Branch T., Pioneers killed, 583
Archer, Branch T., Convention, 635
Archer, Branch T., Prov. Govt., 634
Archer, Branch T., Lamar Admin, 636
Archer, Branch T., Speakers, 639
Archive War, 119
ARCHIVE WAR, 142
Area, Alexander, Veteran, 586
Arkansas River, 134
Armijo, Governor, 127
Arms, Allison, Fannin Massacre, 571
Armstrong, Irwin, S. Jacinto Army, 565
Armstrong, James, Veteran, 586
Armstrong, James C., 620
Armstrong, James, DA's, 638
Armstrong, Robert, 35
Armstrong, William S., Fannin Massacre,
   570
ARMY AT SAN JACINTO BATTLE, 562
Arnold, Hayden, S. Jacinto Army, 567
Arnot, W. S., S. Jacinto Army, 565
Arrington, William W., Gen. Consultation,
   633
Arroyo del Atole, 232
Ashland, 605
Ashley, Robert, 234
Askins, Charles S., Veteran, 620
Askins, Wesley, Veteran, 585
Asphaltum, 445
Atascosa, 652, 653
Atascosa County, 591, 616
Atkins, Joseph, Veteran, 586
Atkinson, Jno, Veteran, 586
Atkinson, John, Veteran, 586
Atkinson, M. B., S. Jacinto Army, 568
Augustin, —, Tx Necrology, 579
Augustin, Henry W., Pioneers killed, 585
Austin, 119, 354, 579, 585, 587, 593,

597, 599, 603, 610, 612, 617, 613, 614, 617, 618, 620, 621, 626, 627, 630, 634
AUSTIN ADDRESS, 1836, 338
AUSTIN AND WHARTON, RECONCILIATION, 89
Austin, Capt. William T., 85
Austin, Col. William T., at Bexar, 220
Austin County, 586, 590, 591, 596, 597, 600, 607, 609, 611, 615, 621, 628
Austin, James Brown, Pioneers killed, 580
Austin, John, 27, 30, 93, 188
AUSTIN, JOHN, 287
Austin, John, Old 300, 557
Austin, John, Pioneers killed, 580
Austin, Municipality of, 633
Austin, Norman, Veteran, 586
Austin Record, 67
AUSTIN'S COLONY, JUDICIAL ORGANIZATION, 175
AUSTIN'S FIRST COLONY, 88
Austin, Stephen F., 23, 68, 74, 87, 191, 192, 194, 645, 656
Austin, Stephen F., Pioneers killed, 580, 583
Austin, Stephen F., Return from Mexico, 191
AUSTIN, STEPHEN F., LETTER FROM 1836, 202
AUSTIN, STEPHEN F., 253
AUSTIN, STEPHEN F., ANECDOTE, 311
Austin, Stephen F., Old 300, 557
Austin, Stephen F., Convention, 635
Austin, Stephen F., Prov. Govt., 634
Austin, Stephen F., Houston 1st Admin, 636
Austin, vessel, 80
AUSTIN, WILLIAM T., 287
Austin, William T., 122, 188, 197, 643
Austin, William T., Tx Necrology, 578
Austin, William, Pioneers killed, 585
Autry, M., 113
Avery, Willis, Veteran, 586
Avoca, Manuel, S. Jacinto Army, 569
Ayish Bayou, 186
Ayres, 113

Ayres, David, Veteran, 586
Ayres, Lewis, Prov. Govt., 634

B

BABE OF THE ALAMO, 116
Bache, Richard, Pioneers killed, 582, 583
Badgett, J. B., 58
Badgett, Jesse B., Convention, 634
Bagly, J. S., Fannin Massacre, 570
Bailess, 113
Bailey, 113
Bailey, Alexander, S. Jacinto Army, 568
Bailey, Eli, Veteran, 589
Bailey, Howard, S. Jacinto Army, 567
Bailey, James B., Old 300, 557
Baker, 113
Baker, Augustus, Fannin Massacre, 573
Baker, Capt., 129, 163
Baker, D. D. D., S. Jacinto Army, 566
Baker, Elias, S. Jacinto Army, 566
Baker, John R., Veteran, 622
BAKER, JOSEPH, 272
Baker, Joseph, 582
Baker, Joseph, S. Jacinto Army, 566
Baker, Mosely, 216
BAKER, MOSELY, 272
Baker, Mosely, S. Jacinto Army, 562, 566
Baker, Mosely, Pioneers killed, 582
Baker, Stephen, Fannin Massacre, 572
Baker, William, Veteran, 620
Balch, John, Veteran, 588
Baldwin, Hiram, Pioneers killed, 582
Balentine, 113
Banks, John B., Pioneers killed, 585
Banks, R., S. Jacinto Army, 565
Banks, Reason, Fannin Massacre, 571
Barbour, James, Pioneers killed, 581
Barclay, Anderson, Veteran, 589
Barclay, David, Veteran, 621
Barclay, James, Veteran, 589
Bardwell, S. B., S. Jacinto Army, 563
Barker, George, S. Jacinto Army, 568
Barkley, J. A., S. Jacinto Army, 568
Barkley, J. H., Fannin Massacre, 573
Barnard, George, 237
Barnard, George, Veteran, 621

Barnard, James H., Fannin Massacre, 570
Barnet, Thomas, Pioneers killed, 581
Barnett, 651
Barnett, G. W., Pioneers killed, 581
Barnett, George W., 58
Barnett, George W., Convention, 635
Barnett, Thomas, Gen. Consultation, 633
Barnett, Thomas, 58
Barnett, Thomas, Prov. Govt., 634
Barnhart, J., Veteran, 587
Barnhill, J. N., Fannin Massacre, 573
Barnwell, J. H., Fannin Massacre, 571
Barr, Robert, Pioneers killed, 581
Barr, William, 233
Barrett, D. C., 634
Barrett, D. C., Gen. Consultation, 633
Barrett, D. C., Prov. Govt., 634
Barrett, William, Old 300, 558
Barry, L. D., Pioneers killed, 583
Barstow, Joseph, S. Jacinto Army, 564
Bartlett, J. C., 587
Barton, Baker, 158
Barton, Jefferson, S. Jacinto Army, 565
Barton, T. B., Fannin Massacre, 572
Barton, Wayne, S. Jacinto Army, 565
Bastrop, 138, 328, 606, 612, 618, 624,
   633, 634
Bastrop County, 588, 590, 592, 595, 596,
   598, 599, 600, 602, 608, 614, 615,
   617, 621, 622, 623, 624, 625, 628,
   629, 630
Bastrop County, geology, 490
Bastrop County, Lignite, 491
BASTROP, BARON DE, 260
Bastrop, Baron de, 580
Bateman, William, S. Jacinto Army, 569
Bates, Anthony, Fannin Massacre, 571
Bates, Silas, 199
Bates, Silas H., Veteran, 587
Battalion, Georgia, Fannin Massacre, 569
Battalion, Lafayette, Fannin Massacre, 569
Batts, —, Fannin Massacre, 570
Baugh, J. J., 113
Bautista, Juan, 234
Baxter, M., S. Jacinto Army, 563
Bayless, Daniel E., Old 300, 561
Baylor, Dr., S. Jacinto Army, 568

Baylor, J. W., 64
Baylor, John R., Veteran, 621
Baylor, R. E. B., Judges, 638
Baylor, Robert E., Pioneers killed, 585
Beachom, John, S. Jacinto Army, 566
Beall, Josias B., Fannin Massacre, 571
Bean, Ellis, 233
BEAN, ELLIS P., 322
Bean, Ellis P., illus., 322
BEAR FIGHT, 313
Bear, —, S. Jacinto Army, 564
Beard, A. J., S. Jacinto Army, 568
Beard, J., 113
Beard, James, Old 300, 557
Beason's Ferry, 193, 205
Beason, Benjamin, Old 300, 557
Beason, Leander, S. Jacinto Army, 566
Beauford, Z. Y., S. Jacinto Army, 564
Beaumont, 586
Beaver Creek, 462
Bebee, Prvt., S. Jacinto Army, 564
Bee County, 589, 597, 609, 612
BEE, BARNARD E., 289
Bee, Barnard E., 582
Bee, Barnard E., Convention, 635
Bee, Barnard E., Houston 1st Admin, 636
Bee, Barnard E., Lamar Admin, 636
Beeman, John S., Veteran, 622
Beeville, 597, 612
Begly, John, Veteran, 588
Beitel, Joseph, Veteran, 622
Bejar, 645
Belden, Prvt., S. Jacinto Army, 564
Belknap, Charles, Old 300, 557
Bell County, 586, 587, 592, 598, 602,
   604, 606, 607, 611, 612, 619, 620,
   624, 626
Bell County, Oil, 498
Bell, A. J., Veteran, 621
BELL, GOVERNOR AND CAPTAIN —,
   312
Bell, J. T., 65
Bell, James, S. Jacinto Army, 566
Bell, Josiah H., 73, 89
Bell, Josiah H., Pioneers killed, 581
Bell, Josiah H., Old 300, 557
Bell, P. H., 623

Bell, P. H., S. Jacinto Army, 564
BELL, P. HANSBORO, 293
Bell, P. Hansborough, Veteran, 589
Bell, T. H., S. Jacinto Army, 566
Bell, Thomas B., Old 300, 557
Bell, Thomas W., Veteran, 622
Bellew, Doc., 185
Bellows, J. F., Fannin Massacre, 570
Bellville, 586, 596, 611, 628
Belton, 586, 602
Bencroft, Benjamin, S. Jacinto Army, 568
Benevides, Placido, 580
Bennett, 651
Bennett, Jake, Veteran, 587
Bennett, Joseph L., S. Jacinto Army, 567
Bennett, Joseph L., Pioneers killed, 582
Bennett, Joseph, Veteran, 588
Bennett, Major, at Bexar, 220
Bennett, Miles, Veteran, 588
BENNETT, VALENTINE, 298
Bennett, William, S. Jacinto Army, 568
Benson, —, S. Jacinto Army, 563
Benson, Ellis, Veteran, 586
Benton, 594
Benton, Alfred, S. Jacinto Army, 563
Benton, Isaac W., S. Jacinto Army, 564
Benton, Jesse, Jr., DA's, 638
Benton, Nat., Pioneers killed, 584
Benton, Prvt., S. Jacinto Army, 564
Berban, Jose, 234
Bernard, Doctor, 170
Bernard, Prvt., S. Jacinto Army, 564
Bernbeck, William, S. Jacinto Army, 566
Berry, A. J., Veteran, 587
Berry, David, 137
Berry, Francis, Pioneers killed, 582
Berry, J. B., Veteran, 588
Berry, Jackson, S. Jacinto Army, 565
Berry, James, Veteran, 620
Berry, Manders, Old 300, 557
Berryhill, W. H., S. Jacinto Army, 565
Bertrand, Thomas, Veteran, 589
Best, Isaac, Old 300, 557
BEST, POEM, 428
Betts, Jacob, Old 300, 557
Betts, Marion, Fannin Massacre, 573
Bevil, 526, 633

Bevil's Settlement, 28
Bevil, John, Gen. Consultation, 633
Bexar, 152, 353, 585, 590, 592, 634, 635,
    646, 648, 649, 650, 652, 653, 654,
    656, 657
Bexar County, 585, 588, 592, 595, 596,
    606, 607, 608, 610, 615, 616, 621,
    622, 624, 625
Bexar Exchange, 122
BEXAR, OFFICIAL ACCOUNT OF
    THE FALL, 218
Bexar, Seige of, 605
Biddle, John, S. Jacinto Army, 567
BIG FOOT, DEATH OF, 124
Big Wichita River, 462
Bigham, Francis, Old 300, 557
Bigley, John, S. Jacinto Army, 566
Billingsley, Jesse, S. Jacinto Army, 565
Billingsley, W. B., Veteran, 621
Billingsly, Jesse, S. Jacinto Army, 562
Billingsly, Jesse, Veteran, 588
Bills, —, Fannin Massacre, 574
Bingham, Francis, Pioneers killed, 582
Bingham, M. A., S. Jacinto Army, 566
Bird, 651
Bird Hunting, 326
Bird's Victoria, 142
Bird, John, 622
Birds in Texas, 475, 479
Birdsall, John, Pioneers killed, 581
Birdsall, John, Houston 1st Admin, 636
Birdsall, John, Jones Admin, 637
Bisbee, Ira, Veteran, 588
Bismuth in Texas, 496
Bissell, Theodore, Veteran, 588
Bissett, Prvt., S. Jacinto Army, 564
Black Jack Springs, 598
Blackbourn, A. J., Veteran, 621
Blackburn, Ephraim, 234
Blackman, Sergeant, 26
Blackwell, Joseph, Fannin Massacre, 573
Blackwell, Thomas, S. Jacinto Army, 564
Blair, 113
Blair, John, Veteran, 587
Blair, Payton, Veteran, 589
Blair, S. C., 113
Blair, W. C., Pioneers killed, 585

Blair, W., Veteran, 622
Blakely, Lemuel, S. Jacinto Army, 562, 565
Blanco County, 603, 609
Blanco River, 232
Blanton, Glover W., Pioneers killed, 582
Blanton, Jacob, Veteran, 588
Blazeby, W., 113
Bledsoe, G. L., S. Jacinto Army, 568
Bledsoe, George L., Veteran, 587
Bloodgood, William, Old 300, 557
Bloodworth, John D., Veteran, 621
Blount, John H., Gen. Consultation, 633
Blount, Stephen W., Veteran, 587
Blount, Stephen W., 206
Blount, Stephen W., Convention, 635
Blue, Uriah, S. Jacinto Army, 565
Boatwright, Thomas, Old 300, 557
Bogart, Samuel A., Pioneers killed, 583
Boles, H., Veteran, 621
Bolivar, 218
Bond, H., S. Jacinto Army, 565
BONHAM, J. B., 270
Bonham, J. B., Pioneers killed, 580
Bonnell, Mount, 326
Bonnett, —, Pioneers killed, 582
Bonzales, Colonel, 654
Booker, —, S. Jacinto Army, 563
Boone, Benj. Z., Veteran, 621
Borden, 587
Borden, Gail, 197
Borden, Gail, Pioneers killed, 585
Borden, Gail, Tx Necrology, 579
Borden, J. P., S. Jacinto Army, 566
Borden, John P., 587
Borden, John P., Lamar Admin, 636
Borden, John P., Houston 2nd Admin, 637
Borden, P. P., S. Jacinto Army, 566
Borden, Thomas H., Veteran, 589
Bosque County, 601, 613
Bostick, Caleb R., Old 300, 557
Bostick, S. R., S. Jacinto Army, 566
Bostick, Sam R., Tx Necrology, 579
Boswell, Rawson P., Veteran, 622
Bottsford, Seym, S. Jacinto Army, 565
Boundaries of Texas, 185

Boundary Hills, 472
Bourn, 113
Bowen, John, 64
Bowen, R., S. Jacinto Army, 567
Bower, John White, 58
Bower, John W., Convention, 635
Bowers, John H., Veteran, 620
Bowie County, ancient sites, 207
Bowie County, geology, 490
BOWIE, JAMES, 269
Bowie, James, 35, 66, 67, 92, 655
Bowie, James, Pioneers killed, 580
Bowie, Rezin P., 35
Bowin, 113
Bowman, J. B., 113
Bowman, James H., Veteran, 588
Bowman, John J., 65
Bowman, John J., Veteran, 588
Bowman, John, Old 300, 557
Bowman, Joseph, 64
Box, James E., S. Jacinto Army, 567
Box, John, S. Jacinto Army, 567
Box, John, Tx Necrology, 579
Box, John, Veteran, 587
Box, Nelson, S. Jacinto Army, 567
Box, Thomas G., S. Jacinto Army, 567
Boyce, Nicholas, Pioneers killed, 582
Boyce, Robert P., Veteran, 587
Boyd, J. C., S. Jacinto Army, 568
Boyle, A. M., Fannin Massacre, 573
Boyle, William, S. Jacinto Army, 568
Bozman, T. B., Veteran, 621
Bracy, L. G. H., Fannin Massacre, 570
Bradberry, James, Veteran, 588
Bradburn, Colonel, 24
Bradford, B. T., Fannin Massacre, 572
Bradford, James A., Fannin Massacre, 572
Brading, Phillilla, S. Jacinto Army, 566
Bradley, Daniel, Veteran, 589
Bradley, Edward R., Old 300, 557
Bradley, J. B., S. Jacinto Army, 564
Bradley, James, S. Jacinto Army, 568
Bradley, John, Old 300, 557
Bradley, Thomas H., 26
Bradley, Thomas, Old 300, 558
Bradshaw Place, 207
Brakey, M. J., S. Jacinto Army, 567

Branch, E. F., S. Jacinto Army, 567
Branch, Edward T., Judges, 638
Brattan, William, Veteran, 589
Bravo, schooner, 153
Brayles, Joseph, Veteran, 589
Brazoria, 21, 188, 191, 607, 610, 628,
    633, 634, 644
Brazoria County, 88, 89, 147, 586, 588,
    591, 594, 607, 610, 615, 616, 624,
    625, 627, 628, 629, 630, 631
Brazoria Volunteers, 222
Brazoria, vessel, 31
Brazos, 635
Brazos County, 591, 595, 597, 603, 609,
    618, 619, 622, 624, 628, 629
Brazos River, 20, 22, 73, 88, 132, 153,
    185, 189, 193, 231, 232, 244, 359,
    465, 466, 472
Brazos Santiago, 78
Brazos Swamp, Tx, 366
Breashear, Isaac W., Pioneers killed, 583
Breece, Capt., at Bexar, 220
Breedlove, A. W., S. Jacinto Army, 568
Breen, Charles, Old 300, 558
Bremond, 590, 621, 628, 632
Brenan, Thomas H., Veteran, 589
Brenham, 487, 585, 590, 600, 609, 614,
    621, 624, 626, 629, 630, 632
Brenham, R. F., 127
Brenham, R. F., Pioneers killed, 581
Brennan, William, Fannin Massacre, 570
Brennan, William, S. Jacinto Army, 568
Breshear, R. C., Fannin Massacre, 570
Brewer, H. M., S. Jacinto Army, 567
Brewster, H. P., Prvt., S. Jacinto Army,
    564
Brewster, H. P., Veteran, 588
Brewster, H. P., DA's, 638
Bridger, Henry, Veteran, 621
Bridges, William B., Old 300, 557
Bridgman, J., Fannin Massacre, 571
Brigance, Alfred F., Veteran, 622
BRIGHAM, ASA, 278
Brigham, Asa, 58
Brigham, Asa, Pioneers killed, 581
Brigham, Asa, Convention, 634, 635
Brigham, Asa, Lamar Admin, 636

Brigham, Asa, Houston 2nd Admin, 637
Brigham, B. R., S. Jacinto Army, 562
Brigham, B., S. Jacinto Army, 566
Brigham, M. W., S. Jacinto Army, 565
Bright, David, Old 300, 557
Bright, John, Fannin Massacre, 571
Brill, Solomon, Veteran, 589
Bringhurst, George H., Veteran, 587
Brisco, Andrew, Pioneers killed, 581
Briscoe, Andrew, 58
BRISCOE, ANDREW, 287
Briscoe, Andrew, S. Jacinto Army, 564
Briscoe, Andrew, Convention, 634
Brister, Adjutant, 220
Brister, Nathaniel R., Fannin Massacre,
    574
Brittan, Forbes, Pioneers killed, 583
BRITTON, FORBES, SPEECH, 1857,
    336
Brockfield, F., S. Jacinto Army, 566
Brooks, A. M., Veteran, 622
Brooks, Bluford, Old 300, 557
Brooks, Daniel B., Fannin Massacre, 571
Brooks, George W., Veteran, 588, 589
Brooks, Gilbert, 587
Brooks, J. S., Fannin Massacre, 570
Brooks, Thomas D., S. Jacinto Army, 567
Brooks, Thomas D., Tx Necrology, 579
Brooks, Z. S., Fannin Massacre, 573
Brotherton, Robert, Old 300, 557
Brown, 113
Brown County, 596
Brown County, minerals, 445
Brown, — (Goliad), 206
Brown, Capt. L., 77
Brown, Col. R. R., 82
Brown, D., S. Jacinto Army, 569
Brown, Edward, Veteran, 621
Brown, G., S. Jacinto Army, 564
Brown, George, Old 300, 557
Brown, George W., DA's, 638
Brown, Gern E., S. Jacinto Army, 565
BROWN, HENRY S., 282
Brown, Henry S., Pioneers killed, 580
Brown, J. S., Fannin Massacre, 571
Brown, John B., Veteran, 621
Brown, John H., Veteran, 621

Brown, John Henry, 188
Brown, John Henry, Veteran, 622
Brown, John W., Pioneers killed, 582
Brown, John, Old 300, 557
Brown, O. T., S. Jacinto Army, 565
Brown, Oliver, Fannin Massacre, 572
Brown, Reuben R., Veteran, 588
Brown, Richard, Veteran, 622
Brown, S. T., Fannin Massacre, 571
Brown, Samuel T., 242
Brown, W. A., Veteran, 622
Brown, W. B., S. Jacinto Army, 569
Brown, William S., Old 300, 557
Brown, William A. J., Fannin Massacre, 571
Brown, William S., 64
Brown, William S., Fannin Massacre, 573
Brown, Wilson C., S. Jacinto Army, 564
Browning, George W., Veteran, 587, 589
Browning, Prvt., S. Jacinto Army, 564
Browning, W. W., Pioneers killed, 584
Brownsville, 487, 596
Bruce, William M., Veteran, 621
Bruce, Willis, Veteran, 587
Bruff, Prvt., S. Jacinto Army, 564
Brush, E., 65
Brush, S. B., Pioneers killed, 585
Brushy Creek, 127, 143
Brutus, vessel, 77, 601
Bryan, 597, 603
Bryan, City of, 591, 609, 618, 624
Bryan, Guy M., 89, 116
BRYAN, GUY M., SPEECH OF, 1873, 181
Bryan, Guy M., Veteran, 588
Bryan, John, Veteran, 587
Bryan, M. A., S. Jacinto Army, 566
Bryan, Morgan, 65
Bryan, Moses Austin, 172
Bryan, Moses Austin, Veteran, 587
Bryan, Moses Austin, Lamar Admin, 636
Bryan, William J., Veteran, 588
Bryant, Luke, S. Jacinto Army, 567
Bryson, John M., Fannin Massacre, 571
Buchanan County, geology, 492
Buchanan, David, 35
Buchel, August, Pioneers killed, 584

Buchman, J., Sr., Veteran, 620
Buckhorn, 590, 596
Buckley, C. W., Pioneers killed, 584
Buckley, Daniel, Fannin Massacre, 573
Buckley, Lyre, Veteran, 588
Buckner, Oliver, Pioneers killed, 582
Bucknor, Aylett C., Old 300, 557
Buffalo, 21, 474
Buffalo Bayou, 25, 59, 193
Buffington, A., 587
Buffington, A., S. Jacinto Army, 569
Bullard, Charles A., Pioneers killed, 582
Bulliner, E., S. Jacinto Army, 567
Bulliner, P., S. Jacinto Army, 567
Bullion, M. D., 443
Bullock, Mr., 315
Bullock, U. J., Fannin Massacre, 571
Bunson, Enoch, Old 300, 557
Bunton, DeSha, Veteran, 622
Bunton, John W., 58, 206
Bunton, John W., S. Jacinto Army, 565
Bunton, John W., Veteran, 588
Bunton, John W., Convention, 634
Buquar, P. L., Veteran, 622
Burbank, Capt. Sidney, 160
Burbridge, Thomas, Fannin Massacre, 573
Burch, James, S. Jacinto Army, 569
Burch, R., S. Jacinto Army, 569
Burdett, William B., Veteran, 589
Burk, David N., Veteran, 589
Burke, David N., Fannin Massacre, 573
Burkham, James, Veteran, 589
Burksville, 603
Burleson, 652, 653
Burleson County, 591, 601, 602, 607, 613, 631
Burleson Springs, 21
Burleson, A., Veteran, 588
Burleson, Aaron, S. Jacinto Army, 566
Burleson, Edward, 23, 86, 92, 133, 157, 204, 620, 630
BURLESON, EDWARD, 268
Burleson, Edward, S. Jacinto Army, 565
Burleson, Edward, Pioneers killed, 582
Burleson, Edward, Convention, 635
Burleson, Edward, Houston 2nd Admin, 637

Burleson, John, Tx Necrology, 579
Burleson, Jonathan, Veteran, 587
Burleson, Joseph, Veteran, 588
Burleson, Lt. Col., 651
Burleson, Ned, 205
Burnam's, 193
Burnell, 113
Burnet, 624
Burnet County, 591, 592, 597, 599, 606, 624, 625, 628, 632
Burnet County, geology, 493
Burnet County, minerals, 21, 445
BURNET ORATION AT WHARTON'S FUNERAL, 315
Burnet Proclamation, March 18, 1836, 213
BURNET PROCLAMATION TO PEOPLE, 1836, 332
Burnet, David G., 190, 212, 441
BURNET, DAVID G., 257
BURNET, DAVID G., ANECDOTE, 1829, 310
BURNET, DAVID G., CHARACTER OF, 441
Burnet, David G., Tx Necrology, 579
Burnet, David G., Pioneers killed, 584
Burnet, David G., Convention, 635
Burnet, David G., Lamar Admin, 636
Burnet, Pumphrey, Old 300, 557
Burnet, Thomas, Old 300, 557
Burnett, David G., 23
Burnham, Jesse, Old 300, 557
Burnham, Jesse, Veteran, 589
Burnham, Jesse, Gen. Consultation, 633
Burnham, Jesse, Prov. Govt., 634
Burnley, A. T., Lamar Admin, 637
Burns Station, 603
Burns, Aaron, Pioneers killed, 585
Burnum, Doc., 185
Buroughs, W. M., Veteran, 621
BURR, AARON, 318
Burr, Robert, Houston 1st Admin, 636
Burroughs, G. H., Veteran, 589
Burroughs, George H. Capt., 166
Burt, James Ross, Veteran, 622
Burt, P., S. Jacinto Army, 565
Burton, 587, 621, 628

Burton, Isaac W., 118
Burton, Stephen J., Veteran, 588
Burton, William, Pioneers killed, 581
Burts, B. F., Fannin Massacre, 573
Bush, Gabriel, Fannin Massacre, 572
Bust, Luke W., S. Jacinto Army, 565
Bustamente, 102, 189
Buster, Claudius, Veteran, 621
Bustilla, Clement, Veteran, 590
Butler, 113
Butler, Bennett, Fannin Massacre, 572
Butler, Moses, Fannin Massacre, 571
Butler, William S., Fannin Massacre, 571
Buttle, Mills M., Old 300, 558
Butts, A. G., S. Jacinto Army, 566
Byerly, Adam, Veteran, 589
Byerly, William, Veteran, 588
Bynum, A., Fannin Massacre, 570
Bynum, J. S. D., Pioneers killed, 581
Byrant, B., S. Jacinto Army, 568
Byrd, James, S. Jacinto Army, 566
Byrd, Micajah, Old 300, 557
Byrn, Rezin, Veteran, 589
Byrne, James, Veteran, 589
Byrne, Matthew, Fannin Massacre, 573
Byrne, William, DA's, 639
Byrom, J. S. D., 58
Byrom, J. S. D., Gen. Consultation, 633
Byrom, J. S. D., Convention, 634

C

Cabler, E. S., Veteran, 623
Caddell, —, S. Jacinto Army, 569
Caddoe Indians, 35, 132, 231
Cadle, Joseph, 65
Cage, B. F., S. Jacinto Army, 568
Cain, J. W., Fannin Massacre, 573
Calder, Judge, 197
Calder, R. J., S. Jacinto Army, 566
Calder, Robert J., Veteran, 590
Caldwell, 591, 601, 602, 607, 613, 631, 651
Caldwell, Colonel, 125
Caldwell County, geology, 490
Caldwell County, 612, 626
Caldwell, James P., Pioneers killed, 583

Caldwell, John, 216
CALDWELL, JOHN, 292
Caldwell, John, Pioneers killed, 584
Caldwell, John, Portrait, 630
CALDWELL, MATHEW, 292
Caldwell, Mathew, Pioneers killed, 581
Caldwell, Mathew, Convention, 634
Caldwell, Pinkey, S. Jacinto Army, 565
Calhoun County, 589, 592, 608, 624
Call, James, S. Jacinto Army, 567
Callagham, J. H., Fannin Massacre, 571
Callahan County, minerals, 445
Callahan, James H., Pioneers killed, 583
Callahan, Morris, Old 300, 558
Callahan, Prvt., S. Jacinto Army, 564
Callahan, Thomas J., Veteran, 590
Callender, Sidney S., Veteran, 592
Callicoatte, John B., Veteran, 592
Callison, J. H., Fannin Massacre, 570
Calvert's Labor, 32
Calvert, James H., Veteran, 623
Calvert, Joseph F., Pioneers killed, 585
Calvit, Alexander, Old 300, 558
Calvit, Joseph F., Tx Necrology, 579
Camergo, 172
Cameron, 597
Cameron County, 596
Cameron, Capt., 129
Cameron, Dr., at Bexar, 223
Cameron, Ewin, Pioneers killed, 581
Cameron, John, Pioneers killed, 583
Camp Colorado, 492
Camp Concepcion, 647
Camp Los Ojuelos, 157
CAMPAIGN OF 1835, 67
Campbell, —, S. Jacinto Army, 563
Campbell, D. W., Veteran, 590
Campbell, David, 141
Campbell, Don, Pioneers killed, 584
Campbell, J., 118
Campbell, J., S. Jacinto Army, 568
Campbell, Jim, Pioneers killed, 583
Campbell, John, Veteran, 591
Campbell, Michael, Veteran, 592
Campbell, Rufus E., Veteran, 591
Campeachy, 356
Canadian River, 469

Candacho Indians, 233
Cane, J., 113
Caney, 593, 603
Cannibalism, 145
Cannon, J. W., S. Jacinto Army, 567
Cannon, William J., Veteran, 591
Canton, 596
Capell, J. B., Veteran, 592
Capital of the Republic, 118
Capitol at Austin, Illus., 120
Captivities, Indian, various, 201-202
Carbajal, Manuel, 64
Carbajal, Manuel, Fannin Massacre, 570
Careron County, 607
Carey, Seth, Veteran, 591
Carlisle, G. W., Fannin Massacre, 572
Carlisle, Robert, Veteran, 592
Carlson, William S., Fannin Massacre, 570
Carnel, Patrick, S. Jacinto Army, 567
Carnes Cavalry Company, 98
Carnes, Col., Goliad, 249
Carnes, Henry, 221
Carnes, Henry, S. Jacinto Army, 563
Carpenter, David, Old 300, 558
Carpenter, J. W., S. Jacinto Army, 567
Carpenter, John, S. Jacinto Army, 564
Carper, W. M., S. Jacinto Army, 565
Carr, Jem, 158
Carravahal, Jose Maria, Pioneers killed, 585
Carriere, C. J., Fannin Massacre, 570
Carrington, D. C., Veteran, 623
Carrol, Michael, Fannin Massacre, 571
Carson, Samuel, 59
CARSON, SAMUEL P., 276
Carson, Samuel P., Pioneers killed, 581
Carson, Samuel P., Convention, 635
Carson, William C., Old 300, 558
Carter, J., S. Jacinto Army, 566
Carter, R. W., S. Jacinto Army, 565
Carter, Samuel, Old 300, 558
Cartmel, Thomas P., Pioneers killed, 583
Cartmell, H. R., Pioneers killed, 584
Cartwright, Jesse, Old 300, 558
Cartwright, M., Veteran, 591
Cartwright, Matthew, Pioneers killed, 584
Cartwright, Thomas, Old 300, 558

Cartwright, W., S. Jacinto Army, 567
Caruthers, A., S. Jacinto Army, 567
Caruthers, Ewing, Fannin Massacre, 572
Caruthers, William, Veteran, 591
Carvier, Matrias, Veteran, 592
Cary, 113
Cash Creek, 620
Cash, —, Fannin Massacre, 574
Cash, Geo. W., 65
Cash, J. L., 129
Cass, J. M., Fannin Massacre, 570
Cassady, Prvt., S. Jacinto Army, 564
Cassillas, Matea, Veteran, 592
Cassillas, Pablo, Veteran, 592
Castleman, Sylvanus, Old 300, 558
Castrillo, General, 108
CASTRO, HENRY, 286
Cathedral at Mexico, illus., 500
Catlett, W. F., Houston 1st Admin, 636
Cattle Industry, early, 21
Cattle Region, 448
Cave, E. W., 535
Cayce, Henry P., Veteran, 591
Cayce, Shadrack, Veteran, 592
Cayuga, 610
Cedar Bayou, 587, 591
Cedar Creek, 491
Central Military Despotism, 83
Central Texan Paper, 334
Centre, 610
Cepton, Cyrus, S. Jacinto Army, 568
Chacon, Carlos, Veteran, 592
Chacta Indians, 233
Chadowin, Thomas, 30
Chaffin, J. A., S. Jacinto Army, 569
Chaffin, James A., Veteran, 591
Chalk, Whitfield, Veteran, 623
Chalmers, John G., Pioneers killed, 582
Chalmers, John G., Lamar Admin, 636
Chamberlain, Willard, Veteran, 592
Chambers Creek, 313, 599, 612
Chambers, George W., Veteran, 623
Chambers, Thomas J., 190, 521
CHAMBERS, THOMAS J., 276
Chambers, Thomas J., Pioneers killed, 584
Chambliss, S. L., Veteran, 590
Champion, vessel, 77

Chance, Samuel, Old 300, 560
Chandler, Capt., 142
Chapman, George W., Veteran, 591
Chappell Hill, 487, 586, 600, 608, 616,
  627
Character of People of Texas, 459
CHARACTERISTICS OF TEXAS, 447
Charencan, M., S. Jacinto Army, 567
Charleston, vessel, 79
Chatham, Thomas, Veteran, 622
Chattam, Tom, Veteran, 590
Cherino, 609
Cherokee County, 588, 591, 602, 604,
  611, 616, 630
Cherokees vs. Wacoes, 237
Cherry, Wilbur, Tx Necrology, 579
Chesher, James, Tx Necrology, 579
Cheshire, Capt., at Bexar, 219
Chevalie, M. M., Pioneers killed, 582
Chevis, John, S. Jacinto Army, 568
Chew, John, Fannin Massacre, 573
CHIEF CLERK OF THE HOUSE,
  REPUBLIC, 639
Child of the Alamo, 117
Childress, B. F., Veteran, 590
Childress, George C., 58
CHILDRESS, GEORGE C., 289
Childress, George C., Pioneers killed, 581
Childress, George C., Convention, 635
Childress, Pleasant, Pioneers killed, 585
Childress, Robert, Veteran, 592
Childs, J. J., S. Jacinto Army, 568
Chireno, 588
Chisem, E. P. G., Fannin Massacre, 570
Chisholm, Enoch P., Veteran, 592
Chism, J. E., Veteran, 623
Chissum, J., Veteran, 590
Choat, David, S. Jacinto Army, 567
Choate, David, Veteran, 591
Choderick, R. T., S. Jacinto Army, 568
Cholera, 1833, 52
Cholwell, Gustavus, 65
Chriesman, Capt. Horatio, 197
Chriesman, Horatio, Veteran, 590
Chriesman, Horatio, Old 300, 558
Christie, Prvt., S. Jacinto Army, 564
Christmas Frolic, 1841, 122

Christy, William, 307
Churchill, Thomas S., Fannin Massacre, 570
Cincinnati, 70
Circleville, 606
Civil Regulations, Austin's Colony, 175
Clare, Abram, Pioneers killed, 584
CLARK, EDWARD, 294
Clark, George Wilson, 623
Clark, Henry, Veteran, 591
Clark, J. H., Fannin Massacre, 572
Clark, Seth, Fannin Massacre, 573
Clark, Stephen, 129
Clark, W., Jr., 58
Clark, William, Jr., Convention, 634
Clarke, Anthony R., Old 300, 558
Clarke, Charles A., S. Jacinto Army, 564
Clarke, J., 113
Clarke, James, S. Jacinto Army, 568
Clarke, John C., Old 300, 558
Clarke, John, S. Jacinto Army, 568
Clarkson, Prvt., S. Jacinto Army, 564
Clarksville, 593, 598, 603, 604
Clary, Francis M., Veteran, 623
Clary, Jesse, Veteran, 590
Clayton, —, S. Jacinto Army, 563
Clayton, Joseph A., Tx Necrology, 579
Clear Creek, 590
Cleburne, 590, 599, 602, 612, 614, 615, 626, 628
Clelens, Joshua, S. Jacinto Army, 569
Clements, J. D., Gen. Consultation, 633
Clements, J. D., Prov. Govt., 634
Clemins, Lewis, S. Jacinto Army, 567
Clemons, Lewis C., Veteran, 590
Clennon, —, Fannin Massacre, 572
Cleveland, —, S. Jacinto Army, 565
Cleveland, J. A. H., Veteran, 591
Climate, 22, 366
Climate, Panhandle, 473
Climatic Divisions, 502
CLIMATOLOGY OF TEXAS, 502
Clinton, 588, 593, 603, 616, 622
Clinton, Veteran, 613
Clopper, —, S. Jacinto Army, 564
Clopton, William A., Veteran, 623
Cloud, 113

Coal, 445
COAL BEDS OF TEXAS, 498
Coal in Texas, 494
Coats, Merit M., Old 300, 558
Cobb, David, 142
Cobble, A., S. Jacinto Army, 568
Cochatethca Comanches, 134
Cochran, Thomas, Veteran, 590
Cocke, James H., Pioneers killed, 582
Cocke, Maj. J. D., 129
Cockran, 113
Cockrill, Simon, Veteran, 592
Coe, J. G., Fannin Massacre, 573
Coe, Philip, Gen. Consultation, 633
Coe, Philip, Prov. Govt., 634
Coffin, A. G., Veteran, 592
Coffman, E. G., S. Jacinto Army, 568
COKE, RICHARD, 297
Coker, John, 98
Coldwell, M., 58
Cole, David, Pioneers killed, 584
Cole, David, S. Jacinto Army, 567
Cole, James, Tx Necrology, 579
Cole, William H., Fannin Massacre, 570
Coleman County, minerals, 445
Coleman, Capt., at Bexar, 219
Coleman, J., Fannin Massacre, 570
Coleman, Jacob, Fannin Massacre, 573
Coleman, R. M., 58
Coleman, R. M., S. Jacinto Army, 563
Coleman, Robert H., Pioneers killed, 581
Coleman, Robert M., Convention, 634–635
Coleman, Young, Veteran, 592
Coles, 25
Coles, B., S. Jacinto Army, 564
Coles, Elleanor, Pioneers killed, 582
Coles, John P., Old 300, 558
Coles, John P., Pioneers killed, 582
Coliant, J. B., S. Jacinto Army, 568
Collard, Elijah, Gen. Consultation, 633
Collard, Elijah, Prov. Govt., 634
Collard, J. H., Veteran, 590
Collard, J. S., Veteran, 590
Collard, Job S., S. Jacinto Army, 567
Collard, L. M., Veteran, 592
Collin County, 312, 614

Collingsworth, James, 58, 93, 149
COLLINGSWORTH, JAMES, 278
Collingsworth, James, Convention, 634, 635
Collins, Bela, Veteran, 590
Collins, Robert, 160
Collins, Willis, S. Jacinto Army, 563
Collinsworth, James, S. Jacinto Army, 563
Collinsworth, James, Pioneers killed, 581
Colonists, First Texas, 185
Colonization, Early Matters, 202
Colorado, 634
Colorado County, 579, 585, 586, 587, 590, 593, 599, 605, 606, 614, 599, 605, 606, 614, 617, 618, 630
Colorado River, 22, 88, 118, 145, 153, 163, 185, 248, 359, 360, 472
COLORADO RIVER FLOODS, 327
Colorado River, Headwaters, 466
Colorado, brig, 79
Colquhoun, Ludovic, Veteran, 622
Colt Firearms, 158
Colton, Prvt., S. Jacinto Army, 564
Columbia, 21, 73, 119, 586, 594, 615, 616, 629, 633
Columbus, 224, 585, 590, 593, 599, 617, 618
Columbus, Schooner, 244
Comal County, 604
Comanche County, 596
Comanche Creek, 489
COMANCHE FIGHT AT SAN ANTO- NIO, 154
Comanche Indians, 35, 134, 158, 233
Comanche Mountain, 489
Come and Take It, 84
Commissary-General of the Army, 1835, 197
Committee of Safety, 1835, 191, 524
Committee of Safety and Corres., 643
Committee of Vigilance, 644
Comstock, William, Fannin Massacre, 572
Conard, Cullen, Fannin Massacre, 572
Concepcion, 601, 652, 653
CONCEPCION, BATTLE OF, 65
Conception Battle, 93, 149
Conception Mission, 228

Concho River, 465
Concho River, Flood, 308
Concrete, 600
Condition of Texas, early, 76
Coney, Thomas F., S. Jacinto Army, 568
Congress Ave., 354
Conley, Preston, Tx Necrology, 579
Conly, Preston, S. Jacinto Army, 565
Conn, J. S., S. Jacinto Army, 564
Connell, Sampson, S. Jacinto Army, 565
Conner, J., S. Jacinto Army, 566
Conner, S., S. Jacinto Army, 566
Conrad, E., 58
Conrad, Edward, Convention, 635
Constitution of State of Texas, 534
Constitution Convention, 189
Constitution of the Republic, 59, 528
Constitution of 1869, 537
Constitutional Advocate, The, 52
CONSTITUTIONAL GOVERNMENT IN TEXAS, 515
Consultation at San Felipe, Nov. 3, 1835, 192
Contis, Julian, Veteran, 592
CONVENTION OF TEXAS, 634
Cook, J. R., S. Jacinto Army, 563
Cook, Lewis P., 118
Cook, Lewis P., Pioneers killed, 582
Cook, William G., Pioneers killed, 582
Cook, William G., 622
Cooke, Capt., at Bexar, 220
Cooke, Col. W. G., 154
Cooke, F. S., S. Jacinto Army, 566
Cooke, Frank J., Veteran, 591
Cooke, James, Old 300, 558
Cooke, John, Old 300, 558
Cooke, Louis P., Lamar Admin, 636
Cooke, T., Fannin Massacre, 570
Cooke, T., S. Jacinto Army, 566
Cooke, W. G., 127
Cooke, William G., 204
Cooke, William G., S. Jacinto Army, 563
Cooke, William G., Houston 1st Admin, 636
Cooke, William G., Jones Admin, 637
Cooley, Solomon, 233
Cooper, — (Fannin), 206

Cooper, D., Fannin Massacre, 573
Cooper, Dillard, Veteran, 590
Cooper, J., S. Jacinto Army, 562
Cooper, William, Old 300, 558, 559
Cooshatta Indians, 227
Copano, 588
Copano, Port, 160, 244
Copeland, George, Veteran, 591
Copino, 656
Copper, 442
Copper in Texas, 495
Corasco, Colonel, 125
Corbys, Thomas H., Fannin Massacre, 571
Coriell, James, 35
Cormana, Cecario, S. Jacinto Army, 569
Corn, 450
Corpus Christi, 498, 596, 610, 625
Corre, Colonel, 172
Corsicana, 590, 623
Corsine, H., S. Jacinto Army, 569
Coryell County, 589, 590, 595, 597
Corzine, Shelby, Pioneers killed, 581
Corzine, Shelby, Judges, 638
Cos, General, 37, 92, 192, 635, 648, 649, 654
COS, SURRENDER OF GENERAL, 218
Coshatties, 132
Cottle, G. W., 113
Cotton, 21, 449
Cotton Gin, 599
Council of War, 649, 650
Courtman, G. F., Fannin Massacre, 573
Courtney, 487, 609, 618, 623, 630
Covington, Charles, Veteran, 591
Cowan, W. J., Fannin Massacre, 572
Cowan, W. N., 129
Cox, Harvey, Fannin Massacre, 573
Cox, John H., Veteran, 622
Cox, Lewis, S. Jacinto Army, 567
Cox, Thomas, S. Jacinto Army, 568
Coy, Alexander, Veteran, 590
Cozart, —, Fannin Massacre, 570
Craddick, John, S. Jacinto Army, 567
Craddock, John R., Veteran, 590
Craft, James A., S. Jacinto Army, 565
Craft, Russell B., S. Jacinto Army, 565
Craig, Harry C., S. Jacinto Army, 564
Crain, J. B., Veteran, 591

Crain, R. T., Veteran, 591
Crane, Capt., at Bexar, 220
Crane, Joel, S. Jacinto Army, 569
Crane, R. T., S. Jacinto Army, 569
Cravens, R. M., S. Jacinto Army, 566
Crawford, A. C., Veteran, 623
Crawford, George W., Pioneers killed, 584
Crawford, Jacob, Veteran, 623
Crawford, R., S. Jacinto Army, 566
Crawford, Robert, Veteran, 591
Crawford, S., 113
Crawford, William C., 58
Crawford, William C., Convention, 635
Crawner, A., Veteran, 591
Creeks in Wichita County, 462
Creeks in Wilbarger County, 462
Crier, John, Old 300, 558
Criminal Regulations, Austin's Colony, 177
Crisswell, William, S. Jacinto Army, 565
Crist, Daniel, Veteran, 591
Criswell, John Y., Veteran, 622
Crittenden, George B., Veteran, 623
Crittenden, R., S. Jacinto Army, 565
Crittenden, William, Veteran, 590
Croce, Colonel, 59
Crockett, 587, 597, 599, 628
CROCKETT, DAVID, 262
Crockett, David, illus., 419
Crockett, David, 579
Crockett, David, Pioneers killed, 580
Crosby, G., S. Jacinto Army, 568
Crosby, Josiah J., Pioneers killed, 582
Cross Timbers, 134, 600
Cross, John, Fannin Massacre, 573
Crossan, R., 113
Crownover, John, Old 300, 558
Cruger, J. W., Pioneers killed, 584
Crunk, Nicholas, S. Jacinto Army, 567
Cruse, Squire, Veteran, 591
Cueves, Antonio, S. Jacinto Army, 569
Cullen, E. W., Veteran, 592
Cullen, Ezekiel W., Judges, 638
Cumberland, —, S. Jacinto Army, 563
Cumbo, James, S. Jacinto Army, 565
Cumming, George Washington, Fannin Massacre, 571
Cummins, James, Old 300, 558

Cummins, John, Old 300, 558
Cummins, Rebecca, Old 300, 558
Cummins, William, Old 300, 558
Cunningham, A. S., Pioneers killed, 582
Cunningham, John D., Fannin Massacre, 573
Cunningham, L. S., S. Jacinto Army, 565
Cunningham, L. C., Veteran, 590
Cunningham, R., 113
CURRENCY DURING THE CIVIL WAR, 344
CURRENCY PLAY, 348
Curtis, Hinton, Old 300, 558
Curtis, Hinton, S. Jacinto Army, 568
Curtis, James, Sr., Old 300, 558
Curtis, James, Old 300, 558
Curtis, James, S. Jacinto Army, 566
Curvis, Maticio, S. Jacinto Army, 569
Curz, Antonio, S. Jacinto Army, 569
Cushney, Wm. M., Pioneers killed, 582
Cypress, 487

D

Daily Bulletin, 122
Daingerfield, William Henry, 216
Daist, Edward, S. Jacinto Army, 568
Daist, R. B., S. Jacinto Army, 568
Dale, Elijah V., S. Jacinto Army, 565
Dale, Elijah V., Veteran, 594
Dale, J. B., 64
Daling, S., S. Jacinto Army, 568
Dallas, 622
Dallas County, 592, 622, 629, 632
Dallas, James L., Veteran, 595
Dallas, W. K., S. Jacinto Army, 567
Dalrymple, Prvt., S. Jacinto Army, 564
Daman, Samuel, Veteran, 594
Dancy, John M., Pioneers killed, 584
Dangerfield, William Henry, Lamar Admin, 636
Dangerfield, William Henry, Houston 2nd Admin, 637
Daniel, G. W., Fannin Massacre, 570
Danlin, William, 233
Darden, Stephen H., Veteran, 594
Darnell, N. H., Veteran, 623
Darnell, N. H., Speakers, 639

Darrel, Prvt., S. Jacinto Army, 564
Dart, schooner, 218
Dasher, Thomas, Fannin Massacre, 574
Davell, L., 113
Davidson, —, S. Jacinto Army, 563
Davidson, R. T., Fannin Massacre, 573
Davidson, Samuel, Old 300, 558
Davie, Tom P., Veteran, 593
Davilla, 590
Davis County, geology, 490
Davis, Abner C., S. Jacinto Army, 565
Davis, Cooper T., S. Jacinto Army, 568
Davis, Daniel, Veteran, 623
DAVIS, EDMUND J., 296
Davis, F., Fannin Massacre, 570
Davis, G. L., Fannin Massacre, 573
Davis, G. W., S. Jacinto Army, 566
Davis, George W., Veteran, 593
Davis, George W., Gen. Consultation, 633
Davis, H. F., 65
Davis, J. K., S. Jacinto Army, 568
Davis, J. P., S. Jacinto Army, 564
Davis, Jackson, Fannin Massacre, 570
Davis, John, Veteran, 592
Davis, Moses, S. Jacinto Army, 567
Davis, Perry, Fannin Massacre, 572
Davis, Samuel, S. Jacinto Army, 566
Davis, Thomas, Old 300, 559
Davis, W. H., S. Jacinto Army, 569
Davis, Walter, W., Fannin Massacre, 571
Davis, William K., Veteran, 623
Davy, Thomas, S. Jacinto Army, 565
Dawess, Isaac, Veteran, 592
Dawnman, H. M., Fannin Massacre, 570
DAWSON AND SIMS, 354
DAWSON'S DEFEAT, 124
DAWSON, FRED, 312
Dawson, Frederick, 79, 354
Dawson, Nicholas, 124
Dawson, Nicholas, S. Jacinto Army, 564
Dawson, Nicholas, Pioneers killed, 581
Dawson, Sarah R., 334
Day, —, S. Jacinto Army, 565
Day, H. B., Fannin Massacre, 573
Day, J. C., 113
Day, Jeremiah, 64
De Bard, E. J., Veteran, 593
De Grijalvo, Jean

De la Garza, Antonio, 220, 646
De la Garza, Antonio, Pioneers killed, 582
De la Garza, Refugio, 234
De Lemos, Manuel Gayoso, 229
De Leon, Ferdinand, Pioneers killed, 582
De Leon, Martin, Pioneers killed, 580
de Leon, Martin, 585
De Madero, Francisco, 187
DE MORSE, CHARLES, SPEECH OF 1874, 204
De Morse, Charles, Lamar Admin, 636
De Nava, Pedro, 229
DE SALIGNY, M., 310
De Saligny, M., 315
De Soto, Father Jose, 18
De Vare, Cornelius, Veteran, 593
De Zavala, Lorenzo, 23, 191
De Zavala, Lorenzo, Pioneers killed, 580
De Zavala, Lorenzo, Gen. Consultation, 633
De Zavala, Lorenzo, Convention, 634
De Zavala, Lorenzo, Convention, 635
DE ZAVALLA, LORENZO, 259
Deaderick, G., S. Jacinto Army, 564
Deadrick, Fielding, Veteran, 594
DEAF SMITH, 278
Deaf Smith's Company, 98
Dean, Alexander, Veteran, 624
Dean, Calloway, Veteran, 593
Dearduff, W., 113
De Bard, E. J., Veteran, 594
Deckro, Daniel, Old 300, 559
Declaration of Independence, 23, 635
DECLARATION OF INDEPEN-DENCE, 1836, 53
DECLARATION OF NOV. 1835, 60
DECLARATION OF DEC. 20, 1835, 61
Decree at Saltillo, Oct. 15, 1827, 202
Decree of October 3, 1835
Decrees of Coahuila, 585
Dederick, Joel, S. Jacinto Army, 568
Dedrick, —, Fannin Massacre, 570
Dedrick, D., S. Jacinto Army, 566
Deffenbaugh, A., Veteran, 593
Deffenbaugh, Anthony, 168
Dehesa, 86
DeLeon, Alonzo, 17

Deleplain, A. C., Veteran, 594
Delevan Creek, 465
Dembrinske, N., Fannin Massacre, 572
De Morse, Charles, Veteran, 593
Demos, Charles, Old 300, 558
Demos, Peter, Old 300, 558
Denham, W. K., S. Jacinto Army, 566
Denmon, Holden, S. Jacinto Army, 568
Dennis, Joseph, Fannin Massacre, 571
Dennis, T. M., S. Jacinto Army, 565
Dennis, T. Mason, 65
Dennis, Thomas M., Veteran, 594
Dennis, Tom, 205
Denton County, 605, 625
Denton, John B., Pioneers killed, 581
Dequello, 110
Deritt, James, S. Jacinto Army, 567
Despalier, C., 65, 113
Devault, 113
Dever, Thomas, Veteran, 594
Dever, William, Pioneers killed, 584
Devereau, Andrew, 64
Devois, Cornelius, S. Jacinto Army, 567
Dewees, Bluford, Old 300, 558
Dewees, William B., Veteran, 593
DeWitt County, 588, 593, 598, 600, 602, 603, 616, 620, 622, 626
DeWitt's Colony, 291
DeWitt, C. C., 594
Dexter, Peter B., 23, 633, 634
Dexter, Peter B., Veteran, 594
Dexter, Peter B., Prov. Govt., 634
Dexter, Samuel, 157, 169
Diaz, Francisco, Veteran, 595
Dibble, H., S. Jacinto Army, 566
Dickens, J., 113
Dickenson, 651
Dickenson, Almiram, 116
Dickenson, John, Old 300, 558
Dickenson, Lieutenant, 111
Dickerson, W., Fannin Massacre, 570
Dickinson, Mrs., 151
Dickinson, Noah, Fannin Massacre, 570
Dickson, A., Fannin Massacre, 573
Dickson, David H., Veteran, 594
Dikes, M. W., Veteran, 594
Dillard, A., S. Jacinto Army, 567

Dillard, J., 113
Dillard, Nicholas, Old 300, 558
Dimit, 656
Dimitt, 654
Dimmit's Landing, 162
Dimmitt, Philip, 65
DIMMITT, PHILIP, 279
Dimmitt, Philip, Pioneers killed, 581
DIPLOMACY, A PIG MEDDLES IN, 315
DISTRICT ATTORNEYS, REPUBLIC, 638
DISTRICT COURT JUDGES, REPUBLIC, 638
Dix, John, Pioneers killed, 584
Dixon, Henry, Fannin Massacre, 572
Dixon, J. W. T., S. Jacinto Army, 564
Dodson, A. B., Veteran, 595
Dolores Mission, 17
Don Onis, 19
Donohoo, John, Fannin Massacre, 570
Dooley, Spirse, 65
Doolittle, B., S. Jacinto Army, 567
Doom, R. C., Veteran, 593
Doren, Jno., Veteran, 594
Dorsett, Theodore J., Veteran, 623
Dorsey, Alfred, Fannin Massacre, 573
Douane, Joseph, S. Jacinto Army, 565
Double Mountains, 465
Doubt, Daniel, S. Jacinto Army, 567
Douglas, Henry L., Fannin Massacre, 574
Douglas, W. C., Fannin Massacre, 573
Douglass, Freeman, Veteran, 593
Douthatt, James, S. Jacinto Army, 564
Doyal, M. A., Veteran, 594
Doyle, Mathew, 35
Dresden, 590, 632
Driscoll, David O., S. Jacinto Army, 564
Dry Region of West Texas, 503
Dubose, William P. B., Fannin Massacre, 572
Duffau, W. T., Tx Necrology, 579
Duffee, William, S. Jacinto Army, 567
Duffield, —, Fannin Massacre, 574
Dugah, J. L., Veteran, 594
Duke, Thomas, Old 300, 558
Duke, Tomas M., 561

Dunbar, William, S. Jacinto Army, 564
Dunbar, William, Veteran, 593
Duncan's Ferry, 29
Duncan, — (Goliad), 205
Duncan, Capt. John, 73, 373
Duncan, Capt., at Bexar, 220
Duncan, Charles R., Veteran, 594
Duncan, J. W., Fannin Massacre, 573
Duncan, Jacob, S. Jacinto Army, 564
Duncan, James, 65
Duncan, John, S. Jacinto Army, 566
Duncan, John, Veteran, 593
Dunham, D. T., S. Jacinto Army, 563
Dunham, D., S. Jacinto Army, 566
Dunham, James H., Veteran, 623
Dunham, Maj. R. H., 129
Dunlap, Richard G., Lamar Admin, 636
Dunlavy, Alexander, Veteran, 593
Dunlavy, W. T., Tx Necrology, 579
Dunlop, Richard G., Pioneers killed, 581
Dunman's, 27
Dunman, James T., 593
Dunn, John, 64
Dunnettell, Henry, Veteran, 594
Duplex, J. B., Veteran, 594
Durrain, E., Fannin Massacre, 572
Durst, E. H., Veteran, 594
Durst, James H., Pioneers killed, 583
Durst, John, Pioneers killed, 582
Dusanque, —, Fannin Massacre, 574
Dusenbury, John E., Veteran, 623
Dust, J., 113
Dutcher, Prvt., S. Jacinto Army, 564
Duty, George, Old 300, 558
Duty, John, Pioneers killed, 583
Duty, Joseph, Old 300, 558
Duty, William, Veteran, 593
Duval and Pig, illus., 371
Duval, B. H., Fannin Massacre, 570
DUVAL, JOHN C., ADVENTURES OF A YOUNG MAN, 368
Duval, John C., Fannin Massacre, 570
Duval, John C., Veteran, 593
Dwenny, N. J., Fannin Massacre, 573
Dwight, J. E., 201
Dyer, Clement C., Old 300, 558
Dyer, Clement C., Gen. Consultation, 633

Dyer, George, Fannin Massacre, 570
Dyer, Leon, Veteran, 594
Dykes, L. P., Veteran, 593
Dykes, Q., S. Jacinto Army, 567

E

Earl, William, Veteran, 595
Earle, Thomas, Old 300, 558
Earle, William, S. Jacinto Army, 568
East Texas Iron Ores, 493
Eastern Texas, 458
Eastern-Union Bayou, 32
Eastland County, minerals, 445
Eastland, Capt., 129
Eastland, N. W., Veteran, 595
Eastland, William, S. Jacinto Army, 566
Eastland, William M., Pioneers killed, 581
Eaton, Thomas H., Veteran, 595
Ebberly, 651
Eberley Firing Off Cannon, illus., 143
Eddy, Matthew, Fannin Massacre, 573
Edenburg, C., S. Jacinto Army, 567
Edens, D. H., Veteran, 595
Edgar, Alexander, Veteran, 595
Edgar, J. S., S. Jacinto Army, 566
Edmonson, James, Veteran, 595
Edrington, James F., Veteran, 624
Edson, Prvt., S. Jacinto Army, 564
Edwards, Capt., at Bexar, 220
Edwards, Charles O., Veteran, 595
Edwards, Col. Hayden E., 92
Edwards, Hayden, 518
Edwards, Isaac, S. Jacinto Army, 567
Edwards, Monroe, 25, 218, 361
Edwards, Munroe, Pioneers killed, 582
Edwards, Pastorus E., Old 300, 558
Edwards, S. M., Fannin Massacre, 573
Edwards, T. C., S. Jacinto Army, 563
Edwards, W. C., 624
Egbert, J. D., S. Jacinto Army, 564
Egenour, Conrad, Fannin Massacre, 573
Egry, C. W., Veteran, 595
Ehrenberg, Herman, Fannin Massacre,
    573
Eiler, Jacob, S. Jacinto Army, 565
Eiser, John, Fannin Massacre, 574

El Blanco, chief, 232
El Paso, 322
El Paso County, 625
Elam, John, Old 300, 558
Elder, James, 65
Elder, Robert, Old 300, 558
Eldridge, John W., Clerk, 639
Eldridge, Prvt., S. Jacinto Army, 564
Elinger, Joseph, S. Jacinto Army, 566
Eliza Russell, vessel, 78
Ellender, Joseph, S. Jacinto Army, 567
Elley, Gustavus, Veteran, 595
Elliot, J. D., S. Jacinto Army, 564
Elliott, Prvt., S. Jacinto Army, 564
Ellis County, 599, 612, 613
Ellis, Devraux, Fannin Massacre, 571
Ellis, J. E., Fannin Massacre, 573
Ellis, Richard, 23, 58
ELLIS, RICHARD, 279
Ellis, Richard, Pioneers killed, 581
Ellis, Richard, Convention, 635
Ellis, Richard, Convention, 635
Ellis, Richard, Pro Tem, 639
Ellis, Willis L., S. Jacinto Army, 568
Ellwood, 621
Ely, John, Fannin Massacre, 571
Elysian Fields, 585
Emigrants, Texan, from Zanesville, Ohio,
    166
Empresarios, 186
English, Capt., at Bexar, 220
English, George, Veteran, 595
English, Joshua, Veteran, 595
English, Robert, Fannin Massacre, 573
Ennis, 599
Ennques, Lucin, S. Jacinto Army, 569
Epidemic Community, 122
EPITAPH OF THE TEXAS DEAD,
    POEM, 440
Erath, G. B., 631
Erath, George B., Veteran, 595
Erath, George, S. Jacinto Army, 565
Erhard, Antonio M., Veteran, 595
Erhard, C., Veteran, 624
Erwin, Dr., 654
ESCAPE FROM THE ALAMO, POEM,
    410

Escott, —, Fannin Massacre, 570
Espada Mission, 228
Espinosa, Ygnacio, Veteran, 595
Esty, E., 129
Etheridge, Howard, Veteran, 595
Eubank, E. N., Veteran, 595
Eubanks, George, Fannin Massacre, 571
Evans, Moses, 361
Evans, T. R., 113
Evens, Musgrove, Lamar Admin, 636
Everett, James, S. Jacinto Army, 567
Everett, S. H., 58
Everett, S. H., Gen. Consultation, 633
Everett, S. H., Convention, 634
Everett, S. H., Pro Tem, 639
Evetts, S. G., Veteran, 595
Ewing, Alexander, S. Jacinto Army, 563
Ewing, George, Veteran, 595
Ewing, J., 113
Executive Ordinance, 1836, 59

F

Fagan, John, Fannin Massacre, 573
Faires, William A., Veteran, 596
Fairfield, 603
Falmash, Charles, Old 300, 558
False Live Oak Community, 239
Falvel, Luke A., Tx Necrology, 579
Fannin County, 587, 589, 595, 602, 617,
    621, 626
FANNIN LETTER, FEB. 28, 1836, 353
Fannin Massacre Survivors, 206
Fannin Massacre, 214
FANNIN'S MASSACRE, 144
FANNIN'S MASSACRE: GEORGIA
    BATTALION, 242
Fannin, Commission, Orders, Correspon-
    dence, 643
FANNIN, J. W., 262
Fannin, J. W., 66, 81, 583, 645, 656, 657
Fannin, J. W., Fannin Massacre, 569
Fannin, James W., Pioneers killed, 580
FANNIN, LIST OF MEN UNDER
    COMMAND OF, 569
Farewell, Joseph, S. Jacinto Army, 567
Faris, Isham, Veteran, 596

Faris, Willis A., Clerk, 639
Farish, Oscar, S. Jacinto Army, 568
Farish, Oscar, Veteran, 596
Farley, Prvt., S. Jacinto Army, 564
Farm country, 449
Farmer, Alexander, Sr., Veteran, 596
Farmer, James, S. Jacinto Army, 567
Farmer, James, Veteran, 596
Farming, 456
Farming Season, 455
Farney, Samuel, Fannin Massacre, 573
Faulkenburg, E. W., Veteran, 624
Faulkenbury, David, 198, 200
Faulkenbury, Evans, 199, 200
Faulkenbury, Plummer, 198
Fayette County, 124, 579, 590, 596, 597,
    598, 599, 603, 604, 605, 610, 611,
    618, 620, 623, 625, 628, 630
Fayette County, Veteran, 629
Fayetteville, 598
Feelcood, Matthias, Pioneers killed, 584
Fees, Legal in Austin's Colony, 177
Feldspar in Texas, 497
Fennell, George, S. Jacinto Army, 565
Fenton, David, Old 300, 558
Fentress, James, Tx Necrology, 579
Ferguson, James, Veteran, 597
Ferguson, Jos., Fannin Massacre, 573
Fero, David, 234
Ferrill, John P. 596
Ferrill, John, S. Jacinto Army, 563
Ferrill, W. F., S. Jacinto Army, 568
Fertilan, William, S. Jacinto Army, 568
Fertility of Soil, 455
Field, James, Fannin Massacre, 570
Field, Joseph E., Veteran, 596
Fields, H., S. Jacinto Army, 566
Fields, Henry, Veteran, 596
Fields, John T., Old 300, 558
Fields, William, Pioneers killed, 583
Filisola, Gen., 249
Finch, William, S. Jacinto Army, 568
Fine, Charles, Fannin Massacre, 571
Finner, Robert, Fannin Massacre, 573
First Congress, 216
Fishbaugh, W., 113
Fisher, Col., 128

Fisher, I. H., Fannin Massacre, 572
Fisher, James, Old 300, 558
Fisher, John, 58
Fisher, John, Convention, 634
FISHER, S. RHODES, 279
Fisher, S. Rhodes, Pioneers killed, 581
Fisher, S. Rhodes, 58
Fisher, S. Rhodes, Convention, 635
Fisher, S. Rhodes, Houston 1st Admin, 636
FISHER, W. S., 279
Fisher, W. S., S. Jacinto Army, 565
Fisher, William S., 205
Fisher, William, S. Jacinto Army, 569
Fisher, William S., Pioneers killed, 582
Fisher, William S., Gen. Consultation, 633
Fisher, William S., Houston 1st Admin, 636
Fisk, Greenlief, Veteran, 596
Fisk, James N., Veteran, 596
Fist, Hezekiah, Fannin Massacre, 572
Fitch, B. F., S. Jacinto Army, 566
Fitsimmons, Edward, Fannin Massacre, 572
Fitzgerald, David, Old 300, 558
Fitzgerald, Capt., 129
Fitzgerald, E. B. W., 64
Fitzgerald, Edward, Pioneers killed, 582
Fitzhuch, —, S. Jacinto Army, 563
Fitzhugh, J. P. T., Veteran, 596
FLAG OF THE LONE STAR, 334
Flag, "Hero of San Jacinto," 166
Flag, Georgia Battalion, 195
Flag, Lone Star, origin, 195
Flag, National, 195
Flanders, J., 113
Flannakin, Isaiah, Old 300, 558
Flatonia, 626
FLETCHER, JOSHUA, 275
Fletcher, Joshua, Prov. Govt., 634
Flick, John, S. Jacinto Army, 566
FLOODS IN TEXAS, 1870'S, 308
FLOODS ON THE COLORADO, 327
Flores, —, S. Jacinto Army, 564
Flores, Gaspar, 561
Flores, Manuel, S. Jacinto Army, 569
Flores, Nep, S. Jacinto Army, 569

Flores, Nepomuceno, 596
Floris, D. Salvador, 653
Flowers, Elisha, Old 300, 558
Floyd, D., 113
Flyn, Prvt., S. Jacinto Army, 564
Foley, A. G., Fannin Massacre, 573
Foley, G. L., Pioneers killed, 585
Foley, S. T., S. Jacinto Army, 566
Follet, Alonzo B., Veteran, 624
Follett, Alexander, Veteran, 624
Fontaine, Henry W., Judges, 638
Forbes, Capt. John, 197
Forbes, Col. John, 205
Forbes, John, S. Jacinto Army, 563
Forbes, John, Veteran, 596
Forbes, R. M., Veteran, 624
Ford, Charles A., S. Jacinto Army, 564
Ford, John S., Veteran, 596
Ford, Simon P., Veteran, 596
Ford, Simon, S. Jacinto Army, 565
FOREIGN RELATIONS REPORT 1845, 340
Forrester, John, Veteran, 624
Forrister, C., S. Jacinto Army, 566
Forsyth, 113
Fort Arbuckle, 133
Fort Belknap, 474, 494
Fort Bend, 153, 248
Fort Bend County, 592, 594, 596, 608, 609, 614, 615, 616, 619, 620, 623, 628, 629
Fort Cobb, 134
Fort Houston, 200, 201
Fort Mason, 490, 588
Fort McIntosh, 160
Fort Parker Massacre, 201
FORT PARKER, OLD, 198
Fort Quitman, 625
Fort Richardson, 133
Fort St. Louis, 17
Fort Worth, 623
Forts in Texas, 505
Foster, Anthony, S. Jacinto Army, 564
Foster, Anthony, Tx Necrology, 579
Foster, B. F., Veteran, 596
Foster, Isaac, Old 300, 558
Foster, J. A., Fannin Massacre, 572

Foster, J. R., S. Jacinto Army, 566
Foster, John, Old 300, 558
Foster, Randall, Veteran, 596
Foster, Randolph, Old 300, 558
Foster, Robert, Veteran, 624
Fowl, Thomas P., S. Jacinto Army, 563
Fowler, —, S. Jacinto Army, 566
Fowler, A. J., Veteran, 624
Fowler, Bradford, Fannin Massacre, 571
Fowler, J. H., Tx Necrology, 579
Fowler, J. H., Veteran, 596
Fowler, John K., Pioneers killed, 584
Fowler, T. M., S. Jacinto Army, 566
Foygnet, Francis A., Veteran, 597
Francis, Miller, Veteran, 596
Franklin, Benjamin C., S. Jacinto Army,
    566
Franklin, Benjamin C., Tx Necrology,
    579
Franklin, Benjamin C., Pioneers killed,
    585
FRANKLIN, BENJAMIN C., 274
Franklin, Benjamen C., 197
Franklin, Benjamen C., Convention, 635
Franklin, Benjamin C., Judges, 638
Franklin, E. B., Fannin Massacre, 573
Franks, Lt., at Bexar, 220
Frazier, Hugh, S. Jacinto Army, 566
Frazier, James, Old 300, 560
Frazier, M. G., Fannin Massacre, 573
Frederich, John, Veteran, 624
Fredericksburg, 588
Fredonia, 102
Fredonian War, 1827, 186
Freeman, T. S., Fannin Massacre, 571
Freestone County, 599, 603, 613, 617
Friel, James, S. Jacinto Army, 566
Frio County, minerals, 445
Frizel, T. B., Fannin Massacre, 572
Frontier Protection, 352
Frost, Robert, 201
Frost, Samuel, 201
Fry, B. F., S. Jacinto Army, 565
Fuga, G., 113
Fulchear, Churchill, Old 300, 558
Fuller, Edward, Fannin Massacre, 572
Fulshear, Churchill, Veteran, 596

Fuqua, Benjamen, Gen. Consultation, 633
Furnaces, Spanish, 444

G

Gafford, John, S. Jacinto Army, 567
Gage, Calvin, S. Jacinto Army, 565
Gage, David, Pioneers killed, 582
Gailan, Victor, Veteran, 597
Gainer, —, S. Jacinto Army, 563
Gaines, James, 58, 227
Gaines, James, Convention, 634
Gaines, W. B. P., Veteran, 597
Galindo, Judge, 234
Gallagher, Dominic, Fannin Massacre, 571
Gallagher, Peter, Veteran, 624
Gallaher, E., S. Jacinto Army, 568
Gallatin, Albert, S. Jacinto Army, 562
Gallatin, Albert, Veteran, 597
Gallatin, Ed., Veteran, 597
Gallitin, Albert, S. Jacinto Army, 567
Galsaspy, James, S. Jacinto Army, 568
Galveston, 80, 87, 119, 221, 357, 579,
    588, 589, 591, 593, 597, 600, 606,
    611, 627, 632
Galveston City, 586, 596, 599, 624
Galveston County, 66, 586, 596, 610
GAME IN TEXAS, 474, 479
Garcia, Luciano, 234
Gardner, G. W., S. Jacinto Army, 566
Garner, —, S. Jacinto Army, 565
Garner, Isaac, Veteran, 598
Garner, John, 99
Garner, John, Veteran, 625
Garner, M. C., Fannin Massacre, 574
GARNERED MEMORY, POEM, 408
Garrett, Charles, Old 300, 558
Garrett, J. C., 113
Garrie, Colonel, 171
Garsear, Francisco, Fannin Massacre, 574
Garwood, Joseph, S. Jacinto Army, 566
Garza, Padre, 648
Gaspar, Gaspar, 88
Gasper, Doc., 185
Gassett, A. E., Veteran, 597
Gaston, J., 113
Gates, Amos, Veteran, 597

Gates, Lewis W., Fannin Massacre, 573
Gates, Samuel, Old 300, 558
Gates, William, Old 300, 558
Gates, Wm. N., Veteran, 598
Gatesville, 590
Gatlin, William, Fannin Massacre, 573
Gaudaloupe River, 655
Gay, Thomas, S. Jacinto Army, 566
Gazeley, Thomas G., 58
Gazley, Thomas J., 84
Gazley, Thomas J., Convention, 634
Gebinrath, Frederick, Fannin Massacre, 572
Gedrie, Lefray, S. Jacinto Army, 567
Gellatley, Robert, Veteran, 598
General Consultation, 23, 148
GENERAL CONSULTATION, 633
General Council, 634
General Land Office, 20
Gentry, F. B., S. Jacinto Army, 567
Gentry, F. B., Veteran, 597
Gentry, George W., Veteran, 624
Gentry, Thomas N., Veteran, 624
Gentry, W. N., Veteran, 624
Geographical Position of Texas, 502
Geography of Texas, 448
GEOLOGICAL RESOURCES OF TEXAS, 488
Geologists, State, 501
George, David, 65
George, Freeman, Old 300, 558
George, H., 64
Georgetown, 587, 619, 623
Georgia Battalion, 161
Georgia Battalion Flag, 195
Geraud, F., 18
Geroge, David, Veteran, 597
Gholson, Albert, 141
Gians, Bazil G., S. Jacinto Army, 568
Gibbs, —, Fannin Massacre, 571
Gibbs, L. C., Fannin Massacre, 570
Gibson, Archibald, Veteran, 598
Giddings, 597, 611
Giddings, G. A., S. Jacinto Army, 565
Gilbert, John F., S. Jacinto Army, 568
Gilbert, Preston, Old 300, 558
Gilbert, Sarah, Old 300, 558

Gilbert, William, Fannin Massacre, 572
Gilkerson, F., Fannin Massacre, 572
Gill, John P., S. Jacinto Army, 568
Gill, W., S. Jacinto Army, 565
Gilland, George M., Fannin Massacre, 570
Gillespie County, 588
Gillespie, James, Pioneers killed, 582
Gillespie, Jo, S. Jacinto Army, 565
Gillespie, R. A., Pioneers killed, 582
Gilliam, James, Pioneers killed, 585
Gilliam, L. W., Veteran, 598
Gilliland, Daniel, Old 300, 558
Gilliland, James, Pioneers killed, 581
Gillmore, 113
Gillmore, Charles, Veteran, 624
Gilmore, Charles, Veteran, 625
Girauds Creek, 465
GIRL WITH THE CALICO DRESS, POEM, 421
Glasscock, George W., Pioneers killed, 584
Gleeson, John, Fannin Massacre, 573
Goff, Felix W., Veteran, 598
Goglan, G. W., Fannin Massacre, 573
Goheen, Capt., 83
Gohoen, M. K., S. Jacinto Army, 568
Gold in Texas, 497
GOLDEN OPPORTUNITY, POEM, 438
Golden, Philip, Veteran, 598
Goliad, 21, 81, 83, 120, 152, 161, 224, 227, 599, 607, 613, 634, 635, 645, 648, 653
Goliad County, 599, 613
Goliad Massacre, 155, 368
Goliad Survivors, 205
Goliad, Battle, 93, 136
Goliad, Battle, Aftermath, 169
GOLIAD, OR LA BAHIA, DESCRIPTION, 135
Gonsen, 651
Gonzales, 65, 153, 291, 594, 601, 602, 603, 607, 610, 615, 633, 634, 635, 655, 657
Gonzales County, 586, 592, 594, 598, 602, 603, 604, 607, 610, 615, 620, 626, 628
Gonzales County, Veteran, 620
Gonzales Retreat, 1836, 93

Gonzales, Battle, 93, 148
Good, Hannibal, Veteran, 597
Goodloe, R. R., Veteran, 597
Goodman, J. B., Veteran, 597
Goodman, Stephen, Veteran, 625
Goodrich, Benjamin B., 58
Goodrich, Benjamin B., Pioneers killed, 583
Goodrich, Benjamin B., Convention, 635
Goodrich, J. C., 113
Goodwin, —, S. Jacinto Army, 564
Goodwin, John, Pioneers killed, 585
Goodwin, Lewis, S. Jacinto Army, 566
Goodwin, William, Veteran, 598
Gorbet, Chester S., Old 300, 558
Gorham, William, Veteran, 598
Gorman, J. P., Veteran, 597
Gossett, A. E., Veteran, 598
Gould, —, Fannin Massacre, 570
Gould, Charles M., DA's, 638
Gould, Wm., 65
Government House Fight, 154
GOVERNORS OF TEXAS, BIOGRA-
    PHIES, 293
Governors of Texas, 24, 121
Grace, John, Fannin Massacre, 570
Grady, Dan, Veteran, 625
Graham, John, S. Jacinto Army, 567
Graham, William, 222
Gramble, Joseph, Fannin Massacre, 572
Grant, Col., 151
GRANT, DOCTOR JAMES, 277
Grant, James, Pioneers killed, 580
Grant, W. W., S. Jacinto Army, 566
Grass Fight, 93, 149, 589, 593, 595, 603,
    605, 606, 613, 614, 615, 617, 619
GRASS FIGHT, 1835, 92
Grasshoppers, 511
Grath County, 610
Graves, Jacob Maybee, S. Jacinto Army,
    565
Graves, Ransom O., Fannin Massacre, 574
Graves, Thomas A., S. Jacinto Army, 566
Gray, E. Fairfax, Veteran, 624
Gray, F. H., Fannin Massacre, 570
Gray, James, S. Jacinto Army, 567
Gray, James, Veteran, 598

Gray, M. B., Pioneers killed, 582
Gray, M. B., S. Jacinto Army, 567
Gray, Peter W., Pioneers killed, 585
Gray, Peter W., DA's, 638
Gray, William Fairfax, Pioneers killed, 581
Gray, William Fairfax, Jones Admin, 637
Gray, William Fairfax, DA's, 638
Gray, William Fairfax, Clerks, 639
Gray, William Fairfax, Sec. Senate, 639
Grayham, James, Veteran, 597
Grayson County, 590, 606
Grayson, Capt. T. W., 122
GRAYSON, PETER W., 270
Grayson, Peter W., Pioneers killed, 581
Grayson, Peter W., 645
Grayson, Peter W., Convention, 635
Grayson, Peter W., Houston 1st Admin,
    636
Great Boiling Springs, 21
Green, B., S. Jacinto Army, 569
Green, Capt. Tom, 173
Green, Col., 128
Green, Gen. Thomas J., 128
Green, George, S. Jacinto Army, 565
Green, George, Fannin Massacre, 570
Green, George, Veteran, 597
Green, J., S. Jacinto Army, 566
Green, James, Veteran, 597
Green, Thomas, Jones Admin, 637
Green, Thomas, Sec. Senate, 639
Green, Thomas J., 587, 594, 595
GREEN, THOMAS J., 270
GREEN, THOMAS J., 276
Green, Thomas J., Pioneers killed, 584
Green, Thomas J., S. Jacinto Army, 563
Green, Thomas J., Portrait, 584
Green, Thomas N. B., S. Jacinto Army,
    563
Green, William J., Fannin Massacre, 573
Greene, D., Fannin Massacre, 572
Greenlaw, A., S. Jacinto Army, 566
Greenwood, James, S. Jacinto Army, 565
Greenwood, James, Veteran, 598
Greer, J. A., Pioneers killed, 583
Greer, John A., Jones Admin, 637
Greer, John A., Pro Tem, 639
Gregg, Darius, Pioneers killed, 584

Gregg, John, Pioneers killed, 584
Grey, Thomas, Old 300, 558
Greynolds, E. J. A., Fannin Massacre, 573
Greyson, Thomas W., 607
Grice, J. B., S. Jacinto Army, 568
Grieves, Prvt., S. Jacinto Army, 564
Griffin, Peter, Fannin Massacre, 570
Griffin, William, S. Jacinto Army, 565
Griffith, L. A., Veteran, 624
Griffith, Leroy, Veteran, 625
Grigsby, Crawf, S. Jacinto Army, 567
Grimes County, 587, 597, 602, 606, 607, 609, 618, 623, 627, 630, 631, 632, 609
Grimes, C., 113
Grimes, Frederick, Veteran, 597
Grimes, George W., Veteran, 597
Grimes, J. E., Fannin Massacre, 574
Grimes, Jesse, 58, 98
GRIMES, JESSE, 280
Grimes, Jesse, Gen. Consultation, 633
Grimes, Jesse, Prov. Govt., 634
Grimes, Jesse, Convention, 635
Grimes, Jesse, Pro Tem, 639
Grimes, Rufus, Veteran, 597
Groce's, 193
Groce, Jacob, S. Jacinto Army, 567
Groce, Jared E., Old 300, 558
Groce, Jared E., Pioneers killed, 580
Groesbeck, 198, 620, 586
Grover, George W., Veteran, 598
Grush, H. L, Veteran, 625
Guadaloupe County, 589, 594, 595, 606, 616
Guadalupe River, 22, 185, 248, 360, 412
Guadalupe River, Indian Antiquities, 238
Guadalupe Swamps, 162
Guaymas, 467
Guaymas Railroad, 467
Guaza Indians, 233
Guest, Martin, Veteran, 625
Guney, Philip M., Pioneers killed, 584
Gunter, William, Fannin Massacre, 574
Gustine, Lem, S. Jacinto Army, 563
Guthrie, Robert, Old 300, 558
Gwyn, 113
Gypsum, 446

Gypsum Formation, 472
Gypsum in Texas, 497

H

Hackberry, 604
Hadden, John, Old 300, 558
Haddon, William, Fannin Massacre, 574
Haddon, Wm., 65
Hady, Samuel C., Old 300, 559
Hagans, Josiah, S. Jacinto Army, 566
Hager, Nat, S. Jacinto Army, 568
Haggard, Squire, Veteran, 599
Hailsborough, 621
Haines, Albert G., Pioneers killed, 584
Hale, J. C., S. Jacinto Army, 563
Hale, John C., S. Jacinto Army, 568
Hale, W., S. Jacinto Army, 566
Haley, Charles Q., Veteran, 599
Haley, Michael, Veteran, 600
Haley, Richard, Veteran, 599
Hall, C. K., Pioneers killed, 585
Hall, Colonel, 644
Hall, George H., Veteran, 600
Hall, Hudson H., Veteran, 600
Hall, J., S. Jacinto Army, 566
Hall, James, S. Jacinto Army, 568
Hall, John W., Pioneers killed, 581
Hall, John, Old 300, 558
Hall, W. D. C., 26, 187, 224, 230, 289, 644, 647, 650, 652
HALL, WARREN D. C., 289
Hall, Warren D. C., Pioneers killed, 584
Hall, William S., 30
Hall, William, Old 300, 558
Halletsville, 616, 627, 632
Hallien, John F., Veteran, 600
Halliet, John, S. Jacinto Army, 566
Hallmark, A. M., Veteran, 599
Hallmark, W. O., Veteran, 599
Hallmask, W. E., S. Jacinto Army, 567
Halstead, E. B., S. Jacinto Army, 566
Ham, E. L., Veteran, 599
Hamilton County, 597
Hamilton Creek, 493
HAMILTON, A. J., 295
Hamilton, David, Old 300, 559

Hamilton, E. E., S. Jacinto Army, 567
Hamilton, Gen. James, 79
Hamilton, J. D., Fannin Massacre, 573
HAMILTON, JAMES, 270, 337
Hamilton, James, Fannin Massacre, 572
Hamilton, James, Pioneers killed, 583
Hamilton, James, Lamar Admin, 636
Hamilton, James, Lamar Admin, 637
Hamilton, John E., Veteran, 625
Hamilton, Nathan, Veteran, 601
Hamilton, R., 58
Hamilton, Robert, Convention, 635
Hamm, Cephas, 35
Hammeken, George L., Lamar Admin, 636
Hammock, Pearce, Fannin Massacre, 571
Hancock Springs, 21
Hancock, G. D., S. Jacinto Army, 569
Hancock, George, Veteran, 599
Hand, John J., Fannin Massacre, 574
Hand, N., Pioneers killed, 584
Handsford, John M., Pioneers killed, 581
Handy, R. Eden, S. Jacinto Army, 563
Handy, Robert Eden, Pioneers killed, 581
Hanks, M. H., 656
Hanks, Wesley W., Veteran, 601
Hanks, Wyatt, Gen. Consultation, 633
Hanks, Wyatt, Prov. Govt., 634
Hanover, Hiram, Veteran, 625
Hansford, John M., Judges, 638
Hansford, John M., Speakers, 639
Hanson, T., 64
Harbour, George W., Veteran, 600
Harbour, James M., Veteran, 600
Hardaway, Samuel G., 242
Hardaway, Samuel G., Fannin Massacre, 571
Hardeman County, 462
Hardeman, Bailey, 59
HARDEMAN, BAILEY, 275
Hardeman, Bailey, Pioneers killed, 580
Hardeman, Bailey, Convention, 635
Hardeman, Capt., West Texas, 464
Hardeman, John, Veteran, 599
Hardeman, Monroe, 373
HARDEMAN, THOMAS J., 289

Hardeman, Thomas J., Pioneers killed, 583
Hardeman, W. P., Veteran, 599
Harden, A. B., Gen. Consultation, 633
Harden, A. B., Convention, 634
Harden, Franklin, S. Jacinto Army, 567
Hardeway, S. G., Tx Necrology, 579
Hardiman, B., 58
Hardiman, T. M., S. Jacinto Army, 566
Hardin County, Sour Lake, 21
Hardin County, minerals, 445
Hardin, A. B., 58
Hardin, Franklin, Veteran, 599
Hardin, W. B., Veteran, 600
Harding, T. B., Veteran, 601
Hardwick, C., Fannin Massacre, 574
Hargrove, W. D., Pioneers killed, 582
Harman, John, S. Jacinto Army, 569
Harmon, Clark M., S. Jacinto Army, 563
Harmon, Clark M., Veteran, 601
Harmonson, Judge, 492
Harnes, Abel, Veteran, 625
Harness, William, S. Jacinto Army, 563
Harper, B. J., S. Jacinto Army, 567
Harper, Peter, S. Jacinto Army, 568
Harper, Prvt., S. Jacinto Army, 564
Harper, William, Fannin Massacre, 570
Harrill, Milvern, Veteran, 626
Harris, 113
Harris County, 586, 587, 590, 591, 593, 599, 601, 602, 605, 608, 609, 611, 613, 617, 618, 623, 624, 627, 630, 631
Harris, A. J., S. Jacinto Army, 565
Harris, Abner, Old 300, 558
Harris, David, Old 300, 559
Harris, Hez, S. Jacinto Army, 568
Harris, Isaac, Veteran, 600
Harris, James, S. Jacinto Army, 568
Harris, Jesse, Fannin Massacre, 572
Harris, John R., Old 300, 559
Harris, P., Old 300, 558
Harris, R. H., 129
Harris, S. M., Veteran, 599
Harris, T. O., S. Jacinto Army, 563
Harris, Temple O., Veteran, 600
Harris, William, Old 300, 558

Harris, William J., Old 300, 558
Harris, William, Fannin Massacre, 573
Harris, William P., Gen. Consultation, 633
Harris, William P., Prov. Govt., 634
Harrisburg, 59, 153, 334, 631, 633, 634
Harrison, 113
Harrison County, 585, 604, 621
Harrison, A. L., S. Jacinto Army, 568
Harrison, E. D., Fannin Massacre, 572
Harrison, George, Old 300, 559
Hart, Timothy, 64
Harvey, John, S. Jacinto Army, 567
Harvey, John, Veteran, 598
Harvey, Prvt., S. Jacinto Army, 564
Harvey, William, Old 300, 558
Harward, John, Veteran, 601
Harwood, B. F., Veteran, 600
Haskell County, minerals, 442
Haskin, T. A., 565
Hassel, J. W., S. Jacinto Army, 566
Hassell, 651
Hasty, Henry, Fannin Massacre, 572
Hatfield, B. M., Pioneers killed, 584
Hatfield, William, Fannin Massacre, 573
Hawford, Henry, Veteran, 598
Hawkins, 113
Hawkins, Capt., 77
Hawkins, Capt. Edward, 218
Hawkins, N. B., Fannin Massacre, 570
Hawkins, W. W., Veteran, 600
Hawkins, William, S. Jacinto Army, 566
Hawkins, Williams, S. Jacinto Army, 567
Hawley, William, Veteran, 600
Hayden, Nathaniel, Veteran, 600
Haye, James, S. Jacinto Army, 568
Hayes, J., 113
Hays County, 159, 583, 588, 597, 605,
    609, 611, 617
Hays, Colonel Jack, 172
Hays, James, Tx Necrology, 579
Hays, W. C., S. Jacinto Army, 565
Hazen, Nat., Fannin Massacre, 574
Heard, S. R., Veteran, 625
Heard, W. J. E., Tx Necrology, 580
Heard, W. J. E., Pioneers killed, 585
Heard, W. J. E., Veteran, 600
Heard, William J. E., S. Jacinto Army, 566

Hearn, Thomas B., Veteran, 598
Hearne, 630
Heaskill, C. R., Fannin Massacre, 570
Heath, E. S., Fannin Massacre, 570
Hec, Charles, Fannin Massacre, 574
Heck, Randle B., Tx Necrology, 579
Hefflefinger, James, Veteran, 625
Helms, Wilson, Fannin Massacre, 571
Hemphill, 600
Hemphill, John, Pioneers killed, 583
Hemphill, John, Jones Admin, 637
Hemphill, John, Judges, 638
Hemphill, William, Fannin Massacre, 574
HEMPHILL, JOHN, 300
Hempstead, 487, 559, 610, 620
Henderson, F. K., S. Jacinto Army, 567
Henderson, J. Pinckney, Pioneers killed,
    583
Henderson, J. Pinckney, Houston 1st
    Admin, 636
Henderson, J. Pinckney, Houston 2nd
    Admin, 637
HENDERSON, JAMES PINCKNEY, 293
Henderson, James W., Veteran, 599
Henderson, James W., DA's, 639
Henderson, John, Veteran, 600
Henderson, Prvt., S. Jacinto Army, 564
Henderson, William T., DA's, 638
Hendersoon, James W., 639
Hendricks, S. B., Veteran, 625
Henern, Pedro, S. Jacinto Army, 569
Henley, James, Fannin Massacre, 570
Henry, Charles M., S. Jacinto Army, 566
Henry, Robert, S. Jacinto Army, 568
Henry, William C., Pioneers killed, 583
Hensley, 651
Hensley, A. J., Veteran, 601
Hensley, James, Old 300, 558
Hensley, John M., Veteran, 600
Hensley, Johnson, Veteran, 599
Hentley, H. H., Fannin Massacre, 573
Herbert, C. C., Pioneers killed, 584
Herder, George, Veteran, 599
Herndon Plantation, Coal, 499
Herndon, John H., Veteran, 625
Herrera, Gen., 225, 227
Herron, John H., Veteran, 600

Herron, John, S. Jacinto Army, 565
Hersie, W., 113
Heth, Joel, Fannin Massacre, 570
Hewitson, Doc., 88, 185
Hewitson, James, Pioneers killed, 584
Hick, C. F., Fannin Massacre, 572
Hick, Charles, S. Jacinto Army, 568
Hidalgo County, minerals, 446
Hieskell, 113
Higginson, 129
High Hill, 599
Highland, Joseph, Veteran, 599
Highsmith, B. F., Veteran, 625
Highsmith, Samuel, Pioneers killed, 582
Hilchard, John, Fannin Massacre, 573
Hill County, 586, 618, 619
Hill, A. W., Veteran, 599
Hill, Ben. F., Pioneers killed, 584
Hill, David, Veteran, 599
Hill, G. B., Veteran, 598
Hill, George B., Old 300, 559
Hill, George W., Houston 2nd Admin, 637
Hill, George W., Jones Admin, 637
Hill, H., S. Jacinto Army, 569
Hill, Isaac L., Veteran, 598
Hill, J. L., S. Jacinto Army, 566
Hill, J. W., S. Jacinto Army, 564
Hill, James M., S. Jacinto Army, 567
Hill, James M., Veteran, 598
Hill, Jeffrey B., Veteran, 626
Hill, Middleton M., Pioneers killed, 582
Hill, T. B. J., Pioneers killed, 585
Hill, William Pinckney, Pioneers killed, 584
Hill, William W., S. Jacinto Army, 566
Hill, Wm. G., 64, 89
Hillsboro, 618
Hinojosa, Lorenzo, 234
HISTORY OF TEXAS, EARLY, 101
HISTORY, TEXAS, early, 147
Hitchcock, A. J., 242
Hitchcock, A. J., Fannin Massacre, 572
Hitchcock, A. J., Veteran, 601
Hobson, John, S. Jacinto Army, 566
Hockley, 618
HOCKLEY, G. W., 272

Hockley, George W., 204
Hockley, George W., S. Jacinto Army, 563
Hockley, George W., Pioneers killed, 582
Hockley, George W., Houston 2nd Admin, 637
Hockley, George W., Houston 1st Admin, 636
Hodge, —, Fannin Massacre, 570
Hodge, Alexander, Old 300, 559
Hodges, James, Pioneers killed, 582
Hodges, James, Gen. Consultation, 633
Hodges, Robert, Tx Necrology, 579
Hoffman, Michael T., Veteran, 600
Hogan, Prvt., S. Jacinto Army, 564
Hogg, James L., Pioneers killed, 583
Hogg, W. C., S. Jacinto Army, 566
Holbrook, Nathaniel, 64
Holden, Prior, S. Jacinto Army, 566
Holeman, S., S. Jacinto Army, 569
Holford, James, 79
Holiday, John, Fannin Massacre, 570
Holland, —, Fannin Massacre, 570
Holland, Francis, Old 300, 558
Holland, J., 113
Holland, S., Pioneers killed, 584
Holland, William, Old 300, 558
Hollaway, S., 113
Holley, Mrs., 188
Hollimen, Kurchen, Old 300, 558
Holman, W. W., Tx Necrology, 579
Holman, William, Pioneers killed, 585
Holmes, Peter W., S. Jacinto Army, 567
Holmes, Thomas, Gen. Consultation, 633
Holstein, H., 88
Holstein, Henry, 185
Holt, David I., 161
Holt, David I., Fannin Massacre, 570
Holt, James J., Pioneers killed, 584
Homan, H., S. Jacinto Army, 564
Hondo Creek, 489
Honey Grove, 587, 589
Hood County, 619
Hood, J. L., Gen. Consultation, 633
Hope, James, Old 300, 558
Hope, Prosper, S. Jacinto Army, 567
Hopkins County, 579, 589, 592, 613
Hopkins, J. E., Veteran, 598

Hopkins, Thomas, S. Jacinto Army, 568
Hopson, Lucien, Veteran, 598
Hornsby, Mrs. Reuben, 139
Horrell, 113
Horry, Thomas, Fannin Massacre, 572
Horse Industry, early, 21
Horsehead Crossing, 446
Horton, A. C., Pioneers killed, 584
Horton, A., S. Jacinto Army, 563
Horton, Albert C., 118
HORTON, ALBERT C., 273
Horton, Alexander, 205
Horton, Alexander, Veteran, 598
Horton, Alexander, Gen. Consultation, 633
Hortonville, 631
Hotchkiss, R., 600
Hotchkiss, R., S. Jacinto Army, 569
HOUSE OF REP, CHIEF CLERK, REPUBLIC, 639
HOUSE OF REP, SPEAKERS, REPUBLIC, 639
House, John, 234
House, Thomas, 234
Houston, 21, 122, 574, 586, 587, 599, 601, 602, 605, 607, 608, 609, 611, 613, 617, 620, 622, 624, 626, 627, 629, 630, 631
Houston and Great Northern Railroad, 22
Houston and Santa Anna, illus., 96
Houston and Texas Central Railroad, 22
Houston County, 579, 587, 595, 597, 599, 628, 631, 632
Houston Issuing Orders, illus., 464
HOUSTON LETTER TO SANTA ANNA, 1842, 331
HOUSTON PROCLAMATION, DEC. 12, 1835, 328
Houston Telegraph And Register, 130
HOUSTON TO SANTA ANNA, 1842, 333
Houston's First Administration, 636
HOUSTON'S INAUGURAL SPEECH, 305
HOUSTON'S SECOND ADMINISTRATION, 637
Houston, Andrew D., Veteran, 601
Houston, Captal, 120
Houston, Sam, 23, 58, 59, 77, 81, 133, 192, 193, 211, 216, 255, 315
HOUSTON, SAM, 255
HOUSTON, SAM, ANECDOTE, 1860, 313
HOUSTON, SAM, ANECDOTE, 1860, 352
Houston, Sam, Gen. Consultation, 633
Houston, Sam, illus., 255, 397
Houston, Sam, S. Jacinto Army, 563
Houston, Sam, wound at San Jacinto, 194
Houston, Sam, Prov. Govt., 634
Houston, Sam, Convention, 635
Houston, Sam , Houston 1st Admin, 636
Houston, Sam, Houston 2nd Admin, 637
Houston, Tx, 119
Howard Association, 488
Howard, Capt., 154
Howard, George T., Pioneers killed, 584
Howard, John C., Veteran, 625
Howard, Philip, Veteran, 601
Howard, T. B., Veteran, 626
Howell, Robert, S. Jacinto Army, 565
Howth, Wm. E., 64
Hoxie, Asa, 172
Hoxie, Asa, Gen. Consultation, 633
Hoxie, Asa, Pioneers killed, 584
Hoxie, Asa, Prov. Govt., 634
Hoxie, Major Bula, 172
Hoyle, Stephen Z., Sec. Senate, 639
Hubble, John, Veteran, 599
Hubert, John R., DA's, 638
Hudson, Charles S., Old 300, 558
Hudson, H. C., Prov. Govt., 634
Hudson, H. C., Convention, 635
Hudson, H. C., DA's, 638
Hudson, H. G., Fannin Massacre, 572
Huff, George, Old 300, 559
Huff, John, Old 300, 558
Hughes, —, Fannin Massacre, 574
Hughes, Isaac, Old 300, 559
Hughes, Thomas M., S. Jacinto Army, 569
Hughs, Wesley, Fannin Massacre, 571
Hughs, Wiley, Fannin Massacre, 571
Humphrey, William, Veteran, 625
Humphreys, P. W., Veteran, 625

Humphreys, P. W., Clerk, 639
Humphries, J. P., Fannin Massacre, 570
Hunt, 651
Hunt County, 605
Hunt County, minerals, 443
Hunt, E. P., Pioneers killed, 584
Hunt, F. M., Fannin Massacre, 571
Hunt, John C., S. Jacinto Army, 567
Hunt, Memucan, Pioneers killed, 582
HUNT, MEMUCAN, 272
Hunt, Memucan, Houston 1st Admin, 636
Hunt, William G., Veteran, 599
Hunter, — (Fannin), 206
Hunter, Eli., Old 300, 558
Hunter, Johnson, Old 300, 558
Hunter, William L., Fannin Massacre, 570
Hunter, William, Fannin Massacre, 573
Hunter, William L., Veteran, 599
Huntsville, 487, 601, 612, 614, 631, 632
Hurd, Capt., 77
Hurd, James G., Veteran, 601
Hurd, Norman, Veteran, 601
Hurd, S. R., Veteran, 626
Hurd, W., Pioneers killed, 584
Hurst, —, Fannin Massacre, 574
Huston and Johnson Duel, 166
Huston, A., Prov. Govt., 634
Huston, Felix, 166, 195, 587, 618
HUSTON, FELIX, 277
Huston, Felix, Pioneers killed, 583
Hutchason, 113
Hutchinson, Anderson, Judges, 638
Hyde, A. C., Veteran, 625
Hyena's Hollow, 122
HYMN OF THE ALAMO, 338
Hynes, John, Veteran, 601
Hynes, Peter, 64

I

I'M THINKING OF THE SOLDIER, POEM, 388
Ijams, Bazel G., Veteran, 601
Ijams, John H., Veteran, 601
Immigrant from other States, 452
Immigrant, European, 452

INAUGURAL SPEECH, HOUSTON'S, 305
Independence, 587
Independence, schooner, 215, 218
Independence, vessel, 77
Indian Artifacts, 239
Indian Escape, Duval, John C., 370
INDIAN FIGHT OF 1831, 35
Indian Graves, 240
Indian Mounds, East Texas, 207
Indian Reservations, 134
Indian sites, 207
INDIAN WARS, 138
INDIAN WARS: BRYANT'S DEFEAT, 141
INDIAN WARS: MORGAN MASSA-CRE, 140
Indianola, 487, 592, 624
Indians, Nassonis, 207
Indians, Near Groesbeck, 201
Indians, Population, 135
INDIANS, TEXAS, 132
Indians, Under Reuben Ross, 228
Indians, Various tribes, 145
Ingraham, Allen, S. Jacinto Army, 566
Ingraham, J., S. Jacinto Army, 567
Ingram, 113
Ingram, Allen, S. Jacinto Army, 562
Ingram, Allen, Fannin Massacre, 572
INGRAM, IRA, 288
Ingram, Ira, 64, 65, 561
Ingram, Ira, Old 300, 559
Ingram, Ira, Speakers, 639
Ingram, John, Veteran, 601
Ingram, Seth, Old 300, 559
Ingram, Seth, Pioneers killed, 583
Innlock, William, 82
International Railroad, 23
Invincible, schooner, 153
Invincible, vessel, 77
Irams, John, Old 300, 559
Irion, Van R., Pioneers killed, 582
Irish, Milton, Fannin Massacre, 570
Irish, Milton, Pioneers killed, 584
Iron, 444
Iron Ore, 490
Irons, John, Old 300, 559

Irven, J. S. P., S. Jacinto Army, 568
Irvine, Josephus S., Veteran, 602
Irvine, W. D., Veteran, 601
Irwin, Doc., 185
Irwin, R. A., Houston 1st Admin, 636
Isaac, Jackson, Old 300, 559
Isaacks, Sam, Veteran, 601
Isaacks, William, Veteran, 602
Isaacs, Samuel, Old 300, 559
Isam, James, Veteran, 626
Isbel, S. H., S. Jacinto Army, 566
Isbell, William, S. Jacinto Army, 566
Isbell, William, Veteran, 601
Islas Negras, 231

J

Jack County, minerals, 445
Jack, James C., Fannin Massacre, 572
Jack, Patrick, 651
Jack, Patrick C., 25
JACK, PATRICK C., 267
Jack, Patrick C., Pioneers killed, 581
Jack, Patrick C., Judges, 638
Jack, Patrick C., DA's, 638
Jack, William H., 25, 187, 216, 651
JACK, WILLIAM H., 267
Jack, William H., S. Jacinto Army, 568
Jack, William H., Pioneers killed, 581
Jack, William H., Convention, 635
Jackson, 634
Jackson County, 292, 600, 602, 606, 618, 619
Jackson County, Veteran, 620
Jackson Creek, 488
Jackson, Alexander, Old 300, 559
Jackson, D., 113
Jackson, E. D., Veteran, 602
Jackson, Humphrey, Old 300, 559
Jackson, John N., Fannin Massacre, 574
Jackson, John, Fannin Massacre, 574
Jackson, Joseph, Veteran, 602
Jackson, T., 113
Jackson, W. R., S. Jacinto Army, 566
Jacksonville, 611, 630
Jacobs, Madison G., Veteran, 602
Jacques, Isaac, S. Jacinto Army, 568
James, —, Fannin Massacre, 570

James, Asbury, Pioneers killed, 582
James, D., S. Jacinto Army, 565
James, John, 65
James, John, Fannin Massacre, 573
James, T. B., Veteran, 626
James, W. F., S. Jacinto Army, 563
Jamison, C. B., 113
January, H., Pioneers killed, 584
January, J. P. B., Veteran, 602
Jaques, W. B., Pioneers killed, 584
Jarman, Asa, Veteran, 602
Jasper, 588, 593, 633, 634
Jasper County, 593, 597, 618
Jasper, L. R. B., Pioneers killed, 582
Jean, James M., Veteran, 602
Jefferson, 21, 633
Jefferson County, 586, 596
Jeffries, A. M., Veteran, 626
Jenkins, John H., Veteran, 602
Jennings, Charles B., Fannin Massacre, 573
Jennings, J. D., S. Jacinto Army, 567
Jenson, Charles, Fannin Massacre, 573
Jett, J. M., S. Jacinto Army, 564
Jett, Steve, S. Jacinto Army, 564
Jewell, George W., 599
Jewett, 603
Jewett, Henry J., Pioneers killed, 584
Jewett, Henry J., DA's, 638
Jewett, Henry J., Sec. Senate, 639
Joeb, Peter W., Veteran, 626
Johns, C. R., Veteran, 626
Johnson County, 590, 599, 600, 602, 612, 614, 615, 619, 624, 626, 628
Johnson, —, Fannin Massacre, 570
Johnson, A. E. C., Prov. Govt., 634
Johnson, A. Sidney, Lamar Admin, 636
Johnson, Benjamin, S. Jacinto Army, 568
Johnson, Col. F. W., 80
Johnson, Colonel, 218
Johnson, David, Fannin Massacre, 572
Johnson, F. W., at Bexar, 219
JOHNSON, FRANK W., 269
Johnson, Frank W., Veteran, 602
Johnson, Frank W., 614
Johnson, H. W. Walker, Old 300, 559
Johnson, Hugh B., 24, 25, 27
Johnson, J. R., S. Jacinto Army, 568

Johnson, J. R., Veteran, 626
Johnson, John, 64
Johnson, L., 113
Johnson, Moses, Pioneers killed, 582
Johnson, Moses, Jones Admin, 637
Johnson, Prvt., S. Jacinto Army, 564
Johnson, Samuel, Veteran, 602
Johnson, T. A., Veteran, 626
Johnson, T. F., S. Jacinto Army, 568
Johnson, Thomas H., Old 300, 559
Johnson, Thomas, Pioneers killed, 582
Johnson, Thomas, Judges, 638
Johnson, Thomas, DA's, 638
Johnson, W., 113
Johnson, W. P., Fannin Massacre, 570
Johnson, William R., Fannin Massacre, 570
Johnson, William, Veteran, 602
Johnston, A. Sidney, Pioneers killed, 583
Johnston, Albert Sidney, 166, 211, 636
JOHNSTON, ALBERT SIDNEY, 271
Johnston, F. W., 25, 30, 65, 151, 187, 197
Johnston, Sidney, 194
Johnstone, G. J., S. Jacinto Army, 566
Jones, —, S. Jacinto Army, 565
Jones, A. H., Veteran, 602
Jones, A., S. Jacinto Army, 563
Jones, Allen, S. Jacinto Army, 566
Jones, Anson, 23, 216
JONES, ANSON, 259
JONES, ANSON, ADMINISTRATION, 637
JONES, ANSON VALEDICTORY ADDRESS, 1846, 339
Jones, Anson, illus., 339
Jones, Anson, Pioneers killed, 583
Jones, Anson, Houston 1st Admin, 636
Jones, Anson, Houston 2nd Admin, 637
Jones, Anson, Pro Tem, 639
Jones, Capt. Randal, 197
Jones, Captain Randal, 28
Jones, D. M., 64
Jones, David J., Fannin Massacre, 570
Jones, Francis, 65
Jones, G. W., S. Jacinto Army, 569
Jones, George W., Veteran, 602
Jones, H. W., Fannin Massacre, 574

Jones, Henry, Old 300, 559
Jones, J., 113
Jones, John B., 216
Jones, John B., Judges, 638
JONES, JOHN RICE, 275
Jones, John Rice, Pioneers killed, 582
Jones, John R., Prov. Govt., 634
Jones, John R., Convention, 635
Jones, John R., Lamar Admin, 636
Jones, Kelton M., Veteran, 602
Jones, Lorenzo, Veteran, 602
JONES, OLIVER, 280
Jones, Oliver, Pioneers killed, 584
Jones, Oliver, Old 300, 559
JONES, RANDALL, 284
Jones, Randall, Old 300, 559
Jones, Randall, Pioneers killed, 585
Jones, Randall, Gen. Consultation, 633
Jones, Randall, Prov. Govt., 634
Jones, Randle, Tx Necrology, 579
Jones, T. L., 129
Jones, William E., Pioneers killed, 584
Jones, William E., Judges, 638
Jones, William J., 628
Jones, William J., Judges, 638
Jones, Wm. J., Veteran, 626
Jordan, A. S., S. Jacinto Army, 564
Jordan, John, Veteran, 626
Jordan, S. W., Pioneers killed, 581
Jose Maria, Chief, 141
Joslyn, James, S. Jacinto Army, 565
JUDGES, BIOGRAPHIES OF DECEASED, 300
JUDGES, DISTRICT COURTS, REPUBLIC, 638
JUDICIAL ORGANIZATION OF AUSTIN'S COLONY, 175
Julius Caesar, vessel, 77
Jurisdiction of Columbia, 643
Justice, Milton M., Veteran, 626

K

Kainer, Prvt., S. Jacinto Army, 564
Kamchatka Community, 122
KARANKAWA INDIANS, 145
Karankaway Indians, 71, 197, 217
Karner, John, 603

Karnes, —, S. Jacinto Army, Tx Spy Co., 569
Karnes, Henry, Pioneers killed, 58
KARNES, HENRY, 281
Kauffman, David S., 637
Kaufman County, 592, 601, 628, 631
KAUFMAN, D. S. — WELCOME TO DE SALIGNY, 335
Kaufman, David S., 216
Kaufman, David S., Pioneers killed, 582
Kauffman, David S., Jones Admin, 637
Kaufman, David S., Speakers, 639
Keachie, 614
Keaghsy, William S., Veteran, 603
Kechi Indians, 133, 237
Kechi Settlement, 232
Keeland, Prvt., S. Jacinto Army, 564
Keenan, C. G., Pioneers killed, 584
Keenan, John, Pioneers killed, 582
Keep, Imla, Old 300, 559
Keizer, B. P., Veteran, 603
Keller, Francis G., Veteran, 602
Keller, John, Old 300, 559
Kelley, Connell O. D., Veteran, 603
Kelley, John, Old 300, 559
Kellogg, A. G., Gen. Consultation, 633
Kellogg, Mrs., 202
Kelly, James, Fannin Massacre, 573
Kelly, John, Fannin Massacre, 573, 574
Kelly, Michael, 65
Kelso, Alfred, S. Jacinto Army, 566
Kelso, Alfred, Veteran, 603
Kemble, G., 113
Kemp, Thomas, Fannin Massacre, 573
Kemper Expedition, 207
Kemper, Col. Samuel, 227
Kendall County, 610
Kendall, George W., 465
Kendall, George Wilkins, Pioneers killed, 584
Kendricks, B. H., Veteran, 603
Kennard, A. D., Veteran, 626
Kennard, Michael, Veteran, 602
Kennard, William E., Veteran, 602
Kennard, Wm. E., Veteran, 626
Kennedy, A. S., Veteran, 603
Kennedy, Samuel, Old 300, 559

Kenney, Allen O., Fannin Massacre, 570
Kennon, Alfred, Old 300, 559
Kenny, J., 113
Kent, A., 113
Kent, David B., Veteran, 603
Kent, J., S. Jacinto Army, 569
Kenyon, A. D., S. Jacinto Army, 568
Kerr County, 605
Kerr, George A., Veteran, 602
Kerr, Hugh P., Pioneers killed, 581
Kerr, James, Pioneers killed, 582
KERR, JAMES, 290
Kerr, James, 60
Kerr, James, Old 300, 559
Kerr, James, Prov. Govt., 634
Kerr, William P., Veteran, 603
Kew, Peter, Old 300, 559
Kew, William, Old 300, 559
Kibbe, W., S. Jacinto Army, 567
Kibby, William, Veteran, 603
Kickapoos, 133
Kimble, H. S., 23
Kimble, H. S., Convention, 635
Kimble, John M., Fannin Massacre, 571
Kimps, Q. P., Fannin Massacre, 570
Kinbo, William, S. Jacinto Army, 569
Kincannon, W. P., S. Jacinto Army, 567
Kinchelve, William, Old 300, 559
Kinchloe, Daniel, Veteran, 603
King, Aaron B., Fannin Massacre, 570
King, Capt., 93, 152
King, Charles, 233
King, John E., Veteran, 626
King, M. P., Fannin Massacre, 573
King, R. B., Veteran, 626
King, W., 113
King, W., S. Jacinto Army, 564
Kingston, William, Old 300, 559
Kinney County, 594
Kinney, Henry L., Pioneers killed, 583
Kiowas, 134
Kirby, Gen. E, 348
Kirby, George, Veteran, 603
Kirk, H. H., Fannin Massacre, 570
Kissam, P. T., Fannin Massacre, 573
Kitrell, W. P., Pioneers killed, 584
Kleburg, R., S. Jacinto Army, 566

Kleburg, Robert, Veteran, 603
Knight, James, Old 300, 561
Knoland, E., S. Jacinto Army, 565
Kohn, —, S. Jacinto Army, Tx Spy Co., 569
Kokernot, D. L., Veteran, 603
Korneky, David, S. Jacinto Army, 567
Kortickey, J., Fannin Massacre, 572
Kosse, 595, 599, 611, 613, 618, 623, 632
Kuykendall Capt. A., 188
Kuykendall, Abner, 28
Kuykendall, Abner, Old 300, 559
Kuykendall, Brazilla, Old 300, 559
Kuykendall, J. H., Veteran, 603
Kuykendall, Joseph, Old 300, 559
Kuykendall, Mat, S. Jacinto Army, 566
Kuykendall, Robert, Old 300, 559

L

La Bahia, 21, 224, 239, 655
La Bahia Mission, 18
La Grange, 125, 605, 620
La Purissima Concepcion de Acuna, 18
La Rais Creek, 231
La Salle, 208
LA SALLE, ROBERT CAVALIER DE, 179
La Vibora Creek, 232
Labadie, —, S. Jacinto Army, 563
Labadie, Dr. N. D., 24
Labadie, N. D., Pioneers killed, 584
Labinski, Victor, Veteran, 604
Lacey, William D., Convention, 634
Lackey, William, 158
Lackie, Sam'l H., Pioneers killed, 582
Lacy, W. D. 58
Ladner, Micolas, Veteran, 627
Ladonia, 617
Lafayette Battalion, 245
LAFITTE, 356
Lafitte, Jean, 87, 217
Laforge, A. B., Veteran, 627
La Grange, 38, 605
Lakey, Joel, Old 300, 559
Lamar County, 585, 596, 597, 612, 619, 620, 621, 625, 626, 627, 629, 631

LAMAR MESSAGE, 1840, 335
Lamar's Administration, 636
Lamar, Mirabeau B., 23, 211
Lamar, Mirabeau B., illus., 226
LAMAR, MIRABEAU B., 258
Lamar, Mirabeau B., S. Jacinto Army, 563
Lamar, Mirabeau B., Pioneers killed, 583
Lamar, Mirabeau B., Convention, 635
Lamar, Mirabeau B., Houston 1st Admin, 636
Lamar, President, 127
Lamar, S. W., S. Jacinto Army, 564
Lamb, George A., S. Jacinto Army, 567
Lamb, Lt., S. Jacinto Army, 562
Lambert, W., S. Jacinto Army, 566
Lambert, Walter, 65
LAMENT FOR A STOLEN PET, POEM, 380
Lamon, John, Veteran, 627
Lampasas County, Sulphur Springs, 21
Lampasas County, 598, 606, 610, 623
Lancaster, J., Pioneers killed, 585
Land in Texas, 457
Land Laws, minerals, 442
Landrum, Capt., at Bexar, 220
Lane, J. S., Prov. Govt., 634
Lane, W. P., S. Jacinto Army, 568
Lane, Walter P., 197
Lane, Walter P., Veteran, 604
Lang, John J., Veteran, 604
Lang, Prvt., S. Jacinto Army, 564
Langerheirmer, William, Veteran, 604
Langley, Campbell, Veteran, 604
Lanio, 113
Lantz, Charles, Fannin Massacre, 572
Lapham, —, Pioneers killed, 581
Lara, Vincente, 233, 234
Larbartare, Prvt., S. Jacinto Army, 564
Laredo, 127, 646, 652
Lasiter, F. B., S. Jacinto Army, 568
LAST TEAR I SHED, POEM, 404
Lathrop, J. K. T., Pioneers killed, 581
Latimer, A. H., Veteran, 604
Latimer, A. H., Convention, 635
Latimer, H. R., Veteran, 604
Latimer, J. W., Pioneers killed, 583
Lattimer, A. H., 58

Laura, steamboat, 122, 607
LAUREL AND CYPRESS, POEM, 386
Lavaca County, 616, 617, 619, 621, 627, 632
Lavaca River, 17, 166, 185, 208, 291, 370, 656
Lavaca River [La Bacca], 248
Lavernia, 632
LAWRENCE, ADAM, RIDE, 342
Lawrence, G. W., S. Jacinto Army, 567
Lawrence, J. W., Veteran, 627
Lawrence, J., S. Jacinto Army, 567
Lawrence, Joe, Veteran, 604
Laws of Austin's Colony, 175
Lawson, J. D., Veteran, 603
Le Grand, Louis, 207
Lead in Texas, 496
Leadbeater, Snead, Fannin Massacre, 570
LEADING CHARACTERISTICS OF TEXAS, 447
LEAVE IT! AH NO—THE LAND IS OUR OWN, POEM, 376
Leayne, Hosea H., Old 300, 559
Ledbetter, 600
Lee County, 588, 597, 601, 611, 613
Lee, Grier, Fannin Massacre, 571
Lee, Isaac, 604
Lee, Pleasant M., Veteran, 627
Lee, Theodore S., Veteran, 604
Leek, George W., S. Jacinto Army, 565
Leftwich, R., 202
Legal Fees, Austin Colony, 177
Legg, —, S. Jacinto Army, 563
Legislature of Coahuila and Texas, 189
Legrand, E. C., S. Jacinto Army, 569
Legrand, E. O., 58
Legrand, E. O., Convention, 635
Leiper, Sam, S. Jacinto Army, 567
Leman, John, Veteran, 603
Lemmans, John, Veteran, 626
Leon, 653
Leon County, 603, 610, 614, 623, 629
Leona, 629
Leonard, William R., Veteran, 627
Lesasseim, A., S. Jacinto Army, 567
Leslie, A. J., Veteran, 627
Lester, James S., S. Jacinto Army, 566

Lester, James S., Veteran, 603
Lester, James S., Gen. Consultation, 633
Leveney, Thomas, S. Jacinto Army, 568
Leverette, O. F., Fannin Massacre, 572
Levy, Dr., at Bexar, 223
Lewis, A. S., S. Jacinto Army, 568
Lewis, A., S. Jacinto Army, 568
Lewis, Capt. W. P., 127
Lewis, Edward, S. Jacinto Army, 564
Lewis, G. K., Pioneers killed, 583
Lewis, G. W., S. Jacinto Army, 568
Lewis, George W., Veteran, 604
Lewis, H. K., 26
Lewis, I. R., Prov. Govt., 634
Lewis, Ira R., Gen. Consultation, 633
Lewis, Ira. R., Pioneers killed, 584
Lewis, Jacob, Veteran, 604
Lewis, John E., Veteran, 604
Lewis, John M., Speakers, 639
Lewis, John S., Veteran, 604
Lewis, John T., Veteran, 605
Lewis, John, S. Jacinto Army, 566
Lewis, M. B., 143
Lewis, M. B., Veteran, 604
Lewis, Washington, S. Jacinto Army, 563
Lexington, 613
Libertador, vessel, 77
Liberty, 21, 24, 25, 66, 487, 593, 633, 634
Liberty County, 593, 594, 599, 607, 613, 616, 618
Liberty, schooner, 153
Liberty, vessel, 77
Lightfoot, William, S. Jacinto Army, 566
Lightfoot, Wilson, S. Jacinto Army, 566
Lightfoot, Wm., 113
Lignite coal, 491
Limestone, 611
Limestone County, 198, 233, 586, 595, 599, 604, 618, 619, 620, 632
Limski, Prvt., S. Jacinto Army, 564
Lincecum, Dr., 494
Lind, Prvt., S. Jacinto Army, 564
Lindheimer, Ferdinand, Veteran, 604
Lindsay, B., S. Jacinto Army, 568
Lindsay, James, 28
Lindsay, James, Veteran, 605

Linley, Charles, Fannin Massacre, 573
Linn, John J., 60, 604
Linn, John J., Prov. Govt., 634
Linn, W., 113
Linsey, Benjamin, Old 300, 559
Linsey, Joseph, Veteran, 604
Lipans, 133
Lipantitlan Battle, 1835, 93
Lipscomb, A. S., Pioneers killed, 583
LIPSCOMB, ABNER S., 300
Lipscomb, Abner S., Lamar Admin, 636
Lipscomb, Abner S., DA's, 639
Liquor, 352
LITTLE BABIES, POEM, 425
Little Llano River, 490, 496
Little River, 142, 494
Little Wichita River, 462
Little, Hiram, Veteran, 603
Little, James, Pioneers killed, 585
Little, John, Old 300, 559
Little, William, 88, 185
Little, William, Old 300, 559
Littlefield, H. B., Veteran, 604
Live-oak County, 595, 598, 600, 612, 617, 619
Livergood, J. H., Veteran, 627
Living, W. H., 65
Livingston, 236
Llano County, 607, 610
Llano County Feldspar, 498
Llano County, geology, 488, 493
Llano County, minerals, 21, 444, 445
Llano Estacado, 464, 466, 470
Llewellyn, Capt., at Bexar, 220
Llewelyn, John, S. Jacinto Army, 565
Lockart, Bird, 615
Lockhart, 588
Lockhart, Byrd, Pioneers killed, 581
Lockhart, J. W., Veteran, 627
Lockridge, William, S. Jacinto Army, 565
LOCUST IN TEXAS, MIGRATORY, 511
Loderback, J. D., S. Jacinto Army, 565
Logan, —, Fannin Massacre, 570
Logan, William M., S. Jacinto Army, 567
Lolison, A., S. Jacinto Army, 568
LONE STAR FLAG, 334
LONE STAR OF TEXAS, 341

LONE STAR OF TEXAS, POEM, 407
LONE STAR OF THE SOUTH, POEM, 399
Long Expedition, 207
Long Point, 487, 624
Long, Dr., 87
Long, Jane H., Old 300, 559
Longcope, C. S., Veteran, 627
Longstreet, 613
Longview, 605
Lonly, J., 113
Lord, George, Veteran, 626
Los Angelos, Coahuila, 586
Los Piedros Creek, 232
Loupy, Victor, 65
LOVE AND LATIN, POEM, 403
Love, D., S. Jacinto Army, 569
Love, G. H., Veteran, 604
Love, John H., 82
Love, Robert, S. Jacinto Army, 568
Love, Wm. M., Tx Necrology, 579
Love, Y. E., Veteran, 627
Lovelace, Edward, 88, 185
Loverly, Alexander J., Fannin Massacre, 571
Loving, Joseph, Fannin Massacre, 571
Low, B. C., Veteran, 605
Lowe, Barney C., Veteran, 604
Lower Spring, 21
Lowrie, Jack, S. Jacinto Army, 568
Lubbock, Francis R., Houston 1st Admin, 636
Lubbock, Francis R., Houston 2nd Admin, 637
LUBBOCK, FRANK R., 294
Lubbock, Thomas S., Pioneers killed, 583
Ludus, Prvt., S. Jacinto Army, 564
Lumkin, John, Fannin Massacre, 572
Lusk, R. O., Veteran, 603
Lusk, Samuel, Pioneers killed, 583
Lyford, John, S. Jacinto Army, 567
Lynch, A. M., Fannin Massacre, 572
Lynch, Alexander, 64
Lynch, James, 559
Lynch, Nathaniel, Old 300, 559
Lynch, Nicholas, S. Jacinto Army, 565
Lynchburg, 487, 593

Lynche's Ferry, 193
Lynd, A. H., Fannin Massacre, 570
Lynn, G. W., 113
Lyon, H. C., Veteran, 603
Lyon, Samuel C., Veteran, 627

M

Mabry, Enos, Pioneers killed, 582
MacGrea, Peter, DA's, 638
MacGreal, Peter, DA's, 638
Mackey, John, Veteran, 606
Macomb, David B., Gen. Consultation, 633
Madden, R. W., Veteran, 605
Madison County, 612, 620, 621
Magee Expedition, 225
Magee, Kemper, Gutierez, Perry Expedition, 87
Magee, Lt., 224
Magill, William H., S. Jacinto Army, 565
Mahan, P., 129
Mahan, P. Jenks, Veteran, 605
Maiden, Isaac, S. Jacinto Army, 568
Mails, 328
Main, G. W., 113
Maldonart, Thomas, S. Jacinto Army, 569
Malone, C., S. Jacinto Army, 566
Malone, Charles, 65
Malone, John, Prov. Govt., 634
Manchaca, Antonio, Veteran, 606
Mangum, Aaron S., Fannin Massacre, 571
Mangum, Aaron S., Veteran, 606
Mann, William, Fannin Massacre, .573
Manomy, J. B., Fannin Massacre, 573
Manor, 587
Manton, Edward, Veteran, 628
Manuel, A. E., S. Jacinto Army, 569
Manufactures in Texas, 461
Maple Springs, 625
Maps of West Texas, 464
Marble in Texas, 497
MARBLE LILY, POEM, 392
Marcy, Capt. R. B., 470
Marin, 172
Marinez, Gov., 185
Marion County, 493

Marion County, geology, 490
Marlin, 611
Marlin, Benjamin, 141
Marlin, Isaac, 140
Marlin, John, 140
Marlin, Mary, 140
Marlin, Miss Adelaide, 140
Maro, Col., 170
Marple, Doc, 185
Marrow, Jacob, Veteran, 628
Marsh, Prvt., S. Jacinto Army, 564
Marsh, Shirbal, Pioneers killed, 584
Marsh, Shubart, Old 300, 559
Marshall, 604
Marshall Mines, 501
Marshall, First of Texas, 197
Marshall, John, S. Jacinto Army, 566
Marshall, John, Veteran, 607
Marshall, Joseph T., Veteran, 606
Marshall, Lewis, Veteran, 606
Marshall, Samuel, Veteran, 607
Marshall, T. W., Veteran, 607
Marshall, W., 113
Martial Law, 654
Martin, B. H., Pioneers killed, 582
Martin, B. H., Pioneers killed, 582
Martin, Harvey, Fannin Massacre, 570
Martin, James, 28
Martin, M. W., Veteran, 628
Martin, Philip, Veteran, 606
Martin, Thomas, Veteran, 605
Martin, Wiley, Pioneers killed, 581
Martin, Wiley, 27, 30, 191, 193, 596
Martin, Wily, Gen. Consultation, 633
MARTIN, WYLIE, 274
Martin, Wyly, Old 300, 559
Martin, Wily, Prov. Govt., 634
Martindale, Daniel, Fannin Massacre, 574
Martinez, Juan Jose, 233, 234
Marton, J. P., Veteran, 605
MARY, POEM, 422
Mason County, 588, 594
Mason County, geology, 490
Mason County, minerals, 445
Mason, Charles, Lamar Admin, 636
Mason, Charles, Houston 2nd Admin, 637
Mason, Charles, Veteran, 607

Mason, G. W., S. Jacinto Army, 565
Mason, Prvt., S. Jacinto Army, 564
Mason, William, Fannin Massacre, 570
Massey, J. W., Veteran, 605
Massie, Prvt., S. Jacinto Army, 564
Masters, Jacob, Veteran, 605
Matagorda, 149, 633, 635, 657
Matagorda Bay, 19, 70
Matagorda County, 593, 603, 609, 610, 618, 620, 628
Matagorda Island, 241
Matamoras Expedition, 1835, 80
Matamoras, 1862, 351
Matamoras, 192
Matamoras Expedition, 1836, 93
Mathis, William, Old 300, 559
Matson, James V., Veteran, 628
Mattern, Peter, Fannin Massacre, 573
Matthews, William H., Veteran, 605
Matthews, Z. W., Veteran, 628
MAVERICK, SAMUEL, 287
Maverick, Samuel A., Pioneers killed, 584
Maxwell, J. M., S. Jacinto Army, 567
Maxwell, Thomas, S. Jacinto Army, 569
Mayer, William, Fannin Massacre, 570
Mayes, J. W., Veteran, 628
Mayfield, James H., 216
Mayfield, James S., Lamar Admin, 636
Mayor, Ambrose, S. Jacinto Army, 568
Mayrie, E. G., S. Jacinto Army, 565
Mays, S. A. J., Fannin Massacre, 571
Mays, Thomas A., S. Jacinto Army, 566
McAllister, Joseph, S. Jacinto Army, 565
McAllister, Joseph, Veteran, 608
McAnnelly, Pleasant, Veteran, 606
McAnnelly, R. D., Veteran, 606
McBride, P. H., Veteran, 606
McCaferty, 113
McCawn, J. W., Sr., Veteran, 627
McCay, A. L., Veteran, 628
McCay, John, Veteran, 607
McCay, Prosper C., Veteran, 607
McClelland, Sam, S. Jacinto Army, 565
McClelland, Samuel K., Pioneers killed, 584
McCloskey, John, Old 300, 559
McCloskey, Robert, S. Jacinto Army, 564

McClure, Robert, 64
McCormack, J. N., S. Jacinto Army, 568
McCormack, M., Veteran, 608
McCormick, Michael, Veteran, 606
McCormick, Arthur, Old 300, 559
McCormick, David, Old 300, 559
McCormick, John, Old 300, 560
McCoy, J., 113
McCoy, John, S. Jacinto Army, 567
McCoy, Simon, 233
McCoy, Thomas, Old 300, 559
McCrab, John, S. Jacinto Army, 566
McCrabb, Joseph, S. Jacinto Army, 566
McCracklin, Jesse L., Veteran, 607
McCraven, William, Pioneers killed, 584
MCCULLOCH, BEN, 271
McCulloch, Benjamin, S. Jacinto Army, 563
McCulloch, Benjamin, Pioneers killed, 583
McCullock, Samuel, Veteran, 607
M'Curdy, Placido, S. Jacinto Army, 568
McCutcheon, William, Veteran, 607
McDade, 588, 596, 621, 623, 624, 630
McDonald, Donald, Veteran, 605
McDonald, Dr.g., Waco, 237
McDonald, J., Fannin Massacre, 570
McDonald, John, Veteran, 628
McDonald, Lt. W., at Bexar, 221
McDonald, Wm., Pioneers killed, 582
McDonough, Edward, 65
McFaddin, D. H., Veteran, 606
McFarlan, A. C., Sec. Senate, 639
McFarlan, Achilles, Old 300, 559
McFarlan, John, Old 300, 559
McFarlane, Dugald, 65
McFarlane, J. B. W., S. Jacinto Army, 564
McGahey, James S., Veteran, 607
McGee Expedition, 207
McGee, J., 113
McGehee, Thomas G., Veteran, 605
McGill, W. H., Veteran, 606
McGloin, John, Fannin Massacre, 573
McGowan, Dennis, Fannin Massacre, 573
McGowen, John, Fannin Massacre, 572
McGown, A. J., Pioneers killed, 584
McGregor, 113
McGrew, William, 142

McGriffin, J. T., Veteran, 606
McHorse, J. W., S. Jacinto Army, 567
McHorse, J. W., Veteran, 606
McIntosh, George S., Houston 1st Admin, 636
McKay, D., S. Jacinto Army, 564
McKay, Daniel, S. Jacinto Army, 567
McKay, Daniel, Veteran, 607
Mckenie, —, Fannin Massacre, 571
McKenney, R., 113
McKenny, Thomas F., Old 300, 559
McKensie, Hugh, Old 300, 560
McKenzie, Hugh, S. Jacinto Army, 566
McKim, 225
McKinney, 614
MCKINNEY, COLLIN, 287
McKinney, Collin, Pioneers killed, 583
McKinney, Collin, 58
McKinney, Collin, Convention, 635
McKinney, Thomas F., illus., 206
MCKINNEY, THOMAS F., 279
McKinney, Thomas F., Tx Necrology, 579
McKinstry, G. B., 26
McKinstry, George B., 188
McKinstry, George B., Pioneers killed, 580
McKneely, — (Goliad), 206
McKneely, Samuel W., Veteran, 605
McLain, A. W., Old 300, 559
McLaughlin, Robert, S. Jacinto Army, 566
McLean, Dugald, S. Jacinto Army, 566
McLennan County, 233, 591, 593, 602, 603, 606, 612, 614, 615, 617, 621, 627
McLeod, Gen. H. D., 127, 154
MCLEOD, HUGH, 276
McLeod, Hugh, Pioneers killed, 583
McLeod, John D., Sec. Senate, 639
McLin, Stephen, S. Jacinto Army, 567
McMahan, Thomas H., Pioneers killed, 584
McManus, R. W. O., Veteran, 607
McMaster, William, Veteran, 605
McMillan, Andrew, Veteran, 606
McMinn, Hugh, 64
McMullen, John, Prov. Govt., 634
McMurray, William, Fannin Massacre, 573
McNabb, John, Veteran, 628
McNair, James, Old 300, 559

McNeel, Pinckney S., Tx Necrology, 579
McNeel, Pleasant, Tx Necrology, 579
McNeil, —, S. Jacinto Army, 565
McNeil, Daniel, Old 300, 559
McNeil, George W., Old 300, 559
McNeil, John G., Old 300, 559
McNeil, John G., Veteran, 607
McNeil, P. D., S. Jacinto Army, 566
McNeil, Pleasant D., 89
McNeil, Pleasant, Old 300, 559
McNeil, Sterling, Old 300, 559
McNelly, Bennett, S. Jacinto Army, 567
McNight, George, Fannin Massacre, 573
McNutt, —, Pioneers killed, 582
McNutt, Elizabeth, Old 300, 559
McSherry, Josiah, Fannin Massacre, 571
McStea A., S. Jacinto Army, 564
McWilliams, William, Old 300, 559
Mechanical Pursuits, 454
Medina, 653
Medina River, 22, 92
Meisenhetter, Emanuel, Veteran, 607
Melrose, 615
Melton, E., 113
MEMORIAL FROM THE CONVENTION OF APRIL, 1833, 38
Menard, M. B., 58
Menard, M. B., Convention, 634
MENARD, MICHAEL, 280
Menard, Michel B., Pioneers killed, 583
Menchasen, Antonio, S. Jacinto Army, 569
Menifee, George, Veteran, 607
Menifee, J. S., S. Jacinto Army, 566
Menifee, Jarrett, 141
Menifee, John S., Veteran, 606
Menifee, Thomas, Veteran, 628
Menifee, William, 58, 118, 206
Menifee, William, Veteran, 605
Menifee, William, Gen. Consultation, 633
Menifee, William, Prov. Govt., 634
Mercer, Eli, S. Jacinto Army, 566
Mercer, Elijah, S. Jacinto Army, 566
Mercer, G. R., S. Jacinto Army, 567
Merchant, J. D., Veteran, 605
Meridian, 100th, 472
Merifield, J. Q., Fannin Massacre, 570
Merrell, Nelson, Veteran, 628
Merriam, Col., 308

Merriman, F. H., Pioneers killed, 584
Merriman, F. H., DA's, 638
Merwin, —, S. Jacinto Army, 563
MESQUIT[E] TREE, 512
Messer, Charles, 65
METEOROLOGY OF TEXAS, 358
Mexia, 604, 613, 617
Mexia, General, 189
Mexican Government, 187
Mexican History: 1800-1834, 517
MEXICAN REVOLUTIONS, 350
MEXICAN WAR, REMINISCENCE OF
   THE, 172
Mexico City, 250
M'Fadden, David, S. Jacinto Army, 567
M'Gary, D. H., S. Jacinto Army, 569
M'Gay, Thomas, S. Jacinto Army, 568
M'Gowan, A. G., S. Jacinto Army, 569
Michael, —, Fannin Massacre, 571
Micheson, 113
Middle Texas, 458
Middleton, Mrs., 495
Middleton, W. B., Veteran, 628
MIDSHIPMAN A. J. BRYANT, POEM,
   426
Midway, 620, 621
Mier Expedition, Sequel, 128
Mier Expedition, Black Beans, 129
Mier Prisoners, 130
MIER PRISONER'S LAMENT, POEM,
   417
MIER, BATTLE OF, 127
Milam, 613, 633, 634
Milam County, 589, 590, 594, 597, 598,
   606, 620, 621
Milam, Ben, 37
MILAM, BENJAMIN R., 260
Milam, Benjamin R., Pioneers killed, 580
Milam, Capt. Benj. R., 86
Milam, Col. B. R., 149
Milburn, David H., Old 300, 559
Miles, A. H., S. Jacinto Army, 565
Miles, Edward, S. Jacinto Army, 565
Miles, Edward, Veteran, 607
MILITARY EVENTS OF TEXAS, 92
Mill Creek, 25
Millard, Henry, Pioneers killed, 581
Millard, Henry, Gen. Consultation, 633

Millard, Henry, Prov. Govt., 634
Millen, W., S. Jacinto Army, 564
Miller, Alsey S., Veteran, 628
Miller, Daniel, S. Jacinto Army, 566
Miller, H., S. Jacinto Army, 565
Miller, James B., 82, 216
MILLER, JAMES B., 267
Miller, James B., Pioneers killed, 582
Miller, Joseph, S. Jacinto Army, 566
Miller, Leroy, Veteran, 605
Miller, S. A., Veteran, 627
Miller, Samuel R., Old 300, 559
Miller, Samuel, Old 300, 559
Miller, Simon, Old 300, 559
Miller, T., 113
Miller, William H., S. Jacinto Army, 567
Millerman, —, S. Jacinto Army, 563
Millerman, Ira, Veteran, 607
Millett, —, S. Jacinto Army, 566
Millican, 487, 628
Millican, Eliot M., Pioneers killed, 583
Millican, James D., Old 300, 559
Millican, Robert, Old 300, 559
Millican, William, Old 300, 559
Mills in Texas, 454
Mills, A. H., Pioneers killed, 581
Mills, Granville, S. Jacinto Army, 566
Miller, James B., Houston 2nd Admin,
   637
Mills, John T., Judges, 638
Mills, Seaborne, Fannin Massacre, 572
Mills, W., 113
Milne, C. C., Fannin Massacre, 572
Mims, B., S. Jacinto Army, 566
Mims, Joseph, 353
Mims, Joseph, Old 300, 559
Mims, W. D., Veteran, 628
Mina, 526, 633
Minchey's, 25
MINERAL RESOURCES OF TEXAS,
   493
Mineral Springs, various, 21
Minerals, 21
MINERALS, 442
Mining, 443
Minor, Perry H., Fannin Massacre, 571
M'Intire, Thomas H., S. Jacinto Army,
   568

Minton, S. F., Veteran, 627
Minuett, Prvt., S. Jacinto Army, 564
Mission Espada, 645
MISSIONS, SPANISH, 17
Missouri, Kansas and Texas Railroad, 23
Mitchell, A., S. Jacinto Army, 564
Mitchell, Asa, 634
Mitchell, Asa, Old 300, 559
Mitchell, Asa, Gen. Consultation, 633
Mitchell, Asa, Prov. Govt., 634
Mitchell, E. T., 113
Mitchell, Eli, Pioneers killed, 584
Mitchell, Isaac, Pioneers killed, 582
Mitchell, J. W., Veteran, 628
Mitchell, James, S. Jacinto Army, 567
Mitchell, N., S. Jacinto Army, 567
Mitchell, Nat, Veteran, 607
Mitchell, S. B., S. Jacinto Army, 566
Mitchell, Warren, Fannin Massacre, 569
Mitchell, Washington, Fannin Massacre, 572
Mixteapan, 20
Mizell, Augustine, Veteran, 607
M'Kenzie, A., S. Jacinto Army, 568
M'Manus, R. O. W., S. Jacinto Army, Tx Spy Co., 569
M'Millan, E., S. Jacinto Army, 568
Moat, John, Fannin Massacre, 571
Mocha, Jose Maria, S. Jacinto Army, 569
Mock, William, S. Jacinto Army, 566
Moffitt, William, Veteran, 608
Money, 651
Money, J. H., S. Jacinto Army, 566
Monks, John, Old 300, 559
Monroe, A. T., Veteran, 628
Monroe, Captain, 124
Montague County Fortification, 207
Monte Grande, 232
Monterey, 172
Monterey, Battle, 173
Montezuma, vessel, 80
Montgomery, 261, 590, 591, 606, 614
Montgomery County, 590, 591, 603, 606, 608, 613, 614, 617, 619, 632
Montgomery, A., S. Jacinto Army, 568
Montgomery, J., S. Jacinto Army, 568
Montgomery, James, Veteran, 605

Montgomery, McGrealy, 607
Montgomery, Prvt., S. Jacinto Army, 564
Montzuma, vessel, 77
Moochakah Comanches, 134
Moody, Edw., Fannin Massacre, 570
Moody, J. W., Prov. Govt., 634
Moody, James A., Pioneers killed, 585
Moody, John W., Pioneers killed, 581
Moody, John W., Houston 1st Admin, 636
Moody, John W., Lamar Admin, 636
Moore, John H., Convention, 635
Moody, Miles W., Veteran, 627
Moore, A. G., Veteran, 607
Moore, Col. John H., 84
Moore, Commodore, 79
Moore, D., Fannin Massacre, 573
MOORE, E. W., 270
Moore, E. W., Pioneers killed, 583
MOORE, FRANCIS, 273
Moore, Francis, Pioneers killed, 584
Moore, J. H., 621, 628, 630, 635, 651
Moore, J. H., Fannin Massacre, 572
Moore, John H., Veteran, 605
Moore, John O., Fannin Massacre, 571
Moore, John W., 58
Moore, John W., Gen. Consultation, 633
Moore, L. V., Veteran, 627
Moore, Lamar, Pioneers killed, 582
Moore, Michael, 234
Moore, Prvt., S. Jacinto Army, 564
Moore, R. B., 113
Moore, Robert, S. Jacinto Army, 564, 566
Moore, T. W., Veteran, 606
Moore, W. J., Veteran, 628
Moore, W. P., S. Jacinto Army, 564
Moore, Z. W., Veteran, 628
Moorehouse, Ed., Pioneers killed, 582
Morales, 602
Moran, Martin, Fannin Massacre, 571
Mordecat, Benjamin H., Fannin Massacre, 571
Mordorff, Prvt., S. Jacinto Army, 564
Moreland, J. N., S. Jacinto Army, 563
Moreland, Joseph, Lamar Admin, 636
Moreton's, 193
Morgan, George, 140

Morgan, George W., Veteran, 608
Morgan, J. F., Fannin Massacre, 572
Morgan, Jackson, 140
Morgan, John D., Veteran, 606
Morgan, John, S. Jacinto Army, 565
Morgan, S. H., Pioneers killed, 584
Morgan, William, 140
Moris, Henry J., 65
MORIS, ROBERT, 278
Mormon Falls, 325
Mormon Mills, 497
Morrel, Z. N., Veteran, 628
Morrill, T. N., 314
Morris, —, Pioneers killed, 580
Morris, George W., Veteran, 608
Morris, F. A., Lamar Admin, 636
Morris, John D., DA's, 638
Morris, Maj. R. C., 81, 220
Morris, Richard, Pioneers killed, 581
Morris, Richard W., Judges, 638
Morrison, — (at Velasco), 31
Morrison, Gwyn, Veteran, 606
Morrison, Moses, Old 300, 559
Morser, David, Old 300, 559
Morton, E., 113
Morton, Prvt., S. Jacinto Army, 564
Morton, William, Old 300, 559
Mosely, Daniel, Pioneers killed, 583
Moses, M. K., Fannin Massacre, 572
Mosier, Adam, S. Jacinto Army, 565
Moss Bluff, 607
Moss, John, S. Jacinto Army, 567
Moss, Matthew, S. Jacinto Army, 567
Moss, Matthew, Veteran, 607
Mosses Spring, 28
Motley, M., Pioneers killed, 580
Motley, W., 58
Motley, William, S. Jacinto Army, 563
Motley, William, Convention, 634
Mott, Samuel, Veteran, 608
Mound Prairie, 207
Mountain City, 588
Mugere Island, 78
Muir, W., S. Jacinto Army, 566
Mukwarrah, Chief, 154
Munger, Nelson H., Pioneers killed, 583
Munoz, Manual, 229

Munson, J. R., Fannin Massacre, 571
Munson, Mordello S., Veteran, 628
Murphy J. B., Fannin Massacre, 572
Murphy, David, S. Jacinto Army, 568
Murphy, William, Fannin Massacre, 574
MURRAH, PENDLETON, 295
Murrah, Pendleton, Pioneers killed, 584
Murray, William, 224
Musquiz, Ramon, 190
Mussulman, R., 113
Mustang Ponds, 465
Muzquiz, Lt. M., journal, 231
MY CHILDHOOD'S HOME, POEM, 377
MY EARLY DAYS, POEM, 420

N

Nabors, William, S. Jacinto Army, 567
Nacogdoches, 1812, 224
Nacogdoches, 21, 87, 189, 227, 230, 231, 596, 602, 611, 613, 617, 629, 633, 634, 656
Nacogdoches County, 586, 588, 604, 609, 612, 613, 615, 616, 617
Nacogdoches Indians, 17
Nacogdoches, Battle, 1827, 92
Nacogdoches, Battle of, 598
Nacogdoches, Campaign, 604
Nacogdoches, Oil, 498
Nacogdoches, Veteran, 628
Nacogdoches, Volunteers, 652
Nail, 651
NAMES OF VETERANS, 585
Nash, J., S. Jacinto Army, 564
Nashville Company, 202
Nassonis Indians, 207
Natchez, vessel, 77
Natchitoches, 17, 224
National Flag, 195
Nautilus, 583
Nautilus, schooner, 1856, 509
NAVAL HEROES, POEM, 405
Navarro County, 313, 587, 590, 601, 604, 606, 623, 632
Navarro, Jose Antonio, 58, 127, 216, 222
Navarro, Jose Antonio, Convention, 634

NAVARRO, JOSE ANTONIO, 289
Navarro, Jose Antonio, Pioneers killed, 584
Navarro, N., S. Jacinto Army, 569
Navarro, Nepomuceno, Veteran, 608
Navasota, 487, 597, 606, 618, 623, 631, 632
Navasota River, 232
Navidad, 600, 619
Navidad River, 370
NAVY, THE TEXAS, 77
Neal, Lewis, Veteran, 608
Neches River, 17, 231
NECROLOGY, 578
Neel, Felding, Veteran, 608
Neighbors, Maj. R. S., 134
Neighbors, Robert S., Pioneers killed, 583
Neil, Colonel, at Bexar, 218
Neil, J. C., S. Jacinto Army, 563
Neil, J., S. Jacinto Army, 564
Neill, Andrew, Veteran, 608
Neill, Andrew, DA's, 638
Nelsom, James, Old 300, 560
Nelson, A. A., Veteran, 629
Nelson, Allison, Pioneers killed, 583
Nelson, David S., S. Jacinto Army, 564
Nelson, James, S. Jacinto Army, 562, 566
Nelson, Wm. G., 113
Nelsonville, 621
Nettles, William, Veteran, 608
Nevin, Patrick, Fannin Massacre, 573
New Braunfels, 604
New Orleans, 70
New Orleans Grays, 222
Newcomb, Thomas, DA's, 639
Newell, 657
Newell, John D., Veteran, 608
Newell, John D., Gen. Consultation, 633
Newland, William, 65
Newman, Joseph, Old 300, 560
Newman, W. G., S. Jacinto Army, 565
Newton County, 602, 603, 604, 605
Nichols, A. B., Pioneers killed, 584
Nicholson, James, Veteran, 629
Niel, Col., 81
Nirlas, Prvt., S. Jacinto Army, 564
Nixon, C., Fannin Massacre, 572

Nixon, Mr., 199
Nixon, N., S. Jacinto Army, 564
Noble, Benjamin, 64
Nobles, Watkins, Fannin Massacre, 571
Noconu Comanches, 134
Noessel, George, Pioneers killed, 584
Nolan Burial, 235
Nolan Trial, 234
NOLAN, PHILIP, 229
Nolan, Throwing Dice, 234
Noland, J., 113
Norris, Thomas, Veteran, 608
North Fork of the Canadian River, 471
Northern Texas, 458
NORTHERS OF TEXAS, 366
Northers, Texas, 506
Northington, M., Veteran, 608
Northwestern Texas, 459
Norton, M. P., Pioneers killed, 583
Norton, M. P., Judges, 638
Norvell, Lipscomb, Veteran, 608
Norvell, William L., Veteran, 608
NOT DEAD—BUT GONE BEFORE, POEM, 436
Nuckels, M. B., Old 300, 560
Nueces, 648
Nueces County, 592, 596, 610, 625
Nueces River, 93, 653, 654
Numlin, John, Fannin Massacre, 573
Nunes, Colonel, 172

O

O'Bannion, Jennings, Veteran, 608
O'Conner, P. B., S. Jacinto Army, 566
O'Connor, C. J., 65
O'Connor, James, 65
O'Connor, Thomas, 65
O'Connor, Thomas, Veteran, 608
O'Daniel, John, Fannin Massacre, 572
O'Donnell, Michael, 64
O'Leary, Patrick, 64
O'Neil, Prvt., S. Jacinto Army, 564
O'Neil, Z., Fannin Massacre, 573
Oakville, 598, 600, 617
Obanion, S. Jacinto Army, 568
OCHILTREE, W. B., 298

Ochiltree, W. B., Pioneers killed, 584
Ochiltree, William B., 216
Ochiltree, William B., Jones Admin, 637
Ochiltree, William B., Judges, 638
ODE TO SAN JACINTO, POEM, 396
Oden, David, S. Jacinto Army, 568
Officers of Provisional Government, 634
Ogden, Frederic W., DA's, 638
Ogden, J. M., 129
Ogden, J. M., DA's, 638
Ogsbury, C. A., Veteran, 608
Oil in Texas, 498
Old Paint, Pioneers killed, 581
OLD THREE HUNDRED, 557
Old Three Hundred, 575
Oldham, W. S., Pioneers killed, 584
Oldum, Benjamin, Fannin Massacre, 570
Oliver, John M., Fannin Massacre, 571
ON THE DEATH OF DAVID CROCKETT, POEM, 419
Onion Creek, 325
Orange County, 589, 611
Orquisaco Indians, 17
Orr, Captain George, 29
Orr, Thomas, S. Jacinto Army, 567
Orrick, James, Old 300, 560
Ortiz, Jose, 646
Osborn, John L., Veteran, 608
Osborn, Nathan, Old 300, 561
Osborn, Thomas, Veteran, 608
Osborne, A. H., Fannin Massacre, 571
Osborne, Benjamin, S. Jacinto Army, 565
Osburn, Patrick, Fannin Massacre, 571
Oso, 605, 623
Ostiner, C., 113
Our Lady of Loretto Mission, 17
Overton, Gen., 224
Owen, Clark L., 611
Owen, Clark L., Pioneers killed, 583
Owen, Harrison, Veteran, 629
Owen, T. D., S. Jacinto Army, 566
Owens, Robert, Fannin Massacre, 570
Owensville, 495, 606
Owensville, Coal, 499
Ownby, James, S. Jacinto Army, 562, 565

P

Pace, Demry, S. Jacinto Army, 565
Pace, James R., S. Jacinto Army, 565
Pace, James R., Veteran, 609
Pace, Robert A., Fannin Massacre, 571
Pace, W., S. Jacinto Army, 565
Pacific Railroad, 467
Pacific Railroad Route, 471
Pacific Railroad Company, 501
Pack Saddle Mountains, 493, 497
Padilla, 646
Padilla, J. A., Prov. Govt., 634
Padilla, Juan Antonio, 60
Page, Calvin, S. Jacinto Army, 562
Paggan, G., 113
Pain, G. W., 65
Pain, George, Fannin Massacre, 574
Paine, John, Veteran, 610
Palestine, 589, 624
Palmer, Isham, Tx Necrology, 579
Palmer, William H., DA's, 639
Palo Pinto County, minerals, 445
Panhandle of Texas, 459
PANHANDLE OF TEXAS, 468
Panhandle, Indians, 133
Pannell, Hugh G., Veteran, 609
Paris, 585, 596, 612, 619, 620, 627, 631
Park, Dr. J., 513
Park, William A., S. Jacinto Army, 563
Park, William, Old 300, 560
Parker County, 609
Parker County, minerals, 443
Parker Rescue, 199
Parker, Benjamin, 201
Parker, C., 113
Parker, C. A., 65
Parker, Daniel, Veteran, 610
Parker, Daniel, Prov. Govt., 634
Parker, Daniel, Gen. Consultation, 633
Parker, Dickins, S. Jacinto Army, 567
Parker, G. A., Pioneers killed, 582
Parker, Granny, 202
Parker, Isaac D., Veteran, 629
Parker, Isaac, Veteran, 609
Parker, J. W., Gen. Consultation, 633
Parker, James W., 200

Parker, John, 201
Parker, John R., Fannin Massacre, 572
Parker, Joshua, Old 300, 560
Parker, Mrs. Silas, 199
Parker, Silas, 201
Parker, William, Old 300, 560
Parker, William S., Fannin Massacre, 572
Parmer, Martin, 58
PARMER, MARTIN, 280
Parmer, Martin, Gen. Consultation, 633
Parmer, Martin, Prov. Govt., 634
Parr, Samuel, Veteran, 610
Parvin, William, Fannin Massacre, 571
Paschal, Frank L., Veteran, 610
Paschal, Ira A., Pioneers killed, 584
Paschal, Prvt., S. Jacinto Army, 564
Pashal, Samuel, Tx Necrology, 579
Pass Caballo, 71
Passe, William, S. Jacinto Army, 566
Pate, William, S. Jacinto Army, 568
Pate, Wm. H., Veteran, 610
Patilla, Juan Antonio, Pioneers killed, 581
Patillo, G. A., Prov. Govt., 634
Patrick, C. H., Veteran, 629
Patrick, George M., 527
Patrick, George M., Veteran, 609
Patrick, George M., Gen. Consultation, 633
Patten, A. B., Veteran, 609
Patten, Wm. G., Veteran, 62
Pattenville, 597, 621
Patterson, Edmund, Fannin Massacre, 572
Patterson, J. S., S. Jacinto Army, 565
Patterson, J. S., Veteran, 610
Patton, Capt., at Bexar, 220
Patton, Charles, Fannin Massacre, 572
Patton, J. M., Veteran, 629
Patton, Prvt., S. Jacinto Army, 564
Patton, St. Clair, S. Jacinto Army, 568
Patton, William H., S. Jacinto Army, 563, 568
Payne, John C., Veteran, 610
Payne, Thomas P., Veteran, 609
Peach Point, 88
Peacock, Capt., at Bexar, 220
Peacock, James T., Veteran, 629
Pearce Boundary Bill, 312

Pearson, Capt., 353
Pearson, William H., Veteran, 629
Pease River, 462
Pease, E. M., 205, 294
Pease, E. M., Veteran, 610
Pease, E. M., Prov. Govt., 634
Pease, E. M., Houston 1st Admin, 636
Pease, E. M., DA's, 638
Pease, L. T., Fannin Massacre, 571
Pebbles, S. W., S. Jacinto Army, 568
Peck, Nathaniel, S. Jacinto Army, 565
Peck, Nicholas, S. Jacinto Army, 566
Pecos County, minerals, 442, 446
Pecos River, 20
Pecos, Tx, 465
Peebles, R. R., Veteran, 610
Pelican Island, 218
Pelican, schooner, 153
Pelone, 113
Pena, Jacinto, S. Jacinto Army, 569
Pendarvis, Caleb, 494
Pennatethca Comanches, 134
Pennington, Elijah, Veteran, 629
Pennington, Sidney O., 58
Pennington, Sidney O., Convention, 634
Penny, George W., Fannin Massacre, 570
Penticost, G. W., S. Jacinto Army, 568
Penticost, George S., Old 300, 560
People of Texas, 459
Perch, Levy, S. Jacinto Army, 567
Perez, Ignacio, Pioneers killed, 582
Perkins, —, Fannin Massacre, 570
Perkins, Austin, Fannin Massacre, 571
Perkins, B. H., 65
Peroti[e], Mex., 127
Perrington, Isaac, Old 300, 560
Perry Expedition, 207
Perry's Landing, 588
Perry, A. G., Prov. Govt., 634
Perry, A. G., Gen. Consultation, 633
Perry, Albert G., Tx Necrology, 579
Perry, C. A., Pioneers killed, 582
Perry, C. R., Veteran, 609
Perry, Emily M., Pioneers killed, 582
Perry, James Franklin, Pioneers killed, 582
Perry, James H., S. Jacinto Army, 563
Perry, M., Veteran, 609

Perryville, 614, 615
Peterson, C. W., DA's, 638
Peterson, John, S. Jacinto Army, 568
Peterson, William, S. Jacinto Army, 568
Petreswich, F., Fannin Massacre, 572
Petroleum in Texas, 498
Petroleum Springs, 446
Pettick, George, Fannin Massacre, 573
Pettus, E. C., S. Jacinto Army, 566
Pettus, Freeman, Old 300, 560
Pettus, John F., Veteran, 609
Pettus, John, S. Jacinto Army, 566
Pettus, W., Pioneers killed, 581
Pettus, William, 25, 188
Pettus, William, Old 300, 560
Petty, George W., Veteran, 609
Petty, George, S. Jacinto Army, 567
Petty, John, Old 300, 560
Petty, R. E., Fannin Massacre, 574
Pevehouse, Preston, Veteran, 608
Peyton, Jonathan C., Old 300, 560
Phelps, J. A. E., Pioneers killed, 582
Phelps, James A. E., Old 300, 560
Phelps, Virgil H., Veteran, 629
Philips, Bennet, Veteran, 610
Philips, Charles, Fannin Massacre, 570
Phillips, Isham B., Old 300, 560
Phillips, Prvt., S. Jacinto Army, 564
Phillips, S., S. Jacinto Army, 568
Phillips, Sam, S. Jacinto Army, 567
Phillips, William, Veteran, 608
Phillips, Zeno, Old 300, 560
Pickering, J., S. Jacinto Army, 568
Picket, Pamelia, Old 300, 560
Piedras, Col., 189
Piedras, Col. Don Je de las, 92
Piedras, Colonel, 28
Pier, J. B., Veteran, 609
Pierce, —, S. Jacinto Army, Tx Spy Co.,
    569
Pierce, Joel J., 233, 234
Pierce, P. R., Veteran, 609
Pierce, Prvt., S. Jacinto Army, 564
Pierce, Stephen, Fannin Massacre, 573
Pierce, W. J. C., S. Jacinto Army, 564
Pierson, J. G. W., Gen. Consultation, 633
Pilant, G. B., Veteran, 629

Pilgrim, Thomas J., Veteran, 609
Pillsbury, Timothy, Pioneers killed, 583
Pilot Point, 605, 625
Pinchback, J. R., S. Jacinto Army, 565
Pipkin, W. R., Veteran, 629
Pitman, James, Fannin Massacre, 574
Pitman, Samuel C., Fannin Massacre, 572
Pittman, Edward W., Veteran, 610
Pitts, John D., Pioneers killed, 583
Pitts, John G., Veteran, 609
Pivey, 651
Placias, Juan J., Veteran, 610
Placido, Chief, 133
Plaster, Thomas, S. Jacinto Army, 563
Pleasanton, 616
Pleasants, George W., Veteran, 609
Plum Creek, 622
Plum Creek Fight, 609
Plummer, James Pratt, 201
Plummer, Mrs., 201
Plunkett, J., S. Jacinto Army, 566
Plunkett, John, Veteran, 609
Pocket, vessel, 77
Poe, George W., Pioneers killed, 581
POEMS, 361, 375
Pohobis Comanches, 134
Polk County, 579, 600
Polk, Thoams, Veteran, 610
Pollan, John, 65
Pollard, Dr., at, 223
Pollard, N., 113
Polley, Joseph H., Old 300, 560
Polly, Doc., 185
Polly, Joseph, 88
Polly, Joseph, Pioneers killed, 584
Pope, Capt., West Texas, 464
Population Statistics, 121
Population, Early Texas, 103
Population, Texas, 22
Porcelain in Texas, 497
Port of Sisal, 153
Port Sullivan, 495
Post, J. C., Veteran, 609
Potatoes, 450
Potomac, vessel, 79
Potsdam rock, 496
Potter's Clay in Texas, 497

Potter, John W., Pioneers killed, 581
Potter, R., 58
Potter, Robert, 216
POTTER, ROBERT, 275
Potter, Robert, Pioneers killed, 581
Potter, Robert, Convention, 634-635
Poveto, Michael, S. Jacinto Army, 567
Powell, J., S. Jacinto Army, 567
Powell, Lewis, 64
Powell, Lewis, Fannin Massacre, 574
Powell, Peter, Old 300, 559
Power, James, 58
Power, James, Prov. Govt., 634
Powers, J. M., Fannin Massacre, 571
Powers, Jackson, 142
Powers, James, Pioneers killed, 582
Prairie Dog Town River, 462
Prairie Lea, 612, 626
Prairie Plains, 627
PRAIRIE SUNSET, 330
PRAIRIE, TEXAS . . . IN SPRING, 330
Prator, William, Old 300, 560
Pratt, Albert, 64
Pratt, Thomas, S. Jacinto Army, 565
Pratt, Thomas, Veteran, 610
PRESIDENTS PRO TEM, SENATE,
  REPUBLIC, 639
Presidio County, minerals, 442
Preusch, William G., Fannin Massacre, 570
Prewett, Elisha, Veteran, 610
Prewett, John M., Veteran, 610
Price, H. W. B., Veteran, 610
Price, Robert, Veteran, 609
Price, William B., Veteran, 609
Prices in Texas, 460
Print, Pleasant, Old 300, 560
Prissick, William, Veteran, 610
PROCLAMATION, HOUSTON, 1835,
  328
Proctor, J. W., S. Jacinto Army, 569
PROMINENT OFFICIAL OF THE
  REPUBLIC, 638
Protectionism, 336
Providence Church, 313
Pryor, William, Old 300, 560
Public Lands in Texas, 460
Puebla, Mex., 127

Putman, Michael, Veteran, 610
Putnam, Mitchell, S. Jacinto Army, 562,
  566

Q

Quahadechaco Comanches, 134
Quail Hunt, 325
Querry, M., 113
Quinan, George, DA's, 639
Quinn, William, 65
Quinn, William, Fannin Massacre, 574
Quirk, Edmund, 64
Quirk, Thomas, Fannin Massacre, 573
Quitman, 613

R

Rabb, Andrew, Old 300, 560
Rabb, Andrew, Pioneers killed, 584
Rabb, John, Pioneers killed, 583
Rabb, Thomas, Pioneers killed, 581
Rabb, Thomas, Old 300, 560
Rabb, William, Old 300, 560
Racoon's Ford, 122
Raglin, H. W., Veteran, 612
Ragsdale, E. B., Veteran, 611
Ragsdale, M. H., Veteran, 612
Ragsdale, Peter C., Veteran, 611
Ragsdale, William J., Veteran, 611
Railey, Charles, Pioneers killed, 585
Railroad in West Texas, 467
Railroads, 22, 184
Rain, V. N., S. Jacinto Army, 566
Rainey, R. R., Fannin Massacre, 570
Rainfall Table, 505
Rains, J. D., Fannin Massacre, 572
Rainwater, E. R., S. Jacinto Army, 564
Raleigh, William, Old 300, 560
Raman, Richard, Veteran, 612
Ramey, Lawrence, Old 300, 560
Ramon, Capt. Don, 17
Ramsdale, M. F., Veteran, 612
Ramsdel, G. L., Veteran, 611
Randall, O. M., Veteran, 612
Randon, David, Old 300, 560
Randon, John, Old 300, 560

Raney, C., S. Jacinto Army, 567
Raney, L., S. Jacinto Army, 568
Ranger Plantation, Coal, 499
Rangers, Texas, 158, 174, 198, 201
Rankin, Frederick, Old 300, 560
Rankin, Frederick H., Veteran, 612
Rapides Parish, 224
Rattan Thicket, Tx, 365
Rawls, Amos, Old 300, 560
Rawls, Benjamin, Old 300, 560
Rawls, Daniel, 73
Rawls, Daniel, Old 300, 560
Ray, —, Fannin Massacre, 571
Ray, Anderson, Fannin Massacre, 571
Raymond, Charles H., Houston 2nd
    Admin, 637
Raymond, James H., Clerk, 639
Raymond, S. B., S. Jacinto Army, 565
Read, Ezra, Veteran, 612
Reamos, S. Y., Veteran, 611
Reaves, D. W., S. Jacinto Army, 564
Record, John, DA's, 638
Rector, Claiborn, S. Jacinto Army, 568
Rector, Claiborne, Tx Necrology, 579
Rector, E. G., S. Jacinto Army, 562, 568
Rector, E. G., Veteran, 612
Rector, Pendleton, S. Jacinto Army, 568
Rector, Pendleton, Veteran, 612
Red River, 20, 469, 635
Red River County, 593, 598, 603, 604,
    621, 625, 628, 631
Red Rock, 622
Redd, — (Goliad), 205
Redd, Capt., 155
Redd, William D., S. Jacinto Army, 564
Reddenson, 113
Redfield, H. P., Veteran, 611
Redfield, Jno. A., Veteran, 613
Redfield, W., 65
Redlanders, 193
Reed, Elijah B., Veteran, 612
Reed, Jefferson, Veteran, 612
Reed, Joseph, 233
Reed, Nathaniel, Veteran, 611
Reed, T. J., Veteran, 611
Reed, William, Veteran, 612
Reed, Wilson, 142

Reel, R. J. L., S. Jacinto Army, 565
Reels, Patrick, Old 300, 560
Reese, C. K., S. Jacinto Army, 566
Reese, Capt., 129
Reese, John, Fannin Massacre, 570
Reese, Perry, Fannin Massacre, 572
Reese, W. P., S. Jacinto Army, 566
Refugio, 608, 611, 630, 634
Refugio County, 239, 594, 595, 608, 611,
    619, 622, 630
Refugio Mission, 81, 144, 146
Refugio Mission Battle, 1836, 93
Register Newspaper, 412
Reid, James, Fannin Massacre, 573
Reid, John R., DA's, 638
Reid, Nathaniel, S. Jacinto Army, 566
Reiley, James, Lamar Admin, 637
REPLY TO LAMENT FOR A STOLEN
    PET, POEM, 382
REPUBLIC DISTRICT COURT
    JUDGES, 638
REPUBLIC DISTRICT ATTORNEYS,
    638
REPUBLIC HOUSE OF REP., SPEAK-
    ERS, 639
REPUBLIC HOUSE OF REP, CHIEF
    CLERK, 639
Republic of Texas, 635
REPUBLIC SECRETARIES OF
    SENATE, 639
Republic, early, 23
REPUBLIC, PRESIDENTS PRO TEM,
    SENATE, 639
RESURGAM, POEM, 423
REVOLUTION OF TEXAS IN 1812,
    224
Revolution, Early Events, 149, 520
Revolution, Early Battles, 192, 527
Revolution, Speech on, 181
Revolution, Texas, 24
REVOLUTION, TEXAS, RELIC OF
    THE, 165
Rheinhart, Prvt., S. Jacinto Army, 564
Rhodes, Joseph, S. Jacinto Army, 565
Rial, John W., S. Jacinto Army, 565
Rice, 449, 587
Rice, James O., Veteran, 629

Rice, Z. B., Veteran, 629
Richards, John, Fannin Massacre, 573
Richards, Mordecai, 230
Richards, Stephen, 233
Richards, William B., Veteran, 613
Richardson, —, S. Jacinto Army, 564
Richardson, Dr., 655
Richardson, J., S. Jacinto Army, 568
Richardson, Prvt., S. Jacinto Army, 564
Richardson, Stephen F., 74
Richardson, Stephen, Old 300, 560
Richardson, W., 651
Richardson, W., S. Jacinto Army, 565
Richmand, 594, 590, 596, 608, 609, 614,
  615, 616, 619, 623, 628, 629
Ricks, G. W., Veteran, 612
Riddell, Samuel, Fannin Massacre, 570
Riddle, Jos. P., Fannin Massacre, 570
Rieves, Thomas, Fannin Massacre, 572
Riley, James, Pioneers killed, 584
Rio Grande River, 17, 18, 20, 22
Rio Tigre, 172
Ripley, H. D., Fannin Massacre, 573
Ripley, Phineas, S. Jacinto Army, 568
Rivers, Principal, 22
Rives, Denmore, 99
Robards, Willis L., Pioneers killed, 584
Robbin's Ferry, 224
Robbins, 113
Robbins, Early, Old 300, 560
Robbins, John, S. Jacinto Army, 564
Robbins, John, Tx Necrology, 580
Robbins, Thomas, S. Jacinto Army, 564
Robbins, William, Old 300, 560
Roberson, Jerome B., Veteran, 611
Roberts, Andrew, Old 300, 560
Roberts, C. H., 129
Roberts, Capt., at Bexar, 218, 219
Roberts, Charles, Veteran, 611
Roberts, D., S. Jacinto Army, 568
Roberts, David, Veteran, 612
Roberts, G. H., Pioneers killed, 585
Roberts, George H., Tx Necrology, 579
Roberts, John S., 58
Roberts, John S., Veteran, 613
Roberts, John S., Convention, 634
Roberts, Joseph P., S. Jacinto Army, 568

Roberts, Moses F., Veteran, 610
Roberts, Noel F., Old 300, 560
Roberts, O. M., DA's, 638
Roberts, Samuel A., Pioneers killed, 584
Roberts, Samuel A., Lamar Admin, 636
Roberts, William, Old 300, 560
Robertson, 624
Robertson Colony, 203, 494, 586, 590,
  604, 606, 621, 628, 630, 632
Robertson County, Veteran, 589
Robertson, Arthur, Sec. Senate, 639
Robertson, E. S. C., Veteran, 611
Robertson, Edward, Old 300, 560
Robertson, H. A., Veteran, 630
Robertson, J. B., 601
Robertson, S. C., 58, 611
ROBERTSON, STERLING C., 288
Robertson, Sterling C., illus., 288
Robertson, Sterling C., Convention, 635
Robertson, William, S. Jacinto Army, 567
Robertson, Wm., 64
Robins, N., Gen. Consultation, 633
Robinson, Andrew, 334
Robinson, Andrew, Old 300, 560
Robinson, Andy, 89
Robinson, Ben W., Veteran, 612
Robinson, Capt. Andrew, 195
Robinson, Col., 656
Robinson, G. W., S. Jacinto Army, 562,
  567
Robinson, George, Old 300, 560
Robinson, George W., Veteran, 612
Robinson, Isaac, 65
Robinson, J. W., S. Jacinto Army, 564
Robinson, J., S. Jacinto Army, 566
Robinson, James W., 23
ROBINSON, JAMES W., 275
Robinson, James W., Gen. Consultation,
  633
Robinson, James W., Pioneers killed, 582
Robinson, James W., Prov. Govt., 634
Robinson, James W., Judges, 638
Robinson, Jesse, S. Jacinto Army, 566
Robinson, Jesse, Veteran, 612
Robinson, Joel W., Veteran, 611
Robinson, John G., Pioneers killed, 580
Robinson, S., 113

Robinson, Sterling C., 202
Robinson, T. J., S. Jacinto Army, 563
Robinson, Zoraster, Veteran, 610
Rockdale, 589, 621
Rockport, 594, 595, 601, 618, 630, 631
Rockwell, C., S. Jacinto Army, 568
Roddy, Anthony, Veteran, 611
Rodgers, A. G., Veteran, 629
Rodgers, J. B., Fannin Massacre, 572
Rodridge, Abro, S. Jacinto Army, 569
Rogers E. W., Pioneers killed, 585
Rogers, H., Fannin Massacre, 572
Rogers, James, Veteran, 613
Rogers, Lieuen M., Veteran, 611
Rogers, S. C. A., Veteran, 612
Rollins, Charles, chief, 227
Rolls, R., Veteran, 611
Roman, Richard, 205
Romans, A. R., S. Jacinto Army, 564
Rooney, Cornelius, Fannin Massacre, 572
Rorder, Louis, S. Jacinto Army, 566
Rose, Gideon, Fannin Massacre, 570
Rose, Moses, 410
Rosenbury, William, Fannin Massacre, 573
Ross Expedition, 207
Ross, Gideon S., Fannin Massacre, 571
Ross, James, Old 300, 560
Ross, Maj. Reuben, 227
Ross, Reuben, Pioneers killed, 581
Ross, Richard, Veteran, 613
Ross, Thomas B., Fannin Massacre, 571
Rough, N., 113
Round Mountain, 609
Round Rock, 602, 614, 628
Round Top, 598
Rounds, George, Fannin Massacre, 572
Rounds, Lyman F., S. Jacinto Army, 564
Rourk, Elijah, Old 300, 560
Routt, Henry T., Veteran, 613
Rowe, James, S. Jacinto Army, 569
Rowe, Joseph, Pioneers killed, 584
Rowe, Samuel, Fannin Massacre, 571
Rowland, Captain John G., 31
ROYAL, R. R., 290
Royall, J. W., Gen. Consultation, 633
Royall, R. R., Pioneers killed, 581
Royall, R. R., Prov. Govt., 634

Rubb, John, Old 300, 560
Ruble, Fielden, Veteran, 612
Rucker, B. F., Veteran, 629
Rucker, Lindsey P., Veteran, 630
Rudders, N., S. Jacinto Army, 565
Ruis, Francis, 58
Ruis, Francis, Convention, 634
Ruiz, Governor, 351
Rumley, Thomas, Fannin Massacre, 571
Rumors, Civil War, 350
Runge, Henry, Pioneers killed, 585
RUNNELS, HARDIN R., 294
Runnels, Hardin R., Pioneers killed, 585
Runnels, Hiram G., Pioneers killed, 583
Runyan, W. J., Veteran, 630
Rupley, William, Veteran, 630
Rusk, David, 611
Rusk, David, S. Jacinto Army, 567
Rusk, T. J., Veteran, 597
Rusk, Thomas J., 58, 59, 65, 623, 625
Rusk, Thomas J., illus., 155
RUSK, THOMAS J., 264
Rusk, Thomas J., S. Jacinto Army, 563
Rusk, Thomas J., Pioneers killed, 583
Rusk, Thomas J., Convention, 634
Rusk, Thomas J., Convention, 635
Rusk, Thomas J., Houston 1st Admin,
  636
Rusk, Thomas J., Jones Admin, 637
Russel, R. B., S. Jacinto Army, 568
Russell, Capt. Wm. J., 90
Russell, R. B., Veteran, 611
Russell, William J., 30, 188, 205
Russell, William J., Veteran, 611
Rutledge, Richard, Fannin Massacre, 572
Ryan, Edward, Fannin Massacre, 573
Ryan, James, Veteran, 612
Ryan, William, Veteran, 629
Ryons, Thomas, S. Jacinto Army, 566

S

S. Fernando, 646
Sabine County, 597, 598, 600, 605, 608,
  613
Sabine River, 20, 22
Sabinetown, 597

Saddler, William T., S. Jacinto Army, 567
Sadler, John, S. Jacinto Army, 567
Sadler, John, Veteran, 613
Sadler, W. T., Veteran, 615
Sal Colorado, 81
Salado, 125, 129, 598, 604, 611, 620,
    624, 626
Salado Battleground, 229
Salado River, 66, 228
Salado, Battle of, 622
SALADO, BATTLEFIELD OF, 136
Salcedo, Gov., 224
Salina's rancho, 653
Salinas, Pablo, Veteran, 615
Salt in Texas, 446, 498
Saltillo, 584
Saltillo Legislature, 1831, 203
Sam Houston, Pioneers killed, 584
Samirer, Eudnado, S. Jacinto Army, 569
San Antonio, 17, 18, 21, 81, 85, 88, 120,
    124, 154, 170, 218, 228, 239, 578,
    583, 584, 585, 586, 587, 588, 589,
    590, 592, 593, 595, 596, 597, 598,
    599, 600, 601, 602, 604, 606, 607,
    608, 610, 616, 618, 619, 621, 625,
    627, 631, 632, 644, 655, 656
San Antonio Battle, 1835, 93, 192
San Antonio de Valero Mission, 17, 18
SAN ANTONIO DE BEXAR, STORM-
    ING IN 1835, 37
San Antonio de Bexar, 229
San Antonio River, 18, 22, 92, 136, 146,
    170, 185
San Antonio Road, 225
San Antonio, campaign of, 593, 614, 617
San Antonio, schooner, 79
San Antonio, Siege of, 606, 608, 610, 613
San Antonio, Veteran, 622, 629
San Augustine, 17, 193, 587, 591, 598,
    605, 608, 633, 634, 635
San Augustine County, 587, 598, 600,
    604, 605, 611, 615, 616
San Bernard, 627
San Bernard Bay, 17
San Bernard Mission, 17
San Bernard, schooner, 79
San Felipe de Austin, 21, 73, 81, 119,

150, 190, 191, 217, 244, 633, 643,
    648, 655, 656
San Fernando, 172
San Fernando Mission, 18
San Francisco Mission, 17
San Ildephonso, 18
San Jacinto, 25
SAN JACINTO, BATTLE OF, 95
San Jacinto, Battle of, 93, 163, 194, 553,
    585, 586, 587, 588, 589, 590, 591,
    592, 593, 594, 595, 596, 587, 598,
    599, 600, 601, 602, 603, 604, 606,
    607, 608, 609, 610, 611, 612, 613,
    614, 615, 616, 617, 618, 619, 620
San Jacinto, Movements before the battle,
    193
SAN JACINTO, REPORT OF RUSK,
    329
San Jacinto, schooner, 79
San Jose del Alamo, 18
San Jose Mission, 18
San Juan, 172
San Juan Batista Mission, 17
San Luis, 624
San Marcos, 159, 605, 609, 611, 617
San Miguel, 127
San Patricio, 81, 249, 634, 635
San Pedro, 18
San Pedro Creek, 231
San Pedro River, 17
San Pierre, Joseph, Old 300, 560
San Saba, 137
San Saba County, 604, 619
San Saba Fort, 496
San Saba Mine, 207
San Saba Mission, 35, 87
Sancedo, 186
Sanders, —, Fannin Massacre, 570
Sanders, J. H., Fannin Massacre, 572
Sanders, John, Veteran, 614
Sandy Creek, 497
Sansberg, John, 129
Santa Anna, 23, 83, 170, 331, 633, 649
Santa Anna, Capture, 164, 171
Santa Anna, illus., 189
SANTA FE EXPEDITION, 1841, 126
Santa Maria de Garcia Creek, 232

Santiago, Mex., 127
Santos, Jose Jesus, 234
Sarby, William A., 614
Sargeant, W., S. Jacinto Army, 565
Saunders, Prvt., S. Jacinto Army, 564
Saunders, Uriah, S. Jacinto Army, 567.
Sauters, J. A., Pioneers killed, 585
Savariego, 648
Savneign, Jo, Veteran, 613
Sawyer, F. A., Convention, 635
Sayers, John, S. Jacinto Army, 568
Scarborough, D. R., Veteran, 630
Scarborough, L., Veteran, 630
Scarborough, Paul, S. Jacinto Army, 566
Scates, W. B., 58, 614
Scates, William B., 206
Scates, William B., S. Jacinto Army, 568
SCENERY, TEXAN, 359
Schelenburg, 590
Scheston, Prvt., S. Jacinto Army, 564
Schubatansville, 122
Schumard, Dr. G. G., 470
Scmnitz, Jacob, Pioneers killed, 585
Scobey, Robert, Old 300, 560
Scolling, J. W., S. Jacinto Army, 568
Scott, James W., 64
Scott, James, Old 300, 560
Scott, James, Pioneers killed, 584
Scott, John, Judges, 638
Scott, Levy P., Veteran, 614
Scott, Philip B., Veteran, 615
Scott, R. J., Fannin Massacre, 570
Scott, W. P., S. Jacinto Army, 566
Scott, William, Old 300, 560
Scrates, William B., 634
Screamersville, 122
Screw-Auger Creek, 122
Scudder, Capt., 487
Scully, John S., Fannin Massacre, 571
Scurlock, — (Fannin), 206
Scurlock, William, Veteran, 613
Scurry, Richardson, S. Jacinto Army, 563
Scurry, Richardson, Pioneers killed, 583
Scurry, Richardson, Judges, 638
Scurry, Richardson, DA's, 638
Scurry, Richardson, Speakers, 639
Scurry, Richardson, Sec. Senate, 639

Scurry, W. R., DA's, 638
Scurry, William R., Pioneers killed, 584
Seargent, Charles, Fannin Massacre, 570
Sears, 113
SEAT OF GOVERNMENT, 118
Seaton, J. N., Fannin Massacre, 574
SECRETARIES OF SENATE, REPUB-
    LIC, 639
Secrets, Fieldings, S. Jacinto Army, Tx Spy
    Co., 569
Secrets, Wash, S. Jacinto Army, Tx Spy
    Co., 569
Secretts, F., S. Jacinto Army, 563
Secretts, W., S. Jacinto Army, 563
Seguin, 589, 594, 615
Seguin's ranch, 646, 647
Seguin, Don Erasmo, 88
Seguin, Erasmo, Pioneers killed, 583
SEGUIN, ERASMUS, 260
Seguin, Juan, 653
Seguin, June N., S. Jacinto Army, 569
Self, George, S. Jacinto Army, 565
Selkirk, William, Old 300, 560
Sellers, Robert, Veteran, 615
Sellers, William Harvey, Pioneers killed,
    585
Sellers, Wm H., Tx Necrology, 580
SENATE, PRESIDENTS PRO TEM,
    REPUBLIC, 639
SENATE, SECRETARIES OF, REPUB-
    LIC, 639
Sennatt, Andrew, S. Jacinto Army, 566
Sermond, A. G., Fannin Massacre, 570
Sesma, Gen., 193
Sessums, Alexander, Pioneers killed, 585
Settle, J. A., Veteran, 631
Sevey, Joseph S., Veteran, 615
Sevey, Manasseh, S. Jacinto Army, 565
Sevey, Ralph E., Veteran, 615
Sewall, 113
Sewell, Andrew J., Veteran, 615
Sewell, Ransom, Veteran, 615
Shackelford, Doctor, 170
Shackelford, F. S., Fannin Massacre, 573
Shackelford, Jack, 242
Shackelford, John, Pioneers killed, 583
Shackelford, W. J., Fannin Massacre, 574

Shadwick, —, Fannin Massacre, 570
Shaine, C. B., Fannin Massacre, 570
Shannon, J. T., Veteran, 631
Sharp, John, Veteran, 613
Sharpe, —, Fannin Massacre, 570
Sharpe, Samuel, S. Jacinto Army, 568
Sharper, J., S. Jacinto Army, 566
Shaw, James, 216
Shaw, James B., Lamar Admin, 636
Shaw, James B., Houston 2nd Admin, 637
Shaw, James B., Jones Admin, 637
Shaw, James, S. Jacinto Army, 564
Shaw, James, Veteran, 613
Shaw, Josiah, Veteran, 630
Shaw, P. V., Veteran, 630
Shearn, Charles, Pioneers killed, 584
Shearn, John, Veteran, 630
Shelby, 633, 634
Shelby County, 588, 609, 610, 614
Shelby, Anthony B., Judges, 638
Shelbyville, 610
Shelly, David, Old 300, 560
Shelly, John, 64
Shelton, William, Fannin Massacre, 571
Sheppard, J. H., Veteran, 614
Shepperd, William M., Houston 1st
    Admin, 636
Sherman, 606
Sherman, Col. Sidney, 155
Sherman, Sidney, 204
SHERMAN, SIDNEY, 268
Sherman, Sidney, S. Jacinto Army, 567
Sherman, Sidney, Tx Necrology, 580
Sherman, Sidney, Portrait, 600
Shingle, Charles, 64
Shipman, Charles Isaac N., Old 300, 560
Shipman, Daniel, Old 300, 560
Shipman, Daniel, Veteran, 614
Shipman, James R., Veteran, 615
Shipman, Moses, Old 300, 560
Shivers, O. L., Veteran, 631
Short, Z. H., Fannin Massacre, 573
Shotts, Lewis, Fannin Massacre, 573
Shreve, John M., Clerk, 639
Shreve, J. M., S. Jacinto Army, 565
Shults, H., Fannin Massacre, 571
Shurlock, William, Fannin Massacre, 574

Sigman, Prvt., S. Jacinto Army, 564
SIGNERS OF THE TEXAS DECLARA-
    TION OF INDEPENDENCE, 58
Siley, Ant., Fannin Massacre, 573
Silsbe, Albert, 65
Silver in Texas, 496
Simmonds, William, Veteran, 614
Simmons, J. B., Veteran, 630
Simmons, James W., Lamar Admin, 636
Simmons, William, S. Jacinto Army, 565
Simons, Thomas, Pioneers killed, 582
Simpson's Spring, 497
Simpson, L. S., Fannin Massacre, 570
Simpson, William R., Fannin Massacre,
    572
Simpson, William, Veteran, 613
SIMS AND DAWSON, 354
Sims, Bartlett, 354
Sims, Bartlett, Old 300, 560
Sims, Bartlett, Prov. Govt., 634
Singleton, George W., Old 300, 560
Singleton, J. H., Veteran, 613
Singleton, Philip, Old 300, 560
Sinickson, John J., Veteran, 630
Sinks, George W., 630
Sirocco, 509
Slaben, John, Veteran, 614
Slack, —, S. Jacinto Army, 565
Slatter, R., Fannin Massacre, 572
Slaves, 184
Sleighston, J., S. Jacinto Army, 567
Smelser, John, Veteran, 630
SMITH ADDRESS TO PEOPLE, 1836,
    332
Smith County, 593
Smith, Erastus (Deaf), S. Jacinto Army, Tx
    Spy Co., 569
Smith, A., 113
Smith, A. M. H., S. Jacinto Army, 566
Smith, Arnold, 223
SMITH, ASHBEL, PART OF ADDRESS
    TO VETERANS, 553
Smith, Ashbel, Veteran, 630
Smith, Ashbel, Houston 2nd Admin, 637
Smith, Ben Fort, Pioneers killed, 581
SMITH, BENJAMIN FORT, 290
Smith, Benjamin F., S. Jacinto Army, 564

Smith, Benjamin W., 651
Smith, C., 113
Smith, Charles, Fannin Massacre, 574
Smith, Christian, Old 300, 560
Smith, Cornelius, Old 300, 560
Smith, Deaf, 38, 95, 193, 223
Smith, Deaf, Pioneers killed, 583
Smith, Edward, Veteran, 615
Smith, Erastus (Deaf), Pioneers killed, 580
Smith, Francis P., 65
Smith, G. W., Pioneers killed, 585
Smith, Gavin, Fannin Massacre, 570
Smith, Henry, Pioneers killed, 582
Smith, Henry, 23, 643, 656
SMITH, HENRY, 274
Smith, Henry, Gen. Consultation, 633
Smith, Henry, Veteran, 614
Smith, Henry, Prov. Govt., 634
Smith, Henry, Houston 1st Admin, 636
Smith, J. C., 113
Smith, J., S. Jacinto Army, 566
Smith, Jackson, Veteran, 630
Smith, Jackson, Lamar Admin, 636
Smith, James, 608
Smith, James, Fannin Massacre, 571
Smith, John M., 26
Smith, John W., 223
Smith, John, Old 300, 560
Smith, John, S. Jacinto Army, 565, 568
Smith, Joseph F., Veteran, 630
Smith, Lemuel, Veteran, 613
Smith, M. C., Veteran, 614
Smith, M. W., Gen. Consultation, 633
Smith, Manaan, Veteran, 614
Smith, Norwich, 223
Smith, Oliver, Fannin Massacre, 572
Smith, Prvt., S. Jacinto Army, 564
Smith, R. W., S. Jacinto Army, 567
Smith, Rev. W. P., 84
Smith, S. R., Veteran, 631
Smith, Siddey, Fannin Massacre, 573
Smith, Thomas I., 242
Smith, Thomas I., Pioneers killed, 582
Smith, Thomas J., Veteran, 614
Smith, Thomas, Fannin Massacre, 571, 573
Smith, W., 113

Smith, William A., Fannin Massacre, 572
Smith, William P., Pioneers killed, 584
Smith, William, S. Jacinto Army, 567
Smithers, Robert, Pioneers killed, 582
Smithers, W., 88, 185
Smithers, William, Old 300, 560
Smithwick, Noah, Veteran, 615
Smoothing Iron Mountain, 488
Smothers, Isaac, Veteran, 631
Smyth, George W., 58
SMYTH, GEORGE W., 273
Smyth, George W., Convention, 634
Smyth, W. A., S. Jacinto Army, 567
Snake Prairie, 595
Snell, M. K., Pioneers killed, 584
Snell, Martin K., S. Jacinto Army, 564
Snively, David, Pioneers killed, 584
Snyder, M., S. Jacinto Army, 564
Socrates, William B., Convention, 634
Sojourner, A. L., Old 300, 560
SOLDIER'S SWEET HOME, POEM, 374
Somerset, 591, 616
Somerville, 635, 651
Somerville Campaign, 615, 624, 625
Somerville, A., 587
Somerville, Alexander, Pioneers killed, 582
SOMMERVILE, ALEXANDER, 277
Sommerville Campaign, 623
Sommerville, Alexander, S. Jacinto Army, 565
Sorzine, Shelby, 638
Sour Lake Mineral Springs, 21
Sour Lake, Oil, 498
South Boulder Creek, Coal, 501
South Fork of the Canadian River, 471
South Winds, 502
Southerland, 645
Southern Pacific Railroad, 23, 466
Southwestern Texas, 459
Southwick, Stephen, Pioneers killed, 584
Souverin, Colonel, 26
Sovereign, Joseph, S. Jacinto Army, 565
Spain, Randolph T., Fannin Massacre, 573
Spanks, S. F., S. Jacinto Army, 567
Sparks, S. F., Veteran, 614

SPEAKERS, HOUSE OF REP, REPUB-
   LIC, 639
Spear, John, Veteran, 615
Spencer, —, Fannin Massacre, 574
Spencer, Jack, 159
Spencer, Nancy, Old 300, 560
Sphon, Joseph H., Fannin Massacre, 573
Spicer, J. A., S. Jacinto Army, 566
Spillers, John T., Fannin Massacre, 571
Spillers, John T., Veteran, 615
Splan, 651
Splane, Captain Peyton R., 29
SPORTS, TEXAS, 325
Sprague, Sam, Fannin Massacre, 574
Spring Creek, 25
Springfield, 233, 235
Spy Company, 569
Squizzlejig County, 122
St. Bernard Bay, 207
St. John, Edward, 65
St. John, Timothy, 64
St. Louis, MO, 70
St. Mark's, 225
St. Mary's, 595
Stafford, Adam, Old 300, 560
Stafford, William, Old 300, 560
Stamans, Horace, 64
Standefer, Jacob L., Veteran, 614
Standefer, Wm. B., Veteran, 615
Standerford, Jacob, S. Jacinto Army, 565
Standerford, William, S. Jacinto Army, 565
Stapp, 651
Stapp, D. M., Veteran, 614
Stapp, E., 58
Stapp, Elijah, Pioneers killed, 581
Stapp, Milton, Pioneers killed, 584
Star, R., 113
Starkley, B. F., S. Jacinto Army, 565
Starn, 113
Starr, James H., Lamar Admin, 636
Starrville, 593
State Gazette,1852, 61
STATISTICAL SECTION, 557
Steamboat, First to Houston, 122
Stebbins, Charles C., Veteran, 614
Steel, Alphonso, S. Jacinto Army, 563,
   568
Steel, Maxwell, S. Jacinto Army, 566

Steele, Alfonso, Veteran, 613
Steele, John, Veteran, 613
Stem, Isaac P., Veteran, 613
Stephens, A. J., Veteran, 631
Stephens, A. R., S. Jacinto Army, 562
Stephens, William, Fannin Massacre, 573
Stephenson, R., S. Jacinto Army, 567
Stepp, Elijah, Convention, 634
Sterne, Adolphus, Pioneers killed, 582
Stevens, A. R., S. Jacinto Army, 563, 567
Stevens, Abraham, Fannin Massacre, 571
Stevens, Thomas, Old 300, 560
Stevenson, J. B., Veteran, 630
Stevenson, R., S. Jacinto Army, 569
Stewart, 113
Stewart, Charles B., Veteran, 614
Stewart, Charles B., 58, 206, 524, 643
Stewart, Charles B., Prov. Govt., 634
Stewart, Charles, S. Jacinto Army, 564
Stewart, Charles, Fannin Massacre, 573
Stewart, J. C., Fannin Massacre, 570
Stewart, Thomas, Fannin Massacre, 571
Stewart, Virgil A., Pioneers killed, 583
Stibbins, Charles, S. Jacinto Army, 565
Stiff, Thomas R., Lamar Admin, 636
Stillwell, W., S. Jacinto Army, 563
Stockbridge, Elam, Veteran, 630
Stockton, 113
Stonfer, H., S. Jacinto Army, 566
Stout, B. O., Veteran, 613
Stout, Henry, Veteran, 613
Stout, J. S., Veteran, 613
Stout, Owen H., Old 300, 560
Stovall, Joseph A., Fannin Massacre, 571
Strange, James, Old 300, 560
Strawsnider, Gabriel, Old 300, 560
Streams in Texas, 453
Stribbling, Thomas H., Pioneers killed,
   585
Stringer, E. N., Veteran, 615
Strode, J. W., S. Jacinto Army, 565
Stroth, Philip, S. Jacinto Army, 566
Stroud, Ethan, 141
Stump, J. S., S. Jacinto Army, 567
Subdivisions of Texas, 458
Sublett, Henry W., DA's, 638
Sugar Cane, 449
Sullivan, Prvt., S. Jacinto Army, 564

Sulphur Springs, 21, 589
Sumerline, J., 113
Summers, W., 113
Summers, W. W., S. Jacinto Army, 564
Sumwalt, Andrew, Veteran, 620
SUNBEAMS, POEM, 428
SUNDAY SCHOOL, FIRST IN TEXAS, 69
Sunrise, 596
SUPREME COURT OF TEXAS, 300
Surface of Texas, 453
Surveyor, First of Austin Colony, 197
Sutherland, George, S. Jacinto Army, 566
Sutherland, George, Pioneers killed, 583
Sutherland, N., 113
Sutherland, Walter, Old 300, 560
Swain, Prvt., S. Jacinto Army, 564
Swearengen, E., Veteran, 615
Swearengen, V. W., S. Jacinto Army, 566
Swearinger, —, S. Jacinto Army, 564
SWEDISH POETRY, 432
Sweeney, W. B., S. Jacinto Army, 564
Sweeny, John, Veteran, 615
Sweman, Frederick, Fannin Massacre, 572
Swift, Hugh M., S. Jacinto Army, 563
Swisher, Capt., at Bexar, 220
Swisher, H. H., S. Jacinto Army, 567
Swisher, J. G., 58
Swisher, J. M., S. Jacinto Army, 567
SWISHER, JAMES G., 287
Swisher, James G., Pioneers killed, 583
Swisher, James G., Convention, 635
Swisher, John M., Veteran, 614
Switcher, 651
Switzer, A. B., Pioneers killed, 581
Swords, —, Fannin Massacre, 572
Swords, A., Fannin Massacre, 573
Sydnor, John S., Pioneers killed, 584
Syers, Daniel, Fannin Massacre, 573
Sylvester, James A., S. Jacinto Army, 565

T

Tabor, James, DA's, 638
Tahuacan Indians, 231, 233
Tahuaya Indians, 232
Talley, David, Old 300, 560
Tandy, A. M., Veteran, 616

Tanner, E. M., S. Jacinto Army, 567
Tanning and the Mesquite Tree, 513
Tarin, Manuel, S. Jacinto Army, 569
Tarlton, James, S. Jacinto Army, 566
Tarrant County, 592, 623, 629
Tarrant, E. H., Pioneers killed, 583
Tarver, B. Ed., Pioneers killed, 584
Tasajo, 145
Tatom, Joseph B., Fannin Massacre, 572
Tatom, Memory B., Fannin Massacre, 572
Taylor, A., S. Jacinto Army, 564
Taylor, Campbell, S. Jacinto Army, 565
Taylor, Campbell, Veteran, 615
Taylor, Charles S., 58
Taylor, Charles S., Convention, 634
Taylor, Charles S., DA's, 638
Taylor, Creed, Veteran, 616
Taylor, E., 113
Taylor, E. W., Veteran, 631
Taylor, Edward, S. Jacinto Army, 565
Taylor, G., 113
Taylor, Gen. Zachary, 172
Taylor, J., 113
Taylor, J. B., S. Jacinto Army, 568
Taylor, John D., Old 300, 560
Taylor, Kneeland, Fannin Massacre, 573
Taylor, Prvt., S. Jacinto Army, 564
Taylor, W., 113
Taylor, William, S. Jacinto Army, 564
Teal, Capt., S. Jacinto Army, 563
Teal, Henry, Pioneers killed, 580
Teale, Col., Goliad, 249
Tecas, 19
Teel, George, Old 300, 560
Tehas, Teja, Tejas, 18, 20, 86
Telegraph Newspaper, 412
Telegraph, schooner, 78
Temperature Ranges, 358
Tenawah Comanches, 134
Tenehaw, 526, 633
Tennell, Benjamin, 25
Teran, Governor, 202
Terrell, E. R., Veteran, 631
Terrill, George W., Houston 2nd Admin, 637
Terrill, George W., Judges, 638
Terrill, George W., DA's, 638
Terrill, Judge, Coal, 500

Terroros Creek, 231
Terry, Benjamin Frank, Pioneers killed, 583
Tewister, —, S. Jacinto Army, 565
TEXAN HYMN, POEM, 395
TEXAN SCENERY, 359
TEXAN SONG OF LIBERTY, POEM, 406
TEXAN SONG OF LIBERTY, POEM, 437
Texana, 606, 618
TEXANS KILLED BY MEXICANS AND INDIANS 1828–1874, 580
TEXAS HISTORY, A COMPEND, 23
TEXAS HISTORY, INCIDENTS OF, 157
TEXAS INDEPENDENCE, 355
Texas Judicial District, 190
TEXAS MINERALS, 442
TEXAS NECROLOGY, 578
TEXAS OUR HOME, POEM, 400
TEXAS RANGER, POEM, 418
Texas Republican, 1836, 61
TEXAS REVOLUTION, BREAKOUT AT GONZALES, 83
TEXAS REVOLUTION, MORE OF, 169
TEXAS SOLDIER'S ADDRESS TO HIS FLAG, POEM, 387
Texas Veteran Association, 204
TEXAS VETERAN ASSOCIATION, CONSTITUTION OF, 574
Texas, Early Government, 1834, 190
TEXAS, GEOGRAPHY OF, 20
TEXAS, HISTORICAL STATISTICS, 120
Texas, Meaning of the word, 86
TEXAS, THE NAME, 19
TEXAS: FROM THE NEW YORK TIMES, 86
Thayer, George, Fannin Massacre, 572
Thomas, Benjamin, S. Jacinto Army, 569
Thomas, Benjamin, Veteran, 616
Thomas, Benjamin R., Veteran, 616
Thomas, David, 58, 59
THOMAS, DAVID, 275
Thomas, David, Convention, 635
Thomas, Evans M., Fannin Massacre, 572
Thomas, Ezekiel, Old 300, 560

Thomas, J. D., Veteran, 616
Thomas, Jacob, Old 300, 561
Thomas, Theophilus, Veteran, 616
Thomas, Wiley, Veteran, 616
Thomason, W. D., Veteran, 615
Thompson, A. P., Tx Necrology, 580
Thompson, Alexander, 202
Thompson, Alexander, Pioneers killed, 584
Thompson, Alexander, Gen. Consultation, 633
Thompson, Alexander, Prov. Govt., 634
Thompson, Algernon, Pioneers killed, 584
Thompson, C. W., S. Jacinto Army, 567
Thompson, Capt., 77, 78
Thompson, Charles, S. Jacinto Army, 566
Thompson, Cyrus W., Veteran, 616
Thompson, Hiram M., Veteran, 616
Thompson, J. M., 129
Thompson, J., S. Jacinto Army, 564
Thompson, Jesse, Old 300, 560
Thompson, Jesse, Veteran, 615
Thompson, Leslie A., Pioneers killed, 585
Thompson, Napoleon, DA's, 638
Thompson, S. J., Veteran, 616
Thompson, Thomas, Veteran, 631
Thompsonville, 602
Thomson, Jesse, S. Jacinto Army, 567
Thorn, John S., Fannin Massacre, 571
Thorn, John S., Veteran, 616
Thornton, 113
Thornton, William, Veteran, 616
Threndgil, J., S. Jacinto Army, 566
THROCKMORTON, J. W., 296
Thruston, J. M., 113
Thurman, Alfred S., Veteran, 631
Thurston, A. S., Houston 1st Admin, 636
Tillage, 456
Tilson, L., Fannin Massacre, 570
Timber, 359, 450, 453
Tindale, D., S. Jacinto Army, 565
Tindall Plantation, Coal, 499
Tindall, Prvt., S. Jacinto Army, 564
Tindall, Thomas P., 495
Tinsley, Isaac T., Tx Necrology, 580
Tinsley, Isaac T., Pioneers killed, 585
Tinsley, James W., S. Jacinto Army, 565

Tiveson, N. W., Pioneers killed, 584
TO MY SLEEPING WIFE, POEM, 390
Tobacco, 21, 449
Todd, John G., Veteran, 631
Todd, Thomas, 64
Toe Nail Community, 122
Toler, Dan J., 82
Toler, R. A., Fannin Massacre, 570
TOLLING BELL, POEM, 378
Tolover, B. W., Fannin Massacre, 570
Tom, Alf, 159
Tom, J., S. Jacinto Army, 562
Tom, John F., Veteran, 616
Tom, John, S. Jacinto Army, 567
Tom, William, Veteran, 616
Tomlinson, Joseph, Veteran, 616
Tompkins, A. M., DA's, 638
Tone, Jameson Thomas, Old 300, 560
Tone, Thomas J., Old 300, 560
Tong, James F., Old 300, 560
Tonkawas, 133
Torrey, David S., Pioneers killed, 582
Torrey, Thomas S., Pioneers killed, 581
Torry, J., 129
Towns, Hanse, Houston 2nd Admin, 637
Townsend, Spencer, S. Jacinto Army, 564
Toy, Samuel, Old 300, 561
Trade with New Mexico, 465
Trahurn, G. W., Veteran, 631
TRANS-MISSISSIPPI DEPARTMENT,
   LAST DAYS, 348
Trask, Olwyn J., S. Jacinto Army, 563
Travel to Texas, 450
Travieso, Justo, Veteran, 616
Travis County, 143, 585, 587, 588, 591,
   593, 597, 599, 603, 606, 608, 609,
   610, 611, 612, 613, 614, 617, 618,
   620, 622, 626, 627, 629
Travis County, minerals, 445
Travis Letter, Feb. 24, 1836, 212
Travis, William B., 25, 646, 648, 653
TRAVIS, WILLIAM B., 261
Travis, William Barrett, Pioneers killed,
   580
Trenay, John B., S. Jacinto Army, 567
Tresvant, L. P., 242
Trevesant, —, Fannin Massacre, 571

Trinity, 25
Trinity River, 22, 180, 186, 198, 229,
   231, 236, 342, 359, 464
Trobough, John, Old 300, 560
Troutman, Mrs., 334
Troutz, C., Veteran, 616
Truehart, James L., Veteran, 631
Trumbull, J., 129
Tucker, James B., Prov. Govt., 634
Tumlinson, Elizabeth, Old 300, 560
Tumlinson, James, Old 300, 560
Tumlinson, John, S. Jacinto Army, 566
Tumlinson, Peter, Veteran, 616
Tunnage, S. C., S. Jacinto Army, 564
Turberville, W. S., Fannin Massacre, 572
Turner, A., S. Jacinto Army, 564
Turner, Amasa, 205
Turner, Amasa, Veteran, 615
Turner, Capt., S. Jacinto Army, 563
Turner, John, 58
Turner, John, Convention, 635
Turtle Bayou, 26, 31
Twohig, John, Veteran, 631
Tyler, 593
Tyler County, 589, 591
Tyler, Prvt., S. Jacinto Army, 564
Tyler, Robert D., S. Jacinto Army, 568

U

Ugartechea, Col., 30, 65, 222
Unappropriated Domain, 23
Underwood, Ammon, Veteran, 616
Union Pacific Railroad, Coal, 501
UNSETTLED REGIONS IN WEST
   TEXAS...., 464
UP! MEN OF TEXAS, POEM, 375
Upper Cross Timbers, 133
Urrea, Gen., 81
Usher, Patrick, S. Jacinto Army, 566
Usphur County, 605
Uvalde County, 622

V

Vail, Albert G., Pioneers killed, 582
Valdez, Gavino, 18

Valentine, 113
Van Bibber, John, Fannin Massacre, 570
Van Dorn, Isaac, Old 300, 561
Van Ness, Cornelius, 216
Van Ness, Cornelius, Pioneers killed, 581
Van Winkle, Prvt., S. Jacinto Army, 564
Van Zandt County, 596
Van Zandt, Isaac, Pioneers killed, 582
Van Zandt, Isaac, Houston 2nd Admin, 637
Vanbibber, John, Veteran, 617
Vanderveer, Log, S. Jacinto Army, 562, 565
Vandyke, Wilson, Veteran, 631
Vanvechten, D. H., Veteran, 617
Varcinas, A., S. Jacinto Army, 569
Varnell, William M., Pioneers killed, 584
Varner, Martin, Old 300, 561
Vasquez, Gen., 142
Velasco, 81, 119, 244, 334, 587, 588, 590, 591, 594, 606, 624, 625, 627, 631, 644, 643
VELASCO, BATTLE OF . . . 1832, 30
Velasco, Battle of, 93, 607, 608, 611, 616, 617, 618
Velasco, Port, 160
Venavides, Placido, 220
Vera Cruz, 644
Vermilion, Joseph, S. Jacinto Army, 566
VETERAN ASSOC, CONSTITUTION OF THE TX —, 574
Veteran Guard of Texas, 575
Victoria, 152, 161, 602, 604, 630, 634
Victoria County, Veteran, 589
Victoria County, 604, 614
Victoria, Guadalupe, 187
Viesca, 526, 633, 654
Viesca, Augustin, 190
Viesca, Governor, 203
Vigal, G. M., Fannin Massacre, 571
VIKING, POEM, 432
Vinater, J., S. Jacinto Army, 565
Vinator, James, Veteran, 617
Vince's Bridge, 95
Vince's Bridge Burning, 1836, 98
Vince, Allen, Old 300, 561
Vince, Richard, Old 300, 561

Vince, Robert, Old 300, 561
Vince, William, Old 300, 561
Vincedor del Alamo, vessel, 78
Vini Gallici, 352
Virginia Point, 626
Virginia Points, 218
Viven, John, S. Jacinto Army, 565
Volckner, J. Q., Fannin Massacre, 570
Volunteer Aid, 645
Volunteer Grays, 654
Voss, George, Fannin Massacre, 570
Votan, Elijah, S. Jacinto Army, 568
Votaw, Elijah, Veteran, 617
Voyel, Andreas, S. Jacinto Army, 566

W

Wanahuila Creek, 146
Wachita Post, 230
Waco, 233, 235, 591, 593, 595, 602, 606, 614, 617, 621, 626, 627
Waco Indians, 35, 133, 237
Waco, 1824, 237
Wade, J. M., 622
Wade, John M., S. Jacinto Army, 563
Wade, John M., Veteran, 617
Wade, John R., Veteran, 618
Wade, Nathan, Veteran, 619
Wadsworth, Capt., 161
Waggoner, William, Fannin Massacre, 570
Walderman, Jesse, S. Jacinto Army, 566
Waldron, C. W., S. Jacinto Army, 565
Walker County, 592, 601, 608, 612, 614, 620, 631, 632
Walker, James, Old 300, 561
Walker, James, S. Jacinto Army, 568
Walker, John, Veteran, 618
Walker, Lt. Col., 173
Walker, Martin, S. Jacinto Army, 562, 565
Walker, Martin, Veteran, 618
Walker, Philip, Veteran, 619
Walker, R. H., Veteran, 617
Walker, Samuel H., Pioneers killed, 582
Walker, Sanders, Veteran, 617
Walker, Tipton, Pioneers killed, 584
Walker, W. S., S. Jacinto Army, 565
Walker, William G., S. Jacinto Army, 562

Wallace, —, Fannin Massacre, 570
Wallace, Benjamin C., Fannin Massacre, 569
Wallace, Caleb, Old 300, 561
Wallace, Col., 197
Wallace, J. W. E., 589
Wallace, J. W. E., Veteran, 617
Wallace, Jesse, 35
Wallace, Lt. Col. J. W. E., 84
Wallace, Samuel, Fannin Massacre, 571
Wallace, William, Fannin Massacre, 572
Wallace, William, Veteran, 632
Waller County, 591, 599, 600, 610, 617
Waller, Edwin, 58, 197, 205, 206, 527
Waller, Edwin, Veteran, 617
Waller, Edwin, Gen. Consultation, 633
Waller, Edwin, Prov. Govt., 634
Waller, Edwin, Lamar Admin, 636
Walling, Elisha, Veteran, 632
Walling, Jesse, S. Jacinto Army, 567
Walling, Vance, Veteran, 632
Walneet, Francis, S. Jacinto Army, 568
Walnut Creek, 138
Walsh, 113
Walters, Alexander, Veteran, 619
Walters, George T., Veteran, 619
Walton, John H., Pioneers killed, 582
Wanderer's Creek, 462
Ward, Col., 144, 152
Ward, John, Veteran, 631
WARD, LT. COL., 277
Ward, Matt, Pioneers killed, 583
Ward, Paul S., Veteran, 619
Ward, Thomas W., illus., 272
WARD, THOMAS W., 272
Ward, Thomas W., Tx Necrology, 580
Ward, Thomas W., Pioneers killed, 584
Ward, Thomas W., 38, 250
Ward, Thomas W., Lamar Admin, 636
Ward, Thomas W., Houston 2nd Admin, 637
Ward, Thomas W., Clerk, 639
Ward, William, 242
Ward, William, Fannin Massacre, 569
Wardryski, Prvt., S. Jacinto Army, 564
Ware, Jefferson, 65
Ware, William, S. Jacinto Army, 567

Warnall, 113
Warner, 113
Warner, Prvt., S. Jacinto Army, 564
Warren, Colonel, 650
Warrenton, 611
Washington County, 585, 586, 587, 589, 590, 594, 595, 597, 600, 602, 608, 609, 614, 616, 621, 624, 626, 627, 628, 629, 630, 632
Washington County Coal, 494
Washington County, Veteran, 625
Washington [on the Brazos], 21, 113, 597, 600, 627, 633, 634, 635, 656
Washington on the Brazos, 59, 89, 119, 217
Washington, Cronican, Pioneers killed, 585
Washington, J., 113
Water in Texas, 457
Waters, George, S. Jacinto Army, 562, 565
Waters, Nicholas B., Fannin Massacre, 572
Waters, T., 113
Waters, William, S. Jacinto Army, 566
Watkins, H. M., Veteran, 632
Watkins, I. E., S. Jacinto Army, 566
Watrous, J. C., Lamar Admin, 636
Watson, D., S. Jacinto Army, 569
Watson, H. E., Veteran, 619
Watson, John, Veteran, 617
Watson, Joseph W., Fannin Massacre, 573
Watts, H. C., Pioneers killed, 581
Waxahachie, 613
Weather, 358, 366, 505
Weathered, F. M., Veteran, 618
Weatherford, 609
Weaver, L. G., Veteran, 618
Webb County, minerals, 445
Webb, Alexander W., 632
Webb, David F., Veteran, 632
Webb, James, 216
WEBB, JAMES, 337
Webb, James, Fannin Massacre, 573
Webb, James, Pioneers killed, 583
Webb, James, Lamar Admin, 636
Webb, Prvt., S. Jacinto Army, 564
Webb, T. H., S. Jacinto Army, 568
Webberville, 328, 583, 588

Weeks, —, Fannin Massacre, 571
Weimar, 614
Wells, Francis F., Old 300, 561
Wells, J. A., Veteran, 632
Wells, Louis, Veteran, 617
Wells, Lysender, S. Jacinto Army, 567
Wells, Major, 170
Wells, Martin J., Veteran, 619
Wells, Samuel G., Veteran, 619
Wells, W., 113
Wells, Waymen F., Veteran, 618
Welsh, James, S. Jacinto Army, 565
Welsh, W., Fannin Massacre, 572
Welshinger, J. G., Houston 1st Admin, 636
Weppler, —, S. Jacinto Army, 566
Wesson, J. M., Veteran, 632
WEST TEXAS . . ., 464
West, —, Fannin Massacre, 570
West, Clae., 58
West, Claiborne, Gen. Consultation, 633
West, Claiborne, Prov. Govt., 634
West, Gilford, Veteran, 632
Westall, Thomas, Old 300, 561
Westall, Thomas, Pioneers killed, 580
Westcott, R. D., Veteran, 631
WESTERN EXPEDITION UNDER
    JOHNSON, GRANT & MORRIS, 80
Western Texas, 458
Westgate, Ezra, S. Jacinto Army, 565
Weston, Thomas, Fannin Massacre, 572
Westover, Adjutant, 93, 150
Westover, Ira, Fannin Massacre, 573
Westover, Ira, Prov. Govt., 634
Whaling, H., 129
Wharton, 591
WHARTON AND AUSTIN, RECON-
    CILIATION, 89
Wharton County, 591, 603, 621
Wharton, (William H.), 635
Wharton, Col. John H., 78
Wharton, James, S. Jacinto Army, 564
Wharton, John A., 216
WHARTON, JOHN A., 267
WHARTON, JOHN A., FUNERAL, 315
Wharton, John A., S. Jacinto Army, 563
Wharton, John A., Pioneers killed, 581, 584

Wharton, John A., Gen. Consultation, 633
Wharton, John A., Prov. Govt., 634
Wharton, John A., Convention, 635
Wharton, vessel, 80
Wharton, W. H., 656
Wharton, William H., 23, 34, 78, 192, 216, 656
WHARTON, WILLIAM H., 267
Wharton, William H., Pioneers killed, 581
Wharton, William H., Prov. Govt., 634
Wharton, William H., Houston 1st Admin, 636
Wharton, William H., Convention, 635
Wheat, 449
Wheeler, Orlando, Fannin Massacre, 573
WHEELER, ROYAL T., 301
Wheeler, Royal T., Pioneers killed, 584
Wheeler, Royal T., Judges, 638
Wheeler, ROYAL T., DA's, 638
Wheeler, S. L., S. Jacinto Army, 564
Wheeler, S. L., Veteran, 618
Wheelock, 604, 624
Wheelock, E. L. R., Pioneers killed, 582
Wheelock, G. R., Veteran, 619
Wheelwright, schooner, 215
Whiskey Creek, 491
Whitaker, M. G., S. Jacinto Army, 567
Whitaker, William, Gen. Consultation, 633
White, Allen, 65
White, Alvin E., Fannin Massacre, 573
White, Amy, Old 300, 561
White, Benj. J., 64
White Cow, Battle of the, 226
White, Francis M., Veteran, 618
White, J., 113
White, J. C., Veteran, 618
White, James Gilbert, Pioneers killed, 582
White, John M., Veteran, 619
White, John, Veteran, 618
White, Joseph, Old 300, 561
White, Joseph, S. Jacinto Army, 563
White, Jr., Benj. J., 65
White, K. B., Veteran, 620
White, L. H., S. Jacinto Army, 568
White, R., 113
White, S. Addison, Pioneers killed, 584
White, Taylor, Pioneers killed, 582
White, Walter C., Old 300, 561

White, Walter C., Pioneers killed, 580
White, William C., Old 300, 561
White-oak, 613
Whitehead, H. S., Veteran, 632
White's Crossing, 26
Whitesides, Boulin, Old 300, 561
Whitesides, E. T., Veteran, 618
Whitesides, E., S. Jacinto Army, 567
Whitesides, Henry, Old 300, 561
Whitesides, James, Old 300, 561
Whitesides, William, Old 300, 561
Whiting, Nathaniel, Old 300, 561
Whiting, S., 122
Whitlock, Robert, Veteran, 618
Whitlock, William, Old 300, 561
Whooping Crane, 476
WICHITA AND WILBARGER COUN-
   TIES, 461
Wichita County, minerals, 442
Wichita Indian Agency, 133
Wichita Indians, 237
Wichita Mountains, 127, 469
Wichita River, 132
Wicksan, Cyrus, Veteran, 619
Wigfall, Lewis T., Pioneers killed, 585
Wightman, Elias R., 69
Wightman, Elias R., Old 300, 561
WILBARGER COUNTY, 461
Wilbarger, Josiah, Scalping, 138
Wilbarger, Josiah, Pioneers killed, 582
Wilbarger, Matthias, Pioneers killed, 581
Wilcox, John A., Pioneers killed, 584
Wilcox, Oswin, Veteran, 617
WILD MAN OF THE WOODS, 361
Wild Man To Wild Woman, 361
Wild Woman to Wild Man, Reply, 362
Wilder, James, S. Jacinto Army, 565
Wilder, James, Fannin Massacre, 574
Wiley, A. P., Pioneers killed, 584
Wiliamson, Bill, 216
Wilkerson, Gen., 230
Wilkerson, William L., Fannin Massacre,
   571
Wilkins, Henry, Fannin Massacre, 572
Wilkins, Jane, Old 300, 561
Wilkinson, F., S. Jacinto Army, 568
Wilkinson, J. G., S. Jacinto Army, 567
Wilkinson, Jem, 159

Wilkinson, John, S. Jacinto Army, 568
Wilkinson, Leroy, S. Jacinto Army, 562,
   566
Wilkinson, Prvt., S. Jacinto Army, 564
Wilkinson, Wm. L., 162
Williams, —, Fannin Massacre, 572
Williams, A. B., Fannin Massacre, 570
Williams, Charles, S. Jacinto Army, 566
Williams, F. F., S. Jacinto Army, 565
Williams, George T., Old 300, 561
Williams, H. R., S. Jacinto Army, 567
Williams, Henry, Old 300, 561
Williams, James, Veteran, 617
Williams, John R., Old 300, 561
Williams, John, Jr., Old 300, 561
Williams, John, Old 300, 561
Williams, John, Fannin Massacre, 574
Williams, Napoleon B., Fannin Massacre,
   574
Williams, Richard, Veteran, 619
Williams, Robert H., 205
Williams, Robert H., Old 300, 561
Williams, Robert H., Veteran, 618
Williams, Samuel L., 203
Williams, Samuel M., 79
WILLIAMS, SAMUEL M., 279
Williams, Samuel M., Old 300, 561
Williams, Samuel M., Pioneers killed, 583
Williams, Samuel M., Lamar Admin, 637
Williams, Samuel M., Houston 2nd
   Admin, 637
Williams, Sol. M., Veteran, 632
Williams, Solomon, Old 300, 561
Williams, Stephen, Veteran, 618
Williams, Thomas, Old 300, 561
Williams, Thomas J., Veteran, 618
Williams, W. F., S. Jacinto Army, 567
Williams, W. R., S. Jacinto Army, 566
Williams, W., Veteran, 619
Williams, Wm. M., DA's, 638
Williamson County, 586, 587, 593, 601,
   602, 606, 607, 614, 619, 623, 628,
   629
Williamson, Capt. R. M., 83
Williamson, R. W., 30
Williamson, R. M., 188
Williamson, R. M., Judges, 638
WILLIAMSON, R. M., 274

Williamson, R. M., illus., 524
Williamson, Robert M., 25, 26
Williamson, Robert M., Pioneers killed, 583
Williamson, Robert M., Gen. Consultation, 633
Willie, James, Pioneers killed, 584
Willis, 590, 603, 606, 632
Willis, P. J., Pioneers killed, 585
Willis, R. S., Veteran, 632
Willoughby, L., S. Jacinto Army, 568
Willoughby, Leiper, Veteran, 619
Wilson County, 616, 632
Wilson, Charles, Gen. Consultation, 633
Wilson, Charles, Prov. Govt., 634
Wilson, D., 113
Wilson, David, 65
Wilson, Hugh, Pioneers killed, 584
Wilson, J., 113
Wilson, J. C., 117
Wilson, J. L., Fannin Massacre, 571
Wilson, J. T. D., Veteran, 617
Wilson, James C., Pioneers killed, 583
Wilson, James, S. Jacinto Army, 567
Wilson, L. J., 113
WILSON, ROBERT, 289
Wilson, Robert, Fannin Massacre, 574
Wilson, Robert, Pioneers killed, 583
Wilson, Samuel, Fannin Massacre, 570
Wilson, Thomas, S. Jacinto Army, 564
Wilson, Walker, S. Jacinto Army, 566
Wilson, Walker, Veteran, 617
Wilson, William, 88, 185
Wilworth, Lewis, S. Jacinto Army, 569
Winburn, McHenry, S. Jacinto Army, 566
Winchester, 603
Wing, M. C., 129
Wingate, E., Fannin Massacre, 572
Winn, Walker, S. Jacinto Army, 565
Winn, Walter, 618
Winner, Christian, S. Jacinto Army, 566
Winningham, William, Fannin Massacre, 573
Winter, A., Fannin Massacre, 573
Winters, Christopher, Fannin Massacre, 571
Winters, J. —, S. Jacinto Army, 567
Winters, J. W., S. Jacinto Army, 567

Winters, James W., Veteran, 618
Winters, William, S. Jacinto Army, 562
Winters, William C., S. Jacinto Army, 567
Wise County, 611
Witesborough, 590
Withered, W. C., Veteran, 619
Witt, Hughs, Fannin Massacre, 574
Wolf, A., 113
Wolf, Thomas H., Veteran, 632
Woll Campaign, 614, 621
Woll, Gen. Adrian, 124
Wolsey, A. W., S. Jacinto Army, 566
Wood, —, Fannin Massacre, 571
Wood, A. H., Veteran, 632
Wood, Edward B., S. Jacinto Army, 567
Wood, Edward B., Prov. Govt., 634
WOOD, GEORGE T., 293
Wood, George T., Pioneers killed, 583
Wood, Isaac, Veteran, 631
Wood, J. B., Gen. Consultation, 633
Wood, J. B., Convention, 634
Wood, James, Veteran, 619
Wood, John H., Veteran, 619
Wood, John, Fannin Massacre, 570
Wood, Robert, S. Jacinto Army, 566
Wood, Samuel, Fannin Massacre, 572
Wood, W. H., Veteran, 632
Wood, W. P., Fannin Massacre, 573
Wood, William Riley, Veteran, 619
Wood, William, S. Jacinto Army, 565
Woodard, W. H., Veteran, 632
Woodland, Henry, Veteran, 632
Woodlief, Devereau J., S. Jacinto Army, 563
Woods, Gonzales, 126
Woods, James B., 58
Woods, Norman, 125
Woods, Prvt., S. Jacinto Army, 564
Woods, Zadoc, 125
Woods, Zeddock, Old 300, 561
Woodville, 591
Woodward, Alvin, 64
Woodward, F. M., S. Jacinto Army, 568
Wooldridge, Thomas M., Pioneers killed, 582
Woollam, J. C., Veteran, 631
Woolrich, —, Fannin Massacre, 570
Worth, —, Pioneers killed, 582

Worth, General, 173
Wren, Allen, Fannin Massacre, 572
Wright, C., 113
Wright, G., S. Jacinto Army, 568
Wright, George W., Veteran, 619
Wright, Isaac N., 572
Wright, Ralph, Veteran, 618
Wright, Rufus, S. Jacinto Army, 565
Wright, Travis G., Veteran, 619
WRITING ON THE WALL, POEM, 413
Wyatt, P. S., Fannin Massacre, 572
Wyley, Samuel, S. Jacinto Army, 568
Wynne, W. II., Veteran, 631

Y

Yamparekah Comanches, 134
Yancy, John, S. Jacinto Army, 567
Yarbrough, S., S. Jacinto Army, 567
Yard, Col., 488
Yeamans, Elias, Fannin Massacre, 574
Yeamans, Erastus, Fannin Massacre, 574
YELLOW FEVER IN TEXAS, 1867, 487
Yellow Stone, Steamer, 193
Yeomans, Horace, Veteran, 620
Yoakum's History, 225
Yoakum, Henderson, Pioneers killed, 583
York, Capt., at Bexar, 220

York, Ellison, S. Jacinto Army, 566
Young County, 474
Young County geology, 494, 491
Young County, Coal, 501
Young County, minerals, 445
Young, C. G., Pioneers killed, 584
Young, Harrison, Fannin Massacre, 571
Young, Hugh F., Veteran, 632
Young, James O., Fannin Massacre, 572
Young, James, Veteran, 620
Young, Michael, Veteran, 620
Young, William C., Pioneers killed, 583
Young, William C., DA's, 639
Young, William, Veteran, 620
Young, William F., Veteran, 620
Young, William F., S. Jacinto Army, 564

Z

Zambrano's Row, 222
Zanesville, Ohio, 166
Zavala County, Coal, 500
Zavala, steamer, 79
Zuber, Abraham, 410
Zuber, William P., Veteran, 620
Zumwalt, Adam, 620
Zumwalt, F. B., Veteran, 620

A

Allan's LONE STAR BALLADS, 374, 376
ALMANAC (?), 92, 442, 461, 464, 488,
  493, 502, 633
ALMANAC 1857, 202, 284
ALMANAC 1858, 175
ALMANAC 1859, 24, 65
ALMANAC 1860, 61, 136
ALMANAC 1861, 83, 98, 138, 334
ALMANAC 1868, 106, 124, 140, 229
ALMANAC 1869, 132
ALMANAC 1870, 286
ALMANAC 1872, 19, 145
ALMANAC 1873, 101, 282, 410
Alsbury, Y. P., 101
Andrews, Edmund, 644
Archer, B. T., 640
Austin City Gazette, 396
Austin Record, 67
Austin Statesman 1874, 165
Austin, Stephen F., 68, 338, 644, 645,
  647, 648, 650, 651, 652, 653, 657
Austin, William T., 223, 640

B

Baker's HISTORY OF TEXAS, 258, 259,
  261, 262, 264, 293
Baker's TEXAS, 268, 269, 274, 276
Baker, D. W. C., 386, 403
Barton, William, 437
Benton, Thomas H., 355
Blewett, W. J., 368
Bowie, James, 67, 644, 647, 651
BRIEF HISTORY OF TEXAS, 19, 95,
  118, 179, 310, 356
Britton, Forbes, 336
Brown, John Henry, 53, 138, 140
Brown, S. T., 250
Brownsville Sentinel, 157
Bryan, Guy M., 89
Bryan, Moses Austin, 172
Buckley, S. B., 488, 493, 498
Burleson, Edward, 220

Burnett, David G., 50
Byars, N. T., 440

C

Coker, John, 101
Collins, Robert, 160

D

Daily Bulletin, 122
Davis, B. H., 440
De Lyle, Dora, 420
De Morse, Charles, 204
Dewees' LETTERS FROM TEXAS, 330
Dexter, Samuel, 157
Dow, J. E., 398
Durham, George J., 474, 479
Duval, Florence, 392
Duval, John C., 368

E

Edward's HISTORY OF TEXAS, 359
Evans, Moses, 364

F

Fannin, J. W., 353, 645, 647
Field's SCRAPBOOK, 116
Forestina, 366
Forshey, C. G., 502

G

Galveston News, 89, 155, 160, 169, 405,
  417, 515
Geijer, E. G., 432
Geraud, Father, 18
Gilleland, William M., 430
Graham, Welthea E., 400, 436
Gray, George H., 142
Green, Thomas J., 129
Groesbeck Argus, 198

H

Hall, W. D. C., 224, 652
Hardaway, Samuel G., 165
Hastings, Thomas, 50
Hemphill, John, 337
Hobby, A. M., 382, 390, 441
Holley's TEXAS, 35, 330
Houston Telegraph, 124, 126, 375, 418, 419
Houston, Nettie Power, 408, 424
Houston, Sam, 331, 413, 656

I

Ingram, Ira, 65

J

J. A. G., 172
Johnson, F. W., 24, 80
Johnston, F. W., 223
Jones, Anson, 339, 645, 654, 655
Josselyn, Robert, 404, 421

K

Kaufman, D. S., 335
Kennymore, J. C. P., 242
Kuykendall, J. H., 145, 238

L

Lamar, Mirabeau B., 335
Land Office, General, 20, 23, 557
Lytle, J. T., 418

M

Martin, Wyly, 52
Mattinson, R. F., 198
McLeod, H. D., 154
Miller, B., 389
Mims, Joseph, 353
Moore, Molly E., 380
Morrill's THIRTY SIX YEARS IN TEXAS, 313

N

New York Times, 86

O

Old Soldier, 86

P

Palm, Swante, 77, 361, 432
Parmenter, J. C., 395
Pease's HISTORY OF TEXAS, 338
Pease, E. M., 147
Potter, R. M., 106, 338

R

Rhodes, William H., 426
Robinson, J. C., 124
Roessler, A. R., 442
Rowe, Horace, 438
Royall, R. R., 657
Rusk, Thomas J., 155, 329
Russell, William J., 91

S

Simcox, Gisborne, 407, 423
Smith, Ashbel, 553
Smith, Henry, 640
Smith, Mary E., 388
Smith, T. F., 419
State Gazette 1849
State Journal, 308
Stewart, Charles B., 640
Stuart, C. D., 406

T

T. J. P., 76
Taylor, William S., 92
Telegraph 1869, 236
Telegraph and Texas Register, 569
Texas New Yorker 1874, 120
Texas Planter, 88

Thrall, H. S., 580
Travis, William B., 212, 262

V

Veteran Association 1874, 204

W

Waco Register, 237
Ward, Thomas, 250
Weaver, W. T. G., 422
West, Mrs. C. S., 392
West, C. S., 298, 300, 325

Weston, 377
Wharton, William H., 50
Whiting, S., 122
Wickeland, H., 468, 473
Wild Woman, 362
Wilke, Herman, 428
Wilson, J. C., 337
Wilson, J. M., 515
Wilson, Mary L., 374

Y

Yoakum's TEXAS, 17, 18, 281
Young, Mary G., 376